palgrave macmillan law masters

constitutional and administrative law

Series editor: **Marise Cremona**

Business Law   Stephen Judge
Company Law   Janet Dine and Marios Koutsias
Constitutional and Administrative Law   John Alder
Contract Law   Ewan McKendrick
Criminal Law   Jonathan Herring
Employment Law   Deborah J. Lockton
Family Law   Kate Standley
Intellectual Property Law   Tina Hart, Linda Fazzani and Simon Clark
Land Law   Joe Cursley, Mark Davys and Kate Green
Landlord and Tenant Law   Margaret Wilkie, Peter Luxton, Jill Morgan and Godfrey Cole
Law of the European Union   Jo Shaw
Legal Method   Ian McLeod
Legal Theory   Ian McLeod
Torts   Alastair Mullis and Ken Oliphant

Series editor: **Marise Cremona**

Economic and Social Law of the European Union   Jo Shaw, Jo Hunt & Chloe Wallace
Evidence   Raymond Emson

palgrave macmillan law masters

constitutional and administrative law

john alder

Emeritus Professor of Law, Newcastle University
Visiting Professor of Law, Bangor University

Seventh edition

Series editor: Marise Cremona
Professor of European Law
European University Institute
Florence, Italy

First edition 1989
Second edition 1994
Third edition 1999
Fourth edition 2002
Fifth edition 2005
Sixth edition 2007

This edition published 2009 by
PALGRAVE MACMILLAN

Palgrave Macmillan in the UK is an imprint of Macmillan Publishers Limited, registered in England, company number 785998, of Houndmills, Basingstoke, Hampshire RG21 6XS.

Palgrave Macmillan in the US is a division of St Martin's Press LLC, 175 Fifth Avenue, New York, NY 10010.

Palgrave Macmillan is the global academic imprint of the above companies and has companies and representatives throughout the world.

Palgrave® and Macmillan® are registered trademarks in the United States, the United Kingdom, Europe and other countries.

ISBN-13: 978–0–230–57662–9
ISBN-10: 0–230–57662–1

This book is printed on paper suitable for recycling and made from fully managed and sustained forest sources. Logging, pulping and manufacturing processes are expected to conform to the environmental regulations of the country of origin.

A catalogue record for this book is available from the British Library.

10 9 8 7 6 5 4 3
18 17 16 15 14 13 12 11 10

Printed and bound in Great Britain by CPI Antony Rowe, Chippenham and Eastbourne

Contents

As in previous editions my aims are firstly to explain the main principles of United Kingdom constitutional law in the context of the political and legal values that influence their development and secondly to draw attention to the main controversies. I hope that the book will provide both a self contained text for those new to the subject and an overview and guide to further research for more advanced students. In this edition, in response to the evolution of Public Law syllabuses, I have expanded the treatment of Administrative Law (judicial review) and Human Rights. There is a new Part IV on Human Rights. Topics related to 'Administrative Justice' such as tribunals and inquiries and ombudsmen are not dealt with in a separate chapter but are included in the appropriate contexts, particularly Chapters 5, 8, 13 ,17 and 18.

Three related themes underlie this book. First there is the tradition that the unwritten constitution of the UK is uncoordinated and relies on informal practices generated by a circle of 'insiders' selected by the government of the day who can therefore easily be manipulated. This can be set against the claim that a constitution should provide an external framework that constrains the power of temporary administrations. The constitutional reforms that have taken place during the last few years have been spasmodic, uncoordinated and relatively minor. They have not seriously addressed the most fundamental problem of the constitution which is the concentration of power in the executive supported by a network of professional, family and business relationships and with little or no power at local level. Of these reforms the most dynamic and democratic are probably the devolution arrangements for Scotland, Wales and Northern Ireland. The Human Rights Act 1998 is also important (but not necessarily for the better) in that it has to some extent strengthened the loose system of checks and balances that holds the constitution together by encouraging an independent judiciary to enter into the political sphere, combating the 'elective despotism' feared by Thomas Jefferson (misquoted by Lord Hailsham, the then Lord Chancellor as 'elective dictatorship' in the context of the UK government).

The second theme is the tension between 'legal' (in the sense of decisions made by our relatively independent judiciary) and 'democratic' controls over government. The Human Rights Act has become a platform from which judges sometimes make grand pronouncements about such matters as democracy, freedom, equality and liberalism. All these notions are highly uncertain and controversial and the Human Rights Act has revealed strong ideological differences within the judiciary as evidenced by frequent dissents. Therefore the third theme is the importance in a free society of keeping alive different points of view and not attempting to impose any particular orthodoxy on the people.

Part I concerns general principles. These include basic constitutional concepts and issues (Chapter 1), a broad account of the moral and political ideals that have influenced the constitution (Chapter 2) and the sources of the constitution (Chapter 3). Chapters 4 and 5 offer an overview of the history and structure of the constitution, aiming to provide a guide to the more detailed discussion in later chapters. Chapter 6 concerns the relationship between the central state, its citizens and the subordinate units of the UK, including legal issues relating to dependent territories. Pervasive legal values and doctrines are considered in Chapters 7, 8 and 9 and Chapter 10 outlines the main principles of European Community (EC) law as far as they affect the UK constitution.

Part II is concerned with the powers of the central government institutions and the relationship between them. No progress has been made since the last edition of this book in reforming the respective powers of the executive and Parliament nor in House of Lords reform and this edition continues the attempt at clearer treatment. The current Constitutional Renewal Bill contains no general or radical principles but deals with miscellaneous and relatively minor matters. Part III deals with judicial review of government action, the core of Administrative Law. Part IV consists of Human Rights both generally and in relation to selected topics that particularly relate to the political freedoms that underpin democracy. These include freedom of expression and assembly, secrecy and national security. In this area selection is exceptionally difficult. In view of the burgeoning of specialist courses on human rights and civil liberties, I have reluctantly excluded discussions of moral freedoms, obscenity and routine police powers since the fragmented and complex nature of these topics makes treatment in a general work of this kind of little value.

I am grateful particularly to Jasmin Naim and Rob Gibson at Palgrave Macmillan for their good advice and encouragement, for the comments of anonymous reviewers of the previous edition and to Barry Hough, Richard Mullender and Ann Sinclair for help with previous editions on which I have built.

I have updated this edition on the basis of material available to me on 31 January 2009.

JOHN ALDER

Note on further reading

Specific references to books and articles in the text are to writings that expand on the point in question. The Further Reading at the end of each chapter discusses fundamental and controversial general issues for those who require greater depth or more ideas and points of view. Short references in the text are to the Further Reading. Unless otherwise stated, the main classical works cited throughout are as follows:

Bagehot, W. (1902) *The English Constitution* (2nd edn) London, Kegan Paul.

Dicey, A.V. (1915 and 1959) *An Introduction to the Study of the Law of the Constitution* (8th and 10th edns) London, Macmillan – now Palgrave Macmillan.

Hobbes, T. (1973) *Leviathan*, in Minogue, K. (ed.) London, Dent.

Locke, J. (1960) *Two Treatises of Government*, in Laslett, P. (ed.) Cambridge University Press.

Mill, J.S. (1972) *Utilitarianism, On Liberty and Considerations of Representative Government*, in Acton, H.B. (ed.) London, Dent.

Montesquieu (1995) 'L'Esprit de Lois' extracted in Stirk, P.M.R. and Weigall, D.W. (eds) *An Introduction to Political Ideas*, London, Cassell.

Paine, T. (1987) *The Thomas Paine Reader*, in Foot, M. and Kramnick, I. (eds) London, Penguin.

Table of cases

Table of statutes

Part I

General principles

Chapter 1

Introduction: constitutional themes and structures

> The effective limitation of power is the most important problem of social order. Government is indispensable for the formation of such an order only to protect against coercion and violence from others. But as soon as to achieve this, government successfully claims the monopoly of coercion and violence it becomes a threat to individual freedom. To limit this power was the great aim of the founders of constitutional government. (Hayek, *Law, Legislation and Liberty*, 1978, Vol. 1, p. 128)

Key words

- Legitimacy
- Red light and green light
- Formal and functional
- Rule of law
- Separation of powers
- Constitutionalism
- Written and unwritten
- Entrenchment
- Conventions, practices and customs
- Positive and negative rights
- Legal and political constitution
- Common law constitution
- Public and private law
- Sovereignty

1.1 What is Constitutional Law?

In this chapter I shall introduce some basic concepts and themes. The general idea of a constitution is relatively simple. A constitution provides the fundamental principles that create the structure and purposes of a human organisation. This has two purposes: firstly to run the organisation efficiently in the light of its goals; secondly to prevent those in charge of the organisation abusing their powers. Conflict between these purposes is at the heart of the law. Any organisation might have a constitution, for example most golf clubs do so. The same basics apply to the constitution of a state such as the UK. Constitutional law therefore concerns the struggle between rival claimants to govern us and how our rulers are chosen, called to account and removed. It is also concerned with how powers are divided, between different institutions or geographically. The constitution might also include the main rights and duties of the people and a statement of the fundamental values of the state.

In the UK the current regime claims to be democratic but a constitution can adopt any form of government. A constitution is valid or 'legitimate' if enough of the people whom it concerns, both officials and the public, recognise it as binding and obey it so that it is broadly viable. UK law takes this pragmatic view in the context for example of recognising the legality of a rebellion (see *Madzimbamuto* v *Lardner-Burke* (1969): legality of a takeover of a British colony by a group of white settlers). Possible reasons for this fact of recognition such as fear, self-interest, apathy, moral fervour and so on are irrelevant, as is the question whether the constitution is morally good. On the other hand, a general sense among the people that the constitution is morally good, or at least that it is in their interests, might help the rulers stay in power. For example Locke thought the people had a right to rebel against an unjust constitution, thus justifying the seventeenth-century English revolution against the Crown.

'Legitimacy' might also refer to an external standard that can be used to assess the constitution. The problem here of course is to identify what this is, if it is to be more than our personal preferences. Lawyers for example might refer to widely accepted community values as identified by themselves. Thus legitimacy depends partly upon what Ward has called 'the popular imagination' (Ian Ward, *A State of Mind? The English Constitution and the Popular Imagination*, Sutton, 2000). This is not confined to formal legal texts and the pronouncement of officials but includes art, drama and literature such as novels and poetry, and the press.

Unfortunately there is no agreed definition of 'law'. For the purposes of studying constitutional law, it is useful to distinguish as a working matter between law and politics. A constitution includes both, law being a branch of politics with its own distinctive features. For the moment it is enough to say that 'law' means rules, principles and standards that are recognised (a) as coming from defined authorities (in the UK's case the courts and Parliament, the law making assembly) and (b) backed by the force of the state ultimately by using violence. 'Politics' comprise all other rules, values, practices and behaviour concerning the exercise of governmental power (below) which call for collective action. They include ideals and practises concerning how power should be divided up and how values such as equality and freedom are understood. They surface in debate, for example in Parliament and the media. They may or may not be translated into legal mechanisms but they are part of the constitution in its broad sense.

There is no single 'correct' recipe for a good constitution or what rules it should contain. A constitution is the result of historical events and personalities. The political and legal concepts that appear in this book have filtered into our culture as a result primarily of different interest groups competing with each other, thereby influencing people to make and accept particular arrangements – all of which are temporary and changeable. Constitutional law is therefore concerned above all with conflicts between groups with different beliefs about the aims and values of the state. There is often no available objective answer as to which of several competing beliefs is correct, for example should religious freedom allow a group to have a dispensation from the normal law? The constitution might therefore be regarded as managing perpetual disagreement. In this respect a dilemma which underlies constitutional law is whether we should rely on a democratic assembly to have the last word or a court comprising a group of independent 'experts'.

A constitution can of course adopt any purposes such as keeping a particular ruling family in power. A constitution which reflects the democratic values which are claimed to apply in the UK aspires to strike a balance between two competing political aims. These have been characterised by Harlow and Rawlings (1997) as 'red light' and 'green light' perspectives. According to the red light perspective, a constitution seeks to control those in power since it is widely acknowledged that people with power over others can easily abuse their power albeit sometimes accidentally or for good motives. Political thinkers over the centuries have worried about the corruptibility of those in power:

> Now it is a universally observed fact, that the two evil dispositions in question, the disposition to prefer a man's selfish interests to those he shares with other people, and his immediate and direct interests to those which are indirect and remote, are characterised most especially called forth and fostered by the possession of power . . . this is the meaning of the universal tradition, grounded on universal experience, of men's being corrupted by power. (J.S. Mill, 1972, p. 242)

John Adams, one of the founders of the United States Constitution asserted that:

> despotism, or unlimited sovereignty or absolute power, is the same in a majority of a popular assembly, an aristocratic council, an oligarchical junta, and a single emperor.

According to the green light perspective, a constitution should create a framework of rules which enable those who run the government to cooperate efficiently in providing public services. In the absence of such rules any cooperative enterprise is doomed to stalemate or chaos. In the context of democracy in particular, it would be impossible to give a group of people or the public in general any kind of voice without ground rules for decision making concerning especially voting and other expressions of opinion. These kinds of rules are particularly open to abuse since it is possible for them to be slanted towards the interests of those who draw them up.

Two closely related ideas characterise the kind of constitution that attempts the balancing exercise between the red and green light approaches. They influence democratic constitutions of the kind found in most European countries. They are 'the rule of law' and 'the separation of powers'. The rule of law is highly ambivalent. Its primary meaning is that it is a good thing to have legitimate rules governing an organisation. This helps the organisation to run effectively by keeping order and producing certainty to some extent. However it ignores the content of the rules, whether they are morally good or bad and the question of who makes them. For example a concentration camp might be subject to the rule of law in this sense. A wider version of the rule of law invokes certain moral and political ideas which are claimed to be especially associated with law in the sense of government by rules. These include justice and fairness, openness, equality and freedom policed by independent courts.

This leads us to the second concept, the separation of powers. This requires that government be divided up into different branches of equal status and importance so as to ensure that power is not concentrated in one person or group. Each branch can restrain the others since any major decision would require the cooperation of all three. The branches concerned are usually threefold, namely the legislature that makes the law, the executive that administers the country day-to-day and proposes laws to the legislature, and the judiciary – the courts that adjudicate on disputes concerning the law. In the case of the UK although we do have the three branches they are not clearly separate according to any systematic plan (Chapter 8).

The separation of powers is not of course foolproof. Firstly in order to avoid stalemate someone must have the last word. In particular there is a long running and unresolved argument as to whether the elected lawmaking branch, Parliament should do so or the unelected but independent courts. Different countries have reached different conclusions. For example in the US, based on eulogising the idea of the rule of law, the Supreme Court has the last word subject only to an elaborate process for changing the constitution

(*Marbury* v *Madison* (1803)). In the UK it is generally thought that Parliament has the last word (Chapter 9). Secondly much hangs on who appoints the leading members of each branch since whoever does so could pack each branch with cronies or sycophants. This is a particularly murky area since most senior appointments are made by the Prime Minister, the party leader who heads the executive branch. However by virtue of the Constitutional Reform Act 2005 there is a relatively independent mechanism for appointing judges (Chapter 8).

Some constitutions make grandiose and broad claims to shared ideals and purposes. For example the Canadian Charter of Rights and Freedoms announces that 'Canada is founded upon principles that recognise the supremacy of God and the rule of law'. The Constitution of Ireland refers to 'seeking to promote the common good with due observance of Prudence, Justice and Charity so that the dignity and freedom of the individual may be assured, true social order attained, the unity of our country restored and concord established with other nations'. The UK constitution makes no such claim, at least explicitly.

Many constitutions contain a list of basic rights of the citizen. These vary from state to state reflecting the political culture of the ruling group in question. In the family of liberal democratic states to which the UK belongs they are primarily 'negative' rights in the sense of rights not to be interfered with by the state. They include the right to life, the right to personal freedom, the right to a fair trial before an independent court, privacy and family life, freedom of expression, assembly and association, freedom of religion, and protection for property. 'Positive rights' such as the right to a decent standard of living, a good environment and medical care might be regarded as equally important but because these require hard political choices between priorities and large scale public expenditure they are often regarded as a matter for the ordinary political process rather than as fully fledged legal rights enshrined in a constitution. Enforcement by a court would be impossible. Nevertheless some positive rights appear in many constitutions, for example those of Germany, Poland and Portugal. Moreover some of the negative rights mentioned above (such as family life) might be interpreted to support some positive claims. Some constitutions, for example that of Switzerland, impose duties on citizens such as military service and voting.

Administrative law deals with the detailed operations of government, especially with the rights of the individual against government. It therefore overlaps with constitutional law. This book does not attempt to cover administrative law comprehensively since the subject has its own separate texts. Chapters 16, 17 and 18 on judicial review of administrative action deal with the core of administrative law. Other matters concerned with administrative law such as special tribunals, public inquiries and ombudsmen are discussed in their context, where they raise general constitutional issues.

1.2   Written and Unwritten Constitutions

Most constitutions are set out in a single document or related group of documents which have the force of law, usually being superior to all other kinds of law in that laws which conflict with the constitution can be struck down by the courts. They also contain provisions which protect the constitution from being changed by the government of the day, for example a referendum of the people or a two thirds majority of the lawmaking assembly. Some constitutions such as that of the US are relatively short and expressed in general terms. Others, like that of Portugal, run to hundreds of detailed pages. The UK has no written constitution in this sense. Its principles and rules, if written at all are to be found in the same documents as the sources of any law, namely Acts of Parliament (statutes) usually dealing with particular issues (such as reforms to the court system) and cases decided by the courts which establish precedents on particular issues often relating to individual rights. Rules from these two sources are automatically binding as law and can be changed in the same way as any other law. The idea of a written constitution in the above sense is a legacy of the revolutionary period in eighteenth- and nineteenth-century Europe when, with mixed success, widespread uprisings challenged traditional aristocratic, colonial and religious regimes. Since the start of the French Revolution in 1789 almost every other nation has adopted a written constitution (Saudi Arabia being an arguable exception), sometimes as a reaction against a hated previous regime and sometimes to mark a new event such as independence from colonial status.

The reason why the UK has no written constitution seems to be historical and cultural since the British people seem in the main to defer to domineering personalities rather than to rely on legal rules. A written constitution in the form of 'articles of government' was introduced in England by the revolutionary regime of Oliver Cromwell in 1653 but after a year was superseded by a military dictatorship. Apart from that, the UK constitution has developed pragmatically, usually out of accommodations struck between different sectional interests. Those who benefit from the arrangements, notably the larger political parties and the legal profession, value the appearance of continuity and tradition as a means of social cohesion (or social control).

The Revolution of 1688 was promoted as a return to ancient values which the Stuart monarchs were supposed to have subverted. In 1688 James II was deposed by a coalition of business and property owning interests centred on Parliament, the main lawmaking body. The settlement drew on existing traditions but modified them by legislation designed to subordinate the monarchy to Parliament (Bill of Rights 1688, Act of Settlement 1701). Thus the revolution sought to assert traditional practices against, on the one hand, radical claims to absolute rule by the king and, on the other, democratic claims by relatively small factions among the ordinary people. A wholesale redesign of the constitution was not therefore politically needed. During the following centuries the aristocracy gradually conceded power to professional and commercial groups. Attempts at popular uprisings were successfully suppressed by a combination of force, buying off leaders and moderate concessions. The UK's unwritten constitution is thus often defended as enabling its people to adjust flexibly and peacefully to changing circumstances. It is also suggested that the complexity and subtlety of the UK's arrangements make it impractical and divisive to reduce the constitution to writing, an argument convenient to those enjoying power.

During the eighteenth century the unwritten constitution was widely admired as a source of stability and justice and the idea of the rule of law was associated with it. Governments usually acted through laws which the system enabled them to change easily. Historians disagree as to how impartial that justice was in practice. Eighteenth- and early nineteenth-century politics is sometimes characterised as aristocratic oligarchy oiled by patronage and bribery with a ruthless enforcement of public order and property rights (for example see Roy Porter, *England in the Eighteenth Century*, Penguin, 1990). Latterly the UK constitution, with its restricted voting system and its concentration of power in the hands of large political parties controlling the executive, has become less admired and is sometimes regarded as the least democratic constitution in western Europe.

The absence of a written constitution has two main consequences. Firstly there is no agreement as to what rules or principles are truly 'constitutional' so as to attract that specially high respect and importance attached to a constitution. There is no doubt that rules concerning the circumstances in which a government should lose office are constitutional but what of local government which exists to provide relatively limited services for local communities? The debate would turn on the political issue of whether Britain's should be a highly centralised or a dispersed democracy. Thus the list of topics on constitutional law courses and in text books varies according to the beliefs of individual teachers and writers.

Secondly a written constitution is normally designed by a group of people working together systematically so as to give it some logical coherence and structure, even though under pressure of events this may not survive long. There is no reason why the UK constitution should have any particular structure or logic behind it. Its institutions and rules have been changed piecemeal over many centuries in response to immediate problems and power struggles. Admittedly some people claim to identify massive underlying abstract forces which guide constitutional change. For example the 'Whig interpretation of history' (see Butterfield, 1931) postulates a gradual evolution towards ever greater democracy and respect for individual rights interrupted by the pretensions of absolute monarchy arising from the Norman conquest but triumphantly restored in 1688 by the revolution which placed Parliament in charge. Certainly the structural features of the UK constitution have historically depended on the emergence of institutions which have taken away powers from monarchs in favour of other groups and institutions, the balance of power constantly shifting between these. Superficially at least, our constitution does have a coherent structure as a Parliamentary or representative democracy (below) which could be enshrined in a written text and indeed has been copied in many written constitutions. However anomalies arise on a more detailed level out of particular changes driven by short term considerations such as the 'West Lothian Question' (Chapter 6). Where this is so, it may be possible to patch together workable machinery by relying on conventions, practices or understandings not written into law but followed in the interests of cooperation (below).

Some claim that the UK constitution is a 'common law constitution' meaning that it is guided by principles laid down by the courts when deciding disputes. It has been suggested that these principles are rational and coherent since they are based on public reasoning by experts supported by the wisdom stored in thousands of decided cases (*Prohibitions del Roy* (1607)). This of course resists radical change. It is difficult to reconcile this with a constitution based on democracy in which the basic principles are decided by elected representatives of the people and anything can be changed. The normal method of reconciling this apparent contradiction is to suggest that the courts will protect the fundamental and permanent liberal values needed for democracy, such as freedom of speech, against the possibility that elected politicians might be irrationally swayed by mob sentiment in favour of giving up democracy for example in response to fear of terrorism. However if the courts do have the last word they can decide anything they like. It has not been established finally in the UK constitution as to who has the last word between the courts and Parliament (Chapter 9).

Those familiar with written constitutions sometimes suggest that the UK does not have a constitution. This is, at least historically wrong in that the term 'constitution', although originally meaning a government enactment, was used in Britain in its modern sense at least by the seventeenth century. More importantly, the substantive content of a constitution can be the same whether or not it is written down. The matter could be regarded as relatively trivial: one of convenience in selecting and storing the information. One might revere a written constitution, as is the case in the US, but the same applies to any symbol. For example Walter Bagehot (1826–77) thought that mystical reverence for royalty was essential to the authority of the UK constitution (or, as he considered it, the 'English' constitution). Dicey (1915) pointed out that a written constitution can be torn up whereas the unwritten constitution of the UK is embedded in the structure of the law as a whole (Chapter 7). It is sometimes said that a written constitution encourages the use of abstract, linguistic, legalistic techniques at the expense of the underlying political realities and human interests. However courts have often emphasised the need for a broad and flexible approach to constitutional interpretation that stresses the underlying moral and political context (for example see *Robinson* v *Secretary of State for Northern Ireland* (2002)). Indeed the language of a written constitution may be very vague, leaving plenty of room for disagreement. For example the US constitution has been interpreted at different times as both justifying and outlawing slavery.

Even without a written constitution, Parliament and the judges give special weight to rights, principles or laws that they consider to be 'constitutional'. For example proposed legislation that Parliament regards as 'of first class constitutional importance' is examined by a committee of the whole House rather than by the normal 'standing committee' (Chapter 15). The courts require the lawmaker to use very clear language in order to exclude constitutional rights (Chapters 7, 9). In *R* v *Secretary of State for the Home Department ex parte Simms* [1999] 3 All ER 400, 412 (right of a prisoner to freedom of speech), Lord Hoffmann stated that we apply 'principles of constitutionality little different from those which exist in countries where the power of the legislature is expressly limited by a constitutional document' (see also Laws LJ in *Thoburn* v *Sunderland City Council* (2002): European Community law). There is authority that compensation can be awarded against a public official who violates a 'constitutional right' even where no loss or damage has occurred (*Ashby* v *White* (1703): right to vote). On the other hand, in *Watkins* v *Secretary of State for the Home Department* (2006): prisoner's access to a lawyer, the House of Lords rejected this argument on the ground that without a written constitution the notion of a constitutional right is too vague. In *Cullen* v *Chief Constable of the RUC* (2004), Lord Hutton (at 46) said that a written constitution does have a special significance. He referred to a right

> which a democratic assembly representing the people has enshrined in a written constitution. In the latter case a person who has suffered harm can recover damages the written constitution being 'clear testimony that an added value is attached to the protection of that right'.

Similarly in *Ghaidan* v *Mendosa* (2004) Lord Millet said [178] that a written constitution would give the court greater legitimacy in reviewing legislation under the Human Rights Act.

If it can be changed only by a special procedure (entrenchment) a written constitution provides some assurance that important rules have the consent of the people outside the control of temporary ruling regimes. A written constitution encourages a rationalistic process of constitutional design, whereas an unwritten constitution tends to develop pragmatically in response to short term factors. It can be argued that, in a matter as large and open to disagreement as a constitution, human beings are not capable of sensible grand designs and that the flexible trial and error approach favoured in the UK is preferable. Edmund Burke (1729–97), a prominent parliamentarian and conservative thinker, claimed that the constitution has special status by virtue of its being rooted in long standing custom and tradition. Burke regarded attempts to engineer constitutions on the basis of abstract reason as ultimately leading to tyranny. This is because he believed that humans, with their limited understanding and knowledge, are inevitably at the mercy of unforeseen events and that reasoning based on abstract general principles, by trying to squeeze us into rigid templates, is a potential instrument of oppression:

> the age of chivalry is gone . . . That of sophisters, economists and calculators has succeeded; and the glory of Europe is extinguished for ever. (Burke, *Reflections on the Revolution in France*, 1790)

On the other hand, an unwritten constitution invites those in power to invent or manipulate 'customs' or 'conventions' to suit their own interests. The claim that the informal constitution can easily adjust to changing politics exemplifies this. Thus Burke's adversary, the democratic activist Thomas Paine (1737–1809), labelled the British government as 'power without right'. In *The Rights of Man*, Paine asserted that without a written constitution authorised directly by the people there was no valid constitution (1987, pp. 220–21, 285–96). Moreover the European Court of Human Rights has recently emphasised the need to justify restrictions on individual rights on the basis of 'considered debate' rather than on 'unquestioning and passive obedience to a historic tradition' (*Hirst v UK* (2004); Chapter 12). Thus there is no 'right' answer and, as is invariably the case with human organisations, different forms of constitution are a mixture of good and bad.

1.3   Conventions, Non-Legal Mechanisms

There are also many rules, practices and customs which are not written down in any authoritative way and cannot be directly enforced by the courts. These get their force only because they are consistently obeyed. The most important of these are known as constitutional conventions (Chapter 3). It is a prominent feature of the UK constitution that many of our most fundamental constitutional arrangements rely on conventions. Some happen to be recorded in writing for example in the Ministerial Code (Chapter 15). Others are informal and haphazard: what the political historian Professor Peter Hennessey has called 'a back of the envelope nation'.

Here is an example of how conventions and law interact. A fundamental group of conventions which would certainly feature in a written constitution concerns the position of the Queen as head of state. In strict law, all government power emanates from the Crown although the Crown's lawmaking power is heavily constrained. The following is the strict legal position. Apart from some special cases known as the 'royal prerogative' the Queen can make law only on the advice of Parliament (Bill of Rights 1688, *Case of Proclamations* (1611)). Crucially she cannot raise taxation nor raise a standing army without the consent of Parliament (Bill of Rights 1688). Moreover the rights of individuals can only be interfered with by law. The Queen can veto laws proposed to her by Parliament. She can dissolve Parliament although her power to summon Parliament is constrained by law. It was established in the seventeenth century in law that the monarch cannot directly interfere with the court process nor with the common law developed by the courts (*Prohibitions Del Roy* (1607)). The Queen appoints any other persons she wishes to form the executive, the leading figures being known as Ministers of the Crown. Within the law she can run the executive as she wishes.

However when the conventions are added, it appears that the monarchy has very limited power, existing mainly as a ceremonial figurehead. The conventions have the effect of making our somewhat medieval arrangements look more democratic. The monarch must apparently assent to all bills (proposed laws) submitted to her by Parliament. She must appoint as Prime Minister (leader of the executive branch) the person with majority support in the elected House of Commons (which together with the unelected House of Lords, the members of which are effectively appointed by the Prime Minister, comprises Parliament). The Prime Minister then advises the Queen what other ministers to appoint, all of whom must also be or become members of Parliament. In respect of this and indeed all her powers she must act on the advice of the relevant minister, usually the Prime Minister. This is particularly important in relation to dissolving Parliament, about which there are further conventions which seek to protect democracy (Chapter 11). In normal circumstances these conventions make the Prime Minister very powerful. In law if the monarch ignored these conventions and appointed a friend as Prime Minister nothing could directly be done. Any solution would be political. Probably Parliament would refuse to support the Prime Minister by not passing laws he or she proposed and refusing to raise taxes to support the executive. However the Queen might be required to exercise her legal powers in a political crisis if for example no leader had the support of Parliament (Chapter 14).

Any constitution or set of formal rules is likely be overlaid by unwritten customs and practices. This is partly because no set of written rules can deal with every possible situation but also because all written documents fall to be interpreted in the light of the practices, assumptions and beliefs, moral and political, of the interpreter. In the case of a constitution there are numerous inputs of thousands of people over time so that the nuances of the constitution are in constant flux. Even so, the UK constitution has relied on convention and practice to an unusually large extent. This can be defended as allowing the constitution to evolve easily to meet changing circumstances. It can be criticised as creating uncertainty but more importantly, because there is no authoritative way of deciding whether a particular convention or practice exists or what it means, as enabling those in power to manipulate the constitution in their own interests. One of the main points of a constitution is that it should be an independent set of rules constraining all those who hold power.

Some practices and understandings are written down by officials in an uncoordinated profusion of 'concordats', 'memoranda', 'codes of practice' and the like (for example the Sewel Convention; Chapter 6). Others are wholly unwritten, residing only in the collective knowledge of those consulted about them. Thus opinions can be sought from those thought likely to come up with the desired answer. These unwritten practices are not legally enforceable and there is no authoritative mechanism for saying what they mean and whether they are valid. Political practices are therefore transmitted through a network of personal, professional and family relationships. For this reason considerable trust must be placed in the integrity, independence and ability of those who hold public office and those who appoint them. The majority of senior public offices, including ministers, heads of public bodies and members of the House of Lords are in practice appointed by ministers. Indeed the same persons are constantly recycled in various public offices and given impressive awards and titles. Moreover senior civil servants and ministers may be valued highly enough on retirement from office as to be offered lucrative positions in private companies with which they had been connected while in office.

The relationship between elected politicians, who are responsible for the exercise of power, and appointed civil servants, other members of official bodies and miscellaneous 'advisers' is mainly outside legal constraint. In recent years for example the government has often been accused of ruling through groups of 'cronies' and bypassing established formal practices in favour of advice from party political advisers and self interested business and media leaders who may have personal links with government members (see Public Administration Committee, 'Lobbying: Access and Influence in Whitehall', HC 36, 2008–9).

Another manifestation of our reliance on non-legal mechanisms consists of miscellaneous bodies that monitor the ethical standards of government or investigate complaints of maladministration with varying degrees of formality but have no direct enforcement powers. Some are statutory, others have no specific legal basis or powers of enforcement. Constitutional issues relating to such bodies concern whether they are genuinely independent and whether they are taken seriously. Examples include various 'ombudsmen' such as the Parliamentary Commissioner for Administration (Parliamentary Commissioner Act 1967), the Committee on Standards in Public Life, the Public Appointments Commission, the Civil Service Commission and the House of Lords Appointments Commission. The Standards Board, a relatively powerful body, has statutory powers to investigate complaints against the conduct of elected members of local government, including a power of suspension (Local Government Act 2000). This raises questions about democratic values and can be contrasted with the lack of enforcement powers available against members of the central government.

Daintith and Page (*The Executive in the Constitution*, Oxford University Press, 1999, Chapter 1) classify those who attempt to understand our unwritten constitution as 'foxes', 'hedgehogs', 'rude little boys' and 'Humpty Dumpties'. A fox regards the constitution as no more than a collection of working practices developed by those who join the government enterprise. A hedgehog looks for a single grand overarching principle such as parliamentary supremacy. It is unlikely that in a matter as complex as government any such principle is credible. A rude little boy therefore asserts that the emperor has no clothes, the constitution being a fiction disguising a power struggle between control freaks. Humpty Dumpties, who probably include most academic commentators, seek to explain the constitution on the basis of vague theories of their own such as liberalism, fairness, social welfare and so on, sometimes claiming that these ideals are inherent in the rules. We shall meet examples of each approach throughout this book.

1.4   The Legal and the Political Constitution

A distinction is sometimes made between the 'legal' constitution and the 'political constitution' (Griffith, 1979). In this context Griffith famously remarked that 'the constitution of the United Kingdom lives on, changing from day to day for the constitution is no more and no less than what happens. Everything that happens is constitutional. And if nothing happened that would be constitutional also' (1979, at 19). On one reading this suggests that there is nothing at all behind the idea of a constitution. However Griffith is stressing the political as opposed to the legal constitution pointing out that, in a society where there is a perpetual political conflict between different interests, the constitution in the sense of the balance between different interests is always changing and any resolution is likely to be only short term (see Gee, 2008).

By the political constitution we mean the actual power relationships between different actors and also the basic values of the community in relation to the government of the country. Politics is therefore wider than law. Law is a specialised tool or manifestation of politics putting political decisions into the authoritative form of enforceable rules. Thus law is defined by its source and the form it takes, not its content which can be anything. The political constitution includes the conventions, practices and understandings discussed above.

The legal and the political constitution are interrelated in various ways. For example:

▶ Politics provides the purposes and values that underpin the constitution and give the law its content.
▶ Law operates as a delivery mechanism for particular political policies written into legislation.
▶ Conversely, values especially concerned with the legal process in the courts which can be summarised as fairness and justice feed into the political process, for example how far immigrants should be protected by the courts.
▶ Within the law itself there is room for political activity arising out of disagreement between different judges and groups of lawyers. Because the limits of language mean that rules can never be entirely clear, judges may be influenced by their political beliefs in deciding between competing arguments. Endless disagreement underlies both law and politics.
▶ Politics determines the actual power relationship between the different branches of government: lawmaker, executive, judges, military and so on. For example even if in law Parliament the lawmaker is supreme, if the culture of members of Parliament is weak, self seeking and subservient the executive is likely to be dominant.

Law can be distinguished from other aspects of politics in at least the following respects. It relies on impersonal and usually written sources of authority in the form of binding general rules. It emphasises the desirability of certainty, coherence and formal, impartial procedures for settling disputes. Most fundamentally, law authorises violence against individuals in the name of the community. Politics is concerned primarily with outcomes, for which law is only one among several instruments, and is more willing than law to use emotions, personal relationships, rewards and compromises in order to achieve those outcomes. Politics also arbitrates as to the limits of the law. For example there is a persistent disagreement running through the subject of constitutional law as to the extent to which unelected courts should interfere with the decisions of elected politicians. The inner resources of the law cannot resolve that type of dispute which questions the very nature of law itself.

Griffith (above) thought that constitutional decisions should be made by political bodies rather than by courts because he thought that judges are likely to be biased in favour of established authority (1997, pp. 335–6). It is also often argued that because there is perpetual disagreement as to the meaning and proper extent of fundamental values such as freedom and democracy, elected bodies representing the public as a whole should decide questions relating to their scope and limits rather than solutions being imposed from above by unaccountable judges. According to this approach, which reflects the separation of powers, the court comes into its own when applying a rule, not in deciding what the rules are.

1.5 Definitions of a Constitution

It is probably not worthwhile attempting to find a precise definition of a constitution, which is more a general idea than a precise legal concept. Many writers have tried to capture the essence of a constitution, each emphasising different aspects. The examples below are intended to illustrate the problem and the variations of approach.

- Professor Dicey (1915, p. 22) gives a bland definition: 'all rules which directly or indirectly affect the distribution and exercise of the sovereign power in the state'.
- Sir John Laws (1996), a contemporary Court of Appeal judge, described a constitution narrowly as: 'that set of legal rules which govern the relationship in a state between the ruler and the ruled'.
- More broadly, Lord Bingham, another leading judge, suggests that 'any constitution, whether of a state, a trade union, a college, a club or other institution seeks to lay down and define . . . the main offices in which authority is vested and the powers which may be exercised (or not exercised) by the holders of those offices' (*R v Secretary of State for Foreign and Commonwealth Affairs ex parte Quark Fishing Ltd* [2006] [12]).
- Friedrich exemplifies an approach that stresses the consent of the community: 'a constitution is the ordering and dividing of the exercise of political power by that group in an existent community who are able to secure the consent of the community and who thereby make manifest the power of the community itself' (Carl J. Friedrich, *Limited Government: A Comparison*, 1974, p. 21).
- Tully ('The Unfreedom of the Moderns', 2002, *Modern Law Review*, 65:204) offers a legally oriented definition capturing the notion that the constitution has a special status: 'the cluster of "supreme" or "essential" principles, rules and procedures to which other laws, institutions and governing authorities within the association are subject'.
- Marshall (2003), a political theorist, identifies four possible meanings of constitution:

  (a) the combination of legal and non-legal . . . rules that currently provide the framework of government and regulate the behaviour of the major political actors;
  (b) a single instrument promulgated at a particular point in time and adopted by some generally agreed authorisation procedure under the title 'constitution' or equivalent rubric such as 'basic law';
  (c) the totality of legal rules . . . (wherever contained) that affect the working of government;
  (d) a list of statutes or instruments that have an entrenched status and can be amended or repealed only by a special procedure.

Nothing much seems to link these four. They say little or nothing about the purpose or content of the rules in question. The UK has a constitution in sense (c) although this tells us little of interest. We do not have a constitution in senses (b) or (d) of a special set of documents (below). Whether we have a constitution in sense (a) depends on whether there is anything coherent enough to be called a framework. This is a matter of opinion.

Whether or not we have a constitution in a strict sense, the term 'constitutionalism' could be applied to the UK. Constitutionalism is the belief that a state should have arrangements that limit the powers of the rulers and which give the ruling regime its moral authority (legitimacy). Constitutionalism includes both legal and political limits on government. It requires government officials to be accountable for their actions to an independent body although not necessarily a court. It requires checks and balances between different governmental organs (Chapter 8) and proper controls within each governmental organ. In a democracy it requires frequent elections open to all and subject to rules which prevent any candidate from having an unfair advantage (Chapter 12).

1.6   Types of Constitution

There are several traditional ways of classifying constitutions. It must be emphasised that these are ideals or models and there is no reason to assume that any real constitution will neatly fit into any category. The types are:

- **Federal and unitary**: In a federal state (such as the US) power is divided between different geographical units and a central government. Each level is protected against intervention by the others. In a unitary state (such as the UK) there may be subordinate units such as the devolved governments of Scotland and Wales but ultimate power is held by the centre. It is often believed that in any constitution there must be some ultimate source of power and authority (sovereignty). In most cases this is the constitution itself or at least the process for changing the constitution. The UK has an extreme unitary constitution since Parliament is usually thought to have unlimited lawmaking power not subject to any higher authority: the doctrine of 'parliamentary supremacy' (Chapter 9). Although in recent years substantial governmental power has been devolved to Scotland, Wales and Northern Ireland (Chapter 6), these remain in law subordinate to the UK Parliament. (However the distinction between law and political reality should be borne in mind in this context.)

  Parliamentary supremacy has been questioned on the grounds that international obligations from above and devolution from below make the idea of a self contained unitary constitution obsolete. It is suggested that there is no need for a single ultimate sovereign body. Different bodies might exercise control in their own spheres with provision for negotiated settlements in the event of conflict. This form of constitution might well put considerable power in the hands of courts as a last resort dispute settler. Indeed it is sometimes suggested that the 'common law constitution' in the keeping of the judges is superior to Parliament so that in the last resort unconstitutional legislation, for example abolishing elections, could be overturned by a court. However the question of what counts as the ultimate authority in a state cannot be answered from within the legal system created by that state but is a political assumption based on community acceptance.

- **Multilayered and unitary:** A contemporary but looser variation of the idea of dispersed power is to contrast a 'multilayered' constitution with a unitary one. In a multilayered constitution power might be fragmented and dispersed not only downwards into units within the state but upwards into international organisations such as the European Union or sideways between different kinds of decision making bodies such as courts and Parliament or between different kinds of mechanisms, legal and political, public and private. Thus the expression 'multilayered' has little value in itself, being no more than a fashionable way of expressing the truism that law and politics take a variety of forms.

- **Written and unwritten:** As we have seen, most constitutions consist at least partly of a special written document or group of documents that sets out what are regarded as the most fundamental principles relating to government. The UK has no such document but still considers itself to possess a constitution in the sense of principles performing the same functions even though these cannot be identified from any single document. This claim has not gone unchallenged (above).

- **Rigid and flexible:** This concerns whether it is easy for those in power to change the constitution to suit their own interests. In legal terms some constitutions are rigid in that a special process such as a referendum of the people may be required to change them. This is known as 'entrenchment'. In the UK no special process is required. However the courts may resist interpreting laws so as to undermine what they regard as constitutionally important matters (Chapter 9). Whether a constitution is easy to change depends more on politics than on law. Any constitution can be ignored or overthrown.

- **Parliamentary and presidential:** In a presidential system there is a split between the legislature (which makes the law) and the executive (which carries out the law) in the sense that each branch is separately chosen and removed. The President is usually both head of government and head of state and might be directly elected by the people. In a parliamentary system the executive is chosen and removed by the legislature and there is a separate head of state usually with little or no political power. The UK is an extreme parliamentary constitution in that the leading members of the executive must also be members of the legislature.

- **Monarchy, aristocracy, democracy:** In a tradition dating back at least to Aristotle, there are three fundamental types of government: monarchy, or rule by one person; aristocracy, literally rule by a group of the 'best' people; and democracy, rule by the many or the people as a whole. According to Aristotle, each form of constitution has its virtues but also corresponding vices or deviations. The virtues exist when the ruler rules for the benefit of others, the vices when the ruler rules for the benefit of him or herself. Modern constitutions draw on these elements but disagree as to the best combination of them. Monarchy is usually inherited within a family so that the holder's power is not dependent on temporary political forces. The main merit of monarchy is its authority and independence since monarchs have a quasi-godlike status. The corresponding defect is despotism. The merit of aristocracy is wisdom, its defect is oligarchy (rule by a selfish group). The merit of democracy is consent of the community, its defect is instability leading to mob tyranny. Aristotle postulated a vicious cycle in which a monarch becomes a despot, is deposed by an aristocracy which turns into oligarchy and is overthrown by a popular rebellion. The ensuing democracy degenerates into chaos resolved by the emergence of a dictator who takes on the characteristics of a monarch and so on. Aristotle therefore favoured what he called 'polity', a 'mixed government' combining all three (but loaded in favour of the middle classes) and with 'checks and balances' between different branches of government. This strategy remains at the heart of modern constitutional design. However a cynical view, 'the iron law of oligarchy', claims that whatever form the constitution takes power will inevitably accumulate in the hands of a group of selfish cronies – a king by whatever name and his courtiers. In contemporary conditions this might well be a political party: 'who says organisation says oligarchy . . . the oligarchical structure of the building suffocates the basic democratic principle' (Michels quoted in Lipset, *Political Parties*, Free Press, 1966).

▷ **Republican:** A republican constitution is more than just a constitution, such as those of France or Ireland which have no monarchy. The idea of republicanism refers to the notion that all citizens deserve equal concern and respect and that the government of the state should be self government by citizens. There is no agreement as to the precise mechanism for bringing this about. There is usually a president as head of state sometimes as in Ireland a largely ceremonial figurehead, sometimes as in the US and France with executive and legislative powers. The separation of powers (above) is consistent with the republican principle that power should not be concentrated in any single person or group. Some republicans favour the notion of deliberative democracy where disputes are settled by ensuring that citizens have the opportunity to participate directly in decision making. This seems to paint an idealised picture of groups of leisured and well informed people with sufficient in common and enough good will to reach agreement. Another version relies on the notion of representative democracy where ultimate power is vested in an assembly chosen by the people in free and fair elections. The UK constitution has a claim to be at least partly republican in this sense, although by no means completely so. For example the House of Lords, which is part of Parliament our supreme legislature, is appointed not elected. Those who support republicanism usually reject the notion that the courts should have the last word and regard the constitution as being safer in political hands (for example Bellamy, 2007).

1.7 Public and Private Law

Constitutional law is the most basic aspect of 'public law'. It is controversial as to whether there is a useful distinction between public law and 'private law'. Broadly public law governs the relationship between the government and individuals and that between different governmental agencies. Private law concerns the relationship between individuals and also deals with private organisations such as companies. For reasons connected with a peculiarly English notion of the rule of law (Chapter 7) the distinction between public law and private law is less firmly embedded here than in the continental legal systems that inherited the distinction from Roman law. It was believed by the likes of Dicey that the liberties of the individual are best secured if the same law, broadly private law, governed officials and individuals alike so that officials have no special powers or status. Attractive though this may be, it is arguably unrealistic given the huge powers that must be vested in the state to meet public demand for large scale public services and government controls over daily life and the movement of the population.

However some writers have rejected the distinction between public and private law at least on the level of fundamental principle, arguing that the same basic values and concepts pervade all law and that any given function could be carried out by the state or a private body (Chapter 18). This is particularly important today when it is politically fashionable to entrust public services to profit making private bodies. Moreover there are numerous bodies not directly connected with the government which exercise large powers over individuals such as sporting and professional disciplinary bodies, trade unions and churches. Outside the core functions of keeping order and defence, there is no agreement in the UK as to what is the proper sphere of the state and which bodies are subject to public law.

At a very general level the rejection of the distinction between public and private law may be defensible. It is difficult to deny that values such as fairness and openness are common to the private and public sector, and organisations such as charities that carry out functions for the benefit of the public on a non-profit basis have elements both of the public and the private. A typical example is that of social housing, which is currently provided by numerous charitable and other housing associations but with powerful government agencies behind the scenes setting standards, dictating objectives and punishing defaulters.

There may however be important distinctions between government and private persons. These include the following:

- The government represents the whole community and its officials have no self interest of their own. By contrast a private company and an individual both have a legitimate self interest including the profit motive. It follows that government should be accountable to the community as a whole for its actions. In the case of a private body, by contrast, accountability might be regarded as an unacceptable intrusion on its freedom.
- The government has a monopoly of force and therefore of lawmaking. It is fundamental that no one can use force against another without their consent unless authorised by law.
- The government has the ultimate responsibility to protect the community against disruption and external threats. For this purpose it must be entrusted with wide powers to use force. As we shall see in Chapter 21 concerning emergencies, it may be difficult or impossible to reconcile this with our belief that all power should be curbed by law.
- The distinction between public and private law has particular implications in two main contexts. First there is the question of the scope of judicial review of decisions made by powerful bodies. This is limited to 'functions of a public nature' (Chapter 18). Secondly the protection of the Human Rights Act 1998 applies mainly against public bodies and bodies certain of whose functions are public functions (Chapter 19). A similar approach is taken in both contexts, the matter depending upon the extent to which the body in question is linked to the central government proper. A pragmatic approach is taken based on all the circumstances such as whether the body in question has special powers, whether it is controlled or financed by the government and the public importance of its functions (see for example R (Weaver) v London and Quadrant Housing Trust (2008), YL v Birmingham City Council (2007)).

Summary

▷ Having read this chapter, you should have a general idea of some basic constitutional concepts and how they relate to the UK. Constitutions deal with the fundamental framework of government and its powers, reflecting the political interests of those who design and operate them and providing mechanisms for the control of government.

▷ The ultimate aim of a constitution is to manage disagreement in circumstances where collective action on behalf of the whole community is required.

▷ Political and legal aspects of a constitution, although overlapping, should be distinguished. The legal aspects of the constitution are a distinctive part of the wider political context each influencing the other. There are also important constitutional principles in the form of conventions and practices operating without a formal legal basis.

▷ There is a tendency in any form of government for powers to gravitate towards a single group so that a primary concern of constitutional law is to provide checks and balances between different branches of government. The UK constitution is a unitary parliamentary system with notionally unlimited lawmaking power vested in Parliament, a central bicameral assembly. Because of the contemporary increase in the political power of the executive, the importance of international influences and the increased role of the courts in the context of fundamental rights, the principle of Parliamentary supremacy is currently subject to question.

▷ The constitution of the UK is parliamentary, unitary, unwritten and heavily reliant on non-legal mechanisms. The distinction between written and unwritten constitutions is of some but not fundamental importance. The UK constitution is an untidy mixture of different kinds of law practices and customs and has a substantial informal element, lending itself to domination by personal networks.

▷ It is questionable whether the UK constitution can be rationalised in terms of consistent general principles. However at the other extreme, it might be more than just 'what happens'.

▷ The distinction between public law and private law is important particularly in the context of the Human Rights Act 1998 and of judicial review of powerful bodies. The courts have adopted a pragmatic approach.

Exercises

1.1 You are discussing constitutional law with an American who claims that the UK has no constitution. What does she mean and how would you respond?

1.2 Which of the definitions of a constitution contained in this chapter best fits the UK constitution?

1.3 Is it useful to distinguish between the 'legal constitution' and the 'political constitution'?

1.4 'It is both a strength and a potential weakness of the British constitution, that almost uniquely for an advanced democracy it is not all set down in writing' (Wakeham Report, Royal Commission on the Reform of the House of Lords, 2000, Cm 4534). Discuss.

1.5 Is there a difference between the idea of federalism and that of the multilayered constitution?

1.6 'The executive is likely to control the legislature in a modern parliamentary democracy.' Do you agree and why?

Further reading

[Note: the further reading for this chapter marked * might usefully be revisited towards the end of the student's course when fuller knowledge of the subject might have been gained]

*Bamforth, N. and Leyland, P. (eds) (2003) *Public Law in a Multi-Layered Constitution*, Oxford, Hart Publishing, Chapter 1.

*Barker, N.(2008) 'Against a Written Constitution', *Public Law* 11.

Bellamy (2007), *Political Constitutionalism*, Cambridge University Press, Chapter 1.

*Ewing, K. (2000) 'The Politics of the British Constitution', *Public Law* 405.

Feldman, D. (2005) 'None, One or Several? Perspectives on the UK's Constitution', *Cambridge Law Journal* 64:329.

Finer, S.E., Bogdanor, V. and Rudden, B. (1995) *Comparing Constitutions*, Oxford University Press, Chapter 1.

*Gee, G. (2008) 'The Political Constitutionalism of JAG Griffith', *Legal Studies* 28:20.

*Griffith, J. (1979) 'The Political Constitution', *Modern Law Review* 42:1.

*Harvey, C. (2001) 'Playing with Law and Politics', *University of Toronto Law Journal* 51:171.

Hennessy, P. (1995) *The Hidden Wiring*, London, Gollancz, Prologue and Chapter 1.

*Hickman, T. (2005) 'In Defence of the Legal Constitution', *University of Toronto Law Journal* 55:981.

*Loughlin, M. (2003) 'Constitutional Law: the Third Order of the Political', in Bamforth, N. and Leyland, P. (eds) above.

*Loughlin, M. (2005) 'Constitutional Theory: a 25th Anniversary Essay', *Oxford Journal of Legal Studies* 25:183.

McIlwain, C.H. (1947) *Constitutionalism Ancient and Modern*, London, Cornell University Press, Chapter 1.

Mc Cormick, N. (2007) *Institutions of Law*, Oxford University Press, Parts I and III.

Munro, C.R. (1999) *Studies in Constitutional Law* (2nd edn), London, Butterworth, Chapter 1.

Poole, T. (2007) 'Tilting at Windmills? Truth and Illusion in the Political Constitution', *Modern Law Review* 70:250.

Walker, D. (2002) 'The Idea of Constitutional Pluralism', *Modern Law Review* 65:317.

Chapter 2

Underlying political values: liberalism

> A free society is premised on the fact that people are different from one another. A free society respects individual differences. (Baroness Hale in *R (Williamson)* v *Secretary of State for Education and Employment* (2005) [72])

Key words

- Different kinds of liberalism
- Autonomy
- Instrumental and intrinsic interests
- Utilitarianism
- 'Public choice'
- Social contract
- Formal and substantive equality
- Positive and negative freedom
- Republicanism
- Different kinds of democracy
  - Representative
  - Deliberative
  - Market
- Accountability

2.1 Introduction

Western European constitutions have been influenced by three broad and overlapping political perspectives. They are loosely termed 'liberalism', 'republicanism' and 'communitarianism'. Each emphasises a different aspect of human nature. Liberalism concentrates on our individuality, focusing on rights and freedom. Republicanism emphasises our social nature as what Aristotle called 'political animals' and concentrates on political involvement as equal citizens in governing ourselves. Communitarianism emphasises our nature as interdependent herd animals who live by copying each other. It emphasises the customs and traditions in which different communities are embedded.

Liberalism stresses tolerance and respect for individual freedom. Despite the efforts of many political philosophers, liberalism is a faith or set of beliefs which, like a religion, cannot objectively be proved or disproved. Liberalism is however the dominant belief system underpinning the UK constitution and is sometimes invoked by the courts. For example according to Lord Steyn in *Roberts* v *Parole Board* (2006) [93]: 'in our system the working assumption is that Parliament legislates for a European liberal democracy which respects fundamental rights'. In *Copsey* v *WBB Devon Clays Ltd* (2005) Neuberger LJ referred to 'enlightened capitalism and liberal democracy' in deciding that an employer could require an employee to work on a Sunday (Chapter 19).

It is difficult to identify concrete principles on which all liberals agree. However, the following might be the main broad principles of liberalism:

- Liberalism emphasises the interests of the individual rather than the collective interests of the community, the latter existing only to protect the interests of the individual.
- The interests of all individuals are worthy of equal concern and respect except those who harm others. This of course begs the question as to what counts as 'harm'.
- Individuals should be free to follow their own chosen way of life ('autonomy').
- The state should not favour one way of life over another. This is particularly problematic, since the state might have to choose between conflicting interests. Similarly, given that the state has to fund itself from taxation, unless it were to tax everyone equally it has to make choices as to whom to tax, thus encouraging or discouraging particular projects.

Liberalism seeks a constitution that free and equal people would rationally support. It recognises that there is likely to be irreducible disagreement even among people of goodwill and so favours caution about state intervention. It attempts to place constraints on government in the interests of individual freedom. It gives the individual an area of private life that is out of bounds for the state. In contemporary society where the activities of government penetrate many areas of everyday life, this distinction between the public and the private is controversial.

Liberalism is not wedded to any particular methods of controlling government. However many liberals place faith in independent courts of law thus linking liberalism with the 'rule of law' (Chapter 7). Some European states empower the courts or a specialised body to override legislation, for example Germany, Spain, Italy and France (Constitutional Council but only prior to enactment). The UK does not do so, preferring informal and political mechanisms. Liberalism also favours democracy, thus conflicting with its liking for courts. However in contrast to republicanism, liberalism is not especially interested in whether citizens directly participate in governmental decision making but accepts government by an elite accountable to citizens.

Liberalism is not universally admired, sometimes being condemned as selfish and uncaring. A modest defence of liberalism is that at least it tries to make room for other beliefs, recognising the 'lurking doubt' in all human affairs. Liberal societies have been relatively stable and peaceful. Even if there is some objective truth as to how to live, it has so far eluded the human race. Indeed the desire for peace was the historical origin of liberalism as a response to the religious conflicts that disrupted Europe during the sixteenth and seventeenth centuries. Once the bond supplied by a dominant religion had been dissolved, it became impossible to govern people of widely different beliefs without either conferring a large amount of individual freedom or resorting to oppression, which would ultimately destroy the community.

There is considerable variation among liberals as to the extent to which the state is entitled to interfere with individuals in pursuit of some public good. In seeking to answer this question, liberals often use the thought experiment of an imaginary agreement, a 'social contract' between free and equal people of goodwill, asking what level of interference could such people reasonably accept. An influential and characteristic modern version is that of John Rawls (1921–2000):

> Our exercise of political power is proper and hence justifiable only when it is exercised in accordance with a constitution the essentials of which all citizens may be reasonably expected to endorse in the light of principles and ideas acceptable to them as reasonable and rational. This is the liberal principle of legitimacy. (*Political Liberalism*, Columbia University Press, 1993, p. 217)

One problem with this is its reliance on the word 'reasonably' since we may disagree as to what is reasonable. Who decides what is 'reasonably expected' in a society made up of people with many different beliefs? Rawls proposed an 'original position' in which a representative group of people ignorant of their own circumstances, including sex, race or wealth, decide what would be a just constitution (*A Theory of Justice*, Oxford University Press, 1972). The purpose of this 'veil of ignorance' is to ensure equality and the removal of self interested influences. However it also reduces the parties to clones, thinking as one and therefore not making an agreement at all in any real sense. Rawls was of course aware of this and later introduced the notion of an 'overlapping consensus'. This is a settlement that people from a wide variety of backgrounds might be prepared to acknowledge as reasonable. However underlying all this is the liberal assumption that people want to agree and might be willing to compromise. It is by no means obvious that this is the case. Rawls acknowledges this, claiming that his arguments are political rather than philosophical and apply only in a community that is broadly sympathetic to liberal values ('Justice as Fairness: Political not Metaphysical', in *Collected Papers* (ed. Freeman), Harvard University Press, 1999).

Rawls' social contract comprises two fundamental 'principles of justice'. First that 'each person is to have an equal right to the most extensive basic liberty compatible with a similar liberty for others'. These liberties include political freedoms, freedom of speech, personal liberty, and the right to hold private property, matters dealt with in charters of rights such as the European Convention on Human Rights (Chapter 19). This has priority over the second principle, 'the difference principle', which is concerned with allocating the resources of society: 'Social and economic inequalities are to be arranged so that they are both (a) reasonably expected to be to everyone's advantage, and (b) attached to positions and offices open to all.' The difference principle involves wide questions of politics outside the scope of this book. However one implication seems to be that fundamental freedoms cannot be overridden in the interests of some other social goal. As we shall see (Chapter 19), this is not the case in the UK.

2.2 Varieties of Liberalism

There are many varieties of liberalism, each applying the basic ingredients of freedom and equality in different ways. The following classical writers exemplify particular points on the map.

2.2.1 Thomas Hobbes (1588–1679): The Impersonal State and Individualism

A fundamental change in political thinking emerged in the sixteenth century when the Church and the state became separated. The idea of the state as an impersonal organisation intended to serve everyone was revived from classical antiquity by republican thinkers such as Machiavelli. Hobbes was one of the earliest English exponents of this approach and, although not a liberal, generated ideas that are basic to liberalism.

Hobbes published his most influential work, *Leviathan*, in 1651 following a time of widespread political unrest when England was in the grip of religious turmoil and civil war between an authoritarian king and an equally authoritarian Parliament dominated by religious interests. He tried to explain the existence of the state without drawing upon religion. Hobbes doubted whether it was possible to discover objective truth about anything. He had a strongly individualistic approach and, in common with modern liberals, believed that human affairs involve endless disagreement and therefore that a constitution has solid foundations only in the minimum on which it is possible rationally to agree. According to Hobbes, this is the preservation of life and therefore a need for someone to settle disputes and keep order.

Hobbes did not believe that humans are inherently wicked but thought that we are self seeking and that our different ideas of good inevitably set us in conflict with each other: a war of 'all against all' so that without government we would destroy each other. According to Hobbes, outside the private sphere of family and personal relationships we are motivated by three impulses: competition, fear and the desire for power over others. We constantly strive to fulfil new desires in a neverending and ultimately doomed search for what he called 'felicity'. Hobbes therefore argued that any government is better than none.

Hobbes' most famous passage encapsulates both his basic principle and the beauty of his language:

> Hereby it is manifest, that during the time men live without a common Power to keep them all in awe, they are in that condition which is called Warre; and such a warre, as is of every man against every man . . . In such condition, there is no place for Industry: because the fruit thereof is uncertain; and consequently no Culture of the Earth, no Navigation, nor use of the commodities that may be imported by Sea; no commodious Building; no Instruments of moving and removing such things as require much force; no knowledge of the face of the Earth; no account of Time; no Arts; no Letters; no Society; and which is worst of all, continuall feare, and danger of violent death; And the life of man, solitary, poore, nasty, brutish and short. (*Leviathan*, p. 65)

Hobbes provided an early example of the 'social contract' device. This asserts that government depends on the consent of the governed which Hobbes thought to be the only rational possibility, hence his relevance to contemporary democratic ideas.

Hobbes believed that humans have certain 'natural' rights based on keeping promises, respect for individual freedom and equality: 'Do not that to another, which thou wouldest not have done to thyself' (1973, pp. 14, 15). However according to Hobbes, these are no more than the rational hopes or expectations of a human being and have no binding force unless the lawmaker chooses to protect them.

Hobbes' hypothetical contract is made between the people, who agree with each other to surrender their natural freedom to a sovereign, and the 'Leviathan', who makes and enforces the laws. The sovereign is not itself a party to the social contract that produces a 'covenant', a one sided promise, to obey. In order to minimise disagreement the sovereign must be a single unitary body, an 'artificial man'. This could be either a monarch or an assembly. Hobbes' sovereign has no special qualifications for ruling but is merely the representative of the community. The obligation of the sovereign derives from its gratitude to the people for the free gift of power.

Hobbes' government has two crucial features. Firstly, because of the uncertainty of human affairs, Leviathan must have unlimited power since otherwise there would be the very disagreement that the sovereign exists to resolve. Hobbes thought that by definition the sovereign can never act unjustly to a subject because the subject has agreed to accept every decision of the sovereign. Secondly the sovereign exists for a single purpose, that of preserving life and has no authority to act for any other purpose: 'When the realm is at peace Leviathan sleeps.' Thus the sovereign should act 'so that the giver shall have no just occasion to repent him of his gift' and 'all the duties of the rulers are contained in this one sentence, the safety of the people is the supreme law'. However Hobbes was clear that it is for the ruler alone to decide whether it needs to exercise its powers and provided no legal remedy against a ruler that exceeded its power.

Hobbes' ideas have an important influence on the modern constitution in that they identify recurring themes and claims. They include the following:

- Government depends on the consent of the people.
- A single sovereign source of absolute power to protect the people particularly in emergencies. This is among the most fundamental problems of constitutional law. Repressive or corrupt governments may use the Hobbesian argument in order to justify restricting individual freedom for example by claiming that there is a threat to security. The contemporary question, contrary to Hobbes, is whether there should be any individual rights that are sacrosanct.
- All citizens are equal. No one should have powers or rights or be subject to special obligations based on factors such as birth, custom, social status or religion.
- Freedom is the natural state of affairs as opposed to a gift bestowed by authority. It is true that the sovereign can make any law but unless it positively does so the individual is free to do what he or she likes: 'freedom lies in the silence of the laws' (*Entick* v *Carrington* (1765)). This is a primary sentiment behind the idea of the rule of law (Chapter 7). Conversely however, there cannot be any guaranteed rights without law.
- The separation of politics from religion, Church from state.
- The distinction between the public and the private sphere. In relation to areas of life not controlled by the state, namely those where public order and safety are not at risk, what I do is not the state's business.

Hobbes was not concerned with republican issues of participation in government. Nor did he tackle the problem of how to make government accountable. Nor did he deal with the problem that in all but the simplest societies, power must in practice be divided up and rulers must rely on advisers thereby creating potential disagreements. Hobbes recognised however that some methods of government might be better than others and in the later part of his work, *The Dialogues*, made many suggestions, such as that the sovereign should act through general laws and should consult Parliament. In a long running dispute with Coke, the Lord Chief Justice, Hobbes attacked the common law made by the judges, believing that laws should made by ordinary common sense. He rejected the view of the judges that law is 'artificial reason' that resides in the learning of an elite group (themselves) as a childish fiction (see Postema, *Bentham and the Common Law Tradition*, Clarendon Press, 1986, pp. 40–48).

2.2.2 John Locke (1632–1704): Individual Rights and Majority Government

Locke is widely regarded as a founder of modern liberalism. Locke's writings (*Second Treatise of Government*, 1690) supported the 1688 revolution, which founded our present constitution against the claims of absolute monarchy. His approach was grounded in the Protestant religion, which stressed individual conscience and self improvement by hard work. Locke believed that individuals had certain natural rights identified by reasoning about human nature and existing, as he saw it, to serve God. These are life, health, freedom and property. For him, the purpose of government is to protect these rights in the exceptional cases where conflicts arise. To this extent Locke's government serves the same function as that of Hobbes. However Locke's government has limited powers.

According to Locke, the people first hypothetically contract with each other unanimously to establish a government and then choose an actual government by majority vote. The government as such does not enter into a contract but takes on a trust, a one sided promise, whereby it undertakes to perform its functions of protecting natural rights and advancing wellbeing. Thus government has duties but no rights of its own, an idea applied by contemporary judges (see Laws J in *R v Somerset County Council ex parte Fewings* (1995)).

Locke's basic principles can be found in modern liberal constitutions. Firstly there is the idea (shared with Hobbes) that government depends on the consent of the people. According to Locke, government should be appointed and dismissed periodically by a majority vote representing those with a stake in the community. However a majority to Locke meant only non-Catholic property owners since he thought that only these have an incentive to loyalty to the community, the loyalty of Catholics being to the Pope. He justified majority voting on the basis that the majority commands most force but recognised that there is no logical reason why a majority should be 'right' in relation to any particular issue.

Secondly Locke was concerned to limit the power of government in order to protect the rights and freedoms of the individual. This is perhaps the most distinctive feature of liberalism, although liberals do not agree how this should be done, for example whether by courts or democratic mechanisms (Chapter 19). Locke himself did not favour detailed legal constraints on government, regarding the contribution of lawyers as 'the Phansies and intricate contrivances of men, following contrary and hidden interests put into words' (1960, para. 12). He relied on dividing up government power so that no one branch can be dominant: the separation of powers (Chapter 8). He also insisted that governments should periodically be held to account by means of elections and upheld as a last resort the right to rebel against a government that broke its trust.

Thirdly Locke promoted 'toleration' of different ways of life provided they did not upset the basic political framework. For example he did not favour toleration of Catholics whom he regarded as subversive. This apparent double standard is one of the alleged contradictions of liberalism.

2.2.3   David Hume (1711–76), Jeremy Bentham (1748–1832), John Stuart Mill (1806–73): Utilitarianism and Welfare Liberalism

Welfare liberalism favours democratic mechanisms rather than the courts. From this perspective, the law is one among several levers of government, others being persuasion and payment. The courts might be presented as in 'partnership' with government to secure good administration (see *R v Lancashire County Council ex parte Huddleston* [1986] 2 All ER 941, 945, and the 'ill tempered outburst' by former Home Secretary David Blunkett asserting that the courts' role was to help the government deliver its policies (2003, *Public Law* 397)).

The most influential version of welfare liberalism is utilitarianism. Utilitarianism is an example of an 'instrumental' moral perspective that evaluates conduct in terms of the results it produces. This of course begs the question of what counts as a good result. In the context of a constitution, this might be anything designated by the lawmaker. In the case of utilitarianism, it is the satisfaction of the preferences of as many people as possible. David Hume was a founder of utilitarianism. He thought that government is a matter of practical compromise. He rejected the social contract as a fiction and regarded ideals of abstract justice as myths useful for persuading people to conform. Hume advocated a pragmatic society based on coordinating individual interests. He believed that our limited knowledge, strength and altruism provided the moral basis for a legal system. He thought that self interest and our natural feelings for others would generate basic principles of cooperation, including respect for private property, voluntary dealings and keeping promises. Hume favoured the common law as a vehicle for this, which he described as a happy combination of circumstances, according to which the law is developed pragmatically in the light of changing social practices and values.

Jeremy Bentham is the most celebrated utilitarian. He gave intellectual respectability to the idea of an all-powerful central government making general laws and accountable to a majority of the people. Using the slogan 'the greatest happiness of the greatest number', Bentham measured utility by counting people's actual demands, giving each equal weight ('each counts for one and none for more than one') and refusing to treat any preference as better than any other: 'pushpin is as good as poetry'. Although utilitarianism could mean authoritarian government by experts, Bentham's version involves strong democratic controls to ensure that the law represents public opinion (see generally Craig, 'Bentham, Public Law and Democracy', 1989, *Public Law* 407). Bentham regarded law and courts as subordinate to utilitarian considerations. In particular he regarded legal certainty and judicial independence, what we call the 'rule of law', as a sham. He thought that the idea of natural rights was 'nonsense on stilts', claiming that rights were simply legal mechanisms, that law is merely a tool of government and public opinion is the ultimate authority.

Although as a crude instrument of policy utilitarianism is much favoured by officials, it is replete with problems particularly in relation to justice and fairness. For example utilitarianism is consistent with slavery in that the standard of living of a majority might be held to outweigh the loss of freedom of a minority. A utilitarian could reasonably think that innocent people could be shot in order to disperse a public meeting or kept in jail even if wrongly convicted in order to preserve public confidence in the police (see *McIlkenny v Chief Constable of the West Midlands Police* [1980] 2 All ER 227, 239–40 per Lord Denning). Utilitarianism also finds difficulty with the notion of rights and obligations. Why should I pay you what I have promised if I now discover a better use for the money, for example by giving it to a disaster fund? Can utilitarianism really give equal weight to all preferences without some non-utilitarian filter to exclude 'irrational' or 'immoral' preferences such as those of paedophiles? These and other problems have been widely discussed without a conclusion.

John Stuart Mill tried to reconcile utilitarianism with liberal individualism by claiming that maximising individual freedom is the best way to advance general welfare since it encourages the virtues of creativity. He believed that happiness could best be achieved by experimenting with different ways of life. This led to Mill's emphasis on freedom of expression and his influential 'harm' principle, namely that the only ground on which the state should interfere with freedom is to prevent harm to others. The state should not normally interfere paternalistically to protect a person for his or her own good. However this begs the question of what counts as 'harm' since harm can be defined as anything we dislike. For example does harm include 'offence' if someone makes fun of my religious beliefs (Chapter 20)?

Mill did not apply his harm principle to those who were unable fully to make rational judgments such as children, a principle that, uncomfortably, Mill seemed to extend to colonised peoples. Moreover distortions creep in. For example Mill was less egalitarian than Bentham, since for Mill preferences were not equal. Mill favoured the 'higher' and more intellectual and artistic capacities of the human mind. He was also a romantic, reminding us that ideas such as justice may not be purely rational, in the sense of being possible to pin down as legal rules, but have an emotional and spiritual dimension (see Ward, 'The Echo of a Sentimental Jurisprudence', 2002, *Law and Critique* 15:107).

Mill preferred political to legal mechanisms, in his case a strong system of checks and balances between different branches of government and a belief in democracy. However he was not a wholehearted democrat. His utilitarian strain led him to favour decision making by experts and he favoured slewing voting rights in favour of the wealthy and educated (below). Mill's utilitarianism also prevents him valuing individual freedom as an end in itself but only as subordinate to the general good. For example it would be consistent with Mill to suggest that it is better for a minority of elite students at Oxbridge to have creative freedom in order to rule the country at the expense of a majority of students trained at 'inferior' universities to perform menial tasks. Moreover, although Mill emphasised that the individual is the best judge of how he or she should live, some ways of life, notably those of the artist or intellectual, are objectively better than others and can be favoured by the state.

2.2.4   Robert Nozick (1938–2002): 'Libertarian' Liberalism

To different degrees liberal individualists treat respect for the equality and freedom of the individual as an end in itself. Thus individual freedom is not regarded as a component of the general welfare as with the utilitarians (above) but requires barriers between the individual and the state. Nozick provides an extreme example. Driven by the idea of minimising state power, Nozick relies on the notion of the natural rights of the individual, deriving these from a view of basic human nature similar to that of Locke (above) but without the religious element. Rather than inventing a social contract that he regards as redundant, Nozick works out what is the minimum amount of government needed to secure basic rights. He argues that rights of personal freedom and property are sacrosanct and the state should not use force against anyone without their consent (*Anarchy, State and Utopia*, Blackwell, 1974). Moreover the role of the state should be limited to providing services that could not be provided voluntarily by private persons. This leads to the minimum or 'nightwatchman' state, the function of which is limited to protecting individuals against force, theft and fraud and enforcing contracts. The state can raise money for these purposes but taxation particularly for redistributing from rich to poor can be equated with theft or forced labour (compare with Rawls above). Nozick therefore provides a model of a hypothetical minimum state that to some extent relates to contemporary ideas of privatisation.

2.2.5   Fredrich Hayek (1899–1992): Economic Liberalism

Closely related to individualism, economic or market liberalism is concerned with harnessing what it regards as the primary human impulse of self interest, in pursuit of the common good. It does so by encouraging competition between free individuals. According to market liberals, the state has neither the knowledge nor the competence to plan people's lives and efficient solutions are best found through free interchange in the market, the price mechanism acting as a store of knowledge of supply and demand. There is no necessary connection between market liberalism and a liberal belief in individual freedom in moral and social matters. A market liberal such as the former British Prime Minister Margaret Thatcher might claim to harness valuable human impulses in the economic sphere while suppressing what he or she regards as harmful human impulses elsewhere. Market liberalism is therefore akin to utilitarianism (above) in that it does not value freedom for its own sake but only as a means to an end, this being wealth maximisation. Moreover market freedom may conflict with personal freedom since the rich may exploit the poor.

Hayek seems to assume, contrary to Hobbes, that within a society which maximises individual freedom, shared understandings will emerge on which enough people agree for life to be harmonious, what he called the 'spontaneous order'. Hayek thought that central government planning was doomed to fail because officials were not capable of acquiring sufficient knowledge of the millions of people going about their individual business to make effective decisions. However he relied strongly on the notion of the rule of law as a framework of certain general rules within which we can be 'free' to plan our lives (Chapter 7). Hayek's approach favours the common law since decisions made by judges could be justified as a step-by-step pragmatic response to problems thrown up by individuals.

Liberals do not usually regard particular economic policies or public service provisions as constitutional matters but treat them as subjects of democratic choice. However, like the other liberalisms, market liberalism influences the underlying values of the constitution, in particular those of accountability and individual freedom. According to 'public choice' theory, public officials in common with other participators in the market are driven by self interest. Thus if left alone, they will try to maximise their incomes, expand their territories and minimise their workloads. There is therefore a tendency to inefficiency in public services. Market liberalism attempts to harness self interest by creating competition in the provision of public services. For example social housing is sometimes allocated on the basis of 'choice based lettings' whereby applicants bid for housing using 'currency' such as housing need, time spent on the waiting list and so on, as determined by officials. Where goods and services cannot actually be competed for, mechanisms are created to simulate competitive price mechanisms, for example by setting targets and standards with accompanying rewards and penalties. Examples are the contemporary practices of privatisation and the splitting up of many civil service operations into semi-autonomous 'executive agencies' run on the model of private business. In terms of accountability, market liberalism favours legal rather than political regulation, hence the creation in recent years of statutory independent regulators for public utilities.

2.2.6   Isaiah Berlin (1907–97): Positive and Negative Freedom

Berlin, a prominent liberal philosopher and historian of ideas, whose family came to Britain as refugees from the Russian Revolution, was concerned to protect liberalism against attempts by those in power to subvert the notion of freedom. The idea of individual freedom is central to liberalism but has different, vague and sometimes conflicting meanings. Some regard freedom as an end in itself: 'he who desires in liberty anything other than itself is born to be a servant' (De Tocqueville, *L'Ancien Regime*, 1856). However it is difficult to regard freedom as an end in itself, let alone the highest end. Do we for example regard Hitler's freedom to pursue his interests as something good in itself, although offset by the harm he did? Moreover freedom may conflict with 'equality' since the strong are free to exploit the weak.

Negative freedom is what most of us understand by freedom: 'By Liberty, is understood . . . the absence of external impediments' (Hobbes, 1973, Chapter 14, para. 1). For our purposes it is narrowly defined to mean that a person is free only if he is not subject to control by others claiming to act under some sort of authority. Thus laws restrict negative freedom although this may be to preserve the freedom of others thus distributing freedom among different people according to the lawmaker's preference, for example by applying Mill's 'harm' principle (above). The wider sense in which we sometimes use the term freedom as meaning the absence of any physical impediment such as 'you are blocking my freedom to use the road' is not relevant here.

A fundamental problem with negative freedom is that some freedoms are obviously more important than others. For example freedom to practice a religion is more important to many people, but not necessarily to everyone, than freedom to smoke. Thus the relative importance of competing freedoms may be controversial such as freedom of the press against privacy. There seems to be no common measure or litmus test to enable us to rank or compare different freedoms although there may be situations where one of them is infringed in a trivial way to prevent a serious infringement of the other, such as a magazine taking pictures of a celebrity in a private situation (*Campbell* v *MGN Ltd* (2004)). The competing notion of positive freedom is therefore attractive to many people.

Positive freedom, a more ancient and wider idea, is freedom not to do what we want as such, but to do what is good for us by exercising the power of reason to make choices that enhance the possibilities of our lives, 'liberating' our higher nature from our animal instincts and allowing us to control our own destinies (autonomy). Thus Plato (*c.* 428–*c.* 348 BC) insisted:

> you are not free when you are slave to your desires. Freedom is mastery by the rational self, mastery by knowledge of what is really good. (Gorman, *Rights and Reason*, Acumen, 2003, p. 33)

The two freedoms sometimes support each other since negative freedom enables us to exercise choices. However positive freedom is in one sense wider since it includes restrictions on freedom caused not just by interference from others but also by social and economic conditions such as poverty or a bad environment. It requires the distribution of resources such as education, wealth and health care to enable people to make genuine choices and so take control of their lives. Thus positive freedom requires the use of public resources which are limited and so must be rationed out according to the state's preferences. In another sense positive freedom is narrower in that it concentrates only on freedom to do good things.

Attitudes of negative and positive freedom towards law therefore differ. Negative freedom regards law as a restriction and concentrates on limiting state power thus reflecting the red light perspective mentioned in Chapter 1. Positive freedom (green light) is open to greater government control since it is consistent with the state designating what are valuable choices. Thus it could well be positive freedom in the minds of judges when they are required to decide which of two rights should prevail or whether some other public interest should outweigh the freedom of the individual (Part IV). In this sense positive freedom allows us to claim paradoxically that obeying the law is 'freedom' in that law gives us a degree of rational choice by providing stability, which enables us to plan our lives (Chapter 7).

Positive freedom also links with republican ideas of democracy (below) since we control our own lives if we participate in collective decision making, what Constant (1767–1830) called 'the freedom of the ancients'. Thus positive freedom might favour compulsory voting. Rousseau (1712–1778) for example famously wrote that we should be 'forced' to be free, meaning that true freedom lies in collective participation by voting in public affairs. He assumed that each person would vote rationally in accordance with the public interest (the 'general will' rather than his or her selfish interests, the will of all) and that the minority who disagree with the outcome must therefore be 'wrong'. (See Rousseau, *The Social Contract*, Book Two).

The distinction between positive and negative freedom sometimes underlies disagreements in the courts. For example in *Tomlinson* v *Congleton District Council* (2003), the claimant had, despite warning notices, jumped into a pool owned by a local authority and broken his neck. The question was whether a local authority was obliged to do more to protect against this risk. Lord Hoffmann remarked from the negative freedom perspective that our liberal individualistic system meant that the nanny state should not be encouraged and given that there was a clear warning notice the claimant should be responsible for his own safety. By contrast Sedley LJ in the Court of Appeal had taken the view, characteristic of positive freedom, that the local authority should have taken precautions to guard people against their own irrationality.

According to Isaiah Berlin, positive freedom has a sinister aspect. Human affairs are prone to disagreement and there are different ideas of what is rational. Who decides what is rational? Berlin was concerned that positive freedom might justify the state claiming that a particular way of life, for example one based on a religious cult, an economic theory or on belonging to the European Union, is 'rationally' better than others and is therefore what the people would 'really' want if they could think properly, just as we say that someone who is drunk is not 'himself'. This justifies coercion in a person's 'own interests':

> Once I take this view I am in a position to ignore the actual wishes of men or societies, to bully, oppress, torture them in the name, and on behalf, of their real selves, in the secure knowledge that whatever is the true goal of man (happiness, performance of duty, wisdom, a just society, self-fulfillment) must be identical with his freedom – the free choice of his 'true', albeit often submerged and inarticulate self. (Berlin, 2002, p. 180).

For example a person detained in a hospital for 'his own good' could be claimed to be not 'detained' at all but freely submitting. Indeed in *HM* v *Switzerland* (2002) the European Court of Human Rights held that placing a child in a foster home was not a 'deprivation of liberty' since it was a responsible measure in the child's own interests. Berlin therefore insists that freedom means negative freedom, the right to do what we like however irrational, and that other values must be distinguished from freedom. 'Liberty is liberty, not equality or fairness or justice or human happiness or a quiet conscience' (ibid.). Berlin of course recognises that the state might sometimes have good reason for interfering with freedom. For example in *HM* v *Switzerland* (above) Berlin's analysis would probably be that there was a deprivation of liberty but perhaps outweighed by a greater good. His point is that by lumping together freedom and other goods we are disguising hard choices and encouraging tyranny. Thus Berlin is concerned that decision makers openly confront difficult choices.

2.2.7   Liberal Pluralism: Group Liberalism

Liberal pluralism, sometimes called 'identity politics' or 'the politics of recognition', requires the state to respect the identities and way of life of different groups such as national, religious, ethnic or sexual minorities as well as political associations, trade unions, vocational groups and the like. At this point liberalism overlaps with communitarianism (above). The groups protected by pluralism might be disadvantaged because of the stereotype of the 'normal' person represented by the ruling group, in our case the white, able bodied, heterosexual, culturally Christian male. Liberal pluralism requires active steps to ensure that all such groups have the leverage to participate fully in the life of the community and to express their own identity against that of the dominant group, for example by being represented in public institutions, using their own language and giving effect to their own law and courts, as in the case of Islamic and Jewish law. It is not enough merely to tolerate or attempt to integrate such groups into the mainstream as is the dominant approach of UK law since this implies only limited acceptance.

Liberal pluralism might conflict with other kinds of liberalism particularly where the values of the group conflict with more individualistic values, for example a religious sect might claim that corporal punishment is part of its religion (see *R (Williamson)* v *Secretary of State for Education and Employment* (2005); Chapter 20). A group might also claim that its way of life should be supported by the state, for example religious schools, or should have special treatment to compensate for past injustices. Most fundamental is the problem of a group whose values are authoritarian: the famous liberal dilemma of 'tolerating intolerance'. Thus according to Lord Walker in *Williamson* [60], 'in matters of human rights the courts should not show liberal tolerance only to tolerant liberals'. For example a common liberal claim is that liberalism contains universal truths derived from reason, so that for example a liberal law should not permit a religious group to prevent its members leaving it (European Convention on Human Rights, Article 9). However such freedom might be unacceptable to a religion which teaches that compulsion is in a person's best interests. Some liberals suggest the proper approach is that the members of any group must accept that the state, in order to protect itself, can override their interests provided the decision process used is fair to all interests. However there may not be agreement as to what fairness means (see Raz, 'Multiculturalism', 1998, *Ratio Juris* 11(3): 193).

In terms of constitutional arrangements, we would expect liberal pluralists to emphasise open and dispersed government, local government and the equal representation of minority groups in public institutions such as the judiciary. The different devolved arrangements in Scotland, Northern Ireland and Wales (Chapter 6) could be presented as embodying this. It is often suggested that one part of the legislature, the House of Lords, might comprise representatives of important interest groups. At present the only such groups represented in Parliament are Church of England bishops (Chapter 11). Liberal pluralism would also favour voluntary mechanisms to enable individuals to participate in society, for example tax breaks for charities and other voluntary bodies ('civil society').

2.3 Republicanism

Originating in ancient Greece, revived in the Renaissance and developed in the seventeenth and eighteenth centuries (Machiavelli, 1469–1527; Harrington, 1611–77; Montesquieu, 1689–1755), republicanism builds on the idea of positive freedom. Its key concepts are limited and balanced government under law and political equality. Republican ideas were widely canvassed during the revolutionary period of the seventeenth century but have not significantly influenced the structure of the UK constitution. However there has been a recent revival of interest in republican ideas stimulated by evidence of widespread apathy among voters and disenchantment with political processes remote from popular experience (see for example Bellamy, 2007; Tomkins, 2005). Thus while liberalism separates the state from the community, drawing a line around state powers, republicanism incorporates the community into the state (red and green light perspectives, Chapter 1).

Republicanism relates to modern democratic ideas but is much wider. It stresses firstly that the state exists for the benefit of all members of the community as free and equal citizens. Thus rulers have no rights of their own (other than as citizens) but only duties to the community. Secondly republicanism is concerned to ensure that no single person or group within the community can dominate others. This applies to private vested interests and democratic majorities, as much as to government bodies. Apart from concern with a separation of powers between different branches of government (Chapter 8) and with protecting basic freedoms, republicanism involves such questions as whether individuals should be able to buy access to political offices or influence.

Thirdly, and this is perhaps where the UK's informal constitution is particularly vulnerable, republicanism stresses that it is not enough that rulers in fact rule wisely and benevolently, affording citizens considerable freedom and not abusing their power. According to republicanism, in the interests of dignity, equality and freedom, all limits on the rulers must be secured by law so that the ruler cannot abuse his or her power. Anything less relies only on hoping that the slavemaster will be kind. For example Parliament, the UK lawmaker, sometimes enacts laws of draconian severity with little discussion, relying on assurances from the government that in practice the laws will be applied only in special and limited circumstances (such as anti-terrorism legislation; see Chapter 22).

Republicans differ as to the best form of constitution to achieve the goal of free and democratic citizenship. Drawing on classical virtues, some advocate direct citizen participation in government along the lines supposed by Rousseau (above). Others regard this as unrealistic in a complex society that depends on specialists and prefer a version of the representative system that applies in the UK today but with important reforms designed to ensure that Parliament the elected lawmaker is not dominated by the executive (see Bellamy, 2007).

2.4 Equality

Liberalism and republicanism presuppose that all people are equal. However 'equality' has no clear meaning. Equality is merely a measure, the real question being 'equality of what?' We distinguish broadly between 'formal' equality and 'substantive' equality. Formal equality relates to the rule of law. It requires that everyone's rights be treated the same in terms of the application of the law, for example the right to a fair trial. It does not mean that the contents of the rights are the same. That is a matter of substantive equality. For example a landlord has greater rights over a house than a tenant. Unless we adopt the difficult position that everyone should be treated identically (which conflicts with freedom), *substantive* equality means only that we should not treat people differently without a good reason. Thus John Stuart Mill, widely regarded as a founder of British liberalism, said that:

> all persons are deemed to have a right to equality of treatment except when some recognised social expediency requires otherwise. (1972, Chapter 5)

We may disagree about what counts as a good reason. This creates further conflicting concepts of equality. For example while there is widespread consensus that we should not discriminate on grounds of personal characteristics such as race or gender, it is controversial whether there should be equality in respect of the distribution of wealth or public services (equality of outcome). Should resource allocation be based on need (equality of opportunity) or on merit (equality of desert)? This raises political questions largely outside the scope of the law. Nevertheless equality is of primary importance in combating governmental action that arbitrarily targets certain groups.

For example in *A v Secretary of State for the Home Department* (2005) legislation authorised the government to imprison without trial foreign terrorist suspects unless they voluntarily left the country. The rationale was that the terrorist threat was an emergency and the action was necessary to protect the public since under the European Convention on Human Rights (ECHR) it would have been unlawful to deport the people concerned who would face torture in their home countries. Nine Law Lords heard the case and by a majority of eight decided that the detention was contrary to the human rights of those concerned. An underlying theme was that of equality. By targeting foreign terrorist suspects in this way, the government had not addressed the equal threat posed by British terrorists. Conversely its measures included people who were not necessarily a threat to the UK.

Equality and freedom are often said to conflict since freedom must sometimes be restricted in order to produce equality. It has also been suggested, notably by De Toqueville (below), that equal voting rights lead to mob rule. However this very much depends on what kind of freedom and what kind of equality we are speaking of. Some kinds of freedom such as market freedom reject the value of equality of outcome but are consistent with equality of desert or of opportunity. Negative freedom is more likely to be consistent with equality of opportunity than positive freedom but not with equality of outcome. In the case of positive freedom the law makes a judgement as to whether a given freedom or a given type of equality is more or less rational and desirable. The interests concerned are compared even though there is no known common measure between them. For example should all children be compelled to have medical treatment even where this violates some ideas of religious freedom?

2.5   Democracy

Liberalism and republicanism share ideals of democracy in a general sense but there are different versions of democracy. Democracy has been defined as:

the people of a country deciding for themselves the contents of the laws that organise and regulate their political association. (Michaelman, 1998, *Californian Law Review* 86:399–400)

According to this definition there is unlikely to be much democracy in the world and yet most states label themselves democracies. Michaelman's aspiration is the republican one of citizen self government by active participation, sometimes called 'deliberative democracy'. This might be practicable in a village where everyone knows each other, but it is unrealistic in contemporary nation states comprising millions of strangers with conflicting goals and interests and where the complexity of society requires decisions to be made by experts.

In the UK's liberal culture, democracy means government with the 'consent' of the people, a more slippery notion. The people cannot consent to anything until there are rules determining who counts as 'the people' and how they express their wishes. For example different voting formulae fixed by those currently in power produce very different outcomes (Chapter 12).

From the earliest times democracy has meant decisions made by a majority. The proposed European Constitution, quoting Thucydides (*c.* 460–400 BC), claims that:

> our constitution is called a democracy because power is in the hands not of a minority but of the greatest number.

The justification for majoritarianism is not that a majority is likely to be 'right' since this is clearly untrue, but that majority voting is fair since it treats everyone equally. However majoritarianism has well known problems. Firstly unless there is a simple choice between only two options, the mathematics of majority voting will not necessarily produce a majority preference. Secondly a majority may oppress unpopular minorities or introduce repressive laws as a panic response to an emergency or become the passive tool of a selfish ruling group. Thus John Adams, one of the founders of the US Constitution, feared 'elective despotism', and De Tocqueville (1805–59), commenting on the newly formed US Constitution, referring to the 'tyranny of the majority', said:

> I am trying to imagine under what novel features despotism may appear in the world. In the first place, I see an innumerable multitude of men, alike and equal, constantly circling around in pursuit of the petty and banal pleasures with which they glut their souls . . . Over this kind of men stands an immense, protective power which is alone responsible for securing their enjoyment and watching over their fate. (*Democracy in America* (trans. Lawrence), Fontana, 1968, Vol. 2, p. 898)

There is therefore a tension between constitutionalism, the rule of law and individual freedom on the one hand, and democracy on the other. This underlies important issues in constitutional law, in particular whether the courts should be empowered to overturn Acts of Parliament on human rights grounds. Liberals are ambivalent about this. On the one hand judges could be regarded as undemocratic. On the other hand liberalism is not tied to democracy. A standard argument in this context is that there are certain fundamental requirements of democracy such as freedom of expression that should be protected by independent courts in case a democratic majority is seduced or panicked into overriding them. A republican answer is that it is those who are affected by the laws in question who should have an equal say in deciding what those laws should be, it being offensive to human dignity not to trust a democratic body (see Waldron, *Law and Disagreement*, Oxford University Press, 1999 and Bellamy, 2007).

Representative Democracy

The characteristic form of modern democracy is 'representative democracy'. The ideal of representative democracy is that of government which the people can choose, call to account and remove. The people choose representatives directly who appoint others to assist them within a clear chain of responsibility. The representatives must explain their actions to the people and must regularly submit themselves for re-election. A famous early statement is that of Chief Justice Sir John Fortescue (*On the Governance of the Kingdom of England*, 1537), who distinguished between *dominium regale*, the rule of the king alone, necessary in certain cases for example to deal with an emergency, and *dominium politicum et regale*, the rule of the king with the assent of representatives of the community after discussion collectively in Parliament. More recently, in *R (Alconbury Developments) v Secretary of State for the Environment, Transport and the Regions* [2001] 2 All ER 929 at 980, Lord Hoffmann informed us that in the UK:

> decisions as to what the general interest requires are made by democratically elected bodies or by persons accountable to them.

Representative democracy favours the more individualistic versions of liberalism since the citizen's only power is to vote as a private solitary act without any requirement for discussion. Representative democracy relies upon a passive population, provided that enough people vote to give those chosen some legitimacy. Republicans and communitarians who favour the active participation of citizens are less comfortable with representative democracy. Mill favoured a greater level of democracy at local level, not because it produced efficient government but in order to develop the abilities of local people to develop themselves by participating in public life. This does not apply to the contemporary UK constitution where local government is substantially constrained by central government so that local elected politicians have little significant power.

Typically the people choose a lawmaking assembly as the highest branch of government. In a presidential system the people also vote for the head of state (below). Bentham and his utilitarian followers recommended that even judges be removable by the people since the people are the final court but this is not the case in the UK. Mill especially favoured representative democracy since it combines popular consent with a utilitarian reliance on experts. However like many contemporary public officials, Mill distrusted 'the people'. He recommended slewing the voting system so that the highly educated had greater voting power. He also suggested that Parliament should include a quota of people with a 'national reputation' and that people on welfare benefits should be disqualified from voting on the ground they might be biased. Fear of democracy remains a significant theme of the constitutional debate in the UK. For example proposals to reform the House of Lords which is currently wholly appointed have foundered largely because of resistance to the idea of a wholly elected legislature (Chapter 12).

The term 'representative' is ambiguous. A representative assembly could be a 'portrait' or microcosm of those it represents, for example being representative in terms of the political balance of opinion or ethnic and racial groupings. Alternatively it could be an *agent* of the people, not having any specified composition but made up of people chosen for their personal qualities or party membership. The practical significance of this concerns different types of voting system designed to produce different outcomes

(Chapter 12). The UK Parliament operates the agency model but the devolved regimes in Scotland, Wales and Northern Ireland combine both models.

Another basic issue is whether representatives in either model are bound by the views of those who voted for them or should vote according to their own consciences. The UK constitution has traditionally taken the attitude that representatives must not be bound by any outside commitments. For example elected local authorities must not bind themselves in law to carry out any political mandate on which they are elected (see for example *Bromley LBC* v *GLC* (1983)). However within Parliament the Whip system encourages MPs to vote blindly for their party. Proceedings in Parliament cannot be challenged in the courts.

Representative democracy provides mechanisms for ensuring that the government is accountable to the electorate. Accountability is an ambiguous idea but basically means that decisions must be explained and justified. The main accountability devices required by representative democracies are as follows:

- Right to question the executive (Chapters 13, 15)
- Policing financial limits on government spending (Chapter 13)
- Internal control mechanisms within government (Chapter 15)
- Judicial review (Chapters 16, 17, 18)
- Public consultation and access to information (Chapters 21, 22).

Each of these depends on a separation of powers between different functions of government (Chapter 8) and on safeguarding basic freedoms, including the freedom to form political parties and freedom of the press to criticise government. The European Court and the UK courts have stressed the special importance of political freedom of speech in connection with the democratic process (for example *Culnane* v *Morris* (2006); *Bowman* v *UK* (1998); *State of Mauritius* v *Khoyratty* (2006)).

2.5.2   Participatory Democracy

Sometimes called 'deliberative democracy', participatory democracy promotes direct participation by individuals and groups in decisions which affect them. Its supporters claim that it can harness 'reason' from a wide range of perspectives. However participants are voiceless without rules and leaders who stage manage their involvement. Such rules may privilege some groups over others, notably the more articulate and those who benefit the rule makers. It is not clear how deliberative democracy can be organised. Notions such as town meetings have been proposed although it is unclear what matters might be appropriate to their remit. Recognising that in a complex society full participation might be impracticable, many have argued (such as Hannah Ahrendt, 1906–75, from a republican perspective) that participation should apply to the smaller units that contribute to the political system such as local government, charities and the workplace (civil society). Habermas suggests a form of deliberative democracy that he regards as appropriate to contemporary circumstances in which the state is merely one among numerous community organisations, each comprising activists 'deliberating' on equal terms. The role of the law is to coordinate these units and to ensure that the discussions are open, fair and equal ('Three Normative Models of Democracy' in *The Inclusion of the Other*, MIT Press, 1996). Liberals, notably Mill, have objected that deliberative democracy is likely to attract busybodies, the self promoting, the corrupt, the ignorant and cranks. However representative democracy is not immune from these.

UK law provides for participation only in a limited and piecemeal way. The devolved regimes of Wales and Northern Ireland contain substantial provision for public involvement. At UK level there is provision for referendums (Political Parties, Elections and Referendums Act 2000). However these are rarely held and are triggered by the government. Referendums were held in 1976 concerning continued membership of what is now the European Union, in 1997 concerning devolution and in 2004 concerning a proposal for a regional assembly in the northeast of England. There are statutory public inquiries into many decisions relating to land development but the outcome is not normally binding on the government. In recent years the courts seem to have adopted a more sympathetic approach to direct participation (compare *Berkeley* v *Secretary of State for the Environment* (2000) with *Bushell* v *Secretary of State for the Environment* (1981)). Participatory democracy shares with representative democracy a concern with freedom of expression, particularly freedom of the press and with public access to information. Thus Lord Bingham pointed out in *McCartan Turkington-Breen* v *Times Newspapers* [2000] 4 All ER 913, 922 that a 'free, active, professional and enquiring press' was all the more important to support a participatory democracy since the majority of people can participate only indirectly.

The jury systems of the UK and the US are sometimes promoted as examples of deliberative democracy, where a randomly chosen panel of citizens deliberates as to the guilt or innocence of those accused of serious offences (Juries Act 1974). This seems a little fanciful since a jury is faced with a predetermined question defined by law and within the rigid institutional framework of the courtroom. There is also some participation in the provision for 'parish meetings' at local government level in small rural villages. However these have little power other than in relation to local amenities such as playgrounds.

2.5.3   Market Democracy: Political Parties

In practice democratic constitutions are dominated by political parties. Political parties publicise and coordinate different opinions and, as Burke somewhat idealistically asserted, make it possible to achieve by discussion a notion of the common good (*On the Present Discontents*, 1770, II). Without them an elected assembly would be a rabble. However when Burke was writing, MPs were usually of independent means as opposed to the paid functionaries of the present day, and party structures were relatively loose. A modern political party can usually exclude independently minded people as candidates for election and ensure that MPs vote in accordance with the party line.

Liberalism regards political parties as self governing voluntary bodies even though they are central to government. In the interests of freedom therefore there is resistance to legal controls over political parties, for example in respect of how they raise funds. On the other hand fair elections require certain controls – a tension characteristic of liberal democracy. For example in the US case of *Buckley* v *Valeo* (1976), restrictions on expenses for election advertising designed to ensure equal competition were held to violate the right to freedom of expression. A different view has been taken in the UK (Chapter 12).

'Market democracy', which is related to market liberalism (above), recognises the role of parties and argues that in contemporary circumstances elections provide only a limited choice. According to Weber (1864–1920) and Schumpeter (1883–1950), the voter's only power is to choose between products offered by competing party leaders who present themselves for election every few years. The vote provides the price mechanism. Market democracy has significant implications for the constitution. No longer is the state the neutral umpire of Hobbes and Locke but is a player in the game offering inducements for votes. In particular there is the danger that political parties will be captured by the vested interests of those who fund them. However supporters of market democracy argue that competition will ensure that one party is unlikely to stay in control permanently, provided that the electoral system properly reflects the range of opinion – a matter which is questionable in the UK (Chapter 12).

It could be argued that contemporary society is too fragmented and diverse to fit into the mould of large scale contesting parties and is represented more accurately by single issue or special interest pressure groups. Modern governments may therefore be chosen not on the basis of broad ideological or class differences but on the basis of the managerial competences of the individuals standing for election. Moreover market democracy encourages government polices to be expressed in terms of outcomes, targets and 'value for money' rather than in terms of 'process' values of fairness and justice. The emphasis on outputs also blurs the divide between the public and private sectors since the means by which outputs are delivered ceases to matter.

2.5.4   Parliamentary and Presidential Systems

Within representative democracy the main distinction is between 'parliamentary' and 'presidential' forms of government. The influential nineteenth century commentator Walter Bagehot remarked:

> The practical choice of first rate nations is between the Presidential government and the Parliamentary: no state can be first rate that has not had a government by discussion, and those are the only two existing species of that government. (1902, Introduction)

In a parliamentary system such as that of the UK and many western European countries (although some countries such as France have a mixture of the two), the people choose representatives who form the legislature, Parliament. The head of government is the Prime Minister (the Chancellor in Austria and Germany) chosen by the Parliament. The Prime Minister chooses and removes ministers who comprise the executive government. Sometimes, as in the UK, these must also be members of the legislature. Parliament scrutinises government activities, consents to laws and provides the government with finance. It can ultimately dismiss the executive by withdrawing its support. Parliamentary government therefore looks strong and accountable. However in practice the executive is likely to be dominant if only because of the human tendency to defer to leaders.

In a parliamentary system there is usually a separate head of state who formally represents the state and is the source of its authority but has little political power except perhaps as a safety mechanism in the event of a serious political breakdown. In some states including the UK the head of state is a hereditary monarchy and thus relatively independent of political pressures. In republican states the head of state is elected either by Parliament or by the people.

In a presidential system such as that of the US the leader of the executive, the President, is elected independently of the legislature and holds office for a fixed period, subject in some countries to dismissal by the legislature. Members of the executive need not and sometimes cannot be members of the legislature. The President is usually also the head of state. Presidential government gives the voter a greater choice. On the other hand, accountability might be confused and when the legislature and President represent different political parties, government might be weak.

The device of a separate head of state has the advantages of separating the authority of the state, in the head of state, from its functional powers. In a parliamentary system the Prime Minister and other members of the executive are merely government employees who cannot identify themselves with the state as such and so claim reflected glory and immunity from criticism. The head of state has a symbolic role and also ensures continuity in the constitution. If the governmental system were to collapse, for example if no leader emerged from the political process, it would be the responsibility of the head of state to ensure that government continued. Conversely apart from this exceptional situation the Queen has little personal political power (Chapter 14), so that any respect due to her as representing the state does not carry the risk of tyranny.

Summary

- ▷ Having read this chapter you should have some general ideas and perspectives which you can use to assess the UK constitution.

- ▷ Constitutions are underpinned by an assortment of sometimes conflicting political values. Of these liberalism has strong contemporary influence. Liberalism separates the individual from the state and emphasises limitations on state power in the interests of individual freedom. Liberalism overlaps with republicanism, however the latter stresses equal participation as citizens and emphasises duties rather than individual rights. Both favour limited government.

- ▷ Liberalism also treats individuals as equal, the two ideas being capable of conflicting. Formal equality relating to fair procedures is a prime concern of the law. Substantive equality relating to the distribution of resources is primarily a matter of pre-legal political choices.

- ▷ A review of significant writers who have influenced liberal ideas reveals different and sometimes conflicting forms of liberalism, depending on the importance and meaning given to individual freedom as opposed to the general public interest. These include liberal individualism, market liberalism, welfare liberalism and liberal pluralism.

- ▷ The distinction between positive and negative freedom illustrates the kinds of disagreements that arise within liberalism. Positive freedom emphasises our ability to choose reason to exercise choice and links with republican ideas of citizen participation in government. It may also lead to authoritarian attempts to impose rational solutions. Negative freedom is the freedom to be left alone. It may be seen as impractical and selfish.

- ▷ Republicanism can be contrasted with liberalism. Republicanism does not separate the individual from the state but favours the notion of the virtuous, politically active citizen. It is associated with positive freedom and treats freedom as the right to participate in government. It also stresses limited government.

- ▷ There are different kinds of democracy including deliberative/participatory democracy, representative democracy and market democracy.

- ▷ There are differences between a parliamentary and a presidential democracy. The former concentrates legal power in the legislature and usually involves a separate head of state with limited power. However in practice the executive may come to dominate the legislature. The latter divides power between the executive and the legislature as equals but the President is both head of the executive and head of state.

Summary cont'd

▶ Democracy may conflict with ideas of constitutionalism and the rule of law. However the courts give particular importance to freedom of speech and of the press in the context of democratic processes.

Exercises

2.1 What would be the main principles of a constitution devised by (a) Hobbes and (b) Locke?

2.2 What are the main principles of a republican form of constitution?

2.3 Sedley (London Review of Books, 15 November 2001) describes a case where a French court upheld a ban on local funfairs where revellers had been permitted to shoot a dwarf from a cannon. The decision was made in the name of public morals and human dignity even though the dwarfs made their living from the spectacle and were among the chief opponents of the ban. Discuss in relation to the views of Nozick, Mill and Bentham.

2.4 Discuss from the perspective of different forms of liberalism the following legislative proposals:
(i) A ban on anyone having more than two children.
(ii) A ban on the NHS providing fertility treatment.
(iii) Provision for a free market in unwanted babies.
(iv) A ban on corporal punishment in schools.

2.5 'A democratic constitution is in the end undemocratic if it gives all power to its elected government' (Sir John Laws, 'Law and Democracy', 1995, *Public Law* 73). Explain and discuss. What would be the main elements of a democratic constitution?

2.6 Compare the merits of the parliamentary and presidential systems of government.

Further reading

Bellamy, R. (2007) *Political Constitutionalism*, Cambridge University Press, Chapters 1,3,4,5,6.

Berlin, I. (2002) 'Two Concepts of Liberty', in Hardy, H. (ed.), *Liberty*, Oxford University Press.

Hayek, F. (1991) 'Freedom and Coercion', in Miller, D. (ed.), *Liberty*, Oxford University Press.

Hickman, T. (2005) 'In Defence of the Legal Constitution', *University of Toronto Law Journal* 55:981

Kymlicka, W. (2002) 'Citizenship Theory', in *Contemporary Political Philosophy* (2nd edn), Oxford University Press.

Laws, J. (1996) 'The Constitution: Morals and Right', *Public Law* 622.

Loughlin, M. (2006) 'Towards a Republican Revival', *Oxford Journal of Legal Studies* 26:425.

Morison, J. (2004) 'Models of Democracy: from Representation to Participation', in Jowell, J. and Oliver, D. (eds) *The Changing Constitution* (5th edn), Oxford University Press.

Pettit, P. (1997) *Republicanism: A Theory of Freedom and Government*, Oxford University Press, Chapters 1–3, 5, 6.

Skinner, Q. (1991) 'The Paradoxes of Political Liberty', in Miller, D. (ed.), *Liberty*, Oxford University Press.

Tomkins, A. (2005) *Our Republican Constitution*, Oxford, Hart.

Further reading cont'd

Tully, J. (2002) 'The Unfreedom of the Moderns', *Modern Law Review* 65:204.

Turpin, C. (2002) *British Government and the Constitution* (5th edn), London, Butterworths, Chapters 19–23.

Wolheim, R. (1969) 'A Paradox in the Theory of Democracy', in Laslett, P. and Runciman, W. (eds) *Philosophy, Politics and Society*, second series, Oxford, Blackwell.

Background reading

Crick, B. (2002) *Democracy: a Very Short Introduction*, Oxford University Press.

Mulgan, G. (2006) *Good and Bad Power: The Ideals and Betrayals of Government*, London, Allen Lane.

Chapter 3

The sources of the constitution

The historian can tell you probably perfectly clearly what the constitutional practice was at any given period in the past, but it would be very difficult for a living writer to tell you at any given period in his lifetime what the constitution of this country is in all respects. (Stanley Baldwin, Prime Minister, 1923–29, 1935–37)

Key words

- Authority and reason
- Convention
- Practices
- Insider self interest
- Law and politics
- Custom
- Codification – two kinds
- Enforcement
- Constitutional 'silences'

3.1 Introduction

As we saw in Chapter 1 the UK is unique among the major nations in not having a written constitution. The UK's unwritten constitution is constructed partly out of the general sources of law. These include Acts of Parliament, the common law in the form of decisions of the higher courts and the 'laws and customs of Parliament' made by each House in order to control its affairs. The conventional view is that as an expression of democracy, statute law is the highest form of law in our constitution. We also saw that the constitution relies heavily upon unwritten rules, practices and traditions the most important of which are known as 'constitutional conventions'. These conventions create what are perhaps the central political tensions in our constitution, namely the concentration of power in the executive and the responsibility of Parliament both to keep the government functioning and to hold the executive to account.

There are also 'practices' which are of constitutional significance even though they are not in any sense binding. The most obvious of these is the existence of political parties through which contenders for power organise themselves. There is no legal or conventional requirement that there be political parties and strictly speaking a political party is a private voluntary organisation, albeit becoming increasingly regulated to prevent parties abusing the electoral process in respect of funding from private sources in particular (Political Parties, Elections and Referendums Act 2000). In a complex society containing many different points of view, parties are an inevitable means of coordinating and organising competing claims and no one would doubt that political parties are a necessary feature of democracy. Because the majority party in Parliament also forms the executive, party leaders can control both the legislature and the executive. Indeed it has been said that:

> parties have substituted for a constitution in Britain. They have filled all the vast empty spaces in the political system where a constitution should be and made the system in their own image. (Wright, quoted in Nolan and Sedley, 1997, p. 83)

Broad cultural values such as 'fairness', 'freedom' and 'equality' are sometimes claimed to be sources of the constitution. Whether these are worth calling sources as such is debatable since they influence most aspects of human life. As we saw in the previous chapter the meaning of these ideas is open to fundamental disagreement which makes them little more than slogans which can be applied to a range of conflicting causes. On the other hand they have driven legal reforms, for example anti-discrimination laws such as the Gender Recognition Act 2004 which allows transsexuals to marry and have new birth certificates. The longstanding debate as to whether the monarchy should be limited as it presently is to white European Protestants is also driven by a belief that our constitution should reflect the value of equality.

The distinction between a written and an unwritten constitution is sometimes expressed as one between a 'formal' and a 'functional' constitution. The UK has no formal constitution but may have a functional constitution in the sense that its separate miscellaneous components may work together to produce a viable system that delivers the basic principles we would expect to find in a constitution. Indeed a formal constitution may not be functional in this sense since its provisions may not actually be applied.

3.2   Statute Law

From the sixteenth century it became increasingly established that Parliament, in the sense of the Queen, the House of Lords and the House of Commons combining to enact statutes (Acts of Parliament), is the supreme lawmaker, although some argue even today that the courts can overturn laws made by Parliament (Chapter 9). The most radical constitutional changes have been made by statute. These include for example the Bill of Rights 1688 which, following the 1688 revolution, defined the relationship between the Crown and Parliament; the Act of Settlement 1700 which regulated succession to the Crown and gave the senior judges security of tenure; the Parliament Acts 1911 and 1949 which made the House of Lords subordinate to the House of Commons and fixed the maximum duration of a Parliament as five years; the European Communities Act 1972 which made European law part of the law of the UK; and the Human Rights Act 1998 which incorporated provisions taken from the European Convention on Human Rights into UK law. Many other statutes raise constitutional issues such as those dealing with elections, complaints against government, immigration, the media, police powers, the security services and freedom of information.

Two things might be noted about these statutes. Firstly they do not add up to a general constitutional code; they deal with specific issues and are usually responses to particular problems. Thus whether a statute is enacted depends mainly on the interests of the government of the day. For example there are no statutes (other than some dealing with incidental matters such as pensions and salaries) limiting the powers of the Prime Minister or regulating the relationship between ministers and civil servants. Exceptionally a statute might be of wide concern and correspondingly used by the courts, such as the Bill of Rights 1688: no taxation without clear parliamentary authority (see *AG v Wilts United Dairies* (1922)).

Secondly some statutes might have a special status both in law and politics as symbolic of great events and important principles. This is true particularly of the Bill of Rights 1688 and also of Magna Carta 1215. Extracted from King John by the leading landowners in order to rectify their grievances, Magna Carta is no longer strictly in force and much of it concerns the particular claims of different groups of medieval property owners. However some of the general principles and sentiments behind it are still invoked in constitutional debate and by the courts. It established that in principle the King is subject to the law, in the sense of the customs of the realm that protected the rights of the landowners and local communities. Magna Carta remains of great symbolic value as capturing the essence of the rule of law and accountable government; for example 'to none will we sell: to no one will we delay or deny justice' (see *R v Secretary of State ex parte Phansopkar* (1976): claimant to right to reside in UK: right to a court hearing prior to deportation); and 'no freeman shall be taken or imprisoned or be outlawed or exiled or in otherwise destroyed . . . but by . . . the law of the land' (see *R (Bancoult) v Secretary of State* (2001)). Magna Carta also includes the principles of no taxation without representation and the right to a fair trial.

In *Thoburn v Sunderland City Council* (2002) Laws LJ, in the context of the European Communities Act 1972, spoke of a 'constitutional' statute, meaning a statute which the courts will not read as overridden by other statutes unless very clear language is used (Chapters 7, 9; see also *Robinson v Secretary of State for Northern Ireland* (2002): devolution legislation). The problem here is that we may not agree as to what counts as a constitutional statute.

3.3   The Common Law

The common law developed by judges on a case-by-case basis claims legitimacy as the embodiment of the values of the community mediated by reason and given order and certainty by precedent. Liberals and communitarians might find it congenial, although republicans would have doubts about whether the common law meets the aspiration of citizen participation in government and might regret the emphasis of the law upon confrontation and rights rather than on compromise (Chapter 2). However from a republican angle it might be claimed that all citizens are on an equal footing in the courts (subject to the obvious objection that the wealthy are at an advantage).

Historically the common law predates Parliament as lawmaker since the common law emerged from customary laws that are sometimes claimed to go back to the ancient Britons. Indeed the idea of an ancient common law constitution is part of the rhetoric of English constitutional debate, designed to instil reverence for existing arrangements. The common law was strengthened from the thirteenth century by the practice of the King's judges touring the country on his behalf as 'the fount of justice', with the main courts later gravitating to London. Although judges are in theory Crown servants, from the seventeenth century it was established that the King cannot act as a judge himself but is bound by the law as made by the judges (see *Prohibitions del Roy* (1607); *M v Home Office* (1993)). This is an important marker establishing a separation of powers of sorts.

There is a tension between the classical common law view of the constitution – advocated with varying degrees of emphasis in the seventeenth century by conservative judges such as Coke (1552–1634), Hale (1609–76) and Mansfield (1709–93) and commentators such as Blackstone (1723–80) – and the modern political notion of the constitution as the application of unlimited democratic power vested in Parliament. Coke claimed that common law was the supreme arbiter of the constitution – an argument still pursued today (Chapter 9). According to Coke, the common law is a matter of reason, but:

> the artificial perfection of reason . . . gotten by long study and experience . . . No man (out of his private reason) ought to be wiser than the law, which is the perfection of reason. (*Institutes*, 1(21))

Artificial reason is apparently the collective wisdom of the judges imposed through precedents. The classical view envisages the common law constitution as the product of the evolutionary development of community practices adapting the law to meet changing circumstances and, importantly, recognising that disagreement requires practical judgements rather than general principles. Hale's famous metaphor of the Argonauts' ship has often been used, where the same ship in the sense of design and purpose returns that had set sail but has been so often mended that no piece of the original remains (Hale, *A History of the Common Law*, 1713, p. 40).

Hobbes (Chapter 2) roundly condemned Coke's claims. He denied that there is anything special about lawyers' reasoning and refused to accept that custom and tradition in themselves carry any legal authority. According to Hobbes, the rule of law derives from authority, subject to 'natural reason' which is available to everyone. He objected to the common law on the ground that disagreement between judges picking over conflicting precedents creates the very uncertainty that the law exists to prevent. Jeremy Bentham (Chapter 2) also objected to the common law on the ground that relying on precedent was irrational. We might also be cynical about the notion that the common law represents community values and may regard it as the creation of professional lawyers, filtering experience through their own self interest even if unintentionally.

Some liberals argue that the courts are the guardians of fundamental freedoms and in extreme cases should have the power to override an Act of Parliament (Chapter 9). A compromise position is a 'twin' or 'bipolar' sovereignty between Parliament and the courts, according to which Parliament makes legislation and the courts interpret it in the light of basic values of justice and respect for individual rights, each respecting the autonomy of the other in its own sphere (*X Ltd* v *Morgan Grampian Publishers Ltd* [1991] 1 AC 1 at 48). Such an accommodation gives the courts considerable scope but requires them to give way to a clear expression of democratic will. The conventional approach characteristic of the UK's reliance on voluntary practices ('constitutional abeyance', below) is that there is an 'understanding' among the personal networks that comprise the institutions of government as to their respective roles and limits.

3.4   Constitutional Conventions

Much of the UK constitution comprises understandings and practices that are not legally binding in that they are not directly enforceable through the courts and have no authoritative sources other than recognition and obedience by those affected by them. Conventions are nevertheless very important and would certainly feature in a written constitution if the UK had one. Examples include the rules that the Queen must act on the advice of ministers and the rule that the government must resign if it loses the confidence of the House of Commons. The 'Sewel Convention' is an example of a deliberately created convention as opposed to one emerging from practice. Formulated in 1999 as a 'Memorandum of Understanding' between the two governments and so without direct legal status, this prohibits the nominally all powerful UK Parliament from legislating in matters devolved to the subordinate Scottish Parliament without its consent.

Conventions deal mainly with the relationship between the different branches of central government, the Crown, the executive and Parliament, ministers and the civil service, the Prime Minister and the Cabinet. There are for example no legal rules requiring there to be either a Prime Minister or a Cabinet and the powers of the Prime Minister are largely conventional. It is sometimes argued that fundamental principles relating to the structure of the constitution such as parliamentary supremacy and the separation of powers are conventions (*R* v *HM Treasury ex parte Smedley* (1985)).

Conventions therefore express the contemporary political morality of the constitution and one argument for their existence is their achievement in continually modernising the constitution. They also raise the question of who decides what the constitution is and how it should be changed. Their existence is an important example of how the UK constitution must be pieced together without a blueprint other than tradition and the opinions of 'important' people. Conventions also show a reluctance to develop the constitution according to principles of abstract reason.

Many conventions relate to the exercise of the prerogative powers that survive as vestiges of the legal powers of the Crown. These powers, if exercised, could have profound political consequences. They are however required to be exercised according to conventions which subject the Queen to Parliament. For example convention requires that the Queen must assent to a bill passed by both Houses of Parliament, and that Parliament must meet annually. There would be no legal impediment if the Queen chose to dismiss all her ministers. However by convention she must appoint as Prime Minister the person supported by a majority of the House of Commons and must then act on his or her advice in appointing and dismissing other ministers. The Prime Minister must appoint only members of Parliament as ministers and the government must resign if it is defeated on a vote of confidence in the House of Commons. These conventions are the core of the fundamental shift of power from a monarchical to a parliamentary system without the controversy that might have been associated with a series of statutory reforms.

However the very existence of conventions generates controversy. If the purpose of a constitution is to impose external limits on government then conventions that are generated *within* government are highly suspect. Some writers argue that the dependence of the UK constitution upon conventions and practices makes it no more than the wishes of those in power. Thus Hennessy (1995) describes the UK constitution as an 'insider's constitution', which is under the control of the government of the day and in particular the unelected officials who secure the continuity of the system at times of political crisis or change. He recounts the Victorian conceit that conventions embody 'the general agreement of public men' about 'the rules of the game' (ibid., p. 37), a proposition that remains significant today. Similarly Bogdanor described the UK constitution as 'a very peculiar constitution which no one intended whereby the government of the day decides what the constitution is' (ibid., p. 165). Horwitz has argued (1997, *Oxford Journal of Legal Studies* 551) that conventions were developed as undemocratic devices to reassure the ruling class that constitutional fundamentals would continue to be developed within government largely beyond the influence of the rising middle classes following rapid extension of the franchise after the Reform Act 1867 . This echoes Mill's utilitarianism in so far as he preferred to leave government to an elite of professionals.

Further, the absence of formal parliamentary debate, or indeed any public and systematic discussion, exposes an important concern about the democratic legitimacy of conventions. Who determines the timing and nature of reforms? Are the voices of persons selected as likely to conform to the wishes of those in power given particular weight (for instance academics anxious for recognition)? Why should not the fundamentals of the constitution such as responsible and accountable government be protected against those they are intended to police? For example the government initially refused to allow either Parliament or the public access to the text of the Attorney-General's legal opinion concerning the legality of the invasion of Iraq in 2003. By convention such advice is normally confidential (although there are precedents for disclosing the advice) but the refusal to disclose was seen as screening government from uncomfortable questions regarding the legality of the use of force. Indeed a successful complaint under the Freedom of Information Act 2000 was upheld in 2006, recognising a public interest in having access to information on how the Attorney-General arrived at his conclusions.

Related to this is the republican argument (Chapter 2) that it is insulting to human dignity to rely on the goodwill of those in power to conform to proper standards of conduct. Respect for the equality of citizens requires that government be constrained by independent rules made democratically and known to all.

3.4.1   Definitions and Binding Force

It is important to distinguish constitutional conventions from other forms of constitutional behaviour such as practices, traditions and legal principles. There is a relatively clear rule of recognition as to what counts as a law, namely a rule interpreted and applied by the courts (even if the courts decide not to enforce it). The crucial point is that in the case of law there is a specific procedure for identifying and applying it. This is not true of conventions. Indeed commentators disagree as to the tests used to identify conventions. This signals doubt about the very nature of conventions and possibly the nature of law. At a practical level, there is inevitable uncertainty as to whether some practices really are conventions (and so become obligatory). There is no consensus as to which practices have constitutional status: for example doubt surrounds the rules for electing the leaders of political parties. Sometimes conventions are contained in written documents along with other rules and pieces of ethical or political advice, for example the Ministerial Code (2005) and the Civil Service Code (2006) issued by the Cabinet Office and the codes of public morality promulgated by the Committee on Standards in Public Life (Chapter 5). The mere fact that a principle has been put in writing does not in itself make it a convention but might be evidence of a convention.

Sir Kenneth Wheare defined conventions as 'a rule of behaviour accepted as obligatory by those concerned in the working of the constitution' (*Modern Constitutions,* Oxford University Press, 1966, p. 102). This emphasises that the crucial matter is the belief of the politicians to whom a convention applies that there is an obligation to act in a particular manner. A convention exists if, as a matter of fact, the belief is present. But it is arguable that a convention ought to engage what politicians *should* consider themselves bound to do and not merely what they actually consider their obligations to be. On the other hand who is to say what this should be?

Dicey famously defined conventions negatively as anything which is not law (1959, p. 24). He stated that apart from laws:

> The other set of rules consist of conventions, understandings, habits, or practices which, though they may regulate the conduct of several members of the sovereign power, of the Ministry, or of other officials, are not in reality laws at all since they are not enforced by the courts.

A further issue concerns the extent to which a practice must be accepted as binding before it is recognised as a convention. Since neither conventions nor non-binding practices are enforced by the courts, Dicey's test does not identify that which is a convention as opposed to non-binding practice (compare Munro, 1999, p. 81, arguing that non-legal rules are best viewed as of one type provided we accept that conventions vary in stringency).

Does *any* disagreement about the status of the practice prevent it from being a convention? This seems unsatisfactory because if unanimity (rather than consensus) is required it suggests that a person whose actions ought to be governed by an existing conventional obligation can apparently destroy that obligation by disputing its existence. As Jaconelli (2005) observes, this places the existence of a convention on a flimsy basis. An alternative approach might be to identify a convention where there was a *consensus* as to the binding nature of a constitutional practice. A consensus may be said to arise informally provided there is substantial support for the proposed convention. Evidence might be found through the collective memory of senior officials or persons recognised as constitutional 'experts', possibly selected on the basis that they are congenial to those in power. Reliance may be placed upon the views of important non-elected officials who represent the continuity of power, such as Peter Hennessy's 'golden triangle' of Cabinet Secretary, the Queen's advisers and the Prime Minister's Principal Private Secretary (PPS). Hennessy (1995) describes how private secretaries, the sovereign's advisers at Buckingham Palace and officials of the Cabinet Office monitor and record practice in a 'Precedent Book', which, characteristically of the UK constitution, is not open to public inspection. Officials and politicians refer to the records contained within this collection to guide future behaviour and this may eventually lead to a consensus that the practice is obligatory.

Jennings offered three tests to identify a convention (*The Law and the Constitution*, London University Press, 1959, p. 136). First, are there any precedents? Second, do those operating the constitution believe that they are bound by a rule? Third, is there a constitutional reason for the convention? This has been accepted by the Canadian courts (*Reference re Amendment of the Constitution of Canada (Nos 1, 2 and 3)* (1982) 105 DLR (3d) 1).

However in the absence of an authoritative decision maker such as a court there are plainly difficulties with precedents because there may be many occasions on which politicians disagree about the precedents they are supposed to follow. This uncertainty clouds even established conventional rules, such as the choice of a Prime Minister. For example King George VI and Neville Chamberlain wanted Chamberlain to be succeeded as Prime Minister by the then Foreign Secretary Lord Halifax (and not Winston Churchill) at a crucial moment for Britain in the conduct of the Second World War. This was notwithstanding the established convention that a Prime Minister should have a seat in the Commons. Sometimes precedent is unnecessary because a convention might be created by agreement, for example by the Cabinet, or even laid down unilaterally by the

Prime Minister. For instance by the Balfour Declaration, made at an Imperial Conference in 1926, a convention was created that no legislation affecting the dominions would be passed by the Parliament at Westminster unless the government of the country affected by it had requested that legislation and consented to it. This convention was substantially placed on a statutory footing by the Statute of Westminster 1931. (See also Sewel Convention, above). The important principles contained in the Ministerial Code (Cabinet Office, 2005) may well furnish an example of conventions laid down by prime ministerial edict. It is arguable however that a convention which is laid down in this way becomes valid only after it has gained general acceptance (see McHarg (2008)). A convention created by an agreement, such as a concordat (below), may perhaps be immediately binding.

Jennings also suggested that a convention exists if those subject to it regard themselves as bound by the rule. It seems odd to say that a rule is binding only as long as it is obeyed, a principle that would undoubtedly be welcomed by criminals. However while conventions are obligatory, they do not all have the same degree of binding force. Some may have exceptions (such as the personal powers of the monarch), some may not be regarded as important. It may be difficult to decide whether a particular pattern of behaviour amounts to a convention. For example is the Cabinet merely a working practice?

It is necessary to distinguish between conventions and practices because practices, however important, are not binding at all. The party system provides an example of a practice fundamental to the workings of the constitution but which has no binding force. There is a logical gulf between practice – what is – and rule – what 'ought' to be – although it must be conceded that well established practices carry at least a presumption that they ought to be continued. This seems to be a basic psychological fact about human motivation. Furthermore a practice ceases to exist if it is broken. If a convention is broken, it ceases to exist only if no criticism follows. To this extent conventions are at the mercy of raw politics.

Jenning's requirement of a reason for the convention is also problematic. Who decides whether such a reason exists? In the absence of an independent judge, the reason for a practice depends upon contested political views as to what the constitution should be like. These are vulnerable to the self interest of the government in power. Indeed a fundamental distinction between convention and law is that there is no authoritative mechanism – a rule of recognition – for settling disputes as to the meaning and application of a convention (below).

3.4.2   Law and Convention

As we have seen, for Dicey the distinction between legal and political rules depended on the absence of direct coercive legal power to enforce conventions. Jennings, by contrast, argued that law and convention share common characteristics, each resting ultimately on public acquiescence. But this does not explain the different attitude of the courts to conventions when compared with laws.

At one level it is possible to understand how laws and conventions differ. A law does not lapse if it becomes obsolete, yet a convention can disappear if it is not followed for a significant period, or if it is broken without objection. Munro (1999) points out that a breach of the law does not call into question its existence or validity. He adds that individual laws do not rest upon consent – an unpopular law or a widely disregarded law is nevertheless a valid law. But a convention is only valid if it is accepted as binding. Another difference is that laws emanate from definite sources – the courts and Parliament – with, crucially, an authoritative mechanism (the courts) for deciding what the rule means and how it applies. In the case of conventions there is no such authoritative source. As Dicey indicated, there is no direct judicial remedy when a convention is breached but this is not so with laws.

Nevertheless Dicey's distinction between law and convention has been criticised as too rigid. Some laws are less binding than others. For example procedural requirements stipulated by statute are sometimes 'directory only'. This means that such requirements need not always be obeyed (Chapter 17). Nor can importance be a distinguishing factor. Both laws and conventions deal with fundamental matters and conventions can be as important as laws; indeed some conventions may be more important than some laws. It must be conceded however that importance is irrelevant to the existence of a law but not to the existence of a convention. It is also sometimes said that conventions are different from laws because they lack certainty. Munro (1999) demonstrates that certainty is not the issue. He argues that some social rules, such as the rules of cricket, can be clearly stated but they are manifestly not laws. Moreover many laws are uncertain and while the courts certainly rely on precedent they are free to depart from precedents in many cases.

Perhaps the crucial distinction between convention and law concerns the attitude of the courts. Many conventions function in a close relationship with laws since they direct how discretionary power will be exercised or prevent the exercise of anachronistic prerogative powers. Conventions provide principles and values that form the context of the strict law, as Jennings famously said 'flesh which clothes the dry bones of the law'.

However the courts do not apply conventions directly. This means firstly that there is no remedy in the courts for breach of a convention as such, and secondly that the views of a court as to whether a particular convention exists and what it means are not binding. The existence and meaning of a convention are matters of fact that must be proved by evidence and not matters of law for the court. On the other hand the courts do not ignore conventions. In particular a convention may form the political background against which a law has to be interpreted.

Two cases may help to illustrate the difference between law and convention in the courts. First, in *Reference re Amendment of the Constitution of Canada* (1982), the Canadian Supreme Court, relying partly on British authority, recognised but refused to apply a convention. Under Canadian law any amendment to the Canadian Constitution required an Act of the UK Parliament following a request from the federal government of Canada. The Canadian government wished to amend the Constitution so as to free itself from this legal link with Britain. The UK Parliament would automatically pass any legislation requested by Canada.

However there were important Canadian conventions on the matter. These required that the governments of the Canadian provinces be consulted about, and give their consent to, any proposed changes in the Constitution that affected federal-provincial relations. Some claimed that this had not been done. The Supreme Court was divided as to whether the convention in question existed. A majority held that it did, and went on to explain in some detail what the convention meant. Some of the judges doubted whether the court should have gone even this far, but as long as we remember that the court's view about the meaning of a convention is not in itself binding, it seems acceptable. In any event a larger majority held that, whatever the convention meant, it could not affect the *legal* rule that empowered the federal government to resolve to seek an alteration to the Constitution. Thus the convention could not be enforced by legal remedies. The judges also denied that a convention can ever crystallise into law, for example by becoming established over a period of years. This seems to be equally true of English law (see Munro, 1999, pp. 72ff.).

The second case is *Attorney-General* v *Jonathan Cape Ltd* (1975). The government sought to prevent publication of the diaries of Richard Crossman, a former Labour cabinet minister. It relied upon the legal doctrine of breach of confidence. This involves balancing the confidential nature of any material against any public interest in favour of its disclosure. The government based its case upon the convention of collective cabinet responsibility, arguing that this necessarily required that cabinet business remain confidential to cabinet ministers. The court refused to apply the convention as such. It held that the convention was relevant only to the problem of deciding where the balance between confidentiality and public interest lay. His Lordship held that the diaries could be published because they dealt only with matters of historical interest and did not concern the activities of cabinet ministers still in office. Thus the convention was a crucial strand in the argument, but not the law itself (see further Jaconelli, 2005).

The courts might also develop common law so as to incorporate principles currently expressed in conventions or convert important practices into rules of law. For instance the law of judicial review has been significantly affected by the convention of ministerial responsibility to Parliament since the courts are reluctant to infringe Parliament's territory (Chapter 15). In *Carltona Ltd* v *Commissioner for Works* (1943) the courts accepted the legitimacy of civil servants taking decisions that are in law the responsibility of the minister without reference to the minister personally. In *R* v *Secretary of State for the Home Department ex parte Ruddock* (1987) it was held that the government practice of publishing the criteria governing the issue of warrants for telephone tapping purposes created a legitimate expectation, enforceable in the courts, that these criteria would be observed before tapping interception was permitted. A counterargument to this kind of incorporation is that if courts enforce conventions their existence becomes 'fixed' as a matter of law, thus taking judges into the political arena and losing the flexibility that is supposed to be a reason for conventions.

3.4.3   The Purposes of Conventions

At the most general level conventions are claimed to ensure that the constitution reflects contemporary political values and so to manage evolutionary constitutional change. More cynically they enable constitutional principles to remain under the informal control of those in power rather than be subject to more open judicial or democratic processes. For example there might have been political dangers in incrementally curtailing the powers of the Crown by repeated legislative means, which might have risked constitutional confrontation. Conventions can also offer advantages in a society in which constitutional reform often finds a low place in the public's (and thus the government's) view of political priorities.

Conventions relating to the monarch ensure that vestigial prerogative powers are normally exercised only in accordance with advice received from ministers who are accountable to Parliament. As we have seen, it is a convention that the sovereign should assent to bills passed by both Houses of Parliament. The royal assent would seem to be automatic, although Marshall (1984, p. 22) has suggested that the assent might be refused if for example a bill purporting to repeal an earlier 'entrenched' enactment had not gone through all the special processes required in the earlier enactment. Related to the convention governing assent is the sovereign's obligation in almost all matters to act on the advice of ministers (whether collective advice or that offered by an individual minister), although even here there are ill defined circumstances in which such advice need not be followed. For example the sovereign might be able to refuse a Prime Minister's advice to dissolve Parliament if a general election would be harmful to the interests of the country, such as might be the case in a national emergency, and an alternative viable government could be formed (Chapter 14). There is considerable debate about the extent to which, and on whose advice, the monarch can exercise personal powers. The chain of conventions embodied in the doctrine of ministerial responsibility to Parliament is of fundamental importance, being intended to ensure that the legal powers of the Crown are subject to democratic control. Dicey (1915) suggests that these conventions reconcile legal sovereignty and political sovereignty. Allan (*Law, Liberty and Justice*, Oxford University Press, 1993, p. 253) concludes that conventions 'give effect to the principle of governmental accountability that constitutes the structure of responsible government'. However the supposed chain of accountability is not complete. Dicey did not anticipate the dominance of the executive in Parliament nor the dispersal of executive power to miscellaneous bodies including private companies outside the central government structure. Moreover if ministerial accountability is to be effective it assumes that members of Parliament will act independently and not through party loyalty. Accountability to Parliament is often accountability to the minister's own party against the background of the adversarial nature of party politics and the government's desire to avoid political embarrassment. Politics is the final arbiter.

Other conventions concern the relationship between the two Houses of Parliament and the judiciary. For example the somewhat uncertain 'Salisbury Convention' (designed in circumstances which no longer apply, where hereditary peers had a built in majority in the House of Lords), requires that the House of Lords should not oppose a measure sent to it by the Commons which was contained in the governing party's election manifesto except perhaps where the matter is the subject of deep public controversy (see Turpin and Tomkins, *British Government and the Constitution* 6th ed. (2007) pp. 643–5 and 652–3).

New conventions are developed and others abandoned. For example the Sewel Convention (above) concerns the new relationship between the UK government and the devolved governments. In the former category may also be the right of the Prince of Wales as heir to the Crown to meet with ministers, to obtain information from them, to comment on their policies, and to argue for alternative policies (Brazier, 'The Constitutional Position of the Prince of Wales', 1995, *Public Law* 401). The former parliamentary convention governing the rules under which the Table Office of the House of Commons refused to allow a written parliamentary question to a minister to be tabled if the minister had earlier refused to answer it has also disappeared, although ministerial conventions on this matter still operate (Second Report of the Public Service Select Committee, HC 313).

A fashionable recent device is the promulgation of 'concordats' agreed between participants and intended to govern the relationship between different organs of government or to set out practices. These may have the status of convention, at least if they are generally acted upon. There are many of these between government departments, agencies and the devolved institutions of Scotland and Wales, which clarify the relationship between these bodies and express their mutual obligations. A concordat made in 2004 between the government and the Lord Chief Justice concerning links between the judiciary and the executive underpins the reforms introduced by the Constitutional Reform Act 2005 (Chapter 8). These could be regarded as expressing new conventions designed to secure the independence of the judiciary. There is another type of 'concordat', an example of which is the 'Enforcement Concordat' dealing with the relationship between regulated commercial interests and enforcement bodies. This merely sets out broad policy goals, for example that enforcement bodies should adopt a helpful and constructive approach and that information should be published in plain language.

Conventions change their meaning incrementally as they are applied – that being one of their alleged advantages. On the other hand there is often doubt about the status of certain practices. For instance since the late 1970s it has become apparent that a government need not resign merely because it suffers a major defeat. A formal Commons vote of no confidence is needed. This makes it very difficult to remove a government. There is uncertainty as to whether there is a convention embodying the 'mandate' doctrine – the idea that governments are bound to attempt to honour election promises. If this doctrine exists it would complete the 'democratic chain' between monarch and people. The status and functions of the Cabinet are also uncertain. Recent prime ministers have preferred to rely upon informal groups of advisers (Chapter 15).

3.4.4   Why Conventions Are Obeyed

The main reason why conventions are obeyed is because of the adverse political consequences that might result from their breach. This is unsurprising since conventions are traditionally regarded as a matter of political ethics. It also produces the circularity that if a convention is not obeyed it may lose its binding force. For example the supposed convention that a minister should resign if there has been a serious wrongdoing in his or her department is usually ignored unless a minister loses political support (Chapter 15). Indeed the adversarial nature of politics means that even political sanctions are far from inevitable. The pressure of political opponents and party, the strength of prime ministerial support and the reaction of the press all play a large part in determining the fate of a minister.

Dicey unsuccessfully tried to link breach of convention to breach of law. He stated (1959, pp. 439 ff.) that conventions are not laws and so not enforced by the courts, but he argued that even the 'boldest political adventurer' would be restrained from breaching conventions because (at least in the case of some conventions) it would eventually lead to the offender coming into conflict with the courts and the law of the land (1959, pp. 445–6). He gave as an example the consequences that might follow if Parliament did not meet at least once a year, or if a government did not resign after losing a vote of confidence. Dicey argued that the government would not have the statutory authority for raising (some) taxes nor for spending money.

However not all conventions can be similarly treated. For example the appointment of a non-member of Parliament as a minister will not lead to a legal violation. The absence of adverse political repercussions may fortify ministers who give inaccurate parliamentary answers but contrary to Dicey this failure is unlikely to lead to a breach of the law. Indeed the absence of political consequences may in part explain why some conventions are not always obeyed. It is however true that if some conventions were breached, Parliament might be compelled to intervene to prevent a recurrence. Most famously this occurred after the Lords refused to pass the Finance Bill 1909, thereby disregarding the conventional principle that the Lords should ultimately defer to the wishes of the elected Commons. The Parliament Act 1911 removed the veto power of the Lords in respect of most public bills. If the sovereign (without ministerial advice) were to refuse to grant royal assent to a bill passed by both Houses, the prerogative power to refuse would soon be removed by legislation.

It also seems that conventions are obeyed because they are part of a shared and respected system of values. This is evident in the commonly accepted definitions of conventions that emphasise the consent upon which they depend for their existence (for example Sir Kenneth Wheare's definition above, and see Munro, 1999, p. 61). Jaconelli (2005) goes further and ventures the possibility that many conventions prescribe behaviour that is implicitly reciprocal. The party in power for the time being accepts the constraints that conventions impose upon its behaviour in the expectation that the opposition parties will do likewise when they attain office, although Jaconelli concedes that this would not furnish an obligatory basis to all conventions, such as those of an inter-institutional rather than inter-party kind. An example of the inter-institutional type would be that obligation of the monarch to assent to bills passed by both Houses. According to Jaconelli, prudence explains why such conventions are observed.

If the values underpinning conventional obligations are shared by those to whom they apply a breach is unlikely. The disregard of a widely shared political ethic might threaten the career of the offender, about which there might also be adverse publicity.

Conventions may apparently be breached or qualified (depending on one's viewpoint) as a safety valve where there is a conflict between what is normally constitutionally expected and current political consensus or expediency. In 1975 the Prime Minister 'suspended' the principle of collective cabinet unanimity to allow ministers to express their views openly in a referendum campaign concerning membership of the European Economic Community (EEC). Any referendum on the future of sterling as British currency might result in a similar temporary modification to collective ministerial responsibility.

3.4.5   Codification of Conventions

The argument surrounding codification of conventions is not unrelated to the arguments for a written constitution for the UK and raises many of the same points. The fact that a set of rules is codified does not in itself determine the nature of the rules. The Ministerial Code (2007) contains a mixture of rules concerning the conduct of ministers. Some may well be conventions. Others, such as duties to reveal conflicts of interest, are applicable to all public bodies. Thus the normal tests for recognising conventions must still be applied. By contrast if the Code was put into the form of a statute, all its rules would automatically have the same authority.

Codification has different meanings. Firstly it includes an authoritative written version of the conventions in question. Strictly speaking this means turning the convention into law in the form of an Act of Parliament, although promulgation as a Standing Order or Resolution of Parliament would give it legal effect within Parliament itself. Conventions might also be codified in a less authoritative sense and not legally binding, for example in the form of a report of a parliamentary committee, a ministerial announcement, a Concordat or a Memorandum of Understanding (see *Report of Joint Committee on Conventions* (2006) HL 1212-1, HC 1212-1 (2005–6)). The case for codification thus involves two distinct positions. The first asserts that conventions should both be codified and given legal force; the second that conventions might be codified within an authoritative text but with no legal status and so remain as non-legal political practices as at present. Even under this version however, which has been adopted in Australia in relation to 34 constitutional practices, it is likely that the courts may cite those conventions that the process codified (see Sampford, '"Recognize and Declare": an Australian Experience in Codifying Constitutional Conventions', 1987, *Oxford Journal of Legal Studies* 369). Such an approach would address the lack of precision in the scope of some conventions and would enable us to say with certainty which usages are and which are not conventional. Establishing the certainty of conventions could safeguard the neutrality of those who apply them. On the other hand this approach might create uncertainty, for example as to the status of any interpretation of a convention that a court might give if the matter arose in litigation.

The more adventurous position involving codification *and* enactment raises a number of concerns. The first is that such a model of codification would damage the flexibility of the constitution and inhibit its evolutionary role in maintaining the relationship between the constitution and contemporary political values. One of the purposes of conventions has been to annul anachronistic law. It would be undesirable if conventions were to become fossilised and so impede further constitutional change. This might even prevent the development of qualifications limiting the scope of some conventions (as in the case of the 'suspension' of collective cabinet unanimity in 1975).

Moreover as conventions are enforced as a matter of political dynamic, some argue that political flexibility might also be curbed if the courts were invited to pronounce on the breach of a conventional obligation. There are strong arguments that the demands of political morality ought to be a matter of collective decision reached through the medium of politics, and so fall outside the proper scope of the judicial function (non-justiciable; see Chapter 18). The codification of conventions might not in any case lead to judicial enforcement. To take the example of ministerial responsibility, we may conclude that apportioning blame is a political matter not a legal one. This means that the question of whether a minister's conduct in office is such that he or she should resign would seem to be a non-justiciable question, depending as it does on party support, the timing of the discovery, the support of the Prime Minister and Cabinet and the public repercussions. But the issue is not so clear if a minister were to deny an obligation to answer *any* questions in the House of Commons. What would prevent the court granting a declaration that such behaviour was unconstitutional? Would the arguments be equally as strong if a minister deliberately misled Parliament where resignation should be automatic? (See Ministerial Code, para 1.5; and the Second Report of the Public Service Select Committee, 1995–6, HC 313, para. 26.)

There might also be practical difficulties in systematic codification. It would be impossible to identify all usages that are currently conventional, and immediately after a code was established there would be nothing to prevent the evolution of new conventions.

The case for a systematic codification of conventions is not self evidently of merit. One possible approach (but one which would not overcome all the difficulties mentioned above) might be to enact some of the most important and widely accepted conventions. This would place those selected outside the scope of the executive and locate more extensive power in Parliament. Constitutional development would then be a matter of statutory reform which itself would follow from more open debate and discussion.

3.5   Constitutional Silence and Abeyance

The absence of a rule set out in a statute or case or embodied in a known convention might also be a source of the constitution in that it may indicate a deliberate choice to leave a question unanswered. Silence might indicate that the constitution prefers to leave an area free for the actors to do what they like, subject perhaps to ordinary private law. The absence of legal or conventional rules governing the organisation of the central executive provides an example, as does the absence of rules controlling government privatisation.

Silence might also encourage the opposite inference that government should have no freedom, for example where a law sets out a list of rights to which it gives special treatment, as is the case with the Human Rights Act 1998 (Chapter 19). Do we assume that this is intended to be a comprehensive list or can other rights be recognised to which we can extend similar protection by analogy? More generally where Parliament has not legislated in a particular area, does this mean that the common law should also refuse to go there, taking its lead from the democratic branch or is this an invitation for common law to fill the gap (see *Cambridge Water Company* v *English Counties Leather* (1994); *Re McKerr* (2004): common law should not fill any gap)?

Constitutional silences are therefore ambiguous. Their most important function might be to discourage us from looking too closely into controversial areas into which it might be wiser not to venture. In other words silence enables us to let sleeping dogs lie and invites disputing factions to take comfort in the belief that the constitution does not rule out their concerns. Examples include the question of whether European law prevails over domestic law, whether Parliament can override certain basic principles of Scottish law (Chapter 9) and the extent of the Queen's personal powers (Chapter 14). This notion of silence is also embodied in the concept of a non-justiciable issue that the court refuses to determine (Chapter 18). Similarly there may be values in the constitution – personal privacy is an example – which cannot easily be embodied in clear rules so that they are best undefined as providing only a general sense of direction or an attitude (see Lord Hoffmann in *Wainwright* v *Home Office* [2003] 4 All ER 969, 979).

The risk of constitutional abeyance is that without established guidelines the pressure of disagreement might eventually erupt into open conflict, with the constitution powerless to resolve the dispute – the Hobbesian nightmare. This was the case in the English Civil War of the seventeenth century against a constitution that did not clearly define the powers of the monarch. However it is arguable that a constitution and indeed the law itself can work only within a broad consensus of beliefs and is irrelevant in situations of fundamental disagreement.

Summary

▷ The UK constitution is embodied in individual statutes and in the common law, which is claimed to derive from the values embedded in the community. Statutes and common law principles that are regarded as 'constitutional' are given special treatment but within a context of considerable uncertainty.

▷ The UK constitution is also embodied in customs and practices, the most important of which are conventions. Conventions are pragmatically intertwined with law but are not directly enforceable in the courts. There is therefore no authoritative mechanism for interpreting, identifying or enforcing conventions.

▷ Conventions are of fundamental importance in the UK constitution. In their best light they enable the constitution to evolve pragmatically in accordance with changing political values. In their worst light they allow the government of the day and its favourites to manipulate the constitution in their own interests, for example by recruiting sycophantic academics to endorse a particular interpretation of a convention.

▷ There is disagreement about the definition of conventions. Accordingly it is not always clear which forms of constitutional behaviour are conventions and which are mere practices. Conventions are binding rules of constitutional behaviour while mere practices are not.

▷ Conventions are distinct from law, firstly in that there are no authoritative formal tests for the validity of conventions and secondly because conventions are not directly enforced by the courts. However there is no inherent difference in the content of laws and conventions and the courts use conventions, as they do moral principles, to help interpret, develop and apply the law.

▷ Some commentators have argued that conventions could be incorporated into the law, but even if this is achieved how many such laws would be justiciable? Codification might offer certainty in respect of those conventions included in the code, but new conventions would be evolved after the code was introduced and some flexibility in adapting existing conventions might be lost. There may be scope for extending 'soft' forms of codification such as the Ministerial Code.

▷ Constitutional silences or 'abeyances' play a useful role mainly by avoiding confrontation in respect of issues that are inherently controversial.

Exercises

3.1 'The British constitution presumes, more boldly than any other, the good faith of those who work it' (Gladstone). 'The constitution is "what happens"' (Griffith). Explain and compare these two statements.

3.2 How are conventions recognised and enforced? Can they be distinguished from 'practices'?

3.3 Are conventions a desirable method of bringing about constitutional change?

3.4 What is the relationship between law and convention? Does it serve a useful purpose to distinguish between law and conventions?

3.5 Should conventions be enacted into law or codified?

3.6 To what extent is silence a valuable constitutional device?

Further reading

Allott, P. (1992) 'The Theory of the British Constitution', in Gross, H. and Harrison, R. (eds) *Jurisprudence: Cambridge Essays*, Cambridge University Press.

Bagehot, W. (1902) *The English Constitution* (2nd edn), London, Keegan Paul, Chapter 1.

Bogdanor, V., Vogenauer, S. (2008) 'Enacting a British Constitution: Some Problems', *Public Law* 38.

Foley, M. (1989) *The Silence of Constitutions*, London, Routledge.

Jaconelli, J. (1999) 'The Nature of Constitutional Convention', *Legal Studies* 19:24.

Jaconelli, J. (2005) 'Do Constitutional Conventions Bind?', *Cambridge Law Journal* 64:149.

McHarg, A. (2008) 'Reforming the United Kingdom Constitution: Law, Convention, Soft Law', *Modern Law Review* 71:853.

Marshall, G. (1984) *Constitutional Conventions*, Oxford, Clarendon Press.

Munro, C. (1999) *Studies in Constitutional Law* (2nd edn), London, Butterworths, Chapter 3.

Nolan, Lord and Sedley, Sir S. (eds) (1997) *The Making and Remaking of the British Constitution*, London, Blackstone, Chapter 2.

Postema, G. (1986) *Bentham and the Common Law Tradition*, Oxford, Clarendon Press, Chapters 1, 2.

Sedley, Sir S. (1994) 'The Sound of Silence: Constitutional Law without a Constitution', *Law Quarterly Review* 110:270.

Wilson, Lord (2004) 'The Robustness of Conventions in a Time of Modernisation', *Public Law* 407.

Background reading

Ward, I. (2000) *A State of Mind? The English Constitution and the Public Imagination*, Stroud, Sutton Publishing.

Chapter 4

Historical outline

> Have you any friends of the same sentiments desirous of securing seats for the next Parliament without trouble, opposition or even attendance? I will enter into arrangements with them to their satisfaction, either for Ilchester, where I have reduced the voted to fifty two or for Grantham, where I own by inheritance and purchase the chief part of the Parish and have the Duke of Rutland at my command. My second question is, whether you can form an idea at what time the promise of the peerage will be realised to me? (Aspinall (ed.) *Letters of King George IV No 271*, Cambridge University Press, 1938)

Key words

- Pragmatism
- Custom
- Power devolving from the Crown
- Patronage
- Religious discrimination
- Political parties
- Reluctant democracy
- Private rights
- Centralisation

4.1 Introduction

The purpose of this historical outline is to highlight themes that have influenced the contemporary constitution. Apart from an abortive draft under Cromwell in the seventeenth century, there has been no attempt to design a comprehensive constitution for the UK. All constitutions reflect myths or stories of how the constitution takes its particular form and how it is justified. Traditionalists claim that the UK constitution is the happy and pragmatic outcome of an evolution towards freedom and democracy ordered by benevolent customs. The story runs that the monarchy, in the shape of the Norman Conquest of 1066, had usurped an earlier, more democratic regime, 'the ancient constitution', in which lay the roots both of the common law and government by a representative assembly. The King gradually gave way to Parliament as representing those worthy to have a stake in the community. Parliament steadily broadened its membership until eventually the people as a whole controlled it with the courts protecting their rights. The collapse of the French Revolution at the end of the eighteenth century was regarded as an awful warning of the dangers of radical constitution building. According to the myth, abuses are unlikely because apart from the odd maverick we can trust our rulers with wide discretionary powers and conflicts of interest since they are persons of high ability and integrity who can vouch for each other. Our rulers are also subject to political pressures to please at least enough of the public to keep them in office. Another view is that the history of the constitution is driven by competition between rival interest groups usually resulting in compromise, against a background of a docile population, chance circumstances and personalities in an endless power struggle. Controls over government fluctuate in response to particular problems and in accordance with changing political beliefs. There is no single driving force: 'everything that happens is constitutional' (Griffith, 'The Political Constitution', 1979, *Modern Law Review* 42(1): 19). In the case of the UK constitution one recurring theme is money – as in the need of the government to ensure the consent of the wealthier sections of the community and the desire of Parliament as representing the community to control government spending albeit with limited success.

4.2   The Medieval Period

The monarchy is the earliest institution dating back to Anglo Saxon times before the Norman conquest in 1066. During that period, after the withdrawal of the Romans in the fifth century, 'England' as a loose unity emerged from rival kingdoms ruled by warlords. Ireland and Scotland were independent Kingdoms and Wales was a collection of Principalities eventually conquered by the English. All legal power and control of the executive derived from the monarchy and in theory still does. Indeed UK residents and citizens remain 'subjects' of the Crown as opposed to being citizens in the republican sense of equal participants in the state. However according to the myth of the 'ancient constitution', the King ruled subject to the consent of a council representing those with a property stake in the community.

The power of the monarchy derived from conquest and was regularised in the hierarchical feudal system of landowning, with the King at its apex and the chief landowners and Church dignitaries (the two often overlapping) as royal advisers. There were systems of local courts and local government to some extent supervised by royal officials such as the Sheriff (an office still surviving in characteristic English fashion as ceremonial and social) and the royal courts. The other branches of government, Parliament and the courts split off from the King and progressively challenged his power. The King claimed jurisdiction over the whole of England and, after the thirteenth century, Wales. England had a centralised but flexible legal regime in the shape of the common law, a system of justice deriving its authority from the King and created by the courts. The army comprised private armies raised by the King and other landowners.

Parliament originated as a meeting of influential persons summoned by the King to give advice. The House of Lords, which dates from Saxon times, was composed of the great landowners. The House of Commons, which began to meet during the thirteenth century, consisted of representatives of the 'people' (in practice being chosen from influential local worthies). They were summoned by the King to legitimate demands for taxation in return for redressing the grievances of subjects. Parliament began to make laws originally on the basis that it was declaring the existing customs of the realm. Parliament also had the status of a High Court, able to give final rulings on the law and to 'impeach' public officials for misconduct. Impeachment, in which the House of Commons brings accusations before the House of Lords, remains possible but depends on a resolution of the House and is unlikely to be used today. Parliament is still summoned and dissolved by the monarch but the modern monarch has very little choice in the matter. During that period the executive branch consisted of the King and his chosen councillors and holders of particular offices. Some offices, notably that of the Lord Chancellor survive today.

Magna Carta (1215), extracted from King John by the leading barons, is widely regarded as a constitutional landmark. Although it is no longer directly in force, its underlying principles have been evoked in modern cases and copied in other constitutions. It was the result of a list of grievances presented by leading landowners and clerics to the King. Many of them concerned local and feudal claims that are now obsolete. Others remain applicable including a right to a fair trial, the protection of the rule of law and the principle of no taxation without consultation of those affected. Magna Carta was altered and dishonoured over the years but remains of great symbolic value in that it embodies the principle that the law is not the will of the king but is contained in the customs of the community. This is one of the foundations of the common law and was the setting for the conflicts between the King and Parliament in the seventeenth century. Magna Carta was also one of the sources of the United States Constitution and of human rights charters.

4.3   The Tudor Period

The Tudor period spanning the sixteenth century saw the emergence in Europe of the modern concept of the nation state as a self contained impersonal structure served by a bureaucracy and with absolute authority within its territory (Chapter 6). This replaced the more complex medieval regime in which Church, state and various interest groups such as landowners and trade groups coexisted uneasily. Throughout Europe the monarchy claimed to embody this absolute notion of the state, although less so in England where the common law and Parliament were established counterforces. By the sixteenth century the two Houses of Parliament met separately, Parliament could make new laws and the King must ask the House of Commons for money in the form of direct taxation. The monarch was entitled to raise indirect taxes such as duties on imports and could also confiscate and sell property and control franchises and monopolies such as the right to pursue certain trades. The monarchy might also borrow money or raise it from investing in overseas adventures such as piracy or through marriages with overseas royalty and so, unlike today, could sometimes rule without help from Parliament.

The Tudor monarchs ruled with relatively little need to summon Parliament, partly by confiscating Church property following the Reformation (1532–6) and partly from the proceeds of naval adventures and levies on overseas trade. This period also saw the emergence of the modern type of executive comprising ministers, the most important of whom were styled secretaries of state; committees, notably the Privy Council comprising the monarch's favourites and exercising the formal powers of the Crown; and a bureaucratic structure of civil servants.

During the sixteenth and seventeenth centuries medieval ideas of limited monarchy within common law clashed with the newer ideas of absolute monarchy and the nation state. Classical republican ideas of equal citizenship also surfaced (for example Sir John Harrington, 1561–1612) although these have not significantly influenced constitutional development in the UK. In the law courts the clash between Crown and Parliament was foreshadowed by controversy about the late medieval notion of the Crown's 'two persons': one (*gubernaculum*) concerned with protecting the realm and which claimed to be above the law, the other (*jurisdictio*) an official whose day-to-day duties primarily concerned the enforcement of private rights which were subject to the law (see *Duchy of*

Lancaster Case (1567)). However it was widely accepted that only in Parliament could the King exercise the fullest lawmaking power.

4.4   The Seventeenth Century Revolution

The seventeenth century was a crucible of ideas, including sovereignty, individual rights, representation and to a limited extent, democracy. The century was dominated by religious and financial conflicts between the Crown and Parliament. These led to the revolution of 1688, the foundation of the present constitution. The Stuart monarchs ran out of money and were under military pressure from Scotland and Ireland. They claimed the right to exercise the royal prerogative to raise certain taxes without Parliament but respected the common law by subjecting their powers to scrutiny by the courts (see *Case of Proclamations* (1611); *R v Hampden* (1637)). The judges were servants of the Crown but asserted their independence from the Crown in deciding cases (*Prohibitions del Roy* (1607)). Nevertheless their position remained ambivalent since they could be dismissed by the King and the outcome of cases was not conclusive. For example Coke CJ's stand against royal interference in *Prohibitions del Roy* was followed by his dismissal for taking a similar stand in 1616 in the *Commendum* case.

From 1629 Charles I attempted to rule without Parliament. However when he attempted in 1639 to impose the Anglican prayer book on the Scots, the resulting uprising forced him to summon Parliament in 1640 (the 'Long Parliament', which continued until 1660 albeit dormant or suspended for most of its life). A shortlived compromise was reached in 1641 when the Star Chamber and other special prerogative courts introduced by the Tudors to support an administrative state were abolished. These events left English legal culture with a deep suspicion of special jurisdictions over governmental matters and a preference for the ordinary courts. From the religious perspective, the Church of England headed by the King was confronted on the one hand by the Catholic Church and on the other by Protestant groups who dominated Parliament. Civil war broke out in 1642, resulting in victory for Parliament in 1646.

There was a wide ranging constitutional debate at Putney between the ruling conservative establishment of landowners led by Oliver Cromwell and the more radical army rank and file represented by the Levellers who proposed a written constitution. This 'Agreement of the People' was based on religious freedom, equality before the law and universal male suffrage (later qualified by excluding servants and beggars). However Cromwell invoked custom and tradition in favour of more limited reforms. The Levellers were defeated by force in 1649.

In 1649 Charles I was executed on the authority of Parliament which was packed with army supporters. The House of Lords was abolished and a republic declared. In 1653 the remnants of Parliament were expelled and a military dictatorship, dominated by Protestants and with Cromwell as 'Lord Protector', was introduced. However after Cromwell's death in 1658 it seemed that chaos could best be avoided by restoring the traditional constitution. A self appointed group of political leaders restored the Crown in 1660 in the form of Charles II, the heir of Charles I. The House of Lords was also restored.

Charles II (1660–85) and his brother James II (1685–88) ruled on the basis that there had been no republic and the republican legislation was expunged from the statute book. Towards the end of Charles's reign, at a time when he was heavily subsidised by the

French, anti-Catholic sentiment was revived. Catholicism was associated in the public mind with absolute monarchy, an association that still scars the constitution by preventing the monarch from being or marrying a Catholic. There was a substantial exodus abroad by Catholics and other religious minorities, thereby sowing the seeds of the American Revolution and adding to the problem of Ireland (Chapter 6). The Exclusion Crisis (1679–81), in which a parliamentary majority attempted to bar Charles's Catholic brother James from the succession to the throne, reactivated the conflict between monarchy and Parliament. Charles used his prerogative power to close the sessions of Parliament and refused to summon Parliament again after 1681.

James II ruled with the support of a Tory dominated Parliament from 1685. However James alienated both Whigs and Tories by favouring Catholics and attempting to override Parliament by virtue of suspending and dispensing powers under the royal prerogative. This had some success at least to meet emergencies (*Thomas* v *Sorrell* (1674); *Godden* v *Hales* (1686)). James suspended the penal laws against Catholics in 1687 and 1688. He also displaced thousands of local parliamentary candidates who would not vote according to his wishes.

During this period the modern two party system appeared in a loose form. Both parties were dominated by the aristocracy. The Whigs, supported by the ideas of John Locke (Chapter 2), were a more populist and progressive party. They favoured a balance of power based on a contract between monarch, Lords and Commons; liberty and religious toleration, except of Catholics; and property rights. The Tories, who drew on biblical authority (for example Sir Robert Filmer, *Patriarcha*, 1680), favoured monarchy, the Anglican Church and paternalistic government. These broad groupings, albeit with considerable splits and regroupings, lasted until the middle of the nineteenth century when the Liberals replaced the Whigs and introduced ideas of market freedom. The Tories became the modern Conservative Party, concern with monarchy and Church being supplemented by ideas of national identity. However contemporary political parties do not fall within any consistent ideological template, all being largely opportunistic and eclectic.

The foundations of the modern constitution were laid by the 1688 'Glorious' revolution when James dissolved Parliament and fled the country. A self appointed 'Convention Parliament' combining Whigs and Tories, landowning and commercial interests, offered the Crown to the Protestant William of Orange and his wife Mary (James's daughter), supported by the Dutch military. In political terms the 1688 revolution was relatively conservative, being a compromise designed to satisfy all influential interests. It was justified in two inconsistent ways. On a Hobbesian premise, James II had abdicated leaving a power vacuum which, according to the common law doctrine of necessity, must be filled in order to avoid chaos. On the other premise, based on Locke, James had broken his contract by misruling so entitling the people to rebel. In Scotland and Ireland, continuing support for the Stuart monarchs was crushed by force.

The Convention also promoted the Bill of Rights 1688 dealing with the grievances against the Stuart kings. It prohibited the Crown from exercising key powers without the consent of Parliament, including the power to make laws, to tax, to keep a standing army in peacetime, and to override legislation. It also protected freedom of speech and elections in Parliament, secured frequent Parliaments, protected jury trial and banned excessive bail. William and Mary then summoned a Parliament which ratified the Acts of the Convention (Crown and Parliament Recognition Act 1689). The Act of Settlement 1700 provided for the succession to the Crown and gave superior court judges security of tenure and therefore independence from the Crown. The Act of Settlement also links Church and state by requiring the monarch to be a member of the Church of England and not to marry a Catholic, contains safeguards to prevent a monarch born 'out of this Kingdom' embroiling the country in a foreign war and prohibits non-citizens from being members of Parliament or the Privy Council (compare Chapter 12). The Meeting of Parliament Act 1694 (the Triennial Act) required Parliament to meet at least every three years (by convention it must meet annually) and limited the life of a Parliament to three years (now five years, Parliament Act 1911).

Thus the 1688 settlement put in place the main legal structures we have today. It was not based on democracy nor the fundamental rights of the individual. If anything it confirmed the principle of aristocratic rule. The House of Lords was a powerful body and the House of Commons was largely made up of landowners and traders dependent on the patronage of the Lords. Thomas Paine, who fled the country in 1792 having been charged with sedition for denying that Britain had a constitution, said in *The Rights of Man* (1791–2):

> What is [the Bill of Rights 1688] but a bargain which the parts of the government made with each other to decide powers. You shall have so much and I will have the rest; and with respect to the nation, it said, for your share, you shall have the right of petitioning. This being the case the Bill of Rights is more properly a bill of wrongs and of insult. (Paine, 1987, p. 292)

The 1688 settlement also led to the creation of the Bank of England in 1694 as a semi-independent institution which guaranteed the currency and through which the government could borrow money. This was an important reason for the successful expansion of the British government and the economy during the following century since it gave the Crown a secure source of funds.

4.5 The Eighteenth and Early Nineteenth Centuries: The Parliamentary System

This period, the Enlightenment, was one of great intellectual and social change. Reason was promoted as replacing revealed religion, custom and traditional hierarchy. During this period the basic political structure of the UK constitution began to develop, mainly through non-legally binding conventions creating the parliamentary system. As is still the case, in law the monarch remained the head of the government with power to appoint members of the House of Lords, to assent to legislation, to appoint and dismiss all ministers and to summon and dissolve Parliament, but unable to raise taxes or make law without the cooperation of Parliament. At first the monarch claimed to run the executive personally although the Commons could dismiss a ministry of which it disapproved. The Crown ran what was in effect a political party known as the 'Court and Treasury Party', which it controlled by giving government jobs to its supporters and manipulating elections. The main parties, the Whigs and the Tories, alternated in forming governments, although during this period the Whigs predominated. Coalition governments were common. A significant difference from the modern Parliament was that the party system was looser and the very existence of parties was controversial (for example lack of independence against rallying support for great causes). About half the MPs were independent of party allegiance and others frequently changed parties. One reason for the relative independence of MPs was that unlike today most MPs had private means and did not depend on their party for career advancement. Indeed an Act of 1710 (9 Anne c.5) imposed a property requirement on membership of the House of Commons (except for the eldest sons of peers and knights and the representatives of Oxford and Cambridge universities).

It was established that the King must act on the advice of ministers and must appoint as Prime Minister the person who commands a majority of the House of Commons. Government policy was made by the Cabinet, a body of senior ministers originally chosen by the King but now on the advice of the Prime Minister. It was also established that the government must resign if it loses the confidence of Parliament. If an alternative government cannot be formed the monarch must dissolve Parliament, leading to an election and the summoning of a new Parliament. The Prime Minister could request the monarch to dissolve Parliament at any time. However the House of Lords was still coequal with the Commons and could veto legislation although the Commons controlled the raising and spending of money by the Crown.

At a time when most European states were absolute monarchies, the British constitution was widely admired from outside as a stable and liberal regime embodying the rule of law and a balance between Parliament and the Crown. The notion of the 'mixed constitution' was promoted in which monarch, Lords and Commons acted as checks on each other in a balanced clockwork-like machine. The leading legal commentator Blackstone (1723–80) announced that the royal assent to legislation meant that the King could not propose evil but could prevent it and went on to eulogise the mutual checks between nobility, King and people that Parliament embodied (Chapter 6). Blackstone also emphasised the importance of the rule of law and the independence of the judges. However in the eighteenth century this was ambivalent (below).

From inside Britain the picture was more blurred. The electoral system was not democratic and bore little relationship to the distribution of the population. Elections were largely controlled by aristocratic families with a power base both in the House of Lords and in local affairs by bribery or by selecting candidates. There was a property qualification to vote in the rural counties. In the boroughs (towns) the right to vote depended on local charters and customs. In many cases this was attached to particular property and could be bought. There were numerous 'rotten boroughs' that only had a handful of electors, sometimes in the gift of particular families. At the other extreme the expanding cities had few representatives. General elections did not necessarily relate to changes in government as is the case today but governments formed and reformed under royal and aristocratic influence.

Judges were politically appointed and were often members of Parliament and the Cabinet. Until the reign of George III (1760–1820) they had to be reappointed on the death of a monarch. The record of the rule of law was mixed. It protected rights in the formal sense that everyone had access to the same courts and whatever rights a person had were usually adjudicated impartially. However it was easy for Parliament to pass harsh laws for the benefit of its supporters which the courts were required by the rule of law principle to apply. These included anti-poaching laws and a tax system that put the overwhelming burden upon consumption as opposed to property, thus penalising the poor (see Thompson, *Whigs and Hunters*, Allen Lane, 1975). The courts protected property rights and personal security strongly (for example *Leach* v *Money* (1765); *Entick* v *Carrington* (1765); *Wolfe Tone's Case* (1798)). Common law rejected slavery within England albeit reluctantly (*Somersett's Case* (1772)). Freedom of expression was less clearly protected other than that of MPs. There were ruthless measures against public disorder, blasphemy and political offences, such as sedition. These measures included the intermittent suspension of habeas corpus (an ancient procedure for ensuring the release of those unlawfully imprisoned). The common law, with its reliance on custom, faced severe challenge by rationalists such as Bentham (Chapter 2) who preferred legislation. Leading legal commentators, notably Blackstone, attempted with mixed success to rationalise the common law but it proved impossible to reconcile it with the developing notion of absolute parliamentary supremacy, a tension that remains today (Chapter 9).

Some contemporary themes are emerging. There is still tension between the House of Lords and the House of Commons and between the courts and Parliament. The Crown still possesses wide legal powers restricted by conventions, the scope of which is unclear. Patronage is exercised by the Prime Minister and political parties who nominate candidates for election and recommend peerages. Then as now, the permanent civil service was caught between two stools. On the one hand, efficiency required it to be distant from day-to-day politics. On the other hand, ministers required loyal servants. Various 'Place Acts' attempted a compromise by barring many categories of public official from membership of Parliament. Today we tackle the problem by barring most public officials from sitting in Parliament and creating a category of 'special adviser' who is a civil servant with party political affiliations (Chapter 5).

Scotland, which had previously been a separate state under the same monarch, was united with England as 'Great Britain' with one Parliament based on the English Parliament (Acts of Union 1706). The Act of Union with Ireland 1800 temporarily united Great Britain and Ireland as the UK. However, by 1921 most of Ireland had become an independent state. Northern Ireland, which from Tudor times had been occupied by Protestant settlers from England and Scotland, remains part of the UK.

4.6   The Nineteenth and Twentieth Centuries: Democracy and the Central State

During the nineteenth century the political and economic circumstances of Britain changed. Rural communities dominated by aristocratic landowners were rivalled by conurbations dependent upon industrial production and overseas trade. This led to a rapidly increasing urban population of wage earners, demands for democratic government and the provision of public services. Between the first Reform Act of 1832 and the Representation of the People Act 1948 which finally introduced equal voting rights for all adults, Parliament gradually and reluctantly extended the right to vote. Many more electoral constituencies were created corresponding to the distribution of the population. Secret ballots were introduced, reducing corruption and intimidation. The balance of power between Parliament and the executive moved in favour of the executive. MPs were becoming professional politicians dependent for their livelihood on party support. Elections became the mass campaigns with which we are familiar today. After the First World War (1914–18) the moderately radical Liberal Party collapsed and the conservative Tories were confronted by the newly emergent Labour Party, then representing working class interests.

Utilitarianism and economics replaced law as the intellectual fashion. For much of the nineteenth century free market ideas were dominant but coupled with strong state activity to provide basic services and remedy injustices. Local authorities were created to provide the roads, utilities and public health services necessary to support business interests but their powers were limited by the courts to prevent them providing more than basic welfare services (for example *Attorney-General* v *Fulham Corporation* (1921)). An important landmark was the Northcote-Trevelyan Report of 1854 which led to the creation of a permanent, professional and non-party political civil service appointed on merit – an ideal retained today albeit increasingly vulnerable.

The extension of democracy led to a debate about the place of common law. Traditionalists regarded the common law as a hedge against tyranny while reformers such as Bentham despised the common law as an enemy of progress, democracy and efficient management. During this period of developing democracy the courts explicitly endorsed the principle of parliamentary supremacy (Chapter 9). In relation to the common law it is arguable that the broad justice-based system that predominated during the eighteenth century was challenged by more formalistic rule-based conceptions of law that suited the development of trade in the nineteenth century. This was underpinned by the dominant religion that extolled the merits of hard work and duty.

During Queen Victoria's reign (1837–1901) the monarchy reshaped itself as a symbolic representative of the nation standing outside party politics. By the end of the nineteenth century it was becoming established that the Prime Minister and most senior ministers must be members of the House of Commons and, it was increasingly claimed, that the unelected House of Lords was subordinate to the House of Commons. Lord Salisbury was the last Prime Minister to sit in the House of Lords (1892).

During the early years of the twentieth century there was persistent hostility between the House of Lords, which had an inbuilt Conservative majority, and the Liberal government. This concerned in particular the question of Irish home rule and the reluctance of the Lords to approve high taxation for welfare purposes. After a long struggle culminating in a general election, followed by King George's reluctant agreement to create enough peers to steamroller the legislation through, the Lords backed down. The Parliament Act 1911 endorsed the supremacy of the Commons by removing most of the powers of the House of Lords to veto legislation. However the House of Lords retains significant influence. Its main function is now that of a revising and delaying mechanism. In view of its relative independence from party politics it could also be regarded as a guardian of constitutional values.

Impelled by the demands of a larger electorate the executive began to increase in size and range of discretionary powers as successive governments provided a wider range of welfare services. These could be delivered only through large bureaucratic organisations making numerous detailed decisions, guided by a plethora of rules and technical specialists. During the twentieth century it became widely accepted that the state could regulate any aspect of our lives and that whether it should do so was a matter not for the constitution but for the everyday political contest. The traditional sources of law, Acts of Parliament and the courts, were supplemented by an array of tools that enabled the executive to act relatively quickly and informally but without detailed parliamentary scrutiny. These included delegated legislation made by government departments under powers given to them by statute and wide discretionary powers conferred on ministers and local authorities. Thousands of administrative tribunals staffed by government appointees were created to deal with the disputes generated by the expansion of state activity. Both raised fears about judicial independence and the rule of law embodying a clash between 'red light' and 'green light' enthusiasts (Chapter 1). Other bodies outside the traditional umbrella of parliamentary accountability were created to run services or to give advice. Executive control over Parliament increased. Parliamentary processes were too amateurish and controlled by government supporters to enable executive action to be thoroughly scrutinised.

The constitution made only limited responses to these developments and it was feared that the executive had outgrown the constraints of both the rule of law and political accountability to Parliament. In the interwar period both ends of the political spectrum were worried. Some believed that the executive had taken over, others that an individualistically minded judiciary would frustrate social reforms. The Report of the Committee on Ministers' Powers (1932, Cmd 4060) concerning delegated legislation and the Report of the Committee on Administrative Tribunals and Inquiries (1958, Cmnd 218, the Franks Committee) recommended marginal reforms. These improved publicity, strengthened the powers of the courts, supplemented parliamentary scrutiny of the executive and introduced a Council on Tribunals to monitor and advise on administrative tribunals and statutory inquiries (Statutory Instruments Act 1946, Tribunals and Inquiries Acts 1958/1992). From the 1960s various 'ombudsmen' were set up to investigate complaints by citizens against government but without enforceable powers.

Recognising the inevitability of executive power and reluctant to appear to be challenging democracy, the courts usually deferred to political decisions. However from the 1960s the courts began to interfere more actively with government decisions in the interests of individual rights, a development supported by the enactment in 1998 of the Human Rights Act. Moreover some judges have revived the old claim that the common law is the basis of the constitution, even suggesting that common law is capable of overriding Acts of Parliament in order to resist executive tyranny (Chapter 9).

There were also concerns about democracy. In 1972 the UK became a member of what is now the European Union (European Communities Act 1972). Much European law has thereby become binding in UK law but is not made by an elected body and is subject only to limited democratic scrutiny (Chapter 10). Concerns were also raised that the electoral system puts minorities into power and enables the large political parties to control both the executive and Parliament. These complaints amounted to fears that the constitution had degenerated into an oligarchy that did little more than allow the people to choose periodically between groups of cronies. Indeed in the eighteenth century the French philosopher Rousseau asserted that the British were slaves except at election time.

In its early years the Labour government which was first elected in 1997 made constitutional changes, some of which strengthen the legal aspects of the constitution, a process sometimes called 'juridification'. These were intended to disperse power and 'modernise' the constitution. They include the following:

- Substantial devolution of powers to new government bodies in Scotland, Wales and Northern Ireland, thereby creating an anomaly as regards England (Chapter 6).
- The removal of most hereditary peers from the House of Lords, leaving its members to be appointed by the Prime Minister subject to a non-statutory vetting committee (House of Lords Act 1999, Chapter 12). Further attempts at reform have stalled largely due to reluctance on the part of many politicians to create a democratically elected chamber that could rival the House of Commons or weaken the power of the executive.

▶ The Human Rights Act 1998 made the main provisions of the European Convention on Human Rights enforceable in the UK courts, albeit subject to Parliament (Chapter 19).

▶ The Freedom of Information Act 2000 confers a limited right of public access to government information but subject to considerable government discretion (Chapter 21).

▶ The Constitutional Reform Act 2005 creates a new Supreme Court as the highest Appellate Tribunal for England, Wales and (except in criminal cases) for Scotland, thus replacing the House of Lords. It abolishes the traditional roles of the Lord Chancellor as head of the judiciary and presiding officer of the House of Lords, leaving the Lord Chancellor with an executive role as Secretary of State for Justice. It also creates an independent Judicial Appointments Commission with power to appoint judges (Chapter 8).

Summary

▶ The historical development of the constitution was driven by the gradual wresting of power from the monarch in favour of other interest groups focused mainly on Parliament.

▶ The 1688 revolution created a settlement that still forms the legal basis of the constitution. It attempts to combine respect for continuity and a balance of forces with the principle of parliamentary supremacy and collective party government.

▶ Despite a tendency to corruption, democratic reforms were introduced during the nineteenth and early twentieth centuries but without there being a complete democratic basis for the constitution.

▶ The common law and independent courts were regarded as important checks on government. In recent years the courts have been more active than previously in challenging government action.

▶ Latterly there have been concerns about the increased power of the executive in relation to Parliament.

Exercises

4.1 To what extent was the 1688 settlement a constitutional revolution?

4.2 Does the history of the UK constitution reveal a march towards greater democracy?

4.3 What historical factors have led to the powerful position held by the executive in the UK constitution?

4.4 'Herein consists the excellence of the English Government, that all parts of it form a mutual check on each other' (Blackstone, 1765). To what extent was this true in Blackstone's time and is it true today?

4.5 What general principles, if any, underpin contemporary attempts at constitutional reform?

Further reading

Budge, I., Crewe, I., McKay, D. and Newton, K. (2004) *The New British Politics* (3rd edn) London, Pearson, Chapters 2, 3.

Chrimes, S.B. (1967) *English Constitutional History* (4th edn) Oxford University Press.

Lyons, A. (2003) *Constitutional History of the United Kingdom*, London, Cavendish.

McIlwain, C.H. (1947) *Constitutionalism Ancient and Modern*, London, Cornell University Press, Chapter 4.

Porter, R. (1990) *England in the Eighteenth Century*, London, Penguin, Chapter 3.

Oliver, D. (2003) *Constitutional Reform in the United Kingdom*, Oxford University Press.

Ward, I. (2004) *The English Constitution: Myths and Realities*, Oxford, Hart Publishing.

Chapter 5

An overview of the main institutions of the UK constitution

Small clusters of self-enclosed, self-serving groups on the peaks, and the public on the plain below. (Anthony Sampson, *Who Runs This Place?*, 2004)

Key words

- Dignified and efficient
- Constitutional monarchy
- Bicameral
- Checks and balances
- Prerogative
- Accountability
- Collective government
- Executive domination
- Civil service impartiality
- Standards
- Voluntary codes
- Patronage

5.1 Introduction: The Dignified and Efficient Constitution

This chapter offers an overview of the contemporary structure of the UK government as a framework for a more detailed discussion of key topics in the following chapters.

It is often said that the glue which holds the unwritten UK constitution together is the propensity of the British to subservience and deference to officialdom. Writing in the mid nineteenth century Walter Bagehot (1902) regarded social class deference and superstition as the 'magic' ingredients that animated the constitution. Bagehot took a jaundiced view of the political sophistication of ordinary people and thought that government could only work effectively if its authority was buttressed by traditional institutions which command people's imagination and make them deferential to the rulers.

Bagehot distinguished between what he called the 'dignified' and the 'efficient' parts of the constitution. The dignified parts give the constitution its authority and encourage people to obey it. They involve the trappings of power and the mystique of ceremonial and ritual. According to Bagehot, the monarchy and Parliament constitute the main dignified elements of the constitution. The efficient part of the constitution, which Bagehot located in the Cabinet and which depends on the political balance of forces at any given time, carries out the working exercise of power behind the scenes. From this perspective all government boils down to an oligarchy of likeminded people in the form of a 'king' and his courtiers.

What is dignified and what is efficient changes over time. For example the eighteenth century Hanoverian kings lost public respect by becoming virtually party politicians.

William IV in 1834 was the last monarch to dismiss a ministry that had the support of Parliament. Towards the end of her reign Queen Victoria 'redignified' the monarchy by distancing herself from political partisanship and introducing the kind of pomp and ceremony that characterises the UK monarchy in modern times. But it remains unclear whether the monarch retains a vestige of political power (Chapter 12).

The distinction between the dignified and efficient performs a useful function in a democracy by preventing working politicians from claiming to embody the state, a technique adopted by tyrants throughout history. For example the monarch and Parliament have authority, the latter because it is elected, while the government has power without authority in its own right.

On the other hand the dignified element can reinforce tyranny by hiding reality. Bagehot thought that it would be dangerous to shed the light of reality upon the constitution. The 'noble lie' postulated by Plato in his *Republic* and designed to keep people happy with their designated roles, was that when humans were formed in the earth the rulers had gold mixed with them, the military silver and the workers lead. Even Plato's pupils found this hard to swallow but they thought that it is sometimes right to lie in the interests of the state. There is an element of the same thinking in the contemporary constitution. In *McIlkenny* v *Chief Constable of the West Midlands Police* [1980] 2 All ER 227 at 239–40, Lord Denning MR took the view that it was better for the 'Birmingham Six' to remain wrongly convicted than to face the 'appalling vista' of the police being found to be guilty of perjury, violence and threats. The Scott Report into the sale of arms to Iraq (1995, HC 115) revealed that ministers and civil servants regarded it as being in the public interest to mislead Parliament, if not actually to lie, over government involvement in arms sales to overseas regimes.

5.2   Legislature and Executive

The constitution comprises the Queen as head of state and the three traditional branches of government:

(1) Parliament is the lawmaker, comprising the elected House of Commons and the appointed House of Lords.
(2) The Crown is the executive branch, known generally as 'the government'. It is accountable to Parliament and its decisions are in the main reviewable by the courts.
(3) The independent judiciary is the third branch, comprising courts and tribunals.

Parliament is widely regarded as the highest branch. Thus in *R (Bancoult)* v *Secretary of State* (2007) Sedley LJ referred to the interlocking but unequal limbs of the state.

Griffiths succinctly identified the basic legal features of the Constitution as follows:

'Governments of the United Kingdom may take any action necessary for the proper government of the United Kingdom as they see it, subject to two limitations. The first limitation is that they may not infringe the legal rights of others unless expressly authorised to do so under statute or the prerogative. The second limitation is that if they wish to change the law, whether by adding to their existing power or otherwise, they must obtain the consent of Parliament' ('The Political Constitution' (1979) *Modern Law Review* 42:1 at 15).

Griffiths has encapsulated the legal constraints upon government. From the point of view of the structure of government it is necessary to provide a more complex description.

We can approach this at three levels: firstly that of the law, secondly widening the perspective to include the main conventions mixed with laws and thirdly identifying political practices and influences that may distort the constitutional structure.

5.2.1   The Legal Level

At the most basic legal level established by the 1688 revolution, the lawmakers are the Queen in Parliament, who (probably) has unlimited legal power and, subject (probably) to Parliament, the judges under the common law. Thus a strict separation of powers does not apply.

The Legislature. Parliament makes primary law in the form of Acts of Parliament (statutes). It also provides the government with money and is meant to hold the executive to account. It is bicameral, comprising an elected lower house, the House of Commons and an upper house, the House of Lords most members of which are appointed by the Queen for life. A Parliament lasts for five years at the end of which there must be a general election for membership of the House of Commons and a new Parliament summoned by the Queen. Within the five year period the Queen can dissolve Parliament whenever she wishes, again leading to a general election. Parliament must meet at least every three years and so cannot be dispensed with by the Queen. The House of Commons is the dominant body. The House of Lords can delay the enactment of statutes but subject to an exception – most importantly a bill to prolong the life of Parliament itself – the House of Lords cannot veto laws proposed by the Commons.

The Executive. The executive comprises the Queen/Crown and her servants. The Queen can appoint and dismiss anyone she wishes as servant or adviser. The Queen cannot raise taxes or make new laws unless authorised by Parliament but her assent is required for laws proposed by Parliament. Most legal powers are conferred by statute on individual ministers. There are also important executive powers vested in the Crown under common law. These are known as the 'royal prerogative' (Chapter 14). This is a residue of the powers of the medieval monarchs. Some prerogatives can be justified as being a necessary aspect of the sovereignty of any state, for example the power to deploy the armed forces and to enter into treaties with other states.

The Crown as the permanent executive is always in being. It can be terminated only by an Act of Parliament. However the legal status of the Crown as such is obscure. It is not clear how far the Crown is a separate legal entity from the Queen personally. As regards technicalities such as the ownership of government property it is common practice to vest property in individual government departments created by statute as separate legal entities for that purpose. In many countries the 'state' is a legal entity but the UK has no legal concept of the state as such, only the Crown.

Apart from implementing the law, controlling public services and handing out jobs, honours and money, the executive makes policy, proposes legislation to Parliament and makes subordinate legislation under powers delegated to it by Parliament. Parliament can of course give executive power to anyone. It has kept historical continuity by preserving the Crown in law as the central executive, although specific executive powers are also given to many other bodies which have been established by statute, notably local authorities. These are not part of the Crown unless the statute provides otherwise. Control of the police is divided between the Crown in the form of the Home Secretary and local police authorities within the local government framework.

The Armed Forces are also Crown servants. Under the Bill of Rights 1688 the existence of a permanent peacetime army requires statutory approval. However control over the armed forces, for example deployment, choice of weapons and declaring war is a royal prerogative power and so does not require parliamentary approval (but see Act of Settlement 1700 s.3). The army is therefore under the control of the civil power in the shape of ministers, on whose advice the prerogative must be exercised, and ultimately Parliament. Some aspects of the armed forces including military discipline and courts martial are directly regulated by statute. There are concerns as to whether military courts are sufficiently independent to satisfy contemporary human rights based notions of a fair trial (see *Findlay* v *UK* (1997), Armed Forces Act (2006)).

In the absence of special statutory powers members of the armed forces, in common with the police have no special privileges in connection with their use of force. They are subject to the same general law that applies to ordinary citizens, namely that the force used must be in self defence or in the defence of others or of property and must be reasonable in the circumstances. This reflects a traditional aspect of the rule of law (Chapter 7). However the pressures of the circumstances, such as being forced to act quickly in a chaotic or dangerous situation is of course part of the circumstances. It is not clear whether there is a defence of obedience to superior orders (Chapter 21).

5.2.2   The Level of Conventions

Once we add in some basic conventions the picture changes particularly in relation to the executive. From this perspective the executive comprises ministers and civil servants. The Queen must always act on the advice of the Prime Minister or other ministers who are the officials responsible for proposing laws to Parliament and putting laws into effect. All ministers must be members of Parliament and collectively they are 'the government'. The most important ministers must be members of the House of Commons. The Queen must appoint as Prime Minister the person chosen by a majority of the House of Commons and she must appoint and dismiss other ministers on the recommendation of the Prime Minister. Ministers are responsible to Parliament for their actions although it is uncertain what this means. If the government loses the support of the House of Commons then unless an alternative leader has the support of the Commons the Queen must dissolve Parliament, leading to a general election. The Queen must also dissolve Parliament on the advice of the Prime Minister. These conventions therefore create a model of representative democratic government in which the government is responsible through Parliament to the 'people' or at least to those of them permitted to vote. Arrangements for elections are a matter for Parliament in the same way as any other law. Thus Parliament both sustains the government and polices it. This leads inevitably to conflict.

Civil servants are employees of the Crown other than the armed forces and ministers. They are governed by an obscure mixture of the royal prerogative, conventions and custom, and practice with some statutory element concerning conditions of employment. Civil servants have two kinds of obligation. The first is that senior civil servants must give impartial advice to ministers. Civil servants are appointed by an independent process supervised by Civil Service Commissioners in order to minimise political bias (see Civil

Service Code 2006). This helps to stabilise the constitution in a system where the political part of government is constantly changing. Unlike the US, senior civil servants are not automatically replaced when a government changes. The second obligation is that all civil servants must loyally carry out instructions from ministers. In law a civil servant is regarded as no more than an extension of the minister. It is obvious that no minister can make every decision in person nor can she or he be aware of the thousands of decisions that must be taken within a government department each year. A minister can act through a civil servant in her or his department without this being an unlawful delegation of power (see *Carltona* v *Commissioner of Works* (1943)). Thus the constitution creates a chain of accountability through ministers to Parliament whoever actually makes a given decision.

5.2.3   Political Practice

The third level is that of political practice, reminding us of Griffith's famous aphorism: the constitution is 'everything that happens' (Chapter 1). Flaws in the above arrangement mean that the straightforward chain of accountability from ministers through Parliament to the people has been distorted and arguably subverted. In practice Parliament is weak; the House of Lords is required to be subordinate to the House of Commons and the House of Commons has allowed the government to dominate it. Political parties are strong. Except on relatively rare occasions when the government has a small majority, most MPs will vote as required by their party perhaps without studying the proposals in question. There is no law or convention requiring them to do this other than one requiring those MPs who are government ministers to be loyal to the government. About one hundred MPs out of a total of about 650 are ministers.

The matter is therefore about the motivation of individual MPs. There are three institutional factors which put pressure on MPs to support the executive without question. Firstly there is the institution of the political party. Strictly speaking the MP's main role is that of a representative of his or her local constituency but party loyalties tend to come first. There is no law or convention requiring political parties to exist. Nevertheless political parties are an inevitable ingredient of a democratic system since elections must be contested by organised groups capable of raising sufficient money to be able to communicate effectively. In practice the Prime Minister is always the leader of the majority political party. Unlike a presidential system the people do not elect the Prime Minister as such, who is simply elected as an ordinary MP by his or her local constituency. Of course at a general election many voters are likely to be thinking of the party leaders when voting for their local MP. If a Prime Minister resigns between elections, the successor is effectively chosen in private under internal party arrangements. Indeed since 1900, among twenty five prime ministers only ten have taken office following a general election. Prime Minister Gordon Brown was elected leader by the Labour Party without opposition following the resignation of Tony Blair under pressure from his party. A strong motivation of candidates for election as MPs is to please the party leaders since these are influential in selecting and reselecting candidates and rewarding them with jobs in government.

Secondly and reinforcing this, there is the voting system for Parliament known as 'first past the post' – technically the 'single relative majority' system. This awards a seat in Parliament to whichever candidate has the largest number of votes in a local area known as a constituency. Other candidates get nothing, whatever their share of the vote. First past the post is therefore unfair to smaller parties. This contrasts with systems of proportional representation used in other countries (including Scotland, Wales and Northern Ireland) under which seats are distributed between the parties according to their share of the total vote. This is likely to weaken the power of the larger parties allowing members of Parliament greater independence. The present system has been justified on the basis that it produces a strong government. Whether that is desirable is a matter for the individual. A related factor is that the geographical constituencies are designated by an independent Boundary Commission according to loose requirements which allow social matters such as travelling distance and cultural affinities to be taken into account. Thus there are variations in the number of voters in different constituencies. Also inevitably some localities traditionally favour a particular party since politics is to some extent based on economic interests.

The third factor is that because ministers are also MPs they are in a position to dominate the procedure of the House using their voting strength to ensure that government proposals have priority, leaving only limited time for other members (backbenchers) to raise and discuss issues. This is reinforced by a system of party discipline known as the Whip system under which the Whips persuade individual MPs to vote for government measures in the House of Commons. The Parliamentary timetable preserves some time each week for MPs to question ministers (who must provide written or oral answers), to propose legislation or to raise issues. However this time is insignificant and without government backing very few have a chance of serious debate.

The chain of accountability between ministers and civil servants has also been distorted in two ways. Firstly since the 1980s, many government functions have been removed from the traditional civil service and transferred either to private bodies operating under contracts with the government or exercised by Executive Agencies, sometimes competing for work with private bodies. Executive Agencies are part of the civil service but are semi independent from their sponsoring government department and partly copy the practices of private businesses. The theory behind these developments is 'public choice' theory (Chapter 2) according to which accountability and efficiency are best served by harnessing self interest in the form of competition. The convention of ministerial responsibility remains but it is unclear how far the agencies or bodies in question are themselves accountable to Parliament or whether ministers must accept the blame where things go wrong. A familiar interpretation of the convention by ministers is that ministers must explain to Parliament what has happened but are to be blamed only if personally involved. This illustrates a weakness of conventions, namely that unlike laws there is no independent authoritative way of deciding what they mean.

Secondly there is the practice of ministers appointing 'Special Advisers'. These are temporary civil servants appointed personally by ministers and working closely with them (see Special Advisers Code of Conduct 2005). Their posts terminate with their minister. Unlike other civil servants they are not required to be politically impartial and need not be selected on merit. Their function is mainly to assist ministers. However some special advisers have been empowered to give orders to established civil servants. There is concern that special advisers may threaten the reputation of the civil service for impartiality and also that permanent civil servants may be denied access to ministers and that their role will be reduced to carrying out orders from special advisers. The distinction between the political and the permanent parts of the executive has therefore become blurred, upsetting an important check and balance. On the other hand special advisers serve as a valuable link between the two elements.

For many years it has been argued that the rights and duties of civil servants and the relationship between ministers, civil servants and special advisers should be put on a statutory basis. In particular special advisers should be defined as a separate category distinct from civil servants and should not normally be given executive powers nor management or disciplinary powers over civil servants. Ministers should be personally accountable for the acts of their special advisers. This has not materialised (see Sixth and Ninth Reports of the Committee on Standards in Public Life, 2000, Cm 4817, 2003, Cm 5964). However the draft Constitutional Renewal Bill (below) includes general provisions governing the civil service and special advisers.

5.3   The Judicial Branch

The third branch of government is the judiciary, which has the distinctive function of resolving disputes impartially. The right to a fair trial before an independent court is a fundamental feature of common law and also the European Convention on Human Rights (ECHR). The judiciary reviews the legality of government action. Under the Human Rights Act 1998 it can scrutinise government decisions and Acts of Parliament for conformity with 'human rights' derived from the European Convention on Human Rights. The 1998 Act does not empower the courts to overturn an Act of Parliament although this might be possible by virtue of the common law (Chapter 9).

In a parliamentary system the distinction between the legislature and the executive is blurred but it is vital that the judiciary be independent of the other branches of government. This section outlines the main constitutional features of the judiciary. Further aspects particularly affecting judicial independence are discussed in Chapter 8. The discussion is concerned primarily with England and Wales as Scotland and Northern Ireland have a separate court system although appeals from Northern Ireland and appeals in civil cases in Scotland are dealt with by the House of Lords.

The main courts are as follows:

▷ **Superior courts** form the Supreme Court of Judicature (to be renamed the Senior Courts when the relevant parts of the Constitutional Reform Act 2005 take effect in October 2009). This includes the High Court which deals with major civil cases and the Court of Appeal which in two divisions deals with civil and criminal appeals. The Administrative Court is part of the High Court dealing with judicial review of public law decisions (Supreme Court Act 1981). These courts are staffed by High Court judges and Lords Justices of Appeal, who enjoy greater independence.

▷ **Inferior courts** include the Crown Court which deals with the more substantial criminal cases, and in certain respects has superior court status (Courts Act 1971), county courts which deal with smaller civil cases (County Courts Act 1984) and magistrates courts which deal mainly with minor criminal cases (Magistrates Courts Act 1980). Professional judges in these courts are circuit judges who hear criminal cases in the Crown Court and civil cases in the county court; district judges and deputy district judges who hear minor county court cases (Courts and Legal Services Act 1990) and magistrates court cases (Courts Act 2003). There are also lay magistrates sitting usually in panels of three supported by a professional justices' clerk who advises them and can also exercise certain judicial functions on their behalf (Courts Act 2003). There are part time professional assistant recorders and recorders who hear criminal cases in the Crown Court. These are normally practising barristers, the post being a road to promotion to higher judicial office.

▷ **The highest appellate court** is the Supreme Court. This hears appeals from all the UK jurisdictions except Scottish criminal cases. Until October 2009 when the relevant parts of the Constitutional Reform Act 2005 take effect, the House of Lords remains the highest court. The Appellate Committee of the House of Lords has an anomalous position. For historical reasons it is part of Parliament. Its members are life peers and as such can sit in Parliament in its legislative role. By convention the Law Lords do not participate in party political debate, although they occasionally speak on law reform matters and those affecting the judiciary. Indeed this kind of structured link between different branches of government is often regarded as desirable. However in 2009 the Appellate Committee is being replaced by a separate Supreme Court, with similar composition, jurisdiction and powers (Chapter 8). Whether this formal change will be merely cosmetic or will stimulate a greater sense of legitimacy in terms of willingness to reshape the law and challenge government action remains to be seen.

5.3.1   The Appointment and Dismissal of Judges

Judges are appointed under particular statutes by the Queen on the recommendation of the Lord Chancellor or in the case of some junior judges and lay magistrates by the Lord Chancellor alone. There is no input from elected bodies, for example along the lines of Senate hearings into the appointment of Supreme Court judges in the US. Other than lay magistrates and tribunal members, judges are appointed from the ranks of professional lawyers. Before the Tribunals, Courts and Enforcement Act 2007, judicial appointments were restricted to those who had rights of advocacy in the High Court for a prescribed period – usually ten or seven years. This contrasts with the position in other European countries where there is a separate judicial profession. The UK system has the advantage of drawing on talented people who are familiar with the workings of the court process. The disadvantage is that this might reinforce the perception of the legal system as a closed elite. The 2007 Act was intended to increase judicial diversity. It allows the Lord Chancellor to specify the 'relevant legal qualification and experience' required for judicial appointments, which allows a wider range of legal experience to be eligible such as legal executives, perhaps academic lawyers and other professionals whose work has not focused on advocacy.

Under the Constitutional Reform Act 2005, except in the case of lay magistrates and some minor offices, a person recommended by an independent Judicial Appointments Commission must be appointed (Chapter 8). This replaces a much criticised informal regime in the hands of the Lord Chancellor and Prime Minister. Prior to the 2005 Act the Lord Chancellor occupied an anomalous constitutional position, being nominally head of the judiciary but also the government minister in charge of the court system and the presiding officer in the House of Lords. Under the Act the Lord Chancellor ceases to be the head of the judiciary, being replaced in that role by the Lord Chief Justice. The Lord Chancellor no longer presides over the House of Lords but remains a cabinet minister in charge of the Ministry of Justice which funds and administers the court system and therefore with a seat in Parliament. The Lord Chancellor's limited role in judicial appointments therefore strikes a balance between judicial independence and political accountability.

Superior court judges, that is judges of the High Court and above (to be renamed 'senior judges') have security of tenure designed to protect their independence. They can be dismissed only for misbehaviour by a resolution of both Houses of Parliament (Chapter 8). The bulk of the judiciary (about 97 per cent) comprises inferior court judges and lay magistrates. They do not have full security of tenure but hold office under various statutes which make different provisions for dismissal (Chapter 8).

5.3.2 Tribunals

Numerous specialised tribunals decide matters allocated to them by particular statutes. These concern specialised areas of law such as taxation as contrasted with the general jurisdiction of ordinary courts and often involving disputes with government bodies. In some cases such as employment tribunals they decide disputes between private persons. They were originally called administrative tribunals thus blurring the distinction between the judicial and executive branches and raising fears that they were not independent (see *Franks Report on Tribunals and Inquiries* (Cmnd 218/1957). Subsequent reforms, the most recent being the Tribunals, Courts and Enforcement Act 2007 have drawn the tribunal system more closely towards that of the ordinary courts.

Tribunal decisions are enforceable through the ordinary courts. They are claimed to have the advantages of economy, speed and expertise compared with the ordinary courts – the price to be paid for this being rougher justice (Franks Report, above). Tribunal procedures are less formal than those of ordinary courts and do not necessarily involve lawyers. They are meant to be accessible to poorer people with whom a substantial part of their work is concerned. However they may deal with complex legal matters and those before them are often without legal representation so that their accessibility is questionable (see Genn, 1993, *Modern Law Review* 56:393). They can also be used to distance decision making from the government itself so as to secure independence or more cynically to avoid responsibility.

The tribunal system is haphazard, numerous tribunals having been established over the years under separate legislation. Tribunals deal with a range of specialised and technical matters. These include education, employment, taxation, health, immigration and asylum, land valuation, title and use, state benefits, transport, trading matters, and the security services (see Report of Council on Tribunals HC 472 (2005–6)). There are some common features (Tribunals and Inquiries Act 1992). They are often presided over by a lawyer chairperson sitting with one or two lay members. They are not bound by strict rules of evidence. Most tribunals must give reasons in writing for their decisions. Tribunals are linked into the judicial system since there is usually a right of appeal from a tribunal to the ordinary court system although again this is somewhat haphazard. The High Court can also review tribunal decisions in the same way as those of other public bodies (Chapters 15–17). Tribunals have limited safeguards for their independence.

Depending on the particular statute, ministers or the Lord Chancellor appoint tribunal judges and in some cases the consent of the Lord Chancellor is required for dismissal. In the case of many tribunals the Lord Chancellor can appoint only a person selected by the Judicial Appointments Commission (see Constitutional Reform Act 2005 s.85, Schedule 14).

There is no conceptual distinction between a tribunal and a court proper. A constitutionally important distinction is whether the body in question exercises 'judicial' functions in the sense of the resolution of a dispute affecting civil rights and obligations. This attracts the right to a fair trial by an independent tribunal under Article 6 of the ECHR as applied by the Human Rights Act 1998. It might also be important to decide whether a body is a court for the purposes of the law of contempt of court, which affects freedom of speech (Chapter 19). In this context it is irrelevant whether the body is called a court or a tribunal. The main question is whether it is exercising judicial functions (see *Attorney-General* v *BBC* (1981); *General Medical Council* v *BBC* (1998)). It is necessary to rely on any definition of a court in a particular statute for a particular purpose, thus illustrating the pragmatic character of the UK constitution. Confusingly some bodies have the status of a court (or 'court of record' meaning a relatively high status court) conferred by statute but are called tribunals, for example the Employment Appeals Tribunal (Employment Tribunals Act 1996).

A Council on Tribunals whose members are appointed by the Lord Chancellor and Scottish ministers has until now supervised both the tribunal system and statutory public inquiries (Tribunals and Inquiries Act 1992). The Council is concerned to implement the basic principles of openness, fairness and impartiality and protect the independence of tribunals from the executive. However characteristically of the UK system, it has only consultative and advisory powers mainly concerning the procedural rules for tribunals made by the Lord Chancellor.

The administration of the tribunal system has recently been overhauled. As a result of the Leggatt Report (2001; see White Paper, *Transforming the Public Services: Complaints, Redress and Tribunals*, 2004, Cm 6243), a Tribunals Service under the Ministry of Justice has been established to administer and coordinate the main tribunals. The basic concerns are to rationalise the tribunal system and to strengthen the independence of tribunals from ministers and other bodies whose decisions they scrutinise and to make the tribunal system simpler and more open and user friendly. The Tribunals Courts and Enforcement Act 2007 gives effect to the main Leggatt reforms:

▷ The Act creates two new generic tribunals which can be grouped in 'Chambers'. These are the First Tier Tribunal and the Upper Tribunal, the latter being mainly an appellate body and having the status of a superior court (s.3). There is a further right of appeal from the Upper Tribunal to the ordinary courts on a point of law (s.13). The Upper Tribunal can also exercise judicial review functions similar to those of the High Court (see Chapter 18). The members of the First Tier Tribunal are appointed by the Lord Chancellor and also include *ex officio* (meaning by virtue of their office) members of certain other tribunals courts (s.4). The Upper Tribunal also comprises persons appointed by the Lord Chancellor and includes *ex officio* other senior office holders (s.5). Judges of ordinary courts are *ex officio* members of both tiers (s.6). Lawyer members of these tribunals will be known as Tribunal Judges. The Lord Chancellor is empowered to transfer the jurisdiction of most of the existing tribunals to the new tribunals thus rationalising and simplifying the tribunal system possibly at the cost of the diversity, flexibility and focus of tribunals. However the new tribunals can be organised in 'Chambers' based on groups of related specialisms. Some tribunals, notably Employment Tribunals and Asylum and Immigration Tribunals, will remain separate.

- The Lord Chancellor's duty to uphold the rule of law under the Constitutional Reform Act 2005 will apply also to tribunals under his jurisdiction.
- There will be a new office, that of 'Senior President of Tribunals' to oversee and lead the tribunal judiciary.
- There is a new Tribunal Procedure Committee to make rules for tribunals.
- The Council of Tribunals is replaced by the Administrative Justice and Tribunals Council. This remains an advisory body but its remit is extended to include the administrative justice system generally, which comprises ombudsmen and dispute resolution mechanisms within government departments and other public bodies.
- The Draft Constitutional Renewal Bill prevents the salaries of judges in the main tribunals being reduced.

5.3.3   Inquiries

Some government decisions, particularly in relation to planning and other land use decisions, are taken in the name of ministers following an inquiry held by an independent inspector. In some cases, notably routine cases under town and country planning legislation, power to make the decision is delegated to the inspector. Unlike tribunal decisions that primarily concern factual or legal issues, the subject matter of such decisions may also concern controversial political issues relating for example to airport building or rural development. The inquiry system is therefore intended to provide an independent element as part of a wider process and is not a self contained judicial process along the lines of a court.

Inquiries are sometimes described as 'quasi-judicial'. They follow a procedure broadly similar to that of a court but are more flexible and less formal. Formal rules of evidence do not apply. People whose interests are affected by the decision in question have a right to appear and give evidence. Others can speak at the discretion of the inspector who can also allow cross examination. This discretion is usually exercised liberally.

The independence and openness of inquiry procedures is partly safeguarded by the Tribunals and Inquiries Act 1992. This requires in particular that evidence must be disclosed in advance, reasons be given for decisions and where the minister overrules the inspector the parties must be given a chance to comment and in the case of disagreement about facts, to reopen the inquiry (see for example Town and Country Planning (Inquiries Procedure) (England) Rules (SI 2000 no. 1624)).

Unlike tribunals, inquiries are primarily part of a larger administrative process and therefore not independent of political influence. Nevertheless provided that judicial review is available, this distinctively British process has been upheld as compliant with the right to a fair trial under the ECHR. The reason offered for this depends on the substantial policy or political element involved which is appropriate for the involvement of a democratic element as opposed to the impartiality expected from a court of law (see *R (Alconbury Developments)* v *Secretary of State for the Environment, Transport and the Regions* (2001)). Furthermore the involvement of ministers and civil servants with their close secretive relationship means that policy advice may not be subject to independent scrutiny at the inquiry (see *Bushell* v *Secretary of State for the Environment* (1981)).

Hiving off important decisions such as those concerning the construction of large projects such as airports to an independent 'expert' Commission under the Planning Act 2008 raises important constitutional issues. These are firstly that such bodies are outside the field of political accountability and secondly that no kind of specialised expertise is especially qualified to choose between such different interests as economic needs, individual rights, nature conservation and the local environment. The balance between these interests requires a collective political choice which according to democratic principles should arguably be made by an elected body.

Special inquiries can be held to investigate events of public concern, for example serious incidents or allegations of misconduct by officials. Under the Inquiries Act 2005 a minister may establish such an inquiry, decide its terms of reference and appoint the person to hold it. Ministers have considerable control. For example a person with a direct interest in the subject of the inquiry or a close association with an interested party cannot be appointed unless the minister considers that impartiality would not reasonably be affected (s.9). Ministers also have powers in relation to public access to the inquiry and to publication of its report. The published parts of the inquiry report must be laid before Parliament (see also Chapter 8). A constitutional difficulty with this type of inquiry arises because senior judges are sometimes asked to hold them (for example the *Hutton Inquiry* (2004) into the death of Dr David Kelly connected with the government's proposal to invade Iraq). This may appear to compromise the independence of the judiciary (see Beatson, 'Should Judges Conduct Public Inquiries?' (2005) *Law Quarterly Review* 121:221). Under the Inquiries Act 2005 s.10 the Lord Chief Justice or the Senior Law Lord must first be consulted when it is proposed to appoint a judge to hold an inquiry.

Another form of inquiry is a Royal Commission. Again this is established by ministers, in this case under the royal prerogative. The report of the Commission is usually laid before Parliament. Royal Commissions have no power to compel attendance or disclosure of information. They are commonly employed to consider general issues, for example the Royal Commission on the House of Lords (Chapter 12). The members are often personally known to ministers. In practice, ministers often prefer to set up informal, non-public inquiries.

5.4 'Ad Hoc Bodies'

Executive powers are also conferred, usually by statute but sometimes informally, on many miscellaneous specialised bodies. These include bodies that regulate important private and public activities such as the Environment Agency (Environment Act 1995), the Financial Services Authority (Financial Services Act 2004), the Charity Commission (Charities Act 2006) and regulators of utility and transport companies (Utilities Act 2000; Railways Act 2005). They have many unofficial labels such as 'ad hoc bodies', 'quangos' (quasi-autonomous non-governmental agencies) and 'non-departmental public bodies' but there is no legal significance in these labels. Specifically constitutional issues are whether a body is part of the Crown, whether it has any democratic element and whether it is a public body for particular purposes (Chapters 17 and 18). Bodies whose powers are conferred by statute may also be subject to special treatment in respect of liability for damage in the sense that they may be immune provided that they do not exceed their statutory powers (see for example *Marcic* v *Thames Water Utilities* (2004); *X (Minors)* v *Bedfordshire County Council* (1995)).

The structure, powers and independence of these bodies depend on the pragmatic concerns of the particular legislation. Their members are usually appointed by a minister, thus providing a source of political favours. In some cases there must be a proportion of elected local councillors, for example regional planning bodies (Planning and Compulsory Purchase Act 2004 s.2). Some must include representatives of particular interests. Ministers may have substantial powers of control over such bodies including providing finance and giving directions. Such bodies have no direct democratic accountability and are vulnerable to abolition if they criticise the executive. For example the Police and Justice Bill proposed merging the Prison Inspectorate, which has been highly critical of prison conditions, into a broader criminal justice inspectorate charged with ensuring the effectiveness of the system as a whole, thereby diluting its purposes. The resulting Act drew back from this (Police and Justice Act 2006).

5.5   Local Government

Unlike the bodies discussed in the previous section, local authorities are elected and have tax raising powers and might therefore be considered to have some constitutional significance. From both liberal and republican perspectives (Chapter 2) local government could be regarded as providing a check and balance on central government in the sense of an alternative source of democratic power. Mill claimed that it is desirable in the interests of democracy and individual self fulfilment for people to have closer contact with governmental bodies than is possible at central government level. In particular local democracy generates different political perspectives and healthy disagreement and debate. However in the UK local authorities are entirely creatures of statute (Local Government Act 1972) and as such are subject to comprehensive central government control. All their powers derive from particular statutes either directly or through central government regulations. Local government in the UK has little political importance, the predominant public image being of elderly councillors arguing over minutiae and apathetic officials.

In as much as they are elected, local authorities might be considered to have a certain independent status (see for example *Secretary of State for Education and Science* v *Tameside MBC* (1977)). However the courts may give little weight to local democracy, regarding local authorities as agencies of Parliament (see *R* v *Somerset County Council ex parte Fewings* (1995)). Moreover local authorities, although having some tax raising powers have little financial independence, more than two thirds of their resources being provided by central government. By contrast some constitutions specifically protect local government autonomy. For example the Italian constitution protects regional and local autonomy according to the 'subsidiarity' principle that decisions should be taken at the nearest possible level to those affected by them. (See also Carnwath, 'The Reasonable Limits of Local Authority Power', 1996, *Public Law* 244.)

Local authorities have executive powers and limited lawmaking powers to make bylaws for prescribed purposes such as keeping order in public places and traffic control. Their geographical boundaries are designated by central government. Their main functions are to provide local political and strategic influence and deliver at an operational level services designated by central government, usually subject to central government power to intervene by means of devices such as injections, 'default powers' to take over a function, and appeals. Some functions such as housing and further education have been substantially removed from local control in favour of separate private and semi-private bodies regulated from the centre.

From a liberal perspective, the weakness of local government threatens the checks and balances required to limit government. There is occasional provision for public consultation but such deliberative democracy (Chapter 2) is normally a matter for the discretion of the authority (see Local Government Act 2000 ss.7, 27; Planning and Compulsory Purchase Act 2004 s.18).

The democratic structure of local authorities and the relationship between elected councillors and appointed officers are controlled by central government (Local Government Act 2000). The ethical conduct of local councillors is policed by the Standards Board for England, a body appointed by central government which has the power to suspend or disqualify local councillors (Local Government Act 2000). In its Tenth Report (2004, Cm 6406) the Committee on Standards in Public Life recommended that the Standards Board should operate on a more local basis and that its composition should be more independent than is currently the case. These proposals were accepted by the government.

5.6 The Police

The police have a claim to special constitutional status since they are authorised to use violence and are closely connected with the judicial process. It is therefore important that the police are seen to be independent of the executive. On the other hand the police service is funded by taxation so that democratic accountability is desirable. An accommodation must be struck between these concerns. The police are not Crown servants. Control over the police has been split three ways, a complex and tension ridden arrangement that can be justified as a liberal mechanism for controlling power.

Firstly there is the traditional status at common law of the 'constable' as an independent officer of the Crown with inherent powers of arrest, search and entry to premises, some common law and others statutory, and owing duties to the law itself to keep the peace (see Police Act 1996 s.10; *R v Metropolitan Police Commissioner ex parte Blackburn* [1968] 2 QB 118 at 136). All police officers and also prison officers are constables. Each police force is under the direction of its Chief Constable (in London the Metropolitan Police Commissioner) with regard to operational matters.

Secondly there is a tradition that the organisation of the police should be locally based and subject to democratic control so as to avoid the concentration of power associated with a 'police state'. Under the Police Act 1996 local police forces are organised on the basis of counties and amalgamations of county units. There are special arrangements in London comprising the Metropolitan Police and the City of London Police Force, limited to the square mile that technically comprises the City (Greater London Authority Act 1999). Each local force is answerable to a local police authority that comprises a mixture of local councillors, justices of the peace and persons appointed by the Home Secretary, with elected members a bare majority. The political balance of the elected members must reflect that of the council as a whole (Criminal Justice and Police Act 2001 s.105). The Chief Constable must have regard to the objects and targets set out in an annual plan made by the police authority (Police Act 1996 s.8). Police funding is a combination of central government grant and a levy (precept) on local taxation. The police authority must maintain an 'efficient and effective police force' (Police Act 1996 s.6(1)). Some argue that this gives the police authority political control since it allows them to specify how policing priorities should be ordered. The more widely held view is that it only requires the authority to provide material resources and fix the budget for whatever policing policies are determined by the Chief Constable. However section 7 enables a police authority to impose 'objectives' on its force consistent with any objectives imposed by the Home Secretary. The plan must also have regard to national objectives and performance targets set out by the Home Secretary. The police authority appoints and removes the Chief Constable and certain other senior officers.

Thirdly the central government has wide and increasing powers over police forces conferred by statute, usually upon the Home Secretary (Police Act 1996 Part II; Police Reform Act 2002). These are subject to no specific constitutional principles but seem to be generated by pragmatic considerations and the desire of particular governments to exercise control. In particular the Home Secretary's approval is needed for the appointment and removal of a Chief Constable and he or she can require a police authority to suspend or remove a Chief Constable. The Home Secretary can also provide funding, set performance targets and make regulations concerning discipline and resources including requiring the use of specified equipment. The Home Secretary can also require the merger of local forces and draw up a national policing plan and a code of practice for chief officers.

Technical support for policing may be too expensive to provide locally and modern crime is no respecter of local boundaries. Therefore there are national bodies, including the National Police Data Bank, the Mutual Aid Coordinating Centre, the National Criminal Intelligence Service and the National Crime Squad (Police Act 1997) which carry out police operations, operating formally by agreement with local forces. They are regulated by central boards, the membership of which strikes a balance between a minority of independent persons appointed by the Secretary of State and nomination by chief officers and local police authorities from among their members. A Central Police Training and Development Authority has also been created (Criminal Justice and Police Act 2001), the objectives of which are decided by the Secretary of State who can also give it detailed guidance and directions. There is therefore a considerable momentum towards a national police force.

Originally the police themselves conducted most prosecutions. However the Prosecution of Offences Act 1985 created a separate Crown Prosecution Service (CPS) which is under the control of the Director of Public Prosecutions (DPP). Crown prosecutors in local areas have powers to prosecute and conduct cases subject to discretion given by the DPP under the Act. The DPP is appointed by the Attorney-General who is answerable in Parliament for the CPS. The CPS has power to take over most criminal prosecutions (s.3) or to order any proceedings to be discontinued (s.23). Except where an offence can only be prosecuted by a person named in the relevant statute (for example the Attorney-General or a specified public authority), any individual may bring a private prosecution but the CPS can take over such a prosecution (s.6(2)). The Police Complaints Authority has an independent role in investigating complaints against the police (Police Reform Act 2002; see *R (Green)* v *Police Complaints Authority* (2004)).

5.7 The Privy Council

The Privy Council is the descendant of the medieval 'inner council' of trusted advisers to the king. Over the centuries most functions of the Privy Council were transferred either to Parliament or ministers. Members are appointed by the Queen on the advice of the Prime Minister and any British citizen is eligible. There are currently over 400 Privy Counsellors including cabinet ministers, senior judges and miscellaneous worthies who have gained the approval of the Prime Minister. The Cabinet is sometimes said to be a committee of the Privy Council although there is no legal basis for this assumption. However cabinet ministers and leading opposition politicians are invariably appointed Privy Counsellors. One reason for such appointments is that Privy Counsellors swear an oath of secrecy, thus assisting government business to be kept out of the public domain.

Apart from its judicial functions (below), the role of the Privy Council is largely formal. Its approval is needed for certain important exercises of the royal prerogative, known as 'Prerogative Orders in Council', including for example the regulation of the civil service and laws for overseas territories, and also for 'Statutory Orders in Council', where Parliament gives power to the executive to make laws in this form. Approval is usually given by a small deputation of counsellors attending the Queen. The Privy Council also confers state recognition and legal personality by granting charters to bodies such as universities and professional, scientific and cultural organisations. It can exercise some degree of supervision over such bodies.

The Judicial Committee of the Privy Council is the final court of appeal for those few Commonwealth countries that choose to retain its services, in which capacity it is familiar with broad constitutional reasoning. It currently hears cases concerning the powers of the devolved regimes of Scotland, Northern Ireland and Wales. However these will be transferred to the new Supreme Court in October 2009 (Chapter 7). It also has jurisdiction in respect of ecclesiastical courts, peerage claims, election petitions and appeals from the Channel Islands and the Isle of Man. Its former appeals jurisdiction in relation to the medical profession is now exercised by the Administrative Court (Chapter 17). The Judicial Committee comprises the Law Lords together with judges of the country under whose laws the appeal is heard. Not being strictly a court, the Judicial Committee can give advisory opinions to the government (Judicial Committee Act 1833 s.4), although this is rare.

5.8   The Church of England

The relationship between Church and state is ambivalent. On the one hand neither Christianity nor any other religion is part of the law as such (*Bowman v Secular Society* (1917)). On the other hand we do not have a formal separation between Church and state such as exists in France or the US. The Church of England is the Established Church in England and the Presbyterian Church of Scotland the Established Church in Scotland. The Church of England has certain links with the state, the result of the historical chance that Henry VIII was the founder of the Church of England. It is sometimes justified even by supporters of other religions on the basis that the Church provides religious services open to all without discrimination and that it helps the state to curb the extremes of religious fanaticism.

There are several particular connections between the Church of England and the state. First the monarch as nominal head of the Church of England must on succession be or become a member of the Church (Act of Settlement 1700 s.3) and must swear an oath to support the Established Churches of England and Scotland (Act of Union with Scotland 1706). Second, Church laws (measures) are legally binding and must be approved by Parliament (Church of England Assembly (Powers) Act 1919). There are also special ecclesiastical courts subject to control by the ordinary courts if they exceed their powers or act unfairly. Third, the Queen, on the advice of the Prime Minister (which as usual is binding on her by convention) appoints bishops (see Ecclesiastical Jurisdiction Measure 1963). Fourth, the twenty six most senior bishops are members of the House of Lords until retirement. Finally everyone has certain rights in connection with baptisms, weddings and funerals. However a Church body is not a public body as such (see *Aston Cantlow and Wilmcote with Billesley PCC v Wallbank* (2003)). However particular Church functions available to the public such as weddings and funerals might be public functions and as such subject to control by the courts. The Anglican Church in Wales is not established (Welsh Churches Act 1914, a measure passed without the consent of the House of Lords).

5.9 Standards in Government

The informal nature of much of the UK constitution makes our arrangements heavily dependent on trusting those in power. A series of scandals from the 1980s onwards have exposed significant corruption, ambivalence and incompetence within central government and Parliament. Most prominent were the Westland affair, where ministers and civil servants appeared to conspire against each other (see Treasury and Civil Service Committee, 1985–6, HC 92), and the 'arms to Iraq' affair, which involved allegations that ministers had tried to cover up breaches of United Nations sanctions against Iraq (see Scott Report, 1996, HC 115). There have also been allegations that MPs, Peers and ministers have received bribes from business interests, worries about manipulation of the voting system by political parties, questions about MPs' expenses, allegations of the sale of peerages and conflicts between media management by government advisers and civil service impartiality.

There are statutory provisions aimed specifically at preventing corruption by public officials. These include the Public Bodies (Corrupt Practices) Act 1889 and the Honours (Prevention of Corruption) Act 1925. The latter was enacted in response to the sale of peerages on behalf of the then Prime Minister, Lloyd George. There are provisions concerning misconduct in elections (Chapter 12) and common law offences of abuse of public office and corruption. However the main mechanism for dealing with the ethical standards of government comprises codes of conduct policed by bodies appointed by the executive and with terms of reference drawn up by the executive.

The Committee on Standards in Public Life was appointed in 1994 by the Prime Minister as a permanent committee to give advice on ethical standards. Its terms of reference included the UK Parliament, UK members of the European Parliament, central and local government and other publicly funded bodies such as the National Health Service (NHS). The Committee reports to the Prime Minister so that there is no independent enforcement mechanism but its reports are published. The Committee does not investigate complaints against individuals.

In its first report (1995, Cm 2850) under the chairmanship of Lord Nolan the Committee promulgated seven 'Principles of Public Life' that are widely regarded as representing the core values of public service. They are 'selflessness, integrity, objectivity, accountability, openness, honesty and leadership'. They are supported by what Nolan called 'common threads', these being mechanisms used to embed the principles into governmental institutions. These are codes of conduct, independent scrutiny and guidance and education. The Nolan principles are enshrined in some codes of conduct such as the Ministerial Code, Local Government Codes, Codes of Conduct for MPs and the House of Lords, Code of Practice for Ministerial Appointments to Public Bodies and Special

Advisers Code of Conduct. The codes are not usually independently enforceable; for example the Civil Service Code is part of the civil servant's contract and so only enforceable by the government itself. The Electoral Commission reviews the conduct of parliamentary and local elections and regulates the funding arrangements of the political parties. The Eleventh Report of the Committee on Standards in Public Life (2007) found the Electoral Commission to be passive and ineffectual.

The Nolan principles regarding public appointments are particularly important. Against the background of a tradition that gives ministers large powers of discretion in appointments, the Committee has promulgated principles of appointment on merit, according to open and published criteria that all public bodies should follow and with independent representation on appointment bodies. Again these are not legally enforceable. There is a non-statutory Commissioner for Public Appointments reporting to Parliament who oversees the appointment process relating to a wide variety of public bodies and publishes a code of practice and annual reports. The Civil Service Commissioners perform a similar role in relation to civil service appointments (above). There is also a non-statutory House of Lords Appointments Commission, which has an advisory role in relation to the Prime Minister's power to select members of the House of Lords.

It is regarded as improper for politicians to interfere with senior public appointments although there are no legal safeguards to this effect. The Committee on Standards has recommended that the rules governing public appointments be made more open and clear in order to combat suspicion of manipulation by ministers. In particular it recommended that ministers should not be able to choose between shortlisted candidates (Tenth Report, 2004, Cm 6407). This proposal was rejected by the government.

There are both advantages and disadvantages in voluntary codes of practice, which might be compared with conventions in this respect (Chapter 3). Firstly voluntary codes of practice could be regarded as democratic and those investigated may be more prepared to cooperate with a non-enforceable code. On the other hand unless there is independent enforcement such codes may not command public confidence. Moreover complaints under the codes may be made for party political reasons as has occurred in local government (see Tenth Report above). The vagueness of many of the codes is also a mixed blessing. On the one hand the codes are flexible and could produce negotiated outcomes which are practical and acceptable to the persons concerned. On the other hand the flexibility of the codes risks attempts to manipulate them for party political purposes or the self interest of ministers.

The work of the Committee on Standards provides a good illustration of the problems of an informal constitution when trust in government is lost. In a consultation paper the Committee on Standards warned that the codes might be undermined by appearing to be overzealous or overbureaucratic and attracting public cynicism (see *Getting the Balance Right: Implementing Standards of Conduct in Public Life*, 2003). The Committee particularly emphasised the principle of 'proportionality' which concerns adjusting processes to the particular context, taking account of the importance of the activity and the risks and costs involved. It also emphasised the importance of the culture of the particular organisation. This can be illustrated by its Tenth Report relating to local government standards.

However the Principles of Public Life have occasionally been incorporated into statute (for example Northern Ireland Act 1998 s.16(4)) and might also be applied as facets of general public law principles such as reasonableness (Chapter 17).

5.9.1   Ombudsmen

There are also mechanisms for investigating complaints against public officials. Popularly known as 'ombudsmen', they share the dominant ethos of UK government by having no power to enforce their decisions but only to report. The Parliamentary Commissioner for Administration (PCA) investigates complaints against central government and certain other bodies controlled by ministers on behalf of MPs and reports to Parliament. An individual can complain to the ombudsman only through an MP (Chapter 13). Commissioners for Local Administration perform a similar function in respect of local government. However where a councillor has failed to do so, individuals can complain directly to them (Local Government Act 1974). Other ombudsmen operate in a similar manner in respect of particular government bodies, for example in respect of the devolved governments of Scotland, Wales (see Public Services Ombudsman (Wales) Act 2005) and Northern Ireland, the NHS, the European Parliament, the police, social housing, the legal profession and judicial appointments (Constitutional Reform Act 2005). The Parliamentary Commissioner for Standards investigates matters concerning the conduct of MPs (Chapter 11).

5.10   Constitutional Reform: Not Seriously On The Agenda

The government which was first elected in 1997 included an agenda for constitutional reform in its programme. This project had the broad aim of modernisation and of dispersing power away from the centre. It included devolution of some powers to Scotland, Wales and Northern Ireland, the enactment of the Human Rights Act 1998 and the Freedom of Information Act 2000, and reform of the House of Lords by ejecting most of its hereditary element. The reforms did not tackle the fundamental issue of electoral reform nor the relationship between the executive and Parliament including the wide prerogative powers wielded by the Prime Minister. The mixture was therefore unsystematic. There have also been suggestions from politicians and pressure groups in favour of enacting a comprehensive Bill of Rights more closely adapted to the needs of the UK (presumably meaning less individualistic) than the European Convention on Human Rights on which the Human Rights Act 1998 is based.

In July 2007 the government published a Green (consultation) Paper on the subject of further constitutional reform (*The Governance of Britain*, Cm 7170). This was in response to widely expressed anxieties that the executive was too powerful. These anxieties came to a head in relation to the Prime Minister's decision to attack Iraq following doubts about whether the government's Law Officer, the Attorney-General (A-G), was acting independently when giving legal advice on the matter. The A-G's control of the Serious Fraud Office also came into question when it withdrew an investigation into possible corruption involving the rulers of Saudi Arabia with whom the government wished to make trade deals. According to the Green Paper reform should 'invigorate our democracy, clarify the role of government, rebalance power between Parliament and government and give Parliament more ability to hold government to account, and work with the British people to achieve a stronger sense of what it means to be British.'

A draft bill, the Constitutional Renewal Bill, was published in March 2008 but it seems to do little to achieve the above aims. There are some reductions in the power of the Attorney-General to intervene in prosecutions in individual cases, counterbalanced by a new power to intervene on national security grounds – a claim which is intended not to be challengeable in the courts. There are some minor and technical changes to the system for appointing judges introduced by the Constitutional Reform Act 2005 of which perhaps the most important is the introduction of an independent consultative panel representing relevant interests. The Bill also places areas currently governed by the royal prerogative concerning the civil service and the ratification of treaties on a statutory footing. An earlier proposal that Parliament should approve any decision to go to war appears to have been dropped as has a proposal that Parliament should consent to the Prime Minister's decision to call a general election. The bill is unlikely to proceed under the familiar qualification of lack of Parliamentary time.

Summary

- To be legitimate a government must be effectively in control. However some commentators suggest that the government must also be supported by a moral basis although the meaning of this is obscure. A distinction can be drawn between the 'dignified' part of the constitution that gives the government its authority and the 'efficient' part that is the practical exercise of power.

- The Crown, traditionally the executive branch of government, must be distinguished from the Queen personally as head of state.

- Parliament the lawmaker is legally supreme and by convention the executive is accountable to Parliament. In practice however the influence of political parties and the power of the Prime Minister mean that Parliament tends to be subservient to the executive.

- Parliament comprises an unelected upper House with limited powers (House of Lords) and an elected lower House (House of Commons). The upper House is currently undergoing reform but there is disagreement as to what form this should take.

- The Queen must appoint the leader of the majority party in the Commons as Prime Minister and must accept the Prime Minister's advice in appointing all other ministers and also senior judges and other public functionaries.

- There are mechanisms to safeguard democracy against both legislature and executive. The executive must have the support of Parliament. Parliament must meet annually. No Parliament can last for more than five years and before then Parliament can remove the executive. The executive can also dissolve Parliament. The dissolution of Parliament triggers the summoning of a new Parliament preceded by a general election. These mechanisms are weakened by the executive domination of Parliament.

- The executive formally comprises ministers of the Crown. Statutory powers are normally given to individual ministers and the central government is therefore fragmented. Permanent civil servants are a source of impartial advice and act in the name of ministers. Special advisers are personal, political appointees of ministers. There are tensions between these groups and the role of civil servants may be unstable.

- According to the doctrine of ministerial responsibility, ministers are responsible to Parliament for the conduct of their departments and for agencies sponsored by their departments. The civil service is responsible to ministers but not directly to Parliament. Ministerial responsibility is becoming weaker and its scope and effect unclear.

- In recent years executive powers have been distributed across a wide variety of public and private bodies.

Summary cont'd

▷ The judiciary is usually regarded as subordinate to Parliament. There is a tension between the judiciary and the executive arising out of the courts' powers of judicial review.

▷ Senior judges have strong security of tenure. The appointment of judges was previously made by the Lord Chancellor and in the most senior cases the Prime Minister. Recent reforms have introduced the safeguard of an independent Judicial Appointments Committee to make binding recommendations.

▷ Tribunals adjudicate relatively small and specialised disputes between government and individual. They are relatively informal but subject to special safeguards to secure their independence and fairness.

▷ Public inquiries form part of the process for making some governmental decisions. They are presided over by independent inspectors and are also subject to special safeguards. Ministers may set up inquiries into particular events or issues. These have limited independence.

▷ The police are regulated by an unstable combination of local and central government.

▷ The Church of England has particular constitutional links with the state but is not a state religion.

▷ Weaknesses in the traditional methods of accountability have led to attempts to formulate standards of ethical conduct for persons holding public office. These do not generally have legal status and are enforced within government itself.

Exercises

5.1 Is it possible to identify the three most fundamental principles of the constitution? If so, what are they?

5.2 What mechanisms enable the executive to dominate Parliament? Are there any counter mechanisms?

5.3 What are the main constitutional differences between the police and the armed forces?

5.4 Assess the arguments for and against abolishing or reforming the monarchy.

5.5 Assess the arguments for and against civil service impartiality.

5.6 Outline the constitutional problems raised by the following:
(i)   Special advisers
(ii) Civil servants
(iii) Ombudsmen
(iv) Inquiries.

5.7 Assess the arguments for and against the Church of England having special constitutional status.

5.8 What is the constitutional significance, if any, of codes of conduct? Should they be legally enforceable and if so how?

Further reading

Bogdanor, V. (2004) 'Our New Constitution', *Law Quarterly Review* 120:242.

Committee on Standards in Public Life website, http://www.public-standards.gov.uk (an excellent resource).

Constitution Committee House of Lords, *Changing the Constitution: the Process of Constitutional Change*, Fourth Report Session 2001–2, HL Paper 69, London, HMSO.

Finer, F., Bogdanor, V. and Rudden, B. (1995) *Comparing Constitutions*, Oxford, Clarendon Press, Chapter 2.

Hazell, R., Masterman, R., Sandford, M., Seyd, B. and Croft, J. (2002) 'The Constitution: Coming in From the Cold', *Parliamentary Affairs* 55.

House of Commons (2003) *Government by Appointment: Opening up the Patronage State*, HC 165, Cm 6056.

Leopold, P. (2004) 'Standards of Conduct in Public Life', in Jowell, J. and Oliver, D. (eds) *The Changing Constitution* (5th edn), Oxford University Press.

Le Sueur, A. (2008) 'Gordon Brown's New Constitutional Settlement, *Public Law* 21.

Loughlin, M. (2003) 'The Demise of Local Government', in Bogdanor, V. (ed.) above.

Nicol, P. (2006) 'Professor Tomkin's House of Mavericks', *Public Law* 467.

Nolan, Lord and Sedley, Sir S. (1997) *The Making and Remaking of the British Constitution*, London, Blackstone, Chapters 1, 3, 4, 5.

Oliver, D. (1995) 'Standards of Conduct in Public Life: What Standards?', *Public Law* 497.

Report of the Power Commission (2006) *Power to the People: An Independent Inquiry into Britain's Democracy*, Rowntree Foundation.

Sampson, A. (2004) *Who Runs this Place?*, London, John Murray, Chapters 1, 2, 3, 4, 7, 8.

Tomkins, A. (2005) *Our Republican Constitution*, Oxford, Hart Publishing.

Tomkins, A. 'Professor Tomkin's House of Mavericks: A Reply', [2007] *Public Law* 33.

Woodhouse, D. (2003) 'Delivering Public Confidence: Codes of Conduct; A Step in the Right Direction', *Public Law* 511.

Chapter 6

The territory and regions of the UK

> The England Team is the only team playing in the World Cup that is not a nation state: there is no political or cultural outlet for England's feeling of national identity. (*Observer*, 13 June 2004)

Key words

- ▶ State, country and nation
- ▶ Statism and non-statism
- ▶ Citizens and subjects
- ▶ Federalism and devolution
- ▶ Asymmetric devolution
- ▶ Multiple crowns
- ▶ Settled and ceded territories

6.1 Introduction: The Notion of the State

The term 'state' derives from 'status' and originally meant a recognised function in the overall scheme of things. In ancient Greece and Rome the 'city state' was regarded as an independent, self governing community existing primarily for military purposes. The contemporary idea of the state has developed from this into what is inaccurately called the 'nation state'. There is no necessary connection between the idea of a nation and that of a state, although sometimes the two terms are used interchangeably, for example the National Health Service. A nation is a cultural, political and historical idea but not a legal concept. It signifies a relatively homogeneous community marked out by a common language, common ethnicity or shared cultural traditions. A state is defined by law and based on geographical boundaries drawn up by officials. However a nation may have a moral claim to be a state with its own laws and government (see Lord Hoffmann in *A v Secretary of State for the Home Department* (2005)). The term 'country' has no legal significance and is often used loosely to refer either to a nation or a state.

The geographical 'nation state' has been the basic unit of political and legal organisation since the seventeenth century (for instance the Treaty of Westphalia 1688 created the now questionable international principle that states are equal and independent in relation to their internal affairs). The notion of the state developed primarily for military purposes in the context of constant territorial conflicts and was a reaction against the loose, medieval political structure of rival warlords (to some extent held together by the Church) and also against the re-emergence in the fifteenth century of republican ideas of citizen self rule. The association of the ideas of nation and state can be used by those in power as a means of inspiring loyalty (for example the Constitution of Ireland Article 9). Most states including the UK have been created by military force, economic circumstances or political bargains. As the history of Ireland, the Balkan states and many African states sadly reveals, the artificiality of state boundaries sometimes generates violence and even genocide.

Throughout mainland Europe the state was represented by a monarch supported by a military and administrative structure and imposing law from above. It is commonly claimed that Britain throughout retained the tradition that the ruler requires the consent of the 'community', although there has been considerable disagreement as to who is included in the 'community'. During the eighteenth century, generated by Enlightenment ideas of scientific reason, secularism and equality, the state developed as an impersonal command structure designed to advance the general welfare. This is broadly the position today, albeit the economic forces of globalisation and the atrocities committed by state governments against their own people have raised doubts as to whether state law should retain its current dominance. Under the influence of democracy, the state has become an all purpose organisation with no limitations as to the functions it might have or any consensus as to the relationship between citizen and state other than the temporary accommodations produced by the balance of powers within the state.

The UK is a state in international law but it is not a nation. Scotland, Wales and England might claim to be nations. Northern Ireland is a province of the UK within the nation of Ireland, part of which is a separate state, the Republic of Ireland. Governmental units are designated by Parliament. The units of the UK, England, Northern Ireland, Scotland and Wales have no international legal status but Northern Ireland, Scotland and Wales have devolved government powers. 'Britain', although identified for some purposes, such as relations with Northern Ireland, has no legal identity but means England, Wales and Scotland collectively. England was a nation state before the union with Scotland in 1707, but now has no legal status. English law applies in England and Wales and is the basis of the law in many former British territories including the US. Scotland and Northern Ireland have their own legal systems which share much in common with English law, although Scotland has also been influenced by French civil law. In all jurisdictions, other than Scottish criminal cases, the highest Appeal Court is currently the UK House of Lords, soon to become the Supreme Court.

Unlike other European legal systems (see for example the Constitution of Ireland Articles 4–6) English law has no legal concept of the state, replacing it with the concept of the Crown. Thus in *R* v *Preston* (1993) at 663, Lord Mustill remarked: 'The Crown as the source of authority means that the UK has never found it necessary to create the notion of the "state" as a single legal entity.' In English law the concept of the state is used loosely to describe any governmental activity (such as state schools). Where legislation refers to the 'state', its meaning depends on the particular context, for example the community as a whole (*Chandler* v *DPP* (1964)), the 'sovereign power' (*General Medical Council* v *BBC* (1998)) or the executive branch of government (*D* v *NSPCC* (1978)).

A significant usage of 'state' concerns the immunity of overseas states from liability in UK courts. Although commercial transactions are not immune, the property of the state central bank or monetary authority cannot be enforced against (State Immunity Act 1978; see *AIG Capital Parties Inc.* v *Republic of Kazakhstan* (2006)).

The non-statist nature of English law has at least the following important consequences:

▶ There is a distinction in statist constitutions between 'public law', which regulates the state itself and its relationship with citizens, and 'private law', which the state uses to regulate the relationship between its citizens. The UK constitution has not historically recognised such a distinction. It has been regarded as a strength of our constitution that a single system of law applies to officials and individuals alike. Thus unless a particular law provides otherwise, officials have no special powers or status and are individually responsible for any legal wrongs they commit (Chapter 7). Thus the doctrine of *raison d'état* as a general justification for government power is not recognised (*Entick* v *Carrington* (1765)). However in order to perform its duties the government often has specific powers not available to other bodies and so should be subject to particular legal controls. Moreover the government's ordinary private law rights such as property ownership must be exercised in the public interest. In this sense private and public law are distinct (see *R* v *IRC ex parte Unilever* (1996), 695; *R* v *Somerset CC ex parte Fewings* (1995), 524).

The increasing powers given to governmental officials and the trend towards privatisation have led to attempts to distinguish between public and private law and between public and private bodies and functions, particularly in connection with judicial review of government action, European law (see *Foster* v *British Gas plc* (1990)), human rights and access to information. A successful definition of a public body or public function has yet to be produced and it cannot be assumed that these terms will be defined in the same way in each context. For example the Freedom of Information Act 2000 (Chapter 21) provides a list of public bodies that can be altered by ministers. The Government Resources and Accounts Act 2000 (Chapter 13) refers unhelpfully to a 'government department or a body exercising public functions' (s.7(3)). The Public Audit (Wales) Act 2004 similarly refers to 'functions of a public nature' but also includes 'a body entirely or substantially funded from public money'. The Civil Procedure Rules 2000 (SI 2000 no. 2092, 54.1(2)), which deals with judicial review, refers to 'a feature or combination of features which impose a public character or stamp'. The Human Rights Act 1998 does not provide a definition (Chapter 19).

▶ One reason why we cannot clearly distinguish between the public and the private is that our non-statist tradition allows us to allocate governmental functions haphazardly between the central government proper (ministers) and other bodies specially created for the purpose and also to transfer functions to private bodies. We regard the distinction between functions that should be carried out by the state and those appropriate to the private sector as a political matter outside the law. There are some advantages in the UK approach. Particular decision making bodies must be openly identified and cannot hide under the general state umbrella. There are also disadvantages in that there seems to be no constitutional principle to prevent public powers being farmed out to bodies that are not democratically accountable. Similarly there are no legal principles governing the question whether and on what terms the government can hand over assets to the private sector. Whether these are sold and at what price, or given away and to whom depends on particular legislation or government practice.

▶ There may be a tension between the duty of a civil servant to the Crown, which is the nearest we have to a general concept of the state, and to particular ministers (Chapter 15). Moreover the civil service must also serve the devolved administrations of Scotland, Wales and Northern Ireland.

▶ Our system of government is fragmented between different bodies and there is no single entity which can hold property or enter into legal transactions on behalf of the public. For legal purposes the Attorney-General represents the government.

Government powers and property are vested by particular legislation or under the royal prerogative either in the Crown or in particular ministers or departments. In *R v Jones (Margaret)* (2006) which concerned an attempt to accuse the government of a war crime in invading Iraq, Lord Hoffmann expressed concern about the theoretical difficulty of the court taking action against the 'state' of which it is a part [65].

▶ In a statist system the state is both a creation of the law and the producer of law. Judges are the authoritative interpreters of the law but not its creators. Judicial opinions are regarded as making more concrete the laws emanating from the state but do not traditionally have an independent lawmaking role. By contrast the historical basis of the common law gives the courts an independent basis of legitimacy. The authority of the common law lies in community values. In the common law system judges are regarded as individuals charged with doing justice. Judicial decisions are normally fully reasoned and dissents are commonplace.

6.2 Citizenship

In its general sense citizenship means full membership of a state. In the civic republican tradition (Chapter 2) citizenship is particularly associated with active participation in public life, whereas 'liberal' citizenship primarily concerns the rights and entitlements of individuals against the state (see Bellamy in Campbell, Ewing and Tomkins (eds), *Sceptical Essays on Human Rights*, Oxford, Hart, 2001). The notion of citizenship as it first emerged in ancient Greece presupposed a small community roughly equal in wealth and from similar social backgrounds. Indeed women, foreigners and slaves – comprising most of the population – were excluded. In today's larger and more diverse communities it is difficult to suppose that common values can be applied uniformly to all. Cultural practices and loyalties such as language and family customs militate against detailed notions of the rights and obligations of citizenship and engage the problems of liberal pluralism (Chapter 2).

The unpleasant side of citizenship is that it entails 'exclusion', in the sense of an unwelcoming attitude to those regarded as non-citizens, who in UK law are labelled 'aliens'. However in *A v Secretary of State for the Home Department* (2005) the House of Lords made it clear that it was unlawful under the Human Rights Act to discriminate between citizens and non-citizens in relation to anti-terrorism measures. Moreover all who are physically present in the UK can claim the protection of the common law and can seek judicial review against the government.

A state can adopt any regime it wishes for its citizens. Although there is a status of 'British citizen' (below), those subject to the jurisdiction of English law are strictly speaking not citizens but 'subjects' of the Crown. A subject includes anyone within the territory of the UK since such a person can lay claim to the protection of the Crown. Despite the word commonly being associated with subservience, the notion of a 'subject' is sometimes said to give valuable protection in that it presupposes a relationship of mutual respect between ruler and ruled which is safeguarded by law. Thus in return for 'allegiance' (loyalty) the Crown is obliged under common law to protect the rights of the subject and keep the peace. In his speech on the scaffold (1649) Charles I announced that:

> I must tell you, that [the people's] liberty and freedom consists in having the government of those laws, by which their life and their goods may be considered most their own; 'tis not for having a

share in government that is nothing pertaining to 'em. A subject and a sovereign are clean different things.

But unless the people can control the lawmaking process, how can they ensure that the laws do in fact protect their rights? On the other hand an extreme view of citizenship such as that of Rousseau proclaims that a citizen must submit to the will of the majority, whatever that might be.

In English law citizenship is mainly concerned with the right to reside, rights concerned with political participation and sometimes access to public services and taxation. Other legal rights and duties depend on presence in the territory or sometimes, particularly in relation to health and welfare services, a more specific connection such as actual residence. In exceptional cases, notably the Channel Islands, non-citizens have restricted property rights.

UK citizenship law is complex due to the many changes that have been made in order to control immigration following the collapse of the British Empire and to assuage post imperial guilt. It can only be sketched here. The British Nationality Act 1981 (BNA) as amended is the main legislation. There is no legal concept of citizenship of any other unit within the UK. There is a notion of citizenship of the EU. However this merely endorses certain rights within member states which under European Law apply to citizens of other EU states.

The following have 'British' citizenship under the Act:

- Those born or adopted in the UK (s.50). However at least one parent must also be either a citizen or settled in the UK. If the parents are not married this must be the mother.
- Those descended from a British citizen (s.2). At the time of birth at least one parent must be a citizen other than by descent or be a citizen working abroad for the British government, having been recruited in the UK, or in certain cases working for the EU having been recruited in a member state.
- Persons who were citizens or who by virtue of specified family connections (patrials) had a right of abode in the UK under the regime that existed before 1983 (s.11).

Citizenship can be acquired by registration or naturalisation:

- Registration is a right available to persons born in the UK or who fulfill certain requirements of residence or parentage and who satisfy the Home Secretary that they are of 'good character' (BNA s.4; Immigration, Asylum and Nationality Act 2006 s.58).
- Naturalisation (BNA s.6) is a matter for the discretion of the Secretary of State and is available to anyone, subject to requirements of residence, language, good character and 'knowledge of life in the UK' as determined in accordance with regulations made by the Home Secretary (Nationality, Immigration and Asylum Act 2002 s.4). Thus a communitarian and potentially illiberal element has been injected into the law.

Certain other categories, although largely obsolete relics of Empire, attract special immigration privileges in specific contexts too specialised to be discussed here. Some require registration; most are subject to immigration control (below). These categories include British subjects, which covers members of previous British territories, Commonwealth citizens, citizens of the United Kingdom and Colonies, British protected persons and British overseas citizens. Most persons connected with British dependencies, other than certain military bases in Cyprus (formerly 'British dependent territories citizens', now 'British overseas territories citizens'), have a right to be full citizens (British Overseas Territories Act 2002). In the case of the Falkland Islands (which Argentina claims), this is automatic (British Nationality (Falkland Islands) Act 1983). Some citizens of Hong Kong, which the UK surrendered to China in 1997, have certain rights to be registration as British citizens (British Nationality (Hong Kong) Act 1997). Others (British nationals overseas) can acquire a British passport although this in itself carries no legal rights, being essentially an identity document (BNA s.12).

All other persons are 'aliens'. Unless statute requires otherwise, while present in the UK, aliens (other than those from countries with whom we are formally at war) have the same rights and duties in English law as citizens. However citizens of the EU and the broader European Economic Area (Norway, Iceland, Liechtenstein: Lisbon Agreement 2004) have substantial rights to reside in the UK.

Citizenship can be renounced by registration with the Secretary of State (BNA s.12). However registration becomes ineffective unless the person in question acquires citizenship of another state within six months.

The Home Secretary can by order remove citizenship (a) on the grounds of public good unless deprivation of citizenship would make the person stateless or (b) where citizenship was acquired by fraud, false representation or concealment of a material fact (Nationality, Immigration and Asylum Act 2002 s.4; Immigration, Asylum and Nationality Act 2006 s.56). There is a right of appeal (below).

Citizenship is legally important mainly in the following respects:

- It confers a right to live in the UK under immigration law. However non-citizens who were ordinarily resident in the UK without restrictions on 1 January 1983 do not need leave to enter and remain (Immigration Act 1971 s.1(2)). The Home Secretary has discretionary powers to give other non-citizens leave to remain either for specific periods or indefinitely. These are guided by Immigration Rules. The Home Secretary can revoke indefinite leave on grounds of public good (Immigration, Asylum and Nationality Act 2006 s.57). Citizens of the European Economic Area and their families have freedom of movement within the UK (Immigration Act 1988 s.7). Citizens of the Republic of Ireland, the Channel Islands and the Isle of Man are not subject to immigration control although passport checks have recently been introduced (Immigration Act 1971 ss.1(3), (9)).

- British, Irish and Commonwealth citizens lawfully resident in the UK may vote in parliamentary and local elections (Representation of the People Act 2000) and in elections for the devolved governments.

- Non-citizens (other than Commonwealth and Irish citizens) cannot be members of either Houses of Parliament (British Nationality Act 1981 Schedule 7).

- Honours cannot be conferred upon non-citizens other than Commonwealth citizens.

- British citizens have a right to call upon the protection of the Crown when abroad, although this is not enforceable in the courts. The main consequence of the Crown's duty to protect British citizens abroad is that the Crown cannot require payment for such protection unless the person concerned voluntarily exposes him or herself to some special risk (see *China Navigation Co. Ltd* v *Attorney-General* (1932); *Mutasa* v *Attorney-General* (1980)).

▶ British citizens abroad are subject to special taxation laws.
▶ British citizens cannot generally be removed from the UK. There are two exceptions:
▶ Anyone can be extradited to another country to stand trial for a criminal offence or serve a sentence.
▶ Under the Terrorism Act 2000 border controls can be exercised over travel between the UK and Northern Ireland.
▶ British citizens owe allegiance to the Crown wherever they are in the world (see *R v Casement* (1917)). Allegiance has two main consequences. Firstly the Crown probably cannot plead the defence of 'Act of State' against a person who owes allegiance (Chapter 13). Secondly the offence of treason is committed against the duty of allegiance. Aliens resident and perhaps even present in the UK also owe allegiance (*de Jager* v *Attorney-General of Natal* (1907)). A person who holds a British passport apparently owes allegiance even if he has never visited the UK and even if the passport has been fraudulently obtained (see *Joyce* v *DPP* (1946)). It seems that apart from renouncing citizenship (above) allegiance cannot be voluntarily surrendered (*R v Lynch* (1903)).

6.3 Federalism

The UK constitution is a 'unitary' constitution with an overriding supreme lawmaker which can devolve power to subordinate units but is free to take the power back. In a federal state such as the US, the constitution divides power between a central government and separate units in such a way that each unit is independent within its own sphere and neither can override the other except as specified by the constitution. Each has its own constitution, legislature and courts.

How powers are allocated varies according to the history and political concerns of the state in question. There may be demarcation problems to be resolved by the courts so that federal constitutions have a strong legalistic element. There is usually a single citizenship of the central state, the federal government being responsible for foreign affairs, defence and major economic matters, while private law issues are the responsibility of the states. Criminal offences, social regulation and public services may be allocated to either level and the lower level may sometimes act as the agent of the centre (such as in Germany). Usually particular matters are given to the federal level with the residue left with the states but the converse sometimes applies (for example in Canada). Federalism is practicable where the component units have sufficient in common economically and culturally to enable them to cooperate, while at the same time each unit is sufficiently distinctive to constitute a community in its own right but not sufficiently powerful to aspire to a role on the international stage. Thus a delicate balance must be struck. The US and Australia are relatively successful federations, whereas Canada with its split between English speaking and French speaking regions is less stable. Yugoslavia with its many ethnic tensions was tragically unsuccessful once Soviet control was removed.

A federal system might also include devolved government such as local government within each federal state. Conversely a unitary state such as Spain may have strongly autonomous regions with significant legal protection. The practical relationship between the units depends of course on the interplay of political forces. Thus federalism is more a matter of degree than of absolutes. Switzerland provides an extreme example of a constitution where both the powers of the federal government and its personnel are severely limited in favour of the autonomy of the cantons. The term 'federal' is not a legal definition but an abstract model. There is no reason why any particular constitution should correspond neatly to the model. It is probably best to regard terms such as 'federal' or 'unitary' not as precise definitions but as a political spectrum ranging from loose associations of countries for particular purposes to simple one-government states.

Federal and devolved governments both respond in different degrees to the idea of group liberalism and particularly of national and local identities (Chapter 2). Federalism also gives effect to republican values of equality and division of power. However John Stuart Mill (1972, Chapter 15) argued in favour of devolved rather than federal government. He suggested that smaller devolved units encourage individuals to participate in public affairs and that the UK constitution did not require the protection of a federal framework since our culture was less obsessed with uniformity than that of continental countries (1972, Chapter 13). This is a political debate relevant to the EU (Chapter 10). On the other hand, Mill would give the most important powers to the centre since there may not be enough serious issues at local level to justify the time of competent public officials or attract the interest of talented people. He also thought that local government was at risk of corruption by small business interests. Dicey (1915, p. 171), the influential Victorian constitutional lawyer, strongly opposed federalism, claiming that it tends to conservatism, creates divided loyalties and elevates legalism to a primary value, making the courts the pivot on which the constitution turns and perhaps threatening their independence. Devolved government is therefore a pragmatic compromise (compare Olowofoyeku, 'Decentralising the United Kingdom: the Federal Argument', 1999, *Edinburgh Law Review* 3(1): 57).

The UK is a union of what were the separate states of England, parts of Ireland and Scotland. Wales is a nation within the UK but has never been a state in its own right. During the late nineteenth century there were some advocates of a federal UK as a way of avoiding home rule for Ireland. Before the introduction of devolved government in 2000 (below), the internal affairs of Scotland, Northern Ireland and Wales were governed by the UK central executive with what has sometimes been regarded as overtones of colonialism. This took the form of 'administrative devolution' to ministers for each territory. There was no specific democratic power base or accountability mechanism linking the ministers to their regions since the relevant minister might have an English constituency. Scotland and Northern Ireland have separate legal systems but the House of Lords and the Privy Council (to be replaced in 2009 by the new Supreme Court, Chapter 8) are final courts of appeal for all the UK jurisdictions.

The *Royal Commission on the Constitution* (1973, Cmnd 5460) argued against a federal constitution for the UK on the following grounds:

- A lack of balance since the units are widely different in economic terms, with England being dominant.
- A federal regime would be contrary to our constitutional traditions in that it would elevate the courts over political machinery.
- The UK was thought to require central and flexible economic management since its resources are unevenly distributed geographically, much of it comprising thinly populated hills.
- Apart from Northern Ireland, regional issues were not high on the agenda of the main parties, which suggested that there was little public desire for federalism.

6.4 Devolution

The Royal Commission (above) asserted that government in the UK was overcentralised and recommended devolved government. Referendums were subsequently held in Scotland and Wales which foundered because they failed to obtain the required two-thirds majorities in favour of change. The Labour government that took office in 1997 was supportive of devolved government. Following further referendums which produced considerable public support for devolution in Scotland and significant but less support for devolution in Wales, legislation was introduced to give devolved powers to a Scottish Parliament (Scotland Act 1998), a Northern Ireland Assembly (Northern Ireland Act 1998) and, to a lesser extent, a Welsh Assembly (Government of Wales Act 1998). The devolution statutes could be regarded as embodying a constitution for the territory in question although they are not comprehensive in the manner of a normal written constitution.

There is no federal element. The devolution arrangements do not affect the unlimited legal power of the UK Parliament to legislate for the devolved regions and to override laws made by devolved bodies. In the cases of Scotland and Northern Ireland they do not specify the powers of the devolved governments but merely specify what they cannot do (for example the Scotland Act 1998 s.29). They can legislate on any other matter. The autonomy of the devolved governments therefore depends on political rather than legal arrangements. In particular under the 'Sewel Convention' (1999) the UK Parliament does not legislate for a devolved territory without the consent of its legislature.

The devolved governments are funded mainly by block grants from the UK Parliament and so have limited democratic legitimacy. The Scotland and Northern Ireland governments have certain limited tax raising powers and only the Northern Ireland government has borrowing powers. The UK government retains ministers responsible for each of the devolved regimes. There are also non-legally binding 'concordats' between each UK government department and the devolved administrations. These put in place principles for coordinating the activities of the governments, for example through a joint ministerial committee, and may buttress the kind of secretive informality characteristic of the UK constitution (see *Memorandum of Understanding and Supplementary Agreements*, 1999, Cm 4444, 2001, Cm 4806, Cm 5420; Poivier, 'The function of intergovernmental agreements', 2001, *Public Law* 134; Rawlings, 'Concordats of the Constitution', 2000, *Law Quarterly Review* 116:257).

The devolution arrangements are different in each region. In the case of Scotland which has the largest amount of power, a concern seems to have been to reduce the likelihood of Scotland attaining national independence. This is achieved by excluding fundamental constitutional matters from the competence of the Scottish Parliament, electoral arrangements that make single party domination (for example by the Scottish Nationalist Party) more difficult than in the case of the UK Parliament and by strengthening the Parliament as against the executive. In the case of Northern Ireland there is an aspiration towards an inclusive form of democracy reflecting the divisive history of the province. Devolution in Northern Ireland raises more fundamental issues than is the case elsewhere. This is partly because the arrangements are concerned with fundamental disputes about the legitimacy of the state itself and partly because they are influenced by the international concerns of relationships with the neighbouring Republic of Ireland. The devolved powers of Wales currently fall below those in the other regions. However there is a mechanism for evolutionary expansion. There are also requirements for substantive economic and social aspirations of a communitarian nature and requirements for participatory democracy. These represent a paternalistic approach to Welsh devolution.

The courts are responsible for ensuring that the limits of the devolved powers are respected. The devolution legislation therefore marks a change of emphasis in our constitutional arrangements away from reliance upon informal and political methods and towards 'juridification' although devices such as the Sewel Convention (above) make this far from complete. This leads to the question of whether the devolution arrangements can be regarded as 'constitutional' and so subject to a special approach to interpretation (Chapter 1). We might invoke matters such as the importance of the devolved arrangements with respect to the fundamental concerns of the particular community. On this basis the Northern Ireland arrangements have a particularly strong claim to be regarded as constitutional. Indeed in *Robinson* v *Secretary of State for Northern Ireland* (2002), Lord Hoffmann [33] asserted that the Northern Ireland Act 1998 is to be construed:

> against the background of the political situation in Northern Ireland and the principles laid down by the Belfast Agreement for a new start. These facts and background form part of the admissible background to the construction of the Act just as much as the Revolution, the Convention and the federalist papers are the background to construing the Constitution of the USA.

6.4.1   Scotland

Scotland was a separate nation state from 1010 until 1706 although after 1603 the Crowns of England and Scotland were united. Since the sixteenth century Reformation there had been some cultural assimilation between the two countries, but also quarrels between Catholics and Protestants. In 1689 Scotland offered its Crown to William and Mary on the same revolutionary terms as in England (Chapter 4). After quarrels between the two Parliaments, the Treaty of Union 1706 abolished the separate Scottish and English Parliaments and created a Parliament of Great Britain. The Union was unpopular but was brought about by economic interest in Scotland and fear of invasion in England. The treaty was confirmed by separate Acts of each Parliament (Act of Union with England 1706; Act of Union with Scotland 1706). Scottish rebellion on behalf of the Stuarts' claim to the throne continued until defeat at Culloden in 1746. The Acts of Union are still in force. They preserve the separate Scottish legal system and Church and safeguard the private rights of Scottish subjects. However section 37 of the Scotland Act 1998 purports to empower the UK Parliament to override the Acts of Union (Chapter 9).

The Scotland Act 1998 creates a devolved government for Scotland. It is modelled broadly on the UK's parliamentary system and the Act gives legal force to provisions similar to those which in England are conventions. There is a Scottish Parliament and a Scottish executive. The Scottish executive has less power in relation to the Parliament than its UK counterpart.

The Crown is the formal head of the Scottish government. Acts of the Scottish Parliament require royal assent (Scotland Act 1998 s.28) and civil servants in Scotland are part of the civil service of the Crown. Since matters such as the appointment and dismissal of ministers and the dissolution of the Scottish Parliament are covered by statute it is not clear whether the Queen has any residual personal power in relation to these matters (Chapter 14). The capacity of the Crown in relation to Scotland is separated from that in relation to the UK, in effect treating the two as separate entities so that they can enter into property transactions with each other, for example (s.99).

The Scottish Parliament can make Acts on any matter other than those specified in the 1998 Act (below). The Parliament comprises 129 members, of which 56 are elected by proportional representation (Chapter 12). Before 1998 Scotland was entitled to at least 71 seats in the UK Parliament, thus making it overrepresented in terms of its population. Section 86(1) of the Scotland Act 1998 abolishes this entitlement and places Scotland under the same regime as England in terms of the criteria for defining constituencies (Chapter 12). This has reduced the number of Scottish MPs to 59. Originally the constituencies for the Scottish Parliament were the same as those for the UK Parliament. However by virtue of the Scottish Parliament (Constituencies) Act 2004, the link between the two has been severed. The Scottish Parliament cannot alter these arrangements.

The Presiding Officer, elected by the House for the duration of the Parliament (s.19) has a formal constitutional role. This includes submitting bills for royal assent (below), recommending the appointment of the First Minister, advising a dissolution (below) and proposing the date of the general election. In relation to devolved matters, royal prerogative powers and powers previously exercised by UK ministers are transferred to Scottish ministers (s.53).

The Scottish Parliament sits for four years when it is automatically dissolved. A general election must be held on the first Thursday in May in the fourth year after the previous ordinary general election, after which the Parliament must meet within seven days (s.2). The Presiding Officer may vary this by up to one month (s.2). The Parliament can also be dissolved by the Queen earlier by a two thirds majority vote – an unlikely event – or following a proposal from the Presiding Officer, where it fails to designate a First Minister within 28 days (below) (s.3). This might arise where an administration finds itself deadlocked because of tensions within a coalition government (more likely than in the UK Parliament because of the proportionate electoral system). Thus unlike the case with the UK Parliament, the First Minister cannot trigger a general election. The electoral system combines the traditional 'first past the post' method with a 'party list' system (Chapter 12).

The Scottish executive comprises the following:

▶ The First Minister is appointed and dismissed by the monarch on the nomination of the Parliament (s.45). Parliament must nominate a First Minister within 28 days of any of the following events: a general election, the resignation of the First Minister, any other vacancy in the office and the First Minister's ceasing to be a Member of the Scottish Parliament (MSP) other than on a dissolution (s.46).

▶ As in the UK government, ministers and the law officers must resign if the executive loses a vote of confidence or if they cease to be MSPs, except after dissolution when they continue in office unless replaced by the new administration (ss.47, 48, 49). If the First Minister ceases to be an MSP, he remains in office until a successor is chosen (s.45(3)).

▶ Other ministers and junior ministers are appointed by the First Minister from MSPs, subject to the formal approval of the monarch and, unlike the UK executive, with the agreement of the Parliament (ss.47, 49, 87). They can be dismissed by the First Minister (ss.47(3)b, 49(4)b).

▶ Scottish civil servants although appointed by Scottish ministers are members of the UK home civil service (s.51), thus there may be a conflict of loyalty. However since the Crown in relation to the Scottish executive is a different entity from the Crown in relation to the UK government (s.91), their primary loyalty may be to Scottish ministers.

▶ Law officers are the Lord Advocate and the Solicitor-General for Scotland. They need not be MSPs. There is also an Advocate-General for Scotland who is responsible for giving advice on Scottish matters to the UK government (s.87). Appointment and removal of the law officers must be recommended to the monarch by the First Minister with the agreement of the Parliament (s.48).

▶ Ministers in the UK government cannot hold office in the Scottish executive (s.44(3)). In relation to the continuing role of the UK government in respect of Scotland, there are special committees in Parliament to examine Scottish affairs and a minister for Scotland accountable to the UK Parliament.

Legislation

The Scottish Parliament can legislate generally subject to the restrictions in the Act (ss.28, 29, Schedule 4). These are substantial and make it clear that this is devolution rather than federalism. Acts of the Scottish Parliament outside these limits are not law (s.29(1)). The UK Parliament retains its full power to legislate for Scotland, thus overriding the devolution provisions (s.28(7)). However this may be politically unreal. Indeed according to the Sewel Convention (above) the UK Parliament will not intervene in a devolved area without the consent of the Scottish Parliament (see (HL Deb vol 592 col 791, (1998), *Memorandum of Understanding and Supplementary Agreements*, 1999, Cm 4444). However where the Scottish Parliament does give its consent, although modish political jargon might call this a 'partnership' the measure in question is scrutinised in depth if at all only by the UK Parliament.

Acts of the Scottish Parliament are strictly subordinate as opposed to primary legislation, owing their validity only to the Scotland Act 1998 (see for example the Human Rights Act 1998 s.21). They can therefore be set aside by the courts. The validity of the procedure leading to an enactment does not affect the Act's validity (s.28(5)), but otherwise Acts of the Scottish Parliament that are outside its competence 'are not law' (s.28). However the democratic character of the devolved lawmaking process provisions suggests that the court will be reluctant to interfere. Moreover where a measure is ambiguous it must be interpreted narrowly in favour of its validity (s.101).

The following are the main limits on the power of the Scottish Parliament (s.29(2)):

▶ Although it can alter UK statutes it cannot, except in minor respects, amend the Scotland Act itself nor various UK statutes including the Act of Union (Schedule 4, s.37).

▶ It cannot alter any law which 'would form part of the law of a country or territory other than Scotland, or confer or remove functions exercisable otherwise than in or as regards Scotland'. The UK government can specify these functions (s.30(3)). This is of particular significance in relation to fishing.

▶ It cannot override European law nor rights binding under the Human Rights Act 1998. UK ministers have the exclusive power to bring EC law into effect (ss.52, 54, 57(2)).

▶ It has taxation powers limited to altering the basic rate of income tax by three pence in the pound (s.73). However most of its finance is derived from the UK government.

▶ 'Reserved matters' on which only the UK Parliament can legislate (s.30, Schedule 5). They include the most basic functions of government and important constitutional matters. The main reserved matters are matters affecting the Crown (but not the exercise of the royal prerogative); the civil service; electoral arrangements (an important control); the registration and funding of political parties; the Union with England; the UK Parliament; the higher Scottish courts; international relations; defence and national security; treason; fiscal, economic and monetary policy; currency; financial services and markets, money laundering; border controls; transport safety and regulation; media policy; employment regulation; certain health matters; the regulation of key professions; social security. Reserved matters can be altered by Order in Council (s.30(2)).

There are provisions for guarding against *ultra vires* legislation. A member of the Scottish Executive in charge of a bill must, on or before the introduction of the bill in Parliament, state that in his view the provisions of the bill would be within the legislative competence of Parliament (s,31(1). The Presiding Officer who submits bills for royal assent (s.32) must decide whether a bill is within the powers of the Parliament (s.31(2)). The Advocate-General, the Lord Advocate or the Attorney-General can require a bill to be referred to the Judicial Committee of the Privy Council (s.33). This jurisdiction will be exercised by the new Supreme Court under the Constitutional Reform Act 2005. Somewhat controversially due to the 'colonial' flavour of such a power, the Secretary of State can prohibit a bill from being sent for royal assent where she or he 'has reasonable ground to believe' that the bill would be incompatible with international obligations, or the interests of national security or defence, or would have an adverse effect on the law relating to reserved matters (s.35). (See also section 58 in relation to the Scottish executive.)

The UK government can make subordinate legislation remedying *ultra vires* Acts of the Scottish Parliament and the Scottish executive (s.107). Moreover additional functions outside devolved matters can be given to Scottish ministers by Order in Council (s.63) for which they are accountable to the UK Parliament. The court can protect people who may have relied on invalid laws by removing the retrospective effect of the invalidity or suspending the invalidity to allow the defect to be corrected (s.102).

The committee system within the Scottish Parliament is more proactive than is the case with the UK Parliament (Chapter 12). Scottish committees can not only scrutinise the executive and revise legislation but can initiate legislation and conduct inquiries that involve direct communication with the people.

After a slow start the Scottish Parliament has enacted a substantial amount of legislation, particularly concerning social matters and public services, which has markedly distinguished the regime from its English counterpart. These include free personal care for the elderly, greater support for students, rescue packages for fisheries and the victims of foot and mouth disease, land reform, mental health and freedom of information.

The Courts

Scotland has its own court system. However civil appeals are decided by the House of Lords which has jurisdiction over the whole of the UK, while criminal appeals are decided within the Scottish courts. Scottish criminal law is markedly different from that in England. However there need not be uniformity in the civil law (see *Mackintosh* v *Lord*

Advocate (1876); *R v Manchester Stipendiary Magistrate ex parte Granada Television Ltd* [2001] 1 AC 300 at 304).

The most senior judges (the Lord President of the Court of Session and the Lord Justice Clerk) are appointed by the monarch on a recommendation from the Prime Minister on the nomination of the First Minister (s.95). Other judges are appointed on the recommendation of the First Minister. In some respects Scottish judges appear to have stronger protection against political interference than their UK counterparts (Chapter 8). Senior judges can be dismissed for inability, neglect of duty or misbehaviour only on a recommendation by the First Minister following a resolution of Parliament (s.95). The resolution can be made only on the basis of a written report from a tribunal, chaired by a member of the Privy Council who has held high judicial office, concluding that the judge is unfit for office on the grounds of inability, neglect of duty or misbehaviour. In the case of the Lord President and the Lord Justice Clerk, the Prime Minister must be consulted.

The courts have a special role in relation to 'devolution issues'. These are (Schedule 6):

- whether the Parliament has exceeded its powers
- whether a member of the executive has acted outside his or her devolved competence or violated the Human Rights Act or European Community law
- any other question about whether a function is within devolved competence
- any other question arising by virtue of the Act about reserved matters.

Devolution issues are ultimately decided by the Privy Council (which will transfer to the Supreme Court) either on appeal or by way of a reference from a lower court. In addition the Lord Advocate, the Advocate-General, the Attorney-General or the Advocate-General for Northern Ireland can directly refer to the Privy Council any devolution issue, including perhaps hypothetical issues, an innovation in the UK.

6.4.2 Northern Ireland

The history of Ireland is complex and raises fundamental political issues about the sharing of political power in Northern Ireland and its relationship with the UK. Disagreements centre on divisions between the Catholic and Protestant communities and on a history of imposed settlement from England and Scotland. Broadly speaking the majority Protestant community prefers to remain an integral part of the UK while the Catholic community would prefer union with the neighbouring Republic of Ireland.

Ireland had been nominally subject to the English Crown from the tenth century. According to English law, laws made by the Irish Parliament had been subject to English statutes and approval by the King in Council since 1494 ('Poyning's Law'). However until Tudor times England effectively controlled only an area around Dublin called the Pale. Henry VIII and Elizabeth I attempted to extend English administration to the whole of Ireland, precipitating rebellion followed by confiscation of land and extensive settlement by English and Scots Protestants in what is now Northern Ireland. Cromwell's regime during the 1650s consolidated this policy with large scale massacres. The conquest of Ireland was completed in 1690 when William III, in alliance with France and supported by the Pope, defeated the deposed Catholic King of England James II at the Battle of the Boyne.

After a series of violent rebellions against Protestant supremacy, the Acts of Union of 1800 joined Britain and Ireland into the UK thus creating the UK Parliament. The Irish Parliament was abolished in favour of Irish representation in the UK Parliament. The Acts of Union declared that the Union was to last 'for ever'. They also protected the United Church of England and Ireland but the repeal of this provision by the Irish Church Act 1879 has been upheld (*Ex parte Canon Selwyn* (1872)).

Unrest punctuated by periods of violence continued throughout the nineteenth and twentieth centuries. In the late nineteenth and early twentieth centuries the question of 'Irish home rule' was among the most important questions in UK politics. It had profound constitutional implications. It weakened the personal authority of the monarch who unwisely took sides in the dispute and generated dispute about the most fundamental principles of the constitution including the nature of the UK Parliament. It was a fundamental reason for the enactment of the Parliament Act 1911 (Chapter 8) which removed the House of Lord's power to veto a bill approved by the Commons. This was because the House of Lords fiercely resisted the Liberal government's desire for Irish home rule fearing that it would destroy the UK. The Government of Ireland Act 1949 duly gave internal home rule to Ireland.

From 1916 there was a period of violent rebellion in favour of complete independence from the UK. The UK attempted to impose a compromise in the form of the Government of Ireland Act 1920. This partitioned Ireland between what is now the Republic of Ireland and the six counties of Northern Ireland. The Act introduced a devolved government in Northern Ireland. Section 75 provided that:

> notwithstanding the establishment of the Parliament of Northern Ireland or anything contained in this Act, the supreme authority of the Parliament of the UK shall remain unaffected and undiminished over all persons, matters and things in (Northern Ireland) and every part thereof.

The Irish Free State (Constitution) Act 1922 purported to give the rest of Ireland internal self government.

Both measures were ignored in the Republic of Ireland which created its own constitution based upon the sovereignty of the people. This constitution applied to the whole of Ireland although it was ineffective in the north. As a result there were conflicting legal orders, each being valid from its internal viewpoint. Eventually the UK recognised the independence of the Republic (Ireland Act 1949) but provided that:

> in no event will Northern Ireland cease to be part of the UK without the consent of the Parliament of Northern Ireland. (s.1(2))

From 1972, following continuing violence resulting from perceived discrimination against Catholics, direct rule from Westminster was imposed and stringent emergency legislation introduced. A series of agreements attempted to engineer a compromise by creating machinery for inter-community negotiations (the Anglo-Irish Agreement 1985; the 'Downing Street Declaration', 1994, Cm 2422). These led to the Belfast or 'Good Friday' Agreement (1998, Cm 3883) between the two governments and the main political parties in Northern Ireland. This provides for the restoration of devolved government, the amendment of the Irish constitution so as to accept that Northern Ireland is currently controlled by the UK, and the creation of various consultative bodies representing the interests of the UK, Northern Ireland and the Republic of Ireland (North/South Ministerial Council, British–Irish Council, British–Irish Intergovernmental Conference).

The Good Friday Agreement was endorsed by 71 per cent of voters in Northern Ireland and 94 per cent in the Republic of Ireland in separate referendums and led to the present devolution arrangements. The Northern Ireland Act 1998 attempts to ensure a balance between the competing communities. It is sometimes characterised as an example of deliberative democracy and liberal pluralism (Chapter 1). It restricts the political freedom of the legislature and executive to a greater extent than is the case in the rest of the UK. The overriding power of Parliament to make law for Northern Ireland is not affected (s.5(6)). Ministers are directly elected by the Assembly in accordance with the balance of the parties within it. Thus the system is very different from the UK's traditional system, which concentrates power in the majority party leader. The Northern Ireland devolution settlement also provides for the people to vote in a referendum to leave the UK and for the Republic of Ireland to participate in the affairs of Northern Ireland. The following are the main provisions of the Act:

▶ Northern Ireland remains part of the UK and the status of Northern Ireland will be altered only with the consent of a majority of its electorate (s.1). If a referendum favours a united Ireland, the Secretary of State is required to 'make proposals' to implement this by agreement with the Irish government (s.1).

▶ The Northern Ireland Assembly is elected by a single transferable vote (Chapter 12). The Assembly's powers are more limited than is the case with Scotland and the Secretary of State has stronger powers. The Assembly sits for a fixed four year term but can be dissolved on a resolution supported by two thirds of its members, or by the monarch on the advice of the Secretary of State, or if a Chief Minister or Deputy Chief Minister cannot be elected within six weeks of the first meeting of the Assembly (ss.16, 32). See also *Robinson* v *Secretary of State for Northern Ireland* [2002] UKHL 32. If thirty members petition the Assembly in relation to any matter to be voted on, the vote shall require cross community support (s.42).

▶ Acts of the Assembly require royal assent and as in Scotland the validity of proceedings leading to an enactment shall not be questioned in the courts (s.5(5)). Unlike the case in Scotland where this is a matter for the Presiding Officer of the Assembly, the Secretary of State submits bills for royal assent (s.14). He can refuse to submit a bill if he thinks it is outside the competence of the Assembly or contains provisions incompatible with international obligations, the interests of defence or national security, the protection of public safety or public order, or would have an adverse effect on the operation of the single market within the UK. The Secretary of State can also make an order remedying an *ultra vires* Act (s.80).

▶ As in Scotland the Assembly can legislate generally except in relation to matters which are excluded (s.6). Similar provisions apply in relation to control by the courts over devolution matters. The Assembly has general legislative power in relation to matters exclusively within Northern Ireland, subject to EC law and to the rights protected by the Human Rights Act 1998. It can raise certain taxes but not the main taxes that apply generally throughout the UK. 'Excepted' and 'reserved' matters are listed in Schedules 2 and 3. The Assembly cannot legislate on excepted matters unless ancillary to other matters. It can legislate on reserved matters and on ancillary matters with the consent of the Secretary of State (ss.6, 8). Discrimination on the grounds of religious belief or political opinion is outside the competence of the Assembly and certain statutes cannot be modified (s.7).

▶ The First Minister lacks the discretionary power of a UK Prime Minister to appoint or dismiss other ministers or dissolve the legislature. Instead there is a bipartisan arrangement ensuring that both unionists and nationalists play a part. The First Minister and Deputy First Ministers are elected jointly by the Assembly from its members. This requires a majority of the Assembly and also separate majorities of unionists and nationalists (s.16). The First and Deputy First Ministers must both lose office if either resigns or ceases to be a member of the Assembly. Subject to a maximum of ten, which can be increased by the Secretary of State (s.17(4)), and to the approval of the Assembly, the First and Deputy First Ministers jointly decide on the number of Northern Ireland ministers heading departments and forming a Cabinet. Ministers are then nominated by the political parties from members of the Assembly in accordance with a formula designed to reflect the balance of parties in the Assembly (s.18). Assembly Committees must also reflect party strengths.

▶ A minister can be dismissed by his or her party's nominating officer and loses office on ceasing to be a member of the Assembly other than after a dissolution (s.18). Ministers collectively lose office when a new Assembly is elected, where a party is excluded on a vote of confidence, where a new determination as to the number of ministers is made or as prescribed by standing order (s.18).

▶ Ministers and political parties can be excluded for up to twelve months (renewable) by the Assembly on the grounds that they are not committed to peace or have otherwise broken their oath of office (s.30). The motion must have the support of at least thirty members (from a total of between 96 and 108) and must be moved by the First and Deputy First Ministers jointly or by the Presiding Officer of the Assembly if required to do so by the Secretary of State. The Secretary of State must take into account the propensity to violence and cooperation with the authorities of the excluded person. The resolution must have cross party support.

▶ Ministers must take a pledge of office which includes a 'Ministerial Code of Conduct' (s.16(10), Schedule 4). The code requires the 'strictest standards of propriety, accountability, openness, good community relations and equality and avoiding or declaring conflicts of interest'. Any direct or indirect pecuniary interests that members of the public might reasonably think could influence their judgement must be registered. The code is similar to the Ministerial Code for UK ministers and requires compliance with the 'Nolan Principles of Public Life' (Chapter 5). In Northern Ireland, unlike the rest of the UK, it might therefore be enforceable in the courts.

▶ There are human rights and equal opportunities commissioners with powers to advise government and support legal proceedings.

6.4.3 Wales

Wales was never a separate state but consisted of a number of principalities. The largest of these passed into English rule in 1084 (Statute of Wales) and the English local government system was imposed by the Statute of Rhuddlan (1284). England had subdued the whole of Wales by the sixteenth century (Act of the Union of Wales 1536). A separate Welsh Assembly was abolished in 1689. English law applied throughout Wales and a single court system was introduced in 1830. Within Wales there are markedly different areas both economically and culturally, so that it is more difficult than in the case of Scotland to regard Wales as a country or a nation. Earlier proposals for Welsh devolution in the Wales Act 1978 were defeated by a referendum and the current proposals were only narrowly approved.

The system originally created by the Government of Wales Act 1998 was a weaker form of devolution than those operating in Scotland and Northern Ireland. It was a hybrid of a local government model based on committees formed out of an elected assembly, a parliamentary model and an administrative model based on the former Welsh Office of the UK government. The Assembly was confined to making subordinate legislation under powers that were previously exercised by UK ministers under particular statutes or are subsequently conferred on it by statute. Latterly statutes have conferred relatively broad powers on the Assembly. All powers were vested in the Assembly itself with flexible powers for delegation to committees and secretaries. Unlike Scotland and Northern Ireland the Assembly can legislate only on prescribed subjects.

The executive comprises a First Secretary, committee secretaries and committees of the legislature. However the Government of Wales Act 2006 has substantially increased the powers of the Assembly and creates a system of ministers responsible to the Assembly. The Act therefore introduces a separation of powers between legislature and executive. It replaces most of the 1998 Act.

Under the 2006 Act the Welsh Assembly can do anything that could be done by an Act of Parliament on any of the subjects designated by the Act. This is subject to EC law and Convention Rights and to restrictions limiting the creation of criminal offences and altering certain statutes. The designated subjects include agriculture, ancient monuments, economic development, education, environment, food, fisheries, health, highways and transport, housing, local government, the National Assembly, public administration, social welfare, sport, tourism, town and country planning, water supply and sewage and the Welsh language. Measures must take effect exclusively within Wales or in the case of enforcement and incidental matters in England and Wales (s.94).

Initially this power will take the form of 'Assembly Measures' each of which will require the consent of the Queen in Council and the approval of Parliament. These must be bilingual unless otherwise prescribed by Standing Order (s78(5)). There is further provision for the Assembly to enact 'Acts of the Assembly' with similar scope (s.106). Acts will require only the formal royal assent as in Scotland. The power to enact Acts is triggered by an Order in Council approved by Parliament requiring a referendum of the Welsh people. The referendum can be triggered either by the UK government or by the Assembly on the proposal of a Welsh minister. In both cases a two thirds majority of the Assembly is required. Following a favourable referendum vote a Welsh minister is empowered to bring the power to enact Acts of the Assembly into effect (sections 103–6). Where the Asssembly initiates the process the Secretary of State can refuse to make the Order for the referendum but must give reasons. Section 114 of the 2006 Act empowers the Secretary of Strate to veto an Asssembly Act on public interest grounds including interference with the English water supply.

The system created by the 2006 Act is closer to the parliamentary system than that put in place by the 1998 Act. The Welsh Assembly of sixty members is elected by a method similar to that in Scotland (see Chapter 12). The Assembly sits for a fixed term of four years but, unlike the position under the 1998 Act, can be dissolved earlier by a two thirds majority (s. 5).

A First Minister is chosen by the Assembly and appoints and dismisses other ministers and deputy ministers from Assembly members on a similar basis to the position in Scotland (ss.46–51). A Council General, responsible for giving legal advice to the government, must also be appointed with the agreement of the Assembly (s. 49). She or he need not be an Assembly member. The total number of ministers and deputy ministers is limited to twelve. Welsh ministers are financially responsible to the Assembly, for which purpose there is an Auditor-General (ss.143, 145). They are also responsible to Parliament through the Treasury, the Comptroller and Auditor-General being effectively in the position of a UK government department for this purpose (ss.132, 136). The UK Secretary of State for Wales represents Welsh affairs at national level and in the Council of Ministers of the EU.

The 2006 Act has a paternalistic edge. Welsh ministers are empowered to promote or improve the economic, social and environmental well being of Wales (s.60) and under the rubric of 'inclusiveness' must consult widely, advance various social and cultural concerns and prepare strategies dealing with sustainable development, the voluntary sector, equal opportunities and the Welsh language. There must also be a 'Partnership Council' comprising ministers and local authority representatives (s.72).

There is no separate Welsh court system although there is a division of the Administrative Court in Cardiff dealing with Welsh governmental issues. This could develop distinctive constitutional principles in the Welsh context. There are provisions similar to those in Scotland and Northern Ireland for the Privy Council and later the Supreme Court to deal with devolution matters. The Council General is responsible for referring devolution issues to the Supreme Court, the provisions being similar to those for Scotland (s.96).

There is a Public Services Ombudsman (Public Services Ombudsman (Wales) Act 2005). This is a stronger version of the ombudsman mechanism than the various English and UK equivalents. The ombudsman can receive complaints directly from the public and has jurisdiction over the Assembly and government, local authorities, health authorities and social landlords. The ombudsman may publish his or her report and the authority concerned must do so unless the ombudsman excludes publication in certain circumstances on public interest grounds (s.21). In the event of non-compliance, the ombudsman can refer the matter to the High Court.

6.4.4 England

England, comprising 85% of the population of the UK, has neither elected institutions of its own nor indeed a legal identity. England is governed by the central UK government. Therefore Scottish, Welsh and Northern Ireland members of the UK Parliament are entitled to vote in debates affecting exclusively English matters for which they are not accountable to their own voters. Similarly a UK government might be kept in power on the strength of Scottish votes. For example in 2004, by a majority of five, the Labour government won the vote in favour of increasing university tuition fees in England by virtue of its Scottish supporters. This problem, often called 'West Lothian question' after the constituency of the MP Tam Dalyell, a relentless pursuer of the matter, is an inevitable result of the UK Parliament having exclusive jurisdiction over English affairs. It can be resolved adequately only by creating a separate lawmaker for England, a proposal for which there is little public interest. Indeed the same problem arose without solution in relation to the Irish Home Rule Bills between 1886 and 1914. One compromise solution of creating a procedure under which Scottish MPs cannot vote on 'English' matters is fraught with problems relating to how English matters are to be identified and disentangled from UK matters particularly in relation to finance (see Hazell (ed) *The English Question* (2006)). Moreover Scottish, Welsh and Northern Ireland voters are represented in the UK Parliament roughly in proportion to their population. This means that the UK Parliament is dominated by English MPs who can vote on Scottish matters including devolved matters such as the amount of money to be given to Scotland from the UK government.

It is often suggested that there should be a devolved assembly for England. Central government powers relating to the English regions such as land use, transport and economic development are divided between different government departments, the names and functions of which are constantly changing. There are nine regional offices of central government charged with a coordinating role. There are also eight Regional Development Agencies (RDAs) comprising boards (mainly of private business people) appointed by the Secretary of State. RDAs are charged with advancing economic development, business efficiency, investment, competitiveness, employment and sustainable development (Regional Development Agencies Act 1998 s.4)). An RDA can do anything which it considers expedient for its purposes (s.5(1)). However general language cannot justify interference with the legal rights of individuals such as compulsorily acquiring property. For this, specific authority is required. An RDA can acquire land compulsorily with the consent of the Secretary of State and can enter property for the purpose of survey or valuation (ss 20, 21). It can also exercise powers delegated by ministers but cannot make laws nor fix charges or fees (s.6). These arrangements are characteristic of the dislike of democracy that pervades political culture in the UK.

There is a limited form of regional devolution for the London region in the form of an elected Mayor and Assembly (Greater London Authority Act 1999). The Assembly is elected on the basis of 'first past the post' (Chapter 12) together with an 'additional member' from a party list in accordance with the party's share of the vote, thereby reflecting public opinion to a greater extent than is the case with local government and Parliament. The Mayor and Assembly have certain executive powers in relation mainly to transport, policing, land use planning, housing and local amenities.

There are provisions for a limited form of devolution to English regions. The Secretary of State has power, after considering the 'level of interest' (which is undefined), to hold referendums in respect of the creation of elected regional assemblies in eight English regions (Regional Assemblies (Preparations) Act 2003). The assemblies would be elected by a mixture of first past the post and an additional member top up on a similar basis to London. They would be funded by central government grant together with limited power to precept from local government taxation and some borrowing powers but would not have lawmaking power. The assemblies would have strategic planning functions currently exercised by local government and unspecified administrative functions, together with targets set by central government (see *Your Region, Your Choice: Revitalising the English Regions*, 2002, Cm 5511). As with local government, it is doubtful whether regional assemblies would have sufficient independence to be of constitutional interest. A referendum for an assembly for northeast England was rejected by 78% in 2004. It is unlikely that English devolution will be implemented – there appears to be little public interest in the matter.

6.5　The Channel Islands and the Isle of Man

The Channel Islands of Jersey, Guernsey and Sark and the Isle of Man have special constitutional status, being neither part of the UK nor British overseas territories. They are subjects of the Crown which makes laws for them in the form of Prerogative Orders in Council. They have their own legislatures, executive and judiciary and can make laws governing their internal affairs. Their status derives from feudal ownership by the Crown as successor to the Duke of Normandy. Sark, with a population of six hundred, is subject to Guernsey law but retains its own feudal structure (the only one in the western world) under which a hereditary ruler, the Seigneur (to whom the Crown granted the right by Letters Patent of 1565 and 1611) owns the land and appoints the main judicial and executive officers. The common law does not apply in the Channel Islands and their internal law is local customary law. As Crown territories, the protection provided by the judicial review powers of the High Court applies to both (see *Ex parte Brown* (1864); *Ex parte Anderson* (1861)).

Parliamentary supremacy was extended to the Channel Islands by a Prerogative Order in Council of 1806. However there is a presumption of interpretation that an Act will not apply to the Channel Islands in the absence of express words or necessary implication. The Channel Islands are not members of the EU but there are special treaty arrangements. Channel Island citizens are British citizens (British Nationality Act 1981 ss.1, 11, 50(1)).

The position of the Isle of Man is broadly similar, although the Crown's rights seem to derive from an ancient agreement with Norway, confirmed by statute (Isle of Man Purchase Act 1765 (repealed)). Legislation made by its elected legislature, the Tynewald, must be assented to by the Queen in Council. (See generally *Royal Commission on the Constitution*, 1973, Part XI and Minutes of Evidence VI, pp. 7, 13, 227–34; *X v UK* (1982).)

6.6　Overseas Territories

In the case of most former UK territories, all ties with UK law have been severed by Acts of Parliament (for example the Canada Act 1982; the Australia Act 1986). However the UK retains a small number of dependent overseas territories. Previously called colonies, they are now 'British overseas territories' (British Overseas Territories Act 2002). Remaining overseas territories include Anguilla, Bermuda, British Indian Ocean Territories (BIOT), British Virgin Islands, Cayman Islands, Falkland Islands, Gibraltar, Montserrat, the Pitcairn Islands, St Helena, South Georgia and South Sandwich Islands (SGSSI), and the Turks and Caicos Islands.

Overseas territories are subject to the overriding principle of parliamentary supremacy in the same way as the UK. However Acts of the UK Parliament do not apply to dependent territories unless they specifically so provide. Moreover under the Colonial Laws Validity Act 1865, legislatures in overseas territories have full lawmaking power, even if this is inconsistent with a UK statute of general effect or with the common law (s.5). This may extend to altering its own constitution but only in the 'manner and form' required by any UK law applying to the territory at the time (see *Bribery Commissioner* v *Ranasinghe* (1965); *R* v *Burah* (1878)).

The application of common law and the mode of legislating for overseas territories depend on historical factors. Royal prerogative powers can be used to legislate for certain overseas territories or colonies but not others. The rules depend on how the territory was acquired and whether formal undertakings were made to the inhabitants of the territory concerning the constitutional arrangements that would be applied. In this context there is an important distinction between 'settled' colonies and 'ceded and conquered' colonies. A settled colony is one in which there were no developed political institutions when British settlers first arrived in the territory (such as SGSSI). In the other category were colonies that were either ceded to Britain (often in a peace treaty following armed conflict) or conquered by force of British arms.

In the case of settled colonies, English common law as it stood at the time of settlement is deemed to have applied to the territory, which means that the limitations placed on the royal prerogative in England apply in that territory. Most significant are the restrictions laid down in the *Case of Proclamations* (1611) after which the King could not introduce new laws without the consent of Parliament. In settled colonies the Crown does not have the power to pass laws for the colony under the royal prerogative, just as it does not in England. The legislative function in the territory can only be exercised under the powers given by an Act of the Westminster Parliament (see British Settlement Act 1837 and *R v Secretary of State for Foreign and Commonwealth Affairs ex parte Quark Fishing Ltd* (2006) below). Such powers are usually expressed as being for the 'peace, order and good government of the territory', a widely used expression in English speaking constitutional law.

In the case of ceded and conquered territories the powers of the Crown are more extensive but are still restricted (*Campbell v Hall* (1774)). Where there is a developed legal and political system, this continues in force until the Crown determines otherwise. By virtue of this local legal system, English common law does not extend to the territory in question which means that the *Case of Proclamations* does not apply. Thus the Crown can make law under the royal prerogative, although this may be implicitly limited by the requirement of 'peace, order and good government' of the territory (above). New laws, including laws imposing new taxes, can be framed for the ceded or conquered territory either by an Order in Council or by letters patent. Similarly governors can be appointed ('commissioned') to make laws within the authority conferred on them by the Crown (in formal 'Royal Instructions' and in subsequent despatches).

However the Crown can deprive itself of this lawmaking power. Lord Mansfield in *Campbell v Hall* (1774) decided that, where there is a local representative legislature, the power is transferred from the Crown to the colony in question and, in the absence of an Act of the Westminster Parliament, cannot be recovered. In *Campbell* the Crown had issued a proclamation empowering a colonial governor to establish a local legislative assembly, although by the date of the action none had been created. Despite the formally announced intention to decentralise government, the Crown had subsequently attempted to impose a new tax directly on the colony and the court held that this was unlawful. Although the assembly had not actually been established it was held that, by promising to create one the Crown had lost its power to pass laws under the prerogative for that colony. The reason for this was that the Crown had sought investment and invited settlers to the colony who would have relied on the promise to create a local assembly. Their private interests would have been better served under this decentralised arrangement than under direct rule. The quandary for Whitehall was that taxes had to be levied if the colonies were not to be a burden on British taxpayers but after *Campbell*, unless it continued with direct rule, the Crown had to rely on local assemblies to agree to the required taxation.

More generally, *Campbell* indicates that prerogative powers are not unlimited and in particular a formal promise governing the future exercise of prerogative powers can bind the Crown. It is unclear whether *Campbell* – the authority of which has never been doubted – is a decision that is now to be confined to its own facts, or whether it establishes a wider principle of constitutional law, the boundaries of which remain unclear.

The judicial review powers of UK courts apply to overseas territories of both kinds – *R v Secretary of State for Foreign and Commonwealth Affairs ex parte Quark Fishing Ltd* (2006) (settled territory) and *R (Bancoult) v Secretary of State for the Foreign and Commonwealth Office* (2001) (ceded territory). This means that the Crown's powers whether statutory or prerogative are limited by a requirement to conform to the laws in force and also by more general notions of fairness and rationality (Chapter 17).

Where a British overseas territory has its own government, even a rudimentary one, the strict position is that the Crown is 'divisible', meaning that the Crown in relation to the territory is a separate legal entity from the Crown of the UK (*R v Secretary of State for the Foreign and Commonwealth Office ex parte Indian Association of Alberta* (1982)). Thus the courts will assess the Crown's actions in relation to the interests of the territory in question. An Act of Parliament is therefore required for the exercise of wider powers. The Crown in the sense of the UK government will of course be closely involved in the affairs of an overseas territory and in political terms it would be difficult to separate the two interests. Nevertheless in each case it is necessary to decide whether the matter concerns the Crown in right of the particular territory or the UK Crown.

In *R (Bancoult) v Secretary of State for the Foreign and Commonwealth Office* (2001), the Commissioner of a ceded territory without its own government, British Indian Ocean Territories (BIOT) which comprised a group of islands, had the normal power under the royal prerogative to make law for the territory. On the instructions of the UK government, he made an order (the Immigration Ordinance 1971) expelling the population of the territory from the islands, resettling them elsewhere. The population consisted mainly of plantation workers, some of whom had lived there for several generations. It was UK government policy to use the territory as a military base jointly with the US and for this purpose it wished to remove the inhabitants, treating them as temporary workers so as to avoid problems with the United Nations. It was held that the decision was unlawful in the sense of irrational since it bore no relationship to the interests of the inhabitants. Laws LJ also thought that the prerogative power could not be exercised so as to exile a permanent inhabitant from the territory in which he has a right to live. Subsequently the Crown made an Order in Council under the royal prerogative which purported to change the Constitution of BIOT by denying the exiled inhabitants a right of abode in the territory.

In *R (Bancoult) v Secretary of State for the Foreign and Commonwealth Office (No. 2)* (2008) the House of Lords held that it had jurisdiction to review the Order in Council but that this Order was valid and was not an abuse of power. A majority held (Lord Bingham and Lord Mance dissenting) that the Crown could make an Order for the benefit of the UK itself and its foreign relations and was not confined to acting in the interests of the inhabitants of the territory. Their Lordships considered that the inhabitants' fundamental rights to their homeland, violated at the previous stage, had been compensated with their agreement. Moreover any right to return was of little practical value unless they were given government funding, a matter not appropriate for the court to determine (Chapter 16).

R v Secretary of State for Foreign and Commonwealth Affairs ex parte Quark Fishing Ltd (2006) concerned a settled territory. The Secretary of State, acting under the British Settlements Act 1837 (above), had ordered the Commissioner of South Georgia and South Sandwich Islands (SGSSI) to refuse a fishing licence to the claimant. His reason for so doing concerned the UK's relationships with neighbouring countries. The claimant sought compensation under the Human Rights Act 1998 which makes the ECHR binding in domestic law (treaties as such are not normally binding in domestic law (below)). Even though SGSSI had no permanent population and its 'government' comprised only a part time civil servant, the House of Lords held that the decision was made on behalf of the Crown as government of SGSSI not of the UK. It was therefore unlawful since it did not advance the interests of SGSSI. However their Lordships also held that the Human Rights Act 1998 did not apply since this has effect only in relation to the UK government. The ECHR as such can be extended to dependent territories (Article 56) but had not been so in this case. However their Lordships did not agree as to whether this would suffice to attract the Human Rights Act. Lords Bingham and Hoffmann took the view that, irrespective of the scope of the treaty, the Human Rights Act applies only to the UK government as such, but Lord Nicholls opined that the matter depended on whether the ECHR applied to the territory. Lady Hale criticised the unreality of the 'two crowns' approach and thought that the Act should apply wherever the territory in question was governed by the UK.

6.7   International Treaties

It is often argued that the state is no longer appropriate as the basic constitutional unit. Pressures from within that favour devolution to areas of regional identity and pressures from outside in favour of globalisation have, according to this view, weakened the legitimacy of the state. It is pointed out that we live in a 'global' economy supported by electronic communication and dominated by organisations that can operate in many countries. These developments can be rationalised by the assumption that states have passively 'consented' to them. However they contain no democratic mechanisms. Indeed it has been suggested that democracy and the rule of law can flourish only at the margins where there is a large measure of stability and consensus (see Harden, *Liberalism, Constitutionalism and Democracy*, Oxford University Press, 1999). Moreover globalisation is a one way street that involves the 'developed' liberal world imposing its ideas on the allegedly 'undeveloped' world but rarely, if ever, the other way round.

Methods of imposing constitutional order on such an unruly world include asserting the rule of law by means of international treaties, which are to a large extent outside democratic scrutiny. In the UK treaties are made and ratified by ministers under the royal prerogative and so are not subject to parliamentary veto (unless of course statute requires this, as with the European Union (Amendment)Act 2008: treaty altering founding treaties of European Union). However under the 'Ponsonby Rule' (a convention), except in urgent cases, a treaty must be laid before Parliament for twenty one days before ratification, which allows some debate. The (shelved) Constitutional Renewal Bill proposes that parliamentary approval be required for the ratification of a treaty.

Furthermore a court cannot enforce nor adjudicate upon the validity of a treaty as such (for example *R* v *Secretary of State for Foreign and Commonwealth Affairs ex parte Rees-Mogg* (1994)). However a treaty cannot alter domestic law unless it is first enacted by Parliament, either by adopting the language of the treaty or by setting out the treaty as a Schedule to the Act (*JH Rayner (Mincing Lane) Ltd* v *Department of Trade and Industry* (1990); compare Lord Steyn in *Re McKerr* (2004)).

A court can ignore a treaty that has not been incorporated into domestic law (see *R (Corner House Research) v Attorney General* (2007) [43]) but it can also take such a treaty into account. If it chooses to do so, it is unclear whether the court is allowed authoritatively to rule upon its meaning (ibid [44]). International principles are often couched in vague language so as to secure the acceptance of communities with different political and cultural perspectives. Where a treaty has been incorporated by statute there is controversy concerning whether the statute should be interpreted literally or flexibly in order to give effect to the intention of the treaty. The latter is the prevailing approach (see *Garland* v *British Rail Engineering Ltd* [1983] 2 AC 751, 771).

Summary

▷ The UK constitution has no unified concept of the state. This leads to a fragmented system of government but may protect individual freedom.

▷ Citizenship entitles a person to reside in the UK and has certain other miscellaneous consequences. There is no legal concept of the citizen corresponding to the republican notion of equal and responsible membership of the community.

▷ The UK constitution does not distribute power geographically as a method of limiting the power of the state. The UK is therefore not a federal state.

▷ Legislative and executive power has been devolved to elected bodies in Scotland and Northern Ireland but without significant tax raising powers. The UK Parliament has reserved the power to legislate in respect of many matters and has a general power to override the devolved assemblies. Their legislation is subordinate legislation, which is invalid if it exceeds the limits prescribed by the devolution statutes. In particular unlike a UK statute, legislation violating the Human Rights Act 1998 is invalid.

▷ A more limited devolution applies to Wales. Executive and subordinate legislative power, delegated by particular statutes, has been devolved to an elected Welsh Assembly. The Welsh language, sustainable development and equal opportunities are specifically protected.

▷ Elections to the devolved bodies are by proportional representation.

▷ The Scottish executive is structured according to the UK parliamentary system. However the balance of power is more in favour of the Parliament than is the case in the UK system. The Welsh system is structured more on local government but this is subject to revision. The Northern Ireland system is primarily concerned to achieve a balance between different political factions and is more restrictive than is the case with Scotland.

▷ There is no devolved government in England. Representatives from the devolved countries can therefore vote in the UK Parliament on purely English matters. Regional Development Agencies have been created but these are appointed bodies charged only with particular economic goals and thus lacking the essential attributes of democratic government.

Summary cont'd

▶ British overseas territories are subject to the jurisdiction of the courts. The Crown is a separate entity in relation to each territory which has its own government. The lawmaking power of the UK government depends on whether the territory in question is a settled territory.

▶ The validity of an international treaty cannot be questioned by the courts but a treaty cannot alter domestic law unless it is incorporated into a statute which therefore falls to be interpreted by the courts in accordance with domestic law.

Exercises

6.1 What are the advantages and disadvantages of the 'state' as a legal entity?

6.2 In what circumstances could a citizen be removed from the UK? What safeguards are provided?

6.3 To what extent is a member of a racial minority protected against deportation?

6.4 What is a federation? Outline the advantages and disadvantages of a federal structure.

6.5 Compare the arguments for devolution within the UK with those in favour of a federal UK.

6.6 To what extent is Wales a 'poor relation' in relation to devolution?

6.7 Compare the balance of power between the legislature and the executive in Scotland with that in the UK government. Which is the more democratic?

6.8 What are the constitutional problems of devolution to the English regions? How would you address them?

6.9 The (imaginary) island of Stark was handed over to the UK by France in the seventeenth century. It has an indigenous population of six hundred. It is governed by a Commissioner employed by the Foreign Office who is advised by an elected Council. The Crown makes an Order in Council requiring all the indigenous inhabitants to relocate to the US. The reason it gives is that it fears the island will soon be devastated by a volcano. George, whose family has lived on Stark for many years, is told by an American friend that the government intends to hand the island over to the US for a naval base. Advise George as to whether he can successfully challenge the Order in Council in the English courts. What difference would it make if a treaty with the US provided that no one can reside in Stark without the permission of the President of the United States? What difference would it make if the Council of Stark passed a law declaring Stark independent of the UK?

Further reading

Bogdanor, V. (2004) 'Our New Constitution', *Law Quarterly Review* 120:242.

Constitution Committee of the House of Lords (2003) *Devolution: Inter Institutional Relations in the UK*, HL 147.

Cornes, R. (2003) 'Devolution and England: What is on Offer?', in Bamforth, N. and Leyland, P. (eds) *Public Law in a Multi-Layered Constitution*, Oxford, Hart Publishing.

Dyson, K. (1980) *The State Tradition in Western Europe*, Oxford, Martin Robertson, Chapters 1, 4.

Hadfield, B. (2005) 'Devolution, Westminster and the English Question', *Public Law* 286.

Further reading cont'd

Hazell, R. (2006) *The English Question*, Manchester University Press.

Hazell, R. and Rawlings R.(eds)(2005) *Devolution, Law Making and the Constitution*, Exeter, Imprint Academic.

Himsworth, C. and O' Neill, C. (2003) *Scotland's Constitution: Law and Practice*, Edinburgh, LexisNexis.

Jowell, J. and Oliver, D. (eds) (2004) *The Changing Constitution* (5th edn) Oxford University Press, Chapters 7, 8, 9.

Merinos, P. (2001) 'Democracy, Governance and Governmentality: Civic Public Space and Constitutional Renewal in Northern Ireland', *Oxford Journal of Legal Studies* 21:287.

O'Neill, M. (ed.) (2004) *Devolution and British Politics*, Harlow, Pearson, Introduction, Chapters 6, 7, 9, 12, 13, 14, 15.

Rawlings, R. (2005) 'Hastening Slowly: the Next Phase of Welsh Devolution', *Public Law* 824.

Rawlings, R. (2001) 'Taking Wales Seriously', in Campbell, T., Ewings, K. and Tomkins, A. (eds) *Sceptical Essays on Human Rights*, Oxford University Press.

Tierney, S. (2004) *Constitutional Law and National Pluralism*, Oxford University Press.

Trench, A. (2006) 'The Government of Wales Act 2006: the Next Steps in Devolution for Wales', *Public Law* 687.

Walker, D. (2000) 'Beyond the Unitary Conception of the United Kingdom Constitution', *Public Law* 384.

Walker, D. (2002) 'The Idea of Constitutional Pluralism', *Modern Law Review* 65:317.

Chapter 7

The rule of law

Key words

- Government by law and government under law
- Republicanism and collective lawmaking
- Law and freedom
- Law and equality
- Law and discretion
- Law and reason
- Law and democracy
- Procedural and substantive
- Fundamental values
- Formalism

7.1 Introduction

The concept of the rule of law is an underlying political value or ideal. It is asserted without definition in section 1 of the Constitutional Reform Act 2005:

> This Act does not adversely affect:
> (a) the existing constitutional principle of the rule of law, or
> (b) the Lord Chancellor's existing constitutional role in relation to that principle.

In its most basic sense the rule of law means that all government power should be subject to general rules. However the idea of the rule of law has been given a wide range of meanings although many of them amount to little more than saying that the law should be fair and just. The rule of law has been widely proclaimed as a pillar of constitutional thought. For example, following Aristotle and many times endorsed, the Massachusetts Constitution (1781) refers to 'a government of laws not men'. However since laws are made and applied by 'men' it is difficult to understand what this means. It seems to assume the existence of objective principles existing in thin air which humans can discover and apply. Aristotle himself seems to have been referring to the customs of his community rather than to legislation as we know it, made by a central authority. Another well known approach is the republican idea that dominating individuals should not make the law which should be made collectively to ensure that all sections of the community can participate in the making of the laws.

Is government by rules a good in itself irrespective of the content of the rules? Are laws made by an evil tyrant and applied without compassion requiring all dissenters to be executed better than a regime that gives absolute discretion to a dictator who might or might not be benevolent? If on the other hand the rule of law means the rule of 'good' or 'fair' or 'democratic' laws, the concept seems to be redundant since few would doubt that these qualities are valuable in any society.

Nor can there ever be complete government by rules since, whatever rules are adopted, someone must have the final say in what they mean and this cannot itself be subject to a law otherwise the process would continue ad infinitum. Nevertheless the rule of law is a significant but not a foolproof means of preventing domination by malicious or capricious rulers.

There is widespread disagreement as to what the rule of law means and whether the concept is of any value. Bellamy (2007) points out that the rule of law has been enlisted in the political debate from opposite perspectives. On the one hand lawyers have used it to assert the importance of the courts meaning that access to the courts should not be impeded, that the courts should be independent of the executive, that the courts should be able to control those in power and that fundamental rights should be respected (for example *M v Home Office* (1993), *R v Secretary of State for the Home Dept ex parte Simms* (1999), *R (Anderson) v Secretary of State* (2002)[27] [39]). On the other hand those favouring political solutions associate the rule of law with the importance of the democratic process as producing valid laws that should be obeyed precisely because they have been through that process. From this perspective the judges have the more limited role of interpreting and applying laws validly made by Parliament but not pronouncing on their wisdom or their conformity to a higher law. The rule of law is sometimes used merely to express the opinion that the powerful should be controlled (see *R (Corner House Research) v Director of the Serious Fraud Office* (2008) (1) [61]). However it does not follow that law is the best or only way to achieve this.

Finally the rule of law is sometimes invoked as meaning that there is a duty to obey the lawful government. Thus the rule of law is two sided since it also requires that there should be protection against government. In *Brown v Stott* [2001] 2 All ER 97, 128, Lord Hope said:

> The rule of law requires that every person be protected from invasion by the authorities of his rights and liberties. But the preservation of law and order on which the rule of law also depends, requires that those protections should not be framed in such a way as to make it impracticable to bring those who are accused of crime to justice. The benefits of the rule of law must be extended to the public at large and to the victims of crime also.

In *Brown* the House of Lords held that the normal right to remain silent was overridden by a requirement to disclose the name of the driver of a car in connection with a drink driving charge. This was because of the social importance of road safety. However it was also emphasised that any specific unfairness should be compensated for by ensuring that the proceedings were fair overall.

There are grandiose claims associating the rule of law with liberal beliefs such as individualism, freedom and democracy – for example in relation to the European Convention on Human Rights (see *Klass v Federal Republic of Germany* (1979); *Young, James and Webster v UK* (1982)) and by the International Commission of Jurists which equates the rule of law with 'the conditions which will uphold the dignity of man as an individual'. (See Raz, *The Authority of Law*, Oxford, Clarendon Press, 1979, 210–11). Thus behind the idea of the rule of law are beliefs about what is good law and that laws should be made in an acceptable way by the right kind of people.

The rule of law is closely connected with 'equality' in its formal sense ('formal' meaning shape or appearance). Thus everyone who falls within a given rule is treated the same under it. However this is procedural and has nothing to do with the substantive equality of a law (Chapter 2). For example a statute which gives a landlord virtually an absolute right to evict a tenant is not contrary to the rule of law.

As John Stuart Mill remarked:

> the justice of giving equal protection to the rights of all is maintained by those who support the most outrageous inequality in the rights themselves. (1972, Chapter 5)

To its supporters the formalism of the rule of law is a valuable achievement of the human mind as an upholder of equality and dignity: a defence not only against tyrants but also against well meaning busybodies. Formalism also supports human dignity by requiring courts and public officials to justify their decisions. For example in *Taylor v Chief Constable of the Thames Valley Police* (2004) the Court of Appeal stressed the fundamental principle that a policeman must give clear reasons for arresting someone, Sedley LJ [58] basing this on the value of human dignity (see also *Christie v Leachinsky* (1947)). However the courts do not claim that the rule of law is an absolute and recognise that it might be outweighed by important public interests, notably security. In *R (Corner House Research) v Director of the Serious Fraud Office*, 2 (2008) the House of Lords held that a prosecuting authority could discontinue a prosecution of alleged corruption involving members of the Saudi royal family on the ground that, had the investigation continued, the Saudi government would have withdrawn cooperation with the UK intelligence services thereby increasing the risk of a terrorist attack.

The rule of law is claimed to be a necessary foundation of democracy in as much as both assume the equality of persons. For example by ensuring that officials keep within the powers given to them by the people and treat people equally, the rule of law is both the servant and policeman of democracy (see Lady Hale's speech in *Ghaidan v Mendoza* (2004) [132]). The rule of law can also protect the values on which democracy depends, such as freedom of speech. However laws can protect other forms of government and historically the idea of the rule of law long predated democracy. In one sense the rule of law seems to be at odds with democracy in that it usually depends on decisions being made by an elite of unelected judges. Thus the ideas of the rule of law and democracy are not inseparable and, if large powers are given to judges, might be conflicting. For example in *R (Countryside Alliance) v Attorney General* (2007) Lady Hale remarked (at 114) that 'democracy is the will of the people but the people may not will to invade those rights which are fundamental to democracy itself.'

Democratic utilitarians such as Bentham argue that the rule of law encourages the rich and powerful to harass people who cannot fight back. If the rule of law were comprehensively applied, then not only would lawyers – a specialised and unelected elite – be in a position to impose their own preferences upon the rest of us but the values of society would be frozen. Bentham was unhappy with what he called 'Judge and Co'. He thought it particularly strange that courts should be bound by precedent since to him this merely reproduces errors. He also thought the common law, which he called 'dog law', was unjust in that we may be ignorant of the wrong until the case is decided (*Truth Versus Ashurst*, 1823; see *R v Rimmington* (2005), [33]). He thought that laws should be no more than guidelines and in the end should give way to his master principle of the greatest happiness of the greatest number.

Nor does the rule of law in its traditional sense easily cater for the diversity of beliefs and values in a modern democracy where people with many different ethnic, religious and social interests live together, each of whom might regard the law differently.

A scene from Shakespeare's *Merchant of Venice* illustrates different aspects of the rule of law. Shylock, a member of a disadvantaged minority, asked the court to enforce his bond against Antonio, a member of the ruling elite. The bond required a pound of Antonio's flesh if he defaulted on payment. Portia, posing as a judge, first made an appeal to mercy which failed. Shylock pointed out that, if mercy was given, people would be less likely to obey the law and disadvantaged minorities would be particularly vulnerable. Portia then opportunistically invoked the rule of law by interpreting the bond literally so as not to include the shedding of any blood, thus making it impossible to enforce. This crude approach ignores the widely held understanding that laws be interpreted in their context and according to their purpose or spirit. From this perspective the shedding of blood was an integral part of the bond. It is a different question outside the scope of the rule of law in its strictest sense whether a law, based on a free market that enforces such a bond, is good or bad.

7.2 Historical Background

The idea of the rule of law was asserted by Aristotle in the third century BC. In England the rule of law is claimed to go back to the Anglo-Saxon notion of a compact between ruler and ruled under which obedience to the King was conditional upon the King respecting customary law. The English version stresses government under law and also the common law as law made by independent courts. Magna Carta (1215) is said to have reinforced the principle that the state can act only through law. By endorsing Magna Carta, the King was forced to commit what were previously unwritten customs to formal writings. Although Magna Carta did not itself hold for long, its symbolic effect was immense:

> no freeman shall be taken or imprisoned or be disseissed of his freehold, or liberties or free customs or be outlawed or exiled or in any wise destroyed . . . but by . . . the law of the land. (see Thompson, *Magna Carta: Its Role in the Making of the English Constitution*, 1972)

The rule of law was famously invoked by the thirteenth century jurist Bracton as 'a bridle on power':

> the King should be under no man but under God and the Law because the Law makes him King. (quoted in *Burmah Oil Co Ltd v Lord Advocate* [1965] AC 75, 147)

This was a conscious break from the Roman law tradition which regarded law as the will of the ruler. Although Bracton accepted that in the sphere of government the King had some autocratic powers (the royal prerogative), he regarded the King as confined by law in respect of decisions concerning the rights of subjects.

The rule of law was asserted against the King in the seventeenth century. This time emphasis was placed on the connection between the common law and reason. According to Coke CJ, the rule of law protected both ruler and subject, the ruler against criticism, the subject against tyranny: 'The golden and straight metwand of the law and not the uncertain and eroded cord of discretion' (*Institutes* Part 4, 37, 41 (*c.*1669); see also *Prohibitions del Roy* (1607) 12 Co. Rep. 63). Later in the seventeenth century John Locke, an ally of Parliament against the King, equated law, reason and freedom, which as we saw in Chapter 1 has its dangers:

> Law in its true notion is not so much the limitation as the direction of a free and intelligent agent to his proper interest and prescribes no further than is for the general good of those under that law . . . for all the power the Government hath being only for the good of the Society, as it ought not to be Arbitrary and at Pleasure, so it ought to be exercised by established and promulgated Laws: that both the People may know their duty, and be safe and secure within the limits of the law, and the Rulers too kept within their due bounds not to be tempted by the Power they have in their hands, to imploy it to such purposes, and by such measures, as they would not have known and own not willingly. (*Second Treatise on Government*, 1690, VI: 57, IX: 137)

During the eighteenth and early nineteenth centuries the constitution was particularly influenced by the rhetoric of the rule of law. The constitution was regarded as a delicately balanced machine held in place by law; as George III put it, 'the most beautiful balance ever framed' (Briggs, *The Age of Improvement*, Longman, 1959, p. 88). The rule of law protected individual rights imagined as being grounded in ancient common law tradition:

> The poorest man may in his cottage bid defiance to all the forces of the Crown. It may be frail, its roof may shake, the wind may blow through it, the storm may enter, the rain may enter, but the king of England cannot enter. (Lord Brougham, *Historical Sketches of Statesmen in the Time of George III*, 1845)

It was widely asserted that the relative stability and economic prosperity enjoyed by Britain during that period was connected with a commitment to the rule of law. By contrast, France with its

> demagoguary, revolt, beheadings and . . . unruly mobs stood in English 'common sense' as a dreadful warning of all that can go wrong, a sort of conceptual opposite to England's altogether more sensible ways. (Pugh, in Halliday and Karpick (eds) *Lawyers and the Rise of Western Political Liberalism: From the Eighteenth to the Twentieth Centuries*, Clarendon Press, 1997, p. 168)

However the eulogies of the rule of law were consistent with harsh and repressive Acts of Parliament, such as the notorious anti-poaching 'Black Acts' (see Thompson, *Whigs and Hunters*, Allen Lane, 1975) and the Corresponding Societies Act 1799 which outlawed radical political and cultural organisations.

With the expansion of democracy that took place from the mid nineteenth century, influential lawyers such as Dicey (below) attempted to reformulate and defend the traditional idea of the rule of law against what they perceived as threats from both democratic ideas and the authoritarian influences of continental Europe. In 1928 Lord Chief Justice Lord Hewart published *The New Despotism* in which he asserted that the rule of law was under threat from the executive. This led to the establishment of the Committee on Ministers' Powers, whose terms of reference were 'to report what safeguards were desirable or necessary to secure the constitutional principles of the sovereignty of Parliament and the supremacy of the law'. Described as having 'the dead hand of Dicey lying frozen on its neck', the Committee's report (1932, Cmnd 4060) gave the constitution a clean bill of health albeit with a powerful dissent from Laski. The Committee recommended some strengthening of the powers of Parliament in relation to delegated legislation and asserted the importance of control by the ordinary courts over the executive. Its report was largely ignored.

Subsequently the rule of law became associated with a belief that conservative and, in recent years, liberal-minded judges were determined to frustrate the more collectivist policies of left wing governments (see Griffith, *The Politics of the Judiciary*, Fontana, 1997). More recently, with the introduction of the Human Rights Act 1998, there has been a revival of interest in the rule of law as a means of bringing together the ideas of law, liberalism and democracy.

7.3   Different Versions of the Rule of Law

A broad distinction can be made between the rule of law as government *by* law (versions 1 and 2) and the rule of law as government *under* law (version 3). This broadly corresponds to the distinction between procedural and substantive versions of the rule of law.

1. **The core rule of law**: This has been outlined above. It means government by law in the form of general rules as opposed to the discretion of the ruler. It also implies 'equality' in the sense that everyone who falls within a given rule must be treated the same in accordance with it. All it requires is that there be rules validly made. It does not specify their content. The core rule of law is therefore consistent with hideously repressive regimes.
2. **The amplified rule of law**: This claims that certain principles relating to fairness and justice are inherent in the notion of law as guiding conduct and that these at least moderate bad laws. It is not claimed that these principles cannot be overridden by other factors. It is primarily *procedural*.
3. **The extended ('thick') rule of law**: This is the most ambitious version and introduces *substantive* values. It claims that law encapsulates the overarching values of the community – assumed to be liberal values such as freedom of expression – in the care of impartial judges (see Allan, 2001). It claims also to link law with republican ideas of equal citizenship. In as much as this version of the rule of law relies upon vague and contestable concepts, it conflicts with the core rule of law. Indeed an action can be lawful but still contrary to the rule of law in the extended sense (see *R (Anderson)* v *Secretary of State* (2002)[39]).

7.4   The Core Rule of Law

As Hayek (1960) asserted of the rule of law:

> stripped of all technicalities this means that government in all its actions is bound by rules fixed and announced beforehand – rules which make it possible to foresee with fair certainty how the authority will use its coercive powers in given circumstances, and to plan one's life accordingly.

At one extreme it has been claimed that the core rule of law is a universal human good irrespective of the content of any particular law since it favours reason, certainty and equality, acts as a restraint to prevent rulers behaving capriciously or maliciously and prevents officials from picking on individuals. In order to be credible even a bad ruler might act through law thereby behaving better than he or she otherwise might have done (see Thompson, *Whigs and Hunters*, Allen Lane, 1975; compare the debate between Kramer and Simpson in (2004) *Cambridge Law Journal* 63, 65, 98). At the other extreme the rule of law could be regarded as mechanical and divisive, allowing officials to hide behind rules to avoid personal responsibility, and ignoring sentiments such as compassion and common sense in favour of ruthless logic or misleading rhetoric (see for instance Hutchinson and Monahan (eds) *The Rule of Law: Ideal or Ideology*, University of Toronto Press, 1987). A legalistic perspective relies on linguistic reasoning turning on verbal definitions and categories perhaps at the expense of the social or moral interests involved and makes compromise and cooperation difficult. Thus we might wish to override a law out of feelings of compassion or other special circumstances.

In *R (Pretty)* v *DPP* (2002) Diane Pretty, who was suffering from an incapacitating terminal illness, challenged the refusal of the Attorney-General to undertake not to prosecute her husband for murder if he assisted her to commit suicide. Suicide as such is not a crime but Ms Pretty was too ill to commit suicide unaided. She claimed among other things that she was fully self aware and was subject to exceptional suffering and that the Attorney-General should therefore make an exception in her case. However the court rejected this argument partly for fear of undermining the general rule.

Moreover the core rule of law can never fully be realised in practice. The meaning or scope of a rule is rarely clear enough or comprehensive enough to be applied to every case that may arise, so that discretion is unavoidable. To self styled 'critical' legal scholars this inherent vagueness of law is a fundamental objection to the idea of the rule of law, which they regard as a mask for naked power. The standard liberal reply is that vagueness is a matter of degree and in some circumstances is to be welcomed (see Kutz, 'Just Disagreement: Indeterminacy and Rationality in the Rule of Law', 1994, *Yale Law Journal* 103: 997). Most laws in practice have a widely accepted meaning. And even where laws are vague, there are widely accepted standards of 'practical reasoning': consequences, moral values, analogy with precedents, appeals to widely shared feelings and so on. In order to be legitimate a judge's interpretation must not diverge far from public opinion. Even though there may be no objective 'right' answer it is possible to justify a solution which would be widely accepted. This is how the common law might be reconciled with the rule of law. It claims to conform to widely accepted community standards: 'ordinary notions of what is fit and proper' (*MacFarlane* v *Tayside Health Board* (2000), 108; *Invercargill City Council* v *Hamlin* (1996), 640–2).

   Indeed discretion may be desirable in many contexts. The rule of law is not the supreme value. It is widely recognised that the provision of public services must involve the exercise of discretion in individual cases where the circumstances are too various, unpredictable or complex to be encapsulated in rules. For example the police do not have to prosecute everyone; the Inland Revenue may release a taxpayer from a tax burden. It would be difficult to lay down detailed rules in advance governing access to health or education. Resources are limited and hard choices have to be made between competing goals. Such choices are for the political rather than the legal process. There must also be wide emergency powers to some extent outside both law and democracy to deal with unforeseen and exceptional threats (see *R (Corner House Research* v *Director Serious Fraud Office 2* (2008) above). Even the European Convention on Human Rights can be derogated from to meet an emergency (Human Rights Act 1998 s.14).

Nor is strict equality necessarily desirable since the interests of justice might call for special treatment for people suffering some kind of disability or disadvantage. Discretion is also desirable to lighten the burden of the strict law. The rule of law may therefore conflict with other valuable impulses such as compassion and mercy, the outcome depending on the preference of the decision maker (see *R (Pretty)* v *DPP* (2002) above).

None of this excludes the rule of law altogether. The law can prescribe broad guidelines within which decisions must be made and in particular lay down procedures policed by the courts that must be followed to ensure that government keeps within the rules it makes and acts fairly and reasonably. Emergency powers can be hedged with legal safeguards, for example a requirement that they lapse after a set period.

7.4.1   The Core Rule of Law and Freedom

It is sometimes asserted that the core rule of law is inherently supportive of freedom. Montesquieu and Locke thought that freedom means doing what the law allows. Since laws can have any content and are enforced by violence, this seems paradoxical. As Hobbes put it, 'freedom lies in the silence of the laws' and in *The Pilgrim's Progress*, Bunyan asks:

> he to whom thou was sent for ease, being by name legality, is the son of the Bond-woman . . . how canst thou expect by them to be made free?

Hayek (Chapter 2) claimed that *in itself* the rule of law guarantees freedom: 'When we obey laws, in the sense of general abstract rules laid down irrespective of their application to us, we are not subject to another's will and are therefore free' (The Constitution of Liberty, pp. 153–4). It is not clear what he meant since a repressive law, such as one that all adults must serve time in the army, is not conducive to freedom but still satisfies the rule of law. Hayek might merely have meant that we are free to plan our lives around laws and so avoid them, in the sense that outside any law there must be a zone of freedom however small, in this case benefiting children. He might also have been defining freedom in a peculiarly narrow sense as meaning not subject to the whims of other individuals directed at us personally. However Hayek seems to be making stronger political claims based on the idea that the rule of law in his sense makes for a very limited kind of government. Firstly Hayek suggested that a government which accepts the rule of law would not enact repressive laws since these would harm its own supporters. Secondly the laws must not pick out individuals for special treatment and this in itself limits government interference. In Hayek's world the law could not for example regulate housing, land use or industry except by means of broad general rules applying equally to everyone. These requirements rule out large areas of state activity involving discretionary economic powers. Hayek recognised that his proposals are likely to lead to economic inequality and perhaps hardship but assumes that these are outweighed by the advantages of individual freedom.

In common with many economic liberals, Hayek also believed that the certainty created by the rule of law would encourage wealth creation through a free market and that the poor would be better off than under alternative regimes. There is no historical evidence either way. Departing from the core idea of the rule of law as rules set out in advance, Hayek favoured the common law as a response to concrete practical problems rather than imposed in the abstract by governments that have neither the skills nor knowledge to plan for the future.

In linking the rule of law to freedom, Hayek might have been thinking of positive freedom in the sense of reason used to expand the possibilities of life (Chapter 2). Indeed he referred to freedom as the absence of *arbitrary* restraint. Reason in the form of applying rules does sometimes expand the possibilities of life by combating confusion and uncertainty. Locke endorses this:

> Law in its true notion is not so much the limitation as the direction of a free and intelligent agent to his proper interest and prescribes no further than is for the general good of those under that law. (*Second Treatise of Government*, VI: 57)

In this sense, by obeying rational laws we are apparently exercising freedom since as rational creatures we are 'obeying laws that we have made ourselves' (Kant, 1724–1804). On the other hand there are different kinds of reason and unless a law has a freedom loving content there is no guarantee that it will offer significant life possibilities. For example a tyrant might use the rule of law to advance some scientific theory involving mass extermination of dissidents.

The rule of law may also protect freedom in the republican sense of non-domination. However kind or reasonable a ruler may be, we are nevertheless at his mercy unless he is bound by rules and so in a sense we are slaves dependent on his goodwill. Thus although in a limited sense it is true that the rule of rule is conducive to freedom, in practice the core rule of law needs to be supplemented by some idea of 'good law' to have any serious chance of protecting freedom.

7.4.2   Dicey's Version of the Rule of Law

Dicey proposed a version of the rule of law similar to that of Hayek and also consistent with republican ideas. Although dating from 1875, this has been of great influence among English lawyers. However although it contains valuable ideas of a republican kind it has limited application to contemporary circumstances. Dicey formulated a threefold version of the rule of law as follows.

1. The absolute supremacy or predominance of 'regular' law

> No man is punishable or can be lawfully made to suffer in body or goods except for a distinct breach of law established in the ordinary legal manner before the ordinary courts.

This means firstly that no official can interfere with individual rights without the backing of a specific law. For example in *R* v *Somerset County Council ex parte Fewings* [1995] 1 All ER 513, Laws J said (at 524) that the principles that govern the application of the rule of law to public bodies and private persons are 'wholly different' in the sense that:

> the freedoms of the private citizen are not conditional upon some distinct and affirmative justification for which he must burrow in the law books ... But for public bodies the rule is opposite and so of another character altogether. It is that any action to be taken must be justified by positive law.

Laws J described this as one of the 'sinews' of the rule of law. However it only applies to acts that interfere with traditional legal rights such as private property. It is therefore ill equipped to deal with the many ways in which modern governments operate. For example in *R* v *Secretary of State for Health ex parte C* (2000) it was held that a government department was entitled to place a man's name on the sex offender's register without giving him a prior right to be heard. Although entry on the register harmed the individual by destroying his job prospects, his legal rights were not infringed since in English law there is no right of privacy as such.

Dicey also believed laws should not give officials wide discretionary powers. For example in *Rantzen* v *Mirror Group Newspapers* (1994) the Court of Appeal condemned the wide discretion given to juries to fix the amount of damages in libel cases as violating the rule of law. We have already suggested that it is impossible and undesirable to avoid discretion. Indeed Dicey did not rule out all discretionary power but only 'wide arbitrary or discretionary power of constraint'. He insisted on limits to and controls over the exercise of discretion. These include guidelines based on the purposes for which the power is given and standards of reasonableness and fairness. This aspiration is to some extent met by the courts' powers of judicial review of government action.

2. Equality before the law

Dicey was not concerned with equality in a general sense. He was concerned with limiting the power of officials in favour of individual legal rights. According to Dicey this is best achieved if everyone is subject to the same law administered by ordinary courts. He did not mean that no official has special powers – this would have been obviously untrue. Dicey had two specific ideas in mind. Firstly he meant only that officials as such enjoy no special protection, so that if an official abuses his power, he is personally liable to anyone whose property rights or personal freedom he violates just as if he were a private citizen. For example officials and private persons alike are liable if they use excessive force in defending others against criminal acts (Chapter 21) and in *M* v *Home Office* (1993) it was held that a minister cannot refuse to comply with a court order on the basis that he is a servant of the Crown (see also *D* v *Home Office* (2006)).

There are exceptions. Judges are immune from personal liability in respect of their actions in court (Chapter 8) and the Crown has certain immunities (Chapter 14). In many cases foreign governments and heads of state are immune from the jurisdiction of the UK courts at least in civil actions (State Immunity Act 1978; see *Jones* v *Ministry of the Interior of Saudi Arabia* (2006): torture; compare *R* v *Bow Street Stipendiary Magistrate ex parte Pinochet Ugarte (No. 3)* (1999) below). Public bodies are sometimes protected against legal liability in the interests of efficiency particularly in cases involving discretionary decisions (see for example *D* v *East Berkshire Community Health NHS Trust* (2005): false accusation of child abuse against parents). Dicey's principle is therefore a presumption that can be overcome by showing some justification for an inequality.

Secondly Dicey meant that disputes between government and citizen are settled in the ordinary courts according to the ordinary law rather than in a special governmental court. In this respect Dicey compared English law favourably with French law, where there is a special system of law dealing with the powers of government (*droit administratif* enforced by the *Conseil d'Etat*). Dicey thought that special administrative courts would give the government special privileges and shield the individual wrongdoer behind the cloak of the state. However Dicey later came to believe that, in view of the increasing power of the executive, he may have been too optimistic about the ordinary courts' ability to protect the individual and began to cast around for other solutions (1915, *Law Quarterly Review* 31).

Nevertheless this aspect of Dicey's teaching has been influential. As recently as the 1970s, there was resistance to the idea of a distinction between public and private law.

Since 1977 however there has been a special procedure for challenging government decisions albeit within the ordinary court system (Chapter 18). However in partial vindication of Dicey, attempts to distinguish between public law and private law have floundered (Chapter 18). There are also numerous special tribunals dealing with disputes between the individual and government. However they are usually subject to the supervision of the ordinary courts and the rule of law requires that attempts to exclude the ordinary courts be strongly resisted (for instance *Anisminic* v *Foreign Compensation Commission* (1969); Chapter 9).

Sometimes Dicean equality backfires. In *Malone* v *Metropolitan Police Commissioner* (1979) it was held that at common law the police are free to tap telephones since there was no legal prohibition against a private person doing so (a gap in the law subsequently closed by statute; Chapter 22). In *Harrow LBC* v *Qazi* (2004) it was held that a local authority can rely on its private property rights as a landlord in order to evict a tenant. It is therefore arguable that a principle of equality is not adequate to remedy abuses of the wide ranging powers of modern government. The housing duties of a local authority have no analogy in the world of private citizens.

3. The constitution is the 'result' of the ordinary law

This derives from the common law tradition. Dicey believed that the UK constitution, not being imposed from above as a written constitution, was the result of decisions by the courts in particular cases and was therefore embedded in the very fabric of the law and backed by practical remedies. According to Dicey this strengthens the constitution since a written constitution can more easily be overturned. Moreover because the common law developed primarily through the medium of private disputes, it biases the constitution against governmental interests by treating private law, with its concentration on individual rights, as the basic perspective. Perhaps Dicey's version of the rule of law shows mainly that he trusted judges and feared democracy.

The seminal case of *Entick* v *Carrington* (1765) illustrates all three aspects of Dicey's rule of law. The Secretary of State ordered two King's messengers to search for Entick, accused of sedition, and to bring him with his books and papers before the Secretary of State. Entick sued the messengers. The court held firstly that the plea of 'state necessity' was unknown to common law because there was no statute or common law precedent from which it could be derived; secondly the practice of issuing general warrants giving officials wide discretion was unlawful and thirdly the messengers had no specific statutory authority regarding the particular papers they seized and so could be sued in ordinary courts just as other private citizens.

On the other hand, in *R* v *IRC ex parte Rossminister Ltd* (1980) Parliament gave a general power to tax officials to enter and search private premises which the courts upheld, rejecting *Entick* v *Carrington* as irrelevant antiquarianism. This illustrates the tension between common law and parliamentary supremacy, which Dicey never succeeded in reconciling (Chapter 9).

7.5   The 'Amplified' Rule of Law

Some writers argue that the notion of law as rules necessarily implies certain moral principles that are inherent in the idea of government by rules. They concern the idea that, in order to guide conduct and be acted on, rules must be clear, look to the future and be applied impartially and publicly. These constitute what is primarily a *procedural* version of the rule of law in the sense that they have little to say about the content of a law as opposed to how it is applied. Inherent in these principles is an overarching requirement that there should be access to independent courts particularly to challenge government action (see Lord Bingham in *A* v *Secretary of State for the Home Department* (2005) [42]; Lord Woolf in *M* v *Secretary of State for the Home Department* [2004] 2 All ER 863, 873).

The American legal theorist Fuller (*The Morality of Law*, Yale University Press, 1969) includes the following moral principles:

- Generality, for example officials not exempt from the rules (*M* v *Home Office* (1993))
- Promulgation so that laws can be known in advance (for example *R (Anufrijeva)* v *Secretary of State for the Home Department* (2003): decision to refuse asylum seeker status took effect from the date when the claimant was informed of it)
- Non-retroactivity: no punishment without a law in force at the time the Act was committed (see ECHR Article 7(1)). However this is not applied generously. For example in *R (Uttley)* v *Secretary of State for the Home Department* (2004) a rape committed in 1983 was prosecuted in 1995. The House of Lords held that a sentence heavier than the maximum available in 1983 could not be imposed but allowed a higher sentence than the *equivalent* in 1983. The requirements of the amplified rule of law are not absolute. For example retrospective law might occasionally be desirable to deal with a particularly serious social problem or an administrative blunder (for example Housing Corporation Act 2006).
- Clarity: a law should be sufficiently clear and certain to enable a person to know what conduct was forbidden before he did it (*R* v *Goldstein* (2006) [32, 33]). This is particularly important in the context of human rights since government action which may override a human right under the Human Rights Act 1998 must be 'prescribed by law', a phrase that has been understood as requiring the law to be clear and accessible (see *R (Gillan)* v *Metropolitan Police Commissioner* (2006) [31],[69],[71]).
- Consistent application (for example *R* v *Horseferry Road Magistrates Court ex parte Bennett* (1994): fair trial not given to person brought before the court by kidnapping even if court process itself is fair; see also *R* v *Grant* [2005] 3 WLR 437 [52]: breach of lawyer– client confidentiality an affront to the rule of law).
- The practical possibility of compliance (for example *R* v *Secretary of State for Social Services ex parte Joint Council for the Welfare of Immigrants* (1996): regulations which deprived asylum seekers of benefits unless they claimed asylum status at the port of entry would frustrate their right of appeal)
- Constancy through time: frequent changes in the law might offend this. For example between 1997 and 2006 more than sixty Acts of Parliament were produced in response to media coverage of incidents in the criminal justice system (see *Independent*, 16 June 2006).
- Raz (1977) includes a right to legal advice (for example *R* v *Lord Chancellor ex parte Witham* (1997): increases in legal fees denied access to courts for low income

people). See also Lord Millett in *Cullen* v *Chief Constable of the RUC* [2004] 2 All ER 237 [67].

▷ Raz also adds 'openness' (for example *R (Middleton)* v *West Somerset Coroner* (2004): victims of a misuse of state power in relation to the death of prisoners entitled to public inquiry, see Lord Bingham [5]).

The amplified rule of law might be criticised as narrow in that by concentrating on procedure rather than substance it gives inadequate protection to the individual and indeed favours those who can enlist the support of the legal profession, that is, the well-to-do. It proponents might respond that the rule of law as such is not meant to address all social problems but is merely one dimension of government (see Sunstein, 1996).

Related to the amplified rule of law is a political version of the rule of law derived from the republican tradition (see Bellamy, 2007, Chapter 2). From this perspective law is a collective enterprise made by numerous people with many different interests, majorities and minorities alike. Indeed any of us might sometimes be part of a majority and sometimes a minority. The focus is not therefore on courts alone but on ensuring that the laws are made by a regular democratic process in which the representatives of all interests in the community have a voice.

7.6   The Extended (Liberal) Rule of Law

This version of the rule of law overlaps with but goes beyond the amplified rule of law. It claims somewhat extravagantly that law provides the overarching values of the community against which acts of government must be evaluated. Thus when Aristotle pronounced that it is better for the law to rule than for any of the citizens to rule (*Politics* III.16, 1087a) he was probably referring to understandings about justice among an elite group with common values and traditions designed to bring about their own collective good. The American philosopher Ronald Dworkin has put forward an influential version of this approach based on the idea that law as determined by the courts should constitute a coherent set of principles, a 'fit' which imposes justice and fairness and gives effect to individual rights against the encroachment of the state (*Law's Empire*, London, Fontana, 1986).

The Dworkinian approach has been enthusiastically taken up on this side of the Atlantic. Labelled as 'the principle of legality', this version of the rule of law claims to restrain 'bad laws' by interpreting legislation and evaluating executive action in the light of common law values – assumed to be liberal – so as to require Parliament to use very clear language if it wishes to override them and therefore be accountable. In this way it claims to support liberal democracy (see Lord Steyn in *Roberts* v *Parole Board* (2006) [93] and *R (Ullah)* v *Special Adjudicator* (2004) [43]).

In *R* v *Secretary of State for the Home Department ex parte Simms* (1999), in the interests of freedom of expression, the House of Lords prevented the government from restricting a prisoner's access to a journalist through whom he intended to publicise his claim that he was wrongfully convicted. Lord Hoffmann said (at 131):

> The principle of legality means that Parliament must squarely confront what it is doing and accept the political cost. Fundamental rights cannot be overidden by general or ambiguous words. This is because there is too great a risk that the full implications of their unqualified meaning may have passed unnoticed in the democratic process. In the absence of express language or necessary

implication to the contrary, the courts therefore presume that even the most general words were intended to be subject to the basic rights of the individual.

The values concerned would include personal liberty, freedom of expression, property rights, non-discrimination (see Lord Nicholls in *Ghaidan* v *Mendosa* (2004) [9]) and fair democratic processes as well as the rights associated with a fair trial included in the 'amplified' rule of law (see *Secretary of State for the Home Department* v *MB* (2008): right to fair trial has core irreducible minimum, but see *Secretary of State* v *AF* (2008); *Culnane* v *Morris* (2006): freedom of political speech).

The suggested link between liberal values, the rule of law and common law seems to be twofold. Firstly the common law is not merely imposed from the top by a lawmaker but is generated by disputes freely brought before the courts by individuals and requires the exercise of power to be rationally justified. Secondly there is the idea that the law must be applied according to the understanding of those subject to it as equal citizens. In this respect common law's independence from government means that it can plausibly claim to represent the values of the community. According to Allan (2001, p. 62):

> The principle that laws will be faithfully applied, according to the tenor in which they would reasonably be understood by those affected, is the most basic tenet of the rule of law: it constitutes that minimal sense of reciprocity between citizen and state that inheres in any form of decent government, where law is a genuine barrier to arbitrary power.

This brings in a republican dimension but, as we saw in Chapter 1, republican and liberal perspectives may conflict – republicanism stressing the desire for citizen participation as equals in decision making. Sir John Laws, a leading contemporary judge, has linked the common law to philosophical principles that appear to combine liberal and republican perspectives ('The Constitution: Morals and Rights' (1996) *Public Law* 622, 623). He asserted that because the courts derive their powers from common law and have no electoral mandate to pursue any particular policy they must fall back on what he considered to be the only possible moral position, namely individual freedom (see also Laws, 'Law and Democracy' (1995) *Public Law* 72; Laws in Forsythe (ed.) *Judicial Review and the Constitution*, 2000):

> The true starting point in the quest for the good constitution consists in . . . the autonomy of every person in his sovereignty. (Laws, 'The Constitution: Morals and Rights' (1996) *Public Law*, 622)

However such philosophical assumptions are controversial and concepts such as freedom and equality are inherently vague and applied differently by different groups. As we saw in Chapter 2, liberalism has several competing forms so that attempts to impose a liberal orthodoxy seem dogmatic. Moreover common law derives its legitimacy not from abstract philosophy but from community values, whatever they happen to be. It is therefore not necessarily liberal. Although confined by the accumulation of precedent, common law arguably tracks the opinions of the dominant group in the legal community at any given time (in particular the judges). While legal education and tradition secure a certain conformity, there is no reason to assume that the precedents are sufficiently clear or the values of the community sufficiently uniform and stable to form a credible basis for coherent liberal principles. The extended rule of law may therefore be no more than the temporary preferences of a fashionable group of lawyers.

Indeed in *R (Bancoult)* v *Secretary of State for the Foreign and Commonwealth Office* (2001), Laws LJ held that the extended version of the rule of law based on the underlying rights and values of domestic common law does not apply to British overseas territories. These have to be content with what he called a 'thinner' rule of law, by which he meant something akin to the core rule of law in the sense of an obligation to conform to the rules. Even so it was held that the UK government acted unlawfully in evicting the inhabitants of the territory from their homes (Chapter 6).

   The extended rule of law may conflict with the ideals behind the core rule of law of certainty and respect for general rules. This is because the nature of fundamental rights and the balance between fundamental rights and other aspects of public interest such as security are inherently uncertain and ultimately depend on a political preference.

An example is *Roberts* v *Parole Board* (2006). The Parole Board has a statutory power to release a convicted prisoner who has served a designated part of his sentence if it considers that he is no longer a public danger. The Parole Board refused to disclose the evidence against him on the ground that it was important in the interests of public safety to protect the identity of its sources who would otherwise not come forward (see Chapter 21). This was arguably in violation of the right to a fair trial. The House of Lords disagreed on the issue. A majority held that it was for the Parole Board to balance public safety against the rights of the prisoner to a fair trial in the circumstances of the particular case and that the matter could not be dealt with in advance as general rules. Lord Steyn, a strong champion of the extended rule of law, dissented on the basis that the prisoner was wholly denied the fundamental right to a fair hearing. Lord Bingham also dissented more moderately on the ground that clear statutory language would be required to allow the Board rather than a court to carry out this balancing exercise and that the overall fairness of the trial must not be compromised.

Lord Bingham (2007), the senior Law Lord, proposed a version of the rule of law which combines elements both of the amplified and extended rule of law. His core notion is that 'all persons and authorities within the state, whether public or private, should be bound by and entitled to the benefit of laws publicly and prospectively promulgated and publicly administered in the courts'. Particular elements are that laws should:

- be intelligible and precise enough to guide conduct;
- minimise discretion recognising that discretion cannot be removed completely;
- apply equally to all unless differences are clearly justified;
- give adequate protection to fundamental human rights (Lord Bingham acknowledges the lack of agreement as to whether this is an appropriate rule of law matter as opposed to a matter of politics);
- include machinery for resolving disputes without excessive cost or inordinate delay;
- provide for judicial review requiring decision makers to act reasonably, in good faith, for the purposes for which powers are granted without exceeding the limits of those powers;
- embody fair adjudicative procedures;
- ensure that the state complies with international law (a controversial proposal).

Lord Bingham's general approach probably represents a widely shared view as to what good law should be like in a liberal society. Whether the label 'rule of law' adds anything is questionable.

7.7 The International Rule of Law

The idea of the rule of law comes under particular stress when there is a clash between different legal regimes, in particular between international and domestic law. International law as such is not automatically part of UK law, which has adopted a 'dualist' approach. An international treaty, if it is to alter domestic law, must first be incorporated by statute into UK law. However customary international law is recognised by common law, albeit not invariably so. A rule of customary law might be rejected if it is incompatible with basic domestic principles. In particular international law cannot create a criminal offence without the endorsement of Parliament since this is regarded as a matter appropriate only to a democratic body.

> In *R v Jones (Margaret)* (2006) the appellants had damaged military equipment in order to obstruct the war against Iraq. Their defence was that they were preventing a crime, namely the crime of aggression, the unprovoked attack on another state, which is an offence in customary international law. The House of Lords held that the defence was available only in respect of crimes under domestic law. Aggression was not a crime in domestic law. The courts were reluctant to interfere with the deployment of the armed forces and it was improper for the courts to create new criminal offences. See also *R (Gentle) v Prime Minister* (2008): violation of international law in relation to decision to attack Iraq not legally relevant.

The idea of the rule of law is represented in international law by the notion of *ius cogens*, that is, certain absolutes that all nations are expected to recognise such as the prohibition against torture (see *R v Bow Street Stipendiary Magistrate ex parte Pinochet Ugarte (No. 3)* (1999), 198–9). Since the Second World War there have been several attempts to draw up internationally binding codes of basic human rights and to promote liberal values under the banner of the rule of law. However such concepts are vague and applied in different ways in different cultures. Indeed in order to command support from as many nations as possible treaties are often written in cloudy language so as to avoid clear commitments thus reflecting the notion of constitutional abeyance (Chapter 1).

For example the Declaration of Delhi (1959), an unofficial pronouncement of the International Commission of Jurists, proclaimed that the rule of law is intended to establish 'social, economic, educational and cultural conditions under which [individuals'] legitimate aspirations and dignity may be realised'. International instruments include the United Nations Universal Declaration of Human Rights (1948) and various regional charters. There is an International Criminal Court to deal with war crimes, crimes against humanity and genocide but the US has not accepted its jurisdiction. Of most direct concern to UK law is the European Convention on Human Rights (ECHR) which drew heavily on the UN declaration. Individuals have a right to petition the European Court of Human Rights in respect of violations by states. Under the Human Rights Act 1998, most provisions of the Convention have belatedly been made binding in UK law, although they do not override

Acts of Parliament (Chapter 19). The rule of law is central to the workings of the ECHR. For example exceptions to the rights protected by the Convention must be 'prescribed by law'. In this context 'a norm' cannot be regarded as a law unless it is formulated with sufficient precision to enable a citizen to foresee the legal consequences of his or her conduct.

R v Bow Street Metropolitan Stipendiary Magistrate ex parte Pinochet Ugarte (No. 3) (1999) illustrates the difficulties of applying international values. Pinochet was the former head of state of Chile making a private visit to the UK. The Spanish government requested that he be extradited to Spain to stand trial in respect of murders and torture that he was alleged to have organised in Chile during his term of office. The Torture Convention 1984, as translated into English law by the Criminal Justice Act 1988, requires a state to either prosecute or extradite an alleged offender. Pinochet relied on the doctrine of state immunity, according to which a head of state cannot be tried in a domestic court. Complete immunity applies to serving heads of state. Immunity also applies to former heads of state but only in relation to 'official' acts committed while they were in office (State Immunity Act 1978 s.20).

The House of Lords, unusually comprising seven judges, held that Pinochet was not entitled to immunity. However their Lordships took different routes to their conclusions. Lords Browne-Wilkinson, Hutton, Saville and Phillips took a relatively liberal, 'core' rule of law approach, which attempted to follow the words of the Act read in the light of the treaty. They held that state sponsored torture violated fundamental principles of international law that Chile had accepted by signing the Convention. Torture was therefore not to be regarded as part of the official functions of a head of state. They held however that Pinochet could only be extradited for offences that were alleged to have taken place after 29 September 1988 when the Act came into force. Lord Millett, supported partly by Lord Hope and Lord Hutton, perhaps reflects the 'extended' rule of law (above). He argued that, irrespective of the Act, torture was an international offence under customary international law and was therefore unlawful at common law whenever and wherever committed. Lord Hutton said that 'certain crimes are so grave and so inhuman that the international community is under a duty to bring to justice a person who commits such crimes' (at 163). Lord Goff, dissenting, took a strict 'core' rule of law approach, holding that the State Immunity Act applies to official acts wherever committed and does not specifically exclude torture as an official act. He emphasised legal certainty, pointing out the difficulty of drawing lines between different kinds of wrongdoing and the problems that might be faced by former heads of government who ventured into countries whose interests they had damaged while in office.

Summary

▶ Constitutionalism means limited government and includes the ideas of the rule of law and the separation of powers as a means of restricting and controlling government. The rule of law is an umbrella for assorted ideas about the virtues of law mainly from a liberal perspective. They centre upon law as reason and law as a means of controlling aggressive government. They do not fit easily with ideas of democracy, nor with government as a provider of welfare services nor with communitarian ideas.

Summary cont'd

▶ The rule of law in its core sense emphasises the importance of general rules as binding on government and citizen alike. The core sense of the rule of law is morally ambivalent since it can also be regarded as an efficient tool of tyranny.

▶ In an amplified sense, the rule of law requires the law to reflect certain basic values derived from the nature of rules as guides to conduct. However these are also consistent with repressive laws.

▶ In an extended sense the rule of law is claimed to be the guardian of the basic liberal values of the community entrusted to the courts because of their role as guardians of impartial reason. It is claimed to be translated into rights such as non-discrimination, freedom of expression, and access to government information. However there is no reason to believe that these values or reason itself are the prerogative of courts and they have to be accommodated against social goals of elected governments. Why courts should do this is a theme to be pursued in later chapters.

▶ The rule of law as expounded by Dicey has significantly influenced the UK constitution. Dicey advocated that government discretion should be limited by definite rules of law, that the same law could in general apply to government and citizen alike, and that Britain does not need a written constitution because, in his view, the common law made by independent courts with practical remedies provides a firmer foundation for individual rights. This has greatly influenced the thinking of the legal profession but may be unsuited to the control of modern government. It is also difficult to reconcile the rule of law in this sense with the principle that Parliament has unlimited power which can be harnessed by a strong executive.

▶ Other modern ideas of the rule of law include the increasing importance of international treaties which attempt to establish codes of fundamental rights and freedoms that governments should respect.

Exercises

7.1 Do you agree with Thompson that the rule of law is an 'unqualified human good'?

7.2 To what extent is Dicey's version of the rule of law of value today?

7.3 'The Rule of Law functions as a clear check on the flourishing of a rigorous democracy. Attempts to characterise the rule of law as the butler of democracy are false and misleading' (Hutchinson and Monahan). Critically discuss.

7.4 To what extent, if at all, is the rule of law conducive to (a) freedom, (b) equality?

7.5 Do the following violate the rule of law?
  (i)   The Queen being exempt from legal liability.
  (ii) A statute banning press criticism of the Prime Minister.
  (iii) A statute which states that an allegation relating to the conduct of the security services cannot be made in the ordinary courts.
  (iv) A statute which gives a discretion to the Education Secretary to decide what courses shall be taught in universities.

7.6 'The rule of law clearly forms an essential element of liberal democracy and plays its part in providing a theoretical basis for an independent judiciary but it forms only one side of a balanced constitution' (Carol Harlow). Explain and critically discuss.

7.7 Is the rule of law a valuable concept from a practical point of view?

Further reading

Allan, T. (2001) *Constitutional Justice: a Liberal Theory of the Rule of Law*, Oxford University Press, Chapters 1, 2, 3, 4.

Bellamy, R. (2007) *Political Constitutionalism*, Cambridge University Press, Chapter 2.

Craig, P. (1997) 'Formal and substantive concepts of the rule of law: an analytical framework', *Public Law* 467.

Bingham Lord, T. (2007) 'The Rule of Law', *Cambridge Law Journal* 66:67.

Endicott, T. (1999) 'The Impossibility of the Rule of Law', *Oxford Journal of Legal Studies* 19:1.

Hayek, F. (1960) *The Constitution of Liberty*, Chicago, Henry Regnery, pp. 133–61, pp. 205–19.

Horowitz, M.J. (1977) 'The Rule of Law: An Unqualified Human Good?', *Yale Law Journal* 86:15.

Michaelman, F. (1988) 'Political Truth and the Rule of Law', *Tel Aviv University Studies in Law* 8:283.

O'Donovan, K. (1989) 'Engendering Justice: Women's Perspectives and the Rule of Law', *University of Toronto Law Journal* 39:127.

Poole, T. (2002) 'Dogmatic Liberalism? T.R.S.Allan and the Common Law Constitution', *Modern Law Review* 65:463.

Poole, T. (2003) 'Back to the Future: Unearthing the Theory of Common Law Constitutionalism', *Oxford Journal of Legal Studies* 66:435.

Poole, T. (2005) 'Questioning Common Law Constitutionalism', *Legal Studies* 25:142.

Raz, J. (1977) 'The Rule of Law and its Virtue', *Law Quarterly Review* 93.

Sadurski, W. (2006) 'Law's Legitimacy and "Democracy-Plus"', *Oxford Journal of Legal Studies* 26:377.

Summers, R.S. (1993) 'A Formal Theory of the Rule of Law', *Ratio Juris* 6:127.

Sunstein, C. (1996) *Legal Reasoning and Political Conflict*, Oxford University Press, Chapter 4.

Tivey, L. (1999) 'Constitutionalism and the Political Arena', *Political Quarterly* 70:175.

Waldron, J. (1989) 'The Rule of Law in Contemporary Legal Theory', *Ratio Juris* 2:79.

Chapter 8

The separation of powers

Political liberty is nothing else but the diffusion of power. (Lord Hailsham)

Key words

- Separation of function and personnel
- Checks and balances
- Judicial independence
- Mixed government
- Democracy
- Parliament and the courts
- 'Partnership'

8.1 Introduction: Montesquieu's Doctrine of the Separation of Powers

The separation of powers, although by no means universal, is widely regarded as one of the pillars of a liberal constitutional democracy. Article 16 of the (French) Declaration of the Rights of Man (1789) states that 'a society where rights are not secured or the separation of powers established has no constitution'. It is widely believed that in all societies there is a tendency for power to gravitate towards a single leader who is likely to abuse his or her power. The separation of powers attempts to combat this by providing mechanisms to make it difficult for any single power group to dominate and to ensure that government action requires the cooperation of different groups, each of which helps to keep the others within bounds. The doctrine is therefore closely associated with the rule of law (see *R (Anderson)* v *Secretary of State* (2002) [27]: executive interference with sentencing process). It is also central to republicanism.

A widely accepted division of power is based on the functions of government. With variations, it can be traced to Aristotle (384–322 BC). Its best known version is that formulated by Montesquieu (1689–1755) who divided government into three branches: the legislature, the executive and the judiciary. The legislature makes the laws, the judiciary settles disputes and imposes sanctions for breaking the law and the executive enforces and puts the law into effect. Thus:

> In the government of this commonwealth, the legislative department shall never exercise the executive and judicial powers or either of them: the executive shall never exercise the legislative and judicial powers, or either of them: the judicial shall never exercise the legislative and executive powers, or either of them: to the end it may be a government of laws and not of men. (Massachusetts Constitution, 1780, Article XXX)

Montesquieu was a leading proponent of the republican tradition (Chapter 2). He was no democrat and placed faith in aristocratic government subject to limits. His idea of limits on power was what he called 'dissonant harmony'. He believed that disagreement was a healthy feature of politics and that the need for different interests to cooperate would prevent any power being used excessively. As he famously stated, 'power must be checked by power'. He thought that if any two of the three functions fall into the same hands the outcome is likely to be tyranny. According to the doctrine of the separation of powers, each branch has different functions but each uses its power to police the limits of the others. Conversely within the limits of its powers, each branch should be independent of the others. As Nolan LJ put it:

> The proper constitutional relationship between the executive and the court is that the courts will respect all acts of the executive within its lawful province, and that the executive will respect all decisions of the court as to what its lawful province is. (Nolan LJ, *M v Home Office* [1992] QB 270, 314)

A balance must therefore be struck between the three powers. Moreover there must be an understanding as to which of them should have the last word in the event of a stalemate since the separation of powers in itself is capable of producing gridlock. The way this is done depends on the political fears and worries of the day. Montesquieu feared the legislature most. He vested the executive in the monarchy, believing that this gave the constitution stability and continuity. The executive and legislature would, according to Montesquieu, check each other. For instance the executive could not make laws or obtain finance without the support of the legislature but in Montesquieu's view the legislature should not be able to remove the executive. Montesquieu thought it appropriate that the executive should summon the legislature as and when needed but did not explain how an abuse of this power might be dealt with. However in the UK constitution the meeting of the legislature is protected by statute and convention and the legislature can remove the executive (Chapter 11).

In the contemporary UK we regard the executive as the most dangerous branch as it commands the resources of the state, including the use of force, and is in a position to dominate the legislature. Indeed by the end of the nineteenth century Mill, influenced by De Toqueville's writing on the emerging American democracy, feared:

> the only despotism of which in the modern world there is real danger – the absolute rule of the head of the executive over a congregation of isolated individuals all equal and all slaves. (*Autobiography*, 1873)

More recently the desirability of an independent judiciary has been emphasised as a check on both an increasingly powerful executive and, apparently, the democratic legislature. Argument rages as to whether the judiciary or legislature should have the last word.

There is disagreement as to importance of the doctrine. Jennings (*The Law and the Constitution*, University of London Press, 1959) argues that there is no important difference between the three functions, the executive and judicial being essentially a more detailed kind of lawmaking. Marshall (1971) argues that the separation of powers is an umbrella for a miscellaneous collection of principles, each of which can be justified on its own terms, for example judicial independence. On the other hand Barendt (1995) and Munro (1999) regard the doctrine as an important organising and critical principle. However this debate may be confused where different protagonists are using the concept of the separation of powers in different senses and for different purposes. In particular separation of powers can mean:

1. Separation of *function* between different units of government
2. Separation of *personnel* in the membership of different units of government
3. *Checks* and *balances* between different units of government.

The strictest version of the doctrine, such as that adopted in the US, would aim at all three, although of course practicalities mean that the reality is likely to fall short of the ideal. As with the rule of law, the separation of powers is no more than an underlying set of values. However some former British territories have a strict separation of powers in their written constitution, which UK judges in the form of the Privy Council must apply (see *Liyanage v R* (1967)).

8.2 The Mixed Constitution

Montesquieu also insisted on a different kind of separation, namely one between class interests. This reflects the 'mixed constitution' based on Aristotle's three forms of government: monarchy, aristocracy and democracy (Chapter 1). Aristotle believed that any single form of government was unstable leading to a permanent cycle of disasters. In particular democracy – in the sense of the rule of the majority – leads to anarchy which is overcome only by the intervention of a dictator who will eventually be overthrown by force in favour of either aristocracy or democracy, each of which in turn will collapse. He therefore favoured a blend of democracy and aristocracy: democracy to provide consent, aristocracy to provide stability and wise leadership. Aristocracy meant literally 'rule by the best', by which Aristotle meant an educated group wealthy enough to be independent.

The early Roman republic adopted similar ideas ('power in the people, authority in the Senate' – Cicero) but was later replaced by dictatorship ('what pleases the prince has the force of law'). To Montesquieu, all three elements of the mixed constitution should be represented in the legislature since this was the supreme body. As with the separation of powers, each element would check the others. The monarch could veto legislation but not initiate it: 'prevent wrong but not do wrong'. The aristocratic and the elected elements would have to agree to make changes in the law.

Montesquieu, an aristocrat himself, believed that an aristocracy based on inheritance produced an independent, educated and leisured class who would protect freedom and curb the democratic element ('liberty is the stepchild of privilege') while the other elements of the constitution could prevent the aristocracy from using their powers selfishly.

Blackstone (1723–80), an influential compiler of English law, also praised the mixed constitution:

> Herein indeed consists the true excellence of the English government that all the parts of it form a mutual check upon each other. In the legislature the people are a check on the nobility and the nobility a check upon the people . . . while the king is a check upon both which preserves the executive power from encroachments. And this very executive power is again checked and kept within due bounds by the two Houses . . . For the two Houses naturally drawing in two directions of opposite interest, and the prerogative in another still different from them both, they mutually keep each other from exceeding their proper limits . . . like three distinct powers in mechanics, they jointly compel the machine of government in a direction different from what either acting by itself would have done . . . a direction which constitutes the true line of the liberty and happiness of the country. (*Commentaries on the Laws of England*, Oxford University Press, 1787, pp. 154–5).

Montesquieu claimed to find both kinds of separation of powers in the British constitution, in that the executive power was centred upon the Crown and the legislature had two parts, one (the House of Lords) being aristocratic. However in Montesquieu's time the conventions that removed power from the Crown in favour of ministers, who were also members of the legislature, had not yet crystallised. Moreover Montesquieu may not have appreciated that the English constitution gave Parliament unlimited power over the Crown (c.f. Claus, 2005).

The mixed constitution remains a significant element of the formal legal structure in the form of the monarchy and the House of Lords. However, politically, the monarchy and the House of Lords are relatively impotent. It is worth remembering that originally aristocracy simply meant government by the 'best'. The hereditary principle which was the historical basis of the House of Lords was rationalised on the ground that inherited landholding gave a powerful interest in the government of the country through which the lower classes enjoyed 'virtual representation'. Today an automatic link between inheritance and political influence is no longer acceptable, at least openly, as giving political power. Indeed anyone can be appointed to the House of Lords as a life peer (Chapter 12). This reform was intended to enlist some of the 'best' into Parliament. However life peerages can be awarded without any reason at all.

There are currently proposals to remove the unelected element entirely from the House of Lords (Chapter 12). However fear of democracy remains alive and many people are attracted by the idea of a non-elected part of the legislature (particularly if it includes themselves). This raises the difficulty of whom we can trust to identify the 'best' so as to avoid Aristotle's corruption of aristocracy into an oligarchy of cronies. Unfortunately it has not proved possible to agree.

8.3 Other Kinds of Separation

There are other kinds of separation of powers which serve the same function of preventing the concentration of power. Examples are:

- Between elected politicians and appointed civil servants providing expert advice (Chapter 15). John Stuart Mill's approach is broadly the form of representative democracy practised in the UK. Mill (1972) thought that most governmental functions should be entrusted to experts, with democracy through elected representatives providing the elements of consent and control. This serves a similar purpose to the mixed constitution of placing a buffer between raw democracy and government. Thus in the UK constitution the people's only legal power is to choose at intervals an individual as a representative for each locality in the House of Commons out of which the executive is formed under conventions over which the people have no control.
- Between the 'dignified' and the 'efficient' parts of the constitution (Chapter 5), for example the Queen and ministers.
- Between geographical areas most effectively in a federal constitution. In the UK there is only a limited form of devolution. However even this can produce political constraints (Chapter 6).

8.4 Judicial Independence

Judicial independence is an aspect of the rule of law in its own right. It overlaps with but goes beyond the separation of powers. Separation of powers concerns the independence of the judicial system from other branches of government. Judicial independence requires the independence of individual judges from any pressures that threaten not only actual impartiality but also the appearance of impartiality. Article 6 of the European Convention on Human Rights (ECHR) includes both elements by requiring 'a fair and public hearing . . . by an independent and impartial tribunal established by law'. For example in *Millar* v *Dickson* (2002) the Privy Council found a violation of Article 6 where the prosecuting authority, the Scottish Lord Advocate, was also responsible for renewing the appointment of a temporary judge even though there was no complaint about the actual impartiality of the judge in question. As Lord Hope stated:

> Central to the rule of law in a modern democratic society is the principle that the judiciary must be, and must be seen to be independent of the executive. (*Millar* v *Dickson* (2002) 3 All ER 1041, [41])

Article 6 of the ECHR, the right to a fair trial, is concerned with judicial independence and the separation of powers. Article 6 does not require a formal separation of powers but requires that in the particular circumstances the court is not only independent but appears to be so (*McGonnell* v *UK* (2000)). Courts of a 'classic kind' must usually sit in public, be fully independent and impartial and there must be a full opportunity to give evidence and challenge witnesses (see *R (Hammond)* v *Secretary of State for the Home Department* (2006)). However sometimes these ideals might be compromised by competing considerations such as security (Chapter 21) and the desire to protect children (Chapter 20). Common law principles of natural justice also require a fair hearing and that a judge should not be vulnerable to personal bias (Chapter 17). In the case of administrative decisions taken within government that involve an element of political policy, full independence and publicity may not be possible. In this kind of case it may be a sufficient safeguard that the decision is subject to judicial review which is confined to basic standards of legality, provided that the reviewing court has sufficient power to investigate the particular defect (see *R (Alconbury Developments)* v *Secretary of State for the Environment, Transport and the Regions* (2001); *Findlay* v *UK* (1997); *Albert* v *Belgium* (1983)).

Judicial independence and the separation of powers overlap particularly in relation to the appointment and dismissal of judges, since judges must be immune from interference by the executive (below). Beyond the separation of powers, judicial independence requires that judges should be protected against attacks on their conduct in court. They are immune from personal actions for damages in respect of acts within their powers or done in good faith (*McC* v *Mullan and Others* (1984); Courts Act 2003 ss.31–35). Superior court judges may enjoy complete immunity (*Anderson* v *Gorrie* (1895)). Anything said in court by judges, advocates and witnesses is absolutely privileged against an action in libel and slander but advocates are not protected against liability for negligence (see *Trapp* v *Mackie* (1979); *Arthur JS Hall* v *Simons* (2000)).

Judicial independence is an uncertain concept. It requires judges to be protected against external pressures but does not mean that they should not be accountable for their actions. Accountability has different meanings. It means firstly that a decision maker must explain and justify his or her actions and secondly that a decision maker might be penalised if his or her actions fall short of required standards. Judges are to some extent accountable in the first sense, which does not conflict with independence. They normally sit in public and judicial decisions are open to scrutiny by the media (Chapter 20). A three tier appeal system and review by the High Court of decisions of lower courts and tribunals contribute to accountability as does the Criminal Cases Review Commission which deals with miscarriages of justice.

Judges occasionally give evidence on general matters to parliamentary committees. However traditionally judges have not participated in public debate (see McMurdo, 'Should Judges Speak Out?' Judicial Conference of Australia 2001; www.jca.asn.au). However in 1987 the Lord Chancellor relaxed the notorious 'Kilmuir' rules made in 1959 by the then Lord Chancellor which restricted such participation and the matter is now left to the discretion of the individual judge.

8.5   The Separation of Powers in the UK

The separation of powers affects the UK constitution in an unsystematic, incomplete and pragmatic way in which the balance of forces is unstable. The separation of powers in Montesquieu's sense has been endorsed by contemporary UK judges (for example Lord Templeman in *M v Home Office* [1993] 3 All ER 537, 540; Lord Hoffmann in *R (Pro-Life Alliance)* v *BBC* [2003] 2 All ER 977, 997) while others have recognised it as applying at least between the legislature and the judiciary (Lords Nicholls and Hope in *Wilson* v *First County Trust* [2003] 4 All ER 97, 116, 130; Lord Diplock in *Duport Steels* v *Sirs* [1980] 1 WLR 142, 157; Sir John Donaldson in *R v HM Treasury ex parte Smedley* [1985] 1 All ER 589, 593). As Lord Steyn put it in *R (Anderson)* v *Secretary of State* (2002) [39]: '(o)ur constitution has never embraced a rigid doctrine of separation of powers. The relationship between the legislature and executive is close. On the other hand, the separation of powers between the judiciary and the legislative and executive branches of government is a strong principle of our system of government'. In the same case Lord Bingham emphasised [27] that '(t)he European Court was right to describe the complete functional separation of the judiciary from the executive as 'fundamental' since the rule of law depends on it'.

The Constitutional Reform Act 2005 (below) is an attempt to strengthen the separation of powers in relation to the judiciary. The Act was influenced by a concordat made in 2004 between the executive and the courts under which the relationship between the courts and the executive was spelt out (see Lord Woolf, *Magna Carta, a Precedent for Recent Constitutional Change*, Royal Holloway College, University of London, 15 June 2005).

Most obviously there are indeed three branches of government, with broadly separate functions: the legislature (Parliament), the executive (the Crown) and the judiciary. All three historically originated with the Crown (Chapter 3) but are now treated as separate institutions.

M v Home Office (1993) concerned whether the court could treat the Home Secretary, a minister of the Crown, as in contempt of court for disobeying a court order. The court rejected the argument that because the courts and ministers were both historically part of the Crown, the Crown would in effect be in contempt of itself. At first instance Simon Brown J ([1992] 4 All ER 97 at 107), citing Montesquieu, pointed out that at least since the seventeenth century the courts had been recognised as an institution separate from the Crown itself and that there were three branches of government with which the Queen had only a symbolic relationship. Moreover a minister exercising powers conferred on him by law was not to be treated as part of the Crown since to do so, as Lord Templeman remarked (at 540), would undo the consequences of the Civil War.

On the other hand the conventions governing the parliamentary system blur the separation between the legislature and the executive since by convention ministers must be members of Parliament. In the UK therefore, depending on the political and personal forces of the day, either the executive is subordinate to Parliament or (more likely) the executive dominates Parliament. Bagehot (1902) claimed that the 'almost complete fusion' between the executive (by which he meant cabinet ministers) and the legislature was the 'efficient secret' of the constitution. However although Bagehot's writings have been highly influential, his analysis is widely regarded as oversimplified ('a television man before his time'). For example there are various devices which attempt to ensure that neither the executive nor Parliament can completely dominate the other. Moreover the functions and processes of the two branches are not fused. Ministers must publicly announce and defend their policies in Parliament whereas executive decisions are taken in secret by self selected groups. Indeed Montesquieu ([1761] 1995) himself recognised that there might be an overlap between the legislature and the executive, although emphasising that there should be some separation between them:

> But if there were no monarch, and the executive power should be committed to a certain number of persons selected from the legislative body, there would be an end then of liberty.

In this context, it is worth remembering that Montesquieu feared democracy. On the other hand the contemporary House of Commons chooses to be subservient to the executive.

8.6   Separation of Function

This assumes that the three functions of government can be conceptually distinguished, in the sense that the activities of lawmaking, judging and carrying out executive tasks are different in significant respects, irrespective of who carries them out. This is a controversial theoretical issue but constitutional thinkers have since the time of Aristotle agreed that there is at least a distinction between the making of general rules, which requires the participation of a wide range of people, and the implementation of those rules in individual cases, which requires professional expertise and impartiality. This idea unites for example Locke, Rousseau and Mill despite their different ideas as to the purpose of government (Chapter 2).

Assuming that in most cases at least we can distinguish between the three functions, a lawmaker issues general rules, the executive implements the law and makes government policy and a judge acts as an independent referee by applying rules to a dispute. The judicial function is associated with courts. There is however no clear definition of a court other than the circular one of a body exercising a judicial function whatever its name (for example Contempt of Court Act 1981 s.19). For instance the Parole Board is a court (*Roberts v Parole Board* (2006)).

The executive function is particularly difficult to define, a matter which raises problems in relation to accountability. It comprises anything that is neither judicial nor legislative. Moreover its functions overlap with the judicial since it resolves disputes and makes copious rules both formally under powers delegated by Parliament (below) and informally in order to implement its general powers. Whether a matter is executive may depend not on any natural quality it has but on the mechanism chosen to deal with it. For example imposing a penalty in connection with a court ruling is part of the judicial function (see Lord Steyn in *R*

(Anderson) v *Secretary of State* (2002)) but arguably an 'administrative penalty' imposed mechanically, such as a parking ticket, is not. Nor arguably is a decision based on government policy such as refusing planning permission for a new building. A grant of planning permission creates a new right but a judicial function, strictly speaking, is meant only to determine existing rights under the law. Decisions which may have serious impacts but which do not strictly affect legal rights, such as placing a person on a register of wrongdoers, are also executive in nature. Unlike a minister or a traffic warden, a court exercising a judicial function cannot initiate action but must respond to disputes which others bring before it. Thus the judiciary is often claimed to be the 'least dangerous branch', having no weapons at its disposal and having no particular axe to grind.

8.6.1 Parliament and the Executive: Delegated Legislation

There is overlap between Parliament and the executive in that while Parliament has no executive functions (except in relation to its own internal affairs) the executive is involved in lawmaking. Parliament does not itself govern and to this extent there is a separation of powers. On the other hand the role of Parliament is mainly reactive, that of scrutinising and criticising measures put to them by the executive. Parliament has neither the time nor the expertise even to scrutinise all the laws that may be desirable. Thus many laws are enacted with no significant parliamentary input, MPs merely voting blindly for their party.

In practice most English legislation consists of delegated or secondary or subordinate legislation (the terms being synonymous) made by ministers and other bodies outside Parliament under powers conferred by Act of Parliament. It is commonplace for a statute to lay down a general principle and then to confer power upon a minister to make detailed rules fleshing out the principle. Delegated lawmaking powers are sometimes very wide, and often permit the minister to implement or alter Acts of Parliament past or future (the 'Henry VIII' clause, for example European Communities Act 1972 s.2(4); Pollution Prevention and Control Act 1999).

Delegated legislation comes under many names including regulations, orders, directions, rules, bylaws. Little hinges on the terminology used. However a compendium term, 'statutory instrument', applies to most delegated legislation made by ministers and to Statutory Orders in Council (Statutory Instruments Act 1946). Statutory instruments must be formally published, and, in accordance with the rule of law, it is a defence in criminal proceedings to show that an instrument has not been published and that it is not reasonable to expect the accused to be aware of it (ibid., s.4). However it seems that failure to publish does not affect validity for other purposes (see *R* v *Sheer Metalcraft* (1954)).

Delegated legislation has often been criticised on constitutional grounds and is an infringement of the separation of powers. It can be made without the public and democratic processes represented, albeit imperfectly, by Parliament. However it is difficult to imagine a complex and highly regulated society that could function effectively if all laws had to be made by Parliament itself (see Committee on Ministers Powers, 1932, Cmd 4060). Most delegated legislation is subject to a limited amount of parliamentary scrutiny by means of being laid before the House although this is usually nominal. There is also a joint committee that scrutinises unusual features of statutory instruments (see Chapter 13).

Unlike a statute the validity of secondary legislation, even if it has been approved by Parliament, can be challenged in the courts if it is outside the powers conferred by its parent Act, according to the grounds of judicial review applicable to all executive action.

It can also be set aside by the courts if it violates the ECHR as applied by the Human Rights Act 1998.

Delegated legislation must be distinguished from what is often called 'quasi-legislation'. This comprises rules, standards, policies, guidance or advice issued for example in circulars by the government without specific statutory authority or under statutory powers which do not involve binding rules. Quasi-legislation is not strictly binding but must be taken into account and is in practice normally followed. Indeed depending on its content it may create a 'legitimate expectation' that the government will comply with it (Chapter 16).

8.6.2 Parliament and the Courts

Our common law system means that the judges are also lawmakers and their function is not confined to interpreting laws made by others. There are certain checks and balances although these depend on the judges restraining themselves. One such is the judges' duty to follow precedent so as to limit the possibility of making up new law according to a judge's personal preferences. Another is the fact that the judges must make their law only in the context of the particular case before them. Another is the supposed principle that a court must ultimately defer to Parliament (Chapter 9). In *WH Smith Do It All Ltd* v *Peterborough City Council* [1991] 4 All ER 193 at 196, Mustill LJ remarked that:

> according to the doctrine of the separation of powers as understood in the UK, the legislative acts of the Queen in Parliament are impregnable.

The highest appellate body is currently the Appellate Committee of the House of Lords and its judges are full members of the House. This has been justified on the grounds of cross fertilisation by injecting a legal perspective into the proceedings of the House and giving judges insight into the legislative process and social and political factors. It is sometimes argued that the Law Lords contribute to the romantic idea of Parliament as a meeting of all the interests of the realm. However by convention the Law Lords do not participate in party political debates and avoid expressing opinions relating to matters likely to come before them in litigation (Hansard HL col. 419, 22 June 2000). Lord Bingham remarked that a member of a legislative chamber is valued for his or her ability to speak out, whereas a good judge is valued for caution and reticence (Constitution Unit Spring Lecture, UCL, 2002).

The Constitutional Reform Act 2005 creates a new Supreme Court as the highest appellate court transferring to it the appeal functions of the House of Lords and in devolution cases of the Privy Council. This takes effect in October 2009. The main reasons are to ensure a separation of powers between legislature and judiciary and to enhance public understanding of and confidence in the judicial system. Devolution and the impact of EU membership mean that the courts have greater political significance than has traditionally been the case. Conversely the House of Lords is increasingly active as a political body. There seems to be no evidence one way or another about lack of public confidence in the present arrangements and it is not doubted that the Law Lords are independent in practice.

The Supreme Court could be regarded as an expensive attempt to achieve a largely cosmetic goal since its composition and powers will remain primarily the same as those of the current Appellate Committee. Indeed the government originally argued in favour of the Law Lords being part of a reformed House of Lords. The court will comprise twelve judges (as now) sitting in panels of at least three; currently five is the norm. It will have some administrative independence, being able to make its own procedural rules, and some financial autonomy. However it has been pointed out that the House of Lords has special protection against the executive by virtue of Parliamentary privilege and that arrangements should be made to protect the new court against such political pressures. The link with the House of Lords may be partly retained in that Supreme Court judges may be appointed to it on retirement.

Parliament and the courts avoid interfering with each other. A court cannot usually investigate parliamentary proceedings or challenge statements made in Parliament (*Pickin v British Railways Board* (1974)). However the courts can decide whether statutory requirements have been complied with even where they relate to parliamentary processes (*R (Jackson) v Attorney-General* (2005); Chapter 9). In relation to its own composition and internal affairs the House of Commons has exclusive power to decide disputes and punish offenders (Chapter 11).

Cases in progress should not be discussed in Parliament except in relation to matters of national importance or the conduct of ministers (see May, *Treatise on the Law, Privilege, Proceedings and Usage of Parliament*, Butterworth, 1997, pp. 383–4, pp. 542–3). Ministers do not answer questions on legal matters. No reflection must be cast on a judge's personal character, competence or motives except on a substantive motion for his dismissal, although backbenchers but not ministers may criticise individual judgments.

8.6.3 The Executive and the Courts

The courts have the power to review executive decisions but are concerned to ensure that they do not enter into the sphere that properly belongs to the executive by deciding questions of economic and social policy, the allocation of resources or pursuing government policy goals in deciding cases. How this balance is struck is a controversial question and various devices are used by the courts to help them in the task (Chapters 16, 17).

The executive sometimes makes judicial decisions when it decides for example whether a given person is entitled to a welfare payment or a school place. Indeed ministers are often required to decide appeals against government decisions, even those in which their own department has an interest. However the practice of ministers determining planning appeals does not violate the right to a fair trial under the ECHR, at least where the decision is one based on policy, provided that there is the safeguard of judicial review (*R (Alconbury Developments) v Secretary of State* (2001) above). Moreover what the separation of powers importantly requires is that each body should have the last word in relation to its particular function. Thus Parliament can approve, veto, or alter laws proposed to it and the judiciary can review executive action and has the last word as to what a law means.

Until recently the separation of powers was violated in that the Home Secretary played a prominent role in the sentencing process. In the case of prisoners serving life sentences he or she could decide the 'tariff' period that must be served before becoming eligible for release on parole. He or she could also control the sentences of young persons imprisoned indefinitely 'at Her Majesty's pleasure'. There is also the royal prerogative of mercy to release or pardon convicted persons, exercisable on the advice of the Home Secretary. In the party political context of the UK, it is easy to believe that these powers are open to abuse (for example *R v Secretary of State for the Home Department ex parte Venables* (1997): use of opinion poll in the *Sun* newspaper). However in a series of cases the European

Court has held that the involvement of the executive in the sentencing process is normally a violation of the right to a fair trial (Article 6; *R (Anderson)* v *Secretary of State for the Home Department* (2002); *Benjamin* v *UK* (2002); *V* v *UK* (1999)). English law has accepted this by removing the Home Secretary's power in most contexts in favour of a judge or the independent Parole Board (for instance in the Criminal Justice and Court Services Act 2000 s.60; Criminal Justice Act 2003 s.269; c.f. *R (Black)* v *Justice Secretary* (2009) [58]). However a distinction can be drawn between increasing and decreasing a sentence on the basis that a residue of compassion is desirable and that the politically accountable executive is the most appropriate body to exercise it. Thus the executive should periodically review an indefinite sentence, at least in the case of a young person, in order to refer it to the relevant body for possible reduction (*R (Smith)* v *Secretary of State for the Home Department* (2006)). The prerogative of mercy remains with the Home Secretary who can refer the matter to the independent Criminal Appeals Board (Criminal Appeal Act 1995 s.16).

Magistrates clerks are members of the civil service (Courts Act 2003) but have certain judicial functions in connection with criminal proceedings and also advise magistrates on the law, participating in their private deliberations. The Act makes some concession to their independence by providing that when exercising judicial functions they are not subject to directions from the Lord Chancellor or any other person (s.29). It has been held that the activities of magistrates clerks do not violate judicial independence provided the clerk advises only on matters of law and procedure and not the actual decision, and any matters that the parties might wish to comment upon are raised in open court (*Clark (Procurator Fiscal Kirkcaldy)* v *Kelly* (2003)). It is difficult to see how these protections are safeguarded given that the deliberations are in private. In *Kelly* the Privy Council relied on the right of appeal, the 'well understood conventions' and the clerk's professional code as safeguards.

Another vital safeguard in the criminal process is that juries should not be vetted by the executive (*R* v *Crown Court at Sheffield ex parte Brownlow* (1980)) and cannot be required to give reasons for their verdicts or punished for giving or failing to give a verdict (*Bushell's Case* (1670)). It is an offence for anyone to publish information as to what was said in a jury room (Contempt of Court Act 1981 s.8(1)).

It is important for judicial independence that judges have no duty to advise the executive. However judges are sometimes appointed to carry out investigations or inquiries into allegations against government or significant incidents. This carries the risk of compromising the independence of the judiciary by making them appear to be involved in politics (such as the Scott Report into arms sales to Iraq, HC 115, 1996; Hutton Report into the death of a government adviser in the context of the decision to invade Iraq, 2003). In some countries such as the US and Australia, the practice of judicial inquiries of this kind is unconstitutional (see Drewry, 'Judicial Inquiries and Public Reassurance', 1996, *Public Law* 368; Woodhouse, 'Constitutional and Political Implications of a UK Supreme Court', 2004, *Legal Studies* 140). As part of the 'concordance' between judges and Parliament entered into in relation to the constitutional reforms of 2005, a senior judge must be consulted on any proposal to appoint a judge of the rank of circuit judge or above to hold an inquiry under the Inquiries Act 2005 section 10(1) (Chapter 5).

8.7   Separation of Personnel

In view of the risk of bias or conflict of interest, the same persons should not be members of more than one of the three branches or exercise more than one function. This principle has traditionally been applied pragmatically and not consistently. We have already seen that the UK constitution does not comply with this, most importantly by its requirement that ministers must also be members of Parliament. In theory this strengthens executive accountability to Parliament. In practice owing to the subservience of MPs, it enables the executive to dominate Parliament. Ambivalence between the minister's two capacities is most notable in connection with the ability of parliamentary select committees to require ministers to give evidence and more generally enables the executive to control parliamentary procedure (see Chapters 12, 13, 15). There is however some separation of personnel. No more than ninety five ministers can sit and vote in the Commons (House of Commons (Disqualification) Act 1975 s.2(1)), thus preventing the government from packing the Commons with sycophants. Other ministers can be members of the House of Lords without apparent limit. However there are limits on the number of ministers who can be paid (Ministerial and Other Salaries Acts 1975, 1997). Certain kinds of officials (judges, civil servants, police, regulators, members of the armed forces and so on) cannot be members of the Commons (ibid. s.1; see Chapter 12).

8.7.1   The Lord Chancellor

Until the Constitutional Reform Act 2005, the office of Lord Chancellor violated the separation of personnel. The Lord Chancellor is in formal status superior to the Prime Minister and has a higher salary and pension than other ministers (Lord Chancellor's Pension Act 1832). However like other ministers the Lord Chancellor is appointed and dismissed by the Prime Minister and has no security of tenure. Often described as a walking contradiction of the separation of powers, the office was created by Edward the Confessor (1042–66). As the King's secretary and the holder of ecclesiastical office ('the conscience of the king'), during the medieval period the Lord Chancellor became primarily concerned with legal processes, being both judge and an administrator. In particular the Lord Chancellor was responsible for most judicial appointments (below). He was the nominal head of the judiciary but during the last few years has not sat as a judge. The Lord Chancellor also presided over the House of Lords but unlike the Speaker of the Commons had no disciplinary powers since the House regulates itself collectively (Chapter 13). The Lord Chancellor is also the minister responsible for the Ministry of Justice, which includes the administration of the courts, legal aid, human rights, constitutional reform and the electoral system.

There was therefore a potential conflict of interest in the Lord Chancellor's functions, in particular between his role as champion of the judges, and the desire for a minister in charge of an important spending department to be democratically accountable. However it is arguable that the overlapping roles of the Lord Chancellor supported rather than infringed the separation of powers by acting as a buffer or lubricant between the three branches. As a member of the House of Lords and therefore unelected, he had a certain independence from party politics. As a spending minister, he could seek to ensure that the courts are properly resourced, and as a judge could defend the judiciary against executive interference.

On the other hand as a member of the Cabinet, the Lord Chancellor is bound by collective responsibility (Chapter 15) and has no security of tenure to stand up to the Prime Minister. Unlike other judicial offices there were no qualifications for appointment. For example, the Lord Chancellor 2003–2007 was a barrister who was formerly a flatmate of the Prime Minister. It has also been argued that our constitution should evolve according to custom and tradition and not be engineered and that the antiquity of the office is evidence that it is good.

The Constitutional Reform Act 2005 removes the Lord Chancellor as Speaker of the House of Lords, which now elects its own Speaker. He also ceases to be head of the judiciary, transferring this to the Lord Chief Justice as President of the Courts of England and Wales (s.7). The Lord Chancellor remains in charge of the Ministry of Justice, which controls the administrative and financial aspects of the courts. The courts must bid for public money just like any other department so that for example legal aid (an essential element of access to justice) competes for resources with other government departments (Access to Justice Act 1999). This could distort the judicial process in favour of taking short cuts. In a 'judicial-centred' model of the separation of powers such as that in the US, the judges themselves are given a budget within which they control the administration of the courts.

The Lord Chancellor need not be a lawyer nor a member of the House of Lords but must be qualified by experience as a minister or member of either House of Parliament, or practising or academic lawyer (s.2). The special access that judges had to Parliament through the Lord Chancellor is replaced by section 5(1), which empowers the Chief Justice of any part of the UK to lay before Parliament or the relevant devolved assembly written representations on matters that appear to him to be of importance relating to the judiciary or the administration of justice. On appointment the Lord Chancellor must swear an oath to protect the rule of law and judicial independence and 'to discharge my duty to ensure the provision of resources for the efficient and effective support of the courts for which I am responsible' (s.17).

Under the Courts Act 2003 the Lord Chancellor has a general duty to ensure an 'efficient and effective' court system (s.1). The Constitutional Reform Act 2005 imposes the following somewhat vague duties (s.3):

(1) The Lord Chancellor, other Ministers of the Crown with responsibility for matters relating to the judiciary or otherwise to the administration of justice must uphold the continued independence of the judiciary.
(2) The Lord Chancellor and other Ministers of the Crown must not seek to influence particular judicial decisions through any special access to the judiciary.
(3) The Lord Chancellor must have regard to
    (i)   the need to defend that independence;
    (ii) the need for the judiciary to have the support necessary to enable them to exercise their functions;
    (iii) the need for the public interest in regard to matters relating to the judiciary or otherwise to the administration of justice to be properly represented in decisions affecting those matters.

The Attorney-General also has conflicting roles, being a member of the government and its chief legal adviser and also playing a part in the judicial process particularly in relation to decisions to prosecute (Chapter 15). The draft Constitutional Renewal Bill proposes to remove most of the Attorney-General's prosecuting powers but adds a power to intervene on grounds of national security.

8.8 Checks and Balances

This involves each branch having some control over the others but also requires each branch to be protected against undue interference by the others, thus entailing the need for pragmatic compromise. The checks and balances concept may therefore conflict with other aspects of the separation of powers. In the UK, in keeping with the 'insider' tradition, but violating republican aspirations of equality and citizenship, many checks and balances such as the various commissions and committees dealing with standards of government are not legally enforceable (Chapter 5). Readers should identify examples of checks and balances throughout the book. Some highlights will briefly be discussed here.

8.8.1   The Executive and the Legislature

- The Prime Minister can advise the Queen to dissolve Parliament but it must meet again within a year.
- The Queen in an emergency could invoke her royal prerogative powers to dismiss the Prime Minister, dissolve Parliament or refuse to dissolve Parliament.
- Individual ministers must appear before and explain the conduct of their departments to Parliament.
- The executive must resign if it loses the support of the House of Commons, leading to a dissolution if an alternative government cannot command the support of Parliament.
- The House of Lords, the composition of which is not dominated by the executive (Chapter 12), could be regarded a partial check over the executive which can usually control the Commons. However under the Parliament Acts 1911 and 1949 the House of Lords cannot veto a bill introduced in the Commons, other than a bill to prolong the life of Parliament and certain other minor exceptions. In *R (Jackson)* v *Attorney General* (2005) the House of Lords disagreed but left open whether there might be exceptional cases – for example where the executive was attempting to subvert fundamental democratic principles or abolish judicial review – where the Parliament Acts could not be used (see [20, 41, 101, 102, 139, 176–8]).

8.8.2   The Executive and the Courts: Judicial Appointments and Dismissals

The executive has an input into judicial appointments on the basis that a democratically accountable element is desirable. A direct legislative input such as the hearings by Congress used in the US would create a risk that judicial appointments and behaviour would be politically partisan. On the other hand since judges make decisions with political consequences and have considerable scope to be influenced by political preferences it is arguable that their political views should be brought into the open.

There are checks and balances to safeguard judicial independence from the executive. These have been put in place by the Constitutional Reform Act 2005, replacing a much criticised informal regime for judicial appointments which was in the hands of the Lord Chancellor and, in the case of appointments to the Court of Appeal and House of Lords, the Prime Minister (see *Peach Report: An Independent Scrutiny of the Appointment Processes of Judges and Queen's Council in England and Wales*, Department of Constitutional Affairs, 2001). However there will still be a limited political input by the Lord Chancellor. The centrepiece of the new process is an independent Judicial Appointments Commission which in substance will make most judicial appointments under the 2005 Act. Appointments are made either by the Queen on the recommendation of the Lord Chancellor or in the case of lay magistrates and certain other junior judges by the Lord

Chancellor directly (Constitutional Reform Act 2005 s.14; Courts Act 2003 s.10). The Lord Chancellor can recommend or appoint only a person selected by the Judicial Appointments Commission or in the case of Supreme Court Judges and certain judicial officers a special commission or panel under the Act.

There are elaborate arrangements to ensure the independence of the Commission. Its fifteen members are appointed by the Queen on the recommendation of the Lord Chancellor. It must comprise a lay chair plus five judges, one of each level, one practising solicitor and barrister, one tribunal member, one lay magistrate and five lay members (Schedule 12). The senior judicial element must be chosen by the Judges' Council which is a representative body. The lay members must be selected by a panel of four persons. These comprise a lay chair (who must not be a lawyer, judge, MP or member of the Commission or its staff) selected by the Lord Chancellor with the agreement of the Lord Chief Justice, the Lord Chief Justice, a person nominated by the chair and the chair of the Commission. Civil servants are excluded from membership of the Commission. The Lord Chancellor, with the agreement of the Lord Chief Justice and subject to the approval of Parliament, can increase the number of members. Commissioners hold office for a fixed term that is renewable but cannot be more than ten years in total. They can be removed on the recommendation of the Lord Chancellor on the grounds of criminal conviction, bankruptcy, failure to perform duties, unfitness or inability.

The Supreme Court which from 2009 will replace the House of Lords as the highest appeal tribunal is subject to special provisions. Its first members will be the present Law Lords. Thereafter its members will be appointed by the Queen on the recommendation of the Prime Minister who must recommend a person notified to him by the Lord Chancellor, who in turn must notify a person selected by a special Selection Commission (ss.26, 28). This comprises the President and Deputy President of the Supreme Court, one non-legally qualified member of the Judicial Appointments Commission and their equivalents in Scotland and Northern Ireland, nominated by the Lord Chancellor on the recommendation of the appropriate body. The Commission must consult the senior judges, the Lord Chancellor and the leaders of the devolved governments. A member of the Supreme Court must be qualified either by holding high judicial office for at least two years or practise in the senior courts for at least fifteen years (s.25). Selection must be solely on 'merit' (undefined) and the judges between them must have knowledge or experience in practice of the law of each part of the UK, thus acknowledging the differences between English law and that of the devolved regimes (s.27). The draft Constitutional Renewal Bill proposes to remove the Prime Minister from the process. Indeed his or her involvement seems to be only a formality.

Appointments of the Lord Chief Justice, Heads of Divisions and Lords Justices of Appeal are made by the Queen on the recommendation of the Lord Chancellor following selection by a panel of four comprising the chair of the Commission, a lay member of the Commission and two prescribed judges (ss.67, 71, 76, 80). Appointments to the High Court and the lower courts are made by the Queen or the Lord Chancellor, in both cases following a selection by the Commission (s.85).

Appointments must be made solely on merit (s.63) subject to the appointee being of 'good character' (undefined). Subject to this, 'diversity' must be encouraged. The Lord Chancellor may issue procedural guidance to the Commission which it must take into account (s.65). Judges of the main courts and some tribunals must be appointed from a pool of experienced practising lawyers or judges. This contrasts with the position in other

European countries where there is a separate judicial profession. The UK system has the advantage of drawing on talented people from outside government who are familiar with the workings of the court process. The disadvantage is that this might reinforce the perception of the legal system as a closed elite.

In relation to all levels of appointment the powers of the Lord Chancellor are similar (ss.29, 73, 82, 90). The Commission or Panel must submit one name to the Lord Chancellor who cannot put forward any other name. He or she can reject a nomination or refer it back for reconsideration but in either case once only. He or she can reject only on the ground that the candidate is not 'suitable' and require reconsideration on the ground of inadequate evidence of suitability or evidence of unsuitability. He or she must give reasons. If the Lord Chancellor rejects a nomination, the same name cannot be put forward again for that vacancy. However where a selection has been referred for reconsideration and not chosen again, he can put forward the original name. In the case of the Supreme Court a reconsideration can also be required if the judges between them would not have knowledge or experience in practice of the law of each part of the UK.

These provisions are designed to make it difficult for any interest group to dominate the appointment process. However given the vagueness of the appointment criteria and the fact that the government system in the UK is pervaded by informal personal networks, it is doubtful whether it is possible to ensure that the appointment process is fully independent or likely to widen the range of candidates.

These provisions do not apply to the appointments of lay magistrates nor to tribunal appointments. Although magistrates deal with relatively minor matters they account for the majority of criminal cases. Magistrates are appointed by the Lord Chancellor (Courts Act 2003 s.10) who may seek advice from the Judicial Appointments Commission and must consult locally (Constitutional Reform Act 2005 s.106).

The changes made by the Constitutional Reform Act can be criticised from three directions. Firstly some might regard them merely as cosmetic tinkering, ignoring wider questions of principle such as the independence and accountability of the judges, whether positive measures should be taken to widen the pool from which judges are selected, whether the Supreme Court should be confined to important constitutional issues and whether it should be able to overrule Acts of Parliament. Secondly traditionalists might regard the reforms as expensive, disruptive and unnecessary in the light of the (to them) successful accommodation achieved by the existing arrangements. Thirdly those with a utilitarian bent might consider the proposals a wasted opportunity for fine tuning of detailed matters such as the reorganisation of the mechanisms for appeals. The draft Constitutional Renewal Bill proposes to alter in minor ways some of the Lord Chancellor's functions in relation to the selection process and more importantly to introduce a consultative panel representing bodies which have an interest in judicial appointments.

8.8.3   Removal of Judges

Superior court judges, that is, judges of the High Court and above (to be called 'senior court judges' in future), have security of tenure designed to protect their independence. As a result of the 1688 revolution they hold office during 'good behaviour' (Act of Settlement 1700, provisions now repealed). In itself this is hardly conducive to independence since what matters is who decides whether they have misbehaved. Today they can be dismissed by the Crown following a resolution of both Houses of Parliament (an important constitutional role for the House of Lords) and probably then only for misbehaviour (Supreme Court Act 1981 s.11(3); Appellate Jurisdiction Act 1876 s.6). An alternative interpretation of these provisions is that the Crown can dismiss a judge for misbehaviour without an address from Parliament, but on an address a judge can be dismissed irrespective of misbehaviour. No judge has been subjected to these provisions since the nineteenth century when a judge was dismissed for embezzling court funds. The Constitutional Reform Act 2005 section 33, which applies similar provisions to the new Supreme Court, continues the ambiguity. In the case of judges of Northern Ireland and Scotland there is the additional safeguard of a Special Tribunal (Constitutional Reform Act 2005 ss.133, 135; Scotland Act 1998 s.95). In exceptional circumstances judges can be removed by the Lord Chancellor on medical grounds (Supreme Court Act 1981 s.11(8)). The Lord Chancellor can also suspend a judge pending an address or on grounds of criminality (s.108). Superior court judges must retire at seventy (Judicial Pensions and Retirement Act 1993).

Other judges do not have full security of tenure. They hold office under various statutes that make different provisions for dismissal. Circuit and district judges can be dismissed by the Lord Chancellor for incapacity or misbehaviour (Courts Act 1971 s.17; County Courts Act 1984 s.11; Courts Act 2003 s.22). Lay magistrates can be removed by the Lord Chancellor for incapacity or misbehaviour, persistent failure to meet standards of competence prescribed by the Lord Chancellor and declining or neglecting their duties (Courts Act 2003 s.11). Justices' clerks, who advise lay justices, are civil servants and have no security of tenure. They are appointed by the Lord Chancellor (Courts Act 2003 s.27), and can presumably be dismissed on the same basis as other civil servants (Chapter 15). Part time judges (recorders) who hear criminal cases are appointed for fixed periods renewable by the Lord Chancellor (Courts Act 1971). Temporary judges comply with the right to a fair trial under the Human Rights Act 1998 provided that there are safeguards to protect their independence (see *Starrs v Ruxton* (2000); *Kearney v HM Advocate* (2006): Scottish cases). Tribunal members are usually appointed for fixed terms either by a minister or the Lord Chancellor and in some cases can be dismissed only with the consent of the Lord Chancellor (Tribunals and Inquiries Act 1992). Most judicial salaries can be reduced only by Parliament (Judges' Remuneration Act 1965; Constitutional Reform Act 2005 s.14).

There is a Judicial Appointments and Conduct Ombudsman empowered to investigate complaints concerning appointments and disciplinary matters and to report to the Lord Chancellor (Constitutional Reform Act 2005 ss.62, 99–105, 110–13). The report is apparently not published.

8.8.4   Judicial Review

The courts provide a check over the executive by means of judicial review in the Administrative Court where they try to draw a line between the legality of government action, which they are entitled to police, and the merits of government action, which is a matter for Parliament. However the limits of judicial review are vaguely defined.

In *R* v *Secretary of State ex parte Fire Brigades Union* [1995] 2 All ER 244, Lord Mustill said at 267:

> It is a feature of the peculiarly British conception of the separation of powers that Parliament, the executive and the courts each have their distinct and largely exclusive domain. Parliament has a legally unchallengable right to make whatever laws it thinks right. The executive carries on the administration of the country in accordance with the powers conferred on it by law. The courts interpret the laws and see that they are obeyed. This requires the courts to step into the territory which belongs to the executive, not only to verify that the powers asserted accord with the substantive law created by Parliament, but also that the manner in which they are exercised conforms with the standards of fairness which Parliament must have intended. Concurrently with this judicial function Parliament has its own special means of ensuring that the executive in the exercise of delegated functions, performs in a way that Parliament finds appropriate. Ideally it is these latter methods which should be used to check executive errors and excesses; for it is the task of Parliament and the executive in tandem, not of the courts, to govern the country. In recent years however, the employment in practice of these specifically parliamentary remedies has on occasion been perceived as falling short and sometimes well short of what was needed to bring the performance of the executive in line with the law and with the minimum standards of fairness implicit in every parliamentary delegation of a decision making function. To avoid a vacuum in which the citizen would be left without protection against a misuse of executive powers the courts have had no option but to occupy the dead ground in a manner and in areas of public life, which could not have been foreseen 30 years ago.

In this case Lord Mustill was in a dissenting minority that refused to intervene with a decision of the Home Secretary not to make an order bringing a new Act into force dealing with criminal injuries compensation, but to introduce another less generous scheme under royal prerogative powers. He considered that this was a matter for Parliament itself. The majority however considered that the matter was appropriate for the court as a check on executive discretion. They held that although they could not require the Home Secretary to bring the Act into force they could quash the prerogative scheme and ensure that he kept the matter under review. Thus different aspects of the separation of powers may conflict.

8.8.5   Parliament and the Courts

According to traditional doctrine Parliament has unlimited lawmaking power and an Act of Parliament cannot be overturned in the courts. However the courts can decide whether a document is a genuine Act of Parliament, a proposition that raises important issues (Chapter 9). The courts also check Parliament since they have power to interpret statutes independently and can do so in the light of the moral values associated with the rule of law (Chapter 7). On the other hand, the intentions of the democratic branch must be respected so that a compromise must be struck based on the limits of interpretation although these are uncertain. An important corrective in this respect is the rule of law idea that an enactment should be read as those subject to it are likely to understand it. In *Duport Steels Ltd* v *Sirs* [1980] 1 All ER 529 at 551, Lord Scarman said:

> the constitution's separation of powers, or more accurately functions, must be observed if judicial independence is not to be put at risk . . . confidence in the judicial system will be replaced by fear

of it becoming uncertain and arbitrary in its application. Society will then be ready for Parliament to cut the power of the judges.

He meant that the judges must observe the law by sticking to the language of legislation even at the expense of their own views of justice or policy.

The Humans Rights Act 1998 attempts to strike a balance between the three branches by requiring the courts to scrutinise acts of all three branches in the light of the main provisions of the ECHR and to interpret legislation if possible to comply with the ECHR. However Parliament can override Convention rights by using very clear language. The court cannot set aside such an Act but can make a non-binding declaration of incompatibility in respect of an Act that it considers to be incompatible with the ECHR (Chapter 19). However some judges have suggested that in extreme circumstances the courts might overturn an Act of Parliament (Chapter 9).

In relation to statutory interpretation *Pepper (Inspector of Taxes) v Hart* (1993) presents problems. The traditional approach based on the separation of powers has been that the courts should not look at what was said in Parliament as an aid to statutory interpretation. The intention of Parliament is assumed to be identified by the language used in the statute itself. However the courts could always consider background material such as official reports as evidence of the policy behind a statute, a distinction that might be regarded as artificial. In *Pepper v Hart* the House of Lords held that, where the language of an Act is ambiguous, the court can look in Hansard (the official record of the proceedings of the House) to discover what the promoters of the Act (usually ministers) intended on the basis of statements made in Parliament. Thus if applied liberally *Pepper v Hart* could threaten the separation of powers by putting the executive in a privileged position over both Parliament and the courts. A statute is the collective enterprise of Parliament over which the executive should not have special control. There is also a rule of law issue in the sense that a statute should be read as understood by a member of the public (see Lord Hoffmann in *Robinson v Secretary of State for Northern Ireland* (2002) [40]).

Later cases have taken a cautious approach to *Pepper v Hart*, emphasising that it is for the courts to decide what a statute means and that the statements of ministers, however explicit, cannot control the meaning. In *R (Jackson) v Attorney-General* (2005) Lord Steyn [97] suggested that trying to discover the intentions of government from ministerial statements made in Parliament is constitutionally objectionable. It has also been stressed that such statements have not generally proved helpful and that *Pepper v Hart* should be applied strictly according to its particular circumstances – namely where the legislation is obscure, ambiguous or would lead to absurd results, and then only if the statements to be used are clear (*R v Secretary of State for Environment, Transport and the Regions ex parte Spath Holme* (2000) [211]; *Wilson v First County Trust* (2003) [58, 59, 139, 140]; *R (Jackson) v Attorney-General* (2005) [40, 98, 172]).

In *Spath Holme* (above) a distinction was made between the meaning of a specific provision, to which *Pepper v Hart* applies, and the general purpose of an Act. Hansard cannot be used to determine the latter unless the executive attempts to enforce a statute in a way that contracts a statement made by the minister when promoting the statute in Parliament. Here the executive might be prevented from contradicting what was said. Lords Nicholls and Cook dissenting found this distinction artificial. In *Wilson* (above) the House of Lords held that, apparently in all cases, Hansard can be used to discover factual policy background to an Act including its likely impact but not to evaluate ministerial statements as to its rationale. For example in *Culnane* v *Morris* (2006) the court was aided by the parliamentary debates in concluding that the Defamation Act 1952 section 10 was not aimed at altering the general law relating to privilege in defamation (Chapter 11). See also *Beckett* v *Midlands Electricity plc* [2001] 1 WLR 281 [30, 34, 38].

The courts cannot interfere with internal parliamentary proceedings, give orders to Parliament or penalise anyone in respect of things said in Parliament (Chapter 11). Conversely Parliament restrains itself from commenting on judicial cases in process although there are no legal safeguards in this respect.

Summary

- The doctrine of the separation of powers means that government power should be divided up into legislative, executive and judicial functions, each with its own distinctive personnel and processes, and each branch of government should be checked so that no one body can dominate the others.

- In Montesquieu's version, the separation of powers is complemented by the idea of the mixed constitution in which different class interests check and balance each other, particularly in the legislature. There is a vestige of the mixed constitution in the institutions of monarchy and the House of Lords. However the idea of the mixed constitution shorn of its historical association with a hereditary aristocracy might still be valuable as providing a check over crude majoritarian democracy linking with the idea of deliberative democracy.

- The question of judicial independence can be regarded as an aspect of the separation of powers but could be considered an issue in its own right irrespective of other aspects of the doctrine. Judicial independence is safeguarded by the right to a fair trial and public trial under the ECHR. This applies more stringently to ordinary courts than to administrative bodies. There is a tension between judicial independence and ensuring that judges are accountable.

- The separation of powers comprises separation of function, institutions and personnel and includes the notion of checks and balances. The particular blend in any given case depends on the preoccupations of the particular country. There is little agreement among writers as to whether the separation of powers is a valuable idea or in what sense it applies in the UK. Separation of powers ideas have influenced our constitutional arrangements but in a pragmatic and unsystematic way.

- In the UK there is no strict separation of personnel particularly between the legislature and the executive. Concern about executive domination is the main driving force.

- The Constitutional Reform Act 2005 attempts to strengthen the separation of powers by creating a Supreme Court to replace the Appellate Committee of the House of Lords, injecting an independent element into judicial appointments and removing the Lord Chancellor's roles as head of the judiciary and Speaker of the House of Lords. It could be that aspects of these reforms, particularly in relation to the Lord Chancellor, strengthen institutional separation but weaken checks and balances.

- The power of the courts to review government action creates a tension between functional separation of powers and checks and balances.

- There are concerns about the relationship between the courts and Parliament, in particular in the context of the use of parliamentary proceedings in the interpretation of statutes.

Exercises

8.1 Does the 'mixed constitution' have contemporary value?

8.2 Distinguish and illustrate the possible different meanings of the separation of powers.

8.3 'In the government of this commonwealth, the legislative department shall never exercise the executive and judicial powers or either of them: the executive shall never exercise the legislative and judicial powers, or either of them: the judicial shall never exercise the legislative and executive powers, or either of them: to the end it may be a government of laws and not of men' (Massachusetts Constitution 1780, Article XXX). Does the UK constitution live up to this?

8.4 It is sometimes said that the UK constitution embodies a 'fusion' between the legislature and the executive. Do you agree? Is it desirable that the composition of the executive and legislature be separate?

8.5 'In some quarters the Pepper v Hart principle is currently under something of a judicial cloud . . . In part this seems . . . to be due to continued misunderstanding of the limited role ministerial statements have in this field' (Lord Nicholls in *R (Jackson) v Attorney General* (2005) [65]). Explain and critically discuss.

8.6 The replacement of the Appellate Committee of the House of Lords will 'put the relationship between the executive, the legislature and the judiciary on a modern footing, which takes account of people's expectations about the independence and transparency of the judicial system' (*Constitutional Reform: A Supreme Court of the United Kingdom*, Department of Constitutional Affairs, 2003). Discuss in the light of the Constitutional Reform Act 2005.

8.7 Does the law relating to the appointment and dismissal of judges adequately safeguard judicial independence?

8.8 Does the present role of the Lord Chancellor comply with the separation of powers?

8.9 Critically assess the roles of (i) the Home Secretary and (ii) the Attorney-General in relation to the separation of powers.

8.10 Bill, a High Court judge, is alleged to have been sexually harassing the junior staff of the High Court Registry. Parliament is not sitting and the Lord Chancellor advises the Queen to make an example of Bill by dismissing him forthwith. Advise Bill. What would be the position if Bill was (i) a circuit judge or (ii) a lay justice?

Further reading

Barber, N. (2001) 'Prelude to the Separation of Powers', *Cambridge Law Journal* 61:59.

Barendt, E. (1995) 'Separation of Powers and Constitutional Government', *Public Law* 599.

Barendt, E. (1998) *An Introduction to Constitutional Law*, Oxford, Clarendon Press, Chapter 7.

Claus, I., (2005) 'Montesquieu's Mistakes and the True Meaning of Separation', *Oxford Journal of Legal Studies* 25:419.

Cooke, Lord (2003) 'The Law Lords: An Endangered Heritage', *Law Quarterly Review* 119:49.

Department of Constitutional Affairs (2006) *Judicial Diversity Strategy*.

Ewing, K.D. (2001) 'The Unbalanced Constitution' in Campbell, T., Ewing, K.D. and Tompkins, A. (eds) *Sceptical Essays on Human Rights*, Oxford University Press.

Legal Studies (2004) Special Issue, *Constitutional Innovation: the Creation of a Supreme Court for the United Kingdom; Domestic, Comparative and International Reflections*, 2, 3, 5, 7, 8, 9, 10.

Kavanagh, A. (2005) 'Pepper v Hart and Matters of Constitutional Principle', *Law Quarterly Review* 121:98.

Le Sueur, A. (2004) 'Judicial Power in the Changing Constitution' in Jowell, J. and Oliver, D. (eds) *The Changing Constitution* (5th edn) Oxford University Press.

McHarg, A. (2006) 'What is Delegated Legislation?', *Public Law* 539.

Marshall, G. (1971) *Constitutional Theory*, Oxford, Clarendon Press, Chapters 5, 6, 7, 9.

Munro, C.R. (1999) *Studies in Constitutional Law* (2nd edn) London, Butterworth, Chapter 9.

Steyn, Lord (1997) 'The Weakest and Least Dangerous Department of Government', *Public Law* 84.

Steyn, Lord (2001) 'Pepper and Hart: a Re-examination', *Oxford Journal of Legal Studies* 21:59.

Steyn, Lord (2002) 'The Case for a Supreme Court', *Law Quarterly Review* 118:382.

Vogenauer, S. (2005) 'A Retreat from Pepper v Hart? A Reply to Lord Steyn', *Oxford Journal of Legal Studies* 25:629. (See also Sales, P. (2006) 'A Footnote to Professor Vogenauer's Reply to Lord Steyn', ibid., 26:585.)

Woodhouse, D. (1998) 'The Office of Lord Chancellor', *Public Law* 617.

Chapter 9

Parliamentary supremacy

> Whoso has sixpence is sovereign (to the length of sixpence) over all men . . .
> A Parliament speaking through reporters to Buncombe and the twenty-seven
> millions, mostly fools. (Thomas Carlyle, 1795–1881)

Key words

- ▶ Political and legal supremacy
- ▶ Internal and external limits
- ▶ The meaning of Parliament as a process
- ▶ Implied repeal
- ▶ Redefinition
- ▶ Common law as foundational?
- ▶ Interpreting or overriding?

9.1 Introduction

The doctrine of the separation of powers which we discussed in the previous chapter leaves open the question of who has the last word when there is stalemate between the three branches of government. The UK constitution answers this by entrusting unlimited power to make law to Parliament. Thus the doctrine of parliamentary supremacy or sovereignty maintains that Parliament has unlimited legal power to enact any law without external restraint. Parliamentary supremacy is a *legal* principle, meaning that a law formally made by Parliament, in the sense of Queen, House of Lords and House of Commons acting together, must conclusively be accepted as valid by the courts (*Pickin* v *British Railways Board* (1974)). It does not mean that it would be *politically* possible for Parliament to pass any law. However we should not take an extreme legalistic position and claim that law and politics are entirely separate, since the fact that Parliament has enacted a law means that the community has indicated that it is politically important enough to justify the use of state force. Indeed judges have recognised that at this level, which is the foundational principle of the constitution, law and politics are inseparable (for example *R (Jackson)* v *Attorney-General* (2005) [126]). Thus we might be concerned if the law is out of step with political reality.

Indeed the doctrine of parliamentary supremacy is increasingly being questioned. In the absence of a written constitution, the foundations of the doctrine of parliamentary supremacy, resting as they do on no more than widespread acceptance, look frail. Challenges include:

- ▶ External legal requirements, notably those of the EU, which have restricted parliamentary supremacy.
- ▶ Pressures from within, such as Scottish devolution, mean that the legal doctrine is out of line with political reality and should be amended.

▶ Parliament might be able to redefine or redesign itself, effectively limiting its own supremacy, for example by requiring a referendum for some legislation.

▶ The claim that the supreme authority is the common law (both historically and because legislation has to be applied by the courts if it is to be enforced) which 'conferred' sovereignty on Parliament and can take it away again.

Even if it is true that political power tends to end up in the hands of a single leader, there is no logical reason why there should be a single *legal* sovereign with unlimited powers. For example in the US power is carefully divided so that no single entity has unlimited legal power. Even the last word, the power to change the constitution, is divided in complex ways between different groups who must agree to make the change. However as Hobbes argued (Chapter 2), it may be necessary as a last resort to give absolute power to a single body to deal with an emergency, including the power to decide whether an emergency exists. Even here safeguards can be put in place (Chapter 21).

9.2   The Meaning of Parliamentary Supremacy

According to Dicey (1915, pp. 37–8):

> The principle of parliamentary sovereignty means neither more nor less than this, namely that Parliament has, under the English constitution, the right to make or unmake any law whatever; and further that no person or body is recognised by the law of England as having a right to override or set aside the legislation of Parliament.

This has three separate aspects:

1. Parliament has unlimited lawmaking power in the sense that it can make any kind of law.
2. The legal validity of laws made by Parliament cannot be questioned by any other body.
3. A Parliament cannot bind a future Parliament.

Dicey tried to split sovereignty into separate legal and political elements, arguing that Parliament was legally sovereign in the sense that the courts must obey it, but not politically sovereign. Dicey described legal sovereignty as 'the power of law making unrestricted by any legal limit' and contrasted this with political sovereignty, as in the sense of the body 'the will of which is ultimately obeyed by the citizens of the state' (1915, p. 70). He recognised both 'internal' and 'external' political limits on the lawmaker. Internal limits are limits inherent in the attitudes of the people who make up Parliament. The political and moral pressures imposed by constitutional conventions, patronage and party discipline are internal limits. The external limits consist of what those subject to the law are prepared to accept. Parliament cannot in practice pass any law it wishes and its laws might be condemned as morally or politically bad or even as unconstitutional in a broad sense. Dicey thought that political sovereignty lay in the electorate and that this would make democracy 'self-correcting' (Craig, *Public Law and Democracy in the UK and the USA*, Oxford University Press, 1991, Chapter 2). However later in life, particularly after the powers of the House of Lords were curbed in 1911, Dicey realised that the executive was increasingly dominating Parliament (1915, Introduction).

Parliamentary supremacy is concerned only with an Act of Parliament (a statute). An Act of Parliament, as the preamble to every Act reminds us, is an Act of the monarch with the consent of the House of Lords and the House of Commons: the Queen in Parliament. In certain circumstances however, the consent of the House of Lords can be omitted under the Parliament Acts of 1911 and 1949 (below). Even if we believe that the House of Commons is the political sovereign, a resolution of the House of Commons has in itself no legal force, except in relation to the internal proceedings of the House (*Bowles* v *The Governor and Company of The Bank of England* (1913); *Stockdale* v *Hansard* (1839)).

Dicey's legal sovereign is therefore divided, comprising three bodies: Queen, Lords and Commons. Only in combination can they exercise the power of Parliament. Thus Blackstone, who defended parliamentary supremacy in the eighteenth century, linked the doctrine with that of the mixed constitution (Chapter 8). Indeed Dicey denied that there was a logical need for an ultimate sovereign (1915, p. 143), merely pointing out that the evidence suggested that we have in fact adopted the doctrine of parliamentary supremacy. However a combination of the convention that requires the Queen to assent to all legislation and the law that subordinates the House of Lords to the House of Commons (below) makes the House of Commons in practice the supreme body.

The courts obey Parliament not as an institution but as a process for producing a valid law. Two questions arise from this. First, what rules create an Act of Parliament? Second, to what extent can the courts investigate whether these rules have been obeyed? There are complex procedural rules for producing statutes but not all of them affect the validity of a statute. Three levels of rule can be distinguished:

1. The basic definition of a statute as a document that received the assent of the three institutions comprising the Queen in Parliament: Queen, Lords and Commons. The royal assent signed by the Queen is usually notified to each House separately as a formality but is sometimes pronounced by commissioners before both Houses assembled in the House of Lords (Royal Assent Act 1967). The preamble to a statute invariably recites that the required assents have been given. A court is not bound by a document that does not appear on its face to have received the necessary assents but conversely must accept the validity of a document that does so appear (*Prince's Case* (1606)). This is called the 'enrolled Act rule' and precludes the courts from investigating whether the proper internal procedures have in fact been complied with (*Edinburgh & Dalkeith Railway* v *Wauchope* (1842)). The official version of a statute was traditionally enrolled upon the Parliament Roll. Today there is no Parliament Roll as such, but two official copies of the Act are in the House of Lords' Library and the Public Record Office.

2. In some cases the basic requirements have been modified by statute. In principle the court can investigate whether statutory requirements have been complied with. In particular under the Parliament Act 1911, if the Commons so decides and subject to important exceptions (below), a bill can become law without the consent of the House of Lords after a delaying period (Chapter 11). The 1911 Act was passed to prevent the Lords from obstructing the will of the elected Commons by vetoing legislation introduced in the Commons. It allowed the Lords to delay a bill for broadly two years. The Parliament Act 1949, itself passed under the 1911 Act, reduced the delaying period to one year. The Parliament Act 1911 partly excludes the courts by providing that a certificate given by the Speaker, to the effect that the requirements of the Act have been complied with, is 'conclusive for all purposes and shall not be questioned in any court of law' (s.3). However this does not prevent the court from deciding the prior question

of whether the bill falls within the 1911 Act at all (see *R (Jackson) v Attorney-General* (2006) (below) [51]). Similarly the Regency Act 1937 provides that the royal assent can be given by a specified Regent, usually the next in line to the throne, if the monarch is under eighteen, absent abroad, ill or in certain other events. In this case the court may also be able to investigate whether the Act has been properly applied.

3. There is a complex network of rules concerning the composition and internal procedure of each House. These include the various stages of passage of a bill, voting procedures and the law governing qualifications for membership of either House. They comprise a mixture of statute, convention and the 'law and custom of Parliament' enforced by the House itself. It is settled that ordinary courts have no jurisdiction to enquire into any matters related to the internal affairs of the House. Quite apart from the enrolled Act rule (above), these are matters of parliamentary privilege and are exclusively within the jurisdiction of the House itself. This is true even if it is alleged that the House has violated a statute or that a bill has been introduced fraudulently (see *Pickin v British Railways Board* (1974)).

9.3 The Three Facets of Parliamentary Supremacy

Freedom to make any kind of law. Dicey claimed that Parliament can make any laws it wishes irrespective of fairness, justice and practicality. The UK courts are bound to obey a statute applying anywhere and whether or not the relevant overseas courts would recognise it is immaterial (for example *Manuel v Attorney-General* (1982)). It has been said that Parliament cannot make a man a woman, or a woman a man, but this is misleading. The so called laws of nature are not rules at all. They are simply recurrent facts. A statute which enacted that all men must be regarded as women and vice versa would be impractical, but would be legally valid. Dicey relied on examples of valid statutory provisions that are arguably grossly unjust. However these do not prove that the courts would apply a statute that they consider even more unjust. Nevertheless modern cases continue to support Dicey. They include retrospective legislation (*Burmah Oil Company Ltd v Lord Advocate* (1965); War Damage Act 1965), statutes conflicting with international law (see *Mortensen v Peters* (1906); *Cheney v Conn* (1968)) or with fundamental civil liberties (see *R v Jordan* (1967)).

Parliament cannot be overridden. Firstly international courts such as the European Court of Human Rights or the European Court of Justice do not have the power in English law to declare an Act of Parliament invalid. Whether they have the power to do so within the terms of their own system is a different question. In this respect a constitution is like a game: the rules depending on which version of the game you are playing. Secondly in the event of a conflict between a statute and some other kind of law, the statute must always prevail. However this leaves open the possibility that a statute itself might authorise some other lawmaking authority to override statutes. This was probably achieved by the European Communities Act 1972 (below) but still leaves it open to Parliament to repeal the Act in question, thereby cutting away the authority of the other body.

Parliament cannot bind its successors. In a sense this is a genuine limit on Parliament although it also means that Parliament cannot be restricted by a previous statute. This is a vital principle closely associated with democracy, that no generation should be able to tie the hands of the future. For example Edmund Burke argued that the 1688 revolution had permanently enshrined a constitution which included the House of Lords. Thomas Paine answered this as follows:

> Every age and generation must be as free to act for itself, in all cases as the ages and generations which preceded it. The vanity and presumption of governing beyond the grave is the most ridiculous and insolent of all tyrannies. (1987, p. 204)

The English courts make it relatively easy to override earlier statutes. They usually apply the 'implied repeal' doctrine according to which a later statute that on an ordinary reading is inconsistent with an earlier statute impliedly repeals the earlier statute to the extent of the inconsistency. The court is not required to attempt to reconcile the two and it is irrelevant that the earlier Act states that it cannot be repealed (see *Vauxhall Estates Ltd* v *Liverpool Corporation* (1932); *Ellen Street Estates Ltd* v *Minister of Health* (1934)). The *content* of the two statutes must be directly inconsistent. For example in *Thoburn v Sunderland City Council* (2002) a 1985 statute which allowed goods to be sold in pounds and ounces did not impliedly repeal section 2(4) of the European Communities Act 1972, which empowered ministers to make regulations altering Acts of Parliament for the purpose of implementing EC law. Regulations were later made requiring only metric units (the 'Metric Martyrs' case).

Lord Maugham in *Ellen Street Estates* v *Minister of Health* (1943) at 597 said that it would be impossible to enact that there shall be no implied repeal. This is questionable. The implied repeal doctrine, although consistent with parliamentary sovereignty, is not essential to it. It is merely a particular approach to statutory interpretation, albeit one attractive from a democratic point of view. There is nothing to prevent a statute from requiring the courts to interpret legislation as overriding another statute only if express or very clear language is used, thus putting a partial brake on change. For example, section 3 of the Human Rights Act 1998 requires all other statutes to be interpreted in accordance with the rights protected by the Act 'if it is possible to do so' (Chapter 19). Another example might be a provision in a statute stating that it shall be repealed only by an Act which expressly states that it is to do so. It has also been claimed that under common law some statutes and some legal rights are so important that they can be repealed only by express words or possibly by necessary implication. In *Thoburn v Sunderland City Council* (above) [62–64], Laws LJ stated that a 'constitutional statute' would be so protected, in the sense of a statute 'which conditions the legal relationships between citizen and state in some general overarching manner, or enlarges or diminishes the scope of what are now regarded as fundamental rights'. *Thoburn* concerned the European Communities Act 1972, which would be difficult to deny is of constitutional importance. In many cases however, our unwritten constitution makes it uncertain what counts as a 'constitutional statute'. Moreover the European Communities Act may enjoy even stronger protection (below).

9.4   Challenging Parliamentary Supremacy

There are various arguments that Parliament can in particular contexts be legally limited. Parliamentary supremacy was a historical response to political circumstances, namely Parliament as the focus for rebellion against the Stuart monarchs. It does not follow that the same response is appropriate today. The Victorian period during which Dicey promoted the doctrine was one of relative stability and prosperity. The people, or at least the majority, were benefiting from the spoils of empire and the belief that Parliament, backed by consensus values, could deliver stability and prosperity was still plausible. Popular revolution as experienced elsewhere had been staved off by cautious reforms. Latterly different forces, both domestic and international, have arisen which have made parliamentary sovereignty appear parochial, politically unreal and intellectually threadbare. These forces include the global economy, devolution, membership of the EU and other international obligations and the increasing powers of the executive over Parliament. There is no longer a political consensus that Parliament should be legally unlimited and no compelling legal reason why it should be. The main challenges to Parliamentary supremacy are as follows.

9.4.1　Grants of Independence

If Parliament were to pass an Act giving independence to a piece of territory currently under UK jurisdiction, such as Scotland, could a later Act revoke that independence? For example the Canada Act 1982 provides that 'no Act of the United Kingdom Parliament passed after the Constitution Act 1982 comes into force shall extend to Canada as part of its law' (s.2). Although as a matter of political reality, the answer is no unless the territory in question either consents or is conquered by force, the legal answer is yes as far as the UK courts are concerned (*British Coal Corporation* v *R* (1935); *Manuel* v *Attorney-General* (1982)). There is however a dictum by Lord Denning in *Blackburn* v *Attorney-General* (1971) that legal theory must give way to practical politics. All his Lordship seems to be saying is that it would be impossible in a practical sense for Parliament to reverse a grant of independence. On the other hand a legal principle that is so out of line with common sense might well be worth reconsidering.

9.4.2　Acts of Union: Was Parliament Born Unfree?

The UK Parliament is the result of two treaties. First the Treaty of Union with Scotland in 1706 created the Parliament of Great Britain out of the former Scottish and English Parliaments. The treaty required among other things that no laws which concern private rights in Scotland shall be altered 'except for the evident utility of the subjects within Scotland'. There were also powers securing the separate Scottish courts and Presbyterian Church 'for all time coming'. The new Parliament was created by separate Acts of the then Scottish and English Parliaments, giving effect to the treaty (see Act of Union with Scotland 1706). Some Scottish lawyers therefore argue that Parliament was 'born unfree', meaning that the modern Parliament cannot go beyond the terms of the Acts that created it. They suggest that the protected provisions of the Act of Union cannot be altered by Act of Parliament. In effect the Union created a new Parliament which, in relation to the protected Scottish provisions, does not necessarily have the quality of supremacy inherent in the former English Parliament (see Munro, 1999, pp. 137–42). A contrary argument is that parliamentary supremacy is an evolving doctrine that developed after the Acts of Union.

In the case of Northern Ireland, there was a Treaty of Union in 1798 which preserved certain basic rights in Ireland including the continuance of the Protestant religion and the permanence of the Union itself. The Treaty was confirmed by the Act of Union with Ireland 1800 which created the UK Parliament. The Act covered the whole of Ireland but what is now the Republic of Ireland later left the Union. It might be argued that the Northern Ireland Act 1998 section 1, which provides for the Union to be dissolved if a referendum so votes, would be invalid as contrary to the Act of Union. The 1998 Act makes no express reference to the Act of Union with Ireland, section 2 merely providing that the Act overrides 'previous enactments'. Political circumstances in Northern Ireland make this ambiguity understandable.

The crucial provisions of the Scottish Union have not been altered but section 37 of the Scotland Act 1998 expressly states that the provisions of the Act are to take priority over the Act of Union. This leaves open the question whether an Act can do this at all. The issue has surfaced in a few cases in all of which an Act of Parliament was obeyed. In *Ex parte Canon Selwyn* (1872) (Ireland) the court denied that it possessed the power to override a statute. In two Scottish cases, *MacCormick* v *Lord Advocate* (1953) and *Gibson* v *Lord Advocate* (1975), the Scottish courts were able to avoid the issue by holding that no conflict with the Acts of Union arose. However in both cases the argument in favour of the Acts of Union was regarded as tenable, particularly by Lord Cooper in *MacCormick*. However his Lordship, with the apparent agreement of Lords Keith and Gibson, suggested that the issue might be 'non-justiciable', that is, outside the jurisdiction of the courts and resolvable only by political means. On this view a statute that flouts the Acts of Union may be unconstitutional but not unlawful. In both cases the courts left open the question whether they could interfere if an Act purported to make drastic inroads into the Act of Union, for example by abolishing the whole of Scottish private law (see also *R (Jackson)* v *Attorney-General* (2006) [105], Lord Hope acknowledging that the Acts of Union might not be repealable). Thus the courts carefully steered around a constitutional abeyance (Chapter 3).

9.4.3   Redefinition Theory

This is an attempt to circumvent the rule that Parliament cannot bind its successors. The argument has various labels, sometimes being called the 'new view', sometimes the 'entrenchment' argument, sometimes the 'manner and form' theory and sometimes the distinction between continuing and self embracing sovereignty. The redefinition argument is essentially that if Parliament can do anything, it can 'redesign itself either in general or for particular purpose', as Baroness Hale put it in *R (Jackson)* v *Attorney-General* (2006) [160]. It can do this so as to make it difficult to change an Act that it 'entrenches', for example by providing that a referendum of the people is required to change certain laws. Whether in any particular case it has done so and what, if any, limits are imposed on the redefined Parliament is a matter of interpretation of the legislation in question. The redefined body can act only within the terms of the law that created it. However as long as it does so within those terms, it may be able to change those terms themselves.

The redefinition argument can be supported as follows:

1. There must be rules of law that tell us what counts as an Act of Parliament and these must be logically prior to Parliament which can speak only through these rules. These rules therefore define Parliament: without them Parliament is merely a rabble of individuals. What these rules currently are is outlined above, namely that an Act of Parliament requires the consent of the Queen, the Lords and the Commons.

2. A document which purports to be an Act of Parliament but which has not been passed according to these basic rules has no legal force so that the courts must ignore it. The same applies if Parliament changes those basic rules which, if it can do anything, must be the case. Suppose for example a statute enacts a bill of rights and goes on to say that 'no law shall be passed that is inconsistent with the bill of rights nor shall this statute be repealed expressly or impliedly without a referendum of the people'. What Parliament has done in this example is to add to the existing requirement of Queen, Lords and Commons a further requirement of a referendum. An entrenched statute can therefore still be repealed but not without the special procedure. In *R (Jackson)* v *Attorney-General* (2006) (above) the House of Lords accepted that the courts had jurisdiction to investigate requirements for enacting statutes which are imposed by statute.

The redefinition argument can be attacked on three fronts:

1. If Parliament were to ignore the special procedure by passing a statute in the ordinary way, the courts would simply obey the most recent Act of Parliament and thus treat the special procedure as impliedly repealed. However this misses the point, since according to the redefinition argument a document that has not been produced under the special procedure is not a valid statute and so must be ignored, just as an ordinary law would be ignored if it did not have the royal assent. Therefore there are no competing statutes for the implied repeal doctrine to engage with.
2. It can be argued that any Act which confers lawmaking power subject to a special procedure is in reality delegating power to a subordinate body since, by definition, subordinate legislation is legislation made under the authority of another body and is inherently restricted by the terms of reference given to it. If this is so, then the superior body can always legislate to override the subordinate. However it is equally possible logically to regard what is happening as a body redefining itself. In both cases the change in the law must be made in accordance with the lawmaking procedure in force at the time. For example if Parliament as Queen, Lords and Commons were to enact a law making the House of Commons alone the primary lawmaker, this does not necessarily make the latter a subordinate.
3. Professor Wade (1955) argues that the meaning of 'Parliament' is 'fixed' by a rule which is 'above and beyond the reach of Parliament': a fundamental constitutional principle which he takes to be common law. Parliament cannot simply make itself supreme so there must be some independent explanation of why it is so. Wade argues that the explanation lies in the 1688 revolution which created the fundamental settlement of Queen, Lords and Commons, a rule that is unique in character, a political principle standing outside and above the ordinary legal system and giving it its validity. Wade argues that because this rule gave Parliament its power, it cannot be altered by Parliament at best producing delegated legislation.

    Wade accepts that the doctrine of parliamentary supremacy could in political reality be abolished but would regard this as a revolution, that is, the introduction of an entirely new basic principle. How will we know whether such a revolution has taken place? Wade would place the matter in the 'keeping of the courts', so that if the courts were to accept the redefinition theory, this would authoritatively signify the 'revolution'. However a change brought about in accordance with the existing law, which was the case with the Parliament Act 1911, is surely worth distinguishing from a revolution that is associated with extra legal activity if not always violence. Indeed it seems a misuse of language not to do so. Moreover even if we accept the idea of Wade's 'higher rule', this does not exclude the redefinition theory. Why should the higher rule, supposedly made by those in charge of the 1688 revolution, not authorise its creature – Parliament – to alter the rule itself?

There is judicial support for the redefinition theory from former UK territories, mainly *Attorney-General for New South Wales* v *Trethowen* (1932), *Harris* v *Minister of the Interior* (1952) (South Africa) and *Bribery Commissioner* v *Ranasinghe* (1965) (Sri-Lanka). *Trethowen* went so far as to suggest that the court could grant an injunction to prevent a bill being submitted for royal assent if it did not comply with the entrenched procedure. This seems unlikely to apply in England since the courts have consistently refused to interfere with the conduct of parliamentary proceedings. The issue would arise in the UK if a court were asked to obey a document that fails to comply with an entrenched provision.

However these cases are unreliable authority. *Trethowen, Ranasinghe* and *Harris* have been explained on the basis that the legislatures in these countries were not truly supreme in the same way as the UK Parliament, since a UK Act had established the powers of the legislatures in question. However in *Harris* the Statute of Westminster 1931 had given the South African Parliament unlimited lawmaking power. Moreover the court stressed that its reasoning did not assume that the legislature was subordinate. Indeed in both *Trethowen* and *Ranasinghe* there were dicta that the same arguments might apply to the UK Parliament. Thus it was said in *Ranasinghe* (1965) at 198 that the legislature can alter the very instrument from which its powers derive.

In *Manuel* v *Attorney-General* (1983) the Canada Act 1982 was claimed to be invalid in that it was enacted without relevant consents as required by the Statute of Westminster 1931 section 4 which at the time applied to Canada as a former UK dominion. The purpose of the 1982 Act was to free Canada from its constitutional links with the UK. The Court of Appeal was prepared to recognise the possibility of redefinition. However, as a matter of interpretation section 4 merely required that the Act had to *state on its face* that it had received the relevant consents. The 1982 Act did so state and the court could not investigate the internal proceedings of Parliament to see whether the statement was true. Obviously the matter depends on the precise terms of the redefinition in question.

The most important case is *R (Jackson)* v *Attorney-General* (2006). The Hunting Act 2004, which outlawed hunting with dogs, had been enacted under the Parliament Acts 1911 and 1949 (above) against persistent opposition from the House of Lords. The Hunting Act was challenged on two main grounds. The first was that Parliament could not redefine itself so that a law passed under the 1911 Act could at best be delegated legislation and therefore challengeable in the courts, power being delegated by Parliament in the 1911 Act to the Commons and Queen. The second argument was that even if Parliament could redefine itself, it could not do so under the Parliament Act procedure. It was argued that there are implied limits inherent in the 1911 Act which prevented the Parliament Act procedure from being used to further reduce the powers of the Lords .Under this argument any laws made under the Parliament Act 1911 would only be delegated legislation. The point of the delegated legislation analysis was that the Hunting Act was passed under the 1949 Parliament Act, which shortened the delaying powers of the House of Lords. The 1949 Act was enacted without House of Lords' consent under the 1911 Act's procedure. It was suggested, and assumed to be correct, that unless there is clear authority to do so from the parent Act, a delegate cannot enlarge its own powers. Therefore the 1949 Act was invalid so that the Hunting Act fell with it.

Nine Law Lords held that the 1949 Act and therefore the Hunting Act is lawful and that Acts passed under the Parliament Acts were not delegated legislation. Thus they endorsed the possibility of redefinition although without confronting Wade's argument (above). Moreover as a matter of interpreting the scope of the 'redefinition' there was nothing to prevent the Parliament Act 1949 from reducing further the powers of the House of Lords. The matter depended on the scope of the redefinition intended by the 1911 Act. Lord Steyn [81–6, 91–3] treated the definition of Parliament as a dynamic matter that Parliament itself could change (see also Lord Bingham [35–6], Baroness Hale [160], Lord Carswell [174], Lord Browne [187]).

However caution is required. It was stressed that the 1911 Act did not transfer power to a body other than Parliament nor limit the power of the democratic House of Commons. It merely constrained the House of Lords [25]. The courts might therefore draw back from accepting a more radical kind of redefinition. Baroness Hale in particular left 'for another day' the question whether Parliament could redefine itself 'upwards', for example by requiring a referendum for a particular measure in addition to the normal procedure [163].

As to the second ground, it was held that since laws made under the Parliament Acts were full statutes, the Parliament Act 1911 was not subject to any implied limitation that would invalidate the 1949 Act. The Hunting Act was therefore valid. However there was disagreement as to whether the Parliament Acts could be used to remove the *express limitations* contained in the 1911 Act, a matter not strictly relevant in this case.

Their Lordships also held that the Parliament Acts applied to bills to alter the Parliament Acts themselves. The 1911 Act *expressly* does not apply to the following (s.2):

- a bill to prolong the life of Parliament beyond five years. This is a safeguard to prevent a government exploiting a Commons majority to avoid an election.
- a private bill, which is a bill concerning specific persons or places, and a bill to confirm a provisional order, a largely unused procedure for approving particular projects
- a bill introduced in the House of Lords.

These limitations arguably set the boundaries of any redefinition. However they could conceivably be overcome in two stages. First, using the Parliament Acts the Commons might alter the 1911 Act itself so as to remove them. It would then, using the altered Parliament Acts, pass a statute, for example extending Parliament's life for ten years. Lord Nicholls [59], Lord Steyn [79], Lord Hope [118, 122] and Lord Carswell [175] suggested that this would be unlawful as subverting the clear intention of the 1911 Act. Lord Rogers [139] was also sympathetic to this view. Lord Bingham [32] and Baroness Hale [159] took the contrary and more logical view, arguing that since Acts passed under the Parliament Acts were full statutes, the courts could not prevent this, however politically undesirable it might be. Lords Walker and Browne did not express a view.

A further issue was discussed. The Court of Appeal in *Jackson* had suggested that a bill which made fundamental constitutional changes such as abolishing the House of Lords altogether or violating basic democratic rights could not be passed under the Parliament Acts. It is not clear why they thought this (although Lord Woolf seemed to support Wade's argument above). Apart from the uncertainty of this notion, the 1911 Act was introduced for the very purpose of enabling important changes to be made against the opposition of the Lords. Their Lordships in *Jackson* did not commit themselves on this point but suggested different views, albeit tentatively. Lord Bingham [32], Lord Nicholls [61], Lord Hope [127] and Baroness Hale [159, 166] thought that there would be no legally enforceable limitations, although Lord Bingham [41] drew attention to the fact that the Parliament Acts weaken the checks and balances over a powerful executive. Lord Carswell [178] and Lord Browne [194] cautiously left open the possibility. Lord Steyn [102] went furthest, taking the view that fundamental changes might be rejected by the courts not merely under the Parliament Acts but also by the full Parliament. This makes the courts the ultimate sovereign.

9.4.4   European Community Law

The EU and its powers were created by a series of treaties between the member states. Member states are obliged under the treaties to give effect to those community laws that are intended by community law to be binding within domestic law. However the law of the EU (strictly speaking, the law of the European Community (EC) which is the institutional backbone of the EU) enters the legal systems of each member state in accordance with the laws of that state. It is sometimes argued that the UK has therefore surrendered part of parliamentary supremacy (see *Blackburn* v *Attorney-General* (1971)). If this is right then a democratic body has committed the sin of trying to bind the freedom of future generations. We shall discuss the EC law in more detail in Chapter 10 but will outline the position as regards parliamentary supremacy here.

A treaty as such cannot change the law but must first be incorporated into an Act of Parliament. The European Communities Act 1972 incorporated EC law into the UK constitution. The European Communities Act 1972 states that 'any enactment, passed or to be passed . . . shall be construed and have effect subject to the foregoing provisions of this section' (s.2(4)). The provisions referred to require among other things that the English courts must give effect to certain laws made by European bodies (s.2(1)). Section 3 of the Act also requires UK courts to follow the decisions of the European Court of Justice (ECJ), the court of the EC. The effect of the above provisions seems to be that a UK statute, even one passed after the relevant EC law, must give way to EC law. Not surprisingly the ECJ, which is part of the internal EC system, favours the supremacy of the EC (see *Costa* v *ENEL* (1964)). However this in itself is not enough since the matter depends on the UK constitution.

Conflict between UK law and EC law may arise where a UK statute is inconsistent with an existing EC law. There are opposing arguments based on differing perspectives as to the effect of the 1972 Act. On the one hand it might be argued along traditional lines that since a statute made EC law binding in the UK, a statute can reverse this. According to this argument it might be conceded that, given the importance of EC law and the clear intention in the Act that it should take priority, it should take very clear words in an Act to override an EC law so that the ordinary implied repeal doctrine is excluded (above). Thus the courts would try to interpret legislation so as to avoid a conflict with a binding rule of EC law. According to Lord Diplock in *Garland* v *British Rail Engineering Ltd* (1983) a statute that unambiguously states that it is to override European law will arguably prevail. Similarly in *Thoburn* v *Sunderland City Council* (2002) Laws LJ attempted to treat the matter as one of a strong presumption against repeal, regarding the 1972 Act as an example of a 'constitutional statute'. However the case of the EC is possibly even stronger in that nothing short of an express statement along the lines of 'this Act is to override EC law' would suffice. On the other hand it could be argued that the 1972 Act had the effect of imposing a European perspective on the UK courts, thus requiring the courts to give priority to EC laws since European law does not recognise our version of parliamentary supremacy. In *Jackson* (above) Lord Hope [105] and Baroness Hale [159] treated EC law as modifying parliamentary supremacy. Independently of both arguments it might be conceded that a UK statute could validly expressly repeal the 1972 Act effectively taking us out of the European Union.

The UK courts have reached an ambivalent solution which is consistent with both the above perspectives. In *R* v *Secretary of State for Transport ex parte Factortame* (1990) there was a clash between the European Treaty and the Merchant Shipping Act 1988. Lord Bridge said at 140, 'By virtue of s.2(4) of the Act of 1972, Part II of the 1988 Act is to be construed and take effect subject to directly enforceable community rights . . . This has precisely the same effect as if a section were incorporated in . . . the 1988 Act . . . which enacted that the provisions were to be without prejudice to the directly enforceable community rights of nationals of any member state of the EC.' Thus his Lordship treated the matter as one of *interpreting* the Act in question so as to conform with the EC rule, not of overriding it. However the House of Lords refused to grant an injunction to prevent the Act being enforced, holding that it had no power to defy an Act of Parliament. The matter was referred to the ECJ, which held that the UK court should enforce the EC law. In *R* v *Secretary of State ex parte Factortame (No. 2)* (1991) the House of Lords fell into line and 'disapplied' the UK statute. This could avoid a direct challenge to Parliamentary supremacy on the basis that to 'disapply' merely means that the statute has no application to the particular case. On the other hand *Factortame* could be taken as supporting the second perspective which modifies parliamentary supremacy arguably signalling Wade's 'constitutional revolution' (see also *Equal Opportunities Commission* v *Secretary of State for Employment* (1994)).

9.4.5 The Common Law

It is sometimes suggested that parliamentary supremacy may be conditional on compliance with fundamental values (see *R (Jackson)* v *Attorney-General* (above) [102], Lord Steyn [107]). These fundamental values relate to the 'extended' notion of the rule of law (Chapter 7). A few cases such as *Dr Bonham's Case* (1610) possibly suggest that a completely unreasonable statute may be overridden but at least since Tudor times there has been no serious challenge to parliamentary supremacy. Nevertheless in the absence of a written constitution we cannot rule out judicial rejection of the doctrine. Indeed the courts themselves inevitably have to decide the limits of their own powers when a case comes before them. Thus it has been said:

> whoever hath an absolute authority to interpret any written or spoken laws, it is he who is truly the lawgiver and not the person who just spoke or wrote them." (Bishop Hoadley's sermon preached before King George I, 1717).

Contemporary judges in the main support ultimate parliamentary supremacy but are sometimes ambivalent. This compromise has been rationalised by claiming that there is 'dual sovereignty', a separation of powers between Parliament and the courts. In *X Ltd v Morgan Grampian Publishers Ltd* (1991) at 13, Lord Bridge referred to the 'twin foundations' of the rule of law, namely 'the sovereignty of the Queen in Parliament in making the law and the sovereignty of the Queen's courts in interpreting and applying the law'. In *Hamilton v Al Fayed* (1999) at 320, Lord Woolf MR referred to 'the wider constitutional principle of mutuality of respect between two constitutional sovereignties'. However it is arguably fallacious to treat interpretation as a sovereign act. Interpretation requires attention to possible meanings of the text to be interpreted and is an inherently limited exercise albeit sometimes with considerable latitude. It is true that there is no further appeal against the interpretation put on an Act by the highest court. But it still makes sense to suggest that the court's interpretation may be wrong in law just as a referee's decision in a sport may be wrong. A rule which says that a decision of a judge cannot be challenged is separate from the question of whether or not that decision is lawful. By contrast in the case of Parliament, if Parliament is a sovereign it is nonsensical to say that its decisions can be unlawful.

The courts can put partial brakes on Parliament's freedom. As we saw in Chapter 7, the courts do not interpret statutes mechanically but will apply them in the context of the rule of law which embodies respect for fundamental values and individual rights. There are many presumptions of statutory interpretation, the overall effect of which is that Parliament must use very clear language if it wishes to override values of fairness and justice developed by the courts. For example in *R v Lord Chancellor's Department ex parte Witham* [1997] 2 All ER 779 at 783, Laws J asserted that:

> In the unwritten legal order of the British State, at a time when the common law continues to accord a legislative supremacy to Parliament, the notion of a constitutional right can in my judgement inhere only in this proposition that the right in question cannot be abrogated by the state save by specific provision in an Act of Parliament . . . General words will not suffice. And any such rights will be creatures of the common law, since their existence would not be the consequence of the democratic process but would be logically prior to it.

It is difficult to draw the line between interpretation or application of and outright disobedience to a statute. *Anisminic Ltd v Foreign Compensation Commission* (1969) is sometimes regarded as a judicial attempt to subvert Parliament under the cloak of interpretation. The applicant challenged a ruling by the Commission refusing it compensation under a statutory scheme. The governing Act included an 'ouster clause' designed to protect the Commission against challenge in the courts. This stated that a 'determination' of the Commission 'under the Act' shall not be questioned in any court of law. Nevertheless the House of Lords, applying a presumption that the jurisdiction of the courts should not be excluded, allowed the challenge on the ground that a ruling which was flawed by an error of law was a nullity and so did not count as a 'determination under the Act'.

The contrary argument is that Parliament legislates in the knowledge of basic common law values, which it can be taken to accept unless it clearly states otherwise. The courts act as a check and balance by ensuring that Parliament does not inadvertently or lightly override basic rights and if it does so it is clearly accountable (Chapter 8); see *R v Secretary of State for the Home Department ex parte Simms* (1999) per Lord Hoffmann (Chapter 7). Far from being radical, the *Anisminic* reasoning was fully documented in the old cases. Therefore Parliament could have anticipated the line that the court might take and have used tighter language if it wanted to exclude challenge, thereby making explicit that it was overriding widely shared values.

Allan (2001) argues that it is inconsistent with the political assumptions of a liberal society on which the rule of law is based that the legislature, or indeed any part of the government, should be all powerful, all being subject to the same overarching principles. Allan claims that in the common law tradition the courts have the duty to protect the fundamental values of the society. Relying on the fact that the court is concerned not with the statute generally but with its application to the individual case, Allan suggests that the court can legitimately hold that a statute which appears to be grossly unjust in the particular context does not apply to the particular case. This approach could be reconciled with parliamentary supremacy on the basis that Parliament cannot foresee every implication of the laws it makes and can be assumed to respect the rule of law. In *Cooper v Wandsworth Board of Works* (1863) Byles J put the matter more strongly when he said that 'the justice of the common law will supply the omission of the legislature'.

Those supporting the courts might argue in favour of the high standard of public reasoned argument practised in the courts and the relative objectivity and independence of judges. A much canvassed argument is that the representative democracy which gives Parliament its legitimacy is an imperfect democracy and does not necessarily reflect the views of a majority of voters (see *R v Secretary of State for the Home Department ex parte Fire Brigades Union* (1995); Chapter 8). In particular Parliament has become dominated by the executive. Thus the usual defence of Parliament, that it can make laws which are informed by a wider range of opinions than are available to a court and which carry the consent of those subject to them, can be presented as hollow. On the other hand, it seems somewhat bizarre to remedy a failure of democracy by suggesting an even more undemocratic mechanism.

Arguments in favour of Parliament point to the indignity of political decisions being made on their behalf by people we have not chosen and also the fact that judges are not accountable. They might also deny that the legal attitude should have a privileged status, whereas Parliament comprises a larger cross section of the community that can make a better informed decision (see Bellamy, 2007). The liberal values that the rule of law embraces are widely accepted but they are not peculiar to law. Moreover ideas such as freedom and equality are the source of much political disagreement which judges are in no better position to resolve than anyone else (see Chapter 19).

9.5 Parliamentary Supremacy and the Rule of Law

Parliamentary supremacy conflicts with the rule of law at least in its amplified and extended senses (Chapter 7). For example Parliament sometimes enacts retrospective laws and often confers wide discretionary powers on the executive even to alter Acts of Parliament. However Dicey (1915, Chapter 3) thought that the rule of law and parliamentary supremacy supported each other. He relied essentially on separation of powers arguments. He argued that Parliament is not a single body but three bodies defined by law, each of which checks the other. He thus relied on the mixed constitution. Secondly he pointed out that Parliament could act only through the medium of law. It has no executive powers and depends on independent courts to apply and interpret its laws. Thirdly the rule of law 'necessitates' parliamentary supremacy in that the executive cannot interfere with the individual without obtaining legal powers from Parliament. A democrat might also argue that the parliamentary rules provided by law ensure that a wide range of opinions can be taken into account as part of the lawmaking process and that Parliament is protected against outside interference. On the other hand Parliament, if it is indeed supreme, could change the law by abolishing all democratic and separation of powers safeguards, including those provided by the courts.

Dicey's view depended on the pivotal role which he thought that the House of Lords played in checking the excesses of democracy and upon his assumption that the common law was the guardian of basic values. Today the House of Lords is subordinate to the Commons and, as we have seen, there is no longer widespread agreement, if there ever was, as to what the values of the constitution should be. In his later years Dicey realised that the power of political parties, an increasingly diverse electorate, external threats and the need for governments to provide expensive public services put the traditional place of Parliament as the centre of the constitution into question.

Summary

- The doctrine of parliamentary supremacy provides the fundamental legal premise of the UK constitution. The doctrine means that an Act of Parliament must be obeyed by the courts, that later Acts prevail over earlier ones and that rules made by external bodies, for example under international law, cannot override Acts of Parliament. It does not follow that Parliament is supreme politically, although the line between legal and political supremacy is blurred.

- Parliamentary supremacy rests on frail foundations. Without a written constitution it is impossible to be sure as to its legal basis other than as an evolving practice which is usually said to depend on the 1688 revolution. It is possible to maintain that the common law is really supreme. The question of the ultimate source of power cannot be answered within the legal system alone but depends on public acceptance.

- Parliament is itself a creature of the law. The customary and statutory rules which have evolved since medieval times determine that, except in special cases, Parliament for this purpose means the Queen with the assent of the House of Lords and House of Commons. However this can be modified as in the case of the Parliament Acts 1911 and 1949.

- The courts can determine whether any document is an Act of Parliament in this sense but cannot inquire into whether the correct procedure within each House has been followed.

- The doctrine has two separate aspects: first that the courts must obey Acts of Parliament in preference to any other kind of legal authority, and second that no body, including Parliament itself, can place legal limits upon the freedom of action of a future Parliament. The first of these principles is generally accepted but the second is open to dispute.

- The implied repeal doctrine is sometimes promoted as an aspect of parliamentary supremacy but is merely a presumption of interpretation. Some statutes can be repealed only by clear language.

Summary cont'd

▷ The doctrine of parliamentary supremacy is subject to considerable attack:
  ▷ Grants of independence to dependent territories: these can probably be revoked lawfully in the eyes of UK courts.
  ▷ The possibility that parts of the Acts of Union with Scotland and Ireland are unchangeable: this is probably outside the courts' jurisdiction.
  ▷ The 'redefinition' argument proposes that by altering the basic requirements for lawmaking, Parliament can redesign itself to impose restrictions on enacting legislation.
  ▷ Parliament limited the freedom of future Parliaments in relation to certain laws made by the European communities.
  ▷ The role of the common law as constituting 'dual sovereignty' through the courts' exclusive power to interpret Acts of Parliament leads to argument that parliamentary supremacy is conditional upon acceptance by the courts. This links with the extended version of the rule of law (Chapter 7).

▷ Dicey attempted to reconcile parliamentary supremacy with the rule of law by pointing out that Parliament is defined by law and can act only through the instrument of law so that independent judges interpret its legislation. This relies on the separation of powers.

Exercises

9.1 Does the doctrine of Parliamentary supremacy have a secure legal basis?

9.2 To what extent can the courts investigate whether an Act of Parliament has complied with the proper procedure?

9.3 'Every age and generation must be as free to act for itself, in all cases as the ages and generations which preceded it. The vanity and presumption of governing beyond the grave is the most ridiculous and insolent of all tyrannies' (Thomas Paine). Discuss with reference (a) to the implied repeal doctrine and (b) to the redefinition argument.

9.4 Marshal the arguments for and against the proposition that the UK Parliament cannot legislate inconsistently with EC law.

9.5 Consider the validity and effect of the following provisions contained in (fictitious) Acts of Parliament:
  (i) 'There shall be a bill of rights in the UK and no Act to be enacted at any time in the future shall have effect, in as far as it is inconsistent with the bill of rights, unless it has been assented to by a two-thirds majority of both Houses of Parliament and no Act shall repeal this Act unless it has the same two-thirds majority.'
  (ii) 'No bill shall be introduced into either House of Parliament which purports to affect the Established Church of England unless it recites on its face that it has the prior approval of the Synod of the Church of England.'
  (iii) 'This Act shall apply notwithstanding any contrary rule of European Community law.'

9.6 'The sovereignty of Parliament and the supremacy of the law of the land – the two principles which pervade the whole of the English constitution may appear to stand in opposition to each other, or to be at best countervailing forces. But this appearance is delusive' (Dicey). Discuss.

9.7 'It is often said that it would be unconstitutional for the UK Parliament to do certain things, meaning that the moral, political and other reasons against doing them are so strong that most people would regard it as highly improper if Parliament did these things. But that does not mean that it is beyond the powers of Parliament to do such things. If Parliament chose to do any of them the courts could not hold Parliament to account' (Lord Reid, *Madzimbamuto* v *Lardner-Burke* (1969) at 723). Discuss whether this is true.

9.8 What, if any, limitations are there on the powers exercisable by Parliament under the Parliament Acts 1911 and 1949?

Further reading

Allan, T. (1997) 'Parliamentary Sovereignty: Law, Politics and Revolution', *Law Quarterly Review* 113:443.

Allan, T. (2001) *Constitutional Justice*, Oxford University Press, Chapter 8.

Bellamy, R. (2007) *Political Constitutionalism*, Cambridge University Press.

Bradley, A. (2004) 'The Sovereignty of Parliament – Form or Substance?' in Jowell, J. and Oliver, D. (eds) *The Changing Constitution* (5th edn), Oxford University Press.

Craig, P. (2003) 'Constitutional Foundations, the Rule of Law and Supremacy', *Public Law* 92.

Ekins, R. (2007) 'Acts of Parliament and the Parliament Acts', *Law Quarterly Review* 123:91

Ekins, R. (2003) 'Judicial Supremacy and the Rule of Law', *Law Quarterly Review* 119:127.

Goldsworthy, J. (1999) *The Sovereignty of Parliament: History and Philosophy*, Oxford University Press, Chapters 1, 2, 9, 10.

Goldsworthy, J. (2001) 'Legislative Sovereignty and the Rule of Law', in Campbell, T., Ewing, K.D. and Tompkins, A. (eds) *Sceptical Essays on Human Rights*, Oxford University Press.

Jowell, J. (2006) 'Parliamentary Supremacy under the New Constitutional Hypothesis', *Public Law* 562.

MacCormick, N. (1978) 'Does the United Kingdom Have a Constitution? Reflections on MacCormack v Lord Advocate', *Northern Ireland Law Quarterly* 29:1.

MacCormick, N. (1993) 'Beyond the Sovereign State', *Modern Law Review* 56:1.

Munro, C.R. (1999) *Studies in Constitutional Law* (2nd edn), London, Butterworth, Chapters 5, 6.

Nolan, Lord and Sedley, Sir S. (1997) *The Making and Remaking of the British Constitution*, London, Blackstone Press, Chapter 7.

Wade, H.W.R. (1955) 'The Basis of Legal Sovereignty', *Cambridge Law Journal* 172.

Chapter 10

The European Union

> Europe has never existed. It is not the addition of national sovereignties in a conclave that creates an entity. One must genuinely create Europe.
> (Jean Monnet, 1888–1979)

Key words

- Federation or confederation?
- Democratic accountability
- Variable geometry
- Politicised court?
- Subsidiarity
- Balance of power between members

In this chapter we shall discuss the main legal principles relating to the European Union as they affect the UK constitution. We shall not therefore discuss the internal workings of the EU except from this perspective. Readers should also refer to Chapter 9 which discusses the impact of the EU on parliamentary supremacy.

10.1 Introduction: The Nature of the European Union

There are few areas of UK law immune from EU influence, which was famously described by Lord Denning as an 'incoming tide' (*Bulmer Ltd* v *Bollinger SA* (1974)). What was originally called the Common Market was created after the Second World War (1939–45) as an aspiration to prevent further wars in Europe and to regenerate the European economies. The prototype was the European Coal and Steel Community created by the Treaty of Paris 1951. The other communities were created in 1957 by two Treaties of Rome. They are the European Community (EC) (formerly called the European Economic Community) and the European Atomic Energy Community. In 1992 under the Maastricht Treaty (Treaty of European Union – TEU) the European Union was created as an umbrella political organisation with aspirations towards 'an ever closer union' (Article 1). It has no legal identity as such but acts through the Communities sharing common institutions.

Democracy was not regarded as the highest value of either the original or the revised union. Democratic government is a requirement of membership but this is envisaged as operating primarily at national level. The EU is a paternalistic concept intended to impose a particular vision of the good life built around a combination of welfare and market liberalism (Article 2 EC Treaty; Article 2 TEU). The unelected European institutions therefore have a larger share of power than the elected European Parliament.

The legal powers of the Communities are exercised through the common institutions of the European Union, the most important being the European Council, the Council of Ministers, the European Commission and the European Court of Justice (ECJ). The most important Community for legal purposes is the EC, which deals broadly with economic, social and environmental matters ('first pillar'). Functions of the EU that are not in the main enforceable through the legal institutions are foreign and security policy, except immigration ('second pillar') and police and judicial cooperation in criminal matters ('third pillar'). Thus the second and third pillars involve primarily intergovernmental cooperation rather than directly binding legal rules. Under the Lisbon Treaty (below) the EC will be fully merged with the European Union which will be given legal personality in its own right.

It is important to be clear that the European Convention on Human Rights (ECHR) (Chapter 19) is not a creation of the European Union but is under the auspices of the Council of Europe which is a completely different organisation with its own court, the European Court of Human Rights. The main connection between the two organisations is that European law takes account of the ECHR and all member states are parties to it. Under the Lisbon Treaty (below) there is provision for the European Union to become a party to the ECHR.

The aims of the EC are as set out in Article 2 of the EC Treaty:

> to promote throughout the Community a harmonious, balanced and sustainable development of economic activities, a high level of employment and of social protection, equality between men and women, sustainable and non-inflationary growth, a high degree of competitiveness and convergence of economic performance, a high level of protection and improvement of the quality of the environment, the raising of the standard of living and quality of life, and economic and social cohesion and solidarity among Member States.

The founder members were France, Germany, Italy, Luxembourg, Belgium and the Netherlands. The UK became a member in 1972 (European Communities Act 1972). There are now twenty seven members including former communist countries, thereby altering the original balance and introducing a wide range of economic, political, cultural and religious perspectives that challenge the old fashioned blend of republicanism and liberalism of the founder members. Members who joined at later dates are Austria, Denmark, Finland, Greece, Ireland, Portugal, Spain and Sweden. The following joined in 2004 under the Nice Treaty (2000): Cyprus, the Czech Republic, Estonia, Hungary, Latvia, Lithuania, Malta, Poland, Slovakia and Slovenia. Bulgaria and Romania joined in 2007.

The objectives of the Communities were originally exclusively economic, primarily to encourage free trade between member states, but the organisation was heavily influenced by a desire to protect agricultural interests espoused principally by France. This has left the EU with a heavy financial burden in that over half of its budget is still devoted to agricultural subsidies. The interests of the EU have steadily widened, partly by a process of interpreting the existing objectives liberally and partly by the member states formally agreeing to extend the areas of competence of the EC. For example the Single European Act 1986 made environmental protection a separate area of competence. The EU has also developed a substantial security and foreign policy perspective.

The Maastricht Treaty (1992) instigated progress towards monetary union, including the creation of an independent European Central Bank. There is now a single European currency, the 'euro', which is regulated by the European Central Bank. The UK does not participate in this. The possible effect of the single currency upon the independence of the UK Parliament is one reason why the decision whether or not to join the euro is widely regarded as raising important constitutional issues. There is also freedom of movement between the mainland EU states under the Schenken Agreement. The UK is not a party to this.

The main treaties, which were amended and consolidated by the Nice Treaty (2003) and would be further consolidated by the Lisbon Treaty if it ever takes effect (below), arguably form a crude constitution. The main treaty is the EC Treaty, the successor to the original Treaty of Rome. (References here are to the EC Treaty unless stated otherwise.) The treaties are 'framework treaties' that allow the institutions to develop laws and policies and indeed other institutions for the purpose of closer integration between member states. In 1991 the European Court of Justice (ECJ), which is charged not only with securing compliance with the law but also with advancing the aims of the communities, described the EC Treaty as a 'constitutional charter' based on the rule of law. It emphasised that individuals as well as states are the subjects of community law, although in fact individuals other than those employed by the EC have only limited rights to instigate proceedings in the court (see *Opinion on the Draft Agreement on a European Economic Area* [1991] ECR 1-6084).

All EC laws and decisions must fall within the powers conferred by the Treaty and cannot go beyond 'what is necessary for achieving the objects of this Treaty' (Article 5). However by virtue of Article 308, the Council acting unanimously can create additional powers:

> if action by the Community should prove necessary to attain, in the course of the operations of the common market, one of the objectives of the Community and this treaty has not provided the necessary powers.

In some cases, notably aspects of agriculture, the EC has 'exclusive competence' in which case member states cannot legislate independently, at least once the EC has decided to intervene (see *Commission* v *UK* (1981)). In other cases there is shared power but EC law is intended to override any inconsistent domestic law (below).

There is a tension between EC law and the independence of member states. This is reflected in the voting arrangements of the Council of Ministers which is the primary lawmaking body comprising ministers from all the member states. There has been a steady movement away from a principle of unanimity, which preserves control by individual states, to majority voting, although unanimity is still required for fundamental matters such as taxation (see the Single European Act 1986; Amsterdam Treaty 1997). However the Amsterdam Treaty introduced safeguards and flexibility arrangements in favour of national governments which can opt out of certain provisions. Involvement in the European enterprise is therefore multilayered, sometimes described as 'variable geometry'. The Lisbon Treaty (below) introduces arrangements for 'enhanced cooperation' under which fewer than all states (at least nine) may 'opt in' to exercise powers. This must not undermine the internal market or economic, social or territorial cohesion.

10.2 Institutions

The Community has lawmaking, executive and judicial powers which are blended in a unique way that does not correspond to traditional notions of the separation of powers nor liberal democracy. The primary concern is to provide a balance between the interests of the Community and those of the member states. There are no clear lines of accountability. Power is divided between institutions, some of which share the same functions. Such democratic accountability as there is takes the forms of (i) a limited degree of accountability to an elected 'European Parliament' and (ii) arrangements made under the constitutions of the individual states. The balance between the different bodies, particularly in relation to the Parliament, varies according to the treaty provision under which a particular issue arises.

The main institutions are as follows.

- Council of Ministers
- European Council
- European Commission
- European Parliament
- European Court of Justice

Other important community institutions include the Court of Auditors and the Committee of Permanent Representatives (COREPER), comprising senior officials who prepare the Council's business and are very influential, and the European Central Bank (Article 8). There are also advisory and consultative bodies, notably the Economic and Social Committee and the Committee of the Regions.

10.2.1   The Council of Ministers

This is the primary lawmaking body. The Council's main function is to approve or amend laws proposed by the European Commission although in some cases it can ask the Commission to make a proposal (Article 208). It also decides the budget, adopts international treaties and is responsible for ensuring that the objectives of the Treaty are attained. The Council is made up of a minister representing each member state who must be authorised to commit the government. The membership fluctuates according to the business in hand. A president holds office for six months, each member state holding the office in turn.

The Council is biased towards national interests rather than towards an overall 'community view'. The community view is represented by the Commission (below), creating a distinct kind of separation of powers and a recipe for political tension. The way in which Council decisions are made is therefore all important. Certain decisions (albeit a shrinking category) must be unanimous, thus permitting any state to impose a veto. An increasing number of decisions are made by a 'qualified majority' whereby votes are weighted according to the population of each state (Article 205). Sometimes a simple majority suffices. According to a convention agreed in 1966 (the Luxembourg Convention), where very important interests of a member state are in issue, the Council should vote unanimously. It is however arguable that given the increasing use of qualified majority provisions in the treaties this convention is losing its political legitimacy.

10.2.2   The European Council

The European Council is a twice yearly meeting of heads of state and the President of the Commission. Its function is to 'provide the Union with the necessary impetus for its development and shall define the general political guidelines thereof' (Single European Act 1986). The Council as such has no lawmaking power but is the most important political influence on the European Union. It is particularly important in relation to foreign and security policies. It seems to tip the balance of power away from the supranational elements of Commission and Parliament towards the intergovernmental element. It makes reports to the European Parliament after its meetings and also a yearly written report on the progress of the Union.

10.2.3   The European Commission

The Commission represents the interests of the communities as such. It is required to be independent 'beyond doubt' of the member governments (Article 213). Its 27 members are chosen by agreement between the member governments and currently comprise one member from each state. Each commissioner is appointed for a renewable term of five years. Prior to the nomination of the other commissioners, the President of the Commission is nominated for a two year term by the member states after consulting the European Parliament. The President has a right to object to individual nominees (Article 217) and the appointment of the commissioners as a whole must be approved by the Parliament (Article 214(2)). The President assigns departmental responsibilities (directorates-general) to the other commissioners who are required to conform to the political direction of the President (Article 219). Individual members of the Commission cannot be dismissed during their terms of office (Article 214) but can be 'compulsorily retired' by the European Court on the ground of inability to perform their duties (Article 216). The whole Commission can be dismissed by the Parliament (Article 201).

The main functions of the Commission are:

- To propose laws or political initiatives for adoption by the Council. The Council or the Parliament can request the Commission to submit proposals (Articles 192, 208).
- To make laws itself either directly under powers conferred by the Treaty or under powers delegated to it by the Council.
- To enforce EC law against member states and the other EC institutions. The EC has no police or law enforcement agencies. It enforces the law by issuing a 'reasoned opinion', negotiating with the body concerned and if necessary initiating proceedings in the EJC (Article 226).
- To administer the EU budget.
- To negotiate with international bodies and other countries (Articles 228, 229–31).

Neither Council nor Commission are directly accountable democratically. Moreover because membership of the Council fluctuates, it is vulnerable to being dominated by the permanent officials of the Commission. The effective operation of the system therefore depends on a threefold informal network of understandings between Commission, Council and Parliament, which has a consultative role (below).

10.2.4   The European Parliament

The European Parliament does not make law but was created as an 'advisory and supervisory' body (Article 189). It injects a limited but increasing democratic element. Its seats (700 maximum) are allocated in proportion to the population of each member state (Article 190). Germany, the largest, has 99; the UK and France are second with 78; the smallest, Malta, has 5. Elections are held every five years. Since 1979 Members of the

European Parliament (MEPs) have been directly elected by residents of the member states, the detailed electoral arrangements being left to each country.

Elections to the EU Parliament in Britain are on the basis of a 'closed party list' (European Parliamentary Elections Act 2002). There are 87 seats divided into electoral regions (nine for England, one each for Scotland, Wales and Northern Ireland, with 71, 8, 5 and 3 members respectively). Each party lists its candidates in order of preference and votes can be cast for either a party or an individual standing separately. The seats are allocated in the order set out on the list by the parties in proportion to the share of the vote achieved by each party.

A Parliament lasts for five years and is required to meet at least once a year. It meets roughly once each month, alternating expensively between Strasbourg and Luxembourg. Its members vote in political groupings and not in national units. Freedom of speech and proceedings within the Parliament are protected but unlike the UK Parliament, the European Parliament does not seem to enjoy privilege against interference from the courts. The ECJ can review the legality of its activities (*Grand Duchy of Luxembourg* v *Parliament* (1983)).

The Parliament's main functions are as follows:

▷ It has the right to be consulted by the Council on many legislative proposals. Under the 'cooperation' procedure, in certain cases a unanimous vote of the Council is required to override its recommendations (EC Art. 252). In some cases under the 'co-decision' procedure (EC Art. 251) it has a right of veto.

▷ It approves the EU budget and can amend the part of the EU budget that is not devoted to compulsory functions. This means that the Parliament has little control over most of the budget and no realistic control over the level of EC spending. It can veto only the whole EU budget (Article 272), a sanction too extreme to be of practical use.

▷ It approves the appointment of the Commission, the admission of new member states and certain other important matters (Arts 7, 49, 107 (5)). It must be consulted on the choice of the Commission's president and the appointment of certain other senior officials.

▷ By a two thirds majority that is also an absolute majority of all members, it can dismiss the entire Commission but not individual members of it (Article 201). Again this sanction is too extreme to be of much use.

▷ It can question members of the Commission orally or in writing. Commissioners often appear before its committees although it has no legal power to compel this.

▷ It can hold committees of inquiry into misconduct or maladministration by other EC bodies (Article 193).

▷ It appoints an ombudsman to investigate complaints by citizens, residents or companies based in member states against EC institutions, other than the ECJ (Article 195).

▷ Any citizen, resident or company based in a member state can petition it on a matter that comes within the EC's field of competence and affects him, her or it directly (Article 194).

Apart from the Parliament's limited powers, the fragmented nature of community decision making makes parliamentary accountability weak, a problem compounded by the fact that the implementation of EC laws and policies is carried out by national governments. The lawmaking processes increasingly require a web of consultation between Parliament, Council and Commission (below). This blurs the lines of accountability. Moreover party organisation is relatively weak. These factors may encourage an ethos of consensus and self interest rather than robust accountability. The accountability of MEPs is itself weak since elections are in large constituencies and there is no relationship between an individual member and the voter. Given its limited powers, it is not surprising that the turnout for elections to the Parliament is low (around 25%).

In some legislative contexts the role of the Parliament has been significantly strengthened (Articles 251, 252). There are two procedures. Firstly, applying mainly to monetary union matters, the *cooperation* procedure permits a parliamentary input at an early stage and requires a unanimous vote of the Council if Parliament either rejects its policy or proposes amendments with which the Commission disagrees. Secondly, relating to most economic, social and environmental matters but not to agricultural matters, the *co-decision* procedure gives the Parliament a veto which it must exercise by an absolute majority. In the event of a deadlock between the Parliament and the Council, there is provision for a joint conciliation committee made up of equal numbers of each, with the Commission as mediator. If agreement still cannot be reached, the parliamentary veto stands.

10.2.5   The European Court of Justice

The ECJ comprises judges appointed by agreement between the governments of the member states. Unlike national judges they have little security of tenure, being appointed for a renewable term of six years and dismissible by the unanimous opinion of the other judges and advocates-general (Statutes of the Court Article 6). As well as the judges there are eight advocates-general who provide the ECJ with an independent opinion upon the issues in each case (Article 222). The opinion of the advocates-general is not binding on the ECJ but is highly influential.

There is one judge from each member state. Appointments must be made from those eligible for the highest judicial office in each member state and also from 'jurisconsults of recognised competence' (EC Treaty Article 223). This permits such persons as academic lawyers or social scientists to be appointed. The judges elect a president for a renewable period of three years. The ECJ sits as a 'Grand Chamber' of eleven. There is also a Court of First Instance sitting in panels of three or five. This hears cases of kinds designated by the Council (unanimity is required). There are no specific qualifications for appointment to the Court of First Instance other than being a person 'whose independence is beyond doubt and who possesses the ability required for judicial office'. The Court of Justice hears appeals on a point of law from the Court of First Instance.

The ECJ's task is to ensure that 'in the interpretation and application of the EC treaty the law is observed' (Article 220). The 'law' consists of the treaties themselves, the legislation adopted in their implementation, general principles developed by the Court, the *acquis communitaire*, which is the accumulated inheritance of community values, and general principles of law common to the member states including the ECHR (Treaty of European Union, Maastricht Treaty Article 2). There is also 'soft law' which is not binding but must be taken into account. Soft law includes 'declarations and resolutions adopted in the community framework; international agreements and agreements between member states connected with community activities' (see Europe Documents No. 1790 of 3 July, 1992, p. 3). It has been suggested that parts of the EU system are 'entrenched' in the sense that not even the Treaty itself could be altered in defiance of them. However in *Grau Gromis* (1995) the ECJ accepted that 'the Member States remain free to alter even the most fundamental parts of the Treaty'.

The main jurisdiction of the ECJ is as follows:

1. Enforcement action against member states who are accused of violating or refusing to implement European law (Article 226). These proceedings are usually brought by the Commission but can be brought by other member states subject to having raised the matter before the Commission (Article 227). The Commission first gives the member state a chance to state its case. The Court can award a lump sum or penalty payment against a member state which fails to comply with a judgment of the Court that the state concerned has failed to fulfill a treaty obligation (Article 228). The EC has no enforcement agencies of its own. The court therefore depends on national law to enforce its rulings.

2. Judicial review of the acts or the failure to act of community institutions (Articles 230, 231, 232). This can be brought by other institutions and by member states. An individual or private body can bring an action only in special circumstances where the community act in question is directed to the individual in person or is of 'direct and individual concern to him or her' (see for example *Salamander v European Parliament* (2000)). In contrast to its reluctance to permit individuals to sue the EC, the Court has been liberal in supporting individual rights against national governments.

3. Preliminary rulings on matters referred by national courts (Article 234). This is the linchpin of the ECJ's role as a constitutional court. Any national court, where it considers that a decision on the question is necessary to enable it to give judgment, may request the ECJ to give a ruling on a question of community law (Article 177). The role of the European Court is confined to that of ruling upon the question of law referred to it. It then sends the matter back to the national court for a decision on the facts in the light of the Court's ruling. A court against whose decision there is no judicial remedy in national law (that is, the highest appeal court or any other court against which there is no right of appeal or review) must make such a request (Article 177). UK courts are required to follow decisions of the ECJ (European Communities Act 1972 s.3(1)). The power to give preliminary rulings does not apply to the Court of First Instance.

It may be difficult to decide whether a reference can or should be made. The parties have no say in the matter (*Bulmer* v *Bollinger* (1974)). A court need not make a reference if it thinks the point is irrelevant or 'reasonably clear and free from doubt' (the *acte-claire* doctrine) nor if 'substantially' the same point has already been decided by the ECJ (see *CILFIT Srl* v *Ministro della Sanita* (1983)). In *R* v *International Stock Exchange ex parte Else (1982) Ltd* (1993) at 422, Bingham LJ said that 'if community law is critical to the decision the court should refer it if it has any real doubt'. The court can take into account the convenience of the parties, the expense of the action and the workload of the European Court (ibid.) (*Van Duyn* v *The Home Office* [1974] 3 All ER 178 at 1986; *Customs and Excise Commissioners* v *Aps Samex* [1983] 1 All ER 1042 at 1055–6).

It may also be difficult to decide whether the law is sufficiently clear to entitle the UK court to decide for itself. Much depends upon how English legal culture responds to the different reasoning methods of the ECJ, that is, whether the UK court approaches the problem by way of our traditional 'literal' approach to questions of interpretation or takes a broader approach, focusing on the 'spirit' as opposed to the letter of the law in the continental manner (below). The same applies to the question of whether a decision in the matter is 'necessary' for the resolution of the case. We may not know this until we know what the relevant community law means.

The ECJ has no jurisdiction over most 'second pillar' matters (foreign and security policy) since apart from immigration these are political matters for the EU (above). Its jurisdiction over 'third pillar' matters (cooperation in criminal matters) depends on the consent of the state concerned but it has no jurisdiction in respect of the operations of the police and other law enforcement agencies. However in other areas, for example freedom of trade, the ECJ can require the police to give priority to EC aims (see *R v Chief Constable of Sussex ex parte International Traders Ferry* [1999] 1 All ER 109 at 155).

It is often said that the constitutional glue that holds together the communities and the member states in a constitutional framework is the rule of law represented by the ECJ. The Treaty itself is not explicit as to the relationship between the ECJ and the law of the member states but the ECJ has developed principles that have enabled it to favour EC law. According to some commentators the ECJ has, in defiance of the normal values of judicial impartiality and democracy, taken upon itself the political agenda of promoting the European enterprise. It has attempted to enlist national courts by requiring them to defer to EC law and by conferring on individuals European law rights that are enforceable in national courts. On the other hand it has injected some democratic principles into EC law, albeit in a sporadic fashion.

10.3 Community Law and National Law

Sections 2 and 3 of the European Communities Act 1972 require UK courts to apply EC law in accordance with the decisions and general principles of the ECJ. We saw in Chapter 9 that the doctrine of parliamentary supremacy has been modified by the 1972 Act to the extent that a binding EC law overrides an inconsistent UK statute unless perhaps the statute specifically states that it is to prevail. There are different ways of approaching the relationship between EC law and national law. One is to regard EC law as a distinct system in which the UK courts must participate by applying European methods as if they were federal courts. On this basis the UK court dealing with an EC matter is effectively a European court. Another would be to regard EC law as 'processed' into English law under the authority of the European Communities Act 1972, to be approached in much the same way as other legislation in the light of the strict reasoning methods of English law. The choice between these two approaches influences the extent to which the courts are willing to subordinate UK law to EC ideas.

There seems to be no consistent practice among the English judges and examples of both approaches can be found. In *Mayne v Ministry of Agriculture, Fisheries and Food* (2001) it was held that UK regulations implementing an EC Directive do not apply to future amendments of the Directive unless they are clearly worded as doing so. However in *Berkeley v Secretary of State for the Environment* (2000) Lord Hoffmann emphasised the importance of giving effect to EC laws' environmental purposes.

There is also a 'spillover effect' whereby rights initially established for European purposes are later extended to domestic contexts on the basis that it would be unjust for domestic law to be more restrictive than EC law (for example *M v Home Office* (1993): interim relief against the Crown). More generally it has been said that involvement with

Europe has accelerated the tendency to approach the interpretation of legislation from a broad purposive perspective as opposed to the narrow linguistic perspective traditionally favoured by the English courts (Lord Steyn in *R (Quintavalle)* v *Secretary of State for Health* (2003)[21]).

It is therefore important to know which EC laws are binding on UK courts. Some EC measures take effect 'without further enactment' (European Communities Act 1972 s.2(1)) and are automatically part of UK law. This is determined by EC law itself (below). In other cases there must be a conversion to UK law, usually in the form of a statutory instrument (ibid. s.2(2)). In the latter case ordinary domestic law applies. Certain measures, including taxation, the creation of new criminal offences and retrospective laws, can only be implemented by an Act of Parliament (ibid. Schedule 2). The relationship between Parliamentary supremacy and EC law was discussed in Chapter 9.

The main kinds of EC legal instrument are as follows (Article 249):

- **The Treaty:** Treaty provisions are sometimes directly enforceable in the UK courts (below).
- **Regulations:** These are general rules which apply to all member states and persons. All regulations are 'directly applicable' and as such are automatically binding on UK courts except where a particular regulation is of a character that is inherently unsuitable for judicial enforcement.
- **Directives:** A Directive as such is not automatically binding but is sometimes so (below). It is a requirement to achieve a given objective but leaves it to the individual states to specify how that objective is to be achieved by altering their own laws. A Directive may be addressed to all states or particular states. A time limit is usually specified for implementing the Directive.
- **Decisions:** These are addressed to specific persons or organisations including member states and are 'binding in their entirety on those to whom they are addressed'.
- **Opinions and Recommendations:** These do not have binding force. However the ECJ has power under Article 228(6) to give an opinion at an early stage of a matter, for example in relation to a proposed treaty.

10.3.1   Direct Applicability and Direct Effect

'Direct effect' must be distinguished from 'direct applicability', which applies only to EC regulations. Regulations are always binding whereas 'direct effect' depends upon the quality of the particular EC instrument. Where the direct effect doctrine applies, the national court must give a remedy which as far as possible puts the plaintiff in the same position as if the Directive had been properly implemented. This might for example require national restrictions to be set aside, national taxes to be ignored or national rules that are stricter than a Directive covering the same ground to be set aside (see for example *Defrenne* v *SABENA* (1976): retirement restrictions; *Pubblico Ministero* v *Ratti* (1979): excessive labelling requirements). It has been suggested that the ECJ developed the direct effect doctrine in order to make use of domestic law enforcement agencies as a means of compensating for the weak enforcement provision offered at EC level through the Commission (see Craig, 1992; Weatherill, 1995, pp. 101ff.).

Direct effect applies to the Treaty and Directives. A Treaty provision that has direct effect is enforceable against anyone upon whom its provisions impose an obligation. Directives however can be enforced only 'vertically', that is, against a public authority or 'emanation of the state', but not 'horizontally' against a private person (see *Marshall* v *Southampton Area Health Authority (No. 1)* (1986); *Faccini Dori* v *Recreb* (1995)). The reason seems to be that the state, which as we saw above has the primary duty to implement a Directive, cannot rely on its failure to do so; an argument that it would be unfair to apply to a private body. It also follows that the state cannot rely on an unimplemented Directive against an individual (see *Wychavon DC* v *Secretary of State* (1994)).

For the purpose of direct effect, any public body seems to be regarded as an emanation of the state (*Marshall* v *Southampton Area Health Authority (No. 1)* (1986)). However the meaning of public body varies with the context (see Chapters 18 and 19). For this purpose a public body must (i) exercise functions in the public interest subject to the control of the state and (ii) have special legal powers not available to individuals or ordinary companies (see *Foster* v *British Gas* (1990)). All the activities of such a body, even those governed by private law, for example employment contracts, seem to be subject to direct effect. The privatised utilities of gas, electricity and water are probably emanations of the state but it is unlikely that the privatised railway companies would be since although they are subject to state regulation and receive state subsidy, they have no statutory obligation to perform public duties nor significant special powers (see *Doughty* v *Rolls-Royce* (1992)).

To have direct effect an instrument must be 'justiciable', meaning that it is of a kind that is capable of being interpreted and enforced by a court without trespassing outside its proper judicial role. In essence the legal obligation created by the instrument must be certain enough for a court to handle. The tests usually applied are as follows (see *Van Duyn* v *The Home Office* (1974)):

1. The instrument must be 'clear, precise and unconditional'. It must not give the member state substantial discretion as to how to give effect to it. For example in *Francovich* v *Italy* (1993) a Directive concerning the treatment of employees in an insolvency was not unconditional because it left it to member states to decide which bodies should guarantee the payments required by the Directive (see also *Gibson* v *East Riding of Yorkshire DC* (2000): Directive about paid leave did not make clear what counted as working time). However the fact that a Directive leaves it to the state to choose between alternative methods of enforcement does not prevent it from having direct effect if the substance of the right is clear from the Directive alone (*Marshall* v *Southampton Area Health Authority (No. 2)* (1993)). The European Court interprets the precision test liberally, bearing in mind that apparent uncertainty could be cured by a reference to the court (see Craig, 1992).
2. The instrument must be intended to confer 'rights'. A problem arises here in respect of purely 'public' interests such as some environmental concerns like wildlife conservation. It is arguable that a body with a public law right sufficient to give standing in national law to challenge the government's action like a pressure group (Chapter 18), could rely on the direct effect doctrine. In other words the 'rights' requirement is no more than an aspect of the general principle that the claimant must have a genuine interest.
3. The time limit prescribed by a Directive for its implementation must have expired.

10.3.2   Indirect Effect

Even where a European law lacks direct effect, the courts must still take account of it. Article 10 requires member states to 'take all appropriate measures' to fulfil European obligations and Article 249 requires that the objectives of Directives be given effect. In *Marleasing* v *La Comercial Internacional de Alimentacion* (1992) the court held that all domestic law, whether passed before or after the relevant community law, must be interpreted 'so far as possible' in the light of the wording and purposes of the Directive in order to achieve the result pursued by the latter. However *Marleasing* involved a law (in the Spanish civil code) that could be interpreted in different ways. It is uncertain therefore whether clear, unambiguous domestic law must give way to a European rule. In *Webb* v *EMO Cargo (UK) Ltd* (1992) Lord Keith said that *Marleasing* applies to laws passed at any time provided that their language is not distorted. In *Ghaidan* v *Mendoza* (2004) [45] which concerned an analogous provision in the Human Rights Act 1998 (Chapter 19) Lord Steyn accepted that *Marleasing* created a strong obligation (compare *Webb* v *EMO Cargo (UK) Ltd* (1992)). Sympathetic interpretation of EC law may avoid confrontation between EC law and the domestic principle of Parliamentary supremacy which was discussed in Chapter 9.

10.3.3   State Liability

Even where a Directive does not have direct effect, an individual may be able to sue the government for damages for failing to implement it. This was established by the ECJ in *Francovich* v *Italy* (above) where the Directive was too vague to have direct effect. Nevertheless the court held that damages could be awarded against the Italian government in an Italian court. The court's reasoning was based upon the principle of giving full effect to EC rights. This is a powerful and far reaching notion. In order to obtain damages:

1. The Directive must confer rights for the benefit of individuals
2. The content of those rights must be determined from the provisions of the Directive (a degree of certainty is therefore needed)
3. There must be a causal link between breach of the Directive and the damage suffered (see also *R* v *Secretary of State for Transport ex parte Factortame (No. 4)* (1996), *(No. 5)* (2000)).

In domestic law damages cannot normally be obtained against the government for misusing its statutory powers and duties (see *Barrett* v *Enfield Borough Council* (1999)). The *Francovich* principle which was subsequently accepted by the House of Lords (*Kirklees MBC* v *Wickes Building Supplies* (1992)) is therefore of great significance. *Francovich* leaves the procedures for recovering damages to national courts but any conditions must not make recovery impossible or excessively difficult. There may also be a developing principle that legal remedies must be equally effective in each member state (below). The *Francovich* principle also avoids the 'vertical' enforcement rule (above). Failure to implement a Directive against a private person would entitle the plaintiff to sue the government.

10.3.4   Effective Remedies

There is a general obligation to give effective remedies to protect rights in EC law. The courts originally took the view that this obligation merely required that the remedies available in European cases should be no worse than in equivalent domestic cases. However it now appears that the courts must sometimes provide better remedies in relation to European rights than would be available domestically. As we saw in Chaper 9, in *R* v *Secretary of State ex parte Factortame (No. 2)* (1991) the House of Lords granted an injunction to prevent a statute being enforced in order to protect an EC right (see also *Johnston* v *Chief Constable of Royal Ulster Constabulary* (1986)).

It remains to be seen how much freedom a member state has in adjusting its remedies to its own circumstances. For example in *Factortame* the court still had a discretion whether to issue the injunction based upon the justice and convenience of the circumstances. The English courts are very cautious about issuing interim injunctions and will do so only as a last resort. The governing principle is that the remedy must be adequate and effective, but member states can choose among different possible ways of achieving the object of a Directive.

10.4   Democracy and the European Union

Although a democratic government is a requirement of membership, perhaps the most fundamental constitutional problem of the EU is the 'democratic deficit'. As we have seen, powers are fragmented between the Council and the Commission, with the latter as the driving force. Neither of these institutions is directly accountable democratically. The European Parliament has a significant role but has limited powers. Some of the founders of the European communities, such as Jean Monnet (1888–1979), a businessman, were paternalistic idealists who had little interest in democratic processes, assuming perhaps that the 'European spirit' could gradually be infused into public opinion by example and propaganda.

Although the goals of the EU have become progressively wider, they are not compatible with the premise that democracy is about governing with the consent of the people and cannot be tied to any particular substantive goals. For example Article 10 of the EC Treaty provides that:

> member states shall take all appropriate measures, whether general or particular, to ensure fulfilment of the obligations arising out of this Treaty or resulting from actions taken by the institutions of the Community. They shall facilitate the achievement of the Community's tasks. They shall abstain from any measure that could jeopardise the attainment of the objectives of the Treaty.

This seems to impose an obligation to place EU goals above democracy (see *Internationale Handelsgesellschaft Case* [1970] ECR 1125 at 1135). It has been described as imposing a moral obligation on member states and even as 'the sort of spiritual and essentially vacuous clause that is more commonly found in constitutional orders such as that of Nazi Germany' (Ward, 1996, p. 65).

The EU relies mainly on the democratic processes of the member states. In the UK proposed EC legislation is scrutinised by Parliament, although it may not have any power of veto or amendment. Council and Commission documents are made available to both Houses, ministerial statements are made after Council meetings, questions can be asked, and in addition to the ordinary departmental committees there are select committees in each House to monitor EU activity. The House of Lords Select Committee is particularly well regarded and in addition to scrutinising new legislation makes wide ranging general reports on the EU.

There may be a convention analogous to the 'Ponsonby Rule' for treaties: that no UK minister should consent to an EC legislative proposal before a debate in Parliament has taken place unless there are special reasons which must be explained to the House as soon as possible. However this is not consistently followed. In practice the volume of EC legislation is greater than the time available and much European business is conducted without MPs having the opportunity to consider it in advance. Ministers in their capacity as members of the Council are probably not bound by resolutions of the House of Commons. There are three specific democratic constraints:

1. By virtue of the European Parliamentary Elections Act 1978, no treaty which provides for an increase in the powers of the European Parliament can be ratified by the UK without the approval of an Act of Parliament (s.6). It is perhaps ironic that this provides protection only against the elected element of the EC.
2. A treaty that alters the founding treaties of the European Union must be ratified by statute (European Union (Amendment) Act 2008, s.5)
3. A Minister of the Crown may not support a decision in the Council of Ministers to alter its voting arrangements without the approval of Parliament (ibid. s.6)

As regards the executive, accountability is weak in that there is no government department specifically dealing with the EU. However the main departments have European sections. The Foreign Office acts as a coordinating body and a junior minister is responsible for 'Europe'. Thus there is a complex network of negotiating machinery involving the competing interests of the UK and the EU, the UK and other member states and interdepartmental rivalries, with Parliament on the sidelines. In keeping with the ethos of UK government, the operation of EU matters relies on informal contacts between unelected officials.

Illustrating the theme of multilayered government, the devolved regimes of Scotland and Wales have some direct involvement at European level. Within their allocated subject areas the devolved governments are responsible for implementing EC law. Although having no right to attend, Scottish and Welsh ministers have sometimes attended Council meetings on behalf of the UK government. Scottish and Welsh ministers have direct representation at lower levels, for example on the Committee of the Regions. Both devolved legislatures have European committees (see Mather, 'The Impact of European Integration', in O'Neill, 2004).

Democracy depends on wide access to information about governmental activity. Article 255 of the Treaty and Regulation No. 1049/2001 have created a limited public right of access to European Parliament, Council and Commission documents including documents both drawn up by them and received by them. This applies to any citizen of the EU (a citizen of a member state) and to any person residing in or having a registered office in a member state. There is however a long list of exceptions relating to most important community activities (Article 4). They include security, defence and military matters, international relations, financial, monetary or economic policy, privacy and the integrity of the individual. Commercial interests, legal matters, inspections, investigations and audits are also excepted, subject to a public interest test. Internal documents are excepted if disclosure would seriously undermine the decision making process, again subject to a public interest test. This is a familiar reason for claiming secrecy and raises the suspicion of self protection (see Chapter 21). No specific enforcement measures are provided.

The Court has taken more a vigorous attitude to the right to information. In *World Wildlife Fund for Nature* v *Commission* (1997) which concerned information about Commission policy on environmental protection, the Court of First Instance held that although at the time there was only a voluntary undertaking to disclose information, having adopted it the Commission is bound to respect it. The Court also held that exceptions should be interpreted restrictively so as not to inhibit the aim of transparency and the Commission must give reasons for refusing to disclose information. The Court has also refused to accept blanket immunity for particular kinds of information and required the Commission to balance the public right to know against a clear public interest in secrecy in the particular case (see *JT's Corporation* v *Commission* (2000); *Van der Val* v *Netherlands* (2000)).

10.5 Federalism and the European Union

The EU is difficult to fit into a coherent constitutional structure. In particular there is a conflict between the ideal of European integration and that of national identity (Article 6). This tension suggests the possibility of a federal model since, as we saw in Chapter 6, federalism is intended to reconcile this kind of tension by marking out spheres of independence for each unit. While some idealists, notably Jean Monnet, pursued the agenda of a federal Europe, the thrust of the original initiative was towards the pragmatic integration of economic policy as the basis of evolution towards what the treaties call 'ever closer union' but with no agreed final destination. The Lisbon Treaty emphasises that the powers of the European Union are conferred on it 'upwards' by the member states. Indeed the German Supreme Court has held that ultimate power remains with the member states (see *Brunner* v *European Union Treaty* (1994)).

At present the EU has perhaps the most important feature of federalism in that the powers of the communities are limited by the Treaty, with member states having residual independence. On the one hand the general commitment to the supremacy of EC law would allow indefinite expansion of the EU thus producing a devolved regime. On the other hand the EU has no elected government or enforcement arm of its own. It cannot raise taxes and depends on the courts and the executives of the member states to enforce its will.

There is a concept of citizenship of the EU that applies to citizens of the member states (Article 17) but this gives only limited rights – namely free movement within the EU – within the requirements of the Treaty, and the right to stand or vote in local government elections and in elections to the European Parliament on the same terms as nationals.

Individual states can sometimes depart from normal community requirements (such as opting out of EC laws on the basis of special circumstances). There are also transitional provisions ('multispeed' or 'variable geometry' arrangements) in which a core of members participate, leaving others to opt in later, if at all (such as monetary union, social welfare provisions and immigration arrangements). In these respects the EU is more like a confederation or an intergovernmental body rather than a genuine supranational body.

On the other hand its laws are directly enforceable against individuals. The EU is therefore best regarded as a unique legal order not reducible into other forms.

The tension between the interests of member states and those of the EU is expressed through the concept of 'subsidiarity'. Introduced by the Maastricht Treaty (TEU Article 2; EC Treaty Article 5), subsidiarity is a vague term with no agreed meaning. It can therefore be enlisted to serve different political interests. Historically it is an authoritarian doctrine used by the Catholic Church to legitimise a hierarchical power structure. Subsidiarity can also be regarded as a pluralist liberal principle that decisions should be made at a level as close as possible to those whom they affect.

The version of subsidiarity in the EC Treaty (Article 5) concerns the distribution of powers between the Community and national governments:

> In areas that do not fall within its exclusive competence, the Community shall take action, in accordance with the principle of subsidiarity, only if and so far as the objectives of the proposed action cannot be sufficiently achieved by the Member States and can therefore, by reason of the scale or effects of the proposed action, be better achieved by the Community . . . Any action by the Community shall not go beyond what is necessary to achieve the objects of this Treaty.

This formulation is vague (for example the notions of 'sufficient' and 'better' and the non sequitur between them). It is unlikely to be directly enforceable in law but may operate at a political level, thereby indirectly influencing the law. However there is another definition of subsidiarity in Article 2 of the Maastricht Treaty that is not only internally contradictory but seems to clash with that in Article 5, namely, 'a new stage in the process of creating an ever closer union in which decisions are taken as near as possible to the citizen' (however Article 2 seems to give priority to the Article 5 version). Moreover doctrines such as those of the supremacy of EC law and pre-emption are difficult to reconcile with subsidiarity.

10.6 The Lisbon Treaty

The Lisbon Treaty (2007, CM 7294) is an attempt to rationalise and consolidate the European Union as a supranational organisation. It replaces the so called Constitutional Treaty which was rejected in 2005 by referendums in France and Germany. Illustrating perhaps the political and symbolic sensitivity of the idea of a written constitution, the Lisbon Treaty reproduces the main provisions of the abortive constitution minus its constitutional rhetoric. Indeed it is drafted as a complex amending treaty overlaying previous treaties. The Lisbon Treaty is intended to strengthen the European Union as an international organisation and to streamline its decision making processes in view of the large increase in its membership. The main changes made by the Lisbon Treaty are as follows (see also House of Lords European Union Committee 10th Report (2007–8).

1. It creates a figurehead leader in the shape of a President of the European Council to be elected by the Council itself for up to two-and-a-half-year terms.
2. It creates a 'High Representative' for foreign and security policy appointed by the Council and replacing two existing officers.
3. It alters the arrangements for voting in the European Council and in the Council of Ministers so as to make it more difficult for individual states to block measures (from 2014).

4. It reduces the size of the European Commission (effective from 2014) thereby weakening state representation.
5. There is some concession to democracy in that the treaty provides for increased involvement by member Parliaments in relation to proposals for European measures. It also increases the policy areas in which the European Parliament has powers in relation to proposed legislation ('co-decision' procedure). However given other pressures on the business of Parliament and the political weakness of its membership it is unlikely that this would make significant difference in practice.
6. It introduces a cumbersome procedure for managing the withdrawal of a member state from the European Union. There is currently no provision for withdrawal at all.

All member states must ratify the Lisbon Treaty. The requirements for ratification differ in the various states. Ireland held a referendum in 2008 which rejected the treaty; the Lisbon Treaty thus remains in limbo. The UK government refused to allow a referendum and the treaty was given parliamentary approval under the European Union (Amendment) Act 2008. Subject to that, ratification is a matter for the royal prerogative which means by convention the Prime Minister. The Treaty has been ratified.

Summary

▷ The EU, and within it the EC, exists to integrate key economic and increasingly social policies of member states with the aim of providing an internal 'common market', creating a powerful European political unit and reducing the risk of war within Europe. The constitution of the EU is an evolving one aimed at increasing integration between its member states. The EU has three main policy areas or 'pillars', these being economic development, common foreign and security policy and cooperation in justice and home affairs. Only the first pillar, together with immigration matters, is regulated by law, most laws being made by the EC. EC law raises conflicts between democratic values and the existing goals of the community, between the independence of member states and the integrationist goals of the EU and between the different legal cultures of the common law and civil law traditions.

▷ EC law has been incorporated into UK law by the European Communities Act 1972, which makes certain EC laws automatically binding in the UK, requires other laws to be enacted in UK law either by statute or by regulations made under the 1972 Act, and obliges UK courts to decide cases consistently with principles laid down by the European Court of Justice. In some cases questions of law must be referred to the ECJ. The ECJ has developed the role of constitutional court and is sometimes regarded as being a driving force for integrationist policies that enlist national courts in the project of giving primacy to European law.

▷ The other main policy and lawmaking bodies are the Council of Ministers, which is the main lawmaking body; the European Council of Heads of State, responsible for policy direction; the appointed European Commission, which proposes laws, makes some laws, supervises the implementation of policy, carries out research and takes enforcement action; and the elected European Parliament, which is mainly a consultative and supervisory body but has certain powers of veto. Taken together these bodies are meant to balance the interests of national governments and those of the EU as such, but not to follow strict separation of power ideas. There is only limited democratic input into the EC lawmaking process.

▶ Law and policy making power are divided between the Council and the Commission, with the Commission as the driving force but the Council having the ultimate control. Voting sometimes has to be unanimous but there is increasing use of qualified majorities where voting is weighed in favour of the more populous states. The Parliament does not initiate laws but has certain powers of veto and can sometimes suggest amendments.

▶ Not all EC law is directly binding on member states. 'Regulations' are binding. Other laws including the Treaty itself are binding if they satisfy the criteria of 'direct effectiveness' created by the ECJ. Directives must also satisfy the criteria of 'direct effectiveness' and can have direct effect only against public bodies (vertical direct effect) but not against private bodies (horizontal direct effect). However the concept of 'indirect effect', which requires domestic law to be interpreted so as to conform to EC law, may alleviate this. The government may also be liable in damages if its failure properly to implement an EC law damages an individual in relation to rights created by the EC law in question.

▶ The doctrine of 'subsidiarity' is ambivalent. It seems to have little concrete legal content and can be applied in favour of giving greater power to the member states or reinforcing the power of central European Union bodies.

▶ Membership of the EU may not have fundamentally altered the doctrine of parliamentary supremacy, but the UK courts have accepted that a statute which conflicts with a binding EC rule must be 'disapplied'. There is a general political principle – perhaps an emerging convention – in favour of the supremacy of EU law.

Exercises

10.1 Explain the constitutional structure of the European Union. To what extent is it federal?

10.2 It is a requirement of membership of the EU that the member state must have a democratic form of government but it has often been remarked that the EU would not satisfy the conditions for membership of itself. Do you agree?

10.3 What powers does the UK Parliament possess in relation to EU policy?

10.4 To what extent are (a) the Council of Ministers and (b) the European Commission accountable for their decisions?

10.5 Explain the relationship between UK courts and the European Court of Justice. To what extent is the ECJ a constitutional court?

10.6 (i) What is the purpose of the direct effect doctrine and what are its main limitations?
(ii) An EC Directive requires member states to ensure that compensation is paid to part time workers who are made redundant. The compensation must be paid by the employer. The UK has not implemented the Directive. Jeff, a part time employee of Dodgy Burgers plc, is made redundant. His employer refuses to pay him compensation. Advise Jeff as to his legal rights, if any.

10.7 Why did the Lisbon Treaty require Parliamentary approval? Is this an effective safeguard for democracy in the UK?

Further reading

Brazier, A. (ed.) (2004) *Parliament, Politics and Law Making*, London, Hansard Society, Chapter 9.

Craig, P. (1992) 'Once Upon a Time in the West: Direct Effect and the Federalization of EEC Law', *Oxford Journal of Legal Studies* 12:453.

Craig, P. (1997) 'Directives: Direct Effect, Indirect Effect and the Construction of National Legislation', *European Law Review* 519.

Craig, P. (2004) 'Britain in the European Union', in Jowell, J. and Oliver, D. (eds) *The Changing Constitution* (5th edn) Oxford University Press.

Harden, I. and McGlynn, C. (1996) 'Democracy and the European Union', *Political Quarterly* 32.

Harlow, C. (2003) 'European Governance and Accountability', in Bamforth, M. and Leyland, P. (eds) *Public Law in a Multi-Layered Constitution*, Oxford, Hart Publishing.

Hartley, T. (1996) 'The European Court, Judicial Objectivity and the Constitution of the European Union', *Law Quarterly Review* 112:411.

Munro, C. (1999) *Studies in Constitutional Law* (2nd edn) London, Butterworth, Chapter 6.

O'Neill, M. (ed.) (2004) *Devolution and British Politics*, London, Pearson, Chapter 11.

Rogers, R. and Walters, R. (2004) 'Parliament and Europe', in *How Parliament Works*, London, Pearson, Chapter 10.

Shaw, J. and More, G. (eds) (1995) *The New Legal Dynamics of European Union*, Oxford, Clarendon Press.

Walter, N. (1995) 'European Constitutionalism and European Integration', *Public Law* 266.

Ward, I. (1996) *A Critical Introduction to European Law*, London, Butterworth, Chapters 1, 2.

Weiler, J. (1993) 'Journey to an Unknown Destination: A Retrospective and Prospective of the European Court of Justice in the Arena of Political Integration', *Journal of Common Market Studies* 31:417.

Background reading

Budge, I., Crewe, I., McKay, D. and Newton, K. (2004) *The New British Politics* (3rd edn) London, Pearson, Chapters 8, 9.

Gallagher, M., Laver, M. and Mair, P. (2004) *Representative Government in Modern Europe*, New York, McGraw-Hill, Chapter 5.

Jones, B., Kavanagh, D., Moran, M. and Norton, P. (2004) *Politics UK* (5th edn) London, Pearson, Chapter 31.

Part II

Government Institutions

Chapter 11

Parliament:
constitutional position

> The virtue, spirit and essence of a House of Commons consists in its being the express image of the feelings of the nation. It was not instituted to be a control on the people. It was designed as a control for the people.
> (Edmund Burke)
>
> The minister, whoever he at any time may be, touches it as with an opium wand and it sleeps obedience. (Thomas Paine, *The Rights of Man*, Pt. 2)

Key words

- ▶ Executive domination
- ▶ Sustaining and controlling government
- ▶ Mixed constitution: the need for a second chamber
- ▶ Freedom of speech
- ▶ Tension between separation of powers and rule of law
- ▶ Conflicts of interest

11.1 Introduction

Parliament comprises two Houses, the House of Lords and the House of Commons. The supreme lawmaker is the Queen in Parliament. The word 'Parliament', which meant a parley or conference, entered into official language about the middle of the thirteenth century. It described a formal meeting summoned by the King between himself and the elite members of society for the purposes of advising him and legitimising his tax demands on the people. A dominant feature of the contemporary UK constitution is its extreme parliamentary system. This is derived from conventions under which the leader of the government (the Prime Minister) is chosen by the House of Commons, the executive depends on the support of the Commons and all ministers must be members of Parliament. The Crown can make law only in conjunction with Parliament and by convention cannot veto any law duly presented by Parliament. The House of Commons controls government finance and the Bank of England, the state bank, is underpinned by Parliament.

The traditional function of Parliament has been to represent the people against the Crown. Its formal functions, as they have gradually emerged, are to enact legislation, sustain the government by choosing and removing it and providing it with money, scrutinise government action and redress the grievances of the people. This reflects Mill's ideal of representative democracy as government by experts subject to control by the people. These functions may well conflict, particularly as in our parliamentary system ministers who head the executive are also MPs. Parliament is also therefore a recruiting ground for ministers and a process for legitimating executive action. Most laws are proposed by the executive so that the activities of Parliament are reactive. Parliament acts as a mechanical way of translating the popular vote into the appointment of an executive, since by convention whoever commands a majority in the House of Commons is entitled to form a government. As we saw in Chapter 5, owing to the distortions of the electoral system, a popular majority does not necessarily translate into a parliamentary majority.

Although the legal supremacy of Parliament probably remains in place, its political power and prestige have declined in recent years. This is the result of an accumulation of factors – some new, others long standing – which together raise doubts as to whether Parliament is still the most important institution of the constitution. These factors include:

- the increasing influence of international lawmaking which in practice restricts national legislatures. Examples are the EU, NATO, the UN, and the ECHR
- at the other end of the scale, the devolution of powers to the nations within the UK, albeit to differing extents
- the increase in the power of the executive
- powerful political parties funded by business interests
- a more assertive and activist judiciary.

The UK version of the parliamentary system gives exceptionally strong powers to the executive, particularly the Prime Minister. Although in law omnipotent, Parliament is correspondingly politically weak. The main reason for the dominance of the executive is the strong two-party adversarial system that has developed in UK politics since the early twentieth century. During the twentieth century the present practice of highly disciplined parties emerged, in which internal differences are suppressed at least when it comes to supporting the leadership in a parliamentary vote. One reason for this is that most MPs are paid professional politicians dependent on party conformity. Another is the media driven nature of modern politics which favours charismatic leadership.

Thus Parliament is the setting of a party/market democracy (Chapter 2). Legal arrangements support this, in that the first past the post voting system which applies to parliamentary elections supports strong large parties by making it difficult for small parties to win seats. The party leaders can pressurise their supporters in the House of Commons partly because, like the eighteenth century aristocracy, they can influence the choice of election candidates and partly because there are many opportunities of patronage through appointments as ministers or to influential committees. Control of parliamentary business and the timetable in the House of Commons are largely in the hands of the government party. Each party has a highly organised 'whip' system dedicated to enforcing party discipline and persuading members to vote in the required way. In some circumstances, usually where matters of personal conscience are at issue, there may be a 'free' vote.

Executive domination of Parliament must not be overstated. Parliament is a separate institution with large powers of its own and it could overcome the executive were it so minded. Its current subservience is voluntary. Government proposals must be publicly explained in Parliament and ministers must justify their decisions in public if required to do so by Parliament. The independent Speaker, who chairs the sittings of the Commons, exercises a certain moderating influence, being responsible for ensuring fair debate and protecting the interests of minorities. The Opposition, the second largest party in the

Commons, is a formal institution protected by the law of parliamentary procedure – a government and Prime Minister in waiting. It has a duty to oppose government policy, short of frustrating the governmental process, and forms a 'shadow Cabinet' ready to take office.

While there is no law to this effect, it is often claimed that an MP has a duty to exercise independent judgement on behalf of all his or her constituents and not merely those who voted for him or her (Chapter 2). However in practice many MPs mechanically support the party that sponsors them. Under the general law, although party political matters can be taken into account it is unlawful for a member of a public body at least when exercising statutory powers to be bound by a prior commitment to party policy (*see R v Greenwich LBC ex parte Lovelace* (1991) and Chapter 14). In the case of an MP however, parliamentary privilege prevents the courts from intervening (below).

There is funding designated by the House of Commons ('Short Money', named after the MP who proposed it) for the parliamentary work of opposition parties. This is determined by a formula based on the number of seats and votes the party received in the previous election. There is also funding for the Opposition leader's office. The funding of the House of Commons and of individual MPs' salaries and support is also determined by the House as a separate charge on public funds and so is relatively independent of the executive. In practice however recent opposition parties have been extremely weak as a result of internal conflicts and failure to recover from damaging election defeats.

11.2 The House of Lords

In common with most larger countries Parliament is bicameral. The purpose of a second chamber is to act as a check on the main chamber by providing an opportunity for second thoughts. The composition and respective powers of the two chambers of course differ from country to country. In the UK the appointed House of Lords is subordinate to the elected House of Commons. This is secured by the Parliament Acts 1911 and 1949 and by conventions, notably the 'Salisbury Convention' which requires the Lords to accept proposals contained in the government's election manifesto. The House of Lords should also defer to the Commons on matters of central government finance since this is a matter between the Crown and the Commons. The government has accepted the recommendation of the Parliamentary Joint Committee on Conventions (*Conventions of the UK Parliament* Cm 6997 (2006)) that these conventions be codified. In relation to reform there is at least a consensus that the powers of the upper house should remain as they are now.

The House of Lords is unusual among second chambers in the following respects:

- Its members are not elected. Most of them are appointed by the Crown (in practice the Prime Minister) including twelve serving Law Lords, on the advice of the Prime Minister. There are also 26 senior Church of England bishops. Thus in many cases membership is compulsory, although attendance is not.
- Members other than the bishops sit for life. Membership is a legal right on appointment as a Peer and can be removed only by Statute.
- Until the House of Lords Act 1999, the bulk of members were hereditary peers whose descendents enjoyed permanent seats. As the first stage of a reform programme, the 1999 Act removed all but 92 hereditary peers.

- Members receive no payment other than expenses.
- Members have no constituencies and are accountable to no one. About 25 per cent of the members are independent of political parties.
- By long standing practice, the proceedings of the House are regulated by the House itself without formal rules or disciplinary sanctions, members being treated as bound by 'personal honour'.

Being undemocratic, the position of the House is controversial. It could be variously depicted as a constitutional abomination, a valuable ingredient of a mixed constitution or a historical survival that, from a pragmatic perspective, might nevertheless have some useful functions. The Parliament Act 1911 (below) removed the power of the House of Lords to veto most legislation. Its preamble stated that this was a precursor to replacing it by a second chamber 'constituted on a popular basis' and for 'limiting and defining' its powers. However there has been no agreement as to how that should be done. In 2000 the Wakeham Report (*A House for the Future: Royal Commission on the House of Lords*, Cm 4534) endorsed the Conservative view that the House of Lords should remain subordinate to the Commons (thus ensuring the clear democratic accountability of the government), that it should provide constitutional checks and balances and that it should provide a parliamentary voice for the 'nations and regions of the United Kingdom'. Despite numerous consultations, government papers and parliamentary debates and reports (see White Paper, *House of Lords Reform* (2007) Cm 7027, for a useful history) no agreed proposals for further reform of the House of Lords have emerged – a pattern that has been repeated since 1911. The most recent government proposal is that there should be a mainly elected House of Lords with the same powers and role as the present House (White Paper 14 July 2008 Cm 7438). However this will not be taken further, if at all, until after the next general election due in 2010.

11.3 The Meeting of Parliament

A crucial check over the executive is that Parliament must terminate after five years. The government must submit to a general election and by convention must resign if it loses its majority. This statutory provision (Parliament Act 1911 ss.2(1), 7) cannot be altered without the consent of the House of Lords so that to some extent it is entrenched against the executive.

Parliament is summoned and dissolved by the Crown under the royal prerogative, the alleged abuse of this power being a major contribution to the seventeenth century revolution. The modern law is overlaid by statute and convention, its foundations being established by the 1688 revolution. The main principles give considerable power to the Prime Minister but also contain important checks over the executive. They are:

- 'Parliament ought to be held frequently' (Bill of Rights 1688 Article 13) and must meet at least once every three years (Meeting of Parliament Act 1694). By convention Parliament meets annually backed by administrative necessity, for example to authorise tax and public spending.
- Parliament automatically ends at the expiry of five years from the date of its writ of summons (below) (Septennial Act 1715; Parliament Act 1911). This triggers a general election (Chapter 12). The five year period is intended to strike a balance between the

desire for MPs to be independent of the temptation to pander to populist pressures and the need to ensure that they do not go native and forget their dependency on the voters.

▷ Within the five years Parliament may be dissolved by the monarch (law) on the advice of the Prime Minister (convention). Dissolution triggers a general election which must be held, according to a complex formula, within about three weeks of the dissolution proclamation (Representation of the People Act 1985 Schedule 1). The same proclamation dissolves Parliament and summons a new one. This is one of the main sources of prime ministerial power. However it is possible that in certain extreme cases the monarch can exercise personal choice whether or not to dissolve Parliament (Chapter 14). A Parliament usually lasts for about four years, dissolution being timed for the political advantage of the Prime Minister. It is sometimes suggested that Parliament should sit for a fixed term, thus removing a Prime Minister's power to call an election to suit his or her own party. This could however paralyse a weak government (see *Royal Commission on the Constitution*, 1969–73, Cmnd 5460).

▷ A Prime Minister whose government is defeated on a vote of confidence in the House of Commons must resign. Unless an alternative leader can be supported by the House of Commons, which is most unlikely, the outgoing Prime Minister must ask for a dissolution of Parliament which the monarch must normally grant. This also gives the Prime Minister power over Parliament, in that Parliament cannot dismiss the Prime Minister without dismissing itself.

▷ A 'Parliament' is divided into 'sessions'. These are working periods of a year, usually running from November (about 170 sitting days). Sessions are 'prorogued' by the monarch under the royal prerogative thus, as usual, being under the control of the executive. Each session is opened by the monarch, with an address from the throne which is written by the government and outlines its legislative proposals. A general debate on government policy takes place immediately afterwards. Within a session, each House can be adjourned at any time by resolution of the House. Adjournments apply to daily sittings and the breaks for holidays and over the summer. The rump of the session following the summer break by convention is used to finish outstanding business. The Speaker can suspend individual sittings of the Commons.

▷ There is machinery for recalling each House by proclamation while it stands prorogued (Parliament (Elections and Meetings) Act 1943 s.34) and also under emergency legislation (Civil Contingencies Act 2004). An adjourned Parliament can be summoned by proclamation (Meeting of Parliament Act 1870) and also by the Speakers of both Houses at the request of the Prime Minister or perhaps at the request of the leader of the Opposition. However it does not seem to be possible for ordinary MPs to recall Parliament in order to debate any crisis that may arise while Parliament is not sitting. This again illustrates the subservience of Parliament to the executive. Government has many powers under the royal prerogative, notably to deploy the armed forces and even declare war, which it can exercise without reference to Parliament.

On the one hand these principles illustrate the constitutional checks and balances that attempt to prevent any single group from being dominant, an objective on which liberals and republicans unite. Each institution can control the other but only at the cost of terminating itself and inviting the people to choose a successor. On the other hand their operation in practice illustrates the limitations of checks and balances when matched against political forces towards oligarchy. Montesquieu, writing in the eighteenth century (Chapter 8), praised this system as a balance of equal constitutional forces. However Montesquieu also relied on the existence of a powerful aristocracy in the House of Lords and did not have to confront the circumstances of modern political parties.

11.4 The Functions of the House of Commons

The main functions of the Commons are as follows:

- **Choosing the government** indirectly by virtue of the convention that the person who commands a majority of the Commons is entitled to form a government. The Commons has no veto over individual appointments nor can it dismiss individual members of the government (another prime ministerial power).
- **Sustaining the government** by supplying it with funds and authorising taxation. The size and complexity of modern government means that parliamentary control over finance cannot be exercised directly. Parliamentary approval of the executive's budget and accounts is largely a formality. Detailed scrutiny and control over government spending takes place mainly within the government itself through the medium of the Treasury (Chapter 15). However a substantial parliamentary safeguard is provided by the National Audit Office headed by the Comptroller and Auditor-General (Chapter 13).
- **Legislating**. Any member can propose a bill but in practice the parliamentary timetable is dominated by government business and legislation is usually presented to Parliament ready drafted by the executive. This is why Bagehot thought that the absence of a strict separation of powers made the UK constitution an effective machine for ensuring government by experts. There are certain opportunities for private members' bills but these rarely become law (Chapter 13).
- **Supervising the executive**. By convention ministers are accountable to Parliament and must appear in Parliament to participate in debates, answer questions and appear before committees (Chapter 13). The House of Commons can require a government to resign by a vote of no confidence. These sanctions are rarely used since the resignation of the government is likely to result in a general election, putting the jobs of MPs at risk.
- **The redress of grievances** raised by individual MPs on behalf of their constituents. There are certain opportunities to raise grievances in debates but they are usually pursued by correspondence with ministers or by the Parliamentary Ombudsman. By convention every constituent has a right of access to his or her MP, which can be exercised by visiting Parliament if necessary.
- **Debating matters of public concern**. Again, there are limited procedural opportunities for such debates.

11.5 The Functions of the House of Lords

A common justification for a second chamber is to represent the different units of a federal system, with the first chamber representing the popular vote as, for example, in the US.

The conventional justification for the existence of a second chamber in the UK is that it acts as a revising chamber to scrutinise the detail of legislation proposed by the Commons and to allow time for second thoughts, thus acting as a constitutional safeguard against the possible excesses of majoritarianism and party politics. According to the Wakeham Report (above), the functions of the second chamber include, and should continue to include, the following:

- **To provide advice on public policy**, bringing a range of perspectives to bear that should be broadly representative of British society and in particular provide a voice for the nations and regions of the UK and ethnic minorities and interest groups.
- **To act as a revising chamber**, scrutinising the details of proposed legislation within the overall polices laid down by the Commons. By convention, supported by the Parliament Acts 1911 and 1949 (Chapter 13), the House of Lords does not discuss matters of government finance, this being a prerogative of the Commons (Brazier, 'The Financial Powers of the House of Lords', 1998, *Anglo-American Law Review* 17(2): 131).
- **To provide a forum for general debate** on matters of public concern without party political pressures.
- **To introduce relatively uncontroversial legislation** or private bills as a method of relieving the workload of the Commons. Any bill other than a financial measure can be introduced in the Lords.
- **To provide ministers**, thus unelected persons can be appointed as ministers. However by convention the Prime Minister and other senior ministers must be members of the Commons.
- **To provide committees** on general topics, such as the European Communities Committee and the Science and Technology Committee. These are highly respected.
- **To permit persons who have made a contribution to public life**, other than party politicians, **to participate in government**. The contemporary House of Lords is dominated by former officials, politicians and leading members of the elite professions and business interests. There have been allegations that seats in the Lords can be bought.
- **To act as a constitutional check** by preventing a government from prolonging its own life, in respect of which the Lords has a veto (Parliament Act 1911, above). The consent of the Lords is also needed for the dismissal of senior judges (Chapter 8).
- **To act more generally as a constitutional watchdog**. It has no specific powers for this purpose but has a Constitutional Committee which examines the constitutional implications of bills brought before the House.

These functions can be pursued in the House of Lords partly because its procedure and culture differ significantly from the Commons. In particular, party discipline is less rigorous and the House of Lords is less partisan than the Commons. Members of the House of Lords other than bishops are removable only by statute and are therefore less susceptible to political pressures than MPs. The House as a whole controls its own procedure, making it relatively free from procedural constraints, and is subject to less time pressure than the Commons. Its members have a considerable accumulation of experience and knowledge. The House of Lords cannot therefore easily be manipulated by the government, is attractive to external lobbyists and can ventilate moral and social issues in an objective way. Occasionally members of the House of Lords will respond to their individual consciences, or to public opinion, and defeat government proposals.

11.6   The Parliament Acts

We have seen statutes without the consent of the House of Lords, thus ensuring that the democratic will prevails. We have also seen that in *R (Jackson) v Attorney-General* (2005) the Law Lords disagreed as to the limits of the Parliament Acts. Introduced mainly to allow important constitutional measures to be passed, the Acts have recently been used to steamroll through government measures such as the Hunting Act 2004 (see Lord Bingham in *R (Jackson) v Attorney-General* (2005) [41]). Before 1991, the 1911 Act was used three times (Government of Ireland Act 1914, Welsh Church Act 1914, Parliament Act 1949). Since then it has been used four times for relatively minor purposes (War Crimes Act 1991, European Parliamentary Elections Act 1999, Sexual Offences (Amendment) Act 2000, Hunting Act 2004).

The conventional view is that subject to the limits specifically mentioned in the 1911 Act – mainly private bills, bills to prolong the life of Parliament and bills introduced in the Lords itself – any statutes can be enacted under the Parliament Acts including an alteration to the Parliament Acts themselves. If this is so then the limits currently contained in the 1911 Act could be removed by repealing that part of the Act then legislating free of those limitations (but see disagreement in the *Jackson* case, Chapter 9). The Parliament Acts do not apply to delegated legislation which sometimes requires the approval of Parliament.

The Parliament Act 1911 as amended by the Parliament Act 1949 gives the House of Lords an opportunity to delay legislation, thus giving the Commons an opportunity to reconsider (s.2). The Lords can reject a bill in two parliamentary sessions provided it is sent to them at least one month before the end of each session and no more than one year elapses between the second reading in the first session and the date the bill passes the Commons in the second session (Chapter 13). After the second session the bill can receive the royal assent without the consent of the Lords. If the Commons amends a bill after it has come back from the Lords in the first session, then it may not count as the same bill unless the amendments were suggested by the Lords. In the case of a 'money bill' the Lords can delay only for one month, provided the bill is sent to them at least one month before the end of a session (Parliament Act 1911 s.1). A money bill is a public bill that in the opinion of the Speaker deals *exclusively* either with central government taxation or central government spending, borrowing or accounts. This definition is narrow since few bills deal exclusively with these matters. The Speaker must certify that the Parliament Act's procedure has been followed and his certificate cannot be challenged (Parliament Act 1911 s.2(20), s.3). However the court can decide whether a bill falls within the limits of the Parliament Act in the first place *(R (Jackson) v Attorney-General* (2005)).

11.7   Parliamentary Privilege

It is important that a legislature can control its own affairs and be protected against disruption and interference both by outsiders and from within its ranks. Interference by the Crown with parliamentary business was an ingredient of the seventeenth century revolution and at the beginning of every Parliament the Speaker symbolically asserts the 'ancient and undoubted privileges' of the House of Commons against the Crown. The House of Lords also has its privileges, which it polices collectively, but does not have the power to punish. The Nicholls Report (Joint Committee on Parliamentary Privilege, HL 43–1, HC 214–1, 1998–9) recommended various reforms but these have yet to be implemented.

Some parliamentary privileges are mainly of historical or symbolic interest. These include the collective right of access of the Commons to the monarch. Members of the Commons also enjoy immunity from civil, as opposed to criminal, arrest during a period from 40 days before to 40 days after every session. In the case of peers the immunity is permanent and seems to be based on their status as peers rather than membership of the House (*Stourton* v *Stourton* (1963)). Now that debtors are no longer imprisoned, civil arrest is virtually obsolete, being concerned mainly with disobedience to court orders. There is no privilege preventing a civil action against an MP in his or her private capacity (*Re Parliamentary Privileges Act 1770* (1958)). Members and officers of both Houses have automatic exemption from jury service (Juries Act 1974) and the House can exempt members from giving evidence in court.

The two most important privileges are (i) the collective privilege of each House to control its own composition and procedure and (ii) freedom of speech. We shall discuss these below. We shall also discuss the conflicts that have arisen between Parliament and the courts over parliamentary privilege. At present there is an uneasy stalemate. Parliament has never accepted that the courts have the power to determine the limits of its privileges. The ordinary courts accept that Parliament has the exclusive power to regulate its own internal affairs but claim the right to determine the limits of other privileges (that is, those affecting the rights of people outside the House) but not to interfere with how established privileges are exercised. Parliamentary privilege has been upheld by the European Court of Human Rights (*A* v *UK* (2003)).

11.7.1   Contempt of Parliament

Breach of a specific parliamentary privilege is one kind of 'contempt' of Parliament. A parliamentary privilege is a special right or immunity available either to the House collectively (for example to control its own composition and procedure) or to individual members (for example freedom of speech). Contempt is a general term embracing any conduct, whether by MPs or outsiders,

> which obstructs or impedes either House of Parliament in the performance of its functions or which obstructs or impedes any member or officer of the House in the execution of his duty or which has a tendency directly or indirectly to produce such results. (May, *Parliamentary Practice*, Butterworths, 1997, p. 108)

This is very wide. It includes for example abuses by MPs of parliamentary procedure, breaching confidences, refusing to obey a committee, causing disruption in the House, improper or dishonest behaviour by MPs, and harassment of, or allegations against, MPs in newspapers. Contempt not only protects the 'efficiency' of the House but also its 'authority and dignity'.

Perhaps the most striking feature of contempt of Parliament is that Parliament accuses, tries and punishes offenders itself. The ordinary courts have no jurisdiction over the internal affairs of Parliament (below) and there are no independent safeguards for the individual. On the one hand this is an assertion of a version of the separation of powers. On the other hand it seems to violate rule of law values and the ECHR concerning the right to be judged by an independent court (see *Demicola* v *Malta* (1992)). The immunity of Parliament from interference by the courts is reinforced by the Human Rights Act 1998 which provides that Parliament, except the House of Lords in its judicial capacity, is not a public body for the purpose of the Act (s.6(3); Chapter 19). This prevents an action being brought against Parliament under the Human Rights Act.

The procedure for dealing with a contempt of Parliament, or a breach of privilege, is as follows (see HC 417, 1976–7):

1. Any member can give written notice of a complaint to the Speaker.
2. The Speaker decides whether to give priority over other business.
3. If the Speaker decides not to do so, the member may then use the ordinary procedure of the House to get the matter discussed. This would be difficult in practice.
4. If the Speaker decides to take up the matter, the complaining member can propose that the matter be referred to the Committee of Standards and Privileges or that some other action be taken, for example an immediate debate. A select committee can in certain cases refer a contempt against itself direct to the Committee (HC Deb. vol. 94, col. 763–4, 18 March 1986).
5. The Committee (seventeen senior members) investigates the complaint. The procedure is entirely up to the Committee. Witnesses are examined but there is no right to legal representation. The accused has no legal right to a hearing nor to summon or cross examine witnesses.
6. The Committee reports back to the House, which decides what action to take. This could range from a reprimand, through suspension or expulsion from the House, to imprisonment for the rest of the session, renewable indefinitely. The House of Lords can imprison for a fixed term and can also impose a fine. The Nicholls Report recommended that punishment of non-members should be a matter for the ordinary courts and limited to a fine.
7. The Speaker also has summary powers to deal with disruptive behaviour in the House or breaches of the rules of debate. He or she can exclude MPs and others from the Chamber until the end of the session (HC Standing Orders 24–6) and make rulings on matters of procedure. The Speaker of the House of Lords has no procedural or disciplinary powers.

The conduct of MPs and the justice and effectiveness of the internal disciplinary process came into the public spotlight during the 1990s when several MPs were accused of accepting payments to give favours to outside interests. The Nicholls Report (1999) recommended that the contempt procedure be reformed in favour of stronger procedural rights including a right of appeal, reflecting contemporary standards of fairness. The Committee on Standards in Public Life has recommended that no party should have a majority on the Standards and Privileges Committee, that ministers' aides should not serve as members, that there should be an investigatory panel with an independent chair, and that full reasons should be published for every decision (Eighth Report, 2002, Cm 5663).

11.7.2   'Exclusive Cognisance'

Although the qualifications for being a Member of Parliament are fixed by statute, each House has the exclusive right to decide who shall actually sit, to regulate all internal proceedings and expel members. In accordance with the separation of powers, no legal process is possible in respect of any matter before the House and no one can be prevented from placing a matter before Parliament (*Bilston Corporation* v *Wolverhampton Corporation* (1942)). The courts cannot order a minister to present a matter to Parliament even where a change in the law is required by European law (*R* v *Secretary of State for Employment ex parte Equal Opportunities Commission* (1992)). Nor can the courts decide whether the procedures within each House of Parliament for enacting legislation have been properly followed (*Pickin* v *British Railways Board* (1974)).

In *Bradlaugh* v *Gossett* (1884) Charles Bradlaugh, a well known freethinker, had been duly elected to the Commons. The House refused to let him take his seat because it deemed that as an atheist he had no statutory right to take the oath. In fact the courts had previously ruled in his favour (*Clarke* v *Bradlaugh* (1881)). Nevertheless the court held that it had no power to intervene since this was a matter exclusively to do with the internal procedure of the House.

On the other hand the courts have claimed that the Commons has no control over those outside the House itself and that Parliament cannot interfere with court processes (*Ashby* v *White* (1703)). Thus there seems to be a stalemate since Parliament has never accepted that the courts can intervene in any of its processes (below).

What counts as an internal proceeding in Parliament? On one view anything that happens within the precincts of the Houses of Parliament (the Palace of Westminster) is protected. In *R* v *Grahame-Campbell ex parte Herbert* (1935) the Divisional Court held that the House of Commons bar was exempt from the liquor licensing laws and so could sell drinks without restriction. However another explanation of this case is that the Palace of Westminster, a royal palace, enjoys Crown immunity from statute law (Chapter 14). Another view is that immunity applies only to the official business of the House. On this view, ordinary criminal offences unconnected with parliamentary business taking place in the precincts should fall within the ordinary law, although the Sergeant at Arms may control the entry of law enforcement officials into the Palace of Westminster. Thus in 2008 the police searched the Parliamentary office of Damian Green, a senior Opposition MP, in connection with an investigation into a leak of information from the Home Office. This may have been politically unwise but since the Sergeant at Arms had apparently given permisison, it was not a breach of privilege.

The privilege only applies to the internal processes of the House. Approval by the House of subordinate legislation or a government decision cannot make valid something unlawful (*Hoffman La Roche* v *Trade and Industry Secretary* (1974)). Resolutions of the House of Commons cannot alter the general law .This requires a statute (*Stockdale* v *Hansard* (1839); *Bowles* v *Bank of England* (1913)).

11.7.3   Freedom of Speech

This is the central privilege of an MP, who must be at liberty to speak and write without fear of interference from outside bodies. On the other hand as with any liberty, the price to be paid is that some MPs might abuse this freedom to make untrue allegations against persons who cannot answer back or to violate privacy as in the 'Child Z' case (HC 1995–6, vol. 252, paras 9, 10) where a child was named in defiance of an order of the Court of Appeal.

Article 9 of the Bill of Rights 1688 (part of the revolution settlement for the purpose of protecting MPs against the Crown) states that:

> The Freedom of Speech or Debates or Proceedings in Parliament ought not to be impeached or questioned in any court or place out of Parliament.

Article 9 has been interpreted widely as not only excluding civil and criminal proceedings against an MP but also preventing parliamentary materials from being used as evidence against an MP in court proceedings (*Church of Scientology of California* v *Johnson-Smith* (1972): MP sued for defamation).

Article 9 does not exclude the use of parliamentary material in court but only prohibits the court from penalising or criticising anything said or done in parliamentary proceedings. For example evidence of something a minister said in Parliament cannot be used to determine whether he is exercising his statutory powers in bad faith (*R* v *Secretary of State for Trade ex parte Anderson Strathclyde* [1983] 2 All ER 233 at 238–9). However it can be used as evidence of the reasons for executive action (*Toussaint* v *AG of St Vincent and the Grenadines* (2008)). Nor can a court say that Parliament has acted for an improper motive. Statements made in Parliament may however be used to ascertain the factual or policy background to a statute and for the limited purposes contemplated in *Pepper* v *Hart* (Chapter 8). In *Pepper* v *Hart* the House of Lords took the view that the purpose of Article 9 was only to prevent MPs from being penalised for what they said in the House.

The Defamation Act 1996 amended the Bill of Rights in order to accommodate Neil Hamilton, a Conservative MP who wished to sue a newspaper for defamation, relying upon parliamentary material for the purpose (s.13). Section 13 permits an MP to use things said in Parliament in evidence provided that the MP waives his or her own immunity (compare *Hamilton* v *Al Fayed* (1999)). This illustrates the frailty of constitutional principle against party political government. Indeed the Nicholls Report (below) pointed out that section 13 was a distortion of the constitution in that Article 9 exists in the public interest to protect Parliament and is not a provision which individual MPs should be able to waive in their own interests. The Committee therefore proposed that Article 9 should be waived only by each House.

'Proceedings in Parliament': The meaning of 'in Parliament' has not been settled. In 1688 it was no doubt thought that the phrase was self explanatory. It certainly includes speeches and written or oral questions by an MP in the House or in committee proceedings. However the work of a modern MP goes beyond this. Much of an MP's time is spent in writing letters and attending meetings in the UK and abroad with pressure groups, local authorities, business organisations, foreign officials and so on. MPs also meet or write to ministers and constituents. Anything said in the Chamber as part of the business of the House and in committees or reports related to the business of the House is certainly protected. Parliamentary committees often visit places around the country and interference with their proceedings wherever they take place is a contempt of Parliament (for example a disturbance at Essex University 1969, HC 308, 1968–9). It is arguable that speech that, even within the House itself, is unrelated to parliamentary business enjoys no privilege (see *Re Parliamentary Privileges Act 1770* (1958)). In 1976 in the Zircon affair, the Committee of Privileges ruled that the showing to MPs, within the precincts, of a film about a secret security project was not protected by privilege and could therefore be the subject of an injunction (see HC 365, 1986–7). In *Rivlin* v *Bilankin* (1953) a libellous letter about a private matter was posted in a letter box within the precincts. It was held in a short unreasoned judgment that the letter was not protected by privilege.

It is clear that statements by an MP to the media are not covered by parliamentary privilege although they may be covered by qualified privilege (below). Nor are statements made in election campaigns. The main area of uncertainty concerns things said or written by MPs outside the House as part of their duties on behalf of their constituents, for example a letter complaining to the Secretary of State about an NHS hospital. In the case of *Strauss* (1956) the House of Commons by a tiny majority (218–213) rejected a recommendation by the Committee of Privileges that such letters should be protected by parliamentary privilege. *Strauss* concerned a complaint about the activities of the London Electricity Board. This was not a central government department so the minister to whom Strauss wrote was not directly responsible to Parliament for its day-to-day activities. It is not clear what the reasons for the Commons resolutions were and the vote may have been on party lines. The *Strauss* view certainly seems narrow and artificial and in later reports the Committee of Privileges has recommended that *Strauss* be overturned. This has not been implemented. On the basis of *Strauss*, a letter from an MP is privileged only if it is to do with a matter currently being debated in the House or is the subject of an official parliamentary question. In 1967 a Select Committee on Parliamentary Privilege (1967–8, HC 34) recommended that privilege be widened to include all official communications by an MP but the Nicholls Report favoured the narrow view. In contemporary circumstances it is likely that any extension of privilege will be made by statute. For example a decision by an MP to refer a matter to the Parliamentary Ombudsman has absolute privilege (Parliamentary Commissioner Act 1967 s.10(5)).

'**Impeached or questioned**': Parliament takes the view that it is contempt even to commence legal proceedings by serving a writ upon an MP in respect of a matter which Parliament considers to be privileged. This is a direct challenge to the courts since if this view is right then the courts have no power to decide the limits of parliamentary privilege. We shall discuss this below.

'**Out of Parliament**': Article 9 prevents interference with the freedom of speech of MPs by any outside body. Legal actions, bribes and threats are the most obvious illustrations (below) but other kinds of pressure also constitute contempt. This could include for example publishing MPs' home telephone numbers (*Daily Graphic Case*, HC 27, 1956), accusing MPs of drunkenness (*Duffy's Case*, HC 129, 1964–5) or making press allegations of conflict of interest by MPs. However Article 9 has not been used against media criticism of political speeches by MPs. Nor does Article 9 prevent courts or other bodies from looking into matters which are also before Parliament, provided that the parliamentary processes or things said in them are not criticised (see *Hamilton* v *Al Fayed* (1999)). The Human Rights Act 1998 might also restrain an expansive interpretation of Article 9. Although an action could not be brought against Parliament itself, the court is required to interpret all legislation including Article 9, 'if it is possible to do so', in a way that conforms to the rights set out in the Act, one of which is freedom of expression (s.3).

Independently of the Bill of Rights, an MP performing his official duties inside or outside the House is protected by qualified privilege. This not confined to MPs and is available to anyone who has a legal or moral duty to make the statement in question and the recipient has a corresponding interest in hearing it. Qualified privilege does give complete immunity but covers only statements made in good faith and taking proper care. It applies only to defamation (the law relating to statements that damage reputation) whereas full or 'absolute' parliamentary privilege covers every kind of legal action. It is a defence to an action so that the MP must subject her or himself to the burden of legal proceedings. Even if she or he eventually wins, the expense and uncertainty of litigation may discourage an MP from speaking freely. It is apparently a contempt of Parliament even to begin legal proceedings against an MP in respect of a matter protected by full parliamentary privilege.

Qualified privilege is particularly important for the press and is discussed in greater detail in Chapter 20 (see *Reynolds* v *Times Newspapers Ltd* (2001)). It could apply to cases such as *Strauss* (above) and to a media interview or press statement (*Church of Scientology* v *Johnson-Smith* above) or to a statement made in an election campaign (*Culnane* v *Morris* (2006): anti-BNP leaflets). Political freedom of expression is regarded as of the highest importance and the scope of qualified privilege correspondingly generous *(Culnane)*. Conversely the limits of full parliamentary privilege are strictly policed. In *Buchanan* v *Jennings* (2005) the Privy Council held that an MP, who in a TV interview endorsed an allegedly defamatory statement he had made in the New Zealand Parliament, could not claim parliamentary privilege but had only qualified privilege.

11.7.4   Publication of Parliamentary Business

A controversial aspect of contempt of Parliament concerns public access to parliamentary information, which arguably should be unrestricted except where the disclosure would harm the public interest. However parliamentary committees often sit in private and 'leaks' of reports of select committees have been prohibited since 1837, although action is only likely to be taken if the leak causes substantial interference with the function of a committee. The House of Commons has waived any more general right to restrain publication of its proceedings and has authorised the broadcasting of its proceedings, subject to a power to give directions. It has also undertaken generally to use its contempt powers sparingly (HC 34, 1967–8, para. 15).

Documents published by order of Parliament such as Hansard have full parliamentary privilege (Parliamentary Papers Act 1840 s.1). The unofficial publication by the press of fair and accurate extracts or abstracts from official reports of parliamentary proceedings also have privilege if published in good faith (s.3) as do broadcasts of parliamentary proceedings (Defamation Act 1952 s.9; Broadcasting Act 1990 s.203(1)).

Other press reports including extracts or parliamentary sketches have qualified privilege protected provided that they are honest and fair (*Wason* v *Walter* (1868); *Cook* v *Alexander* (1974)). This is reinforced by the Defamation Act 1996 s.15 which protects fair and accurate reports of legislative proceedings anywhere. Where the report is embellished with additional material which may flesh it out or comment on it, the privilege is lost unless the ordinary reader can clearly distinguish the reportage from the other material (see *Curiston* v *Times Newspapers* (2007)). The privilege does not in any case apply to the additional material although this may be protected by the more general defence of 'responsible journalism' (see Chapter 21).

None of this affects limitations placed upon members' freedom of speech by Parliament itself, for example by rules of procedure or possibly by party discipline within the House. Indeed these restrictions are themselves immune from control by the courts because of the 'exclusive cognisance' privilege (above). The Speaker, who presides over the House of Commons, has a duty to control procedure impartially. Internal rules exist to prevent MPs misusing their privilege of freedom of speech, for example by attacking people who cannot answer back or by commenting upon pending legal proceedings. For example 'the invidious use of a person's name in a question should be resorted to only if to do so is strictly necessary to render the question intelligible and the protection of parliamentary privilege should be used only as a last resort' and 'in a way that does not damage the good name of the House' (see HC Deb. vol. 94, col. 26, 17 March 1986).

11.8   Standards in the Commons

Following the recommendations of the First Report of the Committee on Standards in Public Life (1995, Cm 2850) there is a Code of Conduct for MPs (HC Session 1996–7, 24 July 1996). In keeping with parliamentary privilege, this is policed by the House itself (below). The protection of parliamentary privilege entails the risk that an MP might abuse his or her privilege for personal gain. It is not clear whether the general law of corruption applies to an MP (see *R* v *Greenaway* (1998)). The traditional role of an MP is to be an independent representative of his or her constituents and to speak in Parliament in furtherance of the general public interest.

However there are obstacles to the freedom of MPs. First and foremost there are party loyalties. Secondly many MPs are sponsored by outside bodies, including trade unions and business interests, who may contribute towards their expenses. Some MPs accept employment as paid or unpaid 'consultants' to businesses and interest groups such as the Police Federation or hold company directorships. MPs are also frequently offered 'hospitality', or gifts, or invited on expenses-paid 'fact finding' trips. There are also 'all party' subject groups of MPs which involve relationships with outside bodies (see HC 408, 1984–5). Except in the case of a private bill, a member is free to vote on a matter in which she or he has a personal interest. There is therefore a risk that MPs are susceptible to lobbying by private interests.

In the *Brown Case* (1947) an MP sponsored by a trade union was dismissed for not advocating the employer's interests in Parliament. The Committee of Privileges voted that a contract could not require an MP to support or represent his or her sponsor's interests in Parliament, nor could the sponsor punish the MP for not doing so. However it was not contempt to dismiss a consultant if for whatever reason the employer or sponsor was unhappy with his or her services. This somewhat evasive compromise does not seem to take the matter much further. It would be a contempt to threaten to dismiss an MP unless she or he took a certain line in Parliament but not, apparently, to dismiss her or him after the event. Arguably pressures from local constituency parties would also be contemptuous.

It is often said that sponsorships and consultancies enable MPs to keep in touch with informed opinion outside Westminster and to develop specialised knowledge. They also enable MPs without private means to supplement their parliamentary salaries. The process of enacting legislation is also helped by consultation with interested parties. There is much 'lobbying' of civil servants and it is desirable that this should be counterbalanced by MPs having their own access to outside interests. On the other hand apart from the risk of corruption, MPs might also spend time in company boardrooms that may generate little understanding of social problems and would be better spent helping their constituents.

Since the seventeenth century, resolutions of the House have declared that certain kinds of external influences are in contempt of Parliament. The latest distinction seems to be between promoting a specific matter for gain, which is forbidden, and acting as a consultant generally, which is acceptable. There have been many resolutions attempting to capture this elusive matter. The latest resolution (1995), which amends a resolution of 1947 (HC 816, 1994–5) and is incorporated in the Code of Conduct for MPs, states that:

> It is inconsistent with the dignity of the house, with the duty of a Member to his constituents, and with the maintenance of the privilege of freedom of speech for any Member of this House to enter into any contractual agreement with an outside body, controlling or limiting the Member's complete independence and freedom of action in Parliament or stipulating that he shall act in any way as the representative of such outside body in regard to any matter to be transacted in Parliament; the duty of a Member being to his constituents and to the country as a whole, rather than to any particular section thereof: and that in particular no Members of the House shall, in consideration of any remuneration, fee, payment or reward or benefit in kind, direct or indirect, which the Member or any member of his or her family has received, is receiving or expects to receive –
>
> (i) advocate or initiate any cause or matter on behalf of any outside body or individual, or
> (ii) urge any other Member of either House of Parliament, including Ministers, to do so by means of any speech, Question, motion, introduction of a bill, or amendment to a motion or a Bill.

A further resolution (1995) restricts the extent to which a member may participate in a delegation to ministers or public officials. A member should not initiate, participate in or attend any such delegation where the problem to be addressed affects only the body with which the member has a relevant paid interest except when that problem relates primarily to a constituency matter.

There are also criminal offences involving members of public bodies. Misuse of public office is a common law offence and there are also offences under the Public Bodies (Corrupt Practices) Act 1889 and the Prevention of Corruption Act 1916. These offences may include cases where MPs are offered bribes (but see Royal Commission on *Standards of Conduct in Public Life*, 1976, Cmnd 6524). However an MP might sometimes be protected by Article 9 of the Bill of Rights (above). Nevertheless in *R v Greenaway* (1998) a Conservative MP had accepted a bribe to use his influence to help a person acquire UK citizenship. The court held that parliamentary privilege did not apply because the offence occurred when the bribe was received and therefore the court did not need to investigate what went on in Parliament. It is arguable that an MP is not a 'public servant' and does not hold a public office as such, so is outside these offences (see *AG's Reference No. 3 (2003)*).

MPs must enter information about their financial interests in a Register of Members' Interests. The register itself has been held (oddly) not to be protected by parliamentary privilege (*Rost v Edwards* (1990)). The categories of interest required by the register have been strengthened to include full details of an employment contract, the provision of services such as consultancy, company directorships, employment or offices, professions and trades, names of clients, financial sponsorships, overseas visits as an MP, payments received from abroad, land or property, shareholdings and 'any interest or benefit received which might reasonably be thought by others to influence the member's actions in

Parliament'. However the precise value of such payments need not be entered. According to the register, only one in five MPs is without an external source of income.

Following the First Report of the Committee on Standards in Public Life (1995, Cm 2850) the House of Commons appointed a Parliamentary Commissioner for Standards empowered to investigate complaints of misuse of the Commons register and to report to the Standards and Privileges Committee of the House of Commons (HC Standing Orders (Public Business) (1995) No. 150). The Commissioner can also investigate complaints by MPs and the public concerning the Code of Conduct and give advice to MPs. Its decisions, being subject to parliamentary privilege, are not subject to judicial review (R v *Parliamentary Commissioner for Standards* (1998)). Parliament can appoint and dismiss the Commissioner. In 2001 Elizabeth Filkin did not have her contract renewed. She had attracted a reputation as an assiduous investigator. In its Eighth Report (2002, Cm 5663) the Committee on Standards recommended that the independence of the Commissioner be strengthened. The Commissioner should be appointed for a non-renewable term of five to seven years, should have the power to call for witnesses and documents and should not be an employee of the House. This has not been implemented.

The Commissioner cannot investigate the interests of ministers acting as such, thus reflecting the separation of powers. There is no independent mechanism for this purpose. Compliance with the Ministerial Code is a matter for the Prime Minister. Independent inquiries in the form of a Royal Commission or under the Inquiries Act 2005 can be held into ministerial misconduct (Chapter 5). However these are set up by ministers. The Tribunals of Inquiry (Evidence) Act under which Parliament could order an inquiry was repealed by the 2005 Act.

11.9 Standards in the House of Lords

There is a 'custom' that the House of Lords should not be subject to formal regulation. It is said by its members that it should rely on their 'personal honour' (see *Seventh Report of Committee on Standards in Public Life,* 2000). However no reason has been offered as to why members of the Lords are more honourable than members of the Commons. The House of Lords has no disciplinary sanctions and, with the possible exception of treason, a member could not be deprived of a peerage or suspended or expelled for misconduct without statutory authority. The Letters Patent from the Crown that create a peerage confer a legal right to sit in the House of Lords. It is customary for membership not to be regarded as a full time commitment and many members have outside interests including full time jobs. Four Labour peers have been under investigation for allegedly selling their Parliamentary services to special interests (*The Times*, 26 January 2009).The current proposals for reform of the House of Lords suggest that members should be paid (see White Paper 2008 above). Indeed payment for public service is an important requirement of a democracy so as to enable anyone to participate.

There is a House of Lords Code of Conduct (2002) embodying the Nolan principles and register of members' interests. This was introduced in 1995 (HL 90, 98, 1994–5). It was originally voluntary in respect of non-financial interests. However as a result of the Seventh Report of the Committee on Standards in Public Life (2000, Cm 4903) it has been made compulsory. It is however less stringent than the Commons register.

11.10   The Courts and Parliament

As we have seen, the courts are not prepared to intervene in the internal affairs of the House. On the other hand, where parliamentary activity involves the rights of persons outside the House, the courts have claimed the power to intervene at least to the extent of deciding whether the privilege asserted by Parliament exists. In a famous eighteenth century controversy that asserted basic rule of law values the courts held that parliamentary officers have no power to deprive citizens of voting rights: 'where there is a right there is a remedy' (*Ashby* v *White* (1703); see also *Paty's Case* (1704)). In *Stockdale* v *Hansard* (1839) it was held that parliamentary privilege did not protect reports published by order of the House from being the subject of libel actions.

The subject matter of these disputes is only of historical interest. Parliament no longer controls elections and *Stockdale* v *Hansard* was soon reversed by statute (Parliamentary Papers Act 1840). Nevertheless the general principle about the power of the courts remains valid.

Parliament has never accepted that *Stockdale* v *Hansard* was correctly decided and has never withdrawn the claim to be the exclusive judge of its own privileges.

In the *Sheriff of Middlesex Case* (1840), which was a sequel to *Stockdale* v *Hansard*, Parliament imprisoned the two holders of the office of sheriff for enforcing the court's judgment in *Stockdale* v *Hansard*. Not surprisingly the sheriffs applied to the court for release but the court, including Lord Denman who had decided *Stockdale* v *Hansard* itself, held that it was powerless to intervene. Parliament had the undoubted right to commit to prison for contempt and it did not have to give reasons. Unless some improper reason was disclosed on the face of the committal warrant, the court must assume that Parliament was acting lawfully even though the judges knew otherwise.

Therefore by relying on the *Sheriff of Middlesex Case* Parliament can arbitrarily imprison anyone it likes. Whether this principle will be taken advantage of in modern times rests with Parliament's – or the courts' – political sense. The courts are unwilling to take action that might be considered as trespassing on Parliament's preserves. Parliament too has shown restraint in asserting claims to privilege (for example the *Strauss* case mentioned above). This standoff between the courts and Parliament could be regarded as an example of the dual sovereignty which it is claimed that the separation of powers requires. Indeed in characteristic fashion it has been claimed that there is a voluntary, mutual respect between the two institutions (*Hamilton* v *Al Fayed* [1999] 3 All ER 317, 333–4).

The Nicholls Report (1999) suggested the enactment of a code of parliamentary privilege to include modest reforms largely intended to clarify the relationship between Parliament and the courts. In addition to the recommendations already mentioned, they include the following:

▷ 'Place out of Parliament' for the purposes of Article 9 should be defined to include courts and tribunals empowered to take evidence on oath but not tribunals of inquiry if both Houses so resolve

- There should be an offence of abuse of public office which should include MPs
- MPs should be subject to the criminal law relating to corruption
- Members of the Lords should be compellable before Commons' committees
- Parliament's 'exclusive cognisance' should be confined to 'activities directly and closely related to the business of the House'
- Contempt by non-members should be dealt with by the ordinary courts
- Freedom from arrest should be abolished.

Summary

- Parliament has developed primarily through the party system. It has the competing functions of sustaining the government and holding the government to account. It scrutinises legislation, provides the executive with finance, debates matters of public concern and redresses grievances. The executive is usually too powerful and complex for Parliament to be effective. However at least Parliament is a public forum in which the executive can be forced to justify its actions.

- There is a network of laws and conventions to ensure that Parliament meets annually and that it can remove the government. However the government can dissolve Parliament subject to the possibility of the overriding powers of the Crown and MPs cannot hold the government to account during the long periods when Parliament is not sitting.

- After the 1688 settlement the House of Lords was regarded as holding the constitutional balance of power but by the twentieth century it had become subordinate to the elected House of Commons. The Lords was given a new lease of life by the introduction of life peers in the 1960s but the constitutional role of the House remains controversial. By convention and law the Lords must ultimately defer to the Commons. It is primarily a delaying and revising chamber. Since the bulk of the hereditary peers were removed in 1999 the House of Lords has become more aggressive in resisting the executive. The House of Lords is less subject to party pressures than the House of Commons. The rules of procedure and party discipline in the House of Lords are more relaxed than is the case with the Commons.

- Because of the control over the Commons exercised by the executive, a second chamber is desirable but there is no agreement as to how the hereditary element in the Lords should be replaced. At present the House of Lords is accountable to no one.

- Parliament can protect itself against interference from without and within through the law of parliamentary privilege and its powers to punish for contempt. Parliament can enforce its own privileges free from interference by the ordinary courts. The Committee on Standards and Privileges which adjudicates on matters referred to it by the House has been criticised on the grounds of lack of independence and a low standard of procedural fairness.

- The main parliamentary privileges are Parliament's exclusive control over its own procedures and freedom of speech. There are difficulties in terms of what counts as parliamentary proceedings. MPs and the media may also have qualified privilege in the law of defamation.

- There are safeguards against conflicts of interest by MPs including the Register of Interests and the (non-independent) Parliamentary Commissioner for Standards. There are similar but less stringent safeguards in the House of Lords. There is no independent mechanism to enforce standards against ministers.

Summary cont'd

▶ There is an unresolved conflict between the courts and Parliament as to who decides whether a claimed privilege or contempt exists. This conflict may depend on the extent of Parliament's power to commit for contempt.

Exercises

11.1 What is the constitutional justification for the House of Lords?

11.2 'It has been a source of concern to some constitutionalists that the effect of the 1911 Act and more particularly the 1949 Act has been to erode the checks and balances inherent in the British Constitution' (Lord Bingham in *R (Jackson)* v *Attorney General* (2005) at 41). Explain and discuss.

11.3 'The virtue, spirit and essence of a House of Commons consists in its being the express image of the feelings of the nation. It was not instituted to be a control on the people. It was designed as a control for the people' (Edmund Burke).

'Parliament really has no control over the executive. It is a pure fiction' (LLoyd George).

To what extent do these statements represent the contemporary constitution?

11.4 'The executive has undue control over the summoning and dismissal of Parliament.' Discuss.

11.5 'It is not unduly idealistic to regard the integrity of Members' judgement, however constrained it may be by the party system, and the devotion of their time to the job to which they have been elected, as fundamental values worth not only protecting but insisted on' (Sedley). Discuss in relation to the outside interests of MPs and peers.

11.6 In what circumstances is an MP immune from legal action in respect of things he or she says or writes?

11.7 Advise in the following cases whether an action in the courts is likely to succeed:
  (i) George is an MP. A constituent sends George a letter accusing the management of a local nuclear power station of negligence in relation to safety standards. George, who is employed as a consultant by a company involved in the promotion of renewable sources of energy, passes on the letter to the minister responsible. The manager of the power station hears about the letter and issues writs for libel against the constituent and George.
  (ii) At a local government election, the English National Party (fictitious) publishes a leaflet accusing Cherie, an MP, of receiving gifts from business interests without declaring them. Cherie brings an action for libel against the publishers.
  (iii) In a speech in Parliament Dave, an MP, alleges that the Prime Minister has been selling peerages for contributions to party funds. Dave is later asked in a TV interview whether he stands by the allegation. He replies that 'you must refer to my speech'.

11.8 Bulldog, MP, asks Fox, the Minister of Health, in the House of Commons a question in which he strongly criticises the manner in which the National Health Board deals with the problem of 'lengthy waiting lists for hospital treatment and allocation of hospital beds'. In a later letter to Fox, Bulldog makes further and more serious allegations concerning the conduct of an individual hospital manager. The NHB issues a writ for libel against Bulldog while Parliament is in session. Contending that this is a matter of parliamentary privilege over which the court has no jurisdiction, Bulldog refuses to enter an appearance or to defend the action.

Exercises cont'd

Meanwhile the House of Commons resolves that any judge, counsel or party who takes part in such proceedings will be guilty of contempt. Discuss the position of Bulldog and any possible action that may be taken against the members of the National Health Board, and any solicitor or counsel who proceeds with the libel action against Bulldog.

Further reading

Archer, P. (2000) 'The House of Lords, Past, Present and Future', *Political Quarterly* 70:396.

Blackburn, R. (1989) 'The Summoning and Meeting of New Parliaments in the United Kingdom', *Legal Studies* 9:165.

Brazier, R. (1989) 'The Constitutional Role of the Opposition', *Northern Ireland Law Quarterly* 40:131.

Dickson, B. and Carmichael, P. (eds) (1999) *The House of Lords: Its Parliamentary and Judicial Roles*, Oxford, Hart Publishing.

Lock, G. (1985) 'Parliamentary Privilege and the Courts', *Public Law* 64.

Munro, C.R. (2000) *Studies in Constitutional Law* (2nd edn) London, Butterworth, Chapter 7.

Oliver, D. and Drewry, G. (eds) (1998) *The Law and Parliament*, London, Butterworth.

Riddall, P. (2000) 'The Second Chamber: In Search of a Complementary Role', *Political Quarterly* 70:404.

Rodgers, R. and Walters, R. (2004) *How Parliament Works* (5th edn) London, Pearson, Chapters 1, 2, 5.

Tomkins, A. (2003) *Public Law*, Oxford, Clarendon Press, Chapter 4.

Wakeham, Lord (2000) *A House for the Future: Royal Commission on the House of Lords*, Cm 4534, London, HMSO.

Background reading

Budge, I., Crewe, I., McKay, D. and Newton, K. (2004) *The New British Politics* (3rd edn) London, Pearson, Chapters 16, 17, 18.

Gallagher, M., Laver, M. and Mair, P. (2001) *Representative Government in Modern Europe* (3rd edn) New York, McGraw-Hill, Chapter 4.

Jones, B., Kavanagh, D., Moran, M. and Norton, P. (2004) *Politics UK* (5th edn) London, Pearson, Chapter 12.

Weir, S. and Beetham, D. (1999) *Political Power and Democratic Control in Britain*, London, Routledge.

Chapter 12

The composition of Parliament and parliamentary elections

Britain has been said to be a party democracy rather than a parliamentary democracy. (Budge et al., *The New British Politics*, p. 450)

Key words

- Mixed constitution
- Different kinds of democracy
- Majorities and representation
- Conflicting functions of elections
- Financial influences
- Relative majorities, proportional representation, alternative votes
- Fair elections and freedom of expression

12.1   Introduction

The composition of Parliament raises questions about the legitimacy of the constitution. Firstly to what extent does Parliament have public consent and confidence in relation to the functions outlined in Chapter 11? Secondly which of the different kinds of democracy outlined in Chapter 2, if any, best captures the UK's arrangements? Can a non-elected element in the legislature be justified on grounds of efficiency? Do the voting rules give adequate representation and cater for the different functions of Parliament? Thirdly there are questions concerning the relationship between democracy and other liberal values. What restrictions should there be on the right to vote, stand for election or participate in an election campaign? Liberal freedoms such as freedom of expression may conflict with the aspiration of equality.

12.2   The House of Lords

Almost anyone can be a member of the House of Lords but in practice it comprises persons close to the ruling elite, linked by education and family or professional connections. The following are disqualified from membership: aliens other than Commonwealth citizens (Act of Settlement 1700 s.3 as amended), persons under 21 (SO2 – Standing Order), undischarged bankrupts (Insolvency Act 1986 s.427(1)) and persons convicted of treason until their sentence is served (Forfeiture Act 1870 s.2). Members can apparently be removed only by statute.

There is no legal limit on the size of the House of Lords. Before the House of Lords Act 1999 there were about 1349 members, making the House of Lords the largest legislative chamber in the world. The 1999 Act reduced this by ejecting 654 of the 746 hereditary peers. This still makes the House of Lords, with about 746 members, one of the largest second chambers in the world – eclipsed, according to Kellner (*Evening Standard*, 8 November 2001), only by Kazakhstan and Burkina Faso. Germany's Bundesrat has 69 members and the US Senate 100. In Europe Italy, with 326, comes nearest to the UK. Small upper chambers could be justified on the basis that they can be more cohesive and more focused. However attendance in the House of Lords is far from assiduous . In practice only about 400 attend regularly. Current reform proposals suggest reducing the membership to no more than 450 (White Paper 14 July 2008, *An Elected Second Chamber*, Cm 7438).

The dominant feature of the House of Lords is that none of its members is elected, all being chosen by the executive in one form or another. Protocol 3 of the European Convention on Human Rights (ECHR) requires states to hold free elections to the legislature. In *Matthieu-Mohun* v *Belgium* (1988) the ECHR held that this requires at least one chamber to be elected. However one of the judges stated that the elected element must comprise a majority of the legislature and the non-elected element must not have greater powers than the elected element. The present House of Lords violates the majority requirement, there being currently 646 members of the House of Commons.

The membership of the House of Lords comprises the following four categories.

The lords spiritual: The lords spiritual comprise the Archbishops of Canterbury and York, the Bishops of London, Durham and Winchester, and 21 other diocesan bishops of the Church of England, these being the senior in order of appointment. Bishops are appointed by the Queen on the advice of the Prime Minister, the practice being that he or she chooses one from a list of nominations provided by the Church authorities. The bishops vacate their seats in the Lords on ceasing to hold office. They are not peers and can vote in parliamentary elections. Dignitaries from other faiths can be appointed to the House of Lords as ordinary peers. Current reform proposals would remove the bishops from an elected chamber but retain them if there is to be an appointed element. It is not proposed that representatives from other faiths be entitled to seats. This might be unworkable in practice given the large number of sects who might claim a seat. On the other hand other than on historical grounds it is difficult to see why the Church of England should be so privileged. Representatives from any sect could be elected or appointed in the ordinary way.

Hereditary peers: Hereditary peers are persons on whom, or on whose ancestors, the monarch has conferred various ranks – dukes, marquises, earls, viscounts and barons – specifying that the peerages can be inherited. Until the House of Lords Act 1999 (below) the hereditary peers formed a majority, thereby biasing the House of Lords in favour of conservative interests and being difficult to justify rationally. The notion of the 'mixed constitution' could be raised in this context (Chapter 8). However this presupposes that the peerage is a powerful economic or political force, neither being the case today, particularly as the historical link between peerage and landholding no longer exists (although some peers such as the Duke of Westminster are among the largest landowners in the UK).

At common law a peer cannot surrender his or her peerage (*Re Parliamentary Election for Bristol SE* (1964)). However under the Peerage Act 1963, a hereditary peerage can be disclaimed for life. The peerage must be disclaimed within 12 months of succeeding to it (one month if the new peer is an MP) or within 12 months of coming of age. The succession to the peerage is not affected. A peer who disclaims his or her title cannot again become a hereditary peer but could be appointed a life peer (below).

As an initial reform measure, the House of Lords Act 1999 provides that no one shall be a member of the House of Lords by virtue of a hereditary peerage. This is subject to an exception, negotiated to prevent the peers from rejecting the Act. Under the exception the House elects ninety peers, together with the Earl Marshall and the Lord Chamberlain who are royal officials. The elected peers comprise 75 peers elected on the basis of party balance, together with 15 elected as deputy speakers and committee chairs. The elected peers sit for life. Other peers can now stand for and vote in elections to the House of Commons. As a result of the 1999 Act, no single party is likely to command an overall majority in the House.

Life peers: Life peers (about 600) are appointed by the Crown on the advice of the Prime Minister with the rank of baron. Originally life peers could not sit in the House of Lords but under the Life Peerages Act 1958 which was enacted in order to regenerate the House of Lords, they can now do so. Life peerages are intended to enable hand picked people to play a part in public life and also to be a way of countering the apparent conservative bias represented by the hereditary peers. In practice a radical element has not emerged. Life peerages are often bestowed on retired public officials who have served loyally or on retired MPs, particularly those who have held high government office. Sometimes a life peerage is created for a person who has performed outstanding public services or whom the Prime Minister wishes to appoint as a minister. This may cause political problems arising out of a lack of perceived legitimacy.

No reason need be given for the conferring of a peerage and it is unlikely that the conferring of honours or titles is subject to judicial review. Allegations are made from time to time that peerages are used to bribe supporters or get rid of dead wood in the House of Commons or even sold. It is unlawful to sell peerages or to offer to do so but this kind of transaction would be very difficult to prove on the standard of criminal liability (Honours (Prevention of Corruption) Act 1925). In an extreme case, where for example a Prime Minister attempts to flood the Lords with his or her cronies, the monarch could perhaps reject the Prime Minister's advice in relation to appointments. Where a Prime Minister seeks to act undemocratically, it is arguable that the monarch has a duty to act as the ultimate constitutional check. On two important occasions the monarch reluctantly agreed to appoint sufficient peers to secure a government majority. These were the Reform Act 1832, which extended the parliamentary franchise, and the Parliament Act 1911, which reduced the powers of the House of Lords. In both cases the House of Lords was threatening to obstruct the Commons. In the case of the 1911 Act George V agreed to appoint the peers only if the government's policy was submitted to a general election.

Pending reform of the House of Lords, the Prime Minister's conventional power to appoint life peers is subject to a non-statutory House of Lords Appointments Commission. Appointed by the Prime Minister in accordance with the principles of the Commission for Public Appointments, it vets all proposals for appointment as a life peer and also administers a new process for non-party political appointments (the so-called 'people's peers'). However its decisions are no more than advisory. The Commission comprises a cross bench peer as chair, together with three peers nominated by the main parties and three 'independent' persons. Its terms of reference embody the Nolan principles of impartiality, integrity and objectivity. Current reform proposals favour a Statutory Commission responsible directly to Parliament.

Any British or Commonwealth citizen over 21 can apply for appointment as a people's peer. The criteria for appointment are a record of 'significant achievement', 'independence of political parties' and 'an ability to contribute to the work of the House'. The last of these criteria invites preference to be given in the manner of a private club to those with whom the existing members feel personally comfortable. Most of the life peers appointed under the new regime have been persons prominent in public life and likely to be personally known to members of the political elite.

Lords of Appeal in Ordinary: These currently comprise 12 judges specifically appointed for the purpose from which are drawn the highest appellate tribunal as the Appellate Committee of the House of Lords. The same judges also sit as members of the Judicial Committee of the Privy Council, which is strictly part of the executive. They are life peers and can sit and vote in the House after they give up their judicial office from which they must retire at 70 (Judicial Pensions and Retirement Act 1993). By convention the Law Lords do not participate in party political debate while holding judicial office but may speak on questions of law reform. Other peers who hold or who have held high judicial office (Court of Appeal or above) can also be invited to sit on the Appellate Committee. Existing Law Lords will remain members of the House but, under the Constitutional Reform Act 2005, the Appellate Committee will be replaced by a separate Supreme Court (Chapter 8).

12.3   Reform of the House of Lords

Attempts to reform the Lords have foundered, mainly because of disagreement as to what proportion of the House should be elected with consequences for the supremacy of the Commons, and also because the matter has not had high political priority. There is substantial agreement that the Second Chamber should remain subservient to the House of Commons with the latter sustaining the government and having the last word on legislation. Mill (1972, Chapter 13) argued that a second chamber should primarily act as a partial check on the majority and should ideally embody

> the greatest number of elements exempt from the class interests and prejudices of the majority, but having in themselves nothing offensive to democratic feeling.

Mill thought that in every constitution there should be a centre of resistance to the predominant power 'and in a democratic constitution, therefore, a nucleus of resistance to the democracy'. He recommended including experts in a second chamber, recruited primarily from persons distinguished in the public professions, such as the judiciary, armed forces and civil service. However although he thought that the question of a second chamber was relatively unimportant, it could be justified (in both liberal and republican terms) on the basis of the corrupting effect of absolute power and as a mechanism for producing compromise. Mill's preferred solution was proportional representation in the House of Commons (below) which would make it more difficult for any majority faction to be dominant.

In a unitary system such as that of the UK, a wholly elected House might either duplicate or rival the House of Commons, thereby weakening the accountability (or power) of the government. On the other hand an entirely appointed Chamber would lack public credibility and reinforce the patronage that currently undermines the constitution.

Furthermore there is no consensus as to who should make appointments to the House and on what basis. The hereditary element is said to have the advantage of independence but at the price of legitimacy. An attractively democratic possibility would be random selection from the whole adult community, as is currently the case with jury service. However, this raises many practical and economic problems and is probably unrealistic (see Phillipson, 2004).

The Parliament Act 1911 began the process of reform by removing the power of the House of Lords to veto most public bills introduced in the Commons (Chapter 13). The Bryce Conference of 1917–18 (Cd 9038) attempted to tackle the problem of the composition of the House of Lords but was unable to agree. In 1958 the introduction of life peers reinvigorated the House to a certain extent, particularly in relation to the work of its committees. In 1968 an all party conference proposed removing voting rights from most of the hereditary element and introducing the concept of 'working peers', mainly life peers, who would form a permanent nucleus of the House. The bill to introduce these reforms was abandoned because of backbench opposition from both sides of the House.

The present Labour government intended to reform the House of Lords in two stages. Stage one comprised the House of Lords Act 1999 (above) the main result of which was to remove most of the hereditary element. Stage two has not taken place. A Royal Commission on the House of Lords (the Wakeham Report, 2000) examined the composition of the House of Lords in isolation from wider questions of constitutional reform and therefore did not question the role and powers of the House of Commons nor those of the executive. Wakeham endorsed the existing roles of the House of Lords as subordinate to the Commons, providing limited checks on the executive, a revising mechanism for legislation and a 'constitutional long-stop' to force the government to have second thoughts. Wakeham's governing principles (Wakeham, 2000, p. 31) seem to be:

> the capacity to offer counsel from a range of sources . . . broadly representative of society in the UK at the beginning of the 21st century . . . It should give the UK's constituent nations and regions, for the first time, a formally constituted voice in the Westminster Parliament.

The electorate is not to be trusted to produce these outcomes but must be paternalistically protected against itself.

Wakeham rejected the extremes of an all elected second chamber and one comprised of 'experts'. Wakeham thought that a wholly elected second chamber might produce the 'wrong sort of people', reinforce party political control, result in 'voter fatigue' and either gridlock or rubber stamp the Commons, thus weakening governmental accountability. Wakeham rejected random selection apparently because of the risk of appointing persons who would not 'fit in'. Wakeham also rejected the notion of a 'council of the wise', recognising that government is about accommodating disagreement and is necessarily political. Perhaps updating the classical 'mixed constitution', Wakeham proposed a balance of representatives from the main interests in the community with about one third elected. Elections would be on a fifteen year cycle, with one third being elected every five years to ensure that the outcome did not duplicate elections to the Commons. An independent statutory commission would appoint all other members, taking account of regional, ethnic, gender and religious concerns.

Subsequent progress of the reforms is one of confusion. Crucial matters have been left open, notably the extent to which there should be an elected element and the method of election. A government White Paper (*The House of Lords: Completing the Reforms*, 2001, Cm

5291) broadly adopted Wakeham's proposals but weakened them in favour of a larger element of government control over the House of Lords. This was not well received and was followed by proposals from the Public Administration Committee (Fifth Report, 2001–2, HC 494–1), the House of Commons and the political parties for different permutations of elected and appointed members. In 2002 a joint committee of both Houses set out seven options ranging from complete election to complete appointment. None of these were approved by the Commons while the Lords voted for an all appointed House (HL 17, HC 171, 2002–3).

The government is still reviewing the composition of the House of Lords with a view to ensuring that the House of Commons remains dominant. Revised proposals were set out in a White Paper in February 2007 which remains of value for its historical summary and references (*House of Lords Reform* Cm 7027). These proposals were not well received. The 2007 White Paper was superseded by the White Paper, *An Elected Second Chamber* Cm 7438 (14 July 2008). This favoured an elected House with the same functions and powers as the existing House of Lords. However it left open the most contentious matters, namely whether there should be an appointed element of 20 per cent and also the voting system to be used. A form of proportional representation would ensure a different political balance to that of the House of Commons. In order to avoid the political balance of the Upper House reflecting that of the Commons, its members would sit for terms of 12–15 years with staggered elections so that one third would be elected at the same time as a general election every four to five years.

A more radical proposal in the White Paper is that of 'recall'. This allows a proportion of the electorate to sign a petition which triggers a special election to remove a sitting member. The recall device has a reactionary tendency against the principle of representative democracy in that opinion can most easily be generated against voices for change.

It is not intended to introduce these reforms before the next election expected in 2010. Moreover existing members will be entitled to remain for life so the main changes will be long postponed. The White Paper was not well received. Given the desultory history of House of Lords reform it is doubtful whether these reforms will be introduced in the foreseeable future.

12.4   Membership of the House of Commons

Anyone can be a member of the House of Commons other than the following:

- aliens other than Commonwealth citizens or citizens of the Irish Republic (Act of Settlement 1700 s.3; Electoral Administration Act 2006 s.18). Resident EU citizens can sit in the devolved legislatures
- people under 18 (Election Administration Act 2006 s.17)
- mental patients (Mental Health Act 1983 – there are provisions for removing MPs under this Act)
- members of the House of Lords (Peers can sit in the devolved legislatures)
- those bishops who sit in the House of Lords (House of Commons (Removal of Clergy Disqualification) Act 2001)
- bankrupts, until five years after discharge unless the discharge certifies that the bankruptcy was not caused by the debtor's misconduct

- persons convicted of election offences (below)
- persons convicted of treason, until expiry of the sentence or pardon (Forfeiture Act 1870)
- persons convicted of an offence and sentenced to prison for more than one year while actually in prison or unlawfully at large (Representation of the People Act 1981, designed to prevent convicted terrorists in Northern Ireland from standing)
- persons holding certain public offices (House of Commons (Disqualification) Act 1975).

The last of these disqualifications is an example of the separation of powers. One element of the seventeenth century conflict between Crown and Parliament was the Commons' fear that the Crown might bribe members by giving them jobs. The Act of Settlement 1700 therefore provided that nobody who held Crown office or a place of profit under the Crown could sit in the Commons. This would of course have prevented ministers from sitting and the constitution would have had a strict separation of powers. This part of the Act was repealed by the Succession to the Crown Act 1707. However there are limits upon the number of ministers who can be MPs, thus giving the Commons a degree of independence. These are as follows:

1. Under the House of Commons (Disqualification) Act 1975, not more than 95 ministers may sit and vote. There are usually about 20 ministers in the House of Lords.
2. The Ministerial and Other Salaries Act 1975 (as amended) fixed the salaries of the various grades of minister and limits the number of paid ministers of the government to 83, plus about 30 other specialised political office holders such as whips and also four Law Officers. However a government can increase its loyalists in the House by appointing unpaid parliamentary secretaries.
3. The House of Commons (Disqualification) Act 1975 debars certain other holders of public office from sitting in the Commons. The main examples are as follows:
   - full time judges of various kinds
   - regulators of privatised undertakings
   - civil servants
   - members of the regular armed services and police (other than specialised forces such as railway police)
   - members of foreign legislatures. However by virtue of the Disqualifications Act 2000 a member of the Irish legislature (the Oireachtas) can be a member of the Commons
   - members of certain public boards and undertakings
   - holders of the offices of Steward or Bailiff of the Chiltern Hundreds or the Manor of Northstead. These are meaningless titles in the gift of the Chancellor of the Exchequer. There are no specific rules entitling MPs to resign or retire but a successful application for one of these offices has the same effect.

In the event of a dispute about a disqualification, the Judicial Committee of the Privy Council may make a declaration on the application of any person (s.7). The House may also refer a matter to the Privy Council for an opinion (Judicial Committee Act 1833 s.4). The House has the statutory power to disregard a disqualification if it has been subsequently removed, for example by the MP resigning from a disqualifying post (s.6(2)).

12.5   The Electoral System

Election law is found primarily in the Representation of the People Acts 1983 and 1985 and the Parliamentary Constituencies Act 1986. Important changes were made by the Representation of the People Act 2000, the Political Parties, Elections and Referendums Act 2000 and the Electoral Administration Act 2006.

12.5.1   The Purpose of Elections

We can assess the electoral system only in relation to its aims. Is it (a) to secure democratic local representation, (b) to produce effective government or (c) to produce 'accountable' governments? No electoral system has yet been thought up that successfully combines all three. Underlying these conflicting aims is the difference between 'representative democracy' and 'market democracy' outlined in Chapter 2. Moreover the process of electing representatives is the only democratic mechanism regularly provided by the UK constitution (referendums on particular issues are occasionally offered by particular governments) so that participatory democracy is excluded. Protocol 1 Article 3 of the ECHR provides a general and vague standard, limited to representative democracy:

> Free elections at reasonable intervals by secret ballot, under conditions which will ensure the free expression of the people in the choice of the legislature.

Until well into the nineteenth century, the prevalent belief was that only landowners had a sufficient stake in the realm to vote, the majority of the population enjoying 'virtual representation' through the property owners. During the nineteenth century the extension of voting rights to non-property owners was slowly and reluctantly conceded, resisted by liberal arguments that the freedom of talented people to develop themselves would be curtailed by the inflated demands of the masses. Democracy was also resisted by the likes of Dicey, who thought that it was unpredictable, and Matthew Arnold (1822–88). Arnold (*Culture and Anarchy*) believed in a grand overarching concept of the public good and recommended an 'authority of culture', by which he seemed to mean a monarchy or the Platonic ideal of a wise ruling class. This approach is still canvassed in the context of reform of the House of Lords. It was not until 1948 that a universal principle of one person one vote was fully adopted (Representation of the People Act 1948).

There is a conflict between the law of the electoral process and practical politics. The legal basis of democracy in the UK is that the electorate in each constituency chooses an individual to represent the constituency in the House of Commons. However as we have seen, by convention, the House of Commons chooses the leader of the executive who is the party leader commanding a majority in the Commons. The party system therefore encourages the electorate to vote for a leader, with the question of effective democratic representation being subsidiary. Elections are therefore fought and funded between the parties on a national battlefield.

The ECHR does not require any particular kind of electoral system, thus endorsing the principle that elections may have different aims. An electoral system must not discriminate against particular groups of citizens although a political party cannot apparently challenge the electoral system on the basis that it is at a disadvantage (see *Lindsey* v *UK* (1979); *Matthieu-Mohun* v *Belgium* (1987); *Liberal Party* v *UK* (1982)). The courts are likely to adopt a low level of review in relation to electoral machinery because of sensitivity to interfering with the province of Parliament (*R* v *Boundary Commission for England ex parte Foot* (1983).

12.5.2   The Electoral Commission

The Electoral Commission was a response to the concerns of the Fifth Report of the Committee on Standards in Public Life (1998, Cm 4057) relating to the financing of political parties. It was created by the Political Parties, Elections and Referendums Act 2000 with wide ranging and disparate functions. These include the following:

1. It has a remit to 'keep under review' and report to the Secretary of State such matters relating to elections and referendums as it may determine from time to time (s.6). It registers political parties and keeps records of their accounts and donations to them thereby bringing what had previously been regarded as private concerns into the open.
2. It provides for public access to information relating to the financial affairs of political parties.
3. It is responsible for periodic reviews of constituency boundaries.
4. It prescribes performance standards for the local authorities who administer elections (Electoral Administration Act 2006).
5. It advises broadcasters in relation to party political broadcasts.
6. It is empowered to facilitate public education relating to current electoral systems in the UK and the EU.
7. It is empowered to arrange schemes for alternative methods of voting such as electronic and postal ballots, making voting facilities available in shops or extending voting times.

The Electoral Commission is independent of the executive. It is appointed by the Queen on an address from the House of Commons which must have the support of the Speaker after consultation with the party leaders (s.3). Its members must not be members, officers or employees of political parties nor holders of elective office. Nor must they have had such connections or been registered party donors (below) within the last ten years (s.3(4)). The Electoral Commission reports to the Secretary of State and is accountable to an advisory Speaker's Committee which comprises relevant ministers and backbench MPs (s.2) and an advisory Parliamentary Parties Panel comprising persons appointed by the parties who must include at least two MPs (s.4).

The Electoral Commission was the subject of the Eleventh Report of the Committee on Standards in Public Life (2007). This was against a background of reduced public confidence in the electoral system as a result partly of the widespread use of postal voting with its opportunities for fraud and partly because of worries about the funding of political parties by private business interests. The Committee found that the Electoral Commission was unclear about its role as regulator as opposed to that of administrator and was passive and timid in investigating abuses. The report pointed out that the Commission's staff lacked relevant expertise and experience, this being due to the requirement that the Commission must be independent thus raising a familiar tension between efficiency and the appearance of fairness. The Report recommended that the Commission's structure and processes should focus more strongly on regulation. In particular its statutory remit as a regulator, as opposed to a monitor, should be clarified.

It suggested that the Commission should be accountable to the Constitutional Affairs Committee of the Commons rather than to the Speaker's Committee which operates on a less formal and therefore less transparent basis. The Report also recommended that the Electoral Commission should no longer be concerned with reviewing constituency boundaries.

12.5.3 General Elections and By-elections

A general election occurs when a Parliament ends. It must be held within about three weeks from the proclamation which summons a new Parliament (Chapter 11). The timetable and other procedural matters are set out in 'Parliamentary Election Rules' in Schedule 1 of the 1983 Act. Writs are sent from the Crown to designated returning officers in each constituency. The returning officers are responsible for the election. There are rules for designating returning officers but where a constituency is a whole county or a whole district, the returning officer is the sheriff of the county or the chairman of the district council. In England this is one of the few remaining duties of the sheriff, who prior to Tudor times was the representative of the Crown in local areas. Registration officers, who are normally local authority chief executives, make the detailed arrangements.

A by-election takes place when there is an individual vacancy in the House. The House itself decides when to fill the vacancy, and by convention the motion is proposed by the party to which the former member belonged. Unfortunately there is no time limit for this. When the House is not sitting, the Speaker can issue the writ (Recess Elections Act 1975).

12.5.4 Candidates

It is important that any law restricting the ability of people to stand for Parliament does not violate the general principle of free election. An individual with an axe to grind or a single interest party should be as free to stand as one of the major national parties, despite the undoubted inconvenience to the latter. The law is therefore concerned with fairness between candidates and with preventing fraud, disruption or confusion.

A candidate must provide a deposit of £500 (forfeited if five per cent of the vote is not won) and be supported by ten signatures (Representation of the People Act 1983 Schedule 1). The nomination paper must state either that the candidate stands in the name of a qualifying registered party under the Political Parties, Elections and Referendums Act 2000 or that they do not purport to represent any party (s.22). The latter applies to candidates standing as independents, to the Speaker seeking re-election or if the nomination paper provides no description. A party is any organisation or person that puts up at least one candidate so that a one person party is possible (s.40). There is nothing to stop a candidate standing in more than one constituency (contrast the devolved regimes).

Each political party must be registered with the Electoral Commission. In order to qualify for registration, the party must provide its name, its headquarters' address and the names of its leader, treasurer and nominating officer, although these can be the same person. It can also provide the name of its campaign officer and if it does so the campaign officer will have some of the responsibilities of the treasurer (s.25). It must also have a scheme approved by the Commission for regulating its financial affairs. It can also provide up to 12 descriptions of itself. The Commission can refuse to register a name or description on the following grounds: having more than six words, being obscene or offensive or where publication would be an offence, being misleading, contradictory or confusing, being in a script other than roman or containing words prohibited by the Secretary of State (s.28; Electoral Administration Act 2006 ss.48, 49). This seems to create a significant possibility of executive censorship. Similar rules apply to party emblems (s.29).

A registered political party is subject to accounting and audit requirements (Political Parties, Elections and Referendums Act 2000 Part III; Electoral Administration Act 2006). Accounts must be lodged with the Electoral Commission and must be available for public inspection (s.46). For the first time the law has acknowledged that political parties are more than private clubs and should be subject to external financial controls. However this creates a risk of state interference with political freedom.

12.6 Eligibility to Vote

In general the law has become progressively more liberal, partly in response to a steady decline in turnout at general elections. At the 2001 election turnout was less than 60 per cent, the government being elected by only 25 per cent of the electorate, thus raising serious questions of legitimacy. Turnout was about two per cent better in 2005.

Under the Representation of the People Act 2000, to be eligible to vote a person must be (s.1):

1. 18 years of age on the date of the poll (the Power Report (2006) recommended reduction to 16).
2. Either a British citizen, a citizen of Ireland or a 'qualifying' Commonwealth citizen (that is, one who is entitled to reside in the UK). Non-citizens can vote in local elections and in elections in the devolved regimes.
3. Registered on the electoral register for the constituency. To qualify for registration, a person must be 18 years of age or due to be 18 within 12 months beginning on 1 December following the date of the application for registration and resident in a dwelling in the constituency on the date of the application for registration.

'Residence' means the person is normally living at the address in question as his or her home. This is a question of fact and seems to focus on whether the dwelling is the applicant's home for the time being as opposed to his being a guest or a lodger for some particular purpose. According to section 3(2) of the Representation of the People Act 2000:

> regard shall be had in particular to the purpose and other circumstances, as well as to the fact of his presence at or absence from the address on that date . . . for example, where at any particular time a person is staying at any place other than on a permanent basis he may in all the circumstances be taken to be at that time (a) resident there if he has no home elsewhere, or (b) not resident there if he does have a home elsewhere.

Temporary absence at work or attendance on a course at an educational institution does not interrupt residence if either the applicant intends to return to the actual residence within six months and will not be prevented from doing so by performance of that duty or the dwelling would otherwise be his or her permanent residence and he or she would be in actual residence (ibid. s.3(3)). Temporary periods of unemployment can be ignored (s.3(4)). A student might therefore choose between two possible residencies (*Fox v Stirk*

(1970)). Under the Political Parties, Elections and Referendums Act 2000 persons in mental hospitals, unconvicted prisoners and the homeless, as an alternative to establishing residence on normal principles, can make a 'declaration of local connection' in relation to another constituency (s.6).

There are special registration provisions for the benefit of certain people who have to be absent for long periods. These include British citizens resident abroad who have been on the electoral register during the last 15 years (Representation of the People Act 1985), persons in mental hospitals, unconvicted prisoners, merchant seamen, members of the armed forces (service voters, Electoral Administration Act 2006 s.13) and certain other public employees. Detained offenders are not resident where they are detained (ss.4, 5). Applicants to be absent voters must provide a signature and date of birth as a protection against fraud (Electoral Administration Act 2006 s.14).

Even if they are on the electoral register, the following have no right to vote:

- Members of the House of Lords other than bishops sitting ex officio.
- Convicted prisoners and persons detained in mental hospitals as offenders (except for contempt of court or refusing to pay a fine), including persons unlawfully at large (Representation of the People Act 2000 s.2). A common law mental capacity test was abolished by the Electoral Administration Act 2006.
- Persons convicted of election offences (corrupt practices – five years; illegal practices – five years in the particular constituency).
- Illegal immigrants and asylum seekers waiting for a decision (Political Parties, Elections and Referendums Act 2000 s.2).

In *Hirst v UK (No. 2)* (2004) the European Court of Human Rights held that the blanket exclusion for prisoners violates the right to free elections (above), depriving some 700,000 people of the right to vote. The court held that an automatic absolute bar was not acceptable, there being no legitimate policy reason for excluding all convicted prisoners, irrespective of such matters as the nature of the offence or length of sentence. The prisoner in question was serving a life sentence and had already served its punitive element; his continuing detention was because he was regarded as dangerous. This in itself should not necessarily disqualify him. The government had argued that decisions as to the franchise were political and should be decided by Parliament. However the court pointed out that there should be a considered debate in the legislature rather than unquestioning reliance on tradition. The government has not yet responded to this ruling.

12.7 The Voting System

As we have seen the vote is for a local representative in the House of Commons. In practice however, due to the convention that the person with majority support in the House of Commons forms a government and that this is likely to be the leader of the largest political party, the voter has the conflicting task of choosing the government and choosing a representative to hold the government to account. This is one reason why the parliamentary system is flawed.

There are problems with the workings of voting systems as reflections of democratic values. Firstly a system that always produces a genuine majority government may be impossible to achieve. For example in an election where there are three candidates, different majorities might prefer A to B, B to C and C to A. Secondly the electoral system for Parliament of 'first past the post', or 'relative majority', is a 'plurality' system, giving the seat to the candidate with the largest number of votes. This need not be an overall majority. Plurality systems are defective in terms of democratic representation in that they ignore the votes for all but the winning candidate so that votes do not translate directly into seats and smaller parties are treated unfairly. For example in 2005 Labour won 356 seats with 35.2 per cent of the vote, the Conservatives won 198 seats on 32.3 per cent and the Liberal Democrats won 10 per cent of the seats with 21 per cent of the vote. In England the Conservatives with 600,000 more votes than Labour won 90 fewer seats.

Another reason why a majority in Parliament may not reflect the majority of the voters is that the constituencies do not contain the same number of voters (below) so that it takes fewer voters to elect a candidate in some seats than in others. About three quarters of the seats are 'safe seats' for either Labour or the Conservatives so that the MP is effectively chosen by party activists. The system broadly favours the Labour Party since Labour votes are more evenly distributed across the country, including the larger cities which have several constituencies with relatively small populations. Conservative seats tend to be concentrated in rural or suburban areas. The Blake Commission on Electoral Reform (Hansard Society, 1976) castigated the voting system as producing flagrant 'minority rule' and at the same time suppressing other minorities. In Parliament itself the members always vote by simple majority in a straight yes/no way between two propositions. The combination of these two forms of voting means that any particular law may command the support of only about 20 per cent of the public.

However the first past the post system is simple and transparent, offering voters a clear choice. It encourages accountable governments that are supported by substantial numbers of voters. A party stands or falls as such at an election and it must answer on its own record. It cannot blame any minority parties and, unlike systems with proportional representation (below), governments cannot change without the consent of the electorate (below).

12.7.1　Other Voting Systems: the Devolved Governments

The choice between voting systems is between the incommensurables of strong government, fairness, reflecting the majority will and protecting minorities. Complex systems of proportional representation (PR) are widely used in an attempt to achieve fairness and protect minorities. They rely on mathematical formulae to make the outcome correspond more closely to the distribution of the vote. All have advantages and disadvantages and no voting system has yet been devised that reconciles the competing demands on it. PR systems favour negotiations between political parties and produce unstable governments held together by shifting alliances between small and large parties, thus weakening accountability. Arguably a degree of instability is desirable in a liberal society where there is no agreement as to the right answer to social and political problems. There are several variations of PR. The main forms are as follows.

The party list. Under the 'closed list system', the voter chooses only the party, individual seats being allocated by the party in accordance with the party's share of the vote. The party list system has been said to destroy the principle of local representation and to put excessive power into the hands of party leaders. In Germany a party must secure at least five per cent of the overall vote or win three constituencies to gain 'list' seats. Thus extremist minorities are prevented from holding the balance of power. This method is used for elections to the European Parliament. A version of it, the **additional member** system, is used for elections to the Scottish Parliament, the Welsh Assembly and the London Assembly (see Scotland Act 1998 ss.1–8; Government of Wales Act 2006 ss.6–9; Greater London Authority Act 1999 s.4). A proportion of candidates (73/129 in Scotland, 40/60 in Wales) are elected on the first past the post principle. This is topped up by a second vote for other candidates on a party list basis, representing eight regions in Scotland and five regions in Wales. Each region is allocated an 'electoral region figure'. In the case of individual candidates, this is simply the total number of votes cast for that person. In the case of a party, the electoral region figure is the number of votes won by that party, divided by one plus the number of seats won by the party in the constituency elections. The candidate or party with the highest electoral region figure wins the first seat. The second and subsequent seats are awarded on the same basis, in each case after a recalculation to take account of seats already won. Thus the fewer the seats won by a party in the constituency elections, the better the chances of winning a seat in the top up election. The second vote can be for either an individual candidate or a registered political party. A person cannot stand for election in more than one constituency.

The single transferable vote. This is probably the method that most reflects voting preferences but loses the single member constituency. It is used for elections in Northern Ireland where, as we have seen, the desire to neutralise conflicting political forces dominates the constitutional arrangements (Chapter 5; see Northern Ireland Act 1998 ss.8, 28, 34). Each constituency can elect a given number of members. Votes are cast for candidates in order of preference. There is an 'electoral quota' for each constituency, calculated according to a formula based on the number of voters divided by the number of seats. The quota is the winning post. A candidate who obtains the quota based on first preferences is elected. Any surplus votes over the quota are transferred to other candidates according to the second preference expressed on the winning candidate's voting slips. This may produce more winners who reach the quota. The process is repeated until all the seats are filled. If no candidate reaches the quota, the candidate with the lowest number of votes is eliminated and his or her votes distributed among the other candidates. This system enables voters to choose between different candidates within the same party since all seats within a constituency could be fought by each party. It also prevents wasted votes and protects minorities.

There are also non-PR voting systems that attempt to produce a candidate with majority support. The main example is the **alternative vote** system. The candidates are voted for in order of preference and there are several rounds. After each round the candidate with the lowest vote is eliminated and his or her votes distributed among the others until a winner with a clear overall majority emerges. If there is still a deadlock, a winner might then be chosen by lot. This system seems unfair in that it takes account of the second preferences only of those who supported losing candidates. It is the system used for elections for the Mayor of London (Greater London Authority Act 1999 s.4).

The alternative vote system was recommended for Britain in 1910 by the Royal Commission on Electoral Systems. In 1998 the Independent Commission on the Voting System (Cm 4090) chaired by Lord Jenkins, a Liberal Democrat victim of the simple majority system, recommended the introduction of a voting system that combined the alternative vote in single member constituencies, topped up from a party list. The Power

Report (2006), into UK democracy (Rowntree Reform Trust) condemned the first past the post system and supported the alternative vote system. It appears that the first past the post system will remain for elections to the UK Parliament for the foreseeable future. It is unlikely to be in the interests of a government to change the electoral system.

12.8 The Constituencies

The outcome of a general election is usually determined by a relatively small number of 'marginal constituencies' in which no one party has a substantial majority. Voting patterns in the UK are significantly influenced by geographical considerations so that the boundaries of the constituencies are crucial, as is the number of constituencies in each region. Moreover the population is not evenly dispersed. Therefore each vote does not carry equal weight.

There is semi-independent machinery for fixing electoral boundaries (Parliamentary Constituencies Act 1986). This is currently the responsibility of the Electoral Commission working through four Boundary Committees for England, Wales, Scotland and Northern Ireland (Political Parties, Elections and Referendums Act 2000 s.14). A wide range of criteria are used and there is considerable discretion. There must be a review of the number and boundaries of constituencies at intervals of between 10 and 15 years. The last review was in 2007. A review may take several years to complete and once made could well be out of date. A report is submitted to the Home Secretary who is required 'as soon as may be' to lay the report before both Houses of Parliament, together with a draft Order in Council giving effect to it (s.2(5)). Each House must approve the order which is then submitted to the Queen in Council. It then becomes law.

The main criteria are as follows (Schedule 2):

1. The total number of seats in the UK but excluding Northern Ireland must not be substantially greater or less than 613.
2. Wales must have at least 35 constituencies and Northern Ireland a minimum of 16 and a maximum of 18, but normally 17. The effect is that Wales is represented more generously than England and Northern Ireland in terms of population. Post devolution Scottish constituencies are on a par with those of England (currently 59 Scottish seats).
3. There must be a separate 'City of London' constituency.
4. Each country has an 'electoral quota'. This is a rough average of voters per constituency. It is calculated by dividing the total electorate by the number of constituencies on the date when the Commission begins its review. It cannot be updated during the course of a review. For England the quota is roughly 65,000. The electoral quota is one factor to be taken into account but because of the many factors that have to be balanced few constituencies correspond exactly to the quota, although in recent years the extent of variation has become less.
5. Other factors to be taken into account are:
    - Conformity to local government boundaries.
    - Local ties.
    - The inconvenience involved in altering boundaries except to comply with local government boundaries.
    - Special geographical considerations including the size, shape and accessibility of a constituency.

These factors may point in different directions and it is a matter for the Commission how to rank them. The Commission is not required 'to aim at giving full effect in all circumstances to the rules' (Schedule 2, para. 7). However the rules relating to the number of constituencies seem to have the highest priority. Inconvenience and local ties can be balanced against any of the rules, but 'special geographical considerations' are related only to the 'local government boundary' and the 'electoral quota' factors.

The report and the Order in Council can be challenged in the courts but the chances of success are small. The time factor is important. As we have seen, no court can interfere with parliamentary procedure so that the Home Secretary could not be prevented from laying an order before the House (*Harper* v *Home Secretary of State for the Home Department* (1955)). A court could perhaps require a Home Secretary to lay an order, in order to prevent her or him delaying a report which does not favour the government party. Moreover by virtue of section 4(7) the validity of any Order in Council which purports to be made under the Act and which recites that approval was given by each House 'shall not be questioned in any legal proceedings' (see Chapter 18).

A report must therefore be challenged before it is submitted to the Home Secretary. Even here the chances of success are slim because of the Commission's wide discretion. The court will defer to the subjective judgement which the Commission is required to make. It does not require equality to be the primary aim nor indeed will it rank the various criteria. Even if the Commission does act improperly, for example by ranking the various factors capriciously, the court out of respect for Parliament would not normally make an order that prevents the report from going to Parliament. At most it would make a declaration (a non-binding opinion). See *R* v *Boundary Commission for England ex parte Foot* (1983)).

12.9   Voting Procedures

Voting is traditionally in person at a designated polling station. However any person otherwise qualified to vote can have a postal vote. 'Absent voters' are permitted to vote by post or proxy (Representation of the People Act 2000 Schedule 4). A person on the register but no longer resident in the constituency can have an absent vote. A proxy vote also applies in special cases. These include service and overseas voters, disabled people, people with work or education commitments and people who have to make a long journey. The government is currently encouraging the use of postal and electronic voting.

The ballot is secret in the sense that the vote itself is cast in privacy. However there is no protection for postal votes and by comparing the registration number on the voting slip with the register of electors, it is possible for officials to discover how a voter cast his or her vote. Indeed this is necessary to prevent multiple voting. There are provisions intended to prevent ballot papers being examined except for the purpose of detecting election offences (Representation of the People Act 2000 Schedule 1). There was substantial evidence of the misuse of proxy and postal votes in the 2005 election. New offences of stealing such votes were created by the Electoral Administration Act 2006 (s.40). The Eleventh Report of the Committee for Standards in Public Life 2007 (above) proposes that registration by households be replaced by individual registration. This is designed to combat fraudulent postal voting whereby one member of a household can return votes on behalf of others.

12.10 Election Campaigns

For most purposes the election period begins with the date of the proclamation announcing the dissolution of Parliament and ends with the date of the poll (Political Parties, Elections and Referendums Act 2000 Schedule 10) but an election campaign may start well before that (ibid. s.72). This chapter is concerned with parliamentary elections but the same principles apply to other elections. The election campaign at constituency level has always been closely regulated by laws designed to ensure fairness between the candidates campaigning in their local arenas. The law was open to the charge that it does not allow for national party politics with its massive financial backing from private donors nor for modern methods of campaigning, including the intensive use of the media. The Political Parties, Elections and Referendums Act 2000 attempts to bring the law up to date by addressing this reality (see *The Funding of Political Parties in the United Kingdom*, 1999, Cm 4443). Reflecting the Nolan Principles of Public Life, the Act attempts to bring greater openness and accountability to the financing of political parties and national campaigns.

12.10.1 Campaign Expenses

There are controls over the money spent on the election campaign. They are intended to ensure that no candidate has an unfair advantage or can buy votes (see *R v Jones* (1999)). In the US restrictions upon election expenses have been held to violate freedom of speech (*Buckley* v *Valeo* (1976)). The counterargument is that equality of resources is a better safeguard of democracy in the long run. The Power Report (2006) suggested, that political parties should be funded by the state so as to avoid being unduly influenced by wealthy individuals. On the other hand state funding attracts state control which may be an equally undesirable prospect. Moreover it is not easy to produce a formula for payments that would be democratically fair and would not favour the status quo. There is no general state funding for political parties. However policy development grants of up to two million pounds are available from the Electoral Commission to parties with at least two MPs and money is provided by each House of Parliament to opposition parties for their parliamentary duties ('Short Money', after the proposer). (See White Paper, *Party Finance and Expenditure in the UK* (2008) Cm 7329.)

The main controls (the Representation of the People Act 1983 applies unless otherwise stated) are as follows:

▷ Every candidate must have an election agent who is accountable for the conduct of the candidate's campaign. A candidate can appoint himself as agent. There are controls over receipts and expenses out of the candidate's own pocket (ss.73, 74).

▷ There is a maximum limit upon the amount that can be spent on behalf of any candidate in respect of 'the conduct or management of a election' (s.75; Political Parties, Elections and Referendums Act 2000 s.132). This can be varied by statutory instrument. It depends primarily on the size of the constituency and amounts to about £10,000 (SI 2005 no. 269). There is a maximum of £100,000 for by-elections where there is less national support. There is no fixed definition of an election expense. Some expenditure, for example to canvassers, on posters (except to advertising agents), on hiring vehicles to take people to vote and on broadcasting from abroad, is banned completely (ss.101–12). Reasonable personal expenses can be incurred (s.18). The Electoral Bill proposes that for the purpose of electoral expenditure the restrictions should be triggered from when a candidate is adopted.

▷ Candidates are entitled to free use of schools and public buildings for meetings (ss.95, 96). Each candidate can send one election address to each voter post-free (s.91).

▷ The Political Parties, Elections and Referendums Act 2000 extended controls over 'campaign expenditure' (s.72) by registered political parties at national level (s.79, Schedule 9). This applies during the 'campaign period', which is 365 days, ending with polling day. Thus the artificiality of distinguishing between promoting the party and promoting the candidate no longer arises. All campaign expenditure must be authorised by the party treasurer, his or her deputy, or other responsible officer delegated by the treasurer (s.75). Campaign expenditure includes party political broadcasts, advertising other than leaflets giving personal information about candidates, market research, rallies, press conferences and transport (Schedule 8). There are overall limits on expenditure based on the number of constituencies contested amounting to £30,000 for each constituency (s.79). The treasurer must deliver a return of expenditure to the Electoral Commission (s.83) which must be made available for public inspection (s.84).

▷ There are provisions regulating payment by third parties, particularly from overseas, on behalf of candidates during the campaign period. No expenditure over £500 can be incurred 'with a view to' promoting a candidate without the authority of the candidate or agent thus counting as part of the candidate's expenses (Representation of the People Act 1983 s.75; Political Parties Elections and Referendums Act 2000 s.131; compare *Bowman* v *UK* (1998): possible restriction on freedom of expression). There are exceptions for newspapers and broadcasting.

▷ At national level it is an offence to incur 'controlled expenditure' above certain limits unless it is made by a 'recognised third party' (s.94). Controlled expenditure is the production or publication of material which is made available to the public and which can reasonably be regarded as intended to promote any candidate (including prejudicing another candidate) even if the material serves some other purpose as well (s.85). For example a leaflet put out by an animal rights pressure group might be controlled expenditure.

The limits are £10,000 for England and £5,000 for the other regions. However a 'recognised third party' registered with the Electoral Commission has higher limits (£793,500 for England, £108,000 for Scotland, £60,000 for Wales, £27,000 for Northern Ireland (Schedule 10)). A recognised third party must be an individual resident in the UK or on the electoral register, or a registered political party, company, trade union, building society, friendly society, partnership or unincorporated association. This could include a pressure group (s.88).

There are certain exceptions to these limits which include newspaper editorial matter, broadcasts, personal expenses and the value of services provided free by individuals (s.87).

▷ Controls also apply to donations, loans and credit facilities of more than £200 to political parties. These controls were tightened by the Electoral Administration Act 2006 as a result of allegations that wealthy individuals were seeking favours in return for loans to political parties. These controls are not intended to outlaw payments as such but to bring them into the open and ensure accountability. Suspicions concerning secret payments particularly from overseas sources have tainted both main parties. 'Donation' is widely defined to include gifts, sponsorship, subscriptions, fees, expenses and the provision of non-commercial services. (s.50). A registered party cannot accept a payment if it is not made by a 'permissible donor' or if it is anonymous (s.54(2); Electoral Administration Act 2006 s. 61).

A permissible donor must be registered to vote in the UK or be a business, trade union or registered political party based in the UK. In the case of a company, the shareholders must have approved the donation and the amount must be disclosed in the directors' report (s.140, Schedule 19). There are some exceptions to the duty of disclosure. These include voluntary services provided by an individual, various payments made under statute, payments to MPs by the European Parliament and the hire of stands at party conferences for a payment deemed reasonable by the Commission.

The party must report relevant donations or loans of more than £5,000 regularly to the Electoral Commission (ss.63, 65, 68, 96; Electoral Administration Act 2006 ss.56, 57). This has caused problems since the person responsible for reporting is not clearly identified. The Commission keeps a public register of controlled expenditure although this must not include the address of a donor who is an individual (s.69). Impermissible payments must be returned or, if the donor or lender cannot be identified, given to the Commission (s.56). The court can order a payment to be forfeited (s.58).

12.10.2   Broadcasting and the Press

There are rules which attempt to ensure that the parties are treated fairly which must be balanced against freedom of speech. Campaign publicity has qualified privilege in the law of defamation so that there is no liability if it is published in good faith (*Culnane* v *Morris* (2006)). The same would apply to the press and broadcasting. There are further controls over the broadcast media, reflecting its power to influence a campaign:

- Political advertising by commercial broadcasters is unlawful except for party political broadcasts made by agreement between the BBC, OFCOM (the Office of Communications) and the main parties (see Communications Act 2003 ss. 319–321; *R* v *Radio Authority ex parte Bull* (1995)). This prevents the worst excesses of wealthy parties. Only registered political parties can make party political broadcasts (Political Parties, Elections and Referendums Act 2000 s.37). Political broadcasting programmes do not count as election expenses (Representation of the People Act 1983 s.75(1)).
- There is a general duty on OFCOM to preserve good taste and balance and impartiality in all political broadcasting (Communications Act 2003 s.6). The BBC is not governed by statute but operates under a royal charter and an agreement with the Home Office. However OFCOM can regulate the BBC in accordance with the charter and agreement (Communications Act 2003 s.198). OFCOM forbids the expression of editorial opinion about matters of public policy excluding broadcasting matters. The independent broadcasters are protected by the European Convention on Human Rights in respect of the right of freedom of expression (Chapter 20). However as a public body the BBC may not be entitled to such protection (Chapter 19). In principle the broadcasters' duties are enforceable by the

courts. However the idea of political impartiality is both vague and complex and the courts are reluctant to interfere in party political matters. For example must there be balance within the context of every specific subject? How much coverage should minority parties enjoy? It is unlikely that a court would intervene with the broadcasting authority's decision except in a case of bad faith or complete irrationality (see *R* v *Broadcasting Complaints Commission ex parte Owen* (1985); *R (Pro-Life Alliance)* v *BBC* (2003)).

▷ Each broadcasting authority in consultation with the parties must adopt a code of practice concerning the participation of the parties in items about the constituency (Representation of the People Act 1983 s.93 as amended).

▷ It is an illegal practice for a person to 'use or aid, abet, counsel or procure' the use of broadcasting stations outside the UK for electoral purposes except where the matter is to be retransmitted by one of the domestic broadcasting companies (ibid.). However this may not prevent overseas stations from directly broadcasting to voters and does not control the internet.

12.10.3 Election Disputes

There is an Election Court comprising two High Court judges. Either a voter or a candidate may within three months of the election lodge a petition to the court. The court can disqualify a candidate, order a recount or scrutiny of the votes, declare the result of the election, void the election and order a fresh election (Representation of the People Act 1983 s.159). The court's decision takes the form of a report to the Speaker which the House is bound to accept (s.144(7)).

Election offences are either 'corrupt' or 'illegal' practices. These involve the offender being disqualified as a candidate or prevented from sitting in Parliament. The extent of the disqualification depends upon whether it is a corrupt practice (ten years everywhere) or an illegal practice (five years in a particular constituency). 'Innocent' illegal practices can be overlooked (s.167). A corrupt practice involves dishonesty, improper pressure on voters or improper expenditure. Illegal practices concern breaches of various statutory requirements relating to agents, premises, advertising, broadcasting and other matters. Where an election offence is involved, separate criminal proceedings may be taken in an ordinary court in relation to the offence. Conviction disqualifies a person from membership of the House and the Speaker must declare the seat vacant. There are also offences concerning misuse of the voting process which are prosecuted in the ordinary courts (Electoral Administration Act 2006).

Summary

▷ The House of Lords is unelected and with nearly 700 members is one of the largest legislatures in the world – this is thought to be inappropriate to its functions. The composition of the House of Lords is to be further reformed. The government has proposed that the House remains mainly unelected but with an elected element of one fifth. A further one fifth should be chosen by an independent commission but most of the House should be nominated by the political parties and appointed by the Prime Minister. As yet no further reforms have been made.

Summary cont'd

▷ The voting system for parliamentary elections is currently the simple plurality, first past the post system. Voting systems must cater for the incommensurables of effective government, accountable government and democratic representation. We asked whether the electoral system is adapted to its modern task of choosing governments, whether it is truly representative of public opinion and whether it is fair to all candidates. We briefly compared different kinds of voting system including the alternative vote and PR. Variations of PR are used in elections to the regional legislatures and the European Parliament. This is likely to create political tensions within the UK.

▷ The machinery for regulating constituency boundaries gives a certain amount of protection against political interference but proposals for changes must be approved by the House of Commons. It is difficult to challenge decisions made by this process in the courts.

▷ The law governing the conduct of elections, which had previously ignored national politics in favour of the individual election at local level, has recently been reformed to regulate campaign expenditure at national level including spending by third parties on election campaigns and sponsorship of political parties. The independent Electoral Commission has wide responsibilities in relation to the finances of political parties and the conduct of elections. This is intended to bring greater openness and accountability to political parties.

▷ Controls over election broadcasting are designed to ensure fairness between the parties in accordance with their popular support and are more stringent than are restrictions over the press.

Exercises

12.1 'The capacity to offer counsel from a range of sources . . . broadly representative of society in the UK at the beginning of the 21st century . . . It should give the UK's constituent nations and regions, for the first time, a formally constituted voice in the Westminster Parliament' (Wakeham Report). To what extent does the House of Lords as it is at present meet these requirements?

12.2 'In a democracy there is no point in an upper house of the legislature. If both houses are elected, there is a problem of duplication. If the upper house is not elected then it is not legitimate.' Discuss with reference to attempts to reform the House of Lords.

12.3 To what extent does the parliamentary electoral system produce a representative democracy?

12.4 Explain the basis on which parliamentary constituencies are designated. Do the present arrangements contain adequate safeguards against political manipulation?

12.5 'There is now an overwhelming case for legislation regulating expenditure on a national (election) campaign' (Rawlings). 'Restrictions on the conduct of elections violate basic rights of free expression.' Do you consider that the Political Parties, Elections and Referendums Act 2000 has adequately addressed these competing concerns?

12.6 A general election is expected to take place within the next year. The Campaign for Free University Education proposes to distribute leaflets and hold meetings during the election campaign in various university towns. Jerry, a wealthy businessman resident in the US, wishes to make an anonymous loan of one million pounds to any political party that will campaign to withdraw the UK from the EU. He also proposes to advertise in the national press and on TV in favour of banning immigration to the UK. Discuss the legality of these proposals.

Exercises cont'd

12.7 'Reforms of the electoral system through the introduction of a single transferable vote . . . would revitalise the operation of political processes and make a major contribution to the development of a more accountable, effective system and a more influential citizenry' (Oliver). Discuss.

Further reading

Bogdanor, V. (1999) 'Reforming the Lords: a Sceptical View', *Political Quarterly* 70:375.

Constitutional Commission (1999) *Options for a New Second Chamber*, London, Constitutional Commission.

Fifth Report of the Committee on Standards in Public Life (1998) *The Funding of Political Parties in the United Kingdom*, Cm 4057, London, HMSO.

Hansard Society (1999) *The Future of Parliament: Reform of the Second Chamber*, London, Hansard Society.

Lardy, H. (2000) 'Democracy by Default: The Representation of the People Act 2000', *Modern Law Review* 64:63.

McClean, I. (2000) 'Mr Asquith's Unfinished Business', *Political Quarterly* 70:382.

Marriot, J. (2005) 'Alarmist or Relaxed: Election Expenditure Limits and Freedom of Speech', Public Law 764.

Phillipson, G. (2004) 'The "Greatest Quango of Them All" ', *Public Law* 352.

Report of the Independent Commission on the Voting System (Jenkins Report) (1998) Cm 4090, London, HMSO.

Report of the Power Commission (2006) *Power to the People*, Rowntree Trust, York Publishing.

Russell, M. (2000) *Reforming the House of Lords: Lessons from Overseas*, Oxford University Press.

Russell, M. and Cornes, R. (2000) 'The Royal Commission on the House of Lords: A House for the Future?', *Modern Law Review* 64:82.

Wakeham, Lord (2000) *A House for the Future: Royal Commission on the House of Lords*, Cm 4534, London, HMSO.

Webb, P. (2001) 'Parties and Party Systems: Modernisation, Regulation and Diversity', *Parliamentary Affairs* 54:308.

Weill, R. (2004) 'We the British People', *Public Law* 380.

Background reading

Budge, I., Crewe, I., McKay, D. and Newton, K. (2004) *The New British Politics* (3rd edn) London, Pearson, Chapters 15, 16, 17.

Gallagher, M., Laver, M. and Mayer, P. (2001) *Representative Government in Modern Europe* (3rd edn) New York, McGraw-Hill, Chapter 11.

Jones, B., Kavanagh, D., Moran, M. and Norton, P. (2004) *Politics UK* (5th edn) London, Pearson, Chapters 8, 12.

Chapter 13

Parliamentary procedure

> . . . As no government is more just in the constitution than that of parliaments, having its foundation in the free choice of the people . . . yet such have been the wicked policies of those who from time to time have endeavoured to bring this nation into bondage that they have in all times, either by disuse or abuse of parliaments, deprived the people of their hopes. (*The Large Petition* 1647)

> In the absence of a written constitution the procedures of Parliament are our constitution. (Simon Carr, *Independent,* 10 March 2006)

Key words

- Adversarial
- Enforcement
- Executive domination
- National Audit Office
- Secrecy
- Standing and select committees
- Supply
- Timetable
- Whips

13.1 Introduction

Parliamentary procedure may seem to be a dry topic but it is of great importance. It is only through procedures for debating, questioning and voting that the voice of Parliament as a collective institution can make itself known. The procedural rules attempt to ensure that the activities of Parliament are public but protected against outside interference and that Parliament as representative of the people can perform its threefold but conflicting task of sustaining the government, holding the executive to account and having the last word on legislation. It is widely acknowledged that the voice of Parliament is to some extent stifled by executive dominance. One reason for this is that the government controls the day-to-day procedures of the House of Commons. Ultimately it is for the House collectively to control its own procedures so that it could, if it so wished, radically transform itself. While ministers command docile party majorities this is unlikely to happen.

Parliamentary procedure is based upon standing orders made by each House, customs and conventions and rulings by the Speaker of the Commons. The authoritative manual of parliamentary procedure is Erskine May, *Parliamentary Practice* (Butterworths, 2004). The finance, administration and staffing of the House of Commons are supervised by the House of Commons Commission which comprises a group of MPs chaired by the Speaker (House of Commons (Administration) Act 1978). It does not have a government majority and is therefore independent of the executive.

Parliamentary procedure is adversarial, presupposing a government and opposition constantly in conflict. The rectangular layout of the Chamber and indeed of the Palace of Westminster itself reflects this. Other European legislative chambers are characteristically semicircular in layout representing a more conciliatory ethos, with the parties, usually elected by proportional representation, merging into each other. The adversarial nature of the procedure is mitigated by what are known as 'usual channels'. These involve informal cooperation between the parties so as to ensure that the procedures operate smoothly and fairly. For example absences from votes may be arranged in 'pairs' so as to maintain party balance. Whips have the responsibility of enforcing party discipline and liaising between the government and backbench MPs. The government Chief Whip, although not a cabinet member, frequently attends cabinet meetings.

Time pressures and its majority mean that the government is usually able to dominate the business of the House of Commons and much business gets through without proper scrutiny. In some countries, influenced by the doctrine of separation of powers, there are provisions which prevent the procedure from being controlled by the executive. In the UK the parliamentary timetable is determined by the government under standing orders which usually give priority to government business. The government also exercises influence over MPs through party discipline and patronage and through influencing the membership of committees. The Chief Whip advises the Prime Minister upon the careers of ministers and MPs.

A report from a Hansard Society Commission, *The Challenge for Parliament: Making Government Work* (Newton, 2001) suggested that there are 'serious gaps in the working of accountability to Parliament'. The Commission recommended in particular that departmental select committees should have greater freedom from government interference and that backbench MPs should have their own career structure to make them independent of government patronage. From 1997 the Modernisation Committee proposed a range of measures to improve the processes of Parliament (see *Modernisation of the House of Commons: A Reform Programme*, HC 1168, 2001–2). These will be mentioned in context. If anything they seem to enhance governmental control. The Power Report (2006, Rowntree Reform Trust) recommended that select committees (below) should get enhanced powers, that there should be limits on the powers of the whips and that Parliament should have greater freedom to initiate legislation, petitions and inquiries independently of the executive.

13.2 The Speaker of the Commons

The office of Speaker, 'the first commoner', symbolises the historical development of the House of Commons. The Speaker presides over meetings of the Commons and is the intermediary between the House and the Crown. The Speaker represents the rights of the House against the Crown, controls the procedure, keeps order and is responsible for protecting the rights of all groups within the House, particularly those of minorities. He or she has considerable discretion. The Speaker makes procedural rulings, decides who shall speak and has summary powers to suspend members or terminate a sitting. In terms of the conduct of particular proceedings, the Speaker need not normally give reasons for decisions (see SOs 31, 42, 45). The Sergeant at Arms is the enforcement agency responsible to the Speaker.

The Speaker is elected from its members by the House at the beginning of each Parliament. The 'father of the house', the longest serving member, runs the election. Traditionally a newly elected Speaker has to be dragged to the chair, a reminder that this was once a dangerous post. The Speaker is required to be impartial between the political parties. He or she cannot therefore represent his or her constituency in debates nor fight elections under a party banner. There is also a Deputy Speaker and deputies to him or her. One of these presides when the House is sitting as a committee.

13.3 Legislative Procedure

Parliament debates each bill in a process that distinguishes between general principles and detail. Parliamentary debates consist of a motion and question proposed by the chair in the same form as the motion. Following debate the question is put and voted upon, the result being expressed as a resolution or order. At any stage there may be amendments proposed but in all cases issues are presented to the House one at a time for a yes or no vote by a simple majority. This reflects the confrontational nature of Parliament and also ensures that the voting is on a majoritarian basis. The main distinctions are between public bills and private bills. There are also special arrangements for financial measures.

13.3.1 Public Bills

A public bill is a bill intended to alter the general law. The formal procedures in the House are only the tip of the iceberg. Any member can propose a bill ('a private member's bill') but almost all public bills are promoted by the government and introduced by ministers. Private members' bills are unlikely to succeed without government support. Twelve Fridays are provided in each session to private members' bills (SO 13(4)). Priority is determined by a ballot held annually, for which only backbenchers are eligible. Only the first six in the ballot have a realistic chance of success because of the twelve Fridays, six are devoted to bills in their later stages. A private member can also get a bill debated under the 'ten minute rule' (SO 19). This involves a motion twice a week that leave be given to present a bill. A short debate takes place. There is little prospect of the matter going any further, the essential aim being to publicise an issue. Nevertheless some important social reforms have been made by private members' bills, including abortion legislation, the abolition of the death penalty and divorce reform. However all had government support in the form of time allocation and drafting assistance.

Before their formal introduction, public bills go through various processes within the administration involving the formulation of policy and principles and consultation with outside bodies. When these have been completed, the bill is sent to the Parliamentary Counsel for drafting. Some bills, particularly those dealing with commercial matters, are drafted with the aid of outside lawyers. The relationship between the draftsmen and the government is similar to that of lawyer and client. The draftsmen work under considerable pressure of time and there is continuous consultation with government departments. Some bills relating to reform of the general law are prepared by the Law Commission. Important bills may be foreshadowed by Green Papers, which are consultation documents, or White Papers, which state the government's concluded opinions, albeit these often leave matters open for further discussion. Both are published. Recently as part of the modernisation programme, important bills have been published as draft bills for 'pre-legislative' discussion by Parliament and with public consultation before the formal process is started. Draft bills are considered by a select or standing committee.

The final version of a bill is approved by the Cabinet and then introduced into Parliament. Except for financial measures, which must be introduced by a minister in the Commons, a bill can be introduced into either House. The same stages apply in each House. Relatively uncontroversial bills are likely to be introduced in the House of Lords. The stages of a public bill are as follows:

- **First reading**: a formality which ensures that the bill is printed and published.
- **Second reading**: at which the main principles of the bill are discussed. In theory once a bill has passed this stage, its principles cannot later be challenged. However 'wrecking' amendments are sometimes introduced (for example by addition of the word 'not'), with a view to neutralising a bill. Occasionally the second reading is dealt with by a special committee.
- **Committee stage**: the bill is examined by a standing committee, with a view to suggesting detailed amendments. Unlike a select committee that exists for the whole of a Parliament, a standing committee is set up only for the purpose of a particular bill. Its membership of around 50 is based upon the strength of each party in the House, so that it is difficult for amendments to be made against the wishes of the government. Opponents of a bill sometimes deliberately cause delays by discussing matters at length in committee. However the chairman has the power to decide which amendments should be discussed and a 'business subcommittee' allocates time for discussion. The parliamentary draftsman may be present and civil servants or experts might be called to give evidence. Sometimes a bill is referred to a committee of the whole House. This might happen for example when the bill is uncontroversial or at the opposite extreme where it is of profound political significance.
- **Report stage**: the bill is returned to the House which can then vote upon the committee amendments and consider further amendments. The Speaker can select the amendments to be debated. The report stage can be dispensed with where the bill has been discussed by a committee of the whole House.
- **Third reading**. this is the final vote on the bill. Only verbal amendments are usually possible at this stage but the bill as a whole can be opposed.
- The bill is then sent to the other House. If the Lords veto the bill or make amendments, it is returned to the Commons. If there is continuing disagreement between the two Houses, the Parliament Act procedure can be triggered (Chapters 9, 11).
- Otherwise the bill is sent for royal assent. This is usually notified by commissioners at the prorogation ceremony that ends each session (Royal Assent Act 1967). By convention the monarch must always assent, except possibly in the unlikely event of the Prime Minister advising to the contrary. In this case however, the government would be at odds with the Commons and so required to resign.

Once a bill has received the royal assent it becomes law. However it is often provided that an Act or parts of it shall take effect only when a minister so orders. A minister's decision whether or not to bring an Act into effect can be subject to judicial review (see *R v Secretary of State for the Home Department ex parte Fire Brigades Union* (1995)). It is also common for an Act to confer power on ministers to make regulations without which the Act itself cannot operate. These might include a 'Henry VIII clause' under which a minister is empowered to alter other statutes.

Private Bills

A private bill is one directed to particular persons or places, for example a bill to build a new section of railway line. It is not subject to the Parliament Acts. It is an antiquated notion and today most powers relating to particular projects are conferred on the executive by general legislation, sometimes with the safeguard of a public inquiry (Chapter 5). Private bill procedure allows both local and national perspectives to be examined and is therefore suitable for very important private schemes. The procedure includes a special committee stage involving an inquiry open to the interests concerned who can be legally represented. Although private bill procedure involves outside elements, it is still wholly within parliamentary privilege. Therefore the courts cannot intervene on the ground that the procedure has not been properly followed or even that there has been fraud (*Pickin v British Railways Board* (1974)).

A public bill with a private element is called a 'hybrid bill'. For example the Aircraft and Shipbuilding Bill 1976 nationalised these industries and was, as such, a public bill but it exempted certain named firms from its proposals. A hybrid bill is subject to the public bill procedure until the committee stage when it is examined by a select committee in the same manner as a private bill.

Private bill procedure has been much criticised, not only because it is slow but because it fails to provide opportunities for the public to be directly involved in debating schemes that may have serious environmental impact, for example new railway lines. There is however a range of alternative procedures. The main examples involving Parliament are as follows:

- The Transport and Works Act 1992 applies primarily to large rail and waterway projects. A Secretary of State authorises projects after consulting local authorities and affected parties and including an environmental assessment. A public inquiry must be held into objections. The Secretary of State can refer proposals of national importance to Parliament for debate.
- Provisional orders made by ministers, again following a public local inquiry, are confirmed by a provisional order confirmation bill, the committee stage of which involves a select committee at which interested parties can be heard. It is not subject to the Parliament Acts. This procedure is rarely used.
- 'Special parliamentary procedure' involves a ministerial order which is subject to a public inquiry and also to a hearing before a special parliamentary committee. It can be debated on the floor of the House. This procedure is less cumbersome than private bills or provisional order confirmation bills. It gives the authority of Parliament to sensitive proposals but is rarely used.

13.4   Government Control over Procedure: Cutting Short Debate

By virtue of its majority and the submissiveness of its supporters, the government is usually in a position to control the timing of debate. Moreover the parliamentary timetable is usually crowded, with the result that many, if not most clauses of a bill are not discussed at all. As part of the 'modernisation' agenda, the committee stage of a bill can be timetabled under a 'programme motion' by the government (see Modernisation Select Committee Report, HC 190, 1997–8; Procedure Committee Report, *Timetabling Legislation*, HC 325, 2003–4: Government's response, HC 1169, 2003–4). This applies to most government bills (this reform arguably increases the government's control over Parliament). If a public bill has not become law by the end of a session, it lapses. However as part of the modernisation programme, the practice has recently been modified to allow some bills to be carried over into the next session (HC 543, 1998). This must be authorised by a resolution of the House which is usually under the control of the governing party. There are other procedural devices available to both Houses, but most importantly in the Commons, to cut short the time spent on debate. The main devices are:

- **Closure**: A motion that the question be now put (SO 35). The Speaker can also cut short debate when she or he thinks there has been adequate discussion (SO 67). Except in the case of private members' bills, closure motions are rare.
- **Guillotine**: A minister may propose a timetable for a bill. The guillotine procedure may prevent parts of a bill being discussed at all. Conversely where a government is weak, a defeated guillotine motion can destroy a bill.
- **Kangaroo** (SO 41): The Speaker at report stage or the chairman of a committee selects clauses or amendments for discussion.

13.5 Financial Procedure

The dependence of the executive on money voted by the people is an essential feature of a democratic constitution. It is a fundamental principle embodied in both law and convention that the House of Commons controls public finance and that proposals for public spending can be initiated only by the Crown: 'The Crown demands money, the Commons grant and the Lords assent to the grant' (May, *Parliamentary Practice*, Butterworths, 1997, pp. 732–6). On the other hand modern government finance is so large and complex that such control may be unrealistic. The Commons scrutinises taxation and expenditure proposals very superficially. In practice the most substantial control over government finance is exercised internally by the Treasury (Chapter 15).

The Crown comes to the Commons to ask for money. Hence financial measures can be proposed only by a minister and the Commons can reduce the estimates but not increase them. The survival of a government depends upon the Commons voting it funds, and the refusal of the Commons to do so is equivalent to a vote of no confidence so that the government must resign. By convention the House of Lords cannot amend measures relating to central government finance and, as we have seen in Chapter 11, can delay bills that are exclusively concerned with raising or allocating central government money only for one month.

Financial procedure is based on an ancient distinction between 'ways and means' – raising money – and 'supply' – allocating money to the purposes of the executive. This is somewhat artificial since the two are closely related. By virtue of the Bill of Rights 1688 the Crown cannot raise taxation without the consent of Parliament. The basis of the principle that the Crown cannot spend money without the consent of Parliament is partly long standing custom endorsed by the common law (*Auckland Harbour Board* v R (1924)) and partly statute, in that payments out of the Consolidated Fund, the government's bank account, require statutory authority (Exchequer and Audit Departments Act 1866 s.11).

Taxation and expenditure – the 'estimates' – must first be authorised by resolutions of the House of Commons. Amendments cannot be made outside the terms of the resolution, thus strengthening the government's hand. The enactment of the legislation is a formality, any serious discussion having taken place months earlier when the government presented its public spending proposals according to a timetable of its choosing.

There are three main financial measures (see Brazier and Ram, 2004, Chapters 1 and 2 for a clear account). Firstly the Finance Act raises taxation. The royal assent to a taxation measure is expressed in the words: *La Reyne remercie ses bons sujets, accepte leur benevolence et ainsi le veult* (the Queen thanks her good subjects, accepts their kindness and thus assents), as opposed to the normal *La Reyne le veult*. Secondly an Appropriation Act, usually in May, allocates amounts out of the Consolidated Fund to the Crown according to the estimates ('votes') presented for each government department for the current financial year, that is, until the following April. It also confirms spending that has been authorised provisionally by other legislation for the current and previous years. Thirdly Consolidated Fund Acts authorise interim spending until the following Appropriation Act and may also authorise additional spending from time to time. The committee stage of these financial measures takes the form of a committee of the whole House.

13.5.1   Taxation Procedure

The key taxation event is the annual 'budget' resolution proposed by the Chancellor usually in March. In recent years however the 'Autumn Statement' made in November has foreshadowed the main features of the budget so that the traditional mystique and prior secrecy of 'budget day' has been reduced. Both speeches set the general economic framework of government policy and proposals for tax changes. The budget resolution is followed by the annual Finance Bill. This includes taxes (notably income tax) that must be authorised afresh each year. These annual taxes are enforced and administered under permanent legislation (Income and Corporation Taxes Act 1988). Some taxes, mainly indirect taxes such as customs duties, are authorised by permanent legislation although their rates can be changed at any time. Constitutional principle is preserved in the case of EC law by the requirement in the European Communities Act 1972 that EC laws affecting taxation, for example VAT, must be implemented by a statute.

The effect of the budget resolution is that the budget's main tax proposals become law with immediate effect, but lapse unless embodied in a Finance Act that becomes law by a specified time. This is 5 August if the speech is in March or April, otherwise within four months (Provisional Collection of Taxes Act 1968). This procedure illustrates the basic constitutional principle that resolutions of the Commons cannot by themselves change the law but need statutory backing (*Bowles* v *Bank of England* (1913)).

Central government money does not come exclusively from taxation. Governments borrow large sums of money in the form of bonds and on the international money market. Money is also raised from landholding, investments both in the UK and overseas and from trading activities. These sources of finance are not subject to detailed parliamentary scrutiny, although statutory authority is required in general terms for borrowing (National Loans Fund Act 1968).

13.5.2 Supply Procedure

Most public expenditure must be authorised annually by the Appropriation Act which approves the government's estimates. These are made under the supervision of the Treasury. They include 'votes' setting out the government's proposed allocation of funds between departments. Thus the Commons approves both the global sum and the executive's broad priorities. However the Appropriation Act is very short and general, merely listing the broad functions of each department to be financed, allocating a global amount, designating a grant from the Consolidated Fund and setting a limit to 'appropriations in aid', that is, money that can be raised from fees and charges and so on. Moreover the Act deals only in cash so that contemporary methods of 'resource accounting' imposed by the Treasury may not fall properly within parliamentary controls (see Daintith and Page, 1999, p. 166).

The Act appears to authorise payment to the Crown rather than to the individual department, thus reinforcing the Treasury's power to control other departments by presiding over the internal allocation of funds. However in *R v Lords Commissioners of the Treasury* (1872) it was said that the Treasury is obliged to pay the sums in question.

The Public Accounts Committee admitted in 1987 that parliamentary control over the estimates is largely a formality (HC 98, 1986–7, para. 2). The Appropriation Act and Consolidated Fund Acts are usually passed without debate. Debates on the estimates have been replaced by twenty 'opposition days' which allow the opposition parties to raise anything they wish, and by special 'adjournment debates' following the passage of the Acts. The latter allow issues to be discussed without a vote.

There is an arcane debate as to whether the Appropriation Act alone is sufficient to make lawful particular items of expenditure that fall within its general provisions. This is worth briefly considering as it raises wider concerns as to the role of internal understandings and influences as against legal constraints in the constitution (see Daintith and Page, 1999, pp. 35, 174, 203–6). One view is that in addition to the Appropriation Act, specific powers must be conferred either by statute or under the royal prerogative. In other words the Appropriation Act is addressed only to the executive. It authorises the Crown to use the government's bank account for purposes that are lawful but does not in itself make any purpose lawful. On the other hand if an act of the Crown does not involve interfering with the legal rights of others, why should the Crown require specific powers since as a person it can do anything that the law does not forbid including, presumably, spending its money? On this argument, the Appropriation Act that puts the money into the Crown's hands should be a sufficient legal basis for spending.

Where a statute does in fact confer specific spending powers, this must be obeyed and cuts down any general power derived from the Appropriation Act (for example *R v Secretary of State for Foreign and Commonwealth Affairs ex parte World Development Movement* (1995); *R v Secretary of State for the Home Department ex parte Fire Brigades Union* (1995)). However a later Appropriation Act could possibly validate past unlawful expenditure. A concordat in 1932 between the Treasury and the Public Accounts Committee (see Treasury, *Government Accounting*, 1989, Annex 2.1) assumed that an Appropriation Act could override limits in other statutes but stated that it was 'proper' that permanent spending powers and duties should be defined by particular statutes. Other government statements are inconsistent (see Daintith and Page, 1999, p. 205). It may be that the courts would be reluctant to read general provisions in an Appropriation Act as overriding specific provisions in other Acts (see *Fisher* v *R* (1901)).

Some items of expenditure are permanently authorised by particular statutes. These are called 'consolidated fund services'. They include judicial salaries, royal expenses, EC payments and interest on the national debt. The Government Trading Act 1990 gives permanent authority to the financing of certain commercial services such as the Post Office by means of a Trading Fund. In practice most government spending is the subject of long term commitments (for example pensions), thus leaving little flexibility.

13.6 Supervision of the Executive

This depends upon the doctrine of ministerial responsibility and relies in the last resort upon the convention that the House of Commons can require the government to resign. In modern times the role of Parliament has been weakened by the party system and the difficulty of obtaining information from the government. It should also be remembered that not all government activity requires formal parliamentary authority. This includes royal prerogative powers, including going to war and other matters concerning foreign affairs (Chapter 14), and commercial and property transactions carried out under private law powers such as buying weapons. Parliamentary scrutiny is also limited by the practice of transferring government functions to bodies outside the central government. The main procedures for scrutiny of the executive are discussed in this chapter. Particular issues of ministerial responsibility are discussed in Chapter 15.

13.6.1 Questions

Questions can be written or oral. About 45 minutes each day are allowed for oral questions to ministers. The Prime Minister has one session of 30 minutes. Any MP can put down a question. In other cases there is a rota of three ministers per day but members must ballot for the privilege of asking an oral question. Except in the case of Prime Minister's Questions, two weeks advance notice must be given but a member may ask one unscheduled supplementary question. Civil servants who brief ministers are skilled in anticipating possible supplementaries, which need only bear a tenuous relationship to the main question. For example, a question might be: 'What are the Prime Minister's engagements for the day?' and the supplementary question could be: 'Why is he not visiting X where another hospital has been closed?' Conversely sycophantic questions by government supporters are frequently asked. Oral questions are probably of value only as a means of ensuring that ministers present themselves in public. They are of limited value as a means of obtaining information. Questions can be put in writing without limit and the answers are recorded in Hansard, the official parliamentary journal. A 'private notice' question can be asked by any member without prior warning, which requires a minister to answer. This must however be of an 'urgent character' and relate either to matters of public importance or to the arrangement of business (SO 8(3)).

A resolution of 1997 (HC Deb., vol. 229, cols 1046–7, 1996–97), incorporated into the Ministerial Code, requires that ministers must be as open as possible with Parliament and give accurate and truthful information to Parliament, correcting any inadvertent error at the earliest opportunity (see also *Guidance to Officials on Answering Parliamentary Questions*, Cabinet Office). However given the government's built-in majority in Parliament, this may carry little constitutional weight. The Ministerial Code is enforceable only by the Prime Minister (Chapter 15). Moreover ministers can refuse to answer on various grounds including cost, government efficiency, commercial sensitivity, confidentiality and the 'public interest' and cannot be pressed upon a refusal to answer. Some specific matters are excluded. These include matters relating to the monarchy and personal criticism of a judge. Matters subject to litigation in UK courts cannot be discussed subject to exceptions ruled on by the Speaker in connection with civil litigation relating to ministerial decisions or matters of national importance. Exemptions in the Freedom of Information Act 2000 (Chapter 21) also apply. Reasons must be given for refusing to answer. However answers might be perfunctory or incomplete, although under the Ministerial Code ministers must not 'knowingly' mislead Parliament and must correct any inadvertent error at the earliest opportunity.

MPs have expressed frustration that ministers are not always prepared to provide full and timely answers to parliamentary questions. Parliament has agreed that MPs should be restricted to asking a maximum of five 'named day' or priority questions a day, which should remove some of the pressure on civil servants in preparing responses to parliamentary questions. For unexplained reasons, it seems that the problem of delay has not been solved by this reduction (see PAC, Second Special Report, 2005–6, HC 853).

The Public Administration Committee (PAC) monitors the government's responses to questions. There is no coercive machinery to compel a minister to offer a prompt, relevant and full answer in Parliament and it is unlikely that Parliament would use its contempt powers to compel ministers to answer questions. The Speaker has recommended that members who receive inadequate departmental responses should press the minister concerned or raise it with the chair of the PAC (HC Deb., 28 November 2001, vol. 375, col. 971). The latter form of redress now seems to have become standard practice for aggrieved MPs (see PAC, 2005–6 above), and the intervention of the chairman of the PAC can be effective.

13.6.2 Debates

There are various opportunities for debating general matters: all involve limited time. However ministers must respond if required and thus debates require government to present itself in public. The different kinds of debates include:

1. **Adjournment debates**: These can be on any matter for which a minister is responsible. The most common is a half hour daily adjournment debate which can be initiated by a backbencher. There is a weekly ballot (SO 9). There can also be adjournment debates following passage of a Consolidated Fund or Appropriation Act (above), emergency adjournment debates (which are rarely permitted) and 'recess' debates in which miscellaneous topics can be debated for up to three hours. Amendments cannot be moved to adjournment motions, so adjournment motions can be used by the government to restrict the Opposition. Adjournment debates do not result in a formal vote and a minister's response cannot be questioned.
2. **Opposition days** after the proceedings on the annual Appropriation Act (above).
3. **Emergency debates**: To open the debate the support of 40 members or a vote of the House is required (SO 20). The Speaker must hold that the matter is urgent and relates to the responsibilities of ministers. Only three minutes are allowed for the application.

4. The debate following the Queen's Speech at the opening of a session.
5. **Censure motions**: By convention a government is expected to resign if defeated on a censure motion (also called a no confidence motion). The government must provide time to debate the motion. Until the 1970s the convention also seemed to include other government defeats on important matters, but the latter seem no longer to require resignation. The possibility that a government can be defeated on a major part of its programme but also remain in office strengthens a weak government by providing a safety valve for dissidents within its party. Since 1964 a government has resigned only once following a censure motion (1979). On that occasion the government was a minority government, again a rare event. A no confidence motion has no particular form. Either government or opposition can declare any vote to be one of confidence. In today's conditions the procedure seems to be essentially a publicity stunt. However such a vote does require the government to publicly defend itself.
6. **The budget debate** (above).
7. **Early day motions.** This procedure allows an MP to put down a matter for debate without a fixed date. Early day motions are hardly ever debated. Their function is to draw public attention to a particular issue. They may be supported by a large number of members across parties, amounting in effect to a petition.
8. **Ministerial statements** which can be followed by questions and discussion. The Speaker can require a minister to attend and make a statement.
9. **Westminster Hall**: Part of the 'modernisation' programme, this sits in a large committee room on three weekdays. It is a supplement to the main chamber as a forum for debates initiated by backbenchers on less contentious business for which time might not otherwise be easily found. Decisions must be unanimous and otherwise are referred to the main House. Ministers must be available to respond every other week, whereas in the main chamber they must respond if required to any debate.

13.6.3   Select Committees

A select committee is appointed from backbenchers for the whole of a Parliament. A select committee must be distinguished from a standing committee, the function of the latter being to scrutinise bills at the committee stage. A select committee is supposed to be independent of government but there is the possibility that committee members would try to curry favour with ministers, for example by discussing proposed committee reports with them.

There are three main kinds of select committee:

1. Committees charged with investigating the expenditure, administration and policy of the main departments and reporting to the House (SO 130). There is no Prime Minister's committee as such but the Prime Minister voluntarily appears twice per year before the Liaison Committee which is composed of the chairs of the other committees. The Security and Intelligence Committee is made up of MPs but is appointed by and reports to the Prime Minister.
2. Committees dealing with important general concerns. These include broadcasting, environmental audit, food standards, European scrutiny, public accounts, public administration and regulatory reform.
3. Committees dealing with matters internal to the House such as standards and privileges, modernisation and procedure. There is also the Speaker's Committee which

deals with electoral matters (Political Parties, Elections and Referendums Act 2000). Some select committees are joint committees of the Lords and Commons. These include human rights, statutory instruments, financial services and markets and reform of the House of Lords.

The work of the departmental select committees is coordinated by the Liaison Committee, which selects the members in proportion to party representation in the House. In practice however the membership is usually selected by the party whips. The chairmanship is a matter for negotiation between government and opposition. However an attempt by the government in 2001 to remove two independently minded select committee members was defeated by the House as a whole, illustrating that ultimately the House does have the power needed to preserve some independence from the executive. Select committees may also recruit outside advisers such as academics. They interview witnesses in public but their decisions are made in private. They have little ability to probe deeply. Time, party discipline, the doctrine of ministerial responsibility and the rules of parliamentary procedure combine to frustrate their activities (see *Shifting the Balance: Select Committees and the Executive*, Liaison Committee, HC 321, 2000–01).

   A select committee can issue a report which is published. The government may make a published response after which nothing is required to happen. A committee has limited powers since enforcement of its report (which the press often misleadingly calls that of a 'powerful' committee depends on a vote of the whole House (see HC 353, 1991–2, paras 20–21). In principle a select committee has power under standing orders to send for 'persons, papers and records' at any time, even when Parliament is not sitting, and failure to attend or refusal to answer questions could be a contempt of the House. Other powers are as follows:

- MPs as such can be compelled to attend and produce evidence. This is explicit as regards the Committee on Standards and Privileges (SO 149(6)). Members of the House of Lords, being protected by their own privilege, cannot be required to attend.
- It is not clear whether ministers as part of the Crown can be compelled to attend. In practice because of the government's majority compulsion is unlikely. However assurances have been given that ministers will attend and give information to committees (HC Deb. vol. 969, col. 45, 1979; see Chapter 15).
- Civil servants attend only with the permission of ministers and cannot be compelled to speak. Their evidence has been limited to describing their 'actions' taken on behalf of ministers as opposed to their 'conduct' generally. Thus civil servants cannot give evidence about the merits of government policy, nor the consultation process within government, nor the advice they gave to government. Indeed ministers have sometimes forbidden civil servants from appearing, in particular on the grounds of national security, 'good government' and 'excessive cost' (see *Departmental Evidence and Response to Select Committees*, Cabinet Office, 2004). There are also conventions that civil servants should not give evidence about the conduct of other officials, matters before the courts and evidence from papers of a previous government of a different political party. As with questions, exemptions in the Freedom of Information Act 2000 also apply. Committees have no power to demand papers from government departments. An address to the Queen (in respect of a Secretary of State) or a formal order from the House may be required.

▷ Other persons, for example former MPs and the heads of public or private bodies, may be compellable. However this raises the unresolved issue of whether the House has power outside its own internal affairs (Chapter 11).

▷ Committee proceedings are open to the public unless the committee resolves to meet in closed session. Strictly speaking, evidence taken by a select committee cannot be published without the consent of the committee, unless and until it becomes part of the formal record of Parliament. However evidence given in public can be published (SOs 135, 136).

Ministers have relied on these limitations as a means of shielding the inner workings of government from publicity, slightly tempered by a general undertaking by ministers to cooperate with committees, for example by explaining why evidence cannot be given. However the backbench composition of select committees and their practice of seeking consensus have given them a certain independent status. They have drawn public attention to important issues and have exposed weaknesses in governmental policies and procedures. Their capacity to do this may have a deterrent effect on government departments. However their reports do not necessarily lead to action or even to debate in Parliament. Relatively minor reforms were made in 2002 to strengthen select committees as a response to a more ambitious agenda from the Modernisation Committee (HC 224, 2001–2). These included paying committee chairs and encouraging committees to monitor the government's response to their reports (see further Chapter 15).

Except for committees of the whole House and some minor committees, all committees in the House of Lords are select committees which can therefore accumulate expertise. Select committees in the House of Lords deal with subjects rather than departments, reflecting the role of the upper House as a forum for the detailed discussion of important issues free of immediate party pressures. The Science and Technology Committee, the European Committee and the Environmental Committee are particularly well regarded.

13.6.4 Supervising Expenditure

As we have seen, money raised by central government goes into the Consolidated Fund. The control of spending from the Consolidated Fund is the responsibility of the Commons but given the size and complexity of modern government this is clearly an impossible task for an elected assembly. In practice direct parliamentary control over expenditure is very limited. More substantial if less independent controls are imposed within the government machine itself. These are based on a mixture of statute, royal prerogative, convention, insider networking, and the inherent power of any employer to administer its workforce, public employees being characteristically conformist and submissive. In medieval times the Court of Exchequer supervised government spending but the modern courts have relinquished this responsibility in favour of Parliament.

The courts are therefore reluctant to interfere with central government spending decisions which are subject to parliamentary scrutiny (see *Nottinghamshire CC v Secretary of State for the Environment* (1986)). However in *R v Secretary of State for Foreign and Commonwealth Affairs ex parte World Development Movement* (1995) a Foreign Office decision to give a large grant to the Malaysian government for the Pergau Dam project was set aside by the Court of Appeal on the basis that the project had no economic justification and that there was an ulterior political motive. The governing legislation required that the decision be based on economic grounds which, crucially, the court equated with 'sound' economic grounds. This has the potential to give the courts a wide and possibly undesirable power of review. On the other hand the matter only came to light because of the intensive adversarial process of the court. The internal process of control had not revealed the misapplication of public funds.

Spending by central departments and other public bodies related to the centre is scrutinised on behalf of Parliament by the Comptroller and Auditor-General. The Comptroller is appointed by the Crown on a motion from the House of Commons proposed by the Prime Minister with the agreement of the chair of the Public Accounts Committee (Exchequer and Audit Departments Acts 1866–1957; National Audit Act 1983 s.1). The Comptroller is an officer of the Commons and has security of tenure similar to that of a High Court judge (see Exchequer and Audit Departments Act 1866). The Comptroller is not directly concerned with the merits of government policy but only with the efficient and economical use of money (National Audit Act 1983, ss.6, 7). However it is difficult to separate these two concerns. The Comptroller reports to the Public Accounts Committee of the House of Commons. This committee carries out an annual scrutiny of government accounts and its report is debated by the Commons (see SO 122). It thus provides a key mechanism for government accountability. The committee's chair is normally a member of the Opposition.

The Comptroller is supported by the National Audit Office (NAO), which is responsible for scrutinising the accounts of central government departments and also those of some outside bodies dependent on government money such as universities. The NAO carries out two kinds of audit. 'Certification audit' is based on financial accounting practice. 'Value for money audit' is based on the wider concerns of the 'economy, efficiency and effectiveness' of government expenditure (National Audit Act 1983 s.6). This is not meant to include the substantive merits of government policy, although the line between them may be difficult to draw. The NAO is also concerned with matters of 'regularity, legality, propriety and probity'.

13.6.5 Scrutiny of Delegated Legislation

Most delegated legislation is detailed and highly technical. It would be impracticable to subject all delegated legislation to detailed democratic scrutiny so that the law is necessarily a compromise. Thus delegated legislation is subject to a limited degree of parliamentary control by being laid before one or both Houses for approval. Unlike a bill, Parliament cannot usually amend delegated legislation.

Originally, the laying process was haphazard, but as a result of public concern about 'bureaucratic tyranny' (see Report of Committee on Ministers' Powers, 1932, Cmnd 4060), limited reforms were made by the Statutory Instruments Act 1946. A statutory instrument made after the 1946 Act came into force is defined as such either if it is made by Order in Council or if the parent Act expressly provides. Thus there is no legal obligation on governments to comply with the controls in the 1946 Act. However in practice most delegated legislation takes the form of a statutory instrument. Moreover a statutory instrument has to be laid before the House only if its parent Act so requires. The laying procedures typically require only that the statutory instrument be 'laid on the table' of the House in draft or in final form for 40 days subject to annulment by a vote of the House – the 'negative' procedure. The fate of the instrument therefore depends upon the chance of a member seeing the document and securing a debate. Some instruments are required to be laid for information only, Parliament having no power to annul them.

A small number of important statutory instruments are made subject to an 'affirmative' procedure under which there must be a positive vote in order to bring them into effect. Such instruments are usually referred to a standing committee. There are also 'super affirmative' forms which require advance consultation.

The 1946 Act also requires that statutory instruments must be published 'as soon as may be' unless there is a special excuse for not doing so (s.3). Failure to publish may not make the instrument invalid but provides a defence to prosecution, provided that the accused was unaware of the instrument and that no reasonable steps had been taken to publicise it (s.3(2); see *R* v *Sheer Metalcraft Ltd* (1954)).

The Parliament Acts do not apply to delegated legislation so that the House of Lords has the power to veto a statutory instrument. It has done so only once in the last 30 years when it vetoed a measure that would deny free mailing for candidates in the election for the Mayor of Greater London (Hansard, HL 20 Feb. 2000, col. 136). The Wakeham Report and the government have proposed that this power be removed in favour of a delaying power only.

The Joint Committee on Statutory Instruments is responsible for scrutinising statutory instruments laid before Parliament. The scrutiny committee is not concerned with the political merits of the instrument but is required to draw the attention of Parliament to specified constitutional matters. These are as follows:

1. Does the instrument impose taxation or other forms of charge?
2. Does it exclude control by the courts?
3. Is it retrospective without the express authority of the parent Act?
4. Has there been unjustifiable delay in laying or publishing it?
5. Is there doubt as to its legal validity or does it appear to make some unusual or unexpected use of the powers under which it was made?
6. For any special reason does its form or purport call for elucidation?
7. Does its drafting appear to be defective?
8. Any other ground other than those relating to policy or merits.

There is also a House of Lords Scrutiny Committee which looks at the merits of statutory instruments laid before the House.

13.7 Redress of Grievances

Overlapping with Parliament's duty to supervise the executive is the duty of members of Parliament and the right of Parliament collectively to seek the redress of the grievances of subjects of the Crown. Procedurally this depends upon opportunities being made available to backbench members to raise individual grievances. One problem is the possibility of conflicts with party interests; another is the lack of resources, including time. No parliamentary time is reserved for the redress of grievances as such. An MP is able to give publicity to a grievance by placing it on the parliamentary record. Apart from that, the process is haphazard.

The main procedures available are questions, adjournment debates, early day motions and, perhaps most effectively, informal communications with ministers, although the latter are not always protected by parliamentary privilege (Chapter 11). All these suffer from the inability of an individual MP to force disclosure of information.

There are other miscellaneous opportunities by way of business questions and points of order, both of which allow members briefly to draw attention to matters which concern them. These must, strictly speaking, relate to the internal procedures of the House but the Speaker customarily gives considerable latitude. Finally there are public petitions that members can present on behalf of their constituents. These are published in Hansard. However there is no formal machinery for giving effect to them.

These examples suggest that a sophisticated knowledge of the procedures of the House can be used tactically to some effect. However it is easy for an MP to avoid following up a complaint from a constituent by passing it to another agency. Members habitually deal with grievances outside the formal parliamentary framework, acting in effect as generalist welfare offices. A letter from an MP is likely to be dealt with at a higher level in the civil service hierarchy than would otherwise be the case.

13.8   The Parliamentary Commissioner for Administration

The Parliamentary Commissioner for Administration (PCA) investigates on behalf of Parliament complaints by citizens against the central government and certain other bodies controlled by the central government (Parliamentary Commissioner Act 1967; Parliamentary and Health Services Commissioners Act 1987; Parliamentary Commissioner Act 1994). Popularly known as the 'ombudsman', the PCA enjoys similar salary and security of tenure to a superior court judge. The PCA has a discretion whether or not to investigate any particular case. This is subject to judicial review (see *R v Parliamentary Commissioner ex parte Dyer* (1994)). Investigations are private (s.7(2)). This may be advantageous by encouraging greater frankness by those being investigated. The PCA can see documents and interview civil servants and other witnesses and the normal plea of government confidentiality cannot be used (s.8(3)). However cabinet documents can be excluded (s.8(4)) and the PCA must not name individual civil servants.

There are considerable limitations on the powers of the PCA:

- Important areas of central government activity are excluded from its jurisdiction. These include foreign affairs, state security (including passports), legal proceedings, criminal investigations, government contracts, commercial activities other than compulsory purchase of land (but statutory powers exercised by contractors under privatisation arrangements are within the ombudsman's jurisdiction), civil service employment matters and the granting by the Crown of honours, awards and privileges.
- The PCA can investigate allegations of 'injustice in consequence of maladministration' (s.5(1)). Maladministration is not defined but means broadly some defect in the *process* of decision making as opposed to its substance: 'bias, neglect, inattention, delay, incompetence, inaptitude, perversity, turpitude, arbitrariness and so on' (the 'Crossman Catalogue' 734 HC Deb. 1966, col. 51). The PCA cannot directly question government policy nor the merits of the exercise of a discretion (s.12) (see *R v Local Commissioner for Administration ex parte Bradford City Council* (1979)).
- Complaints must be in writing within 12 months of the decision complained of.
- Complaints must be made to an MP who can decide whether to take the matter to the PCA. This is intended to preserve the constitutional principle that the executive is responsible to Parliament. There has been considerable criticism of this rule on the ground that MPs may be reluctant to refer to the PCA in order to claim credit for

themselves. Conversely MPs may be unclear about the PCA's power and refer inappropriate cases or even pass the buck by referring cases indiscriminately.

▷ The PCA should not investigate a matter that is appropriate to a court unless in all circumstances it would be unreasonable to expect the complainant to do so. The ombudsman can take into account the complainant's personal circumstances but not the likelihood of success (*R* v *Local Commissioner for Administration ex parte Liverpool City Council* (2001)).

▷ The PCA has no power to enforce its findings. Its must report to the MP who referred the case. If it has found injustice caused by maladministration and considers that it has not been remedied, it may also lay a report before Parliament. The Public Administration Committee monitors the PCA. Reflecting the convention of ministerial responsibility, it is for the minister concerned to decide whether to give effect to the recommendations, for example by compensating the victim of the injustice or improving departmental procedures. The executive sometimes refuses to accept the PCA's findings (see Kirkham, 'Challenging the Authority of the Ombudsman: the Parliamentary Commissioner's Special Report on Wartime Detainees', 2006, *Modern Law Review* 69:792). This happened in 2006 when the PCA ruled that the government had given misleading advice to people transferring from state to private pension schemes (see *Memorandum to the Public Administration Select Committee*, 26 June 2006, www.ombudsman.org.uk/news/hot topics).

13.9 House of Lords Procedure

The House of Lords regulates its own procedure which is less adversarial and party dominated than the Commons. There is also less reliance on formal procedural rules. The Speaker is elected by the House but does not have the disciplinary powers available to the Speaker of the Commons, the only power being to put a question to the vote (SO 18). The House of Lords has no power to suspend or expel a member. A bill other than one involving government taxation or expenditure can be introduced in the House of Lords. It is not subject to the Parliament Acts. A bill introduced in the House of Commons and passing all its stages goes to the House of Lords. The procedure is broadly similar except that the committee stage usually takes place before a committee of the whole House. The House can call upon considerable specialist expertise from among its membership even if some of it may be out of date. This is often regarded as a justification for an appointed upper house. Reports of select committees of the House of Lords, notably those of the European Union Committee and the Environment Committee, command considerable respect.

Summary

▷ Procedure in the House of Commons is regulated by standing orders and the Speaker who has a duty to safeguard all interests. We outlined the lawmaking procedure as it applies to public bills and private bills. We then looked at the procedural framework within which the Commons attempts to make legislation, hold the government to account, control public finance and redress citizens' grievances. The timetable is largely under the control of the government as are procedural devices for cutting short debate. However there are opportunities for backbenchers and the Opposition to intervene.

Summary cont'd

▶ There are mechanisms for approving government spending and taxation proposals and scrutinising government expenditure, notably the office of Comptroller and Auditor-General and the Public Accounts Committee. In general however the House of Commons is not equipped for the detailed control of government expenditure. In recent years the emphasis has switched to internal controls over expenditure through the Treasury (Chapter 15).

▶ Other devices for parliamentary control of the executive include specialist select committees and the Parliamentary Commissioner for Administration. These devices have implications for ministerial responsibility. This is because they involve investigating the activities of civil servants and they raise questions about the relationship between ministers and the House of Commons. Select committees provide a valuable means of publicising issues but have weak powers and are subject to influence by the executive. The extent to which select committees can scrutinise the activities of executive agencies is unclear.

▶ Delegated legislation is often required to be laid before the House although unless the affirmative procedure is used it may not get serious scrutiny. The Joint Committee on Statutory Instruments monitors delegated legislation on constitutional grounds.

▶ The House of Lords regulates its own procedure. The Lord Chancellor presides but does not have the disciplinary powers available to the Speaker. Subject to these considerations, procedure in the Commons is dominated by the government through its power to propose business and its control of a majority of votes. Government proposals take up most of the available time. Members of Parliament have no privileged access to government information so that their debate is not especially well informed.

▶ The conventional assessment of Parliament is that it has become subservient to the executive, primarily because its members have capitulated to party loyalty, reinforced by the electoral system and the dual role of ministers as members of both executive and Parliament. Parliament, according to this view, is at its worst as a method of controlling government finance, poor at supervising the executive and lawmaking but better at redressing individual grievances, although this owes a lot to the work of members outside the formal parliamentary procedures. On the other hand Parliament provides a forum where the executive must defend itself in public and expose the strengths and weaknesses of its leaders. The possibility of defeat in an election may encourage members to distance themselves from an unpopular government and act as a limited constitutional check.

Exercises

13.1 To what extent has the modernisation programme made Parliament more democratic?

13.2 'The main democratic service provided by Parliament is that it forces the government to defend itself in public.' Discuss.

13.3 'The key to democracy is the power to control public finance.' Are the powers of Parliament adequate in this sense?

13.4 A group of Opposition MPs believes that a senior government minister has been holding secret discussions with a company making defence equipment concerning the possibility of engineering a uprising by anti-Western elements in an African state so as to sell weapons to the government of that state. In an answer to a question in the House, the minister denies that the government has any involvement with the state in question. Advise the group as to their chances of obtaining a thorough parliamentary investigation into the matter.

13.5 Compare the strengths and weaknesses of parliamentary questions and select committees as a means of controlling the executive.

13.6 'Parliament in principle can do what it likes but lacks a mechanism independent of the party system controlled by government, in particular to initiate independent inquiries'. Explain and critically discuss.

13.7 Compare the procedures of the House of Commons and House of Lords. To what extent do these reflect the different constitutional functions of the two Houses?

13.8 To what extent can backbench MPs play an effective role in Parliament?

Further reading

Blackburn, R. and Kennon, A. (2003) *Parliament: Functions, Practice and Procedures* (2nd edn), London, Sweet & Maxwell.

Brazier, A. (2004) *Parliament, Politics and Law Making*, London, Hansard Society, Chapters 1, 2, 3, 4, 5, 6, 13.

Brazier, A. and Ram, V. (2004) *Inside the Counting House*, London, Hansard Society.

Brazier, A., Flinders, M. and McHugh, D. (2005) *New Politics, New Parliament? A Review of Parliamentary Modernisation since 1997*, London, Hansard Society.

Cowley, P. and Stuart, M. (2001) 'Parliament: a Few Headaches and a Dose of Modernisation', *Parliamentary Affairs* 54(3):442.

Daintith, T. and Page, A. (1999) *The Executive in the Constitution*, Oxford University Press, Chapter 4.

Davies, P. (2007), 'The Significance of Parliamentary Procedures in Control of the Executive: a Case Study: The Passage of Part 1 of the Regulatory Reform Act 2006', *Public Law* 677

Flinders, M. (2002) 'Shifting the Balance: Parliament, the Executive and the British Constitution', *Political Studies* 50.

Jowell, J. and Oliver, D. (2004) *The Changing Constitution* (5th edn) Oxford University Press, Chapter 15.

Judge, D. (2004) 'Whatever Happened to Parliamentary Democracy in the United Kingdom?' *Parliamentary Affairs* 57(3).

Maer, L. and Sandford, M. (2004) *Select Committees under Scrutiny*, London, The Constitution Unit UCL.

Oliver, D. (2001) 'The Challenge for Parliament', *Public Law* 666.

Oliver, D. (2006) 'Improving the Scrutiny of Bills: the Case for Standards and Checklists', *Public Law* 219.

Rogers, R. and Walters, R. (2004) *How Parliament Works* (5th edn) London, Pearson, Chapters 6, 7, 8, 9, 10, 11, 13.

Tomkins, A. (2003) 'What is Parliament For?', in Bamforth, M. and Leyland, P. (eds) *Public Law in a Multi-Layered Constitution*, Oxford, Hart Publishing.

The fool had stuck himself up one day, with great gravity, in the King's Throne; with a stick, by way of sceptre in one hand, and a ball in the other: being asked what he was doing? He answered 'reigning'. Much of the same sort of reign I take it, would be that of our Author's Democracy. (Jeremy Bentham, *A Fragment of Government*, 1776, Chapter 2, para. 34)

Key words

- Crown and Queen
- Crown and government
- Personal and political powers
- Special and ordinary powers
- Justiciability
- Democratic accountability
- Legal immunities

14.1 Introduction: The Nature of the Crown

We saw in Chapter 6 that UK law has no concept of the state as such and sometimes uses the notion of the Crown as a substitute but that the Crown is an ambivalent concept. It includes the Queen as head of state and is also used as the collective term for the central executive. As head of state, the Queen is:

- part of the legislature, albeit with at most a veto
- formal head of the executive for the UK, the devolved governments and dependent territories. In relation to each government, the Crown is a separate legal entity (Chapter 6)
- head of the Church of England
- head of the armed forces
- source of the authority of the judiciary, although since *Prohibitions del Roy* (1607) it has been clear that the Queen cannot interfere with judicial proceedings
- prosecutor of criminal offences. By statute, the independent Crown Prosecution Service carries out this role under the Director of Public Prosecutions who is accountable to the Attorney-General (Prosecution of Offences Act 1985).

As head of state, the Queen also has the undefined responsibility of being the ultimate guardian of the constitution. No minister appears to have this responsibility. The fundamental problem about the monarchy is therefore that it is difficult to see how there can be legitimacy and public confidence in the important role of head of state where it is held by a person who is neither elected nor appointed on merit. Furthermore as we shall see, the monarch inherits the role subject to conditions of religion and blood ties based on the controversies of the seventeenth century.

By convention the Queen must act on the advice of ministers, particularly the Prime Minister, thereby separating the 'dignified' from the 'efficient' constitution and preventing the Prime Minister from pretensions to the role of head of state and ministers from sheltering behind the dignities and privileges of the Crown. Thus when Sir Robert Armstrong, the then Cabinet Secretary, said that 'for all practical purposes, the Crown is represented by the government of the day' (Hennessy, 1995, p. 346), he was not referring to the legal position.

The historical process of removing power from the monarch (Chapter 4) has left us with ambiguities and confusions concerning the legal nature of the Crown and its relationship with the executive. It is not clear whether the 'Crown' means the Queen as an individual or a corporate body with one member, namely the Queen – a corporation sole; or a kind of company synonymous with the executive (corporation aggregate); or merely a 'brand name' with no legal identity as such. For example, for purposes of civil liability the defendant is a designated government department (below and see McLean, 'The Crown in Contract and Administrative Law', 2004, *Oxford Journal of Legal Studies* 129). The Crown is probably separate from the individual who holds it at any given time (*Calvin's Case* (1608)).

For legal purposes the most important question is whether a particular function is vested in the Crown as such or in a minister. The principle that the Queen must almost always act on the advice of ministers is not relevant in this respect since this is only a convention. The Crown has a range of important powers collectively known as the 'royal prerogative'. These are common law powers and derive historically from the monarch's personal command of the government and also from the monarch's feudal powers over property. Some of the more draconian prerogatives were abolished in the seventeenth century (Chapter 4) and all prerogative powers are subject to parliamentary supremacy. However as the ultimate source of power, the Queen might exercise her residual personal powers in time of crisis (below).

Statutory powers are usually conferred directly on ministers who cannot then claim to be acting on behalf of the Crown. In *M v Home Office* (1993) the Home Secretary attempted to rely on Crown immunity in order to deport an immigrant in defiance of a court order. The House of Lords held that he was liable in his official capacity for contempt of court. In that case Parliament had conferred the power in question directly upon the Secretary of State. Sometimes however statutory powers are conferred on the Crown as such (for instance Bank of England Act 1998 s.1(2): appointment of governor of Bank). Property is usually vested in the Crown as such, since not all government departments have their own legal personality.

In *Town Investments Ltd v Department of the Environment* (1977) the House of Lords disagreed as to the legal nature of the Crown. The question arose whether an office lease taken by a minister, using the standard formula 'for and on behalf of Her Majesty', was vested in the minister or the Crown, since in the latter case it would be immune from taxation. The House of Lords held that the lease was vested in the Crown. Lord Diplock thought that the Crown was a fiction describing the executive. Lord Simon of Glaisdale said that the expression 'the Crown' symbolises the powers of government that were formerly wielded by the wearer of the crown and reflects the historical development of the executive as that of offices hived off from the royal household. He stated that the legal concept best fitted to the contemporary situation was to consider the Crown as a corporation aggregate headed by the Queen and made up of 'the departments of state including ministers at their heads'. His Lordship added two riders: 'First the legal concept still does not correspond to the political reality. The Queen does not command those legally her servants. On the contrary she acts on the formally tendered collective advice of the Cabinet.' Secondly, 'when the Queen is referred to by the symbolic title of "Her Majesty" it is the whole corporation aggregate which is generally indicated. This distinction between "the Queen" and "Her Majesty" reflects the ancient distinction between "the King's two bodies", the "natural" and the "politic"' (see *Duchy of Lancaster Case* (1567) 1 Plow 325 at 327).

Moreover there is not one Crown but many: the divisibility of the Crown. Even though the same individual holds each office, there is a separate Crown and therefore separate responsibilities in relation to each government where the Queen is head of state, whether this is an independent state such as Australia or a British dependent territory or the devolved parts of the UK (see Government of Wales Act 2006 s.89; Scotland Act 1998 s.91). This raises questions as to the nature of any advice on which the Crown's powers should be exercised (see Twomey, 2008, *Public Law* 742). The Queen is also Head of the Commonwealth, a title of symbolic importance that carries no legal powers, but probably still has political significance. Indeed a conflict could arise between the Queen's role as Head of the Commonwealth and her duty to accept the advice of the British government.

If we were to abolish the monarchy, then a different explanation would have to be found as to the basis of legal power. This could lead to a written constitution. Thus even though the role of the monarch herself is relatively insignificant, the monarchy remains the keystone of the constitution.

14.2 Succession to the Monarchy

Under the 1688 settlement Parliament obtained the power to designate who shall be the monarch. The Act of Settlement 1700 (applying to Scotland and Northern Ireland by the Acts of Union 1707 and 1800) provides that the Crown is to be held by the direct descendants of Princess Sophia (the granddaughter of the deposed James II). The monarch does not apparently have to be a British citizen. However there are provisions designed to prevent a monarch dragging the country into foreign disputes. If the monarch is not 'a native of this kingdom of England', any war for the defence of a foreign country needs the consent of Parliament (s.3). The holder of the Crown must be or become a communicating member of the Church of England and must not be nor marry a Catholic (ibid.). Under the Royal Marriages Act 1772, a member of British royal family directly descended from George II cannot marry without the consent of the monarch, subject, if over the age of 25, to an appeal to Parliament.

The rules of descent are based upon the medieval law governing succession to land. Preference is given to males over females and to the elder over the younger. The land law rules required sisters to hold land equally (co-parcenaries). However in the case of the Crown the first born prevails (although the matter has not been litigated). The succession was last altered when Edward VIII abdicated in 1936 and his brother, the next in line, succeeded (His Majesty's Declaration of Abdication Act 1936). It is not clear whether the monarch has the power to abdicate without an Act of Parliament. Since monarchy is a status conferred by law and without a voluntary act, the answer is probably not. The Crown's titles are also determined by statute (Royal Titles Act 1953).

It is often suggested that the Act of Settlement should be reformed to remove the religious restrictions on the ground that they are inappropriate in modern conditions and might violate the Human Rights Act 1998 being discriminatory in relation to religious freedom and the exercise of property rights (the succession being arguably a property right). This worthy but limited reform is characteristic of proposals for constitutional change in the UK in that it leaves unquestioned the more fundamental matter of why the head of state should be defined according to a primitive concept of blood line.

When the monarch dies, the successor immediately and automatically becomes monarch. A special Accession Council, composed mainly of members of the House of Lords proclaims the successor. This is confirmed by the Privy Council. Whether these bodies have a power of veto is unclear. One view is that the Accession Council reflects the mythical 'ancient constitution', according to which the monarch was appointed with the consent of the 'people'. The monarch is also required to swear a coronation oath of loyalty (Act of Settlement 1700) although the Coronation Ceremony has no legal significance.

If the monarch is a minor, ill, or absent abroad, the royal functions are exercised by a regent or councillors of state. These are the persons next in line to the throne (see Regency Acts 1937–53). In such cases certain bills cannot be assented to – most importantly a bill for altering the succession to the Crown.

14.3 Financing the Monarchy

Even in her private capacity the Queen is exempt from taxes unless statute specifically provides otherwise. The Queen has however entered into a voluntary agreement to pay tax on current income and personal capital. The expenses of the monarchy and of those members of the royal family who perform public duties are funded from the Civil List in return for the monarch surrendering to Parliament the hereditary income from Crown property. The Civil List is an amount granted by Parliament at the beginning of each reign. It consists of an annual payment that can be increased by statutory instrument made by the Treasury, subject to veto by the House of Commons (Civil List Acts 1952–75). However under the Civil List Act 1975, the Treasury can make additional payments, a practice that would make the monarchy equivalent to an ordinary government department. Many of the royal expenses are funded directly by government departments, such as the upkeep of Crown buildings, security, travel and entertaining political dignitaries.

14.4 The Personal Powers of the Monarch

Since 1688 the personal powers of the monarchy have gradually been reduced by the emergence of conventions that require the monarch to act on the advice of Parliament and ministers. The 1688 revolution left the monarch in charge of running the executive but dependent upon Parliament for money and lawmaking power. The monarch retained substantial personal influence until the late nineteenth century, mainly through the power to appoint ministers and influence elections in the local constituencies. Until after the reign of George V (1910–34), monarchs occasionally intervened in connection with ministerial appointments and policy issues. The abdication of Edward VIII (1936) probably spelt the end of any political role for the monarch.

The modern functions of the monarchy can be outlined as follows:

1. **To represent the nation**. For this purpose the monarch participates in ceremonies and public entertainments. It is often said that the popularity and public acceptance of the monarchy is directly related to the fact that the monarch has little political power and is primarily an entertainer. It is not clear why a modern democracy requires a personalised 'leader'. There is a strong element of superstition inherent in the notion of monarchy, hence the importance of the link between the monarch and the Established Church.

2. **To 'advise, encourage and to warn'**. The monarch has access to all government documents and regularly meets the Prime Minister. The monarch is entitled to express views in private to the government but there is no convention as to the weight to be given to them.

3. **Certain formal acts**. These include:
   - Assent to statutes
   - Orders in Council
   - Appointments of ministers, ambassadors, bishops and judges
   - Proclamations, for example dissolving and summoning Parliament or declaring a state of emergency
   - Ratifying solemn treaties
   - Granting charters to universities, professional bodies and so on. These bestow the seal of state approval and also incorporate the body in question so that it can be treated as a separate person in law
   - Awarding peerages, honours and medals.

In certain cases it is believed that the monarch can and indeed must exercise personal power. There is little precedent and no principles as to whose advice she should take. There are internal Cabinet Office guidance documents on the matter but the fact that unpublished sources have any weight at all is a sad reflection on the culture of those who exercise power. The governing principle seems to be that the head of state is the ultimate guardian of the constitution and must intervene where the normal machinery of government has broken down. The most basic principle here is that the government must have the support of the House of Commons. Important occasions calling for the intervention of the monarchy are as follows:

  The appointment of a Prime Minister. The Queen must appoint the person supported by a majority of the House of Commons. This usually means the leader of the largest party as determined by a general election. Nowadays each party elects its leader. In the unlikely event of a majority not being found, the existing Prime Minister must probably be permitted to attempt to form a government. Failing that, the Queen should summon the leader of the next largest party. If that fails, there is disagreement as to what should happen, and in particular as to whether the monarch has any personal discretion. The Queen should attempt to find someone else capable of commanding a majority, but it is not clear who, if anyone, she should consult. For example should she consult the outgoing Prime Minister? Alternatively the Queen should dissolve Parliament, causing another election. The guiding principle seems to be that she must try to determine the electorate's preference.

▶ **The dismissal of a government and the dissolution of Parliament.** If a government is defeated on a vote of confidence in the House of Commons but refuses to resign or advise a dissolution, the Queen could probably dismiss the government. This has not happened in Britain since 1783, but happened in Australia in 1975. In such a case the Opposition, if it could form a majority, could be placed in office or the Queen could dissolve Parliament, thus putting the case to the people through an election. It has been suggested that the Queen could dismiss a government that violates a basic constitutional principle, for example by proposing legislation to abolish elections. In order to dissolve Parliament, the Queen would require a meeting of the Privy Council. It would therefore be convenient as a temporary measure for her to appoint the Leader of the Opposition as Prime Minister, who would then formally advise her in favour of a dissolution (see *Adegbenro* v *Akintola* [1963] AC 614 at 631).

▶ **Refusing a dissolution.** This possibility arises because of the convention that the Prime Minister may advise the monarch to dissolve Parliament. The Queen might refuse a dissolution and appoint another Prime Minister if the Prime Minister is clearly acting unconstitutionally, for example if he or she lost a general election and immediately requested a dissolution or where a Prime Minister falls personally foul of his or her party. Unfortunately there are no clear cut precedents. It is likely that the Queen could refuse a dissolution only where there is a viable alternative government and a general election would be harmful to the national interest, although it seems difficult for anyone, let alone the Queen, to make such a judgement. A dissolution has not been refused in Britain in modern times but one was refused by the Governor-General of Canada in 1926. The Governor-General's decision was later rejected by the electorate.

▶ **The Queen might refuse a prime ministerial request to appoint peers to the House of Lords** where the reason for the request is to flood the Lords with government supporters. The precedents (1832 and 1910–11) suggest that the monarch would have to agree to such a request but only after a general election. This matter is therefore closely connected with the power to dissolve Parliament.

▶ **The royal assent.** The monarch has not refused assent to legislation since 1709. It appears to be a strong convention that royal assent must always be given. However the Queen might conceivably refuse assent where the refusal is on the advice of the Prime Minister, for example in the unlikely event of a private member's bill being approved by Parliament against the wishes of the government. Here two conventions clash. It is submitted that the better view is that she must still give assent because the will of Parliament has a higher constitutional status than that of the executive. It has also been suggested that the Queen has a residual discretion to refuse consent to a statute that violates fundamental constitutional principles such as abolishing democracy (see Twomey, 'The Refusal or Deferral of Royal Assent,' 2006, *Public Law* 580).

14.5   Crown Immunities

The Crown has special privileges in litigation. At common law no legal action would lie against the Crown in respect of its property rights and contracts, or in respect of injuries caused by the Crown (torts). This gap in the rule of law was avoided by the Crown's practice of voluntarily submitting to the jurisdiction of the courts. In the case of actions involving property and contract, this was through a procedure called a 'petition of right'. In the case of a tort, the individual Crown servant who committed the tort could be made liable. Where it was not clear who was responsible, the Crown would nominate a defendant, for example where a visitor to military premises was accidentally injured. In either case the Crown would pay the damages.

There is also the obscure maxim: 'the king can do no wrong'. This goes beyond the still existing rule that the monarch cannot be made personally liable. It means that wrongdoing or bad faith cannot be attributed to the Crown. For example the Crown at common law could not be liable for wrongs committed by its employees because unlawful acts of its employees were necessarily committed without its authority. However the maxim has never prevented the courts from deciding whether a particular action falls within the lawful powers of the Crown. Invalid acts as such are not wrongful acts (see *Dunlop* v *Woollahra Municipal Council* (1982)).

The Crown Proceedings Act 1947 subjected the Crown to legal liability as if it were a private person, for breaches of contract, for the wrongs of its servants and for injuries caused by defective Crown property. Section 1 permits action for breach of contact against the Crown; section 2 permits action in tort but only where a private person would be liable in the same circumstances. However the Act still leaves the Crown with several special privileges. The most important are as follows:

- **No court order can be enforced against the Crown**, so that the claimant's right to damages depends upon the Crown voluntarily paying up. Similarly no injunction lies against the Crown or against a Crown servant acting on behalf of the Crown (Crown Proceedings Act 1947 s.21). However this applies only in civil law cases involving private rights. In judicial review cases where the legality of government powers are in issue and in cases involving the enforcement of EC law ministers cannot claim Crown immunity (*M* v *Home Office* (1993), *R* v *Secretary of State for Transport ex parte Factortame No 2* (1991)).
- **In an action for breach of contract the Crown can plead 'executive necessity'**. This means that it can refuse to comply with a contract where it has an overriding power to take some action in the public interest (*Amphitrite* v *The King* (1921); *Commissioners of Crown Lands* v *Page* (1960)). There must either be some definite prerogative power that overrides the contract or the contract must conflict with a statutory duty. Governments cannot cancel contracts without compensation merely because of policy changes.
- **The Crown is not liable in tort for the acts of its 'officers'** unless the individual officer was appointed directly or indirectly by the Crown and paid wholly from central government funds (s.2(6)). (The term 'officer' includes all Crown servants and ministers.)
- **The Crown is not liable for wrongs committed by 'judicial' officers** (s.2(5)), that is, judges or members of tribunals. A person exercising judicial functions also enjoys considerable personal immunity (Chapter 8).

▷ Until 1987 a member of the armed forces injured on duty by another member of the armed forces or while on military property could not sue the Crown if the injury was pensionable under military regulations (s.10). This caused injustice because it was irrelevant whether or not the victim actually qualified for a pension. The Crown Proceedings (Armed Forces) Act 1987 abolished this rule but the Secretary of State can restore it in times of war or national emergency (see *Matthews* v *Ministry of Defence* (2003)).

▷ **The Crown is not bound by an Act of Parliament** unless it expressly or by necessary implication binds the Crown. Necessary implication is a strict notion. It is not sufficient to show that the Crown is likely to cause unfairness and inconvenience or even that the exemption is against the public interest (*Lord Advocate* v *Dumbarton District Council* (1990)). It has to be established that the statute would be unworkable unless the Crown were bound (see *Cooper* v *Hawkins* (1904): speed limit did not bind Crown). It is debatable whether the Crown can take the benefit of statutes, even though it is not bound by them. For example the Crown can evict a tenant free of statutory restrictions, but could the Crown as a tenant resist eviction by a private landlord by relying on the same statutory rights that it can ignore as a landlord?

▷ **Act of State**. The Crown is not liable for injuries caused in connection with bona fide acts of government policy overseas, provided that the action is authorised or subsequently ratified by the Crown (for example *Nissan* v *Attorney-General* (1970): British troops billeted in Cyprus hotel; not an act of policy; *Buron* v *Denman* (1848): British naval officer set fire to barracks in West Africa in order to liberate slaves; Crown subsequently confirmed the action).

The defence of Act of State cannot apply within the UK except against 'enemy aliens', that is, citizens of countries with which we are formally at war (*Johnstone* v *Pedlar* (1921): US citizen maltreated; Crown liable). This is because the Crown owes a duty to protect anyone who is even temporarily on British soil. Indeed for the same reason the defence may not be available against a British subject anywhere in the world. In *Nissan* the House of Lords expressed divided views (see also *Walker* v *Baird* 1892); *Johnstone* v *Pedlar* (above)). However, it seems unfair to favour people with no substantial link with the UK merely because they happen to hold British passports. The Human Rights Act 1998 applies to acts done by the UK government in overseas territory under its direct control (*R (Al-Skeini)* v *Secretary of State for Defence* (2007): treatment of prisoners in Iraq) but not in respect of waging war (*R (Gentle)* v *Prime Minister* (2008)), nor it seems in relation at least to some dependent territories (see Chapter 6).

Certain high level policy acts directed at other countries are also called Acts of State, for example making treaties, declaring war, recognising governments or granting diplomatic immunity (see Diplomatic Privileges Act 1964). These are exercises of sovereign powers with which the courts will not interfere. British subjects along with others may be incidentally affected by this kind of Act of State. For example in *Cook* v *Sprigg* (1899) the Crown annexed Pondoland and refused to honour railway concessions granted to British subjects by the former government (see also *West Rand Central Gold Mining Co.* v *R* (1905)). This kind of Act of State may affect rights in domestic law, for example a formal declaration by the Crown as to the existence of a state of war (*R* v *Bottrill ex parte Kuechenmeister* (1947)), the recognition of a foreign government (*Carl Zeiss Stiftung* v *Rayner & Keeler Ltd (No.2)* (1967)) and the conferring of diplomatic immunity (*Engelke* v *Musmann* (1928)).

14.6   The Royal Prerogative

The royal prerogative comprises special powers, rights and immunities vested in the Crown at common law. Identifying each of these powers and their scope is problematic since there is no authoritative source. This uncertainty is a concern because as a matter of constitutional principle those exercising power should be able to identify authority justifying its exercise. The modern prerogative can be explained as the residue of the special rights and powers conferred on the monarch by medieval common law. Some aspects might also be justified in Hobbesian terms (Chapter 2) on the basis that a residue of discretionary power is always needed to protect the community against unexpected dangers.

Lord Denning in *Laker Airways Ltd* v *Department of Trade* (1977) considered that the Crown had a general discretionary power to act for the public good in certain spheres of governmental activity for which the law had otherwise made no provision. This interpretation is however inconsistent with *Entick* v *Carrington* (1765). Here the court emphatically rejected a claim of 'executive necessity' that officers of the state had a general power to enter and search private property in the absence of express statutory or common law powers. Lord Denning's views were not supported by the other members of the Court of Appeal. They are also fundamentally inconsistent with ideas of limited government. The better view is that although the Crown has certain discretionary powers in relation to emergencies, such as the requisitioning of property (below), the prerogative comprises a finite number of miscellaneous powers rather than one general power to act for the public good.

Some of these powers were based upon the position of the monarch as chief landowner within the feudal system. Others derived from the responsibility of the monarch to keep the peace and defend the realm. This duality may have corresponded to the distinction drawn in seventeenth century cases between the 'ordinary' and the 'absolute' prerogatives, the latter being discretionary powers vested in the King and arguably beyond the reach of the courts (see *Bates Case* (1606)). From the sixteenth century, theories of absolute monarchy became dominant in Europe but were less influential in England.

In 1611 it was made clear that the King could legislate only within areas of prerogative allowed to him by the general law (*Case of Proclamations* (1611)). The debate therefore shifted to exploring the limits of the prerogative. The Stuarts attempted to extend the prerogative and to impose taxes and override the ordinary law. However even they submitted themselves to the courts and in a series of famous cases punctuating the political conflicts of the time the scope of the prerogative was inconclusively argued (*Bates Case* (1606); *R* v *Hampden* (1637); *Godden* v *Hales* (1686)). Given that the judges were dismissable by the Crown, these cases were not always consistent.

The outcome was revolution culminating in the 1688 settlement (Chapter 4), which provides the framework of the modern law. This can be summarised as follows:

- In principle the royal prerogative remains but must give way to statute.
- No new prerogatives can be created (*British Broadcasting Corporation* v *Johns (Inspector of Taxes)* (1965))

▷ The prerogative can be controlled by the courts, although the extent of such control depends upon the type of prerogative power in question and the context (below).

Prerogative powers can be exercised either directly by ministers or by Prerogative Orders in Council. The latter require a formal meeting of the Privy Council (a quorum of four) in the presence of the monarch. The Bill of Rights 1688 outlawed certain aspects of the prerogative including the power to suspend laws without parliamentary consent. The Bill of Rights also banned taxation under the royal prerogative. Modern judges have taken this further by refusing to imply a power to tax directly or indirectly unless very clear statutory language is used (see *Attorney-General* v *Wilts United Dairies* (1921); *Congreve* v *Home Office* (1976); *Macarthy & Stone (Developments) Ltd* v *Richmond upon Thames LBC* (1991)).

14.6.1   Modern Prerogative Powers

There is no authoritative list of prerogative powers. However in October 2003 the Public Administration Committee (PAC) of the House of Commons published a list supplied by the government of what it believed to be the main prerogatives (Fourth Report, Session 2003–04). It also took the view that some prerogative powers, for example the power to press men into the navy, may have lapsed through disuse. Similarly the ancient writ of *ne exeat regno*, which prevents persons from leaving the country, is sometimes regarded as obsolete. However there is no doctrine of obsolescence in English law.

The PAC's list includes the following. Firstly in relation to domestic affairs:

▷ Appointment and dismissal of ministers
▷ The summoning, prorogation and dissolution of Parliament
▷ Royal assent to bills
▷ The appointment and regulation of the civil service
▷ The commissioning of officers in the armed forces
▷ The deployment of the armed forces in the UK
▷ The appointment of Queen's Counsel (senior barristers). The Crown appoints judges by statute (Chapter 8)
▷ The prerogative of mercy (used to remedy errors in sentence calculation)
▷ The granting of honours
▷ The granting of royal charters to bodies such as universities, learned societies, charities or professional associations that gives the body the status of a legal person and signifies state approval of its activities
▷ Crown immunities (above).

Secondly in relation to foreign affairs where considerable flexibility is needed so that these prerogatives are not generally subject to legal control (below):

▷ The making of treaties
▷ The declaration of war
▷ The deployment of the armed forces on operations overseas
▷ The recognition of foreign states
▷ The accreditation and reception of diplomats.

The PAC's list did not mention certain other established prerogatives. These include the governance of some overseas territories (Chapter 6), the granting and revoking of passports and the Attorney-General's prerogative power to institute legal proceedings in the public interest and to stop criminal proceedings by issuing a *nolle prosequi*. The Constitutional Renewal Bill proposes to abolish the latter power. There is also the possibility that the Crown has a residual power to keep the peace within the realm, for example by issuing the police with weapons (*R v Secretary of State for the Home Department ex parte Northumbria Police Authority* (1988)) and similarly to enter upon, take and destroy private property in an emergency, although compensation may be payable if the property is taken in peacetime for public use (see *Burmah Oil Co.* v *Lord Advocate* (1965); War Damage Act 1965). In relation to emergencies however, the prerogative has largely been superseded by statute (Chapter 21). The security services also operate within a broad statutory framework, but many of their powers were formerly prerogative powers. Similarly immigration control, the administration of charities and the care of children and mental patients are now governed by statute.

Finally there are miscellaneous prerogatives based on feudal landholding. The most important of these are the Crown's ownership of the seashore and tidal waters and the Crown's rights to ownership of certain living creatures, notably swans.

14.6.2 Two Kinds of Prerogative Power?

There is ambiguity as to what a prerogative power is. Blackstone (1723–1780), whose view seems to be technically correct, regarded the prerogative as confined to the special powers of the Crown. Dicey (1915, p. 429) however described the prerogative as including *all* the non-statutory powers of the Crown, including the 'private law' powers of ownership, employment, contracting and so on apparently possessed by the Crown as a legal person in common with everyone else. These are sometimes called 'third source' powers and it is controversial whether they exist in their own right (see *Shrewsbury and Atcham Borough Council* v *Secretary of State* (2008); *R* v *Secretary of State for Health ex parte C* (2000): creating sex offenders register).

Blackstone's distinction seems unreal in as much as all Crown powers are important politically, and in the way they are exercised are indistinguishable from powers that Blackstone would regard as genuine examples of the prerogative. For example the Crown has enormous economic power (sometimes called *dominium* power); a defence contract or health service contract made with the Crown could affect the livelihoods of millions. The Crown may be a property owner in common with others but its economic and political power surely put it in a special position and call for additional controls, particularly if, following Locke (Chapter 2), we believe that government holds all its powers subject to public duties. There is much to be said for Dicey's view and for treating all non-statutory powers of the Crown alike.

The modern cases seem to support Dicey. In *Council of Civil Service Unions (CCSU)* v *Minister for the Civil Service* (1985) (also known as the GCHQ case) the House of Lords treated the control of the civil service as part of the royal prerogative, holding that they could review the validity of an Order in Council varying the terms of employment of certain civil servants. Lord Diplock expressed the view that the distinction between special and ordinary powers of the Crown is artificial and would regard all common law powers of the Crown as part of the prerogative. In *R* v *Criminal Injuries Compensation Board ex parte Lain* (1967) a government scheme to pay compensation to the victims of crime was treated as a matter of prerogative, thus enabling the court to review errors of law made by the board set up to run the scheme. The scheme was financed out of money provided by Parliament but was not then statutory. Since anyone can give away money, this scheme would not count as royal prerogative under the Blackstone definition.

14.6.3   Political Control over the Prerogative

Most prerogative powers are exercised by ministers. These powers include some that are among the most significant powers possessed by government, for example a decision to deploy troops and the power to make a treaty. The constitutional problem concerns a lack of democratic control over officials claiming to act under the prerogative. As common law powers, prerogative powers do not need to be approved by Parliament so that there is a gap in democratic accountability. Decisions taken under the prerogative are essentially decrees with no formal accountability other than the limited possibility of judicial review.

There was for instance no legal requirement for the government to gain parliamentary approval to send British troops to Iraq in 2003, although since approval was in fact sought on that occasion there may now be a convention requiring this. Whether the convention extends to the deployment of troops in a peacekeeping role as opposed to armed conflict is unclear. The absence of any statutory requirement for parliamentary approval thus raises profound questions in a modern democracy (see Fourth Report of the Public Administration Committee, HC 422, 2003–04, *Taming the Prerogative: Strengthening Ministerial Accountability to Parliament*). Similarly there are few democratic safeguards in relation to the treaty making power: a ministerial signature, without parliamentary approval, is all that is legally required to make a treaty. However under the 'Ponsonby Convention' a treaty is laid before both Houses for 21 days before ratification so as to invite a debate. The Constitutional Renewal Bill (now postponed) proposed to give this statutory force albeit in a weak manner. Under the Bill, if Parliament rejects a treaty the Secretary of State may then lay a statement indicating that it should be ratified anyway. This can be overridden by a vote of the House of Commons. The Secretary of State can also exclude these provisions by stating that in his opinion, 'exceptionally', the treaty should be ratified without being laid before Parliament.

The UK constitution is perhaps unique in allowing government such extensive and imprecise powers that are not granted by the legislature. In some cases however the exercise of a prerogative power must be confirmed by statute. These include treaties that alter the existing law and certain EU treaties (Chapter 10).

Some parliamentary control is possible, firstly because all government functions depend on money which must be authorised by Parliament and secondly through the doctrine of ministerial responsibility. These methods of control are inherently weak since Parliament has insufficient resources adequately to investigate government spending and there is in any case normally an automatic majority for the executive. Moreover government spending is usually authorised by a blanket departmental allocation or met out of a general contingency fund or a retrospective vote (Chapter 13). Although conventionally ministers are responsible to Parliament, at least one Prime Minister has expressed the view that 'it is for individual Ministers to decide on a particular occasion whether and how to report to Parliament on the exercise of prerogative powers' (HC Deb. 1 March 1993, col. 19W).

By convention the Prime Minister cannot be questioned about advice given to the sovereign concerning certain prerogative powers, such as the granting of honours and appointments and the dissolution of Parliament. The reason is that these powers are exercised personally by the monarch even though the monarch must usually act on the advice of the Prime Minister. In addition ministers sometimes refuse to be questioned about prerogative powers relating to foreign relationships, national security matters and the prerogative of mercy. However Parliament, if it wished, could insist on investigating these. Whether their exclusion is justifiable upon any basis other than the mystique that has traditionally attached to the prerogative is debatable. They involve wide discretionary powers, but that in itself could be an argument *for* rather than against political accountability.

14.6.4   Judicial Control

Historically the courts exercised only limited control over the prerogative. If a prerogative power was disputed, a court could determine whether it existed and (if it existed) what it empowered the executive to do, but the monarch was the only judge of how to exercise the power. For example in the *Saltpetre Case* (1607) the King had the power in an emergency to enter private land and was held to be the sole judge both of whether an emergency existed and what measures to take (see also *R* v *Hampden* (1637); *Attorney-General* v *De Keyser's Royal Hotel* (1920); *Chandler* v *DPP* (1964)).

The courts have developed sophisticated rules for judicial review of the exercise of statutory powers based on notions of fairness, reasonableness and relevance (Chapter 16). These do not (in theory at any rate) entitle the courts to make the government's decisions for them but are designed to ensure that government keeps within the limits of its powers and complies with basic moral standards. Is there any reason why the same should not apply to the prerogative?

As a result of the speeches in the House of Lords in *Council of Civil Service Unions* v *Minister for the Civil Service* (1985) the courts have asserted a jurisdiction over executive power, including a prerogative power. They held that decisions made under the authority of prerogative powers are in principle reviewable on the same basis as decisions made under a statutory power. But this does not mean that this jurisdiction will always be exercised. The power must be of a 'justiciable' nature, which means that it must be suitable for the courts' scrutiny. This is no longer resolved by looking at the source of the power (statute or prerogative) but upon its subject matter and its suitability in the context of the facts of the case, the particular grounds of review and the political role, expertise and knowledge appropriate to the court. This will be considered in Chapter 18 in the context of judicial review generally. In summary, in cases where there is a high degree of political discretion without guidelines, or where there are considerations outside the powers or expertise of the courts, such as in relation to foreign affairs, the threshold of successful challenge is likely to be high. At the other extreme a more intensive standard of review is likely where human rights are at issue. It is noteworthy that the courts seem to be increasingly reluctant to treat any power as wholly non-justiciable but to take the view that the matter is one of judicial restraint in relation to the particular issue (see *R (Gentle)* v *Prime Minister* (2008)). Nevertheless a characteristically non-justiciable power is likely be a royal prerogative power, such as the power to deploy the armed forces or make treaties.

14.6.5 Prerogative and Statute

Since Parliament is sovereign, statute can abolish a prerogative power. How easily can this be achieved in the light of the courts' approach to interpretation? Express words or necessary implication certainly do so. It is less clear whether repeal of that statute may revive the prerogative (see *A-G v De Keyser's Royal Hotel* (1920) at 539; *Burmah Oil Co. v Lord Advocate* (1965) at 143).

Problems arise where Parliament has enacted statutory provisions dealing with the same subject matter as the prerogative without clearly abolishing the prerogative powers. Where an area of governmental activity is subject both to a statutory and a prerogative power, the statutory power may supersede the prerogative power (see *A-G v De Keyser's Royal Hotel Ltd* (1920); *Laker Airways Ltd v Department of Trade* (1977)). Whether or not it does so is a matter of interpretation of the statute. Firstly it depends on whether the statute is intended to bind the Crown (see above) and secondly whether the statute is intended to replace the prerogative. If the entire area of governmental activity that was regulated under the prerogative is covered by a statute, the statute probably prevails.

In *A-G v De Keyser's Royal Hotel Ltd* (1920) the question concerned whether the property owners were entitled to compensation after their hotel was occupied by the armed forces in wartime. The Crown took possession ostensibly under a statute that conferred an enforceable legal right to compensation. It was nevertheless argued on behalf of the Crown that it had a prerogative power to take possession of land during an emergency and that no compensation was payable as of right under this prerogative power. The House of Lords upheld the property owner's claim, holding that the occupation of the hotel had taken place under statutory powers. The prerogative had been superseded by a comprehensive statute regulating this field of governmental activity and it would be meaningless for the legislature to have imposed limitations on the exercise of governmental power if these could merely be bypassed under the prerogative.

On the other hand in *R v Secretary of State for the Home Department ex parte Northumbria Police Authority* (1988) the prerogative was not put into abeyance where an apparently comprehensive system of statutory powers existed. Here it was held that the Home Secretary could use a prerogative power to supply the police with weapons even though statute placed local authorities in charge of providing police resources. The court said that the prerogative power was suspended only when its exercise was actually inconsistent with a statutory power. *De Keyser's* was treated as an example of inconsistency. Purchas LJ also suggested that the *De Keyser's* principle is qualified where executive action is designed to benefit or protect the individual. In such cases the exercise of prerogative power for this purpose will be upheld unless statute unequivocally prevents this.

This decision was somewhat surprising since the relevant statute contained no saving for the prerogative. Vincenzi (1996) is critical of it, arguing that the decision is an unprecedented example of the courts' permitting the Crown to disregard statutory provisions in its perception of the public interest. He identifies a tension with the Bill of Rights that prohibits the Crown from suspending or dispensing with statute.

> *R v Secretary of State for the Home Department ex parte Fire Brigades Union* (1995) may indirectly support Vincenzi's view. The Secretary of State had power to make a commencement order bringing legislation into force intended to establish a particular regime for compensation for victims of crime. It was held that he could not refuse to bring the statute into effect in order to establish a different scheme under the prerogative. However, as their Lordships remarked, the case is not strictly an example of a conflict between statute and prerogative. The statute was not yet in force and the gist of their Lordships' reasoning was that by committing himself to the prerogative scheme the minister had disabled himself from bringing the statute into force. However prerogative power is subject to the important limitation that it must not be exercised in a manner which, in substance, conflicts with the intention of Parliament. Thus in *Shrewsbury and Atcham Borough Council v Secretary of State* (2008) the Court of Appeal held that the common law powers of the Crown could not be exercised where Parliament legislated comprehensively covering that ground. However in the circumstances the Act had retrospectively validated the Crown's action which had been to make preparations for a reorganisation of local government in advance of the coming into force of the relevant Statute. It might have been different if the use of the common law power had seriously disadvantaged the claimant.

14.6.6 Prerogative and Human Rights

The Human Rights Act 1998 provides that an Order in Council made under the royal prerogative is 'primary legislation' for the purposes of the 1998 Act (s.21). This means that, although like any other executive action an Order in Council can be challenged in the courts on other grounds, the court cannot set aside an Order in Council that conflicts with a right protected under the ECHR but would be limited to making a Declaration of Incompatibility (Chapter 19). However ministers have the power to amend Orders in Council as they think fit anyway.

A further consequence of section 21 is that a public authority is only bound to act in accordance with convention rights unless conflicting primary legislation requires it to act otherwise (s.6). Since an Order in Council is deemed by section 21 to be 'primary legislation', a public authority that acts in accordance with its terms would appear to act lawfully even if in breach of a convention right (see further Billings and Ponting, 'Prerogative Powers and the Human Rights Act: Elevating the Status of Orders in Council', 2001, *Public Law* 21).

Summary

▷ In this chapter we first discussed the meaning of the term 'Crown'. The Queen as head of state must be distinguished from the Crown as the executive. It is not clear whether the Crown is a corporation sole or a corporation aggregate. The Crown is a separate entity in respect of each government of which it is the head.

▷ Succession to the Crown depends on statute, thus reinforcing the subordinate nature of the monarchy.

▷ The monarch has certain personal political powers which should be exercised in times of constitutional crisis. These include the appointment of a Prime Minister, the dissolution of Parliament and the appointment of peers.

▷ At common law the Crown was immune from legal action. Some of this immunity has been reduced by the Crown Proceedings Act 1947, but the Crown is still immune from enforcement and has certain special defences including 'Act of State' and 'executive necessity' in contract. There is however no general doctrine of state necessity as justifying interference with private rights. Certain acts of the Crown give rise to immunity from legal liability.

▷ The Crown's executive powers derive from three sources:
1. Statutes
2. The royal prerogative, that is, the residue of special common law powers peculiar to the monarch
3. Powers possessed by virtue of the fact that the Crown is a legal person with basically the same rights and duties as an adult human being. The Crown can therefore make contracts, own property, distribute money and so on. There is a dispute as to whether this kind of power is part of the royal prerogative and whether it exists at all.

▷ The prerogative cannot be used to make law or raise taxation.

▷ No new prerogative powers can be created.

▷ Prerogative powers can be reviewed by the courts unless they concern a 'non-justiciable' subject matter or issue such as foreign relationships.

▷ While prerogative powers are subject to some parliamentary scrutiny, in practice political control over prerogative power is limited.

▷ The prerogative must give way to statute although the scope and extent of this is unclear.

Exercises

14.1 Compare the royal prerogative with parliamentary privilege (Chapter 11), with reference to (i) its purposes; (ii) its history and sources; and (iii) the extent to which it can be controlled by the courts.

14.2 'For all practical purposes, the Crown is represented by the government of the day' (Sir Robert Armstrong, former Cabinet Secretary). Is this a correct statement of the law?

14.3 To what extent are royal prerogative powers subject to control by Parliament?

14.4 To what extent does the Crown enjoy special privileges or immunities in litigation?

Exercises cont'd

14.5 Advise the Queen in the following cases:

   (i)   There has just been a general election in the UK. The existing government has obtained the largest number of seats in the Commons but without an overall majority. The Opposition is negotiating with a minority party to form a government. The Prime Minister refuses to resign.

   (ii) What would be the position if the Opposition had obtained the largest number of seats in the Commons, and the government was negotiating with the minority party?

   (iii) The government is defeated in a vote on the Annual Finance Act. The Prime Minister refuses to resign.

   (iv) The Prime Minister has just been sacked as party leader. However due to an agreement with the Opposition and a minority party, he could still command a small majority in the Commons.

14.6 Critically discuss proposed reforms of the prerogative powers.

14.7 The Government of Carribia, an independent Commonwealth country, is overthrown by a rebel force, 'The People's Front'. Cane, the displaced Prime Minister of Carribia, requests the aid of the British government. British troops are sent to Carribia and are authorised under an agreement between the British government and Cane to 'use all necessary measures to restore the lawful government of Carribia'. During the British troops' campaign on the island they requisition buildings owned by Ford, an American citizen, for use as a military depot, and destroy the home of Austin, a British citizen, in the belief that it is being used as a base by the rebels. Ford and Austin sue the British government for compensation. Discuss. Would your answer differ if Carribia was a British overseas territory?

14.8 Ruritania is an independent member of the Commonwealth. The UK Queen is the Queen of Ruritania. Last week a military coup in Ruritania succeeded in capturing the palace occupied by the Governor-General who represented the Queen. The military commander requests the Queen to abdicate in favour of himself as King. The situation in Ruritania is currently uncertain and forces loyal to the Queen are attempting to secure control. The British government advises the Queen not to abdicate. The Commonwealth Secretary-General advises her to abdicate. What would you advise?

Further reading

Blackburn, R. (1999) 'Monarchy and the Royal Prerogative', in Blackburn, R. and Plant, R. (eds) *Constitutional Reform*, London, Longman.

Bogdanor, V. (1995) *The Monarchy and the Constitution*, Oxford University Press.

Brazier, R. (1999) *Constitutional Practice* (3rd edn) Oxford University Press, Chapter 9.

Harris, B. (2007) 'The Third Source of Authority for Government Action Revisited', *Law Quarterly Review* 123:225.

Hennessy, P. (1995) *The Hidden Wiring*, London, Gollancz, Chapter 2.

Jones, B., Kavanagh, D., Moran, M. and Norton, P. (2004) *Politics UK* (5th edn) Harlow, Pearson, Chapter 16.

Loveland, I. (2003) *Constitutional Law, Adminstrative Law and Human Rights: a Critical Introduction* (3rd edn) London, Butterworths, Chapter 4.

Munro, C.R. (1999) *Studies in Constitutional Law* (2nd edn) London, Butterworths, Chapter 8.

Sunkin, M. and Payne, S. (eds) (1999) *The Nature of the Crown: a Legal and Political Analysis*, Oxford, Clarendon Press.

Further reading cont'd

Tomkins, A. (2003) *Public Law*, Oxford, Clarendon Press, Chapter 3.
Vincenzi, C. (1998) *Crown Powers, Subjects, Citizens*, London, Pinter.

Background reading

Nairn, T. (1988) *The Enchanted Glass: Britain and its Monarchy*, London, Hutchinson.
Sampson, A. (2004) *Who Runs this Place?*, London, John Murray, Chapter 3.

Chapter 15

Ministers and departments

Institutions tend to protect their own and to resist criticism from wherever it may come. (Lord Hope in *R* v *Shaylor* [2002] 2 All ER 477, 509)

Provided that ministers act 'in good faith' ministerial responsibility for gross errors of judgment is written in water – except at election time. (Anthony Lester QC, *Guardian*, 3 August 2004)

Key words

- ▶ Fragmented government
- ▶ The pre-eminence and vulnerability of the Prime Minister
- ▶ Collective and individual responsibility
- ▶ Accountability and responsibility
- ▶ Chain of accountability: policy and operations
- ▶ Disclosure
- ▶ Civil service impartiality
- ▶ Select committees

15.1 Introduction

There are few legal controls over the organisation of government departments or the relationship between ministers, civil servants and Parliament (see Chapter 5). Some provisions are made under the royal prerogative by Orders in Council. There are statutes dealing with particular matters usually of a technical nature. The more important aspects of these relationships are governed by conventions or internal understandings. Some very general published principles are contained in the Ministerial Code (revised 2005) and the Civil Service Code (revised 2006). The core relationship is governed by the conventions of collective and individual ministerial responsibility to Parliament but there is no consensus as to what these mean and no independent method of enforcing them. The shelved Constitutional Renewal Bill proposed to put the general principles governing the civil service, now contained in the Civil Service Code as a mixture of royal prerogative rules and non-legally binding conventions and practices, onto a statutory footing but no significant substantive changes were proposed.

15.2 The Powers of the Prime Minister

The powers of the Prime Minister have evolved since the middle of the eighteenth century, corresponding to the decline in the powers of the monarch. The office, which dates from the early eighteenth century, was originally that of cabinet chairman deputising for the monarch, and acting as an intermediary between the monarch and the government. The Prime Minister is appointed by the Queen and by convention must be a member of and enjoy the support of the House of Commons. In practice the Prime Minister is always the leader of the party with the largest number of seats in the Commons. However should a prime minister resign or retire during the course of a Parliament there may be no clear alternative candidate. In such a case the matter seems to fall within the discretion of the Queen (Chapter 14). It is not clear what action she should take nor whom she should consult (see Vennard, 2008). Her first course would probably be to seek a consensus among the senior members of the majority party.

The powers of the Prime Minister are mainly derived from convention. They are also scattered in statute, custom and practice, royal prerogatives and 'nods and winks' derived from the instinct to obey a leader supported by the conformist cast of mind of the majority of persons working in public life. The Prime Minister exercises important prerogative powers. Apart from political powers (below) these include overall responsibility for security, control of the civil service and the mobilisation of the armed forces. The Prime Minister also has statutory powers in sensitive political areas (such as Police Act 1997 s.9; Intelligence Services Act 1994 s.2; National Minimum Wages Act 1998; National Audit Act 1983 s.1). In recent years prime ministers have also assumed control over foreign policy, which has the attraction of providing opportunities for self promotion without the chore of detailed administration.

The main conventions that secure the pre-eminent power of a Prime Minister are as follows:

- The Prime Minister appoints and dismisses all government ministers and determines their status and pecking order. She or he also has powers of appointment in relation to many other important public posts (a mixture of statute and convention).
- By convention the Prime Minister controls the cabinet agenda, formulates its decisions and allocates government business. In this way cabinet discussion can be bypassed and matters entrusted to selected prime ministerial supporters, smaller groups of ministers or advisers or indeed anyone since there is no constraint on a Prime Minister taking advice from anyone.
- Except for the unlikely event of intervention by the monarch, impeachment by Parliament and removal by his or her party under its rules for electing a leader, there is no formal machinery to get rid of a Prime Minister. A vote of no confidence in the House of Commons can only bring down the government as a whole.
- The Prime Minister may advise the Queen to dissolve Parliament. Thus the Prime Minister can choose the date of a general election, holding his or her colleagues' careers to ransom.
- The Prime Minister is also Minister for the Civil Service.
- The Prime Minister is head of the internal security services.
- The Prime Minister is the channel of communication between Queen and government.
- The Prime Minister is the main spokesperson for the nation and as such has unique access to the media. The Prime Minister's press office holds a key position. There is a danger that, in terms of public perception and therefore legitimacy, the Prime Minister is perceived as a head of state, thereby eclipsing the monarchy. Ministers' energies are centred upon their own departmental interests. Few have the time or knowledge to concentrate upon issues outside their departmental concerns.

The main limits upon the power of a Prime Minister lie in the checks and balances that prevent the Prime Minister using powers arbitrarily. These include:

- The Queen's power to intervene in extreme cases (Chapter 14).
- The risk of dismissing cabinet ministers who may enjoy political support in their own right. In practice, a Prime Minister's freedom to appoint ministers may be limited by party considerations. The Cabinet is full of rivals for power. A Prime Minister could not impose his or her will over a united Cabinet that enjoys substantial support in the Commons. If a Prime Minister requested the Queen to dissolve Parliament in such circumstances, she might be entitled to refuse the request.
- The absence of a separate prime ministerial department (apart from a Private Office). However prime ministers may have a substantial staff of independent special advisers brought in from outside the regular civil service. Under Tony Blair three of these had executive powers. They no longer do so but have significant influence particularly in relation to the press.
- A Prime Minister could be deposed as party leader and therefore lose the support of the Commons. The influence of senior backbench MPs may be significant. The resignation of Margaret Thatcher in 1989 provides an example.

153   The Cabinet

The Cabinet is the policy making body comprising all secretaries of state and certain other senior ministers which formally coordinates the work of government departments (see Haldane Committee, 1917, Cmnd 9230). It is doubtful whether it is underpinned by convention or is merely a creature of practice. Its proceedings are confidential (Chapter 21). In recent years it has been sidelined in favour of the Prime Minister and informal groups selected by the Prime Minister whose decisions it usually supports without extended discussion or full information (see Butler Report, *Review of Intelligence on Weapons of Mass Destruction*, HC 898, 2003–4, para. 610). The Cabinet no longer appears to be an effective political force, having deteriorated in recent years from being the primary policy making body to a role which seems largely that of confirming decisions made elsewhere.

The Cabinet originated in the seventeenth century as a group of trusted Privy Counsellors called together to give confidential advice to Charles II. The term was originally one of abuse and referred to the King's 'closet' or anteroom. An attempt was made in the Act of Settlement 1700 to prevent 'inner caucuses' from usurping the functions of the Privy Council, but the provisions were never implemented and were later repealed. George I (1714–27) leaned particularly heavily on party leaders and from his reign onwards the monarch ceased to attend cabinet meetings, substituting the Prime Minister. During the reign of George III (1760–1820) the convention emerged that the monarch should generally consult the Cabinet. The eighteenth century Cabinets served the vital purposes of ensuring that the executive could command the support of the Commons and as a means of presenting the monarch with a united front. From a mid-nineteenth century perspective, Bagehot regarded the Cabinet as the 'buckle' that holds the government together.

The Cabinet has no legal powers as such. However statute law recognises the status of the Cabinet by protecting cabinet secrecy (Health Service Commissioners Act 1983 s.12;

Parliamentary Commissioner Act 1967 s.8(4)) and sometimes powers can be exercised only by a minister of cabinet rank (for example Data Protection Act 1998 s.28(10)).

According to the Ministerial Code (below) the business of the Cabinet and ministerial committees consists in the main of (i) questions which significantly engage the collective responsibility of the government because they raise major issues of policy or are of critical importance to the public and (ii) questions on which there is an unresolved argument between departments. Cabinets usually comprise between 20 and 30 ministers including the heads of the main government departments and certain other senior office holders. Other ministers and civil servants often attend cabinet meetings for particular purposes, notably the Chief Whip who forms a link between the government and its backbench supporters.

Cabinet business is frequently delegated to committees and subcommittees or informal groups of ministers and other persons such as civil servants and political advisers. This is an inevitable consequence of the complexity of modern government and is an important method by which the Prime Minister can control the decision making process. There are two kinds of formal cabinet committee: (i) ad hoc committees set up on a temporary basis to deal with particular problems and (ii) named permanent committees, for example defence and overseas policy, economic strategy and legislation. The names and membership of these committees are published (www.cabinet.office.gov.uk). The Butler Report (above) criticised the contemporary practice of policy making by informal groups and individuals selected by the Prime Minister without written records and without the Cabinet being fully informed.

Collective cabinet responsibility (below) ensures that every member of the government is bound by decisions approved by the Cabinet whether or not the full Cabinet has discussed them. Thus it is sometimes said that the Cabinet has become merely a rubber stamp or 'dignified' part of the constitution. The secrecy surrounding the workings of the Cabinet is also an aspect of collective responsibility and makes objective analysis difficult. Other practical limits upon cabinet power are that its meetings are relatively short (about two hours per week), its members have departmental loyalties and its agenda and procedure are controlled by the Prime Minister.

The Cabinet Office services and coordinates the work of the Cabinet and records its decision for implementation by departments. It comprises about 100 civil servants headed by the Cabinet Secretary who also coordinates other Whitehall committees, designates most of their chairmen and, as head of the civil service, reports to the Prime Minister. Arguably these three roles create fundamental conflicts of duty. The Ministerial Code (2005) issued by the Cabinet Office provides a general framework for the conduct of ministers which we shall draw upon in context.

15.4 Ministers

A minister is defined by the Ministers of the Crown Act 1975 as an office holder under Her Majesty. It is for the Queen on the advice of the Prime Minister to designate the number and titles of ministers and to appoint and dismiss ministers. Some ministers have separate legal personality as corporations sole. By convention a minister must be a member of Parliament and most ministers, particularly those in major spending departments and the Treasury, must be members of the House of Commons. In principle any number of ministers can be appointed. However as we saw in Chapter 8, there are statutory limits on the number of ministers who can sit in the Commons and also the number of paid ministers in either House. There are about 100 ministers, ranked as follows:

- **Cabinet ministers**: Most cabinet ministers head departments but some offices are traditionally without departments and can be assigned to special or coordinating work by the Prime Minister. These include the Chancellor of the Duchy of Lancaster and the Lord President of the (Privy) Council. The Leader of the House of Commons is responsible for managing government business in the House. The most important departments are traditionally headed by secretaries of state. These are the successors of the powerful officials created by Henry VIII to control the central government.
- **Ministers of state and parliamentary under-secretaries of state** (where the head of the department is a Secretary of State). The two law officers, the Attorney-General and the Solicitor-General, who deals primarily with internal matters, are also of this rank.
- **Parliamentary secretaries**: These are mainly recruited from the House of Commons and assist more senior ministers with political and administrative work.
- **Parliamentary private secretaries**: These are members of Parliament who act as unpaid assistants to individual ministers.

Whips control party discipline and provide a channel of communication between government and backbenches. They are formally officers of the royal household. The Chief Whip is not a member of the Cabinet but attends cabinet meetings and consults with the Prime Minister on matters such as the appointment of ministers.

15.5 Government Departments

By convention a minister must head each department in order to ensure ministerial responsibility to Parliament. Ministers are often appointed for their political or parliamentary skills or for reasons of political balance and reward for loyalty. They do not necessarily have the skills, interest or experience to run complex departments. Unlike the position with most other parliamentary systems there is a practice in the UK of 'reshuffling' ministers at roughly yearly intervals so that only exceptionally does the same person hold office for the duration of a Parliament. During a reshuffle ministers may be sacked or reallocated and junior ministers or backbench MPs promoted. This is a prime minsterial tool to enforce party loyalty and perhaps to deflect public attention from policy failures. It also underpins incompetent government by inexperienced politicians who are likely to leave office without taking responsibility for the consequences of their failings.

The senior civil servants whose advice contributes to policy making are selected according to the supposition that a highly educated person is good at everything. Their role is to provide expertise, continuity and balance in the system of government. In recent years there has been some recruitment from the private sector but most senior civil servants have spent their whole careers in the civil service. Against the background of a political ethos which favours private business practices and competition, ministers and civil servants may therefore lack the technical, financial and business skills and knowledge for example to evaluate complex procurement issues relating to defence equipment or IT systems or to assess the quality of external consultants. Coupled with the traditional mindset of civil servants against change and in favour of their own convenience there is an underlying momentum towards fragmented and incompetent government against a background of limited and blunt accountability mechanisms.

There are no constitutional requirements relating to the organisation of government departments. They can freely be created, abolished or amalgamated by the Prime Minister. The only statutory limitations concern restrictions upon the number of ministers who can sit in the House of Commons (Chapter 12) and miscellaneous provisions relating to particular offices, notably the Lord Chancellor (Constitutional Reform Act 2005). The organisation of departments is sometimes regarded as one of 'royal prerogative' but could also be the right of the Crown, as of any private organisation, to organise itself as it wishes, thus illustrating a possible weakness in our non-statist constitution. In the nineteenth century committees of the Privy Council or special bodies were set up to deal with new governmental responsibilities but as the work of government increased separate permanent departments headed by ministers were created. These have been expanded, abolished, split up or combined as circumstances dictated without apparent constitutional constraints.

Some government departments and ministers, notably the Treasury and the Lord Chancellor, trace their origins back to medieval times. The Home Office and Foreign Office are nineteenth century creations of the royal prerogative. Other departments are either statutory or more commonly set up by using the prerogative to create a Secretary of State (see below). Some departments such as the Inland Revenue – now combined with Customs and Excise – have substantial administrative and financial independence with powers conferred directly upon them. They are known as non-ministerial departments. However a minister remains constitutionally responsible for them.

Because English law has no umbrella concept of the state (Chapter 6), provision must be made for transferring rights and liabilities between different departments. These problems are dealt with by standardised legislation (for example Ministers of the Crown Act 1975; Deregulation and Contracting Out Act 1994). Under the Civil Service (Management Functions) Act 2002 a minister can transfer the management of civil servants to any other Crown servant. This is intended to allow ministers to create semi-independent executive agencies headed by a Chief Executive. For the purposes of litigation a list of appropriate departments is maintained by the Treasury. In cases of doubt the Attorney General represents the Crown (Crown Proceedings Act 1947 s.17). There is a curiosity that since the office of 'Secretary of State' is in law a single office, the various secretaries of state can interchange functions and assets without the need for legislation. In addition all ministers can delegate the exercise of their powers to any civil servant within their department but not to other ministers (*Carltona* v *Commissioner for Works* (1943); *Lavender & Son* v *Minister of Housing and Local Government* (1970); see Chapter 17).

15.5.1   The Treasury

The Prime Minister is the First Lord of the Board of the Treasury, a body that never meets. By convention the Chancellor of the Exchequer is the responsible minister. The Treasury is an overlord and coordinating department in that it is responsible for the economy as a whole, allocates finance to government departments, supervises their spending and is responsible for the tax gathering agencies – the Inland Revenue and the Customs and Excise Commissioners.

The Treasury has special constitutional significance and its activities provide a good illustration of the mix of legal and informal controls that typify the UK constitution and make the exercise of power obscure. There is a general 'understanding', the basis of which lies in internal practices based on 'ancient authority', that the Treasury both authorises and polices departmental expenditure (see Daintith and Page, 1999, pp. 109–26). The support of the Public Accounts and Public Administration Committees of the House of Commons also authorises Treasury power. Article 10 of the Ministerial Code requires government departments to consult the Treasury in relation to spending proposals. Thus the Treasury can strongly influence if not control the spending priorities of other departments.

The Treasury also plays the role of gatekeeper to Parliament in which it authorises and presents government spending and taxation proposals. Parliament depends on an initiative from the Treasury since the Crown's (by convention) recommendation is required for all taxation and public expenditure. Moreover it is arguable that Parliament votes money to the Crown rather than to any particular department (Chapter 13). This gives the Treasury a powerful lever since it can approve allocations to individual departments. The Treasury fixes the overall levels of expenditure for each department and can set objectives against which the effectiveness of spending is measured. It approves spending proposals by departments either in general or in relation to especially sensitive items.

Treasury pre-eminence is backed by specific legal powers. Firstly the Treasury has statutory power to approve payments from the Consolidated Fund and the National Loans Fund (the government's main bank accounts) and to place limits on other sources of income such as fees and charges (Government Resources and Accounts Act 2000 ss.2, 3). Secondly the Treasury approves the form and method of the accounts of government departments (ibid. ss.5, 7). Under these powers the Treasury is in a position to decide what counts as public assets and expenditure and thereby to determine the extent to which public bodies can raise private money. Thirdly the Treasury can authorise additional payments to departments (ibid. s.6) and many items of expenditure require Treasury consent under particular statutes. It is unlikely that in the absence of a plain violation of statute matters of economic policy would be subject to judicial review (see *R v HM Treasury ex parte Smedley* (1985): payments contrary to statute).

The Treasury appoints an accounting officer for each department who is responsible for the management of the department (Exchequer and Audit Department Act 1866 s.22). This is usually the head (Permanent Secretary) of the department and in the case of an executive agency, its chief executive. The Comptroller and Auditor-General examines departmental accounts and reports unauthorised expenditure to the Treasury which can either authorise it or report the matter to Parliament (Exchequer and Audit Departments Act 1921 s.1).

The Bank of England has some independence. A statutory body, it administers the government's bank account and in conjunction with the Treasury and the Financial Services Authority regulates other banks (Bank of England Act 1998). Subject to the statutory objectives of maintaining price stability, supporting the economic policies of the government and complying with inflation targets set by the Treasury, it is responsible for monetary policy (primarily fixing interest rates) and for issuing currency. Its directors are appointed by the Crown and can be dismissed on prescribed grounds with the consent of the Chancellor of the Exchequer and 'in extreme economic circumstances' it is subject to directions from the Treasury. The Bank is also subject to scrutiny by the Treasury Select

Committee and is required to publish the minutes of its monetary policy committee, an annual report and an annual inflation report.

15.6   The Law Officers

The Attorney-General is the chief law officer and is assisted by the Solicitor-General. As party politicians, the law officers raise questions about the separation of powers. They are entitled to consult other ministers but by convention act independently. The Attorney-General has the following functions:

1. Representing the government in legal proceedings, including intervening in any legal proceedings to put the government's view.
2. Giving legal advice to the government which the government claims to be entitled not to make public on the questionable analogy of a lawyer–client relationship.
3. Political responsibility for the Crown Prosecution Service and under various statutes to consent to the prosecution of certain offences; under the prerogative to interfere to prevent a prosecution (*nole prosequi*). Most of these powers were proposed to be abolished under the Constitutional Renewal Bill, to be replaced however by a wide power to intervene on national security grounds.
4. To bring legal proceedings on behalf of the general 'public interest', either on his or her own initiative or on the application of any member of the public (a relator action). This might include an action against a public authority. The Attorney-General's decision whether or not to intervene cannot be challenged in the courts (*Gouriet* v *Union of Post Office Workers* (1978)).
5. To refer questions of law to the Court of Appeal where an accused person has been acquitted of a criminal offence or to request a more severe sentence for a convicted person.

The extent to which the Attorney-General (A-G) is influenced by political considerations is obscure. For example in relation to prosecutions of government officers and government attempts to suppress the media, the A-G's two roles as government lawyer and representative of the public interest are potentially in conflict. We have only the predictable assertions of successive A-Gs that they can be trusted. In 1924 the government fell because the A-G acted on instructions from the government in relation to a prosecution of an anti-government journalist. The Scott Report (HC 115, 1996) revealed an official culture in which the advice of the A-G was treated as if it had legal force, a practice condemned by the court in *R* v *Brown* (1993). Moreover the A-G is regarded as having a private lawyer–client relationship with the government so that his or her advice can be made public only with the consent of the government. The combination of these principles for example allowed the current government to claim that it was lawfully entitled to invade Iraq in 2002 on the basis of advice from the A-G over which he changed his mind. The government has no obligation to obtain independent legal advice. At first the Attorney-General doubted the legality of the invasion but subsequently became confident that it would be lawful having accepted advice from one of a minority of international legal experts who supported that view. As if advising a private client on the basis of information given by the client the Attorney-General sought assurances from the Prime Minister that Iraq possessed weapons of mass destruction that threatened the UK. These assurances later turned out to be untrue. Lord Bingham, recently retired as the senior Law Lord, has now made public his view that the invasion of Iraq was clearly unlawful and that the Attorney-General's advice was fundamentally flawed (Grotius Lecture, British Institute of International and Comparative Law, 17 November 2008).

15.7 Ministerial Responsibility

Ministerial responsibility is traditionally a central principle of the constitution, defining both the relationships between ministers and Parliament and that between ministers and civil servants. It is entirely a matter of convention. Comparable principles operate in the devolved institutions on a statutory basis (Chapter 6). However it is arguable that the doctrine is so nebulous and so damaged by executive domination of Parliament that it has little value as a constitutional principle. Parliament may from time to time make grand pronouncements in its favour but these are seldom translated into action (see Tomkins, 2003, p. 134, who is more optimistic). In particular Tomkins identifies three 'fault lines' in the doctrine. These are firstly a lack of openness in government, secondly 'ownership' in the sense that the government itself can influence the meaning and enforcement of the doctrine, and thirdly and most importantly, the pressures of party domination. These work together to weaken Parliament.

Ministerial responsibility has two aspects that are not entirely consistent, these being collective and individual responsibility. 'Responsibility' is sometimes used interchangeably with 'accountability'. Both terms have a range of meanings (see Second Report of the Public Service Committee, HC 313, 1995–6, paras 14–21, 32). They include obligations to provide an explanation, information, acknowledgement, review and redress. Sometimes resignation may also be expected. The particular combination appropriate to any given case depends on the circumstances. In addition to ministerial responsibility as such, there are instruments such as the Freedom of Information Act 2000 (FOIA), the Codes of Conduct for MPs and civil servants and the *Guidance to Officials on Drafting Answers to Parliamentary Questions*, which inform the notion of openness and accountability. More generally the openness and accountability of government is required by the fourth and fifth Principles of Public Life, namely accountability and openness, set out by the Committee on Standards in Public Life (Chapter 5).

Ministerial responsibility does not mean that Parliament (except in its capacity as lawmaker) can give orders to ministers or lay down policies. Parliament does not itself govern and to this extent there is a separation of powers. Ministerial responsibility means only that ministers must discharge their duties in a manner that has the continued support of the Commons and they must give an account of their actions and decisions. If the Commons so votes on a motion of confidence, the government must resign. Opposition MPs as well as those of the minister's own party influence ministers in their decisions and exert pressure for changes in government policy. Ministerial responsibility also provides information to arm opponents in the adversarial conduct of British political debate. Indeed it is a characteristic of the parliamentary system of government that there is a continuing struggle on the part of MPs to gain more information than ministers are willing to provide.

The doctrine of ministerial responsibility developed during the eighteenth and nineteenth centuries, corresponding to the rise of the House of Commons and the decline in the power of the Crown. Its original purpose was as a weapon against the monarch by achieving coherence among politicians holding divergent views. On its face the convention can be acclaimed as a device to ensure accountable government. An alternative view is that the convention favours 'strong' government because it allows ministers to govern with little effective parliamentary supervision or interference since Parliament has neither the will nor the resources to hold ministers effectively to account (see Flinders, 2000). Ministerial responsibility may also be out of line with the practices of modern government, in particular the techniques of privatisation and devolved public management. In this context the convention actually shields government from public accountability because the impugned decision may have been taken in an agency that has been hived off from central government. Although in principle the minister remains fully responsible, the vague meaning of responsibility enables ministers more easily to evade blame the further away they are from the location of decision making. The party system and the tradition of secrecy within the civil service have also played a part in breaking the chain of accountability through Parliament to the electorate.

15.7.1 Collective Responsibility

Collective responsibility applies to the Cabinet and probably to all government ministers. It was developed originally so that government and Parliament could put up a solid front against the King. It suggests collegial government that is at odds with the legal basis of government with powers given to individual ministers. Collective responsibility has four aspects:

1. It requires all ministers to be loyal to the policies of the government whether or not they are personally concerned with them (solidarity). Collective responsibility therefore applies even though many important decisions are made by subcommittees or informal groups selected by the Prime Minister (which can include unelected persons, indeed anyone) and are not fully discussed by the Cabinet as a whole.
2. It requires the government as a whole to resign if defeated on a vote of confidence in the House of Commons or if the Prime Minister resigns.
3. It requires that Cabinet and government business be confidential.
4. It protects ministers against personal responsibility since collective responsibility can be used to justify individuals avoiding blame. For example the Butler Report into intelligence failures relating to Iraq (2004, www.butlerreview.org.uk) absolved all ministers and civil servants from blame for misleading the public on the basis that the various falsehoods were 'collective' (Butler himself was a former head of the civil service). Collective responsibility and individual responsibility (below) are therefore in conflict. It can also be argued that the doctrine of collective ministerial responsibility could contribute to a general public disenchantment with politics if ministers are seen to vote in support of policies they are believed not to support (Winetrobe, 2003).

The drastic sanction of a vote of confidence is the only method by which Parliament can enforce collective responsibility but governments have rarely been defeated in this way in modern times. In 1924 Ramsay MacDonald's Labour government resigned and in 1979 so did James Callaghan's Labour government. Both were minority governments.

Modern ideas of party solidarity make collective responsibility virtually meaningless as a method of control over governments but very important as a method of asserting prime ministerial power and ensuring secrecy within the government since cabinet discussions are confidential (see Ministerial Code, Cabinet Office 2005, para. 6.17). Resignation is also required before a minister can speak out on a particular issue. Nevertheless as a convention collective responsibility may be adapted to new circumstances. The Prime Minister can apparently modify it over a particular issue (such as membership of the EEC in 1975).

The relationship between Prime Minister and Cabinet has an important impact on how well collective responsibility works in practice. There are tensions between a collegial style and a prime ministerial style of government. The collegial model of government, which emphasises the participation of all cabinet ministers in decision making, disguises the dominance of the Prime Minister in the formulation of policy (above) which tends to blur the difference between a parliamentary and a presidential system. There are no formal checks and balances. The extent to which the Prime Minister can exercise an authoritarian style depends on the composition and mood of the Cabinet, the attitude and cohesion of the party and that of the Commons, the temper of the electorate and not least the personal style of the Prime Minister. If undue reliance is placed on a select group of senior ministers (the 'inner cabinet') or unelected 'cronies', if too many 'private deals' are struck with individual ministers, or if too many controversial policies are effectively formulated in cabinet subcommittees, ministers may feel less inclined to loyalty. Some consensus among ministers may be necessary if only to avoid political embarrassment or ministerial resignations. Serious embarrassment can result where senior ministers resign having concluded that the workings of the Cabinet have strayed unacceptably far from the collegial model. Michael Heseltine resigned during the Westland affair in 1986. Similarly Geoffrey Howe's resignation over EC policy in 1990 resulted from his concern about the Prime Minister's apparent distaste for collective decision making. This resignation played a pivotal role in ending Mrs Thatcher's tenure of No. 10 Downing Street.

It is uncertain how far collective responsibility applies to those junior ministers who have no legal status as ministers of the Crown and who do not even nominally participate in the decision in question. It would appear however that the same 'conform or go' rule can be applied by a Prime Minister. Thus the government is assured of the 'payroll vote' from about 100 MPs who hold government office and from the whips. It seems that a junior minister cannot accept individual responsibility for departmental errors because this is a responsibility that lies with the Secretary of State. Junior ministers account to Parliament on behalf of the minister.

It could be argued that collective responsibility is no different from the solidarity expected within any organisation. Ministers can discuss policy differences in private, confident that all will support the decision which is eventually reached. The presentation of a single view also adds authority to the government's position because it disguises the coalition nature of many governments. This argument begs the question whether government can be compared with, say, a large private sector company. Given that an important value of democratic government is to manage disagreement without suppressing it, it may be desirable for government not to speak with a single voice but to recognise the provisional nature of any decision reached.

15.7.2 Individual Responsibility

Sir Edward Bridges, the Permanent Secretary to the Treasury, expressed the classical interpretation of the doctrine in 1954 after the Crichel Down affair (see Second Report of the Public Service Committee, HC 313, 1995–6, para. 8). He stated that a minister is responsible to Parliament for the exercise of all executive powers and every action taken in pursuance of those powers. This emphasises that a minister must always answer questions and give a full account of the actions of his or her department. This is so whether or not the minister is personally at fault for what has gone wrong and has been subject to only limited exceptions related among other things to commercial confidence, national security and some macroeconomic issues.

Individual ministerial responsibility is concerned with a chain of accountability from Parliament through ministers to civil servants. Ministerial responsibility protects civil servants from direct public responsibility since they owe their loyalty to the government and especially to the minister in charge of their department (see *Notes of Guidance on the Duties and Responsibilities of Civil Servants in Relation to Ministers*, 1985 – the Armstrong Memorandum). Thus civil servants appear before Parliament only with the permission of ministers and on terms set by ministers.

Beyond that, its meaning and scope are unclear; firstly in respect of what 'responsibility' entails and secondly in respect of what actions the minister is responsible for. Ministerial responsibility is primarily enforced by Parliament. Most specifically it requires that ministers provide information to Parliament by means of answers to parliamentary questions, evidence to select committees, formal ministerial statements and letters to MPs. Within the executive the Prime Minister is responsible for enforcing ministerial responsibility and therefore, indirectly, of defining it.

Ministers have attempted to limit their responsibility by making various distinctions. Firstly it has been claimed that responsibility applies only to 'policy' mistakes as opposed to 'operational' errors, which are deemed to be failures properly to implement policy. This has particularly been evident following the radical restructuring of government, with the majority of civil servants working in semi-detached executives or Next Steps agencies under the day-to-day direction of chief executives with only limited departmental control (below). This restructuring has tended to confuse lines of accountability. Similar problems can be identified where a quango stands between the minister in charge of policy formulation and the delivery of a service, such as was the case with the Qualifications Agency and the examination boards in assessing A-level qualifications during the so-called 'exams crisis'. It seems however that ministers do not always escape blame where serious errors occur in such cases (see McCaig, 'School Exams: Leavers in Panic', 2003, *Parliamentary Affairs* 56(3): 471).

The policy/operational dichotomy is a vague one. Indeed the two are often inextricably interconnected. The effect has been to make it more difficult for Parliament to find out who is to blame when problems arise. For example, is prison overcrowding policy or operation? Furthermore even if a matter can be classified from the outset as 'operational', as soon as adverse political consequences arise, the same matter may mutate into one of policy, causing confusion as to whether (and if so when) responsibility shifts from a chief executive to a minister. An example of this concerned the deaths of immigrant workers in Morecambe Bay in 2004, which was connected with ineffective administration of immigration controls. The example of the Child Support Agency illustrates some ministerial reluctance to accept blame where inadequate agency performance is partly attributable to such matters as inadequate funding (a matter for ministers under *Taking Forward Continuity and Change*, 1995, Cm 2748). Conversely ministers can exploit confusion by intervening where they perceive electoral gains, as in the events leading up to the dismissal of Derek Lewis, the head of the prison service, following allegations of interference by the Home Secretary in the detailed administration of the service (see the Learmont Report, 1995, Cm 3020; the House of Lords Public Service Committee Session, 1997–8, 55, para. 341). Ministers may also interfere in 'operational' matters while declining to answer questions about them, claiming that such matters fall within the responsibility of the chief executive. Moreover since it is the minister who decides what is policy and what is operation, ministers can effectively determine the extent of their constitutional responsibilities. The House of Lords Select Committee (above) concluded that it was not possible effectively to separate policy from operations and that such a division was not desirable (ibid. para. 348).

Secondly ministers have distinguished between 'accountability' and 'responsibility'. This seems to divorce the circumstances in which a minister must give to the House an explanation of the actions of their department (accountability) from cases in which a minister must accept the blame for departmental mistakes and resign (responsibility). In *Taking Forward Continuity and Change* (pp. 27–8) the government stated that Parliament can always call a minister to account for all that goes on in his department but it added that a minister cannot be responsible in the sense of having personal knowledge and control of every action taken and cannot be personally blameworthy when delegated tasks are carried out incompetently or errors of judgement are made at an operational level.

The accountability / responsibility distinction was rejected in 1996 by the Public Service Committee of the Commons (above) but accepted by the Scott Report on the 'arms to Iraq' affair (HC 115, 1995–6). It demands that ministers must be prepared to offer a complete explanation of any error to Parliament. The duty embraces an obligation to offer reasons by way of justification in the face of criticism. This is so even if there is no obligation to resign. Experience reveals however that ministers have not always been willing to give a full account of their actions. Notoriously the conclusion of the Scott Inquiry (above) was that there were numerous examples of ministers failing to give full information about the policies, decisions and actions of government regarding arms sales to Iraq (K8.1, para. 27) and that this had undermined the democratic process (D4.56–D4.58). Answers to parliamentary questions in the affair had been 'designedly uninformative' because of a fear of adverse political consequences if the truth were revealed (D3.107).

Following revelations of this kind, it became clear that there should be a renewed commitment to the doctrine of individual responsibility combined with a need to clarify the obligations entailed by it and in particular to ascertain the matters about which ministers must answer questions. This led to resolutions of the House of Commons and House of Lords on ministerial accountability (HC Debs, vol. 292, cols 1046–7, 19 March 1997; HL Debs, cols 1055–62, 20 March 1997).

These resolutions led to the adoption by the government of the Ministerial Code (Cabinet Office, 2005) which now incorporates a 'Ministerial Code of Ethics'. The Code reminds ministers that their conventional duties are part of a matrix of overarching obligations, including the obligations to uphold the law, the integrity of public life and the seven Principles of Public Life. It then sets out the following principles of ministerial conduct (which are mostly in the terms of the resolutions):

1. Ministers must uphold the principle of collective responsibility.
2. Ministers have a duty to Parliament to account, and be held to account, for the policies, decisions and actions of their departments and Next Steps agencies.

3. It is of paramount importance that ministers give accurate and truthful information to Parliament, correcting any inadvertent error at the earliest opportunity. Ministers who *knowingly* mislead Parliament will be expected to offer their resignation to the Prime Minister.

4. Ministers should be as open as possible with Parliament and the public, refusing to provide information only when disclosure would not be in the public interest, which should be decided in accordance with the relevant statutes and the FOIA 2000.

5. Ministers should similarly require civil servants who give evidence before parliamentary committees on their behalf and under their direction to be as helpful as possible in providing accurate, truthful and full information in accordance with the duties and responsibilities of civil servants as set out in the Civil Service Code.

However there is no independent method of enforcing the Code which has no legal force. It states that it is not an enforceable rule book (para. 1.3). It is not policed by the Cabinet Secretary nor by the Parliamentary Committee on Standards since this has jurisdiction only over MPs as such. Part 1 of the Code reminds ministers that they can only continue to hold office for as long as they have the support of the Prime Minister. The Code states that the Prime Minister 'is the ultimate judge of the standards of behaviour expected of a Minister and the appropriate consequences of a breach of those standards'. This suggests that the Code envisages that the Prime Minister is both a setter of standards and responsible for their enforcement. For that reason the statement reads rather oddly in the light of the resolutions.

The respective resolutions of each House are of fundamental importance because ministerial responsibility is no longer an unwritten convention which can be varied at will by the government of the day; ministerial responsibility is now a rule of Parliament. The terms of the resolutions are not however without difficulty. As Woodhouse (1997) observes, satisfying them may not be unduly burdensome. Ministerial judgement will still govern what it means to be 'as open as possible' and when disclosure 'would not be in the public interest'. This means that the problems of interpretation remain and that the doctrine of ministerial responsibility is still somewhat elusive.

What is the effect of the statement that the Prime Minister is the ultimate judge of the appropriate standards of behaviour? Does this merely restate the political reality that loss of office inevitably follows the loss of prime ministerial support for a beleaguered minister or does it hint at a diminished role for Parliament? Could a future Prime Minister amend the Code in a manner inconsistent with the resolutions?

The Code of Practice on Access to Government Information was revised in 1997 to create a clear statement of the presumption in favour of disclosure of information and included revisions to limit the scope of the exemptions under which information could be withheld. The government accepted a recommendation of the Public Service Committee that the relevant exemption from that Code (such as defence, security and international relations, immigration and nationality, information of economic sensitivity, and internal discussion and advice such as cabinet papers) should be specified when departments failed to provide an answer to a parliamentary question. This was important because it emphasised that information could only be withheld on limited grounds. Paradoxically the introduction of the Freedom of Information Act (Chapter 21) has led to the abandonment of this practice and the government appears reluctant to require ministers and civil servants to reinstate it by referring to the applicable exemption under the FOIA.

The Public Administration Committee (PAC) in its Second Special Report for the Session 2005–6 (HC 853) recommended that this refusal should be reconsidered (see also Chapter 13).

Accountability may be more effective in the devolved Parliaments. The Scottish Parliamentary Standards Commissioner Act 2002 permits the Parliamentary Standards Commissioner to investigate complaints that a Member of the Scottish Parliament (MSP) has breached the Code of Conduct and report the findings to the Scottish Parliament. A complaint by an aggrieved MSP that a minister has breached the Scottish Ministerial Code by improperly refusing to disclose information may be made to the First Minister. If this avenue is not fruitful, the complaint can be referred by the MSP to the Presiding Officer as a dispute between MSPs. If the Presiding Officer were either unwilling or unable to resolve the matter, he or she may decide to refer it to the Scottish Parliament's Standards and Public Appointments Committee, which could by motion recommend that a member's rights and privileges be withdrawn if the complaint were upheld. However ministerial openness seems less controversial than in Westminster.

In Wales the Committee on Standards of Conduct receives and investigates complaints referred to it by the Presiding Officer relating to the conduct of any member of the National Assembly for Wales. If the complaint is substantiated, in its report to the Assembly, the Committee may 'recommend' action in appropriate cases. In addition the Code of Practice on Members' Access to Information (2004) confers on members of the National Assembly for Wales more extensive rights of access to information than those available under the FOIA. The National Assembly Commissioner for Standards can investigate complaints that any Code of the Assembly has been breached.

More generally the relationship between ministers and civil servants can cause an 'accountability gap'. This is because accountability can break down where a minister blames a civil servant for some failure and subsequently directs that individual not to appear before a select committee (this is permitted under the Cabinet Office document *Departmental Evidence and Response to Select Committees*; Chapter 13). Notoriously the Secretary of State for Trade and Industry refused to allow the civil servants involved in aspects of the Westland affair to appear before the Commons Defence Select Committee (see HC 519, 1985–6, 1986, Cmnd 9916). This problem has in part been addressed in the parliamentary resolutions. Although civil servants still give evidence to select committees under the direction of ministers, the minister must insist that civil servants be as helpful as possible in providing accurate, truthful and full information (HC resolution para. iv). As we have seen however, Parliament still lacks power to compel ministers to answer questions and cannot require civil servants to give evidence to select committees.

15.7.3   Resignation

Ministerial resignation engages both collective and individual responsibility. This is because where resignation takes place it saves fellow ministers from having to offer support for the beleaguered minister under the principle of collective responsibility. The classical doctrine does not resolve the question of when, as a constitutional requirement, a minister's 'responsibility' also entails a duty to take the blame for departmental errors if necessary by resignation. One interpretation of the convention is that resignation is required for every serious departmental error regardless of the personal blame of the minister. Characteristically of conventions, such a convention if it ever existed seems to have been destroyed by disuse. The Crichel Down affair (1954, Cmd 9220), which involved serious official misconduct in relation to government appropriation of land, was once thought to have required resignation but is not now considered to support such a wide proposition. Sir Thomas Dugdale's resignation in that case probably owed more to political misjudgement and a lack of parliamentary support.

Of 27 cabinet resignations since 1982, 13 were the result of misconduct or corruption in office, seven misconduct in private life, five political disagreement, one voluntary and only one, Lord Carrington (following an intelligence failure in relation to the Falkland Islands), apparently as a response to the convention of formally accepting responsibility for departmental errors. The following are characteristic:

▷ Norman Lamont kept his post as Chancellor of the Exchequer after sterling was withdrawn from the exchange rate mechanism in 1992, notwithstanding that this was a serious reversal of government policy. Perhaps it is significant that Parliament was not sitting at the time. James Callaghan, his predecessor during the 1967 devaluation crisis, was less fortunate.
▷ David Blunkett, the Home Secretary, remained in office following a number of serious breaches of security at Buckingham Palace since he was not personally to blame but resigned in 2004 as a result of personal accusations.
▷ Stephen Byers eventually resigned in 2002 after a series of criticisms of his department, culminating in his misleading Parliament concerning the abolition of Railtrack.
▷ Beverley Hughes resigned in 2004 after wrongly denying that she knew about the scale of bogus visa applications. Her denial appears to have been an unwitting error, which means that she was not obliged to resign under the Code. However there were signs of a withdrawal of prime ministerial support as the issue was seized on by the Opposition (*Telegraph*, 2 April 2004).
▷ Charles Clarke's offer in 2006 to resign as Home Secretary was refused by the Prime Minister, notwithstanding grave concerns about the effectiveness and political management of the Home Office. The minister lost his job just two weeks later following a 'reshuffle' but only after public confidence had ebbed away.

It seems that resignation is only *constitutionally* required in two categories of case:

1. Where a minister has *knowingly* misled Parliament (except in the very limited cases where this is justified: Public Service Committee, Second Report, HC 313, 1995–6, para. 32).
2. The minister is personally to blame for a serious departmental error (Sir Richard Butler in evidence to the Scott Inquiry, 9 February 1994, Transcript pp. 23–4).

An honest even though unreasonable belief in the accuracy of information given to Parliament can be a lifeline to beleaguered ministers. The Scott Inquiry found that Mr Waldegrave unreasonably clung to the view that government policy governing the sale of arms to Iraq had been reinterpreted but that it had not changed (HC 115, 1995–6, D4.1–7). Waldegrave did not resign. Similar questions arose after Lord Falconer's refusal in 2001 to resign in respect of the funding and sale of the Millennium Dome.

The second case embraces both serious personal misconduct and serious error in the minister's department in which the minister is implicated. Examples of the former include

Peter Mandelson who in 1998 did not disclose that he had received a substantial private loan from a fellow minister whose business affairs were subject to investigation by Peter Mandelson's department (see also the Blunkett resignation (2004) concerning the giving of favours for personal reasons). Private misconduct unrelated to a minister's duties might also lead to resignation but perhaps only where the minister becomes politically vulnerable (for example David Mellor in 1992 following adverse publicity about his private life). Woodhouse argues that personal indiscretions fall within the ambit of conventional requirements because they affect the public credibility of the minister concerned ('Ministerial Responsibility in the 1990s: When do Ministers Resign?', 1993, *Parliamentary Affairs* 46:277).

Raw politics and media attention rather than constitutional obligation may therefore be the best explanation of ministerial resignations. Even in cases of personal misjudgement or serious policy failure, resignation will be influenced by pragmatic concerns of the gravity of the issue, party support for the beleaguered minister, the timing of the discovery of the error, the support of the Prime Minister and Cabinet and the public repercussions of the fault.

15.8   Civil Servants

The civil service is a professional, permanent and independent part of the executive, giving the constitution continuity and stability. Its purpose is to assist the government in formulating its policies, to carry out decisions of the government and to administer services for which the government is responsible. There is no authoritative legal definition of a civil servant. The Constitutional Renewal Bill following the Tomlin Commission on the Civil Service (1931, Cmnd 3909) unhelpfully refers to 'the civil service of the State'. This may include every person who serves the Crown in a civil capacity as opposed to a military capacity, other than holders of judicial or political office, and who are paid wholly and directly out of moneys provided by Parliament. The armed forces are of course also Crown servants paid from parliamentary funds but are subject to a distinctive legal regime. The police may 'serve' the Crown but are not civil servants because they are paid partly out of local funds. Thus the best definition of a civil servant is partly negative, meaning a Crown servant other than those falling into special categories (see Sandberg, 'A Whitehall Farce? Defining and Conceptualising the British Civil Service', 2006, *Public Law* 653).

There is particular tension from two directions. On the one hand the civil service must offer impartial advice and expertise to governments of all political colours (Civil Service Code 2006, paras 1, 13). On the other hand it is required loyally to carry out government instructions. The argument that UK civil servants should have wider duties to the Crown as distinct from duties to the government of the day has not succeeded (see House of Commons Public Services Committee, *Ministerial Accountability and Responsibility*, HC 313, 1995–6, para. 169). Ministers (perhaps weak ones) may complain that they are dominated or subverted by their civil servants. Civil servants may draw attention to the risks of political interference with the impartiality and influence of the civil service, particularly through ministerial involvement in appointments and also through the influence of special advisers and other persons recruited informally by ministers.

15.8.1   Legal Status of a Civil Servant

Apart from specific statutory provisions dealing with the transfer of functions and certain employment matters, there is no statutory regime governing the civil service. The position of a civil servant is governed primarily by the royal prerogative and by conventions. Following persistent recommendations by the Committee on Standards in Public Life (see First Report, 1995, Cm 2850–1; Sixth Report, 2000, Cm 4557–1; Ninth Report, 2003, Cm 5775) the Constitutional Renewal Bill proposed to codify the main principles regulating the civil service. Rules controlling the civil service are sometimes made by Prerogative Orders in Council, which have the status of law but may also take the form of instructions issued by ministers (see Civil Service Order in Council 1995, as amended; Civil Service Management Code; Civil Service Code, revised 2006). Management of the civil service is vested in the Prime Minister as Minister for the Civil Service. The Cabinet Office and the Treasury supervise the civil service with each department or agency being managed by its accounting officer. The accounting officer's activities can be directly examined by Parliament by means of the Public Accounts Committee and the Comptroller and Auditor-General.

The independent Civil Service Commission regulates the appointments process and disciplinary matters and hears complaints brought by civil servants under the Civil Service Code (Civil Service Order in Council 1995 Article 4(5)). It has no direct enforcement powers. It makes an annual report to Parliament. General statements regarding impartiality, objectivity, honesty and duties of confidentiality are set out in the Civil Service Code. This is enforceable as part of the civil servant's terms of employment. The Code makes no reference to accountability and treats openness as incidental to integrity and honesty rather than as important in itself.

15.8.2   Appointments

Following a practice dating from the nineteenth century and designed to replace a tradition of patronage and nepotism, permanent civil servants must be appointed on merit in a fair and open competition (Civil Service Order in Council 1995, Article 2, 5). In the case of senior appointments ministers can be consulted but by convention do not make the decision. Senior appointments must be approved by the Civil Service Commission (Article 5). However there are exemptions from the principle of appointment on merit (Article 3, 6). They include special advisers (below) and appointments made directly by the Crown, such as the Governor of the Bank of England. Other exceptions include temporary appointments and appointments in special circumstances of persons of 'proven merit' must be approved by the Commissioners (Article 6). There is a convention that ministers should not influence civil service appointments.

Members of public bodies outside the civil service are also appointed on merit by a process requiring independence and open competition (see First, Fourth and Sixth Reports of Committee on Standards in Public Life). There are concerns relating to ministerial patronage and interference in relation to such appointments and the sycophantic tendencies of the objects of such patronage. Some 11,000 appointments made by ministers to non-departmental public bodies, public corporations and regulatory bodies are monitored by a Public Appointments Commission under the royal prerogative (Order in Council July 16 2002), which has drawn up a Code of Practice (2004); there is also a commissioner for NHS appointments. The principles include independent assessors and 'proportionality' which enables simplified procedures to be used in the case of less important appointments (see Fourth Report of Public Administration Select Committee Session 2002–03, *Government by Appointment: Opening up the Patronage State,* HC 135; *Getting the Balance Right,* Committee on Standards in Public Life, 2004).

15.8.3　Discipline

According to one view, a civil servant being subject to the royal prerogative has no contract of employment and cannot enforce the terms of his employment other than those laid down by statute. At common law the Crown can dismiss a civil servant 'at pleasure', that is, without notice and without giving reasons (*Dunn* v *R* (1896)). This is consistent with the view that there is no contract. On the other hand it has been held that there can be a contract between the Crown and a civil servant but that as a matter of public policy the contract can be overridden by the Crown's power to dismiss the civil servant at pleasure (*Riordan* v *War Office* (1959), but see *Reilly* v *R* (1934)). On this second analysis the terms of employment such as pay and conditions are enforceable against the Crown.

Modern cases have stressed that there is no inherent reason why the relationship cannot be contractual (see *Kodeeswaren* v *Attorney-General for Ceylon* (1970); *R* v *Civil Service Appeals Board ex parte Bruce* (1988); *R* v *Lord Chancellor's Department ex parte Nangle* (1992)). The Employment Act 1988 deems there to be a contract between the Crown and a civil servant for the purpose of making a civil servant liable for industrial action (s.30). Whether or not there is a contract it seems clear that the Crown can still dismiss at pleasure and that a contractual term which says otherwise is not enforceable. This can be regarded as a matter of public policy.

Civil servants like other citizens may be protected by judicial review. However in *Nangle* (above) it was held that judicial review did not apply to internal disciplinary decisions unless a formal adjudicative process is involved (compare *Bruce* (above) and *R* v *Civil Service Appeals Board ex parte Cunningham* (1991)). Moreover internal remedies must be used before resorting to the courts. Most civil servants are also protected by statutory unfair dismissal rules administered by industrial tribunals (Employment Rights Act 1996 s.191). Special machinery applies to security issues. A minister can, by issuing a certificate, remove any category of Crown employee from the employment protection legislation on grounds of national security (Employment Rights Act 1996 s.193). A civil servant who is suspected of being a security risk is given a special hearing, but without the normal rights of cross examination and legal representation, before a panel of 'three advisers'. These usually comprise two retired senior officials and a High Court judge.

Problems arise when a civil servant considers that his or her integrity is compromised, for example by being required to act for politically partisan purposes or possibly to break the law. Obeying the orders of a superior is not a defence in English law. The orthodox doctrine is that civil servants owe an absolute duty of loyalty to ministers (above) and the Civil Service Code imposes a lifelong duty not to disclose official information without authority (Article 6). There are internal mechanisms to enable civil servants to express issues of conscience. These include a right of appeal to the independent Civil Service Commission (above) and special provisions relating to the Official Secrets Act (Chapter 21). Judicial review may also be available (see *R* v *Shaylor* (2002)).

The political activity of civil servants is restricted according to the level of the individual in the policy making hierarchy. The majority are unrestricted except while on duty or in uniform or on official premises. An 'intermediate' group can take part in political activities with the consent of their head of department. This includes clerks, typists and officials performing specialist non-political jobs. A 'restricted' group of senior officials directly involved in policy making cannot take part in national politics at all but can indulge in local politics with the consent of their head of department. However whole departments can be exempted. Civil servants are also prohibited from taking gifts or doing other things that could create a conflict between their private interests and their official duties. A retired civil servant requires government approval before accepting employment with private sector organisations that are likely to have dealings with the government (see Civil Service Pay and Conditions Code, Fifth Report of Treasury and Civil Service Committee, HC 1989–90).

15.8.4 Special Advisers

Special advisers are party political advisers appointed directly by ministers and working closely with them. They were formally recognised by a government announcement in 1974 but have probably always existed. In 2006/7 there were 68 special advisers of which 20 worked for the Prime Minister (compared to about 3000 senior civil servants). They are temporary civil servants whose posts terminate with their minister (see Code of Conduct for Special Advisers, amended 2006). They are appointed for the purpose of providing 'assistance' to ministers, a purpose which goes beyond advice (Civil Service Order in Council 1995 Article 3 (as amended)). Unlike other civil servants they are not required to be appointed on merit (ibid. Article 3). They have no executive powers, these having been removed in 2007 (Civil Service (Amendment) Order in Council (No .2) (2007)).

Special advisers therefore serve as a link between the political and the permanent parts of the government. There is a concern that their activities, particularly in relation to communication with the media, may threaten the reputation of the civil service for impartiality. There is also a concern that permanent civil servants may be denied access to ministers and their role will be reduced to carrying out orders from special advisers (see Report of Select Committee on Public Administration (2001) H.C. 293 and HL Deb.7 Nov. 2005 col. 482–98). On the other hand special advisers serve as a valuable link between the two elements. In its Ninth Report (2003) the Committee on Standards in Public Life recommended that both the civil service and special advisers should be subject to a statutory regime which clarifies their respective constitutional roles and duties. In particular special advisers should be defined as a separate category distinct from civil servants and should not normally be given executive powers nor management nor disciplinary powers over civil servants. Ministers should be personally accountable for the acts of their special advisers. The recent Constitutional Renewal Bill proposed to put special advisers onto a statutory footing but without significant changes to the regime.

15.8.5 Civil Servants and Ministerial Responsibility

Under the *Carltona* doctrine (*Carltona* v *Commissioner for Works* (1943)) a minister can lawfully exercise any of his statutory powers through a civil servant in his department and need not personally exercise any power unless statute specifically so requires (for example Immigration Act 1971 s.13(5); Regulation of Investigatory Powers Act 2000 s.59). The decision remains that of the minister – the civil servant and the minister being indivisible in law (see also *Bushell* v *Secretary of State for the Environment* (1981); *R (Alconbury Developments Ltd)* v *Secretary of State for the Environment, Transport and the Regions* (2001)). It is not clear how far this principle depends on the power of control over civil servants available to ministers, the convention of ministerial responsibility itself or simply the unreality of ministers being capable of acting personally in every case. Possible limits to the principle might be influenced by such matters. In *Oladehinde* v *Secretary of State for the Home Department* (1990) the House of Lords held that a deportation decision could be made by an immigration officer on behalf of the Secretary of State. However Lord Templeman remarked (at 397) that the person exercising the power must be 'of suitable seniority in the Home Office for whom the minister accepts responsibility' (compare *Re Golden Chemical Products Ltd* (1976): denying judicial control).

The classical doctrine of ministerial responsibility has been that as civil servants have no powers of their own and so cannot take decisions or do anything except and in so far as they are subject to the direction and control of ministers, a civil servant has no direct responsibility to Parliament and cannot be called to account by Parliament. Civil servants are therefore accountable to ministers, and ministers accountable to Parliament. In particular advice given to ministers by civil servants cannot be disclosed without the permission of ministers and, according to the government, civil servants appear before parliamentary committees only with the consent of their ministers. Ministers therefore shield civil servants from outside scrutiny. In return civil servants are loyal to ministers and owe no other allegiance, thus emphasising the minister's own accountability to Parliament (see also Chapter 13). However in 1994 the Permanent Secretary in the Overseas Development Department disclosed to the Public Accounts Committee that ministers had overridden his advice (*The Times*, 18 January 1994). Conversely the head of the civil service was exposed to public ridicule in 1987 in the 'Spycatcher' affair when he was sent by the government to persuade an Australian court to suppress publication of the memoirs of a former member of the civil service.

The Scott Inquiry (above) revealed how in practice civil servants have sometimes acted independently of ministers or in the expectation of subsequent ministerial ratification of their actions (Scott, 1996, HC 115, para. D3.40). This exposed the constitutional fiction that civil servants only give advice to ministers. Civil servants concealed important questions from ministers and may even have defied ministerial instructions. Moreover as we saw above, ministers have attempted to pass responsibility to civil servants, firstly by distinguishing between policy and operational matters and secondly by distinguishing between 'accountability' as a duty to explain and 'responsibility' as liability to take the blame (Fifth Report of Treasury and Civil Service Select Committee, *The Role of the Civil Service*, HC 27, 1993–4, para. 120).

It has long been accepted that as accounting officer the permanent head of a department must appear before the relevant parliamentary committee. It has never been settled whether select committees can require other civil servants to attend to answer questions. In 1986 the Defence Select Committee claimed the absolute right to secure attendance from civil servants (HC 519, 1985–6). However a compromise has been arrived at whereby ministers are enjoined to permit civil servants to appear but subject to restrictions (see para. 37, *Departmental Evidence and Response to Select Committees*, Cabinet Office, January 1997, replacing the so-called 'Osmotherly Rules'). This document exhorts civil servants to be as forthcoming as possible in providing information under the Code of Practice on

Access to Government Information. Information can however be withheld in the public interest which should be determined in accordance with the law and the exemptions set out in the Code. Moreover civil servants cannot disclose or discuss the advice they gave to ministers, only the action they took on behalf of ministers.

The reorganisation of government departments into a fragmented model copied from private business, coupled with the privatisation of some governmental activities (the 'hollowing out' of the state), has further placed the classical model under strain. This is most notably the case in the relationship between ministers and chief executives of executive agencies (EAs). Ministerial responsibility was intended to apply equally to the work of EAs. However the principle underlying the respective functions of the agencies and the departments is that autonomy for service delivery should reside with the agency, while policy matters should be reserved for the department acting under ministerial control. Framework agreements made between the agency and the sponsoring department (sometimes with the Treasury as a party) constitute the relationship between the two. The framework agreement contains the corporate strategy and financial arrangements under which the agency will work.

A chief executive is appointed (as a temporary civil servant) to be responsible for the day-to-day management of the agency. The chief executive is responsible to the minister but as accounting officer also appears before select committees to answer MPs' questions about the functioning of the agency. Controversially this suggests that a convention *may* have been emerging under which agency chief executives are directly responsible to Parliament in their own right (but see below). MPs have also been encouraged to approach chief executives directly on behalf of their constituents and chief executives answer written parliamentary questions. The answers are published in Hansard to avoid the bypassing of Parliament which might have occurred if chief executives responded directly to individual MPs (for example Fifth Report of the Treasury and Civil Service Committee (above) col. 53, para. 170).

In 1997 the House of Commons Select Committee on Public Service identified a need for a re-examination of the relationship between ministers and civil servants and in particular a clarification of the respective roles of ministers and agency chief executives. It expressed the view that there should be no distinction between the constitutional responsibilities of chief executives and other civil servants. This would mean that when they answer written parliamentary questions or appear before select committees they do so on behalf of their ministers. The Committee stated emphatically that ministers remain accountable for what goes on in agencies just as in their departments. However there remain concerns that when chief executives appear before select committees they are subject to the direction of their minister which would limit their competence as witnesses and Parliament's ability to investigate (see Second Report of Public Service Committees, HC 313, 1995–6, paras 84–91, 109–123; Cabinet Office, *Modernising Government,* 2002, Cm 4310).

Finally the *Carltona* principle (above) may not apply to civil servants in executive agencies who are not directly under the control of a minister (see Freedland, 'Government by Contract and Public Law', 1994, *Public Law* 86). In *Williams v Home Office (No. 2)* (1981) the court drew a distinction between acts done by civil servants in the exercise of statutory functions conferred on ministers and routine management matters, saying that the latter are not to be regarded as the act of ministers. This is questionable in terms of the traditional doctrine of ministerial responsibility but perhaps represents a more realistic view of the nature of modern government.

Summary

- The Prime Minister has large powers under the royal prerogative, pre-eminently to dissolve Parliament, appoint and dismiss ministers and control the government agenda. However these are largely convention and determined political opposition could control a Prime Minister.

- As a body the Cabinet has been reduced in power in recent years with decisions effectively being made by smaller groups within and outside the Cabinet and by departments of the executive.

- There are few constitutional laws or conventions concerning the detailed distribution of functions between departments. Political and administrative considerations rather than constitutional principle determine the number, size, shape and interrelationship of government departments. The creation of bodies outside the framework of the Crown is of greater constitutional and legal significance.

- The convention of ministerial responsibility is central to the UK constitution. Collective responsibility means that all members of the government must loyally support government policy and decisions and must not disclose internal disagreements. Individual responsibility means that each minister is answerable to Parliament for all the activities of the department under his control. It also means that civil servants are not personally accountable. From these principles follow (i) the traditional notion of the civil service as anonymous and politically neutral, having a duty to serve with unquestioning loyalty governments of any political complexion and (ii) the secrecy that pervades the British system of government.

- The traditional doctrine of ministerial responsibility may be out of line with the practices of modern government and effectively shields the government from accountability. In particular: (i) cabinet decisions are rarely made collectively; (ii) many government bodies are not directly controlled by ministers, the creation of executive agencies reinforcing this; (iii) civil servants are increasingly expected to make political decisions and to be responsible for the financial management of their allotted activities; (iv) public functions are increasingly being given to special bodies or private bodies. Thus the traditional chain of accountability between Parliament, ministers and civil servants is weakened.

- In law civil servants are servants of the Crown. They can be dismissed 'at pleasure', that is, without notice and without reason being given. However the modern cases suggest that there can be a contractual relationship between the Crown and a civil servant and that a civil servant can be protected by the law of judicial review.

- In the light of the convention relating to ministerial responsibility civil servants are regarded as servants of the government of the day with an absolute duty of loyalty to ministers. Their advice to ministers is secret and they appear before Parliament only with the consent of ministers. They are supposed to be non-political and neutral, responsible for giving ministers objective advice and for carrying out ministerial orders. However 'special advisers' need not be neutral nor appointed on merit. Their existence creates tensions within the civil service.

- The internal arrangements for the carrying out of government business involve entrusting individual civil servants with considerable decision making responsibility and in recent years with financial accountability within the government machine. Many civil servants work in executive agencies, hived off from the central departmental structure and outside the direct control of ministers. This has led to tensions between traditional ideas of ministerial responsibility and the actual channels of accountability and has raised problems in connection with the supposed distinction between policy and operational matters.

Exercises

15.1 Consider whether the relevant laws and conventions support Bagehot's view that the Cabinet is the central institution of the UK constitution.

15.2 George, a civil servant, is told by a journalist that the Prime Minister intends to appoint Lionel, the chairman of a large film company, as a special adviser. In return Lionel is to make a donation to the party and has promised to arrange for the Prime Minister to have a starring role in one of his films when he ceases office. Advise George as to the constitutional position and what action he might take.

15.3 'Ministerial responsibility is, in practice, an obstacle to the availability of information and to the holding of government to account' (Oliver). Discuss.

15.4 To what extent can Parliament and the public scrutinise the activities of a civil servant?

15.5 When should a minister resign?

15.6 Critically evaluate the constitutional significance of special advisers.

15.7 The government creates an executive agency to regulate motorway service areas. The Secretary of State for Consumption delegates to the agency his statutory powers to ensure the 'adequate provision of motorway services'. Under a contract made with the Secretary of State the agency promises to achieve certain 'targets', including a clean environment. The agency employs Grasper plc to run the Crusty Group of service areas. Due to cuts in its funding from the Secretary of State the agency does not check Grasper's performance but increases its chief executive's annual 'performance bonus' by 100 per cent. A newspaper subsequently discovers that many of the catering staff employed by the Crusty Group are illegal immigrants and several of them have contracted food poisoning. In response to a parliamentary question, the Secretary of State asserts that the matter is no concern of his and he knows nothing about it. He also refuses to permit the agency chief executive to appear before the Select Committee for Consumption. Discuss.

Further reading

Benn, T. (1980) 'The Case for a Constitutional Premiership', *Parliamentary Affairs* 33:7.

Bogdanor, V. (ed.) (2003) *The British Constitution in the Twentieth Century*, London, British Academy, Chapter 8.

Brazier, R. (1999) *Constitutional Practice* (3rd edn) Oxford University Press, Chapters 5, 6, 7.

Brazier, R. (1991) 'Reducing the Power of the Prime Minister', *Parliamentary Affairs* 44:453.

Daintith, T. and Page, A. (1999) *The Executive in the Constitution*, Oxford University Press, Chapters 1–6.

Drewry, G. (2004) 'The Executive: Towards Accountable Government and Effective Governance?', in Jowell, J. and Oliver, D. (eds) *The Changing Constitution*, Oxford University Press.

Flinders, M. (2000) 'The Enduring Centrality of Individual Ministerial Responsibility within the British Constitution', *Journal of Legislative Studies* 6:73.

Harden, I. (1993) 'Money and the Constitution, Financial Control, Reporting and Audit', *Legal Studies* 13:16.

Hough, B. (2003) 'Ministerial Responses to Parliamentary Questions: Some Recent Concerns', *Public Law* 211.

Further reading cont'd

McEldowney, J. (2004) 'The Control of Public Expenditure', in Jowell, J. and Oliver, D. (eds) *The Changing Constitution*, Oxford University Press.

Thompson, B. and Ridley, F. (eds) (1997) *Under the Scott-Light: British Government seen through the Scott Report*, Oxford University Press.

Tomkins, A. (2003) *Public Law*, Oxford, Clarendon Press, Chapter 5.

Vennard, A. (2008) 'Prime Ministerial Succession', *Public Law* 302

Winetrobe, B. (2003) 'Collective Responsibility in Devolved Scotland', *Public Law* 24.

Woodhouse, D. (1997) *In Pursuit of Good Administration: Ministers, Civil Servants and Judges*, Oxford, Clarendon Press.

Background reading

Budge, I., Crewe, I., McKay, D. and Newton, K. (2004) *The New British Politics* (3rd edn) London, Pearson, Chapters 5, 6.

Foster, C. (2004) 'Cabinet Government in the Twentieth Century', *Modern Law Review* 67:753.

Hennessy, P. (1995) *The Hidden Wiring*, London, Gollancz, Chapters 3, 4, 5, 8.

Sampson, A. (2004) *Who Runs this Place?*, London, John Murray, Chapters 6, 7, 8, 9, 18.

Part III

Administrative Law

Chapter 16

The grounds of judicial review, I: Illegality and ultra vires

> In modern Britain, where no agreement exists on the ends of Society and the means of achieving those ends, it would be disastrous if courts did not eschew the temptation to pass judgement on an issue of policy. Judicial self-preservation may alone dictate restraint. (Lord Parker LCJ, 1959)

Key words

- Legality and merits
- Ultra vires
- Justiciabilty
- Void and voidable
- Law, fact and policy
- Reasonably incidental
- Respect for democracy
- Context-sensitive review
- Legitimate expectation
- Substantive and procedural

16.1 Introduction: The Constitutional Basis of Judicial Review

Judicial review, sometimes called the 'supervisory jurisdiction', is the High Court's power to police the legality of decisions made by public bodies. As usual an accommodation must be struck between competing aspects of the separation of powers. On the one hand the rule of law has been said to require that the legality of government action be

> subject to review by independent and impartial tribunals . . . The principles of judicial review give effect to the rule of law. They ensure that administrative decisions will be taken rationally in accordance with a fair procedure and within the powers conferred by Parliament. (per Lord Hoffmann in *R (Alconbury Developments Ltd) v Secretary of State for the Environment, Transport and the Regions* [2001] 2 All ER 929, 981)

On the other hand judicial review operates within the context of parliamentary accountability of the executive and the doctrine of the separation of powers. The checks and balances aspect of the separation of powers requires the courts to check misuse of power by the executive. The functional separation of powers pulls in the other direction by requiring the court to avoid trespassing into the political territory of the government and Parliament. Judicial review is regarded as a last resort method of challenge and there are procedural barriers intended to prevent it being too easily taken up (Chapter 18).

The courts claim not to be concerned with the 'merits' of government action, that is, whether it is good or bad, but only whether governmental decisions fall within their authorising legislation and meet legal standards of fairness and 'reasonableness' (see Laws J in *R v Somerset County Council ex parte Fewings* (1995)). However as *Fewings* illustrates (disagreement as to whether morality should be taken into account in relation to a decision to ban hunting), these principles are vague, shading into questions of merit and there is considerable room for debate as to the proper limits of the courts' powers.

Judicial review cases are decided by the Administrative Court, part of the Queen's Bench Division of the High Court. Also the Tribunals, Courts and Enforcement Act 2007 s. 15 confers judicial review jurisdiction upon the Upper Tribunal created by that Act (Chapter 18). The court follows a special flexible procedure designed to cater for the public interest that actions against the government should be dealt with quickly and without trespassing into the legitimate area of government freedom. However following the 'Woolf' reforms of civil procedure (2000) that were designed to increase the efficiency of ordinary litigation, the difference between the Administrative Court and other proceedings, while still significant, is less than was previously the case.

Judicial review applies to all public bodies other than the High Court itself and Parliament. However some matters are 'non-justiciable', meaning not appropriate for judicial review (see *Council of Civil Service Unions (CCSU) v Minister for the Civil Service* (1985)). This is firstly due to judicial restraint where the courts lack the expertise or practical competence to deal with the matter, or where the legal process is unsuitable owing to the nature and range of matters involved, and secondly where legally irrelevant matters are involved. Examples, mostly involving the royal prerogative, include the dissolution of Parliament, the appointment of ministers, the granting of honours, the making of treaties and the decision to go to war (see Chapter 18). The court's constitutional role concerns focused disputes between particular parties and it is not equipped to deal with wide ranging questions concerning the public as a whole or a large range of interests which may not be represented in court. Those matters are the concern of elected assemblies or those who act on their behalf.

The judicial review principles are flexible in that the intensity of review, the range of grounds available and the selection of remedies varies with the context. While not excluding review entirely as with the non-justiciable cases (above), the courts may allow a wide discretion to the government decision maker particularly where subjective decisions by or on behalf of elected bodies are concerned. There is no definitive list; the matter depends on the particular circumstances. For example the courts apply strict standards to judicial bodies, such as tribunals that determine legal rights, but are less willing to interfere with a decision that involves the discretionary allocation of scarce resources, for example whether or not to treat an NHS patient (see *R v Cambridge Health Authority ex parte B* (1995) and contrast *R (Rogers) v Swindon Primary Health Care Trust* (below)). The same applies to national security cases, although since the advent of the Human Rights Act the courts have been more willing to intervene in national security matters (Chapter 22). The courts also respect the sphere of Parliament, although some judges are more deferential to this than others (see the disagreement in *R v Secretary of State for the Home Department ex parte Fire Brigades Union* (1995), Chapter 8). As early as 1911 one judge at least was expressing doubts about ministerial responsibility (see *Dyson v Attorney-General* (1911)). In the interests of the separation of powers the courts are also reluctant to interfere with the decisions of independent prosecutors but will do exceptionally where the grounds for doing so are strong and clear (see *R (Corner House Research) v Director of the Serious Fraud Office (No. 2)* [2008] UK HL 60 [30] [32]).

The legal basis of judicial review is disputed and reflects the wider debate as to the nature of our constitution and of the rule of law. There is a large but somewhat repetitive literature on this issue (the main viewpoints are collected in Forsythe, 2000). One perspective bases judicial review upon the common law, according to which powerful bodies must act in accordance with rule of law values of fairness and rationality (*Dr Bonham's Case* (1610); *Bagg's Case* (1615); *Cooper* v *Wandsworth Board of Works* (1863)). This draws inspiration primarily from liberal and republican ideas (Chapter 2). The other perspective gives greater emphasis to parliamentary supremacy, democracy and the separation of powers. It assumes that because most government powers are created by Act of Parliament, the courts' role should be confined to ensuring that powers do not exceed the limits set out by Parliament: the ultra vires doctrine. This requires the court to respect democratic principles. Rather tediously, both approaches can be made to fit the facts and the historical evidence is inconclusive. Both approaches conform to possible meanings of the separation of powers and the rule of law. The ultra vires approach is more heavily biased towards the functional aspect of the separation of powers, the common law approach towards checks and balances.

The ultra vires approach accepts that the judges are developing their own principles in accordance with the 'amplified' or 'extended' versions of the rule of law (Chapter 7). It claims that Parliament intends these to be implied into the exercise of statutory powers because Parliament can be assumed to respect the rule of law as developed by the courts. In other words the ultra vires doctrine concerns an *assumed* intention of Parliament as opposed to a *specific* intention as to the meaning of given legislation. Forsythe (1996) therefore suggests that the ultra vires doctrine is a useful 'fig leaf' which gives constitutional respectability to what is happening and at least reminds us that Parliament has the last word. There are many presumptions of statutory interpretation which require courts to assume that Parliament intended to act fairly while allowing the court considerable room to decide what this means (Chapter 9). Judicial review may be regarded as an application of this.

Forsythe's fig leaf could be taken to hide something we would prefer not to see, namely that the ultra vires doctrine is an empty vessel for whatever happens to be the prevailing judicial fashion. The common law version claims to be more honest. It does not ignore the intention of Parliament. Firstly a decision which is ultra vires in the sense that it violates a particular statutory requirement or limitation or is based on irrelevant considerations is invalid under both theories. Secondly the common law approach would claim that broader grounds of review such as unreasonableness or unfairness (below) are freestanding, but that by using clear language, Parliament can exclude any ground of review just as Parliament can change any common law rule. There is therefore no inconsistency with parliamentary supremacy. Indeed neither the ultra vires approach nor the common law approach necessarily commits us to any particular attitude on the question of parliamentary supremacy. The difference between them is that according to the common law view, Parliament *tolerates* judicial review, whereas on the ultra vires view, Parliament somehow *authorises* judicial review.

The common law approach also frees up judicial review so that its principles might apply to bodies whose powers do not derive from statute. For example it is settled that royal prerogative powers and other non-statutory powers exercised by public bodies are subject to judicial review (*CCSU* v *Minister for the Civil Service* (1985); *R* v *Panel on Takeovers and Mergers ex parte Datafin plc* (1987)). The common law might also be the basis for extending judicial review principles, similar to those applied to government, to powerful private bodies (such as sports regulatory bodies, powerful commercial companies and so on) which exercise control over aspects of public life (for example *McInnes* v *Onslow-Fane* (1978)). Proponents of the ultra vires doctrine accommodate this possibility by suggesting that there need not be a single basis for judicial review. Thus the practice of judicial review depends on political choice rather than an abstract conceptual theory.

There are substantial judicial dicta in support of the ultra vires doctrine as the basis of judicial review (for example *Boddington* v *British Transport Police* [1998] 2 WLR 639 at 650, 655, 662; *Credit Suisse* v *Allerdale Borough Council* [1996] 4 All ER 129 at 167; *Page* v *Hull University Visitor* [1993] 1 All ER 97 at 107). On the other hand in *CCSU*, Lord Diplock famously abandoned the ultra vires doctrine by classifying the grounds of judicial review under the three broad heads of 'illegality, irrationality and procedural impropriety', claiming that the law should not pursue 'fairy tales'.

16.2   Appeal and Review

Judicial review must not be confused with an appeal. An appeal is a procedure which exists only under a particular statute or, in the case of a voluntary body, by agreement. An appeal allows the appellate body to decide the whole matter again unless the particular statute or agreement limits the grounds of appeal (see Tribunals and Inquiries Act 1992 s.11: questions of law only). An appeal therefore may involve a thorough reconsideration of the whole decision, whereas judicial review is concerned only with ensuring that legal standards are complied with. Depending on the particular statute, an appellate body might be a court, tribunal, minister or indeed anyone. A claim for judicial review is possible only in the High Court or the Upper Tribunal.

An appellate body can usually substitute its decision for the first instance decision, although in some cases its powers are limited to sending the matter back to be decided again by the lower body. In judicial review proceedings, unless there is no doubt as to the right decision, the court cannot make the decision itself but must send the matter back to the decision maker with instructions as to its legal duties.

Unlike a right of appeal which can be raised only in the body specified, the invalidity of government action can be raised not only in the Administrative Court but also, by way of 'collateral challenge', in any proceedings where the rights of a citizen are affected by the validity of government action (for example *Boddington* v *British Transport Police* (1998): defence to prosecution for smoking contrary to railway bylaws alleged to be ultra vires). This is because an unlawful government decision is of no effect in law (void/nullity) and can be ignored, thus vindicating the rule of law (*Entick* v *Carrington*) (Chapter 7). In the case of an appeal, the offending decision is fully valid until the appeal body changes it.

16.3   Nullity: Void and Voidable Decisions

According to the rule of law and also the ultra vires doctrine, an invalid government act should be a nullity: void, and have no legal consequences. Indeed this has been emphasised by the courts (see for example Lord Reid in *Ridge* v *Baldwin* (1964) and *Anisminic* v *Foreign Compensation Commission* [1969] 2 AC 147, 171, 195, 207; *Lord Irvine LC in Boddington* (above); see also *Secretary of State for the Home Department* v *JJ* (2008) [27]). The 'red light perspective' strongly supports this. On the other hand it may be impractical simply to ignore a decision since its invalidity can be exposed only once a court has ruled as much. In that sense a decision is only voidable – valid – until set aside by a court. This is reinforced by the fact that all the judicial review remedies are discretionary so that the court does not have to set aside even an ultra vires decision (*Credit Suisse* (above)). By contrast where a decision is challenged collaterally, for example as a defence to a prosecution, the court has no discretion (ibid.) so that a different outcome is possible depending solely on which route is taken to challenge.

If a decision is held in judicial review proceedings to be a nullity then in principle it will be treated as never having had legal effect and its consequences will be unwound. For example in *Ridge* v *Baldwin* (1964) a Chief Constable dismissed without a hearing was held still to be in office and so entitled to his pension rights. Also in *Secretary of State for the Home Department* v JJ (2008) it was held that a void Control Order made by the Home Secretary under anti-terrorist legislation could not be amended to make it lawful but must be set aside.

The concept of nullity does not always lead to a just solution. In *DPP* v *Head* (1959) a woman was improperly detained in a mental hospital as a result of an invalid medical procedure. A man charged with having sexual relations with a patient 'detained' under the Mental Health Acts was able to argue that because the patient's detention order had not been made according to the required formalities, she was not 'detained' under the relevant Acts. On the same analysis the officials who administer the hospital would have made numerous decisions affecting the detainee on the assumption that the initial order was valid. If, due to the initial infection of the invalid decision, all consequential acts had to be unpicked the result would be chaos. In *Credit Suisse* v *Allerdale Borough Council* (1996) a local authority successfully relied on the argument that a guarantee which it had given was ultra vires so as to prevent the guarantee being enforced against it (see Local Government (Contracts) Act 1997). Similarly would everyone granted a driving licence under a regulation which later turned out to be invalid for some procedural reason find themselves guilty of an offence?

There are various ways of attacking this problem, none of them entirely satisfactory.

1. To argue that only the most serious defects make a decision void, while others make it only voidable in the sense that it might be set aside for the future only (see *Bugg* v *DPP* [1993] QB 473, 493; Lord Denning *in DPP* v *Head* (above) who later recanted treating the matter as semantic only (*Lovelock* v *Minister of Transport* (1980)). This was rejected by the House of Lords in *Anisminic* (above) who took the view that all defects make the decision a nullity (compare Lords Browne Wilkinson and Slynn in *Boddington* (above)).

2. To claim that there is a 'presumption of validity', meaning that until it is set aside a decision must be treated as valid but if successfully challenged it can be set aside retrospectively, that is, treated as if it never existed (see *Hoffmann-La Roche* v *Secretary of State* (1974)). In that sense all decisions would be 'voidable'. This does not address the problem of third parties who rely on a decision before it is set aside.

3. Craig suggests that careful use of judicial discretion is the answer (*Administrative Law* 5th ed. (2003) pp. 698–704). This sits uncomfortably with the rule of law.

4. Treating the matter as one of statutory interpretation in the particular context (see *Seal* v *Chief Constable of South Wales Police* (2007)). Of course a statute can prevent a decision being treated as void but this approach abandons any general principle and could be

as discretionary as Craig's approach. This approach was favoured by Lord Hoffman (dissenting) in *Secretary of State* v *JJ* (2008) (above).

5. Professor Wade deals with the conundrum by using the concept of 'relative nullity', meaning that an invalid decision is indeed a nullity but only if challenged in the right court by the right person in the right way (1968, *Law Quarterly Review* 84:95). For example a claimant may be out of time in which case the decision must stand and a third party can rely on it. Again this does not deal with the position of third parties who rely on the decision if it is set aside (see also *Agricultural Training Board* v *Aylesbury Mushrooms Ltd* (1972)).

6. Forsythe suggests a distinction between an act valid in *law* and an act that exists in *fact* (in Forsythe and Hare (eds) *The Golden Metwand and the Crooked Cord*, Oxford University Press, 1998). This refers to the situation where an invalid decision has a chain of consequences where it is relied upon by other officials or citizens – the 'domino effect' and 'the theory of the second actor', that is, an official who makes a decision on the assumption that the previous decision is valid (see also Beatson and Matthews, *Administrative Law: Text and Materials* 3rd ed., Oxford University Press, 2005 pp. 94–101). According to Forsythe the crucial question is whether the validity *in law* of the first act is a precondition to the validity of the following or whether a decision *in fact* is sufficient. For example in *R* v *Wicks* (1998) the House of Lords held that a developer could be prosecuted for disobeying a planning enforcement notice even though the notice was invalid since the statutory requirement was only for a notice that existed in fact, that is, one that appeared to be valid. This approach (which harks back to an ancient notion of a document which is defective 'on its face' (see *Smith* v *East Elloe RDC* ((1956)) begs the question of how we know which category applies to the given case.

7. Another approach is to distinguish between a decision with legal consequences and the preliminary steps leading to it. These need to be treated as void (see *Shrewsbury and Atcham Borough Council* v *Secretary of State* (2008) [57] [58]).

16.4 Classification of the Grounds of Review

Unfortunately there is no general agreement on how to classify the grounds of review and textbooks take different approaches. The grounds themselves are broad, vague and overlapping, a conspicuous example of this being *Wheeler* v *Leicester City Council* (1985) (Chapter 17). In the following sections I shall organise the grounds of judicial review on the basis of Lord Diplock's classification in *CCSU* (above), that is, under the three heads of 'illegality, irrationality and procedural impropriety'. However the Diplock categories tell us little in themselves and do not avoid overlaps. Indeed the House of Lords has emphasised that the heads of challenge are not watertight compartments but run together (*Boddington* v *British Transport Police* (1998)). It might however be helpful at this point to provide a checklist:

1. **Illegality**
   - 'Narrow' ultra vires or lack of jurisdiction, in the sense of straying beyond the limits defined by the statute.
   - Errors of law and (in certain cases) errors of fact.
   - 'Wide' ultra vires or acting for an ulterior purpose, taking irrelevant factors into account or failing to take relevant factors into account.
   - Fettering discretion.

2. **Irrationality**
   - *Wednesbury* unreasonableness. This could stand alone or be the outcome of taking an irrelevant factor into account.
   - Proportionality at least under the Human Rights Act 1998.
3. **Procedural impropriety**
   - Violating important statutory procedures.
   - Bias.
   - Lack of a fair hearing.
   - Failure to give reasons for a decision.

In this chapter, we shall discuss illegality. The other grounds are discussed in Chapter 17.

16.5   Illegality: 'Narrow' Ultra Vires

A decision is ultra vires if it is outside the language of the statute. In the case of courts and judicial tribunals, the terminology of 'lack' or 'excess' of jurisdiction means the same as ultra vires. A distinction is sometimes made between lacking jurisdiction at the outset, so that the decision maker has no power to deal with the matter at all, and straying outside jurisdiction by some subsequent defect. In most cases however, this distinction does not matter (see *Anisminic Ltd* v *Foreign Compensation Commission* (1969)).

A famous example of ultra vires that raises its main issues is *Attorney-General* v *Fulham Corporation* (1921). A local authority had power to provide a 'wash house' for local people. It interpreted this as authorising the provision of a laundry service for working people who could leave washing to be done by staff and delivered to their homes. This was held to be unlawful in that 'wash house', according to the court, means a place where a person can do their own washing. This raises questions as to the assumptions that the courts bring to the task of interpreting statutes. For example the court might have been influenced by a prejudice against local bodies spending taxpayers' money on welfare services. If the court had read the statute against an assumption of democratic freedom, the outcome might have been different. More recently in *Bromley London Borough Council* v *Greater London Council* (1983) the House of Lords held that an obligation to provide an 'efficient and economic' public transport service meant that the Council could not subsidise the London Underground for social purposes. Among other lines of reasoning, it was held that 'economic' meant that there was an obligation to break even financially (see also *Prescott* v *Birmingham Corporation* (1955): free transport for pensioners held ultra vires under a power to charge such fares as the Council thought fit). *Roberts* v *Hopwood* (1925): 'wages' should not include a social welfare element, is a similar case where the court might be suspected of political bias.

As we saw in Chapters 7 and 9, where the scope of a statute is unclear, the courts rely on presumptions of interpretation. They can reflect the courts' perception of community values, although this does not necessarily reflect public opinion. Many of these presumptions appeal to individualistic liberals (red light) but some of them have been criticised by 'welfare liberals' as attempts to counter policies based on the collective public interest (green light). Examples include *R* v *Secretary of State for the Home Department ex parte Simms* [1999] 3 All ER 400 at 412: freedom of expression; *Congreve* v *Home Office* (1976); *Macarthy & Stone* v *Richmond upon Thames LBC* (1991): no taxation without statutory authority; *R* v *Secretary of State for the Home Department ex parte Pierson* (1998): retrospective use of powers; *Raymond* v *Honey* (1983): prisoner's rights; *Anisminic* v *Foreign Compensation Commission* (1969); *R* v *Lord Chancellor's Department ex parte Witham* (1997): access to the courts. They have been reinforced by the Human Rights Act 1998 which imposes a strong obligation to interpret all legislation so as to conform with rights embodied in the ECHR (Chapter 19).

There is some leeway in the ultra vires doctrine in favour of the government. The courts will permit an activity that, although not expressly authorised by the statute, is 'reasonably incidental' to something that is expressly authorised. The Local Government Act 1972 (s.111) applies a similar principle to local authorities. For example in *Akumah* v *Hackney London Borough Council* (2005) the House of Lords held that it was lawful to clamp cars in a car park attached to a block of local authority flats under a scheme which required tenants to obtain parking permits at a cost of £2. The Council had statutory power of 'management, regulation and control' over the 'dwelling houses' and this should be interpreted broadly to include the regulation of car parking since this affects the quality of life of the residents. This was the case even though the Council could have made parking regulations under other more specific legislation. However the House of Lords was not asked to rule on the legality of the particular scheme, thus leaving it open whether making a charge or clamping were themselves lawful.

A narrow approach was taken in *Macarthy & Stone* v *Richmond upon Thames LBC* (1991) where a charge for giving advice in connection with planning applications was held not to be incidental to the authority's planning powers. Giving advice was not expressly authorised and was itself an incidental function. The House of Lords took the view that something cannot be incidental to the incidental. Moreover there is a presumption dating from the Bill of Rights 1688 that taxation cannot be imposed without clear statutory authority (but is a charge for a service taxation?).

See also *Attorney-General* v *Crayford Urban District Council* (1962): voluntary household insurance scheme reasonably incidental to the power to manage council housing because it helped tenants to pay the rent; *Hazell* v *Hammersmith and Fulham London Borough Council* (1992): interest swap arrangements – made by several local councils to spread the risk of future changes in interest rates – were not incidental to the Council's borrowing powers because they concerned debt management rather than borrowing as such.

16.6 Illegality: Errors of Law and Fact

The question whether the court can review decisions on the ground of legal or factual errors has caused problems. There is a clash of principle. On the one hand if the court can intervene merely because it considers that a decision is wrong, it would be trespassing into the merits of the case and violating the separation of powers. From this perspective the question is not so much whether there was a mistake but who should have the last word in deciding whether a mistake has been made. It is not obvious for example that a reviewing court is in a better position than the original decision maker to decide what the facts are or who is telling the truth (see *R* v *Nat Bell Liquors* (1922): false evidence not reviewable). On the other hand the rule of law surely calls for a remedy if a decision maker makes a clear mistake. The courts have therefore adopted a compromise. Almost all errors of law and some errors of fact can be challenged. However they have reached this position only after much technical wrangling.

A rationale that was popular in the nineteenth century is the doctrine of the 'jurisdictional' or 'collateral' or 'preliminary' question. According to this doctrine, if a mistake relates to a state of affairs which the court thinks that Parliament intended should exist objectively as a condition of the official having power to make the decision, then the court will interfere if it thinks that the required state of affairs does not exist. For example in *White and Collins* v *Minister of Health* (1939) the Secretary of State had power to acquire land 'other than a garden or parkland'. It was held that the court could interfere if it thought that the minister had wrongly decided whether the claimant's land was parkland. The doctrine can be justified on the rule of law ground that a minister should not be allowed to expand his own powers (see Farwell J in *R* v *Shoreditch Assessment Committee ex parte Morgan* [1910] 2 KB 859 at 880). However there seems to be no logical way of deciding which of many issues that a decision maker has to decide are 'preliminary' in this sense. Nevertheless the doctrine still exists (below).

A second device that flourished during the 1960s but has largely been superseded is the doctrine of 'error of law on the face of the record' or patent error (*R* v *Northumberland Compensation Appeal Tribunal ex parte Shaw* (1952)). This allows the court to quash a decision if a mistake of law can be discovered from the written record of the decision without using other evidence. This could not be squeezed into the ultra vires doctrine and decisions tainted by patent error may only be 'voidable', that is, valid unless and until formally quashed by the court (above). The face of the record principle provides a practical compromise by allowing obvious mistakes to be rectified without reopening the whole matter. Many bodies were required to give written reasons for their decisions as part of the record (now Tribunals and Inquiries Act 1992 s.10) and the courts were liberal in what material they regarded as part of the record. However mistakes of fact could not be challenged at all.

Most importantly as a result of the speeches of the House of Lords in *Anisminic Ltd* v *Foreign Compensation Commission* [1969] 2 AC 147 (above), notably that of Lord Reid, the older doctrines have been made largely redundant in relation to errors of law. *Anisminic* appears to have made all errors of law reviewable, at least in principle. The Foreign Compensation Commission (FCC) adjudicated on claims to compensation for war damage in connection with an Arab–Israeli war. Under the regulations, which were densely drafted, the owner of the damaged property and its 'successor in title' must be British subjects. The FCC had interpreted the term 'successor in title' as including a purchaser. This led it to refuse compensation to the claimant who had sold its property to an Egyptian company. The House of Lords held that as a matter of law a purchaser was not a successor in title. Therefore an irrelevant matter had been taken into account that Parliament did not intend, namely the Egyptian company. According to a majority of their Lordships, this made the decision not just wrong but outside the FCC's jurisdiction.

Anisminic has been widely taken as deciding that any mistake of law makes a decision ultra vires in that all such mistakes could be presented either as taking an irrelevant factor into account or failing to take a relevant factor into account. It therefore invites the courts to investigate the decisions of public bodies in considerable depth. However there are dicta denying that all errors of law should be jurisdictional and it is not clear that their Lordships in *Anisminic* intended to go so far (see *South East Asia Fire Brick Sdn*

Bhd v *Non-Metallic Mineral Products Manufacturing Employees Union* (1981); *Pearlman* v *Governers and Keepers of Harrow School* (1979)). However, the wide reading of *Anisminic* has been endorsed at least as a general principle by the House of Lords in *Re Racal Communications* (1981), *O'Reilly* v *Mackman* (1982) and *Page* v *Hull University Visitor* (1993).

The courts have to some extent drawn back. They have used the argument that some questions raise specialised issues or involve a mixture of matters of law, fact and opinion with which the courts should not interfere unless the approach taken by the decision maker is completely unreasonable. For example in *Re Racal Communications* (1981) Lord Diplock suggested that *Anisminic* did not apply to decisions of courts where questions of law and questions of fact were inextricably mixed up. In *Page* v *Hull University Visitor* (1993) it was held that the specialised rules of universities should be conclusively interpreted by the university visitor. More generally *Anisminic* has not been applied to mistakes of fact which arguably should not be reviewable because the primary decision maker is usually in a better position than the court to discover the facts.

It is not always easy to distinguish between questions of law, questions of fact and questions of opinion. A question of law basically involves the meaning and usually the application of a rule. A question of fact involves the existence of some state of affairs or event in the world outside the law and depends on evidence. A question of opinion is where on the same evidence more than one view can reasonably be taken (*Lord Luke of Pavenham* v *Minister of Housing and Local Government* (1968): whether a building 'harmonised' with its surroundings). However the courts may treat some apparently legal questions of interpretation as matters of fact or opinion where they concern broad everyday notions or involve value judgments or matters of degree where no sharp line is possible. The following are characteristic: *Pulhoffer* v *Hillingdon Borough Council* (1986): 'homeless'; *R* v *Monopolies and Mergers Commission ex parte South Yorkshire Transport* (1993): 'substantial' part of the UK; *Edwards* v *Bairstow* (1956): 'trade'; *Brutus* v *Cozens* (1973): 'insulting'; *R* v *Radio Authority ex parte Bull* (1997): 'political nature'; *Shah* v *Barnet London BC* (1983): 'ordinarily' resident; *BBC* v *Sugar* (2007): 'journalism, art or literature'.

Errors of *fact* are not normally reviewable since the courts regard the initial decision making body as in the best position to find the facts. However there are exceptions:

▷ The doctrine of the preliminary question (above) applies to errors of fact where it is sometimes called the 'precedent fact' doctrine. This allows the court to decide the question of fact itself. For example in *Khawaja* v *Secretary of State for the Home Department* (1983) the Home Secretary could deport an 'illegal immigrant'. The House of Lords held that the court could decide whether the appellant was in fact an illegal immigrant and was not limited to deciding whether the minister's decision was unreasonable. The problem is to decide what kind of case falls within the doctrine. This depends upon the statutory context. In *Khawaja* the court was influenced by the fact that the decision involved personal freedom, so that a high level of judicial control was required. By contrast in *Bugdaycay* v *Secretary of State for the Home Department* (1987) the question was whether the applicant was a genuine asylum seeker. Here the decision was heavily laden with subjective political judgment and the court was not prepared to treat the matter as one of precedent fact.

▷ A finding of fact which is completely unreasonable in the sense that it has no evidential basis is reviewable (*Ashbridge Investments* v *Minister of Housing and Local Government* [1965] 1 WLR 1320, 1326). In *R* v *Criminal Injuries Compensation Board ex parte A* [1999] 2 AC 330, 344, Lord Slynn said that 'misunderstanding or ignorance of an established and relevant fact' is reviewable but emphasised that this is no more than an application of ordinary review principles (see also *Secretary of State for Education and Science* v *Tameside Metropolitan Borough Council* [1977] AC 1014 at 1017). By contrast judicial review does not include a reinvestigation of *disputed* facts unless the decision is perverse (*Adan* v *Newham London Borough Council* (2002)). In other words the courts will not attempt to investigate factual disagreements or to weigh evidence but will intervene in clear cases.

16.6.1   Errors and the ECHR

Article 6 of the ECHR which applies to UK law under the Human Rights Act 1998 confers a right to a fair trial where 'civil rights and obligations' are in issue (see also Chapter 8). This includes a right to challenge an administrative decision before a body with 'full jurisdiction'. In deciding whether there has been a fair trial, the court will look at the process as a whole including any right of judicial review (*Albert* v *Belgium* (1983)). The question arises whether the limited review on questions of fact available in an English court satisfies this.

The first question is what is meant by a 'civil right and obligation'. Although some judges, notably Lord Hoffmann (*R (Alconbury Developments)* v *Secretary of State for the Environment, Transport and the Regions* (2001), prefer to confine the term to disputes about private law rights such as property rights, the courts have taken a broader view including some public law rights. The scope of this is not clear. The underlying principle seems to be that the decision in question must have a serious effect on existing individual interests or must involve a claim to some kind of entitlement. For example in *Feldbrugge* v *The Netherlands* (1986) a claim to health insurance from the state on proof of certain facts was held to concern a civil right. In *Tre Tractorer Aktebolag* v *Sweden* (1989) it was held that the revocation of a liquor licence engaged a civil right. In *Runa Begum* v *Tower Hamlets London BC* (2003) the House of Lords assumed but specifically did not decide that a discretionary decision by a local authority whether to provide accommodation for a homeless person engaged civil rights. By contrast if a government decision involves a refusal to award a benefit that was not enjoyed before or one involving a wide discretion in which the which the citizen has no special claim, or if a decision is purely advisory in its effect, a civil right may not be engaged (see also *R (Hammond)* v *Secretary of State for the Home Department* (2006) [11, 28]; *R (Wright)* v *Secretary of State for Health* (2009)).

The limited scope of judicial review in relation to findings of fact has sometimes been held to satisfy Article 6. The courts have reduced the notion of 'full jurisdiction' to the virtually meaningless 'full jurisdiction to deal with the case as the nature of the decision requires' (see *Runa Begum* v *Tower Hamlets London BC* [2003] 1 All ER 731, 736 per Lord Bingham). They have made a distinction between, on the one hand, a decision where a citizen has a definite entitlement on proof of certain facts (for example to a pension based on prescribed contributions) and, on the other hand, a decision where the facts are part of a larger policy or politically oriented process where the decision maker has to balance facts against competing considerations and has a discretion as to the outcome, for example a decision to widen a motorway (*Alconbury*, above).

In the first 'factual' kind of case, judicial review is not normally a sufficient safeguard and unless the initial decision is made by a body fully independent of government, such as a tribunal, an independent procedure is required which can examine all questions of fact (*Runa Begum*, above). In the second 'policy' kind of case, it has been held that the interests of democracy and respect for the machinery chosen by Parliament require a more flexible and less formal approach. In this case judicial review may suffice as a safety net (see *Alconbury*, above: land use planning decisions). It can be decided which category a case falls within only by looking closely at the particular decision making process and its goals. It is clear however that the wider the view taken on the question of the meaning of 'civil right' (above), the more likely it is that the case will fall within the 'policy' category.

Irrespective of Article 6 however, in cases where specific human rights are engaged such as the right to respect for home and family life (Article 8), the limited scope of judicial review in relation to findings of fact has been held to provide inadequate protection (*Connors* v *UK* (2004); *R (Wright)* v *Secretary of State for Health* (2009).

16.7 'Wide' Ultra Vires: Improper Purposes and Irrelevant Considerations

These aspects of illegality arise in the context of discretionary powers and are sometimes labelled 'abuse of discretion'. Even though the decision maker keeps within the express language of the statute, its motive may be improper, it may be influenced by irrelevant factors or it may overlook relevant factors. This applies even where the statute appears to give the decision maker an unrestricted, subjective discretion using such expressions as 'if the minister thinks fit', since even the widest discretionary power is in principle reviewable. It is for the court to decide what factors are relevant and what are the purposes of the Act (*Padfield* v *Minister of Agriculture, Fisheries and Food* (1968): a minister acting under a particular statutory power must not be influenced by wider political considerations that do not advance the policy of the Act). However it is for the claimant to establish that irrelevant considerations have been taken into account.

As always the starting point is the language of the statute but where wide discretionary powers are concerned this may not be helpful. Sometimes it will be clear from the statutory context what factors are relevant. This was the case in *Padfield* (above) where the statute concerned pricing arrangements for agricultural products. Sometimes the legislation is unhelpful. For example the Town and Country Planning Act 1990 requires decision makers to have regard to 'material considerations' without saying what these are (see *Tesco Stores* v *Secretary of State* (1995): apparently taking the view that anything could be relevant unless clearly irrelevant). The courts therefore have leeway to impose their own view as to the purpose of the statute. Much may depend for example on the approach of the judge to the question of individual freedom.

In *R* v *Somerset County Council ex parte Fewings* (1995) the Council had banned hunting on its land for ethical reasons. Laws J held that freedom could not be interfered with by a public authority without clear statutory language and that the statute in question, which was for land management purposes did not explicitly authorise ethical factors to be taken into account. The Court of Appeal took a different view, holding that the Council could take ethical factors into account unless barred by the statute. However they agreed with Laws J that the decision was flawed since the Council had not taken the statute into account at all but had assumed that they could do what they liked on their own land. It is of course fundamental that a statutory authority can act only in accordance with statute.

In *R v City of Westminster Housing Benefit Review Board ex parte Mehanne* (2001) legislation required the housing benefit authority to reduce a claim when it considered that the rent was unreasonably high, 'having regard in particular to the cost of suitable accommodation elsewhere'. The board interpreted this as preventing it from taking into account the claimant's personal circumstances, including his wife's pregnancy and his reduced income as an asylum seeker. The House of Lords held that personal circumstances were relevant, pointing out that the phrase 'in particular' invited other factors to be considered. Lord Bingham said (at 617) that 'in the absence of very clear language I would be very reluctant to conclude that the board were precluded from considering matters which could affect the mind of a reasonable and fair minded person'.

In deciding what factors are relevant, the court can look at background evidence, for example official reports that influenced the legislation in question and also things said in Parliament as to government policy. However statements made in Parliament cannot be used as evidence that a minister has acted in bad faith since this would violate the protection given to parliamentary proceedings by Article 9 of the Bill of Rights 1688 (Chapter 11). An unequivocal statement as to the scope of a provision might however prevent a minister subsequently from attempting a different explanation (*R v Secretary of State for the Environment, Transport and the Regions ex parte Spath Holme* (2001)). A decision maker must also take into account all relevant government policies and guidance even though these do not necessarily have the force of law. Indeed such policies might create a 'legitimate expectation' (below) that they will be followed. Moreover if a policy refers to 'exceptional circumstances', the authority must be able to indicate what these might be (*R (Rogers) v Swindon Primary Health Care Trust* (2006): refusal to provide drug).

The relevant consideration doctrine can be used to protect important interests. In *R (Bulger) v Secretary of State for the Home Department* (2001) the court, drawing on international obligations, held that in fixing the length of time a convicted child offender must serve, the Secretary of State must take into account the welfare of the child and keep its progress and rehabilitation under review. In *R v Secretary of State for the Home Department ex parte Venables* (1997) it was held that public opinion, in the shape of an opinion poll in the *Sun* newspaper, was not relevant where the Secretary of State was charged with the judicial duty of reviewing the sentence in a notorious child murderer case, since his judicial function must be exercised by his independent judgment. The courts have also held that local authorities should concern themselves with local issues as opposed to general issues of national or international politics (see *R v Lewisham LBC ex parte Shell UK Ltd* (above)). The courts are therefore policing the boundaries of the democratic process. In earlier cases the courts appeared to be restricting the powers of local authorities in order to compel them to conserve taxpayers' money by adopting 'business principles' in fixing wages, fares and prices at the expense of local democratic freedom (*Roberts v Hopwood* (1925); *Prescott v Birmingham Corporation* (1955); *Bromley LBC v GLC* (1983)). However it has also been stressed that the scope of what is relevant should be responsive to changing community values (see *Pickwell* v *Camden London Borough Council* (1983)).

In *R* v *Secretary of State for Foreign and Commonwealth Affairs ex parte World Development Movement* (1995) the court perhaps went too far into the merits of government action. The government had statutory power to give financial aid to other countries for 'economic' purposes. It decided to give a grant to Malaysia for the Pergau Dam project. The Court of Appeal held that Parliament must have intended the word 'economic' to include only 'sound' economic decisions so that the court was entitled to infer that the decision had been made primarily for an ulterior purpose (perhaps of facilitating an arms sale arrangement). This seems to come near to interfering with the merits of the decision since the court could deepen its investigation into any statutory function by saying that Parliament must have intended that function to be carried out 'soundly'. On the other hand parliamentary scrutiny had been ineffective so that the court's role may be justifiable as the only available constitutional check.

The relevance principle does not mean that the decision maker must give any particular weight to a given matter. In general the appropriate weight to be given to a factor is a political matter that is not for the court. The decision maker can choose which of the competing factors to prefer, provided that a relevant consideration is not completely ignored. For example in *Tesco Stores* v *Secretary of State for the Environment* (1995) the House of Lords held that in accordance with a government circular, a planning authority must take into account an offer from Tesco to contribute to the building of a new road in the area in return for planning permission. However it could give the offer 'nil' weight in influencing its decision. On the other hand the court is not entirely excluded from matters of weighting.

1. A statute might expressly or implicitly indicate that special weight be given to some factors
2. The courts themselves have decided that special weight must be given to the fundamental rights of the individual (for example *R* v *Secretary of State for the Home Department ex parte Simms* (1999)).
3. Similarly matters falling within the Human Rights Act 1998 attract the 'proportionality' principle which is essentially one of weighting, requiring as it does a strong reason to override a human right.
4. A legitimate expectation might also be given special weight (below).
5. More generally the court can interfere if the decision maker has acted irrationally in relation to matters of weighting (Chapter 17).

There is some flexibility. Firstly the court will not set aside a decision if the irrelevant consideration would not have made any difference to the outcome. In this sense the line between legality and merits is blurred (see *R* v *Inner London Education Authority ex parte Westminster City Council* (1986); *R* v *Secretary of State for Social Services ex parte Wellcome Foundation* (1987)). In the context of improper purposes, this is sometimes expressed as the 'dominant purpose' test. The following are illustrations.

In *Westminster Corporation* v *London and North Western Railway* (1905) the local authority had power to construct public lavatories. It incorporated a subway into the design of its lavatories and it was objected that this was its real purpose. This was held to be lawful on the basis that the subway was merely incidental. Although it could be used by people to cross the street, it was also an appropriate method of reaching the lavatories. By contrast in *Webb* v *Minister of Housing and Local Government* (1965) the local authority had power to construct coast protection works. It incorporated a promenade into a scheme, compulsorily acquiring a number of houses for the purpose. This was held to be unlawful on the ground that more land was acquired than was needed for a coastal protection barrier. The whole scheme was invalid and the good part could not be separated from the bad.

In *R* v *Lewisham London Borough Council ex parte Shell UK Ltd* (1988) the Council decided to boycott Shell's products on the ground that Shell had interests in South Africa which at the time was subject to apartheid. It was held that the policy could have been lawfully justified on the ground of promoting good race relations in the borough. However as the Council had tried to persuade other local authorities to adopt a similar policy, it had gone too far, its purpose being to put pressure on Shell.

In *Porter and Another* v *Magill* (2002) a local authority had embarked upon a policy of selling off its housing. It concentrated sales in marginal electoral wards with a view to attracting votes. The House of Lords held that the policy could not be justified on the basis of legitimate housing purposes. A democratic body can hope for an electoral advantage as the incidental outcome of its policies (and probably choose between alternative legitimate policies for electoral reasons), but it cannot distort policies in order to seek electoral advantage.

Secondly in relation to some very general factors, unless the statute plainly requires otherwise, the decision maker may have discretion to decide what is relevant in the particular circumstances particularly where the statute confers power in broad terms. The court will interfere only where the authority exercises its discretion unreasonably. For example in *R* v *Somerset County Council ex parte Fewings* (above) the Court of Appeal took the view that had the Council properly addressed the statute, it could – but did not have to – take into account the moral question of cruelty (see also *R (Khatum)* v *Newham London BC* (2004)).

16.8　Fettering Discretion

Officials fetter their discretion by binding themselves in advance, for example by a general rule, without being prepared to consider departing from the rule in an individual case. Unless the rule is enshrined in a statute or subordinate legislation, this is unlawful (*R* v *Port of London Authority ex parte Kynoch* (1919)). Officials are of course bound by rules contained in legislation but where legislation gives them a discretion as to how to decide a particular case, they must consider the case on its merits. An official can take into account guidelines drawn up within the government but cannot be rigidly bound by them. Indeed government would be impracticable without them. Moreover fairness requires that people be treated equally, thereby requiring general guidelines. As stated in the previous section, it is not usually for the court to decide the weight to be given to a factor such as a general guideline. No more is required than that the decision maker must always keep an open mind by considering whether in any given case an exception to the guideline should be made. This is a vital protection for the individual against official intransigence. As Lord Reid put it in *British Oxygen Co.* v *Ministry of Technology* [1971] AC 610, 625:

> a Ministry or large authority may have had already to deal with a multitude of similar applications and then they will almost certainly have evolved a policy so precise that it could well be called a rule. There can be no objection to that, provided that the authority is always willing to listen to anyone with something new to say.

For example in *R* v *Secretary of State for the Home Department ex parte Hindley* (2000) a 'whole life tariff' set by the Home Secretary for a convicted murderer was lawful, provided that it was open to periodic review.

Examples of unlawful fetters include the following:

- Rigid application of government policies or party political policies without making an independent judgment (*R* v *Waltham Forest London Borough Council ex parte Baxter* (1988)).
- Electoral mandates (*Bromley LBC* v *GLC* (1983)).
- Agreements and contracts that contradict a statutory obligation (*Ayr Harbour Trustees* v *Oswald* (1883); *Stringer* v *Minister of Housing and Local Government* (1971); compare *R* v *Hammersmith and Fulham LBC ex parte Beddowes* (1987)).
- Advice given by officials (*Western Fish Products* v *Penwith District Council and Another* (1981)). Thus the doctrine of estoppel, under which in certain circumstances a person is bound by a promise or statement on which another relies, does not apply to governmental decisions made under statute. However this must be distinguished from the case where the decision making power has been validly *delegated* to the official in question (see below). Here the decision will of course be binding. Moreover while not absolutely binding, a statement made by an official may create a *legitimate expectation* entitling the person to whom it was made to at least a hearing and perhaps more (below).
- Acting under the dictation of another body (*Lavender & Son Ltd* v *Minister of Housing and Local Government* (1970)) but consulting another body and even relying on the decision of another body unless an objection is raised is lawful (see *R* v *GLC ex parte Blackburn* (1976)).

16.9   Legitimate Expectations

By ensuring that the decision maker takes all relevant factors into account, the fettering discretion doctrine sometimes protects the citizen. However it also protects the general public interest by allowing a public body to change its mind or put right a mistake if the public interest so requires. This is one of the most important democratic principles. On the other hand it may be unjust to the individual if the decision maker disregards a previous promise or announced policy particularly where the individual has re-arranged his or her affairs in reliance on the undertaking. Suppose for example a student gives up a job or pays fees for a course on the strength of a government announcement that a student of her category will be given a grant. The government later withdraws the announcement. Thus the law creates a dilemma in which fairness to the individual and legal certainty are in conflict with the public interest in democratic freedom.

The developing concept of 'legitimate expectation' confronts this dilemma. There is much uncertainty about its rationale and limits. First recognised by Lord Denning in *Schmidt* v *Secretary of State for Home Affairs* (1969), a legitimate expectation arises where the citizen has been led to believe by a statement or other conduct of the government that he is singled out for some benefit or advantage of which it would be unfair to deprive him. The expectation might be generated by a promise or assurance either announced generally (*R* v *Secretary of State for the Home Department ex parte Khan* (1985): Home Office circular stated that adoptions of children from abroad would be allowed in certain circumstances) or given specifically to an individual (*Preston* v *IRC* (1985): letter concerning tax affairs). The distinction between the two may be significant (below). A legitimate expectation might also be generated by a consistent practice whereby people in the same position as the applicant have been given a benefit in the past (*CCSU* v *Minister for the Civil Service* (1985)).

A legitimate expectation must single out the claimant or a group of which the claimant is a member. It usually depends on a particular statement or promise and cannot be inferred merely from the general context (*Re Westminster City Council* (1986)) nor from unofficial statements such as an election address or media interviews (*R* v *Secretary of State for Education ex parte Begbie* (2000)). There may be a legitimate expectation that the government will honour an international treaty obligation (*R (Abassi)* v *Secretary of State* (2002) but compare *R* v *DPP ex parte Kebeline* (1999)). Although Article 9 of the Bill of Rights 1688 prevents the courts from holding a minister liable for anything said in Parliament, a statement made in Parliament might be used as evidence in judicial review proceedings and might also create a legitimate expectation (see *Wilson* v *First County Trust* [2003] 4 All ER 97 [140]). Article 9 does not seem to be violated since the minister is not being penalised for anything said).

The statement that gives rise to the expectation must be clear and unambiguous and it must be reasonable for the claimant to rely upon it (see *Preston* v *IRC* above). Where an assurance is given to an individual, the individual must have disclosed all relevant information (*R* v *IRC ex parte MFK Underwriting Agents Ltd* (1990)). Moreover where the individual is relying on a general government policy, the statutory context might exclude a legitimate expectation being directed to concerns other than the interests of the claimant (for example *Findlay* v *Secretary of State for the Home Department* (1985): change in parole policy).

A legitimate expectation cannot arise if the decision in question is one that the official has no power to make (see *Rowland* v *Environment Agency* (2003) [78] [81]). In this case the ultra vires doctrine (above) prevents the statement having any legal consequences. Thus the legitimate expectation doctrine is about a valid government statement or practice which the government subsequently withdraws either because it was made by mistake or because it has changed its mind. However where personal freedom or property rights are in issue, this domestic rule of English law might violate the wider principles of the ECHR since it is clearly unfair that that public body should be able to rely on its own illegality so as to override the interests of the individual (see *Stretch* v *UK* (2004)).

16.9.1   Reliance

It is sometimes suggested that the individual must rely on the statement that creates the legitimate expectation by incurring expense or other detriment. In practice this will often be the case. However the need for reliance has been denied (see *R v Minister of Agriculture, Fisheries and Food ex parte Hamble (Offshore) Fisheries* (1995)). Indeed in the Australian case of *Minister of State for Immigration ex parte Teoh* (1995) it was suggested that the individual need not even know of the statement (but see *R v MoD ex parte Walker* (2000)). This raises the question of what the purpose of the doctrine should be (see also *R (A) v Secretary of State for the Home Department* (2006)). In support of *Teoh* it might be suggested that the matter is about good administration and accountability. It is simply wrong for government to disregard serious assurances that it has given. On the other hand the purpose of the doctrine could be to redress injustice suffered by the individual. On this basis the principle of equality indicates that the individual should not get special treatment without a good reason, namely that he or she has suffered in some way as a result of the government statement.

Perhaps a distinction can be drawn between statements made to particular individuals and statements made more generally. Where the undertaking in question is given to a particular individual, there is a strong argument that his or her interests deserve special consideration even if he or she has not suffered in reliance upon it. However an expectation is often generated by a general policy announced in a circular or a general practice. It is arguable that where the claimant relies on an announcement or practice directed to the public at large, the claimant must show that she or he can be distinguished from the public at large by acting on the expectation so as to incur expense or other detriment (see *R v Jockey Club ex parte RAM Racecourses* [1993] 2 All ER 225 at 236–40). Perhaps detrimental reliance may be one aspect of a wider principle of fairness, something to be taken into account but not conclusive (see *R v Secretary of State for Education ex parte Begbie* (2000); *R (Bibi) v Newnham London Borough Council* (2002); *R (Bancoult) v Secretary of State (No. 2)* (2008)).

16.9.2   Consequences

The legitimate expectation doctrine does not prevent a policy from being changed for the future. It concerns only the possible injustice to those who have already been affected by it. A legitimate expectation looks similar to the private law doctrine of estoppel according to which a person can be held to a statement or undertaking. Applying estoppel in public law can be said to be unconstitutional since it fetters official discretion (above). It is clear that a legitimate expectation does not create an enforceable right (*O'Reilly v Mackman* (1982)). What are its consequences?

1. A legitimate expectation is a relevant consideration which must be taken into account in making a decision (*R (Theophilus) v Lewisham BC* (2002): student grant to study abroad). In *R (A) v Secretary of State for the Home Department* (2006) Collins J said [29]:

> Legitimate expectation is grounded in fairness. The courts expect government departments and indeed all officials who make decisions affecting members of the public to honour statements of policy. To fail to do so will . . . mean that the decision maker has failed to have regard to a material consideration.

On this basis, as long as the expectation is taken in account, the court will interfere only if the decision is completely unreasonable (see *R v North and East Devon Health Authority ex parte Coughlan* (2000), [57]).

2. A legitimate expectation will also entitle the claimant to a fair hearing and perhaps reasons to be given before the benefit is refused or withdrawn (*R v Secretary of State for the Home Department ex parte Khan* (above)). Indeed as in *Attorney General for Hong Kong v Shiu* (1983), the expectation itself may be only to be given a hearing (see also *R v Liverpool City Council ex parte Liverpool Taxi Fleet Operators Association* (1975)). This is called a 'procedural' expectation. It may however be that some other factor for example national security might override the duty to give a hearing (see Chapter 17).

3. Where the expectation is that of an actual benefit (a substantive expectation) it is becoming established that in some cases the court may go further and require the authority to give the citizen the benefit itself (substantive protection). However the circumstances where this will be so are unclear. In any event a substantive expectation will give the individual a right to be heard as above in order to persuade the authority either to change its mind or to make a special exception to its new policy or practice. This is sometimes but misleadingly called a procedural expectation (see above). For example in *R v Secretary of State for Health ex parte US Tobacco International Inc.* (1992) it was held that a legitimate expectation could not override the government's statutory discretion. The government had encouraged the company to manufacture snuff in the UK. After the company had incurred expense on its investment, the government withdrew its permission on medical advice. However the company was entitled to a hearing on the health issue and an opportunity to persuade the government to change its mind.

The following cases support giving substantive effect to a legitimate expectation.

In *Khan* (above), where the government stated by letter that certain policies concerning overseas adoptions would be followed, Lord Parker CJ suggested (at 48)

> that vis-à-vis the recipient of such a letter, a new policy can only be implemented after such recipient has been given a full and serious consideration whether there is some overriding public interest which justifies a departure from the procedures stated in the letter.

In *R v Minister of Agriculture, Fisheries and Food ex parte Hamble (Offshore) Fisheries (1995)* Sedley J suggested that a legitimate expectation creates a binding obligation that could only be overridden if the objectives of the statute could not otherwise be achieved, a matter to be assessed by the court. The case concerned a claim to retain a fishing licence on the basis of a previous announcement in the face of a change in a policy designed to conserve fishing stocks (compare *R v Secretary of State for the Home Department ex parte Hargreaves (1997)*).

In *R v North and East Devon Health Authority ex parte Coughlan* (2000) the Court of Appeal held that a severely disabled resident of a local authority nursing home could hold the local authority to a previous assurance that it would be her home for life. The authority proposed to close the home in order to transfer nursing care to the local authority. It was held that the assurance created an enforceable legitimate expectation that only an overriding public interest could displace. The scope of this is not clear. In particular the right to respect for home and family life (ECHR Article 8) was in issue, thereby raising the threshold of review. Moreover although the decision to close the home had financial consequences, it did not raise general policy issues.

It is not clear what the level of review is in relation to substantive protection. At one extreme we have seen that there can be no absolute right. At the other extreme the test is more than the general tests of relevance and reasonableness (the latter to be discussed in the next chapter). The best approach may be that indicated by Lord Parker in *Khan* (above), according to which the government must show a strong public interest in support of its decision to override the expectation. In *Coughlan* (above) Lord Woolf suggested that the court should weigh the expectation against any overriding interest required by the change of policy. This balancing exercise invites the court to scrutinise the merits of the decision beyond the usual limits of judicial review. However he also formulated a more conventional test, namely where 'to frustrate the expectation is so unfair that to take a new and different course will amount to an abuse of power' (ibid.). Lord Woolf also distinguished between on the one hand statements made to a few individuals or to a group with a common interest and on the other hand statements made to large numbers of people or to diverse groups. Substantive protection may be less appropriate in the second kind of case. A variation of this would be to argue that substantive protection should apply only to undertakings given to individuals as opposed to general policy statements, although such a distinction, even if convenient to the legal mind, might be too crude to do justice since it ignores the actual interests at stake.

In *R v Secretary of State for Education ex parte Begbie* (2000) Laws LJ took the view that that decisions that affect wide ranging policy issues or affect indefinite numbers of people should not be overridden since the court would be usurping the democratic process and would not be sufficiently aware of the consequences of its decision. In *R (Rashid) v Secretary of State* (2005) the Court of Appeal condemned as 'conspicuous unfairness' [52] a refusal to give asylum to a group of Kurds fleeing from Iraq, where the officials concerned were apparently unaware of a government policy that relocation to an apparently safe part of Iraq should not defeat an asylum claim. Even though the policy had later been withdrawn, the court held that the claimants were entitled to be treated under it. Dyson LJ identified circumstances where it would be 'an abuse of power' to override an expectation [50]. In particular the court should not usually interfere where the matter raised issues in the 'macro political field' that affected large numbers of people or with long term consequences. Even here however, a seriously unfair decision would probably be invalid. These cases therefore seem to take the courts beyond the normal limits of judicial review.

The legitimate expectation debate therefore sets the individual claim to respect against the majoritarian public good. The law cannot combine these and so reaches an untidy accommodation, usually by offering the individual a hearing that might persuade the authority to change its mind. Another compromise solution would be to pay compensation to the victim. Unfortunately there is no right to compensation in UK law for unlawful administrative action as such.

16.10   Duty and Discretion

The converse problem to that of fettering discretion sometimes arises. This is where an authority claims to have a discretion when the statute appears to impose an absolute duty. It arises most frequently when a local authority fails to provide a benefit, for example a welfare payment, medical treatment or housing, on the grounds that it does not have sufficient resources and must prioritise between different kinds of needs. If the court were to order the authority to perform the duty, the rule of law would be asserted and political pressure put on the government to come up with the necessary resources. There may also be inequity where different standards are applied in different local areas. On the other hand the court cannot command the impossible. Moreover the imposition of a duty inhibits democratic choice. Different priorities between areas reflect the workings of democracy. Thus in *Southwark LBC* v *Tanner* [2001] 1 AC 1, 9, 10, Lord Hoffmann warned against judicial intervention in

> a field which is so very much a matter for the allocation of resources in accordance with democratically determined priorities.

The courts are required to interpret the statute in order to determine whether the duty is intended to be absolute (mandatory) or permissive. Words such as 'shall' or 'may' are indicative but not conclusive and the whole statutory context must be examined. The importance of the matter, the desirability of uniformity and resource implications are taken into account (see *R (M)* v *Gateshead Council* (2007)). For example in *R (G)* v *Barnet London Borough Council* (2004) the House of Lords held that the duty imposed on local authorities by the Children Act 1989 to safeguard and promote the welfare of children in need, provided only broad aims which the authority should bear in mind. This is sometimes labelled a 'target duty', reflecting the fact that all needs cannot realistically be met in full. The Act therefore gave the authority a discretion to choose between competing demands and to take cost into account and the court will interfere only if the discretion is exercised unreasonably (Chapter 15). By contrast in *R (Conville)* v *Richmond on Thames London Borough Council* (2006) the Court of Appeal held that a statute which required the Council to give a tenant a 'reasonable opportunity' to secure other accommodation did not allow it to take its own circumstances into account in deciding what was reasonable (see also *R* v *Gloucestershire County Council ex parte Barry* (1997); *R* v *East Sussex County Council ex parte Tandy* (1998); *R* v *Sefton Metropolitan BC ex parte Help the Aged* (1997); *R* v *Newham London Borough Council ex parte Begum* (2000)).

Summary

▷ Judicial review is constitutionally ambivalent. On the one hand it supports the rule of law, parliamentary supremacy and democracy by enabling the courts to police the limits of government power. On the other hand the courts are open to the complaint based on the separation of powers that they are interfering with the decisions of democratically elected bodies. The basis of this complaint is that the courts interpret the legislation in question in the light of their own values and presumptions of interpretation which are not necessarily democratic.

Summary cont'd

▶ Judicial review is not concerned with the merits of a government decision but whether the decision maker has kept within legal limits and followed broad principles of fairness and rationality. The grounds of judicial review are loosely classified under the heads of illegality, irrationality and procedural impropriety. This chapter concerns illegality which includes ultra vires in a narrow sense, errors of law, taking irrelevant considerations into account or failing to take relevant considerations into account and fettering discretion.

▶ The constitutional basis of judicial review is contested. According to one view, it depends on the ultra vires doctrine. The alternative view is that judicial review is a freestanding part of the common law but subject to parliamentary supremacy. Proponents of the ultra vires doctrine cater for the fact that much of the law is actually judge made by claiming that Parliament intends legislation to be interpreted according to principles of the rule of law.

▶ Review for mistakes of fact is limited since this might involve a reviewing court going outside its proper sphere. Clear errors of fact may be reviewable and an error of fact might also fall within one of the other grounds, for example irrationality (Chapter 17). The interpretation of broad subjective terms in a statute may be classified as mixed questions of law and fact to limit review. Limitations on review for mistakes of fact may raise the question of the right to a fair trial under the ECHR.

▶ Fettering discretion concerns the application of a self created rigid rule, policy or undertaking in a case where, under a statute, the decision maker must exercise a discretion. A decision maker can adopt guidelines but cannot treat them as absolutely binding.

▶ The doctrine of 'legitimate expectation' attempts to deal with the injustice arising where a decision maker departs from a lawful undertaking, policy statement or practice which the citizen relies upon. Basically a legitimate expectation does no more than entitle the individual to a hearing to persuade the decision maker to give effect to its previous statement. In some cases the court may require the authority to honour its previous statement by weighing the interests of the individual against the public interest

▶ There is also an issue as to whether a statute confers a discretionary power or an absolute duty. Where a decision involves the use of scarce resources, the courts may use the concept of a 'target duty' which allows an element of discretion.

Exercises

16.1 'The simple proposition that a public authority may not act outside its powers (ultra vires) might fitly be called the central principle of administrative law' (Wade and Forsythe, *Administrative Law*). Discuss.

16.2 In what circumstances can a mistake of fact made by a government official be challenged in the courts?

16.3 Pleasantville District Council has statutory power to 'manage dwelling houses designed for elderly persons'. The Council owns a block of ten flats with accommodation for a warden on the outskirts of Pleasantville that it lets to persons over the age of 60. Experiencing financial difficulties, it makes the following arrangements:
(i) It advertises the sale of three of the flats to persons under 60.
(ii) It bans all car parking in the precincts of the flat unless a residents' parking permit is purchased at £50 per annum or a visitors' permit at £20 for 10 visits.

(a) Advise the residents of the flats who object to both these arrangements.

(b) Advise George who is 58 and has purchased one of the three flats and transferred it to Clare who is 60.

16.4 The (imaginary) Higher Education Act 2009 provides that local authorities 'may award grants to university students in accordance with criteria approved by the Secretary of State'. In March 2009 the Secretary of State issues guidance in a circular sent to all secondary schools stating that grants will be awarded to anyone whose family income is less than £15,000 or if there is evidence of hardship. Peter who has read the guidance and Wendy who has not, decided to leave their current employment to take up university places in September 2009. Their family incomes are £10,000 and £12,000 respectively. Fi wishes to undertake a university course in Surfing Studies from September 2009. Her family income is in excess of £15,000 but her family refuse to support her as they want her to study Law. An official from the local authority writes to Fi informing her that this constitutes hardship and that she is eligible for a grant.

In June 2009 the Secretary of State issues new guidance. This states that 'due to a funding shortfall, grants will be awarded only where family income is less than £8000 or where there is evidence of 'exceptional hardship'. The official now writes to Fi telling her that her circumstances do not constitute exceptional hardship and that she will not receive a grant. Peter and Wendy are also refused grants.

Advise Peter, Wendy and Fi as to the likelihood of a successful challenge to these decisions in the courts and whether they are entitled to grants.

16.5 Under the Sports Act 2002 (fictitious) the Minister of Sport has power 'where he considers it necessary in the interest of public safety and good order, to require the admission of paid spectators to any sporting event to be subject to showing membership cards at the entrance'. The Minister, interpreting 'sport' as including any activity that is competitive, has made an order requiring entrance to chess competitions to be subject to the showing of membership cards. There has been some evidence of disorder at the events. The Minister has been advised that chess events are an important source of the opposition party's finances. In another case the Minister has revoked the membership cards of all the members of a football club because the club has failed to provide an all seater stadium. The club is in the third division and the present stadium is very rarely more than half full. Discuss.

Further reading

Allan, T. (2003) 'Constitutional Dialogue and the Justification for Judicial Review', *Oxford Journal of Legal Studies* 23:129.

Atrill, S. (2003) 'The End of Estoppel in Public Law?', *Cambridge Law Journal* 3.

Barber, N. (2001) 'The Academic Mythologians', *Oxford Journal of Legal Studies* 21:369.

Craig, P. (2004) 'The Common Law, Shared Power and Judicial Review', *Oxford Journal of Legal Studies* 24:237.

Craig, P. and Bamforth, N. (2001) 'Constitutional Principle, Constitutional Analysis and Judicial Review', *Public Law* 763.

Craig, P., Tomkins, A. (eds)(2006) *The Executive and Public Law*, Oxford University Press.

Forsythe, C. (1996) 'Of Fig Leaves and Fairy Tales: the Ultra Vires Doctrine, the Sovereignty of Parliament and Judicial Review', *Cambridge Law Journal* 55:122.

Forsythe, C. (ed.) (2000) *Judicial Review and the Constitution*, Oxford, Hart Publishing (includes some articles cited here).

Further reading cont'd

Forsythe, C. and Elliot, M. (2003) 'The Legitimacy of Judicial Review', *Public Law* 286.

Halpin, A. (2001) 'The Theoretical Controversy Concerning Judicial Review', *Modern Law Review* 64:500.

Hannett and Busch, (2005) 'Ultra Vires Representations and Legitimate Expectations', *Public Law* 729

Hare, I. (1998) 'Separation of Powers and Error of Law', in Forsythe, C. and Hare, I. (eds) *The Golden Metwand and the Crooked Cord*, Oxford, Clarendon Press.

Harlow, C., Pearson, L.(2008) *Administrative Law in a Changing State*, Oxford, Hart.

Jowell, J. (1999) 'Of Vires and Vacuums: the Constitutional Context of Judicial Review', *Public Law* 448.

Oliver, D. (1998) 'A Negative Aspect to Legitimate Expectations', *Public Law* 558.

Poole, T. (2005), 'Legitimacy, Rights and Judicial Review, *Oxford Journal of Legal Studies* 697.

Sales, P. (2006) 'Legitimate Expectations', *Judicial Review* 186.

Sales, P. and Steyn, A. (2004) 'Legitimate Expectations in English Public Law: An Analysis', *Public Law* 564.

Steele, I. (2005) 'Substantive Legitimate Expectations: Striking the Right Balance', *Law Quarterly Review* 121:300.

Williams, R. (2007) 'When is an Error not an Error? Reform of Jurisdictional Review of Errors of Law', *Public Law* 793.

Woolf, Lord (1998) 'Judicial Review: The Tensions Between the Executive and the Judiciary', *Law Quarterly Review* 114:579.

Chapter 17

The grounds of judicial review, II: Beyond ultra vires

> The indispensable requirement of public confidence in the administration of justice requires higher standards today than was the case even a decade or two ago.
> (Lord Steyn, *Lawal* v *Northern Spirit* (2004) [22])

Key words

- Process and outcomes
- Varying intensity of review: heightened and super-*Wednesbury*
- Proportionality
- Minimum content of fairness
- The appearance and reality of justice
- Minimum levels of protection

This chapter continues the discussion in Chapter 16 but concentrates on grounds of review that are less directly linked to the notion of ultra vires and which therefore raise issues of the proper limits of the courts' role.

17.1 Irrationality/Unreasonableness

Irrationality or 'unreasonableness' is an overriding ground of review. It can be used to challenge the exercise of discretion or findings of law and fact. Although the question of what is reasonable must, as always, be decided in the context of the particular statutory power, this ground of review operates as an external control in that it draws on values not directly derived from the statute itself. Indeed the notion of 'unreasonableness' is so vague that it seems to invite the court to impose its own opinion of the merits for that of the decision maker. As against this, the separation of powers coupled with practical considerations suggests that the courts should be cautious in interfering with the decisions of the executive on vague grounds such as unreasonableness. The former Lord Chancellor Lord Irvine (1996) suggested that three broad reasons lay behind this: firstly respect for Parliament which had conferred decision making power on the body in question, secondly limited judicial expertise in matters of policy concerning the general public interest and thirdly what he called the 'democratic imperative', namely that government is judged by the electorate every few years. (Lord Irvine's third rationale seems ludicrous in that the electorate cannot vote in respect of individual decisions and his first begs the controversial question as to whether ultra vires is the basis of judicial review and if so what Parliament intends; see Chapter 16).

The courts have struggled to give the notion of unreasonableness a limited meaning. The main result has been to create a multi-level approach in which the intensity of judicial scrutiny varies with the context, the main factors being the seriousness of the decision in relation to the rights of the individual and, pulling in the other direction, the extent to which the decision maker's powers involve controversial social, economic, political or moral judgments.

The starting point and baseline is usually called 'Wednesbury unreasonableness' after Lord Greene's speech in *Associated Provincial Picture Houses Ltd* v *Wednesbury Corporation* (1948). Lord Greene MR emphasised that the court will interfere only where a decision is so unreasonable that no reasonable authority could have made it, not merely because it thinks it is a bad decision. Another way of putting it is that the decision must be 'beyond the range of responses open to a reasonable decision maker' (*R* v *Ministry of Defence ex parte Smith* [1996] 1 All ER 257 at 263; see also *R* v *Chief Constable of Sussex ex parte International Traders Ferry Ltd* [1999] 1 All ER 129 at 157). In *Council of Civil Service Unions (CCSU)* v *Minister for the Civil Service* (1984) at 951, Lord Diplock said that the courts will interfere only where a decision has no rational basis or 'is so outrageous in its denial of accepted moral standards that no sensible person who has applied his mind to the question to be decided could have arrived at it'.

Lord Diplock's test is often used to justify not interfering with a decision. For example in *Brind* v *Secretary of State for the Home Department* (1991) the government banned live media interviews with supporters of the Irish Republican Army (IRA). The House of Lords held that although the ban was probably misguided it had some rational basis as a means of denying publicity to terrorists and was therefore valid (see also *R* v *Radio Authority ex parte Bull* [1997] 2 All ER 561, 577). On the other hand although successful challenges for unreasonableness are rare, they seem to fall short of irrationality in the extreme sense suggested above. For example in *Hall & Co. Ltd* v *Shoreham-By-Sea Urban District Council* (1964) a local authority planning condition required the plaintiff to dedicate a road to the public. This was held to be 'unreasonable' because it amounted to the confiscation of property without compensation. However the condition was hardly perverse or irrational, given that the plaintiff stood to make considerable profit out of the permission.

A more flexible approach to unreasonableness is to ask whether a reasonable decision maker *in the light of the material properly before him* could reasonably justify his decision; or whether a decision shows 'conduct which no sensible authority acting with due appreciation of its responsibilities would have decided to adopt' (see Lord Cook *in R* v *Chief Constable of Sussex ex parte International Trader's Ferry* ({199} 2 AC 418, 452). This formula seems to give little practical guidance but enables the court to apply different levels of scrutiny in different contexts and to make value judgements as to the adequacy of the decision maker's reasoning (see for example *R (Rogers)* v *Swindon and District NHS Trust* (2006): decision to withhold drug treatment not based on financial considerations but no alternative rationale given). However this approach carries the risk of interference with the merits.

Where important interests of the individual are at stake, the level of review is sometimes called 'heightened *Wednesbury*'. It requires the decision maker to show that it has placed particularly close attention – 'anxious scrutiny' – to the interests in question (see *Bugdaycay* v *Secretary of State for the Home Department* [1987] 1 All ER 940, 952; *R* v *Ministry of Defence ex parte Smith* (above); *R* v *Lord Saville of Newdigate* (1999)). Heightened *Wednesbury* in itself does not mean that the court will intervene. For example in *R* v *Ministry of Defence ex parte Smith* (above) the Court of Appeal refused to interfere with a decision to ban practising homosexuals from serving in the army. The court recognised that the decision affected fundamental rights and therefore called for 'anxious scrutiny' but also thought that the court was not in a position to assess the specialist needs of military service and should therefore defer to the views of the military establishment. The decision of the UK courts was later held to violate the ECHR (below). In *R v Secretary of State for the Home Department ex parte Daly* (2001) Lord Cooke [32] described the *Wednesbury* case as 'an unfortunately retrogressive decision in English administrative law, in so far as it suggested that only a very extreme degree (of unreasonableness) can bring an administrative decision within the scope of judicial invalidation'. He emphasised that the level of interference should vary with the subject matter: 'It may well be, however, that the law can never be satisfied in any administrative field merely by a finding that the decision under review is not capricious or absurd.'

At the other end of the scale where a decision depends on controversial social, economic or political factors or matters 'remote from ordinary judicial experience', the court should as a matter of practical reality be cautious in interfering. In cases of this kind, at least where human rights interests are not an issue, the courts may move to a standard even lower than Lord Diplock's rationality test, interfering only where a decision is entirely capricious – an approach sometimes called 'super-*Wednesbury*. This also applies where separation of powers issues are at stake, in particular where the decision in question is one that has been approved after a debate in Parliament.

In *Hammersmith and Fulham LBC v Secretary of State for the Environment* (1990): central grants to local government, Lord Bridge said: 'since the statute has conferred a power on the Secretary of State which involves the formulation and implementation of national economic policy and which can only take effect with the approval of the House of Commons, it is not open to challenge on the ground of irrationality short of the extremes of bad faith, improper motive or manifest absurdity. Both the constitutional propriety and the good sense of this restriction seem to me to be clear enough. The formulation and implementation of national economic policy are matters depending essentially on political judgment. The decisions which shape them are for politicians to take and it is in the political forum of the House of Commons that they are properly to be debated and approved or disapproved on their merits. If the decisions have been taken in good faith within the four corners of the Act, the merits of the policy underlying the decisions are not susceptible to judicial review by the courts and the courts would be exceeding their proper function if they presumed to condemn the policy as unreasonable'.

It must be emphasised that Lord Bridge's remarks apply only to unreasonableness. Where a decision is ultra vires on some other ground, then approval by Parliament (other than in the form of a statute) does not validate it nor prevent the court scrutinising it in the ordinary way. Thus the separation of powers works in both directions, (see *R v Secretary of State for the Home Department ex parte Fire Brigades Union* (1995)) and *Nottinghamshire County Council v Secretary of State for the Environment* (1986)).

Sometimes the statute itself may require that a decision maker must act 'reasonably' or 'have reasonable cause' to believe or do something. In this kind of case the court may sometimes decide for itself what is reasonable in the ordinary, non-*Wednesbury* sense, in effect treating the matter as one of ordinary ultra vires (see for example *Nakkuda Ali* v *Jayaratne* (1951). On the other hand if a wide subjective discretion is involved or the matter is politically controversial the court may apply the *Wednesbury* approach. The matter depends on the particular context (see for example *Secretary of State for Education and Science* v *Tameside MBC* (1977)).

The flexible approach to unreasonableness is an aspect of the wider issue of how far the courts should respect the decisions of other branches of government. This is sometimes called 'deference'. It arises particularly in relation to human rights issues in connection with the concept of proportionality (below). It could be regarded as a matter of the separation of powers or pragmatic concern for the particular institutional expertise and knowledge available to the court. It arose in Chapter 16 in connection with errors of law and fact and is discussed further in Chapters 18 and 19.

Unreasonableness may overlap with other grounds of review. In *Wheeler* v *Leicester City Council* (1985) a local authority refused to allow a rugby club to use its playing field. This was because the club had not prevented certain of its members from touring in South Africa during the apartheid era. The House of Lords held that the Council had acted unlawfully. This could be regarded as an unreasonable infringement of individual freedom, as a decision based upon an improper political purpose, or as an unfair decision in that the matter had been prejudged. Today *Wheeler* would probably be explained on human rights grounds, a perspective that was raised in the Court of Appeal but which the House of Lords avoided.

17.1.1   Proportionality

At least in cases subject to the Human Rights Act 1998 (Chapter 19) and in EC law, a more stringent standard of review applies in the form of the doctrine of 'proportionality'. Broadly speaking a decision is proportionate only if it meets an important public goal (a 'pressing social need') and in doing so violates the right in question as little as possible. As Lord Diplock ponderously put it in *R* v *Goldsmith* (1983) at 155, proportionality 'prohibits the use of a steam hammer to crack a nut if a nutcracker would do'.

The requirements of proportionality set out by the Privy Council in *De Freitas* v *Ministry of Agriculture, Fisheries and Housing* (1999) have been widely adopted. These are whether:

- The legislative objective is sufficiently important to justify limiting a fundamental right. It is a difficult question as to whether the court or an elected body should decide this but under the Human Rights Act, unless the language of the statute makes it impossible to interpret it other than as violating the right, the court has the last word (Chapter 19).
- The measures designed to meet the legislative object are rationally connected with it.
- The means used to impair the right or freedom are no more than is necessary to accomplish the objective. An important matter would be for example whether there are alternative safeguards for the right in question.

Before the new climate of opinion generated by the Human Rights Act 1998 English judges had objected to proportionality on the ground that it takes the court too far into the political merits (see *Hone* v *Maze Board of Prison Visitors* [1988] 1 All ER 321 at 327–9; *Brind* v *Secretary of State for the Home Department* (1991); *Tesco Stores* v *Secretary of State for the Environment* (1995)). Therefore English law sometimes fell foul of the ECHR because it failed to reach the standard of necessity required by the proportionality doctrine. For example *Smith* (above) was condemned by the European Court of Human Rights in *Smith and Grady* v *UK* (2000). It was held that even the heightened *Wednesbury* threshold was too low to satisfy the ECHR because it excluded any consideration of whether the interference with the applicant's rights answered a pressing social need or was proportionate to the national security and public order aims pursued.

Illustrations of proportionality will be given in Chapter 19. Proportionality overlaps with unreasonableness but will sometimes produce a different outcome as in *Smith* (above). In many cases however the two are likely to produce the same outcome. For example in *R* v *Barnsley Metropolitan Borough Council ex parte Hook* (1976) a market trader was dismissed by the market manager for the relatively minor wrong of urinating in the street. This was held to be an unreasonably severe penalty.

In *R* v *Secretary of State for the Home Department ex parte Daly* (2001) it was government policy that a prisoner's confidential correspondence with his lawyer could be examined in the prisoner's absence in order to ascertain that it was genuine. The House of Lords held that although the policy satisfied the bare rationality test and was administratively convenient it was contrary to Article 8 of the ECHR (respect for correspondence). A reasonable minister could not have concluded that the policy was necessary for the legitimate goal of keeping order in prisons. The House emphasised that the court must 'anxiously scrutinise' the decision to ensure that the minister gave proper weight to the right at stake. Lord Bingham based his reasoning firstly on the common law, heightened *Wednesbury* approach that there was no reasonable justification for the policy. However he also said (at 455) that under the Human Rights Act:

> domestic courts must go beyond the ordinary standard and themselves form a judgment whether a convention right has been breached, conducting such an inquiry as is necessary to form that judgment.

Lord Steyn applied the proportionality test, emphasising that it went beyond traditional Wednesbury approaches by requiring the court itself to decide whether the right 'balance' had been struck between the conflicting interests. Lord Steyn also said that there has not been a shift to merits review, the respective roles of judges and administrators remaining 'fundamentally distinct' (although how the distinction should be drawn seems elusive to the point of being without meaning).

It is sometimes suggested that proportionality should not be confined to human rights cases but should be considered as an aspect of unreasonableness. It is generally accepted sometimes reluctantly that the two approaches, although overlapping are not merged. Thus in *R (Alconbury Developments)* v *Secretary of State for the Environment, Transport and the Regions* [2001] 2 All ER 929 at 976, Lord Slynn emphasised that proportionality was different from *Wednesbury* but that 'the difference in practice is not as great as is sometimes supposed'. He thought that proportionality and *Wednesbury* should not be kept in separate compartments and that 'even without reference to the 1998 Act the time has come to recognise that this principle is part of English administrative law, not only when judges are dealing with community acts but also when they are dealing with acts subject to domestic law'. (See also *Council of Civil Service Unions (CCSU) v Minister for the Civil Service* [1984] 3 All ER 935 at 950 per Lord Diplock; *R (Association of British Civilian Internees; Far East Region) v Secretary of State* [2003] QB 1397 [35]–[37]: suggesting *Wednesbury* be replaced by proportionality but bound to apply *Wednesbury* meanwhile.) This leaves unexplained what other situations might attract the proportionality test. On such might be the case of a 'substantive' legitimate expectation (see Chapter 16).

17.2   Procedural Impropriety: Statutory Procedural Requirements

This topic illustrates the elastic nature of contemporary judicial review. Failure to comply with a procedural requirement laid down by statute (such as time limits, consultation or giving required information or notice) could make a decision ultra vires and so void. However the courts are reluctant to set aside a decision on purely technical grounds. Traditionally the courts have tried to rationalise this by distinguishing between 'mandatory' (important) and 'directory' (unimportant) procedural requirements by reference to the language of the governing statute (see for example *R v Clarke and McDaid* (2008)). They also take a flexible response to the particular context. Using their discretionary power to withhold a remedy, the courts will set a decision aside for procedural irregularity only if the harm or injustice caused to the applicant by the procedural flaw outweighs the harm to the government or to innocent third parties in setting the decision aside (see for example *Coney v Choyce* (1975); *London and Clydesdale Estates Ltd v Aberdeen District Council and Another* (1979); *Wang v IRC* (1995); *R v Immigration Appeal Tribunal ex parte Jeyeanthan* (1999)).

The courts may not allow administrative efficiency to override a statutory right of the public to be consulted. In *Berkeley v Secretary of State for the Environment* (2000) the House of Lords held that a local authority was required to make environmental information relating to a planning application for a football stadium available to the public even though the council successfully argued that it already had adequate environmental evidence to enable it to make a proper decision. Lord Hoffmann in particular, reflecting the broad concept of democracy, suggested that public consultation was an end in itself and not merely an instrument of effective decision making.

Another important statutory procedural requirement is the rule against delegation. An official (or indeed anyone) who is entrusted with power to make a decision affecting the rights of individuals should not transfer that power to someone else (*delegatus non potest delegare*; *Barnard v National Dock Labour Board* (1953)). Applying this principle strictly would cause administrative breakdown and many exceptions have been made. Nevertheless public bodies have sometimes ignored the requirement. For example the Housing Corporation had done so for more than 40 years until the matter was put right by retrospective legislation (Housing Corporation Act 2006).

Exceptions to the rule against delegation are as follows:

▷ The *Carltona* doctrine that a minister can act through a civil servant in her or his department (Chapter 15). This can be rationalised as not a true exception in that constitutionally the minister and civil servant are one and the minister is responsible to Parliament for the act of the civil servant (see *R (Alconbury Developments) v Secretary of State* (2001)). On the other hand why should political responsibility affect the legal position, particularly as we have seen that ministerial responsibility is weak and uncertain (Chapter 15)? Nevertheless unless the method of delegation is entirely unreasonable it seems that the courts cannot interfere (*Re Golden Chemical Products* (1976); *R v Secretary of State for the Home Department ex parte Olahinde* (1991)). The *Carltona* principle applies to Executive Agencies (Chapter 15) unless possibly the arrangements are such that the minister is not accountable to Parliament (see *R v Secretary of State for Social Services ex parte Sherwin* (1996)). It does not of course apply to government agencies outside the central civil service such as the police or the local government or independent statutory bodies (but see R *(Chief Constable of the West Midlands Police)* v *Birmingham City Justices* (2002): basing the rule on a wider rationale of implied statutory authority and distinguishing between normal decision making within the organisational hierarchy and cases where the statute requires a named official to act personally).

- Many local authority functions can be delegated by statute to committees, subcommittees, officers and other authorities but not to individual councillors or outside bodies unless authorised by statute (see Local Government Act 1972 s.101; *R v Port Talbot Borough Council ex parte Jones* (1988)).
- Many governmental functions can be transferred to private bodies (Deregulation and Contracting Out Act 1994 ss.61, 69).
- Functions involving little independent discretion can be delegated. Indeed the courts seem ready to imply statutory authority to delegate in cases where it would be inconvenient for the decision maker to do everything her or himself (*Provident Mutual Life Assurance Association* v *Derby City Council* (1981); see also R(*Chief Constable of the West Midlands Police*) v *Birmingham City Justices* (above)).
- Fact finding, making recommendations and giving advice can be delegated but the decision maker must not merely 'rubber stamp' the advice she or he is given. They must have enough information before them, for example a summary of evidence, to make a genuine decision (*Jeffs* v *New Zealand Dairy Production and Marketing Board* (1967)).

17.3 Procedural Impropriety: The Right to a Fair Hearing

This ground of review is of ancient common law origin and is central to the idea of the rule of law. Until the early twentieth century the courts applied a broad principle, traceable to the seventeenth century and usually labelled 'natural justice', namely that anyone whose rights were affected by an official decision was entitled to advance notice of a decision and a fair hearing before an unbiased judge (for example *Bagg's Case* (1615); *Dr Bonham's Case* (1610); *Cooper* v *Wandsworth Board of Works* (1863)). The advance of the democratically supported administrative state produced a more cautious judicial approach. *Local Government Board* v *Arlidge* (1915) marks a turning point where Dicey felt that even the rule of law was at risk. In *Arlidge* the House of Lords held that in the case of administrative decisions (in that case a house closure order), provided that it complies with minimum standards of fairness, the government can decide for itself what procedures to follow, the citizen's protection lying not in the courts but in ministerial responsibility to Parliament (see also *Board of Education* v *Rice* (1911) 182, but contrast *Dyson* v *Attorney-General* (1911)).

The courts then refused to apply natural justice to decisions other than those which they labelled 'judicial'. For this purpose 'judicial' means the impartial application of rules to settle a dispute about the parties' existing rights, narrowly defined; essentially what a court does. Thus the courts took a crude separation of powers approach that removed natural justice from political, discretionary and policy oriented decisions which the court labelled 'administrative'. This excluded much of the welfare state from natural justice since the conferring of benefits such as education and housing does not strictly affect existing rights. It also excluded government powers such as planning, compulsory purchase and other forms of licensing which, although they affect rights, are usually discretionary. The main area left for natural justice was where a formal tribunal or inquiry determined a specific dispute but even this caused problems in the case of public inquiries held as part of a larger discretionary process leading to a political decision, for example to build a new road (see for example *Franklin v Minister of Town and Country Planning* (1948)).

However in *Ridge v Baldwin* (1964), a landmark case that marks the beginning of the contemporary renaissance of judicial review, the House of Lords returned the law to its older rationale. The Chief Constable of Brighton had been dismissed by the local police authority without a hearing. The authority had statutory power to deprive him of his position for incapacity or misconduct but not otherwise. The House of Lords held that he was entitled to a hearing for two reasons: (i) he had been deprived of an important right; (ii) the power to dismiss was limited by statute so that the authority did not have a complete discretion. Lord Reid emphasised that irrespective of whether it is judicial in the above sense a government decision that causes serious harm to an individual ought in principle to attract the right to be heard. Moreover it was emphasised that the right to be heard applies irrespective of how clear cut the outcome appears to be. Indeed the protection of a hearing may be most necessary in what seems to be an open-and-shut case.

Since *Ridge v Baldwin*, the right to a hearing is no longer limited to judicial functions. The courts have extended it into most areas of government, including for example prison management (*R v Hull Prison Visitors ex parte St Germain* (1979); *Leech v Parkhurst Prison Deputy Governor* (1988)). Although the expression 'natural justice' is still sometimes used it has become interchangeable with 'fairness' (see *Re HK* (1967)). The concept of 'judicial' is still relevant since a judicial decision will certainly attract a right to a hearing and this may be of a higher procedural standard than in the case of an administrative decision (below). However a legitimate expectation (Chapter 16) is also ground for a right to be heard in order to persuade the decision maker to honour the expectation (*A-G for Hong Kong v Ng Yuen Shiu* (1983); *R v Secretary of State for the Home Department ex parte Khan* (1985)). As we saw in the previous chapter a legitimate expectation may give no more than a right to be heard although sometimes there is an entitlement to the substantive benefit unless the government can show a strong countervailing public interest.

The courts have however introduced limits to the right to be heard. These are based on pragmatic factors and include the following:

▷ 'Fairness' concerns the protection of persons who are adversely affected by government action and not the idea of democratic participation in government. Thus the right to be heard may not include access to policy information (see *Bushell* v

Secretary of State for the Environment (1981); *Hammersmith and Fulham LBC v Secretary of State for the Environment* (1990)). Similarly advisory or preliminary governmental decisions do not attract a right to be heard unless the decision has direct adverse consequences for the individual's rights (*Norwest Holst v Trade Secretary* [1978] Ch 201: decision to start an investigation, no right to be heard; compare *Furnell v Whangarie High Schools Board* [1973] AC 660: suspension of teacher pending investigation, hearing required).

▷ A judicial decision to remove existing legal rights usually attracts a hearing but the refusal of a discretionary benefit in the public interest, where the claimant has no specific entitlement, may not (see *Schmidt v Secretary of State for Home Affairs* (1969): extension of immigration permit; *McInnes v Onslow-Fane* (1978): refusing a referee's licence; *Findlay v Secretary of State for the Home Department* (1985): parole, change in policy). However a decision to refuse a benefit that can only be made on limited grounds or involves accusations of misconduct or bad character or affects a legitimate expectation will attract a hearing (see *R v Gaming Board ex parte Benaim and Khaida* (1970); *R v Secretary of State for the Home Department ex parte Fayed* (1997)).

▷ Other factors might override or limit the right to a hearing, in particular national security considerations (*Council of Civil Service Unions (CCSU) v Minister for the Civil Service* (1985); see Chapter 21). The need to act quickly under pressure of circumstances will also exclude at least a prior hearing (*R v Secretary of State for Transport ex parte Pegasus Holidays Ltd* (1989): air safety; *Calvin v Carr* (1980) (below)). A hearing might be excluded where large numbers compete for scarce resources, for example applications for university places, or in respect of general decisions such as school closures. On the other hand where a policy decision, for example to close an old people's home, directly affects the existing rights of the persons concerned there may be a collective right to be consulted although not necessarily a hearing in individual cases (see *R v Devon County Council ex parte Baker* (1995)).

▷ Although the courts have sometimes warned against this (for example *Ridge v Baldwin* (above); *John v Rees* (1969)) a hearing may be excluded when the court thinks that the outcome of the decision was not affected so that a hearing would be futile (*Cheall v Apex* (1983)). In *Cinnamond v British Airports Authority* (1980) the Court of Appeal upheld a decision to withdraw licences without a hearing from a group of Heathrow airport taxi drivers who had been repeatedly warned about allegations of misconduct but had not responded.

The same flexible concept of 'fairness' also determines the ingredients of a hearing. There are no fixed requirements. Subject to any statutory requirements, a decision maker can fix its own procedure provided that it is 'fair' in the circumstances of the particular case (see *Lloyd v McMahon* (1987)). Perhaps the law has become too flexible, with the disadvantage that 'fairness' does not necessarily imply a definite right to a hearing. For example in *Calvin v Carr* (1980) the plaintiff, a racehorse trainer, was suspended from the course because of accusations of tampering with the horses before a race. The Privy Council held that a combination of factors meant that he was not entitled to be heard. These included the need to act quickly to preserve the integrity of the sport, the fact that he could appeal when he would be given a full hearing and the fact that he had agreed to the regulations under which the decision was made.

The following factors are particularly important:

▷ The more serious the consequences for the individual, the higher the standard of hearing that is required. To this extent the notion of a judicial decision (above) remains important. At one end of the scale preliminary or advisory investigations at best entitle a person to be told only an outline of any accusations against him or her and answer them (*Maxwell* v *Department of Trade and Industry and Others* (1974); *R* v *Commission for Racial Equality ex parte Cottrell and Rothon* (1980)). At the other end of the scale a person accused of misconduct or whose rights are in issue is normally entitled to see all the evidence and cross examine witnesses (*R* v *Army Board of the Defence Council ex parte Anderson* (1992)). This is endorsed by the right to a fair trial under Article 6 of the ECHR (see for example *Roberts* v *Parole Board* (2006)). Administrative convenience cannot justify refusing to permit a person to call witnesses, although the tribunal does have a residual discretion in the matter (*R* v *Hull Prison Visitors ex parte St Germain (No. 2)* (1979)).

▷ Fairness is a *minimum* standard to be balanced against the government's right to decide its own procedure. An oral hearing is not necessarily required even under the ECHR, although an absolute rule excluding an oral hearing is not permitted (*Lloyd* v *McMahon* (1987)). The importance of the matter and the nature of the particular issues should be taken into account to decide whether the matter can fairly be determined without an oral hearing (see *R (Smith)* v *Parole Board* (2005); *R (Dudson)* v *Secretary of State for the Home Department* (2006)). Formal rules of evidence are not required. Fairness demands only that the evidence be relevant and that the parties have a chance to comment on it (*Mahon* v *Air New Zealand* (1984)). There is no automatic right to legal representation but the decision maker must not adopt an absolute rule on the matter and must allow representation where a person cannot effectively present his or her own case (*Hone* v *Maze Prison Board of Visitors* (1988); compare *Enderby Town Football Club* v *Football Association* (1971)).

▷ Problems arise where an individual is confronted with those who claim inside knowledge but are reluctant to have this challenged. An expert decision maker can rely on his own accumulated experience without having to disclose this to the parties. Expert assessors are sometimes used to help judges and other decision makers; these need not disclose their advice in advance. However where the judge disagrees with an assessor on an important matter he should give the parties a chance to comment (*Ahmed* v *Governing Body of Oxford University* (2003)). If an inquiry is held the decision maker cannot subsequently take new evidence or advice received from an outside source into account without giving the parties an opportunity to comment (see *Elmbridge BC* v *Secretary of State for the Environment, Transport and the Regions* (2002); *AMEC Ltd* v *Whitefriars City Estates* (2005)). However advice given to a minister by a civil servant in his or her department does not count as outside advice and by virtue of the doctrine of ministerial responsibility need not be disclosed (*Bushell* v *Secretary of State for the Environment* (1981)).

17.4 Procedural Impropriety: Bias

An impartial and independent judge is a fundamental aspect of the rule of law. However complete impartiality is impossible to realise. Not only is bias inherent in human nature but many kinds of decision making processes inevitably involve conflicts of interest. The law therefore has to compromise, and has done so by distinguishing between different kinds of decisions and different kinds of biases.

The decision maker need not actually be biased – this would fall under the head of irrelevant considerations (Chapter 16). The bias rule is importantly concerned with the risk or appearance of bias, hence the dictum of Lord Hewart in *R v Sussex Justices ex parte McCarthy* [1924] 1 KB 256 at 259 that 'justice must not only be done but must manifestly and undoubtedly be seen to be done'. The rationale is not only that of fairness to the parties but also of public confidence in the integrity of the decision making process. A decision maker who becomes aware that he or she is subject to a biasing factor must disqualify him or herself, irrespective of the cost, delay or inconvenience that may result (*AWG Group* v *Morrison* (2006)). However the parties can consent to the bias in question (waiver) (see *Smith* v *Kvaener Cementation Foundations Ltd* (2006)). The main principles are as follows:

17.4.1   Financial interests

A direct personal financial interest, however small, will *automatically* disqualify the decision maker, the law conclusively presuming bias (*Dimes* v *Grand Junction Canal Co.* (1852): Lord Chancellor held shares in company appearing before him; *R v Hendon Rural District Council ex parte Chorley* (1933): local councillor had financial interest in development for which planning permission was sought; see also *R v Camborne Justices ex parte Pearce* (1955) at 47).

17.4.2   Parties to the case

In *R v Bow Street Stipendiary Magistrate ex parte Pinochet Ugarte (No. 2)* (1999) the House of Lords extended automatic disqualification to a case where a judge is a member of an organisation that is party to the case even though there is no financial element. Lord Hoffmann, a Law Lord, was an unpaid director of a charitable subsidiary of Amnesty International, a human rights pressure group, which was a party to an appeal concerning whether to extradite the former President of Chile to Spain to face charges of torture and genocide. *Pinochet* has been criticised on the ground that there is an important distinction between 'interest', where the judge stands to gain personally so that he is a judge in his own case and should automatically be disqualified, and 'favour', where the judge might prefer a particular outcome and where a more flexible approach may be appropriate (Olowofoyeku, 2000). Other common law jurisdictions have confined automatic disqualification to strictly financial interests (ibid.) and bearing in mind that *Pinochet* was a case of special political significance it is unlikely that its rationale will be extended (see *Locobail (UK) Ltd* v *Bayfield Properties Ltd* (2000)).

17.4.3   Other personal connections

These are too various to list. Examples include social, family or professional relationships with the parties, previous involvement with the same decision making process, the holding of opinions or the membership of groups related to the issues. Here a more flexible approach is taken. The courts have tried to find a form of words which on the one hand reflects the interest of public confidence in the impartiality of the decision maker and on the other hand blocks challenges for flimsy or ill informed suspicions. The current formula asks whether in the view of a 'fair minded and informed observer' taken as knowing all the circumstances, there is a 'real possibility' or 'real danger' of bias (*Porter and Another* v *Magill* (2002)).

This formula emerged from *R* v *Gough* (1993) which replaced two earlier tests (albeit often producing the same outcome). These were firstly a strict 'reasonable suspicion' test according to which any suspicious factor as it appeared to a reasonable hypothetical observer might disqualify the judge, even though if all the circumstances were known the observer might be reassured; secondly the more liberal 'real likelihood' test allowed the reviewing court to decide for itself whether in all the circumstances bias was likely. *Gough* tried to compromise between the two. It did not include the device of the hypothetical outsider but nor did it require an overall balance, only a 'real danger' of bias. However *Gough* seemed to be out of line with the ECHR and the practice in other English speaking countries (see Olowofoyeku, 2000). In particular the court might be too trusting of other decision makers, sharing the 'insider' view of public life which is endemic among the clannish professional and official elite.

The *Gough* test was modified by *Medicaments and Related Classes of Goods (No. 2) in Re* (2001) which reintroduced the standpoint of the imagined attitude of a hypothetical outsider. It is questionable whether this makes any difference since the outsider's opinion is made up by the court. Each case depends on its particular circumstances. For example in *Gough* the accused's brother was a neighbour of a jury member who did not however recognise him. The jury was not disqualified. It was perhaps crucial that the accused had accepted the juryperson's explanation since, unlike the other grounds of review, bias can be waived by the claimant. In *Porter* v *Magill* (above) a local government auditor investigating allegations of bribery had made a provisional press announcement endorsing the allegations. His later formal report confirmed his findings. The House of Lords held that he was not disqualified since the reasonable observer could assume that an experienced professional was capable of being impartial. In *Medicaments* a *lay* member of the Restrictive Practices Court was applying for a job with a firm, one of whose members often appeared as an expert witness before the court. The Court of Appeal held that she was disqualified even though she had taken steps to minimise the conflict of interest.

The decisions seem largely impressionistic, although a basic principle is that the bias must relate to the particular circumstances or parties.

In *Locobail (UK)* v *Bayfield Properties* (2000) the Court of Appeal stressed that general objections based on religious, racial, ethnic or national characteristics, gender, age, class, political views, membership of organisations, income, and sexual orientation would not normally disqualify. Specific connections might include personal friendships or animosity but making adverse remarks on a previous occasion would not in itself be sufficient. The court disqualified a judge who had written polemical articles in legal journals attacking the practices of insurance companies in circumstances similar to those in the case before him. However it did not disqualify a judge who had been a member of a solicitors' firm acting for one of the parties since he had not been personally involved, nor a decision to give a licence to a betting shop where the judge was a director of a company of which the shop was a tenant. Nor did the court disqualify the chair of a tribunal that had decided both a preliminary application to proceed in a sexual harassment case and the full case later.

On the other hand in *R (Al-Hasan) v Secretary of State for the Home Department* (2005) a deputy prison governor who had been present while the governor gave an allegedly unlawful order to carry out an intimate body search on a prisoner was held to be disqualified from participating in the hearing into the complaint. (See also *AMEC Ltd v Whitefriars City Estates* (2005): reappointment of same adjudicator to redetermine previous flawed arbitration constituted bias; *Gillies v Secretary of State for Work and Pensions* (2006): prior experience and specialist knowledge not a disqualification).

Allegations of bias are sometimes met by the claim that professional practices ensure integrity, in other words we should trust those in power. In *Taylor v Lawrence* (2002) it was held that a judge was not disqualified where a solicitor appearing before him had recently transacted family business on his behalf. Lord Woolf remarked [61–4] that an informed observer can be expected to be aware of 'the legal traditions and culture of this jurisdiction', with the implication that this would be reassuring. Similarly in *R v Abdrocar* (2005) it was held that the presence of a policeman and a CPS solicitor on a jury were acceptable in the light of the normal understandings of what citizenship entailed. However *Lawal v Northern Spirit* (2004) suggests a less complacent approach. The claimant appealed to the Employment Appeal Tribunal in respect of an allegation of racial discrimination by his employer. The senior counsel for the employer had previously sat as a part time judge with one of the lay members of the Tribunal. The House of Lords held that the reasonable outsider might well suspect that the relationship could bias the lay member. Lord Steyn [22] warned against complacent assumptions of professional integrity, pointing out that:

> the indispensable requirement of public confidence in the administration of justice requires higher standards today than was the case even a decade or two ago. The informed observer of today could perhaps be expected to be aware of the legal traditions and culture of this jurisdiction . . . But he might not be wholly uncritical of that culture.

The bias rule is overridden where no other decision maker is qualified to act, in which case Parliament must be taken to have impliedly authorised the bias (*Wilkinson v Barking Corporation* (1948); see also Supreme Court Act 1981 s.11: judges as taxpayers). In the case of administrative decisions taken by politicians, conflicts of interest arising out of political policies or competing responsibilities may be built into the system by statute. The same applies in organisations such as prisons and universities where officials have a mixture of administrative and disciplinary functions. A personal interest will of course disqualify on the principles discussed above. However conflicting interests inevitably built into the structure do not invalidate the decision unless the decision maker actually acts unfairly by closing his mind to relevant factors (for example *R v Frankland Prison Board of Visitors ex parte Lewis* (1986): prison visitors having both judicial and investigatory roles; *R v Secretary of State for the Environment ex parte Kirkstall Valley Campaign Ltd* (1996): local authority had interest in developing land for which it also had to decide whether to grant planning permission). This approach has been held to satisfy the ECHR (below). A decision may also be upheld if there is no unbiased decision maker available (see *R v Barnsley Licensing Justices* (1960): all justices members of the local Co-op).

17.5   Procedural Impropriety: Reasons for Decisions

There is no general duty to give reasons for decisions, although many statutes impose such a duty (see *R* v *Criminal Injuries Compensation board ex parte Moore* (1999); *Stefan* v *General Medical Council* (1999); Tribunals and Inquiries Act 1992 s.10). This has been justified on the grounds of cost, excessive formality, the difficulties of expressing subjective reasons and because in the case of collective decisions it may be impossible to identify specific reasons (see *McInnes* v *Onslow-Fane* (1978); *R* v *Higher Education Funding Council ex parte Institute of Dental Surgery* (1994); *Stefan* v *GMC* (1999)). However these concerns do not meet the main justification for the giving of reasons and treat the recipients of decisions as objects. The primary justification for the giving of reasons is respect for human dignity and equality so that those who purport to exercise power must be accountable. Even an admission that a decision is based on subjective judgment fulfils this requirement. The giving of reasons also strengthens public confidence in the decision making process, strengthens the rationality of the process itself and helps to challenge decisions.

However the courts have required reasons to be given in certain cases based on the principle of fairness which allows the court to take all the circumstances into account. In *R* v *Secretary of State for the Home Department ex parte Doody* [1993] 3 All ER 92 at 107, Lord Mustill referred to 'a perceptible trend towards an insistence upon greater openness in the making of administrative decisions'. The dominant view seems to be that a duty to give reasons must either be expressed or implied in the relevant statute or there must be some special justification for giving reasons. In *R* v *Higher Education Funding Council* (above) Sedley J held that arguments which applied to all cases were not sufficient, for example the difficulty of challenging a decision in the absence of reasons. Examples of cases where there is a duty to give reasons include the following:

- Judicial decisions analogous to those of a court (*R* v *Ministry of Defence ex parte Murray* (1998)).
- Cases that involve very important interests where if reasons were not given the individual would be at a disadvantage (for example *Doody* (above): fixing of minimum sentence for life prisoner; *Stefan* (above): risk of loss of livelihood, unrepresented defendant).
- Cases where the particular decision is unusual or a severe penalty is involved (for instance *R* v *Civil Service Appeals Board ex parte Cunningham* (1991): compensation award out of line with that given in analogous cases by industrial tribunal; *R* v *DPP ex parte Manning* (2000): decision not to prosecute after coroner's finding of unlawful killing).
- A legitimate expectation might also generate a duty to give reasons for overriding the expectation (*R* v *Secretary of State for Transport ex parte Richmond upon Thames Borough Council (No. 4)* (1996)).
- If an appeal is provided this may point to a duty to give reasons where the appeal would otherwise be pointless (*Stefan* above). On the other hand a comprehensive appeal that reopens the whole case may point against a duty to give reasons at first instance.
- In *Padfield* v *Minister of Agriculture, Fisheries and Food* (1968) the House of Lords suggested that if a minister refuses to give reasons, the court can infer that he has no proper reasons for his decision. However in *Lonrho* v *Secretary of State for Trade and*

Industry (1989) the House took the view that a failure to give reasons does not in itself justify the drawing of an adverse inference but is at most supportive of other evidence that the decision is improper.

Reasons need not be detailed or comprehensive, provided that they enable the parties to understand the basis of the decision (see *South Bucks DC v Porter* (2004)).

A duty to give reasons arises after the decision is made and should be distinguished from failing before the decision is made to disclose *grounds* in the sense of allegations against the applicant. Failure to disclose such grounds would normally be unfair as a breach of the right to a hearing. Moreover once an applicant has obtained leave to apply for judicial review there is a duty of full and frank disclosure. The authority 'owes a duty to the court to cooperate and make candid disclosure of the relevant facts and the reasoning behind the decision challenged' (*Belize Alliance of Conservation NGOs v Department of the Environment* (2003) per Lord Walker; *R v Lancashire County Council ex parte Huddlestone* (1986)). However this is of no help in finding grounds for challenge in the first place.

17.6   Natural Justice and the European Convention on Human Rights

The main provisions of the ECHR are enforceable in UK courts under the Human Rights Act 1998, thus adding a further layer to the law of judicial review. Article 6(1) states that

> in the determination of his civil rights and obligations . . . everyone is entitled to a fair and public hearing within a reasonable time by an independent and impartial tribunal established by law.

The requirements of Article 6(1) are usually sufficiently flexible to be satisfied by the common law of procedural propriety (see *Bentham v Netherlands* (1986); *R v DPP ex parte Kebeline* (1999)). However an irreducible core of fairness is required by Article 6 whereas the common law duty is less strict, involving a broader balance between fairness and the public interest (*Re Officer L* (2007)), *Secretary of State for the Home Department v MB* (2008)). Thus, except in connection with the right to a hearing in public which can be excluded in certain circumstances (Article 6(1)) the right to a fair trial cannot be overridden by other factors, although particular aspects might be modified to deal for example with security matters (Chapter 21) or a grave social problem (*Brown v Stott* (2001)). The common law does not necessarily require a public hearing. Under Article 6 there are additional requirements in criminal cases including a right to legal representation.

As we saw in Chapter 16, although the European Court takes a broad approach not every decision of a public authority affects civil rights and obligations. For example in *R (M) v Secretary of State for Constitutional Affairs* (2004) it was held that a district judge could make an interim Anti-Social Behaviour Order against certain youths suspected of drug dealing without notice or a hearing. Because the order only had temporary effect and was subject to review and confirmation at a later hearing, it did not affect civil rights (contrast *R (Wright) v Secretary of State for Health* (2009): placing on Child Abuse Register). Apart from Article 6 some convention rights may require a hearing in themselves. In cases involving deaths in government custody that the relatives of the victims have a right under Article 2 (right to life) to an open and public investigation to establish blame, a matter closely related to the rule of law (see *R (Middleton) v West Somerset Coroner* (2004); *R (Amin) v Secretary of State for the Home Department* (2002)). This may also apply to Article 3: torture and inhuman and degrading treatment). Compare *R (Gentle) v Prime Minister* (2008): no right to inquiry concerning military deaths in Iraq war.

As regards the bias rule, there is a distinction between policy decisions and judicial decisions.

In *R (Alconbury Developments) v Secretary of State for the Environment, Transport and the Regions* (2001) a variety of decisions made by the Secretary of State were challenged as violating Article 6 on the ground of bias. These included decisions to confirm compulsory purchase orders relating to road and rail schemes in which the government had an interest. Apart from the Human Rights Act, the arrangement could not be challenged because it was authorised by statute. The House of Lords held that in order to satisfy the test of impartiality the process as a whole should be examined including the protection given by judicial review. Overruling the lower courts, the Lords held unanimously that the process satisfied Article 6. They held that the jurisprudence of the ECHR supported a fundamental democratic distinction between policy or political decisions, for which the minister is answerable to Parliament, and judicial decisions made by courts and similar bodies. Provided that there is judicial review, 'a government minister can be both a policy maker and hear appeals without violating Article 6 (per Lord Hutton at 1018). The position is otherwise where a decision turns on findings of law or disputed facts as opposed to policy, where further safeguards such as independent fact finding might be necessary (see Lord Hoffmann at 992). Thus the House of Lords endorsed the traditional English approach against a stricter application of the separation of powers.

Finally as regards the giving of reasons the ECHR has confined itself to holding that the courts, as the citizen's last protection, must give reasons for their decisions (*Van de Hurk v Netherlands* (1984); see also *Helle v Finland* (1998): detailed reasons not necessary).

Summary

> The doctrine of *Wednesbury* unreasonableness comes near to interfering with the merits of a decision. The threshold of unreasonableness varies with the context on a sliding scale determined by the impact of the decision on the individual and whether the decision involves political factors with which a court should not interfere. At one extreme a bare 'rationality' test is applied. At the other extreme where the Human Rights Act 1998 applies the court itself may weight the competing considerations, exercising what is effectively an appeal function. Between these extremes the test appears to be whether the outcome is within the range of reasonable responses to the particular context. In effect the court is drawing upon widely shared social and moral values.

> The principle of proportionality is applied in the human rights context and may extend to other contexts. This requires the court to weigh the competing factors on the basis that the interference with the right must be no greater than is necessary to achieve a legitimate objective (in the case of some rights protected by the ECHR, 'a pressing social need').

Summary cont'd

▶ Natural justice or fairness requires that a person adversely affected by a decision be entitled to a hearing. The requirements of a hearing are flexible and depend on the circumstances. In order to respect the interests of government efficiency, fairness is regarded as the minimum necessary to do justice. The courts are increasingly requiring reasons to be given for decisions.

▶ A decision maker must also be free from the appearance of illegitimate bias. This too depends on the circumstances. A direct financial interest automatically disqualifies the decision maker as perhaps does membership of an organisation which is a party to the case. Apart from that the test is whether a hypothetical, reasonably informed observer would consider there to be real danger of bias.

▶ The rules of natural justice or procedural fairness are underpinned by the Human Rights Act 1998, although what amounts to a fair trial depends on the context and in particular the extent to which the decision is a policy oriented political decision.

Exercises

17.1 'I think the day will come when it will be more widely recognised that the Wednesbury case was an unfortunately retrogressive decision in English administrative law' (Lord Cooke in *R* v *Secretary of State for the Home Department ex parte Daly* (2001)). What does he mean and do you agree?

17.2 'The difference in practice (between Wednesbury unreasonableness and proportionality) is not as great as is sometimes supposed…even without reference to the 1998 Act the time has come to recognise that this principle is part of English administrative law, not only in when judges are dealing with community acts but also when they are dealing with acts subject to domestic law' (Lord Slynn). Do you agree?

17.3 'Since the statute has conferred a power on the Secretary of State which involves the formulation and implementation of national economic policy and which can only take effect with the approval of the House of Commons, it is not open to challenge on the ground of irrationality short of the extremes of bad faith, improper motive or manifest absurdity. Both the constitutional propriety and the good sense of this restriction seem to me to be clear enough. The formulation and implementation of national economic policy are matters depending essentially on political judgment. The decisions which shape them are for politicians to take and it is in the political forum of the House of Commons that they are properly to be debated and approved or disapproved on their merits. If the decisions have been taken in good faith within the four corners of the Act, the merits of the policy underlying the decisions are not susceptible to judicial review by the courts and the courts would be exceeding their proper function if they presumed to condemn the policy as unreasonable'. Lord Bridge in *Hammersmith and Fulham LBC* v *Secretary of State for the Environment* (1990).

Explain and evaluate critically. Would Lord Mustill in *R* v *Secretary of State ex parte Fire Brigades Union* [1995] 2 All ER 244, at 267 (see Chapter 8) agree with Lord Bridge?

17.4 The (fictional) Environmental Penalties Act 2009 provides that 'the Secretary of State may make regulations for the purpose of ensuring that household waste is recycled on a sustainable basis'. The Secretary of State makes the following regulation: 'Each household must produce if required to do so by an authorised officer a standard sized bin containing a reasonable amount of recyclable waste. Failure to do so will incur a penalty at the discretion of the authorised officer.

(a) Alf fails to produce a bin. He claims that his bin was recently stolen. The authorised officer tells him that he has no choice but to impose a penalty.
(b) Bill produces a bin containing only a small amount of waste. He explains that he has recently been absent abroad. The officer who considers that Bill is lying and who has fallen behind with his performance target imposes a penalty on Bill.
(c) Clara's bin is filled to overflowing. The officer imposes a penalty on her on the ground that the amount of waste produced is unreasonable.

Advice Alf, Bill and Clara as to any grounds on which they can challenge the regulations and the decisions in their individual cases.

17.5 The Sports Commission is a (fictitious) statutory body. It is required to 'encourage and assist the provision of sporting facilities in local communities'. The statute requires that the Commission comprises a panel of five people chosen by the Secretary of State on the basis of their 'established international reputation in sporting activities'. The Commission decides to set up a scheme to give grants to darts clubs based in public houses. It delegates the power to award the grants to local agents chosen from pub landlords. Advise as to the legality of the scheme. Are there further facts you need to know?

17.6 Does the bias rule strike a reasonable balance between efficiency and justice?

17.7 Under the (imaginary) Landlords Act 2008 no person can do business as a residential landlord without first obtaining a licence from the local authority certifying that he or she is a 'fit and proper person' to be a landlord. Ed applies to the local authority in writing for a licence giving the required information including the fact that he has no criminal record. An official writes to him informing him that there 'will be no problem' with his application. However when the relevant committee of the local authority considers his application they are informed by one of their members (a competitor of Ed's) that the police once charged Ed with intimidation. Another member of the Committee remembers Ed as a pupil at the school of which she was head teacher and that he was a 'trouble maker'. Ed's application for a licence is refused .Ed wishes to explain that the charge against him had been withdrawn as being without evidence. The Committee refuses to reconsider the matter. Ed now seeks judicial review. Advise him.

Further reading

Allan, T. (1998) 'Procedural Fairness and the Duty of Respect', *Oxford Journal of Legal Studies* 18:497.

Hickman, T. (2004) 'The Reasonableness Principle: Reassessing its Place in the Public Sphere', *Cambridge Law Journal* 63:166.

Hunt, M. (2003) 'Sovereignty's Blight: Why Contemporary Public Law Needs the Concept of Due Deference', in Bamforth, N. and Leyland, P. (eds) *Public Law in a Multi-Layered Constitution*, Oxford, Hart Publishing.

Irvine, Lord (1996) 'Judges and Decision Makers: the Theory and Practice of Wednesbury Review', *Public Law* 59.

Jowell, J. (2000) 'Beyond the Rule of Law: Towards Constitutional Judicial Review', *Public Law* 671.

Jowell, J. (2003) 'Judicial Deference: Servility, Civility or Institutional Capacity, *Public Law* 592.

Further reading cont'd

Olowofoyeku, A. (2000) 'The Nemo Judex Rule: The Case Against Automatic Disqualification', *Public Law* 456.

Poole, T. (2008) 'The Reformation of English Administrative law', *Cambridge Law Journal* 67.

Rivers, J. (2006) 'Proportionality and Variable Intensity of Review', *Cambridge Law Journal* 174.

Taggart, M. (2003) 'Reinventing Administrative Law', in Bamforth, N. and Leyland, P. (eds) *Public Law in a Multi-Layered Constitution*, Oxford, Hart Publishing.

Tomkins, A. (2003) *Public Law*, Oxford, Clarendon Press, Chapter 6.

Walker, P. (1995) 'What's Wrong with Irrationality?', *Public Law* 556.

Wong, G. (2000) 'Towards the Nutcracker Principle: Reconsidering the Objections to Proportionality', *Public Law* 92.

Chapter 18

Judicial review remedies

For this is not the liberty which we can hope, that no grievance ever should arise in the Commonwealth, that let no man in this world expect; but when complaints are freely heard, deeply considered, and speedily reformed, then is the outmost bound of civil liberty attained that wise men look for. (Milton, *Areopagitica*, 1644)

Key words

- Protection of governmental interests
- Streamlining remedies
- Discretion
- Public and private rights
- Public and private functions
- Presumptions against excluding courts
- Justiciabilty

18.1　Introduction

It could be argued that the courts provide the only open and universal means by which the individual can challenge government action. Ministerial responsibility to Parliament is of little use to the citizen directly in that it can be called upon only by members of Parliament who are unlikely to be independent. The work of the Committee on Standards in Public Life plays a valuable monitoring role but has no enforcement powers. The 'ombudsman' institution which investigates citizens' complaints against government is free to complainants and its powers of investigation into facts more extensive than those of the courts. However its jurisdiction is limited to maladministration and many public bodies are excluded, it has no enforcement powers and does not hold a public hearing (see *R v Local Commissioner for Administration ex parte Liverpool City Council* (2001)).

Before 1977 there was no distinctive legal process for judicial review. The powers of the courts to review government action developed historically in different courts through a variety of remedies, some of which were general remedies applying also to private disputes. As we saw in Chapter 7, one aspect of the 'rule of law' emphasised by Dicey was that the common law does not distinguish between public law and private law but applies the same principles to government and citizen alike, so that an official is in no better position than a private individual. However since Dicey's day the powers of government have expanded enormously and this approach has become inadequate, both to protect the citizen and to reflect the democratic interest in the effective delivery of government policy.

Since 1977 the various remedies have been concentrated in a single section of the High Court, part of the Queen's Bench Division and now called the Administrative Court. Some flexibility is added by the Tribunals, Courts and Enforcement Act 2007 under which the Upper Tribunal, which also hears appeals from the main tribunals, has a judicial review jurisdiction in types of case (other than those concerning the Crown Court) designated by the Lord Chief Justice or another judge designated by him or her (ss.15, 18). The Upper Tribunal has the same status as the High Court but includes other senior judicial officers.

There is a unified procedure for all the remedies. This replaces numerous technical rules which had developed over the years in relation to individual remedies. These had made challenge to government action complex and sometimes unjust, with litigants having to traverse a minefield of procedural niceties and sometimes being frustrated by choosing an inappropriate remedy in the wrong court. A Law Commission Report in 1976 (Law Com. 6407) led to the main reforms. A further Law Commission Report (No. 226, 1994) led to further relatively minor changes.

The law is governed by the Supreme Court Act 1981 section 31 and the Civil Procedure Rules 1998 (CPR) Part 54 (see *Practice Direction* [2000] 1 WLR 1654). A claim for judicial review means a claim to review the lawfulness of (i) an enactment or (ii) a decision, action or failure to act in relation to the exercise of a public function (CPR 54.1). The procedure as a whole is characterised by wide discretionary powers which allow the court to choose the most appropriate remedy from the whole range (below). It also embodies principles concerned with the special nature of disputes between government and citizen. These principles are of three kinds:

1. The remedies are designed to set aside unlawful government action and to send back the matter to the decision maker or to restrain an unlawful act but not, normally, to allow the court to make a new decision itself, thus complying with the separation of powers. However the court might exceptionally correct a drafting mistake made for example in a statutory instrument, where it is plain that the mistake was inadvertent and when the purpose of the instrument is clear (*R (Confederation of Passenger Transport (UK))* v *Humber Bridge Board* (2004)). Moreover where it considers there is no purpose to be served in sending it back, the court can take the decision itself (CPR 54.19). This would apply in the rare case where there is only one possible decision that could lawfully be made.
2. The procedure reflects the limited role of the courts. In particular the procedure is normally based on written statements since the court is not primarily concerned with factual disputes.
3. The procedure contains safeguards designed to represent the public interest in protecting government against improper challenges (below). To a certain extent judicial review could be regarded as part of the political process since it provides a public platform for grievances against the government so that, to a well-funded partisan, even hopeless litigation might be attractive as a means of publicising a cause. On the other hand any restriction on the right to go to court might be seen as an affront to the rule of law. However in cases where a person's ordinary private rights are at stake, for example if a public authority interferes with private property, an action or defence can be brought in any court, thus reflecting the traditional idea of the rule of law.

18.2   The Range of Remedies

Historically there are two groups of remedies suitable for judicial review. Firstly from the seventeenth century the courts developed the 'prerogative orders' (so called because in theory they issue on the application of the Crown). These were *mandamus, prohibition* and *certiorari*. They enabled the High Court to police the powers and duties of 'inferior bodies', that is, lower courts and government officials. *Mandamus* ordered a body to perform its duty. *Prohibition* was issued in advance to prevent a body from exceeding its jurisdiction. *Certiorari* summoned up the record of an inferior body to be examined by the court and the decision to be quashed and sent back if it was invalid. These orders remain the basis of the modern law of judicial review but are now called *mandatory orders, prohibiting orders* and *quashing orders* respectively (CPR 54.1). The judicial review procedure must be used when applying for the above remedies (CPR 54.2).

The second group of remedies comprises declarations, injunctions and damages (Supreme Court Act 1981 s.31(2)). These are also available in other courts and are primarily private law remedies, a matter which causes problems (below). A claimant may apply for these in a claim for judicial review and must do so if he or she is seeking these remedies in addition to a prerogative order (CPR 54.3). A declaration is a statement of the legal position which declares the rights of parties – for example 'X is entitled to a tax repayment'. Declarations are not enforceable but a public authority is unlikely to disobey one. Indeed a declaration is useful where an enforceable order would be undesirable, for example a draft government order before it is considered by Parliament or an advisory government opinion. It might for example be used to avoid offending the sensibilities of Parliament (see *R* v *Boundary Commission ex parte Foot* (1983)). The former prerogative orders do not lie against the Crown as such but the declaration does. However this is relatively unimportant because most statutory powers are conferred on ministers and the prerogative orders lie against individual ministers.

An injunction restrains a person from breaking the law or orders a person to undo something done unlawfully (a mandatory injunction). An interim injunction can restrain government action pending a full trial. In *M* v *Home Office* (1993) the House of Lords held that an injunction can be enforced against a minister of the Crown (see also *R* v *Minister of Agriculture, Fisheries and Food ex parte Monsanto plc* (1998)). This overturns a long tradition that the Crown and its servants cannot be the subject of enforceable orders (see Crown Proceedings Act 1947 s.21, which still applies to ordinary civil law actions involving contract, tort or property issues). However it was stressed that injunctions should be granted against ministers only as a last resort. Injunctions cannot be granted against the Crown itself.

Claimants often apply for more than one of the remedies which may well overlap. For example a quashing order has the same effect as a declaration that the offending decision is void. The court can issue any of the remedies in any combination and is not limited to those for which the claimant has applied (Supreme Court Act 1981 s.31(5)).

A claimant cannot seek a financial remedy, damages, restitution, or the recovery of a debt alone in judicial review proceedings but must attach it to a claim for at least one of the other remedies (CPR 54.3(2)). Moreover even in the Administrative Court damages are not available in respect of unlawful government action as such but can be awarded only in respect of conduct and losses which are not authorised by statute and which would be actionable in an ordinary civil action (Supreme Court Act 1981 s.31(4), Tribunals, Courts and Enforcement Act 2007 s. 16 (6)). In other cases damages must be sought in an ordinary civil action.

The law relating to the liability for damages of public authorities is complex and cannot usefully be discussed without prior knowledge of the law of tort. We will not attempt to discuss the matter here other than to remark that the courts are reluctant to impose liability in damages upon government bodies on the basis of failure of a public duty (see for example *X (Minors)* v *Bedfordshire County Council* (1995); *Marcic* v *Thames Water Utilities Ltd* (2004); *Cullen* v *Chief Constable of the RUC* (2004); *Anufrijeva* v *Southwark London Borough Council* (2004)). This is because the risk of paying damages might inhibit the decision maker from exercising its powers independently. In four kinds of cases however damages may be awarded on the basis of unlawful government action:

1. Under the *Francovich* principle in EC law (above, Chapter 10).
2. The tort of 'misfeasance in public office' where an authority is motivated by a specific intention to injure or knowingly acts outside its powers being reckless as to the consequences and causes material damage (see *Dunlop* v *Woollahra Municipal Council* (1982); *Calverley* v *Chief Constable of Merseyside Police* (1989); *Racz* v *Home Office* (1994); *Three Rivers District Council* v *Bank of England (No. 3)* (2003); *Watkins* v *Secretary of State for the Home Department* (2006)).
3. Where a right protected by the Human Rights Act 1998 is infringed (see *D* v *East Berkshire Community Health NHS Trust* (2005)).
4. Where there has been a misuse of power coupled with negligence or a breach of a duty specifically intended to be enforced by the person to whom it is owed. However the courts are reluctant to interpret statutes as imposing such enforceable duties on a public authority (*Marcic* v *Thames Water Utilities Ltd* (2004)).

There is also the ancient prerogative writ of habeas corpus ('produce the body'). Habeas corpus is not part of the judicial review procedure, although the grounds for issuing it are probably the same as those of judicial review. It requires anyone detaining a person to bring the prisoner immediately before a judge to justify the detention. According to Dicey (1959, p.199) habeas corpus is 'worth a hundred constitutional articles guaranteeing civil liberty'. However habeas corpus may be of little practical importance today when judicial review can provide a speedy way of challenging unlawful detention. Indeed because it cannot be used to challenge facts, habeas corpus has been held not to provide an effective remedy under Article 5 of the ECHR: right to liberty (*X* v *UK* (1982)). (See Le Sueur, 'Should We Abolish the Writ of Habeas Corpus?' 1992, *Public Law* 13; Shrimpton, 'In Defence of Habeas Corpus', 1993, *Public Law* 24.)

18.3 The Judicial Review Procedure

The judicial review process contains mechanisms designed to protect the public interest against improper challenges. In attempting to do this, it is vulnerable to objections relating the right of access to the courts and the right to a fair trial under Article 6 of the ECHR. As so often, a balance between competing values must be struck and the court has a wide discretion. The judicial review process must also be set in the wider context of the 'Woolf' reforms in civil procedure introduced in 1999 (Woolf, *Access to Justice: A Final Report to the Lord Chancellor*, 1996). These reforms include the following general aspirations in respect of which the parties are under an obligation to assist the court (CPR. 1.1):

(a) ensuring that the parties are on an equal footing
(b) saving expense
(c) dealing with the case in ways which are proportionate
   (i) to the amount of money involved
   (ii) to the importance of the case

(iii) to the complexity of the issues
(iv) to the financial position of each party
(d) ensuring that it is dealt with expeditiously and fairly
(e) allocating to it an appropriate share of the court's resources while taking into account the need to allot the resources to other cases.

The main distinctive features of the judicial review procedure are as follows:

▷ Permission to apply is required from a judge before proceedings can be commenced in or transferred to the Administrative Court (Supreme Court Act 1981 s.31(3); CPR 54.4). The procedure is ex parte, that is, the government side need not appear although it must be given the opportunity to do so. At this stage the applicant merely shows that she or he has a chance of success, so as to discourage spurious challenges and help the court to manage an ever increasing caseload by filtering out hopeless cases. There is a right to renew the application for permission before another judge in open court, and in the case of a refusal in open court, before the Court of Appeal then with leave to the House of Lords. If the Court of Appeal gives permission it often then proceeds to deal with the matter as a full hearing. After permission has been granted, interim relief preventing the implementation of the government action in question can be granted pending the full hearing either by injunction (above) or under Supreme Court Act 1981 section 31.

▷ At the full hearing the court has a discretion in relation to procedural matters. The case is normally decided on the basis of affidavits (sworn written statements) but the court may order discovery of documents, witnesses and cross examination 'where the justice of the case so demands' (CPR 54.16(1)). In *Tweed* v *Parade Commission For Northern Ireland* (2007) it was held that this was a broad principle which should take account of all the circumstances and that there may be a greater need to examine evidence in cases where the doctrine of proportionality applies. Moreover the government is obliged to make full and frank disclosure of all relevant material (see *R* v *Secretary of State for Foreign and Commonwealth Affairs ex parte Quark Fishing Ltd* (2006); *Belize Alliance of Conservation NGOs* v *Department of the Environment* (2003) per Lord Walker).

Procedural flexibility is enhanced in that the administrative court can transfer cases to the ordinary trial process and vice versa (CPR 54.20). Also with the agreement of the parties, the court can decide the whole matter without a hearing (CPR 54.18). It is arguable that, in view of the broad policy issues that may arise in judicial review cases particularly under the Human Rights Act, it would be desirable that a more expansive process be used, at least in cases of major importance. One suggestion has been to appoint an Advocate-General or Director of Civil Proceedings with the duty of representing the public interest before the court.

▷ There is a shorter time limit than the periods of three or six years applicable to ordinary civil litigation. The law is contained in a somewhat confusing combination of the Supreme Court (Senior Courts) Act 1981 s.31 (6) (7) and CPR 54.5(1)(b). The former is without prejudice to any enactment or rule of court which specifies a time limit (compare Tribunals, Courts and Enforcement Act 2007 s.16 (4) (5) which seems to be comprehensive). Under s.31 (6) the court may refuse leave to make the application or refuse to give a remedy if 'undue delay' results in 'substantial hardship to any person, substantial prejudice to the rights of any person, or would be detrimental to good administration'.

But by virtue of CPR 54.5(1) the claim must be filed (a) promptly and (b) not later than three months after the ground to make the claim first arose. In the case of a quashing order, this means the date of the decision. The time limit cannot be extended by agreement and is subject to any shorter time limit in a particular statute (CPR 54.6). The time limit can however be extended by the court (CPR 3.1(2)).

The combined effect of these provisions is that a failure to apply for permission promptly even within three months is undue delay. The court might then extend the time limit. If it does so it can still refuse relief but only on the grounds specified in s.31(6) above)). In practice these considerations are usually examined at the full hearing stage (see *Caswell* v *Dairy Produce Quota Tribunal for England and Wales* (1990)).

▷ The court can refuse to grant a remedy in its discretion even when a decision is ultra vires and strictly speaking void. By contrast in ordinary litigation an ultra vires decision is treated as a nullity (*Credit Suisse* v *Allerdale Borough Council* (1996); see Chapter 16). The court will not set aside a decision where for example no injustice has been done, where the interests of third parties would be prejudiced or where intervention would cause serious public disruption (for example *R* v *Secretary of State for the Home Dept ex parte Swati* (1986); *R* v *Secretary of State for Social Services ex parte Association of Metropolitan Authorities* (1986)); *Coney* v *Choyce* (1975)). The court might also prefer a declaration to an enforceable order, where enforcement might be impracticable or hinder the governmental process (see for example *R* v *Panel on Takeovers and Mergers ex parte Datafin plc* (1987); *Chief Constable of North Wales Police* v *Evans* (1982); *R* v *Boundary Commission for England ex parte Foot* [1983] 1 All ER 1099, 1116). The court will also take into account whether the claimant has made full disclosure of all relevant circumstances (*R* v *Lancashire County Council ex parte Huddleston* (1986)).

▷ A particularly important aspect of the court's discretionary power is that judicial review is intended as a remedy of last resort, so that the court will not normally permit judicial review if there is another remedy which is at least equally appropriate. The court's approach is flexible and pragmatic. It will take account not only of the interests of the parties but whether the matters to be decided raise issues of general importance in which case judicial review would be more appropriate. The rule of law and the general presumption in favour of access to the courts is of particular concern. The matter can be decided at the application for permission stage but might also be considered at the full hearing (see for example *R* v *Chief Constable of the Merseyside Police ex parte Calverley* (1986); *R (G)* v *Immigration Appeal Tribunal* (2004); *R (Weatherspoon)* v *Guildford Borough Council* (2007)).

18.4 Standing *(Locus Standi)*

The applicant must show that he has 'sufficient interest' in the matter to which the application relates (Supreme Court Act 1981 s.31(3)). Before the 1977 reforms the law was complex and diffuse depending primarily upon which remedy was being sought. In some cases standing was limited to a person whose legal rights were affected by the decision in question.

However, in *IRC* v *National Federation of Self-Employed and Small Businesses Ltd* (1982), sometimes called 'Fleet Street Casuals', the House of Lords, although holding that the applications had no standing on the facts, significantly liberalised the law. The applicants were members of a pressure group representing certain business interests. They challenged a decision of the Inland Revenue not to collect arrears of tax from casual print workers on the ground that the decision was politically motivated. The following propositions were laid down:

1. The question of standing must be decided both at the preliminary leave stage, with a view to filtering out obvious busybodies and troublemakers, and at the full hearing where the entitlement to a particular remedy is in issue.
2. Standing is not limited to a person whose legal rights are affected by the decision in question.
3. A majority held that 'sufficient interest' depends on the nature of the interests relevant to the statute under which the decision was made. Here the applicants failed since under the tax legislation a taxpayer's affairs are confidential and not the concern of other taxpayers, whether individuals or groups. Lord Diplock, with some support from the others, took a broad approach based on the importance of the matter from a public interest perspective, suggesting that the more important the matter the more generous should be the standing requirement. In some cases affecting the whole community, any citizen should have standing.
4. Standing should not be separate from the substance of the case. It is not clear what this means since the two matters are conceptually distinct. It probably means that the stronger the merits, the more generous the standing test. Indeed Lord Diplock would have given the applicants standing had they produced evidence in support of their allegations.
5. Upholding the rule of law is also important so that a low threshold might be appropriate if there is no other way of calling the decision maker to account (see *R (Bulger) v Secretary of State for the Home Department* (2001) per Rose LJ).

Standing has become substantially a matter of discretion and it may be that standing will be given to anyone with a serious issue to argue and where a useful purpose would be served (for example *R (Feakins) v Secretary of State for the Environment, Food and Rural Affairs* (2004); *R v North Somerset District Council ex parte Dixon* (1998)). The narrower approaches taken in *R v Somerset County Council ex parte Garnett* (1998) and *R v Secretary of State for the Environment ex parte Rose Theatre Trust* (1990) are probably now unreliable.

The courts have given standing to pressure groups certainly when they are 'associational' (see Cane, 2004) meaning that they represent people as a group who have an interest in the matter (see *R v Inspectorate of Pollution ex parte Greenpeace (No. 2)* (1994); (*R (Edwards) v Environment Agency* (2004)). By contrast what Cane calls 'surrogate' groups, representing others who themselves could have standing, are less likely to succeed (see *R v Legal Aid Board ex parte Bateman* (1992)), although even here an important matter might succeed (for example *R (Quintavalle) v Human Embryology and Fertilisation Authority* (2005): pressure group representing a patient, but standing not contested).

A third category according to Cane (above) comprises groups and individuals representing the general public interest. These have standing at least where there is no other way of challenging the decision (for instance *R v HM Treasury ex parte Smedley* (1985): taxpayer; *R v Secretary of State for Foreign and Commonwealth Affaires ex parte World Development Movement* (1995): campaigning organisation; *R v Secretary of State for Foreign and Commonwealth Affairs ex parte Rees-Mogg* (1994): concerned citizen (former editor of *The*

Times); *R (Quintavalle)* v *Secretary of State for Health* (2003): anti-abortion group). However where a contribution can more effectively be made by others, standing may be denied (for example *R (Bulger)* v *Secretary of State for the Home Department* (2001)). Indeed the contribution of pressure groups has been welcomed as adding a valuable dimension to judicial review (*R* v *Secretary of State for Trade and Industry ex parte Greenpeace* (1998)).

The particular remedy is also a factor. For example in *R* v *Felixstowe Justices ex parte Leigh* (1987) a newspaper editor had standing for a declaration that magistrates should not hide behind anonymity, but not *mandamus* to reveal the identity of magistrates in a particular case.

In many cases (such as *Bulger* and *Rose Theatre* above) even where the claimant lacks standing the court considers the substantive issues albeit without granting a remedy. Moreover even where a person has no standing in their own right the court has a discretion in an action brought by someone with standing to hear any person, thereby broadening the scope of the process and allowing interest groups to have a say (CPR 54.17).

18.5 Choice of Procedure: Public and Private Law

The special features of the application for judicial review raise two questions. When is the procedure available? When must it be used in place of other methods of approaching the courts? Before the judicial review procedure was created in 1977 the prerogative orders were available only in the Divisional Court of the Queen's Bench Division and are now available only in the Administrative Court. The other remedies – declaration, injunction and damages – were and still are available in any court. Neither the Supreme Court Act 1981 nor the Civil Procedure Rules expressly require a person to use the Administrative Court.

Until the 1980s it was accepted that a citizen could apply to any court for a declaration or injunction and could raise the invalidity of a government decision in any relevant legal proceedings. Indeed the right to contest government action wherever and however it arises is a basic aspect of the rule of law. Nevertheless in *O'Reilly* v *Mackman* (1982) the House of Lords held that apart from in exceptional cases a 'public law' matter must be brought in the Administrative Court since this ensures that safeguards designed to protect the government and therefore the public against improper challenges are in place. Two distinct questions must be separated: firstly what is a public law matter? If a matter is not one of public law then the Administrative Court procedure is irrelevant. Secondly the 'exclusivity' question, namely what 'exceptional' public law cases fall outside the special procedure?

18.5.1 Public Law Matters: Scope of the Judicial Review Procedure

The judicial review procedure applies only to 'public functions' (CPR 54.1). This implies that not all activities of government bodies are necessarily public functions and opens the possibility that some functions carried on by bodies outside government might nevertheless be public functions. Indeed contemporary political fashion favours using private bodies to deliver public services. It seems anomalous that a body carrying out functions on behalf of government should not be subject to judicial review (see the dissenting speeches of Lord Bingham and Lady Hale *in YL* v *Birmingham City Council*

(2007)). There is no clear definition of 'public'. Indeed it is often suggested that judicial review is about controlling any concentration of power rather than government as such.

The remedies provided by the Human Rights Act 1998 are also triggered by a 'public function' (Chapter 19). The courts have warned that the meaning of public function in the two contexts is not necessarily the same since the purpose of the Human Rights Act is the narrower one of applying certain provisions of the ECHR in domestic law. On the other hand cases in either context can be used as guidance (*YL* v *Birmingham City Council* (2007); *Hampshire County Council* v *Beer* (2003)). The courts have taken a relatively flexible if cautious approach. It is relevant but not enough that the function in question is exercised in the public interest nor that the body is important nor that the decision has serious consequences for those affected by it. The courts have refused to apply a single test but have indicated a number of factors which make a function 'public':

▷ Firstly where a power exercisable for public purposes is conferred directly by statute or royal prerogative it will normally be regarded as a public function (see *R* v *Panel on Takeovers and Mergers ex parte Datafin plc* (1987); *Scott* v *National Trust* (1998)). However the fact that a body, like an insurance company, which exercises commercial functions of a kind similar to those exercised by private bodies, is created by statute and has statutory powers does not in itself make its functions public functions (*R (West)* v *Lloyds of London* (2004)).

▷ Secondly a function which is intermeshed with or 'underpinned' by government may be public in the sense that government bodies have control over its exercise or participate in its activities (*Poplar Housing and Regeneration Community Association Ltd* v *Donoghue* (2001): housing association formed by local authority). How much government involvement is required is a matter of degree in the particular circumstances, making this approach highly uncertain.

In *R* v *Panel on Takeovers and Mergers ex parte Datafin plc* (above) which is the seminal case it was held that the Takeover Panel, a self regulating voluntary body which acted as a city 'watchdog', was exercising public law functions. This was because it was set up in the public interest, it reported to the government and although not having statutory powers itself was supported by the statutory powers of the Department of Trade. In *Hampshire County Council* v *Beer* (2003) the Court of Appeal held that a farmers' market run by a farmers' cooperative was exercising public functions both for human rights and judicial review purposes. This was for two reasons, each of which alone would have apparently sufficed. Firstly it had control over a public space in the street; secondly it had previously been run by the local authority which had now handed it over to the cooperative.

At the other end of the scale in *YL* v *Birmingham City Council* (2007), a human rights case, a majority of the House of Lords held that a privately run for-profit care home was not exercising a public function in relation to a resident who was placed there and financed by the local authority. The particular relationship between the home and the resident was the same as that between the home and a resident funded by self or family. Relevant factors are the degree of involvement of government through finance, control or regulation and the extent to which the body in question has special powers. The matter might have been different if the state had financed and regulated the home as opposed to the individual patient. There were however strong dissents from Lord Bingham and Lady Hale. Both thought it straightforward that the home was exercising public functions. This was because the state had taken on itself the responsibility of caring for the elderly and from this perspective it was immaterial that it had done so through a private agency.

By contrast in *Weaver* v *London and Quadrant Housing Trust* (2008) Richardson J held that a publicly funded housing association when attempting to evict a tenant was exercising public functions both for Human Rights Act and judicial review purposes. His lordship took into account the fact that the association was a non-profit charity operating for community benefit, that it was subject to intensive government regulation as to its purposes, in effect taking the place of a local authority, that it received state subsidy and implemented government policy and that it was under a statutory duty to cooperate with local authorities.

▶ It has been held, sometimes reluctantly, that a power which is based exclusively on contract or other agreement to submit to the jurisdiction, for example the disciplinary power exercised by sports or professional associations, is a private law power (see *R* v *Disciplinary Committee of the Jockey Club ex parte the Aga Khan* (1993); *R* v *Football Association ex parte Football League* (1993); *R (Heather)* v *Leonard Cheshire Foundation* (2002): retirement home owned by a charity). This seems artificial since many such bodies exercise their powers for the purpose of protecting the public in much the same way as the Takeover Panel. In such cases, for example the Jockey Club (above), the reality is that the individual has no choice but to submit to the jurisdiction since the alternative is to be excluded from an area of public life. However the contract test is not conclusive. Where there is an additional element of statute or governmental policy or if the decision affects persons beyond the contractual relationship the court may treat the matter as one of public law (*McLaren* v *Home Office* (1990)). Compare *R* v *East Berkshire Health Authority ex parte Walsh* (1985): nurse employed under contract, with *R* v *Secretary of State for the Home Department ex parte Benwell* (1985): prison officer employed directly under statute.

▶ Another possible test is whether if the body in question did not exist the government would have to intervene (see *R* v *Advertising Standards Authority* (1990); *R* v *Chief Rabbi ex parte Wachmann* (1993)). However this is not reliable nor conclusive since there is no agreement on what functions are necessary in this sense (see for example *Aga Khan* above). Indeed it could apply to anything of importance. For example if all food shops closed, no doubt the government would intervene.

18.5.2   Exclusivity

Assuming that a decision is one of public law, must the judicial review procedure always be used? Because the judicial review procedure is more restrictive than an ordinary action there is a school of thought that the rule of law is threatened by forcing people to use it. As against this the judicial review procedure is geared to the special concerns of challenging government action and in many cases is clearly appropriate in view of the remedies available and the relative speediness of the proceedings.

In *O'Reilly* v *Mackman* (1982) prisoners sought to challenge a decision not to give them remission for good behaviour. They were outside time for judicial review and attempted to bring an ordinary civil action for a declaration. Lord Diplock emphasised that a prisoner has no legal right to remission, which was an 'indulgence' from the government, but at most a legitimate expectation that his or her case would be considered fairly. The House of Lords struck out their claim as an abuse of the court's process. Lord Diplock said that the judicial review procedure should normally be used because of its safeguards which protected the government against 'groundless, unmeritorious or tardy harassment'. Lord Diplock suggested that there should be exceptions to the exclusivity principle but did not fully identify them. He did however suggest that the judicial review procedure would not be exclusive in cases of 'collateral' challenge, where the validity of government action arises incidentally in litigation, for example where a local authority resists a claim to pay a debt by arguing that the decision to incur the debt was ultra vires (*Credit Suisse* v *Allerdale Borough Council* (1996)). Similarly a citizen can raise a defence in any relevant proceedings against an unlawful government claim (*Wandsworth London Borough Council* v *Winder* (1985); *Boddington* v *British Transport Police* (1998)). An ordinary civil action might also be appropriate if the issues are mainly factual or where the public law aspects are peripheral (*Mercury Communications* v *Director General of Telecommunications* (1996)).

The most fundamental exception to the *O'Reilly* principle may be where existing private law rights are in issue. In *Cocks* v *Thanet District Council* (1983) the House of Lords applied *O'Reilly* to hold that a claimant under homelessness legislation must use judicial review rather than a more convenient action in a local county court. This was because the legislation gave him no absolute rights but required a discretionary government decision before a claimant became entitled to housing. Similarly in *Roy* v *Kensington, Chelsea and Westminster Family Practitioner Committee* (1992) a doctor was seeking a discretionary 'practice allowance' from the NHS. He had established entitlement to some kind of allowance but not as to how much. The House of Lords suggested that whenever a litigant was protecting a 'private law right', he or she need not use the judicial review procedure. Alternatively it was held that the circumstances were so closely analogous to a private claim that as matter of discretion the action should go ahead.

A private law right includes any right arising in contract or tort or property law that can be protected by damages (for example *Clark* v *University of Lincolnshire and Humberside* (below)). It also includes a case where a person can establish a definite entitlement against the government. For example, in *Cocks* (above), had the claimant been allocated accommodation, a private right would have arisen (see also *Trustees of the Dennis Rye Pension Fund* v *Sheffield City Council* (1997); *British Steel* v *Customs and Excise Commissioners* (1997) illustrating that this may turn on complex questions of statutory interpretation).

These cases seem to leave *O'Reilly* v *Mackman* little to bite on because in the absence of a 'private law right', judicial review, with its flexible standing requirement, would in any event be the only possible procedure. Indeed in *Kay* v *Lambeth London Borough Council* (2006), concerning the eviction of a former tenant, the House of Lords held that methods of redress available in other courts can be used where appropriate but that in some cases no other forum is available [30, 31]. This respects the principle that judicial review is a last resort and that other means of redress should first be exhausted. Cases where there is no alternative to judicial review include government decisions to grant benefits or permissions, many immigration, prison and homelessness claims, and challenges to government investigations or inquiries that do not produce legal consequences. However sometimes there may be a circular element where the existence of a private law right is influenced by the court's view as to whether judicial review would provide an adequate remedy, for example where it has to be decided whether the breach of a duty imposed on a public authority by statute gives rise to a claim for damages (for example *Cullen* v *Chief Constable of the RUC* (2004): failure to give prisoner access to a lawyer).

The courts have emphasised that the matter is one of discretion and that unless the procedure chosen is clearly inappropriate they will not disturb it. In *Clark* v *University of Lincolnshire and Humberside* (2000) a student brought an ordinary action for breach of contract against a decision by the University to fail her. It was argued that she should have brought a judicial review claim within the three months' time limit. The Court of Appeal held that she was entitled to bring a civil action. Even if judicial review were appropriate, as was the case here because the University also had statutory powers, the court would not strike out a claim merely because of the procedure that had been adopted unless the court's processes were being misused or the procedure chosen was unsuitable (for example *D* v *Home Office* (2006): ordinary trial appropriate where factual matters in issue). Moreover cases can be transferred between the Administrative Court and other courts at any stage.

The tendency to relax the *O'Reilly* principle has been encouraged by the Woolf reforms (above), which have narrowed the gap between judicial review and other civil actions by giving the courts wider powers to control the civil process by requiring the parties to cooperate with the court in expediting proceedings. Although permission to apply is not required in an ordinary civil action, Part 24 of the Civil Procedure Rules empowers the court to strike out a civil action at an early stage if the defendant can show that it has no reasonable chance of success. In judicial review proceedings however the *claimant* must establish a reasonable chance of success.

18.6 The Exclusion of Judicial Review

18.6.1 Justiciability

Some matters are non-justiciable, meaning that they raise issues the courts consider unsuited to judicial resolution, either because they are outside judicial expertise or because they do not raise issues of domestic law. Examples include fundamental political questions appropriate for democratic resolution such as the appointment of ministers and the dissolution of Parliament, wide ranging social and economic issues where there are few if any concrete rules, foreign relations and the international rules of war and bodies of equal status to the courts in accordance with the separation of powers. We have already seen that the courts will not rule on the validity of international treaties (Chapter 6) nor interfere in the internal proceedings of Parliament (Chapter 11) nor adjudicate on certain 'acts of state' (Chapter 14).

Before *Council of Civil Service Unions (CCSU)* v *Minister for the Civil Service* (1985) it was widely believed that royal prerogative powers were non-justiciable. The House of Lords rejected that approach holding that it was the *content* rather than the source of the power that mattered (see Lord Roskill at 418). In that case the prerogative power to control the civil service was used to ban strikes at GCHQ (the base for intelligence interception of overseas broadcasts) without complying with an established practice of consulting the trade unions. The House held that the power was reviewable and that the unions had a legitimate expectation of consultation. However because the matter was one of national security, the court would not interfere since the government must be the judge of what national security requires. It is noteworthy however that the court did not regard the matter as wholly non-justiciable. It was held that the government must prove supporting evidence that the matter was genuinely one of national security, which in that particular case was of course easy to do.

The underlying principle may be not that some subjects are inherently non-justiciable but that the court will not interfere *with a particular issue* where for a variety of pragmatic reasons the court considers that it is not qualified to do so. This relates to the issues of 'deference' and reasonableness discussed in other chapters. For instance in the case of error of law (Chapter 16) the courts have refused to interfere with findings in respect of which the decision maker's expertise is greater than that of the court but will interfere on grounds of irrationality and unfairness. Similarly the level of scrutiny given to complaints of unreasonableness and human rights violations varies with the context (Chapters 17 and 19). The courts are reluctant to interfere with matters appropriate to the democratic process such as priorities in allocating resources where there are no objective rules or with professional judgments in controversial areas such as medical treatment (for example *R v Cambridge Health Authority ex parte B* (1995); compare *R (Rogers) v Swindon Primary Care Trust* (2006). On the other hand the greater the violation of individual rights, the more likely are the courts to intervene.

The courts seem to be increasingly reluctant to treat a matter as wholly non-justiciable. The prerogative of mercy has been held to be reviewable (*R v Secretary of State for the Home Department ex parte Bentley* (1993); *Attorney-General of Trinidad and Tobago v Lennox Phillips* (1995)). A Prerogative Order in Council was held to be reviewable in *R (Bancoult) v Secretary of State (No. 2)* (Chapter 6). The power to issue a passport was held to be reviewable because it is merely an administrative decision affecting the right of individuals and their freedom of travel (*R v Secretary of State for Foreign and Commonwealth Affairs ex parte Everett* (1989)). Other prerogative powers held to be reviewable are the powers to make ex gratia payments to the victims of crime (*R v Criminal Injuries Compensation Board and Another ex parte P* (1995)) and to farmers affected by the foot and mouth epidemic (*National Farmers Union v Secretary of State for the Environment, Food and Rural Affairs* (2003); the issue of warrants for telephone tapping (*R v Secretary of State for the Home Department ex parte Ruddock* (1987) – see the Regulation of Investigatory Powers Act 2000 which replaces the prerogative in this respect); and the policy of discharging homosexuals from the armed services (*R v Ministry of Defence ex parte Smith* (1996)).

The courts accept that some cases still fall within 'forbidden areas'. The disposition of the armed forces and the Attorney-General's powers to commence legal actions remain unreviewable at present (see *Chandler v DPP* (1964); *R v Jones (Margaret)* (2006); *Gouriet v Union of Post Office Workers* (1978)). However the Privy Council has hinted that the court's jurisdiction in relation to the Attorney-General's powers might be reconsidered (*Jeewan Mohit v DPP of Mauritius* [2006] UKPC 20 [21]). The court will not consider whether a treaty making power has been unlawfully exercised nor review the content of a treaty (*R v Secretary of State for Foreign and Commonwealth Affairs ex parte Rees-Mogg* (1994); *Blackburn v Attorney-General* (1971)). The main reason for this is the unsuitability of the judicial process to matters of 'high policy concerning the nation as a whole, particularly in the sphere of international relations where objective rules are not appropriate. For example in 2002 when diplomacy was still proceeding in the run up to the 2003 war with Iraq, the court would not determine whether UN Resolution 1441 authorised states to take military action in the event of non-compliance by Iraq with its terms, lest its decision would have compromised Britain's negotiating position (*CND* v *Prime Minister of the United Kingdom* (2002)).

Similarly the powers mentioned by Lord Roskill as non-justiciable in the CCSU case (above), relating to matters such as the dissolution of Parliament and the appointment and dismissal of ministers, are central to the democratic process and in law are the prerogative of the head of state. They are unlikely be justiciable in the absence of a fundamental remodelling of the separation of powers (see Harris, 2003, 'Judicial Review, Justiciability and the Prerogative of Mercy', *Cambridge Law Journal* 62: 631).

However the law is evolving. The courts have gone so far as to hold that the Foreign Office's power to make diplomatic representations on behalf of a British subject could be reviewable (*R (Abbasi)* v *Secretary of State for the Foreign and Commonwealth Office* (2002): indefinite detention by the US at Guantanamo Bay without access to either a lawyer or a court).

In *R v Jones (Margaret)* (above) the House of Lords was influenced by the reluctance of the courts to investigate the deployment of the armed forces in holding that the international war crime of aggression was not an offence in domestic law. Lord Bingham took the view that the courts would be slow to interfere with matters relating to the conduct of foreign policy or the deployment of the armed forces but did not rule it out altogether [30]. Lord Hoffmann treated it as a 'constitutional principle' that the Crown's discretion to go to war was not justiciable [65].

The courts will review a prerogative matter which falls within a right protected under the Human Rights Act 1998. However whether the matter in issue is suitable for judicial resolution will influence the court in deciding the scope of the right.

In *R (Gentle)* v *Prime Minister* (2008) the House of Lords held that the legality of the decision to go to war against Iraq did not engage Article 2 of the ECHR (right to life). This was because the rules of international law which governed the matter were not relevant to the ECHR. Furthermore the risk of a soldier dying was no greater because the war was illegal. Moreover the likelihood of death was not great enough to engage the government's duty to protect its citizens against death.

18.6.2   Statutory Exclusion of Review

Sometimes a statute attempts to exclude judicial review thereby confronting a fundamental tenet of the rule of law. The courts are reluctant to accept this and construe such statutes narrowly. For example a provision stating that a decision shall be 'final' does not exclude review but merely prevents the decision maker from reopening the matter and excludes any right of appeal that might otherwise apply (*R v Medical Appeal Tribunal ex parte Gilmore* (1957)). Even a provision stating that a 'determination of the tribunal shall not be questioned in any court of law' is ineffective to prevent review where the tribunal exceeds its 'jurisdiction' (powers). This is because the tribunal's act is a nullity and so not a 'determination'. Given that a government body exceeds its jurisdiction whenever it makes an error of law (Chapter 16) this neatly sidesteps the 'ouster clause' (*Anisminic v Foreign Compensation Commission* (1969)).

However given Parliament's ultimate supremacy, a sufficiently tightly drafted 'ouster clause' could surmount *Anisminic*. A clause often found in statutes relating to land use planning and compulsory purchase allows challenge within six weeks and then provides that the decision 'shall not be questioned in any court of law'. The courts have interpreted this provision literally, on the ground that review is not completely excluded and that the policy of the statute is to enable development of land to be started quickly (see *R v Cornwall County Council ex parte Huntingdon* (1994)). Similarly a provision stating that a particular act such as entry on a register or a certificate shall be 'conclusive evidence' of compliance with the Act and of the matters stated in the certificate may also be effective since it does not exclude review as such but makes it impossible to prove invalidity. However this may leave open the possibility of review for unfairness or unreasonableness (see *R v Registrar of Companies ex parte Central Bank of India* (1985)).

The court will take the policy of the Act into account. Under the Anti-Terrorism, Crime and Security Act 2001 an asylum seeker can appeal to the Immigration Appeal Tribunal against a decision of an adjudicator but only with the permission of the Tribunal (s.101). A decision to refuse permission to appeal can be challenged by a 'paper review' by a High Court judge which is significantly more limited than the normal judicial review. It was held in *R (G) v Immigration Appeal Tribunal* (2004) that in the absence of express words in a statute, judicial review could not completely be excluded. However given the intention of Parliament to deal with the serious problem of delays arising from the processing of asylum cases, the court would permit judicial review only in exceptional cases. A similar position might be taken under the same Act where there is a right of appeal to the Special Immigration Appeals Commissioners (who include a High Court judge) against a decision of the Home Secretary to certify that a person is an 'international terrorist'. The proceedings of the commissioners are in private and evidence is sometimes not revealed to the complainant. The Act provides that any action taken by the Home Secretary in connection with or in reliance on the certificate may be questioned in legal proceedings only by this method (s.30).

Statutes dealing with the surveillance and the security services feature a clause stating that a decision cannot be challenged even on jurisdictional grounds (see Security Services Act 1989 s.5(4); Regulation of Investigatory Powers Act 2000 s.67(8)). These may exclude judicial review completely although they do provide a right to complain to special commissioners.

Where judicial review is completely excluded, Article 6 of the ECHR may be invoked on the ground that the ouster clause prevents a fair trial in relation to a person's 'civil rights and obligations'. The fairness of the proceedings must be considered as a whole including the judicial review stage. It is arguable that the limited rights of challenge conferred by legislation dealing with security matters would be regarded as a proportionate response, since 'fairness' is a flexible concept. Nevertheless in *Re MB* (2006): control order over a suspected terrorist, the Administrative Court held that section 3 of the Prevention of Terrorism Act 2005 violated Article 6. It was conspicuously unfair in limiting judicial review to the lawfulness of the Secretary of State's decision on the basis only of the material before the Secretary of State which the claimant was unable to see or challenge.

Summary

> There is a special procedure for challenging decisions of public bodies in the Administrative Court. It is highly discretionary. The procedure provides the citizen with a range of remedies to quash an invalid decision, prevent unlawful action and require a duty to be complied with. Damages may sometimes be available but under restricted circumstances. It provides machinery for protecting government against improper or trivial challenges. Leave to apply is required and judicial review will be refused where there is an equally convenient alternative remedy.

> Standing is flexible and increasingly liberal although a third party may not be given standing where others are in a better position to challenge the decision.

> Judicial review applies only to public law functions, which usually include powers exercised by a wide range of bodies connected to the government or exercising statutory powers but does not usually exclude powers derived exclusively from contract or consent. In some cases the citizen may challenge public law powers outside the judicial review procedure on the basis of the rule of law principle that, where private rights are at stake, unlawful government action can be ignored.

> The remedies and procedure for judicial review are discretionary so that even though an unlawful government decision is strictly speaking a nullity, the court may refuse to intervene. Delay, misbehaviour, the impact on third parties and the absence of injustice may be reasons for not interfering. Public inconvenience or administrative disruption are probably not enough in themselves but they might be relevant to the court's discretion, coupled with another factor such as delay.

> Some kinds of government power are inherently non-justiciable. This depends on the political content and level of the particular power, its impact on the rights of the individual, the knowledge and expertise of the respective bodies and the appropriateness of the judicial process.

> Sometimes statutes attempt to exclude judicial review. The courts are reluctant to see their powers taken away and interpret such provisions strictly. The Human Rights Act 1998 reinforces this.

Exercises

18.1 What are the advantages and disadvantages of the judicial review procedure from the point of view of the citizen? When may government action be challenged in the courts by means of an ordinary action?

18.2 'The expressions "private law" and "public law" have recently been imported into the law of England from countries which unlike our own have separate systems concerning public law and private law. No doubt they are convenient expressions for descriptive purposes. In this country they must be used with caution for, typically, English law fastens, not upon principles but upon remedies' (Lord Wilberforce in *Davy* v *Spelthorne* BC [1984] AC 262, 276). Discuss.

18.3 '*O'Reilly v Mackman* is effectively a dead letter.' Discuss.

18.4 James, a civil servant working in the Cabinet Office, has evidence that the Prime Minister has been selling peerages to rich businesswomen in return for promises to make donations to charities specified by the Prime Minister's wife. He informs the head of his department who replies that 'it's not possible old boy'. James now seeks judicial review. Advise him.

18.5 Snobville District Council has statutory power to acquire, within its area, land which in its opinion it 'is desirable to set aside as a public park'. The Council makes a compulsory purchase order in respect of a row of houses owned by Fred, who lets them at a low rent and who has frequently been prosecuted by the Council under public health legislation for offences involving overcrowding in the houses. The governing statute provides that a compulsory purchase order may be challenged in the High Court within six weeks of its confirmation by the minister on the ground of ultra vires but 'thereafter a compulsory purchase order shall not be questioned in any court of law'. Fred does not challenge the order but, nine months after its confirmation by the minister, John, one of the residents in Fred's houses, learns that the Council had agreed with another landowner, X, to acquire Fred's land rather than X's on the ground that 'since Fred's houses were unhealthy this would kill two birds with one stone'. Advise John.

18.6 Forever Open Housing Association provides sheltered accommodation for vulnerable people. It is a charity owned by a religious sect and is part funded and regulated by the Housing Corporation, a government agency. Mary lives in a residential home owned by Forever Open, her accommodation being paid for by the local authority under its statutory obligation to arrange for care provision for the elderly. When Mary took up residence Forever Open told her that she 'now has a home for life'. Forever Open now proposes to close the home. Advise Mary whether she can challenge this proposal in the Administrative Court.

18.7 By statute (fictitious) the NHS is required to provide 'an effective healthcare service for all UK residents'. The statute also provides that 'the actions of any NHS hospital in relation to the provision of any service to the public shall not be questioned in any court on any ground whatsoever'. St Tony's hospital is short of money and trained staff because of government financial cuts. The Secretary of State has issued a circular to all hospitals stating, among other things, that no further patients be admitted for sex change operations, and that hip replacement operations should normally be performed only on patients who play an active part in the economic life of the community.

   (i) The Holby Transsexual Rights Society, a local pressure group, objects to the circular. It discovers the contents six months after it came into effect. Advise the Society as to its chances of success in the courts.

   (ii) Frank, who is an unemployed resident in a hostel for the homeless, is refused a hip replacement operation. He wishes to bring an action in his local county court. Advise St Tony's Hospital.

Further reading

Cane, P. (1995) 'Standing up for the Public', *Public Law* 276.

Cane, P. (2003) 'Accountability and the Public/ Private Distinction', in Bamforth, N. and Leyland, P. (eds) *Public Law in a Multi-Layered Constitution*, Oxford, Hart Publishing.

Cane, P. (2004) *Introduction to Administrative Law* (4th edn) Oxford, Clarendon Press, Chapter 3.

Craig, P. (2004) 'The Common Law, Shared Power and Judicial Review', *Oxford Journal of Legal Studies* 24:129.

Further reading cont'd

Fordham, M. (2001) 'Judicial Review: The New Rules', *Public Law* 4.

Fredman, S. and Morris, G. (1995) 'The Costs of Exclusivity: Public and Private Re-examined', *Public Law* 68.

Halliday, S. (2004) *Judicial Review and Compliance with Administrative Law*, Oxford University Press.

Harlow, C. (2000) 'Export, Import: the Ebb and Flow of English Public Law', *Public Law* 240.

Le Sueur, A. (1992) 'Applications for Judicial Review: The Requirement of Leave', *Public Law* 102.

Miles, J. (2003) 'Standing in a Multi-Layered Constitution', in Bamforth and Leyland (eds) (above).

Richardson, G. and Genn, H. (eds) (1994) *Administrative Law and Government Action*, Oxford University Press, Part 1.

Taggart, M. (ed.) (1997) *The Province of Administrative Law*, Oxford, Hart Publishing, Chapters 1, 2, 10.

Woolf, Sir H. (1995) 'Droit Publique, English Style', *Public Law* 57.

Part IV

Human Rights

Chapter 19

Human rights and civil liberties

> The absurd device of a bill of rights. (Michael Oakeshott)

> Democracy is the will of the people but the people may not will to invade those rights which are fundamental to democracy itself. (Lady Hale in *R (Countryside Alliance) v Attorney General* (2008))

Key words

- Law and democracy
- Interest balancing
- Constitutional dialogue
- Individual and community
- Positive and negative duties
- Proportionality
- Deference
- The limits of interpretation
- Horizontality

19.1 Introduction: The Bill of Rights Debate

The concept of human rights concerns attempts to identify fundamental human interests which have a special status in the sense that they should not be violated, either at all or only in extreme circumstances. They concern basic needs such as personal freedom, privacy and freedom of religion; political interests such as freedom of expression and association; fairness and justice such as the right to a fair trial before an independent judge. Many of them conflict with each other and may also conflict with social goals such as security and the fair distribution of wealth. Human rights are strongly favoured by liberals but less so by communitarians among whom they may be regarded as divisive, selfish and frustrating community values. Human rights are also favoured by many lawyers because they raise the political importance of courts substituting authoritative pronouncements by judges within a limited framework of formal argument for the wider ranging discussions and compromises of the political forum.

Human rights did not become a prominent legal issue in the UK until the aftermath of the Second World War which produced a worldwide reaction against the atrocities of the Nazis.

There are three interrelated issues. Firstly what is a human right? Is it anything other than a political claim? The classic Enlightenment writers, notably Locke (Chapter 2) thought that there were certain natural rights given by God which it is the state's duty to protect. In his case these were life, health, liberty and property. For Hobbes by contrast there are no rights other than those created and enforced by law. Natural rights are based on the universal human interests of gain, safety and reputation and are essentially rational reasons for action rather than rights as such. They include primarily self defence, 'do-as-you-would-be-done-by' and the honouring of promises. From a utilitarian perspective, Bentham regarded the notion of rights as 'nonsense on stilts' except in the sense of interests protected by particular laws.

There is no agreement as to how we identify human rights. Some claim that they are revealed by God, others that they are based upon the idea that humans have a special 'dignity', others that they are self evident, being derived from basic human needs. For example the UN Universal Declaration of Human Rights (1948, Cmd 7226) is founded on the 'inherent dignity . . . of all members of the human family', equality, rationality and 'brotherhood' (Preamble Article 1). However in the absence of a religious belief it is difficult to see where this 'dignity' comes from. Some, for example Hume (Chapter 2), claim that human rights are driven by our natural sympathy for others and that we create conventions underpinning particular ways of life which we desire to preserve. Others, following Kant, derive them from apparently self evident rational truths such as 'equality' or 'autonomy'. For example Dworkin (*Freedom's Law*, Oxford University Press, 1996) argues that certain interests such as freedom of expression and the right to a fair trial are non-negotiable conditions of a democratic society because they underpin equality, this being the nearest we can get to a bedrock principle.

Such grandiose assertions face the difficulty that they may be too vague to be applied in practice. Indeed politicians and officials drafting laws or international treaties might take refuge in vagueness as a way of producing agreement, while leaving the hard questions to be decided by others such as the courts. Indeed this was the case with the European Convention on Human Rights (ECHR) (see Marston, 'The UK's Part in the Preparation of the ECHR', 1993, *International and Comparative Law Quarter*ly 42:796). Moreover claims to universality face the problem of multiculturalism. Some rights, for example private property, may not be recognised in every culture and different cultures may understand particular rights and their limits in different ways. In the UK this feeds into a debate as to whether our human rights law should be confined by the limits of the ECHR or whether we should develop our own notion of human rights (which might be more or less liberal than the ECHR). At present the UK courts stick closely to Strasbourg jurisprudence.

This leads to the second issue. What is the legal basis for a statement of fundamental rights? The UK relies on the ECHR and the European Court of Human Rights. This came into force in 1953 as an international treaty under the auspices of the Council of Europe, which was established in 1949 and has 41 members. It derives from the Universal Declaration of Human Rights, a resolution of the UN General Assembly (1948) which is not in itself legally binding. As a response to Nazi atrocities the ECHR concentrates on the protection of individual freedom against state interference rather than what are known as 'second and third generation rights', these being respectively social claims such as housing and collective interests such as environmental quality. The ECHR is something of a bland compromise with many exceptions.

The third issue is who should have the last word in disputes relating to fundamental rights? In particular should a bill of rights be protected against being overridden by the democratic lawmaker? Even if we accept that the concept of human rights is meaningful and should be embedded in the law, nothing follows automatically from this as to what is the best mechanism for protecting it. The ultimate decision maker might for example be a court as in the US, an elected lawmaker as in the UK or a special body as in France.

Human rights disputes differ significantly from those with which the courts traditionally deal. There is fundamental and apparently never ending disagreement about the meaning and application of human rights concepts. Rather than requiring the application of an existing rule human rights cases often require the judge to assess the validity of a legal rule or government decision against a vague aspirational concept such as 'freedom of expression' and to decide the extent to which a right should be sacrificed to some important public goal, for example personal freedom against the suppression of terrorism. Thus a human rights dispute often raises wide issues affecting society as a whole going beyond the interests of the particular parties. As we saw in Chapter 2 there are different perspectives upon political values which are incommensurable, lacking any overriding principle against which they can be assessed. For this reason it is often doubted whether the legal process with its limited sources of information, its authoritative solution imposed from above and its formalised narrowly focused participants is an appropriate way of deciding human rights disputes. The legal process is vulnerable to the republican attack that it gives the judge the power of arbitrary domination. In other words human rights might be understood as basic conditions of our collective life and as such pervading all spheres of activity. From this perspective it could be wrong to give the legal sphere a special status.

It is often claimed that the courts are most likely to produce the 'best' outcome, being independent, open and guided by intense rational analysis as a forum for public debate. However arguments about what is the best outcome merely repeat the disagreement. Unless we agree as to what counts as a best outcome, we could not agree what mechanism is most likely to produce it. A court is attractive to those who wish to impose philosophical master principles on others but less so to those who rely on a pragmatic accommodation between competing interests. A court is limited by the circumstances and parties in a particular case and the legal process is not comfortable with wide ranging debate. While judges may be good at interpreting and applying linguistic formulae, conflicts between fundamental rights and other important interests go beyond legal rules into territory where judges have no special expertise, requiring them either to be political philosophers or politicians or to resort to semantic evasion. For example, in *Secretary of State for the Home Department* v *JJ* (2008) disagreement in the House of Lords turned upon the semantic question of the line between a 'deprivation of liberty' and a restriction on liberty, the former but not the latter being a violation of a Convention right.

The main role of a court based on the separation of powers is to apply a legal rule made by others to a specific case using methods which enjoy substantial public agreement. Of course many, if not all, everyday legal principles are to some extent vague and therefore the subject of disagreement. For example does the term 'vehicle' include a child's scooter? This kind of difficulty can usually be resolved pragmatically by reference to the context and purpose of the legislation in question. In human rights cases these are the very matters on which there is often unresolvable disagreement. Moreover in a human rights case the public interest supported by the right usually has to be 'weighed' against a competing public interest. Since there is no objective way of doing this, or at least one which commands widespread support, the task may be more appropriate to a democratic body which may be able to negotiate a solution acceptable to most of those involved rather than to a court.

In *Marper* v *UK* (2008) the European Court condemned the UK practice of retaining DNA samples indefinitely from people arrested or charged with offences irrespective of whether they were subsequently convicted. The House of Lords had upheld the practice under the Human Rights Act (*R (S)* v *Chief Constable of South Yorkshire Police* (2004)). The difference between the two courts seems to lie mainly in that the English judges placed less importance on the offence to human dignity involved (Lady Hale dissenting), gave greater weight to the policing advantages of the practice and had greater confidence in the integrity and competence of the police not to misuse the power. Is it possible objectively to choose between these two approaches?

The favourite liberal argument in favour of a court is fear of what De Toqueville called 'the tyranny of the majority'. The argument runs that 'democracy' is more than just the will of the majority and must be policed by certain basic rights of equality and freedom protected against the volatility, corruption or foolishness of the majority. It is argued that handing over power to a court is not anti-democratic but a prudent 'pre-commitment' of a majority anxious to guard against its own weaknesses, for example a panic overreaction to a supposed threat such as that of terrorism. By removing fundamental rights from its control, the majority lessens the risk that it will misuse its power. In particular a court can protect unpopular minorities.

However Waldron draws on the republican argument (Chapter 2) that we sacrifice dignity, equality and control over our lives by letting unelected judges decide whether laws are valid. The appropriate question is what mechanism can most appropriately manage disagreement? Arguably this should be a democratic assembly in which the whole community can participate on equal terms (see Waldron, 1999).

The Human Rights Act (HRA) 1998 recognises this irreducible disagreement by trying to accommodate both sides. It uses the advantages of the courts in applying the law even to the extent of scrutinising statutes for compatibility with the ECHR. On the other hand the Act upholds democracy by leaving the final word with Parliament while empowering the courts to put pressure on Parliament, thereby creating an accommodation in accordance with the separation of powers. In this way the HRA is sometimes said to create a 'constitutional dialogue'.

19.2   The Common Law

English lawyers have traditionally used the terminology of negative freedom (Chapter 2) and civil liberties rather than the positive language of rights. The traditional common law standpoint has been that everyone is free to do whatever the law does not specifically prohibit. In Hobbes' language, 'freedom lies in the silence of the laws'. However in a constitution based on unlimited parliamentary power the problem lies in ensuring that the laws are indeed silent. Moreover the notion of negative freedom assumes that all freedoms are of equal value. For example, Dicey (1915, p.500) may appear complacent:

> English law no more favours and provides for the holding of public meetings than for the giving of public concerts . . . A man has a right to hear an orator as he has a right to hear a band or eat a bun.

The common law's residual approach therefore depends on trusting the lawmaker not to enact intrusive laws and trusting the courts to interpret laws in a way sympathetic to individual liberty. This violates republican ideas by treating us as 'happy slaves' content with a kind master. We have met the presumption of statutory interpretation, known as the 'principle of legality', that clear language or necessary implication is required to override fundamental rights (Chapters 7 and 9). However this cannot surmount the creeping erosion of liberty by the accumulation of statutes which, taken individually, are relatively innocuous but which add up to a formidable armoury of state powers. Numerous Acts were passed from 1997 restricting individual liberty in order to combat antisocial behaviour and latterly terrorism (see *Guardian*, 2 April 2006). Moreover legislation enacted to deal with a particular problem may be used for other purposes. The Terrorism Act 2000 for example was used to remove an octogenarian heckler from the 2005 Labour Party Conference and the Serious Organised Crimes and Police Act 2005 to arrest a demonstrator for possession of an article in *Vanity Fair* critical of the government (see HL Deb. 1 Feb. 2006, cols 231, 239; *Guardian*, 29 June 2006).

It is claimed that the common law, being open to any argument and treating all parties as equals, is especially suitable for a liberal society (Allan, *Constitutional Justice*, Oxford University Press, 2001). Indeed until the Human Rights Act 1998 the UK had resisted incorporation of the ECHR on the basis that the common law provided equivalent protection (see *Brind* v *Secretary of State for the Home Department* (1991) and *Attorney-General* v *Guardian Newspapers (No. 2)* (1998) at 660 (Lord Goff)). However the two approaches are different in important respects. Firstly the ECHR requires special justification to override a right, whereas in the common law any sufficiently clearly worded statute will do. Secondly the common law, sometimes described as unprincipled, is multifactoral in the sense that it depends on accumulating factors pointing to or against a particular conclusion without necessarily organising these within a formal hierarchy of principles.

19.3 The European Convention on Human Rights

The ECHR imposes duties on the state to comply with the rights embodied in it. A few of the rights are absolute but most can be overridden in certain circumstances by other rights or by the public interest. It is frequently asserted that a principle of 'fair balance' between individual rights and the wider interests of society runs through the whole Convention (for example *Kay* v *Lambeth London Borough Council* (2006) [32] Lord Bingham; *Sporrong and Lonnroth* v *Sweden* (1982) [52]). Thus even the 'absolute' rights might be qualified. It has also been proclaimed that the ECHR is a 'living instrument' to be interpreted in the light of changing values and circumstances (for example *Tyrer* v *UK* (1978)).

The ECHR has three roles under the UK constitution.

1. Individuals can petition the European Court of Human Rights in Strasburg alleging that the state has violated their rights under the Convention. The court may award compensation and require the state to change its law. However its decisions are binding only in international law under the Convention itself and have no direct binding force in domestic law. The court sometimes gives a 'margin of appreciation' to the state. This acknowledges the liberal value of diversity and allows the convention to be applied flexibly in the light of particular variations in the values and needs of different countries. Without this room for manoeuvre it would be difficult to obtain general

acceptance of the court's jurisdiction (see *Handyside* v *UK* (1976): pornography; *Leander* v *Sweden* (1987): security). The margin of appreciation is of course limited and does not amount to acceptance of cultural relativism. States cannot disregard fundamental values and standards supported by a consensus among member states and the court will review the reasonableness of the state action (see for example *Funke* v *France* (1993) [55]–[57]; *Marper* v *UK* (2008), [102]).

2. As a treaty the Convention should be taken into account by domestic courts when interpreting statutes at least where they are ambiguous. The common law should probably also be developed in the light of the Convention (see *Attorney-General* v *Guardian Newspapers Ltd (No. 2)* (1998)).

3. The Human Rights Act 1998 which came into force in October 2000 incorporates the main provisions of the Convention, but not the Convention as such, into UK law and provides a special mechanism for applying them. 1 and 2 (above) are not affected by the Human Rights Act. As Lord Bingham pointed out in *R (Al-Skeini)* v *Secretary of State* (2007) [10], rights *under* the Convention differ from rights created by the 1998 Act *by reference to* the Convention. The most significant feature of the Human Rights Act is that it empowers the courts to assess whether an Act of Parliament is compatible with a Convention Right. However the court has no power under the Act to overturn an Act of Parliament so that the traditional doctrine of parliamentary supremacy is preserved. Arguably this is a quibble since a court ruling that a statute does not comply with the Convention has great political force particularly where the government lacks moral authority.

The ECHR is primarily concerned with 'negative' rights protected against state interference as opposed to positive rights requiring state action to give effect to the right. There are two kinds of positive right. The first is where the right requires the state to provide some positive benefit or facility such as welfare services or formal acceptance of a minority status (see *Rees* v *UK* (1986): transsexuality). In a democracy courts are reluctant to impose this kind of duty on the state since it may involve choices about public spending that are regarded as more appropriate to an elected body. Moreover liberals may object to the impact of positive rights on the free market and the likely conflict with individual liberty and initiative (see Sunstein, '*Against Positive Rights*' 2/1 *East European Constitutional Review* 35 (1993)). This raises the irreducible clash between positive and negative freedom which we met in Chapter 2. Only in cases of extreme destitution does the ECHR enter the territory of positive rights in this sense. There are however other international treaties dealing with social and political rights of a positive kind, notably the UN International Covenant on Economic, Social and Cultural Rights (1976). These have not been incorporated into domestic law and contain no enforcement machinery. Some constitutions, notably those in states associated with the former Soviet Union contain a range of economic and social rights.

The second kind of positive right is where the state is required to ensure not only that itself but also that private bodies respect the right in question. It is not enough that the state does not interfere with the right. It must also take active steps to protect the right (see Lord Steyn in *R (Ullah)* v *Special Adjudicator* (2004) [34]; Fredman, 'Human Rights Transformed: Positive Duties and Positive Rights', 2006, *Public Law* 562). Such positive obligations are unlikely to be absolute and the state will be afforded a margin of discretion in carrying them out (below; see *R (Pretty)* v *DPP* (2002) [15]). Particular examples include the right to life, respect for privacy and family life and press freedom. Thus the state must ensure not only that the media is free to inform the public but also that the privately owned press respects the privacy of individuals.

The following provisions of the ECHR are incorporated into the Human Rights Act 1998 (s.1):

Article 2: Right to life.
Except for capital punishment following criminal conviction, defence against unlawful violence, lawful arrest or prevention of unlawful escape, lawful action for quelling riot or insurrection. This requires the state not to take life without qualification and to provide a positive framework of laws to protect life. It must also hold an open, effective and thorough investigation into an unexplained death involving the state (see *R (Middleton)* v *West Sussex Coroner* (2004); *R (Hurst)* v *North London District Coroner* (2007); see also *R (D)* v *Secretary of State for the Home Department* (2006): supervision of suicide risk; *Thompson and Venables* v *News Group Newspapers Ltd* (2001); *Van Colle* v *Chief Constable of Hertfordshire Police* (2006): protection of witness). However this duty is not absolute but only to take reasonable precautions. In so far as there is a duty to prevent loss of life it is narrow, requiring a real and immediate risk objectively verified (*Re Officer L* (2007); *R (Gentle* v *Prime Minister* (2008): right to life not engaged by decision to go to war in Iraq). In another respect Article 2 has been interpreted narrowly so as not to authorise voluntary euthanasia (*R (Pretty)* v *DPP* (2002): the right to life is the right not to be killed, not to have control over one's own life). The court emphasised that the Convention is not meant to intervene in controversial moral issues around which there is no consensus. This is one way in which the court deals with the problem that it lacks democratic legitimacy.

Article 3: Torture or inhuman or degrading treatment or punishment.
This is an absolute right which cannot be overridden (see for example *Tyrer* v *UK* (1978); *Costello-Roberts* v *UK* (1993): severe corporal punishment; *Ireland* v *UK* (1978): interrogation of suspected terrorists; sensory deprivation not torture but inhuman treatment). Article 3 was applied to a government decision to withdraw welfare support from asylum seekers where to do so would result in destitution thereby imposing a positive duty (*R (Limbuela)* v *Secretary of State for Social Security* (2007)). However it was emphasised that Article 3 does not confer a right to be provided with welfare services as such. In *Limbuela* the inhuman treatment resulted from a specific exclusion of failed asylum seekers from the normal provision. The House of Lords emphasised that Article 3 was engaged only when, taking account of all the claimant's circumstances, age, health, gender, other means of support and so on, the claimant was reduced to a sense of despair and humiliation for example by having no access to toilet or washing facilities. The prohibition of torture means that the UK government cannot use evidence which might have been obtained by torture in other countries in legal proceedings here (*A* v *Secretary of State for the Home Department (No. 2)* (2005); Chapter 21). However it seems that the government might still use evidence obtained by torture overseas as part of its investigations. The government has a positive duty to ensure that private persons do not violate Article 3 rights, for example child beating (*A* v *UK* (1998)).

Article 4: Slavery, forced or compulsory labour.
Exceptions are prison or parole, military service, emergency or calamity and 'normal civic obligations'.

▶ **Article 5: Liberty and security of person**.
This relates to deprivation of liberty. Except in prescribed cases in accordance with a procedure prescribed by law, this is an absolute right that cannot be overridden. The main exceptions are criminal convictions, disobedience to a court order, control of children, infection, mental health, alcoholism, drug addiction, vagrancy and in order to prevent illegal immigration or with a view to deportation or extradition. There are safeguards to ensure a speedy trial and adequate remedies against unlawful detention. A person arrested must be informed promptly of the reasons for the arrest, shall be brought promptly before a court and 'shall be entitled to take proceedings by which the lawfulness of his detention shall be decided speedily by a court and his release ordered if the detention is not lawful' . The right to personal liberty is given especially high importance (see for example *Secretary of State for the Home Dept* v *JJ* (2008)[37] [107]).

Article 5 has been weakened by drawing a distinction between deprivation of liberty and restrictions upon liberty. The latter does not fall within Article 5 (but could fall within Articles 3 or 8).

In *Austin* v *Metropolitan Police Commissioner* (2008) the Court of Appeal held that detaining a crowd for two hours within a cordon on the road was only a restriction on liberty and so not protected by the ECHR (see *Guzzardi* v *Italy (1980)*). It was stated rather curiously that a detention which is justified is not 'detention' at all within Article 5 ([102]–[105]). If this is so, it is difficult to see why the specific exceptions outlined in the previous paragraph are included. Thus and perhaps echoing the distinction between positive and negative freedom discussed in Chapter 2, the ECHR has held that the placing of a child in a foster home was not a deprivation of liberty since it was done by a responsible authority in the child's own interests (*HM* v *Switzerland* (2002)).

'Control Orders' made by the government under anti-terrorism legislation impose severe restriction of movement upon terrorist suspects including confinement in the home for many hours. These have also been treated as only restricting liberty. The matter is one of degree depending on all the circumstances but particularly upon the impact on the victim's ability to live a normal life (compare *Secretary of State for the Home Dept* v *JJ* (2008); *Secretary of State for the Home Dept* v *MB* (2008); *Secretary of State for the Home Dept* v *E* (2008)).

▶ **Article 6: Fair trial**.
'In relation to civil rights and obligations and the determination of any criminal charges against him there is a right to a fair trial in public before an independent and impartial tribunal established by law'. 'Civil rights and obligations' has a wide meaning including loss of employment opportunities and other important social and economic interests (*R (Wright)* v *Secretary of State* (2009): placing on Child Abuse Register). In a criminal case there must be further safeguards. These include a right 'to be informed promptly and in a language he understands and in detail, of the nature and cause of the accusation', adequate time and facilities to prepare a defence, a right to choose a lawyer and free legal assistance 'when the interests of

justice so require', a right to call witnesses and to examine opposing witnesses on equal terms and a right to an interpreter. However 'charged with a criminal offence' has been defined narrowly to exclude matters relating to sentencing and bail (*Phillips* v *UK* (2001); *R (DPP)* v *Havering Magistrates Court* (2001)).

Judgment shall be pronounced publicly. The press and public may be excluded from all or any part of the proceedings in the interests of morals, public order, national security in a democratic society, where the interests of juveniles or the protection of the private lives of the parties so require, or the extent strictly necessary in the opinion of the court in special circumstances where publicity would prejudice the interests of justice.

The right to a fair trial as a whole is not subject to exceptions and cannot be overridden by public interest concerns. However *individual ingredients* can be overridden as long as the trial overall is fair. For example in *Brown* v *Stott (Procurator Fiscal Dunfermline)* (2001), the Privy Council held that the requirement of the Road Traffic Act 1998 section 172(2) to disclose the name of the driver was not in breach of the right against self incrimination. The reason for this was the clear public interest in reducing the high rate of death and injury on the roads. Nevertheless the trial overall must be fair so that any shortfall in one respect must be compensated by scrupulous fairness in others. The court will look at the entire process. Thus where a decision maker is not itself independent and impartial, as in the case of administrative policy decisions, then as we saw in Chapters 16 and 17 judicial review may provide a sufficient safeguard (see *R (Alconbury Developments)* v *Secretary of State* (2001)). In cases involving claims to state secrecy evidence may sometimes be withheld from an accused person but if the safeguards for fairness are insufficient the trial may not go ahead (see Chapter 22).

Article 6 is primarily concerned with procedural matters. It may sometimes be difficult to distinguish procedural matters from matters of substantive law which might engage other parts of the Convention but not Article 6. For example in *Z* v *UK* (2002) a local authority was held to be in breach of Article 3 for failing to protect children but not in breach of Article 6. The domestic law of negligence had failed to protect the children, not because of any procedural immunity, but because of the limited scope of negligence law itself in relation to the duties of public bodies (Chapter 18). The same applies to the non-liability of the Crown in certain cases (*Matthews* v *Ministry of Defence* (2003); Chapter 14). The immunity of an MP, however, is arguably of a procedural nature (Chapter 11).

Article 7: No retrospective criminal laws.

Except in respect of acts which were criminal when committed according to the general principles of law recognised by civilised nations.

The following Articles are subject to being overridden by state actions taken in the public interest on a variety of grounds. As we shall see in the following chapter the court is required according to the principle of 'proportionality' to weigh the importance of the right in question not only to the person who is being interfered with but also to the public interest, against the public interest claimed by the state to justify overriding the right. Moreover this group of rights is vague and difficult to define. For these reasons the judicial process is especially problematic in this area.

▶ **Article 8: Respect for privacy, family life, home and correspondence.**
This is especially vague. Indeed unlike other rights which are phrased as definite entitlements Article 8 gives only an entitlement to 'respect' whatever that means. Article 8 is very wide and susceptible to the different traditions and values of individual states. The court therefore often gives a 'margin of appreciation' to each state (*Rees* v *UK* (1986): transsexual; *Olsson* v *Sweden* (1988): child care; contrast *Marper* v *UK* (2008): DNA samples from innocent people). Article 8 has two aspects. Firstly it protects against intrusion and surveillance. Secondly it embraces respect for personal autonomy and identity and has a social dimension including family and community relationships, culture and lifestyle: 'those features which are integral to a person's identity or ability to function socially as a person' (Lord Bingham in *R (Razgar)* v *Secretary of State for the Home Department* (2004) [9]; see for example *Wainright* v *Home Office* (2003): strip searches; *Pretty* v *UK* (2002) 35 EHRR 1 [61]: serious disability; *R (G)* v *Barnet London Borough Council* (2004) [69]; *Chapman* v *UK* (2001): ethnic group). It protects parenthood, gender and sexual preferences. Article 6 broadly reflects Mill's version of liberalism, namely that in the context of the good of society as a whole, people are happier when they choose for themselves what form of life and lifestyle to adopt (Chapter 2).

However the UK courts are reluctant to treat Article 8 liberally. In *M* v *Secretary of State for Work and Pensions* (2006) [24–9], Lord Nicholls and Lord Mance took the view that 'family life' did not include same sex couples on the ground that there was no European wide consensus on this matter. Article 8 does not confer a general right to self determination.

In *R (Countryside Alliance)* v *Attorney-General* (2008)) it was argued that the Hunting Act 2004, which makes hunting foxes and other wild mammals with dogs a criminal offence, violated Article 8 in that there was a right to participate in hunting as an aspect of countryside life and as a social activity integral to the personality. The House of Lords held that Article 8 was not engaged. It was accepted that in principle sporting and cultural activities, such as playing music could fall within Article 8 since these were an important aspect of human nature and self development. Hunting as traditionally carried out in the UK fell outside Article 8 because it was carried out in public and was a spectator sport open to all. At the heart of Article 8 is the idea of the personal and intimate. Moreover hunters were not a distinctive group so as to claim an identity analogous to an ethnic group. Some of the claimants were workers who serviced the hunt. It was held that Article 8 can apply to loss of livelihood but only where the loss of a job seriously impinges upon other aspects of Article 8 protection affecting the person's social relationships and status in society as a whole or involving loss of a home.

Article 8 applies to nuisances and environmental pollution although the courts are likely to give considerable weight to the limited resources of public authorities in this context (see *Guerra* v *Italy* (1998); *Hatton* v *UK* (2003); *Marcic* v *Thames Water Utilities* (2004)). Article 8 also applies to the restriction of employment at least where there are wider social consequences of social exclusion (*R (Wright)* v *Secretary of State for Health* (2009): placing on Child Abuse Register).

Article 8 protects the inviolability of the home but does not normally confer a positive right to be provided with a home or welfare benefits but only a right to be protected as to the use of an existing home against eviction for example, thus illustrating that the Convention's primary concern is with privacy interests rather than acting as a welfare agency (*Kay* v *Lambeth London Borough Council* (2006) [191–3]; *Harrow London Borough Council* v *Qazi* (2004) [50]; *N* v *Secretary of State for the Home Department* (2005)). However in serious cases Article 8, referring as it does to 'respect', may impose a positive duty to provide a benefit. This may arise in respect of vulnerable groups (for example *Chapman* v *UK* (2001): gypsies; *R (Bernard)* v *Enfield London Borough Council* (2002): disabled with children; *Anufrijeva* v *Southwark London Borough Council* (2004): asylum seekers). However there must be culpability in the sense of a deliberate or negligent failure to act which has foreseeably serious consequences *(Anufrijeva)*.

There may also be a positive obligation on the state to enable the expression of personal lifestyles and to protect Article 8 rights against violation by private bodies (see Lord Hope in *Harrow LBC* v *Qazi* (2004); *Campbell* v *MGN* (2004): press intrusion; Chapter 20). In *YL* v *Birmingham City Council* (2007) Lady Hale emphasised that the state has such a positive duty. However as we saw in Chapter 18 she was in the minority in her view that, partly for this reason, a private care home should be treated as having public functions so as to bring it directly within the ambit of the Human Rights Act. The state might however be required to regulate private care homes so as to ensure that they respect the Article 8 rights of their residents.

In one respect Article 8 may be weaker than the other protected rights. In *Harrow LBC* v *Qazi* (2004) a majority of the House of Lords held that property rights, in that case a right to evict a tenant, always overrode a right based only on Article 8 and that personal circumstances were not relevant. However Lord Steyn (dissenting) remarked [27]:

> It would be surprising if the views of the majority . . . withstood European scrutiny . . . The basic fallacy in the approach is that it allows domestic notions of title, legal and equitable rights and interests, to colour the interpretation of Art. 8 (1). The decision of today does not fit into the new landscape created by the 1998 Act.

And so it proved. In *Connors* v *UK* (2004) the European Court held that a decision by a local authority to evict gypsies from a site that it owned was contrary to Article 8. In *Kay* (above) the House of Lords modified *Qazi* to the extent that, in exceptional cases, personal circumstances could be taken into account. *Connors* was such a case since gypsies are vulnerable minorities. Another might be where the victim has special personal circumstances such as ill health. However Lord Bingham emphasised that personal circumstances which were catered for by statutory welfare services should not be relevant [38]. There shall be no interference by a public authority with an Article 8 right except such as is in accordance with the law and is necessary in a democratic society in the interests of national security, public safety or the economic well being of the country, for the prevention of disorder or crime, for the protection of health or morals, or for the protection of the rights and freedoms of others.

▷ **Article 9: Freedom of thought, conscience and religion.**
This includes a right to manifest religion or belief in worship, teaching, practice and observance. In order to avoid intolerance the courts have not attempted to define religion, which includes any kind of spiritual belief such as vegetarianism and pacifism, nor to assess the validity of a religious belief beyond deciding whether it is genuinely held. However while the 'holding' of a belief is entirely subjective, the 'manifestation' of belief has been subject to a broad objective threshold based on 'seriousness, coherence and consistency with human dignity' (see *R (Williamson)* v *Secretary of State for Education and Employment* (2005)). Thus despite the importance of respect for minority beliefs there is a tendency towards imposing orthodoxy by assessing the claimant's practices against those of dominant groups within the sect in question (for example *R (Begum)* v *Head Teacher and Governors of Denbigh High School* (2007): extreme version of Muslim dress lawfully forbidden in school); or by giving a broad margin of distinction to the majority opinion represented by Parliament, for example *R (Williamson)* v *Secretary of State* (above [50] [51]): 'light' corporal punishment in school in pursuance of fundamentalist Christianity outlawed; *Otto Preminger Institut* v *Austria* (1994): majority Catholic susceptibilities protected against offensive film. Moreover although in the *Denbigh case* (above) at 111, Lord Bingham emphasised the pluralistic, multicultural nature of our society, religion although important is regarded – as in the protestant tradition but certainly not universally – as essentially a private matter (see *Williamson* (above) [15]–[19]).

In the employment sphere the right to manifest religion has been held to be violated only where the employer fails to take reasonable steps to accommodate the religious requirements of the employee with its own interests. In *Copsey v WBB Devon Clays Ltd* (2005) an employee was dismissed for refusing to work on a Sunday. The employer had compelling economic reasons for Sunday working, had engaged in a long consultation process on the matter and had offered the employee an alternative position which was refused. The Court of Appeal held that in these circumstances Article 8 had not been violated. Mummery LJ appeared to go further, indicating that Article 8 was not engaged at all by requiring work which interfered with the manifestation of religion. Freedom to manifest one's religion or beliefs shall be subject only to such limitations as are prescribed by law and are necessary in a democratic society in the interests of public safety, for the protection of public order, health or morals or for the protection of the rights and freedoms of others. *Copsey* (above) illustrates that it may not be clear whether the matter concerns the extent of the right itself or whether an override should prevail. This will be discussed in the next chapter.

▷ **Article 10: Freedom of expression.**
This includes freedom to hold opinions and to receive and impart information and ideas without interference by public authority and regardless of frontiers. This article shall not prevent states from requiring the licensing of broadcasting, television or cinema enterprise. The exercise of these freedoms, since it carries with it duties and responsibilities, may be subject to such formalities, conditions, restrictions or penalties as are prescribed by law and are necessary in a democratic society in the interests of national security, territorial integrity or public safety, for the prevention of disorder or crime, for the protection of health or morals, for the protection of the

reputation or rights of others, for preventing the disclosure of information received in confidence or for maintaining the authority and impartiality of the judiciary.

Freedom of expression is discussed in greater depth in Chapter 21.

Article 11: Freedom of assembly and association.

This includes the right to form and to join trade unions. No restrictions shall be placed on these rights other than such as are prescribed by law and are necessary in a democratic society in the interests of national security or public safety, for the prevention of disorder or crime, for the protection of health or morals or for the protection of the rights and freedoms of others. This article shall not prevent the imposition of lawful restrictions on the exercise of those rights by members of the armed forces, of the police or of the administration of the state.

Freedom of assembly is discussed in Chapter 21.

Article 12: The right to marry and found a family according to national laws governing the exercise of the right.

In *R (Baiai)* v *Secretary of State for the Home Department* (2007) it was held that the courts must be vigilant to protect the right to marry but that it carries less weight than the fundamental rights of personal liberty, freedom of expression and access to the courts. In that case a requirement of Home Office consent for non-Anglican marriages by immigrants was held invalid on the basis that the immigration authority could only interfere with the right to marry in the case of a sham marriage and it must be shown that the marriages targeted made substantial inroads into the scheme of immigration control. Moreover 'marriage' has been narrowly interpreted as referring only to traditional marriages between biological men and women (*Rees* v *UK* (1986): transsexuals), leaving it to individual states to determine policy on this sensitive issue (for example *Wilkinson* v *Kitzinger* (2006): civil partnerships).

Article 14: Non Discrimination

'The enjoyment of the rights and freedoms set forth in this Convention shall be secured without discrimination on any ground such as sex, race, colour, language, religion, political or other opinion, national or social origin, association with a national minority, property, birth or other status.

Article 14 is not freestanding. It applies only where discrimination takes place in relation to one of the other convention rights, although no such right need actually have been violated. For example although there is no right to be housed, refusing housing for discriminatory reasons is unlawful (*R (Morris)* v *Westminster City Council* (2005): refusal of housing because dependent child had no immigration rights; *Ghaidan* v *Mendoza* (2004): inheritance by gay partner). However a tenuous link will not suffice (*M* v *Secretary of State for Work and Pensions* (2006): differential maintenance payments).

Article 14 was described by Lord Nicholls in *Ghaidan* v *Mendosa* (2004) [9] [19] as fundamental to the rule of law and calling for close scrutiny and by Lady Hale in the same case as 'essential to democracy which is founded on the principle that each individual has equal value' [132]. Although Article 14 has no express overrides, discrimination can nevertheless be justified on the basis of the overrides relevant to the Articles on which it is parasitic (see *Belgian Linguistics Case* (1968)). One way of rationalising this is to argue that 'discrimination' in itself means making an *unjustified* distinction so as to violate the principle of equality. However this has the danger of confusing whether discrimination has taken place with whether it should be overridden (see Baker, 'Comparison Tainted by Justification: Against a Compendious Question in Article 14 Discrimination', 2006, *Public Law* 476). Another is to rely on the principle of balance which is said to underlie the Convention as a whole (above).

The courts have often applied the following guidelines in Article 14 cases (see *Wandsworth London Borough Council* v *Michalack* (2002); compare *R (Carson)* v *Secretary of State for Work and Pensions* (2006)) recognising however that they overlap:

1. Do the facts fall within the ambit of one or more of the substantive convention provisions?
2. If so, was there differential treatment as respects that right between the complainant on the one hand and the other persons put forward for comparison (the chosen comparators) on the other?
3. Were the chosen comparators in an analogous position to the complainant's situation?
4. If so, did the difference in treatment have an objective and reasonable justification in accordance with proportionality?

In *A* v *Secretary of State for the Home Department* (2005) a statute failed the fourth test. The Anti-Terrorism, Crime and Security Act 2001 authorised the indefinite detention of a foreign national, whose presence in the UK the Home Secretary reasonably believes is a risk to national security and whom he reasonably suspects is a terrorist, unless the person voluntarily leaves the country. The government claimed that these powers were necessary because a non-national could not be deported to a place where he or she would be at risk of torture or inhuman or degrading treatment (*Chahal* v *UK* (1996)). The government argued that it would otherwise be impossible to deal with suspects who were too dangerous to be at large but against whom no criminal charges could be brought. The House of Lords held by an 8 to 1 majority that the derogation was discriminatory and without justification in singling out foreign nationals since the threat was no less from British terrorists. In response to *A*, the Prevention of Terrorism Act 2005 put restrictions of movement, 'control orders', on non-nationals and nationals alike (see Chapter 22).

Article 14 extends to forms of discrimination other than those listed (for example *Ghaidan* v *Mendoza* (2004): sexual orientation; *R (Douglas)* v *North Tyneside DC* (2004): age; *Wandsworth LBC* v *Michalack* (2002): family membership). It is not easy to identify its limits. In *R (S)* v *Chief Constable of South Yorkshire Police* (above) the House of Lords took the view that the discrimination must relate to a 'personal characteristic or status' shared by the disadvantaged group as opposed to a matter of behaviour only. Article 14 was therefore not engaged by a policy of retaining DNA samples taken lawfully from suspects who were later found to be innocent since the general category of 'innocent persons' was not capable of being a protected category. In another instance 'rough sleeper' was held not to be a protected category

(*M* v *Secretary of State for Work and Pensions* (2006)) nor was the hunting community (*R (Countryside Alliance)* v *Attorney-General* (2008)). Similarly a policy towards releasing prisoners on licence which was geared to the seriousness of the offence did not fall within Article 14 but fell only within Article 5 (*R (Clift)* v *Secretary of State for the Home Department* (2007). On the other hand 'overseas resident' and 'person responsible for a child under a residence order' have been held to be protected as having different legal rights and duties to UK residents and natural parents respectively (*R (Carson)* v *Secretary of State* (2006): claim to pension; *Francis* v *Secretary of State for Work and Pensions* (2006): maternity grant). A protected category can therefore be something voluntarily assumed. It is difficult to see an underlying rationale such as protecting a sense of identity. However certain 'suspect categories', race and sex being pre-eminent, which are central to identity and over which the victim has no choice, enjoy a high standard of protection in that especially strong reasons are required to justify discrimination on those grounds (see *R (Carson)* v *Secretary of State* (above), Lord Walker, see also Lord Carson [15–17, 32]; *Walker* v *UK* (2006)).

Article 15: Derogation
States can derogate or reserve from many rights under the Convention 'in time of war or other public emergency threatening the life of the nation' but only to the extent strictly required by the exigencies of the situation. This does not apply to Article 2: right to life, except in respect of a lawful act of war; nor to Article 3: torture and inhuman or degrading treatment or punishment; nor to Article 4(1): slavery or servitude; nor to Article 7: retrospective punishment.

Article 16:
Articles 10, 11 and 14 shall not prevent a state from imposing restrictions on the political activities of aliens.

Protocol 1, Article 1:
Every natural or legal person is entitled to the peaceful enjoyment of his possessions. No one shall be deprived of his possessions except in the public interest and subject to the conditions provided for by law and by the general principles of international law. The preceding provisions shall not, however, in any way impair the right of a State to enforce such laws as it deems necessary to control the use of property in accordance with the general interest or to secure the payment of taxes and or other contributions or penalties.

This protects property rights against confiscation without compensation but does not confer a positive right to acquire property (see *Marckx* v *Belgium* (1979)). Restrictions on the *use* of property imposed in the public interest, for example environmental and rent controls are valid without compensation, although the line between use and confiscation may be difficult to draw (*Mellacher* v *Austria* (1989); *Fredin* v *Sweden* (1991)). Moreover the courts are not willing to use the Convention in cases where a property right is restricted by the exercise of other property rights (see *Aston Cantlow and Wilmcote with Billesley Parochial Church Council* v *Wallbank* (2003): charge to repair church roof taking effect as a common law right). Property rights probably have a lower level of protection than the other human rights and the rights the state to override them are wider and less specific (see *R (Countryside Alliance)* v *Attorney General* (2008).

▷ **Protocol 1, Article 2: Education.** This is a limited right. It does not confer a right to be educated as such. Its primary purpose is to combat state discrimination and indoctrination. It does not require the state to provide education. It means only a right not be excluded from whatever education the state chooses to provide (*A v Head Teacher and Governors of Lord Grey School* (2004)). Nor does it include a right to state funding (*R (Douglas) v North Tyneside DC* (2004)).

> The State shall respect the right of parents to ensure such education and training in conformity with their own religious and philosophical convictions.

This raises the conflict between individualistic liberalism and liberal pluralism (Chapter 2) since religious education might favour repression against individuals. It also treats the right as that of the parent rather than that of the child itself, an attitude that could be regarded as misplaced. It probably prevents the state from outlawing 'faith schools' but is subject to the limits on the manifestation of religion mentioned above (*R (Williamson) v Secretary of State for Education and Employment* (2005)). Moreover the UK has made a reservation:

> only so far as compatible with 'the provision of efficient instruction and training and the avoidance of unreasonable public expenditure'.

▷ **Protocol 1, Article 3: Free elections to the legislature** at reasonable intervals by secret ballot (see *Hirst v UK (No. 2)* (2004)).

▷ **Protocol 6: Abolishes the death penalty in peacetime**. The Human Rights Act 1998 abolished the last remaining death penalty provisions in the UK (s.21(5)).

Summary

▷ The human rights debate involves attempts to accommodate competing and incommensurable values without any coherent overarching principle to enable a choice to be made. It is therefore arguable that an elected body rather than a court should have the last word. The Human Rights Act 1998 has attempted a compromise by leaving Parliament the last word but giving the court power to influence Parliament.

▷ Freedom in the common law is residual in the sense that one can do anything unless there is a specific law to the contrary. I suggested that this is an inadequate method of safeguarding important liberties. There is a debate as to the extent to which the common law embodies the principles of the ECHR and it is suggested that there are important differences in the approaches of the two systems.

▷ The ECHR as such is not strictly binding upon English courts but can be taken into account where the law is unclear or where a judge has discretionary powers. The individual can petition the European Court of Human Rights the decisions of which are binding in international law but unlike those of the European Court of Justice (in relation to European Union law) are not legally binding in domestic law.

▷ The HRA 1998, while not incorporating the Convention as such, has given the main rights created by the ECHR effect in domestic law. UK legislation must be interpreted to be compatible with convention rights but parliamentary supremacy is preserved.

Summary cont'd

▶ Most convention rights are negative rights which restrain the state from interfering with them. Some have a positive aspect by imposing a duty on the state to ensure that the right in question is respected.

▶ Some of the rights are absolute and cannot be overridden by public interest considerations although they might be defined narrowly in the light of the public interest. Other rights are subject to being overridden on prescribed grounds of public interest or of other rights.

▶ Some rights, notably deprivation of liberty are narrowly defined, others, notably privacy and family life are broad and vague.

▶ Some rights, notably the right to life, protection against torture, deprivation of liberty, freedom of expression and non-discrimination have an especially high status. The right to property may have a lower level of protection than other rights.

Exercises

19.1 'Human Rights are permeated with irresolvable disagreement as to what they mean, how they apply, and as to the nature of disputes about them. The courts are therefore a hopelessly inadequate mechanism for resolving human rights problems'. Discuss.

19.2 Explain the scope of Article 14 of the ECHR. Does it go far enough in combating discrimination?

19.3 'Democracy is the will of the people but the people may not will to invade those rights which are fundamental to democracy itself.' Lady Hale in *R (Countryside Alliance)* v *Attorney General* (2008) Discuss.

19.4 Compare the legal effect of the ECHR with that of the European Union (Chapter 10).

19.5 What is meant by a deprivation of liberty under the ECHR?

19.6 You are the leader of a pressure group representing the hunting community. What arguments could you raise to challenge the decision of the Law Lords in *R (Countryside Alliance)* v *Attorney General* (2008)?

Further reading

Alder, J. (2006) 'The Sublime and the Beautiful: Incommensurability and Human Rights', *Public Law* 697.

Amos, M. (2006) *Human Rights Law*, Oxford, Hart Publishing.

Campbell, T., Ewing, K.D. and Tomkins, A. (eds) (2001) *Sceptical Essays on Human Rights*, Oxford University Press, Chapters 3, 6, 7.

Gearty, C. (2006) *Can Human Rights Survive?* Cambridge University Press (Hamlyn Lectures).

Harvey, C. (2004) 'Talking about Human Rights', *European Human Rights Law Review* 500.

Hill, M, Sandberg, R., (2007), 'Is Nothing Sacred? Clashing Symbols in a Secular World', *Public Law* 488.

Jowell, J. (2003) 'Judicial Deference and Human Rights: a Question of Competence', in Craig, P. and Rawlings, R. (eds) *Law and Administration in Europe*, Oxford University Press.

Further reading cont'd

Leader, S. (2007) 'Freedom and futures: Personal Priorities, Institutional Demands and Freedom of Religion', *Modern Law Review* 70:713.

Mahoney, P. (1998) 'Marvellous Richness of Diversity or Invidious Cultural Relativism', *Human Rights Law Journal* 19:1.

Poole,T. (2005) "Of headscarves and heresies: *The Denbigh High School* case and public authority decision making under the Human Rights Act", *Public Law* 685.

Symposium (2007) 'Can Human Rights Survive?', *Public Law* 209.

Tomkins, A. (2002) 'In Defence of the Political Constitution', *Oxford Journal of Legal Studies* 22:157.

Waldron, J. (2006) 'The Core of the Case against Judicial Review', *Yale Law Journal*, 115(6):1346.

Williams, A. (2007) 'Human Rights and Law: Between Sufferance and Insufferability', *Law Quarterly Review* 123:133.

Chapter 20

The Human Rights Act 1998

General Scope of the Act

The extent to which the Human Rights Act (HRA) is radical is controversial. On the one hand according to Lord Hoffmann (*R* v *Secretary of State for the Home Department ex parte Simms* (1999) 412, 413) the Human Rights Act does little more than reinforce the existing law. It has three aims. These are firstly to provide a specific text, much of it in his view reflecting existing common law principles; secondly to enact the existing 'principle of legality' (Chapter 7), according to which fundamental rights can be overridden only by explicit statutory language or necessary implication; and thirdly to force Parliament to face squarely what it is doing. Similarly in *R* v *Secretary of State for Health ex parte C* (2000) he remarked that the Act 'was no doubt intended to strengthen the rule of law but not to inaugurate the rule of lawyers'. (See also his speech in *R (Alconbury Developments)* v *Secretary of State* (2001) emphasising a desire to relate the Act to the characteristics of UK parliamentary government.) In *R* v *Lambert* (2001) at 603, Lord Hope emphasised

> the need (a) to respect the will of the legislature so far as this remains appropriate and (b) to preserve the integrity of our statute law so far as this is possible.

On the other hand in *R* v *DPP ex parte Kebeline* (1999) Lord Hope emphasised that a generous approach should be taken to the scope of fundamental rights and freedoms, and in *R* v *Lambert* [2001] 3 All ER 577 at 581, Lord Slynn remarked:

> it is clear that the 1998 Act must be given its full import and that long or well entrenched ideas may have to be put aside, sacred calves culled.

However a conservative approach has been predominant. In *R (S)* v *Chief Constable of South Yorkshire Police* (2004) the House of Lords considered that the application of the ECHR should be decided on a uniform basis throughout member states. This rejected the approach taken in the Court of Appeal that English law might develop its own higher standard of human rights. Their Lordships' actual decision was rejected in *Marper* v *UK* (2008) (above p. 375). In *R (Begum)* v *Head Teacher and Governors of Denbigh High School* (2006) [29] it was said that the purpose of the Act was not to enlarge human rights but to apply the Convention in domestic law, and in *R (Pretty)* v *DPP* (2002) that the purpose of the Convention was to reflect a European consensus and not to lead opinion.

The Human Rights Act does not incorporate the European Convention on Human Rights as such. By virtue of section 1 it gives the rights outlined above the status of 'convention rights', having specific consequences in UK law. Decisions and opinions of the European Court of Human Rights must be taken into account although they are not binding on the UK court (s.2(1)). However the House of Lords has consistently emphasised that the European Court must be followed unless there are special reasons not to do so (*R (Clift)* v *Secretary of State* (2007); *R* v *Secretary of State ex parte Quark Fishing Ltd* (2006) [34]; *R (Gentle)* v *Prime Minister* (2008)). Thus the Act does not entitle the UK to develop its own bill of rights. On the other hand the ECHR allows for a 'margin of appreciation'. Within limits based on the importance of the particular right and the extent of consensus among member states this allows a state to apply the Convention in accordance with its own values and constitutional traditions (see Lord Hoffman in *R (Alconbury Developments) v Secretary of State* 2001). Moreover except perhaps where the whole rationale of the previous case has been undermined, courts below the House of Lords must follow domestic cases even if they are inconsistent with Strasbourg rulings (*Lambeth LBC v Kay* (above) [43, 44, 45]).

The HRA has not incorporated Article 1: duty to secure to everyone within the jurisdiction the rights and freedoms under the Convention, nor Article 13: effective domestic remedies for breach of the Convention; it being argued that the Act itself achieves these aims even though convention rights must give way to Acts of Parliament.

The HRA is sometimes described as a 'partnership' between the three branches of government. It respects the separation of powers by making specific provisions concerning the relationship between the three branches (see Lord Hobhouse in *Wilson v First County Trust* (2003)).

1. As regards the legislature, the court cannot override an Act of Parliament (s.3(2)(b)) thereby preserving parliamentary supremacy. If an Act of Parliament violates a convention right, the court must enforce it but can make a 'declaration of incompatibility' (s.4) which invites Parliament or the executive to change the law (below). This is often described as a 'constitutional dialogue' between the two branches but if so it is a limited and formalised one. Thus as with other aspects of the separation of powers the practical relationship between the courts, Parliament and the executive depends on political forces and the relative moral authority each is able to command. It has been suggested that this kind of 'Parliamentary' Bill of Rights differs little in its effect from an 'entrenched' bill of rights that empowers courts to overturn legislation. The court is likely to enjoy greater public respect than the government and legislation is likely to be drafted with judicial review in mind (see Hiebert, 'Parliamentary Bills of Rights: An Alternative Model', (2006) *Modern Law Review* 69:7).

2. The courts are required to interpret all legislation if it 'is possible to do so' in order to comply with convention rights (s.3). This evasive formula means that the balance between the courts and Parliament depends upon how radical the courts are prepared to be in manipulating or departing from statutory language when applying the Human Rights Act to other legislation.

3. A 'public authority' including the executive and the courts is liable in the courts for failing to comply with a convention right unless this is required by a statute or other primary legislation (ss.6, 7).

4. Under section 19 a minister of the Crown in charge of a bill in either House of Parliament must, before the second reading of the bill (a) make a statement to the effect that in his or her view the provisions of the bill are compatible with convention rights (a 'statement of compatibility'); or (b) make a statement to the effect that although he or she is unable to make a statement of compatibility, the government nevertheless wishes the House to proceed with the bill. The statement must be in writing and published in such manner as the minister making it considers appropriate.

Apart from putting political pressure on the government, it is not clear what is the effect of a statement of compatibility. As a statement of the opinion of the executive, the courts should not defer to it when interpreting the legislation in question (*Wilson v First County Trust* (above)). Indeed a statement of compatibility means little where the statute in question confers a wide discretion on the executive or the police. Moreover because the statement applies only to the second reading it does not cover amendments that might be included at later stages. There is a Joint Parliamentary Committee on Human Rights which considers all bills having human rights implications and this might give some reinforcement to section 19.

The HRA applies to legislation made both before and after it came into force in October 2000 (s.3(2)(a)). However the Act is not in general retrospective. It applies only to events that occurred after it came into force. This seems to be strictly applied (see *R (Hurst)* v *North London District Coroner* (2007): death occurring before Act came into force but a decision not to resume inquest made after Act came into force: Act not applicable (Lady Hale and Lord Mance dissenting)). There is an exception in the case of a defence to proceedings brought by a public authority. Here it applies whenever the action complained of took place.

<h3>20.1.1   Extraterritorial Application</h3>

It is unclear how far the HRA applies in respect of actions outside UK territory. The ECHR imposes a duty on states to secure the rights in respect of everyone 'within their jurisdiction'. There is an argument that international relations might be destabilised if the courts interfere with matters occurring abroad. In *R (Al-Skeini)* v *Secretary of State for Defence* (2007) the House of Lords took a cautious approach. It was held that the Act could in principle apply outside UK territory (Lord Bingham dissenting) but that it applied only where the UK was exercising powers of a kind associated with government including perhaps diplomatic and other activities recognised in international law as having extra territorial jurisdiction. Thus Article 2 (right to life) applied to the death of a prisoner in territory under the control of the British Army but not to deaths in the course of a military campaign (see also *R (Gentle)* v *Prime Minister* (2008); *R (Al Saadoon)* v *Secretary of State* (2009)). As we saw in Chapter 6 the House of Lords disagreed as to the circumstances in which the HRA applies to British dependent territories (*R* v *Secretary of State ex parte Quark Fishing* (2006)).

Under the UN Refugee Convention (1951) a person cannot be deported to a country where he or she is likely to suffer torture or degrading or inhuman treatment or punishment (Article 3). In *R (Ullah)* v *Special Adjudicator* (2004) the House of Lords extended this to the risk of serious violations of other convention rights (see *Chahal* v *UK* (1996)). This raises problems most obviously in relation to Article 8 – respect for family life – and Article 9 – religion – because of the cultural and social differences involved. In *R (Wellington)* v *Secretary of State* (2008) the House of Lords held that Article 3 should be construed less strictly in cases involving extradition in that case to the US. Otherwise extradition arrangements might be at risk. There is also the consideration that the HRA should not impose a positive duty on the government to provide medical or other welfare services. Contrast *R (Razgar)* v *Secretary of State for the Home Department* (2004): serious mental illness if Kurdish refugee returned to Germany; upheld under Article 8 (Baroness Hale dissenting), with *N* v *Secretary of State for the Home Department* (2005): likelihood of earlier death from AIDS if deported to Uganda due to lower level of treatment available; refused under Article 3. The fact that medical treatment or other support are worse than in the UK does not engage convention rights except in exceptional cases (for example *D* v *UK* (1997): final stages of AIDS and no family support). According to Lord Steyn in *Ullah*

[50] in cases other than Article 3 there must be a 'real risk of a flagrant violation of the very essence of the right' (see Wilde, 'The Extraterritorial Application of the Human Rights Act', 2005, *Current Legal Issues* 65:47).

20.2 The Interpretative Obligation

At the heart of the Act is the requirement that:

> so far as is possible to do so, primary legislation and subordinate legislation must be read and given effect in a way which is compatible with Convention rights. (s.3 (1))

For this purpose primary legislation includes statutes, measures of the Church Assembly and the General Synod of the Church of England and delegated legislation that brings into force or amends primary legislation. A Prerogative Order in Council is also primary legislation even though the courts can set it aside on other grounds in judicial review proceedings (*R (Bancoult)* v *Secretary of State for Foreign and Commonwealth Office (No. 2)* (2008)). Acts of the Scottish Parliament and Northern Ireland Assembly are not primary legislation (s.21). The court cannot set primary legislation aside but can set aside subordinate legislation unless primary legislation makes it impossible to do so (s.3(2)).

The limits of the section 3 obligation to interpret in line with the Convention are not precise and depend primarily on the judges' attitude to the constitutional limits on their function. The court has to keep to the right side of the border between interpretation and legislation. The government did not introduce a strong formula of the kind used in Canada under which a statute must expressly state that it overrides the Bill of Rights (Cmnd 3782, 2.10). Nevertheless section 3(1) was apparently intended to be a strong provision. The court is not confined to cases where the provision is ambiguous (*R v A* (2001); *Ghaidan* v *Mendoza* (2004)).

In *Wilson* v *First County Trust* (2003) the House of Lords emphasised that the normal assumption of statutory interpretation, namely that the court is seeking the intention of Parliament, does not apply and that it is for the court to make an independent judgment as to whether the language of the statute can be read in a way to make it compatible with the Convention (Chapter 8). Nor does the court apply the normal principle that the ordinary meaning of the statute must prevail. In *Harrow LBC* v *Qazi* (2004) Lord Bingham said [23]:

> The court has to arrive at a judicial choice between two possibilities, a choice which transcends the business of finding out what the legislation's words mean.

In *Ghaidan* v *Mendoza* (2004) a statutory provision entitled a person who had lived with a tenant 'as husband and wife' to succeed to the tenancy on the tenant's death. A majority of the House of Lords held that a homosexual relationship fell within the phrase 'living as husband and wife', which they made Convention-compatible by inserting the words 'if they were' after 'as'. The House held that even if the ordinary meaning of the statute is clear, the court could still distort its language or read in additional wording in order to achieve a meaning that complied with the Convention. The court should take a broad purposive approach. The boundary of the court's power depended on two factors. Firstly the interpretation must not go against the grain of the legislation in the sense of contradicting its underlying purpose. The courts must look beyond the language itself and consider the policy context and legislative history of the statute in order to identify the essential features of the statutory scheme in question which they must not violate. Secondly the courts must not make decisions for which they are not equipped in the sense of producing an interpretation that raises social or economic issues that are best left to Parliament.

The language of the statute is however a side constraint. The courts can strain, supplement but not contradict the statutory language and have been warned to refrain from 'judicial vandalism' (*R (Anderson) v Secretary of State for the Home Department* [2002] 4 All ER 1089, 1102–3: power given to Home Secretary to interfere with sentencing process could not be circumvented; see Nicol, 'Statutory Interpretation after Anderson', 2004, *Public Law* 273; Kavanagh, 2004). In *Ghaidan* Lord Millett gave the example of the word 'cat' in a statute [72]. In some circumstances 'cat' might be read to include 'dog' for example where the care of pets was the underlying concern. However if the legislation had originally stated 'Siamese cats' and later been amended to 'cats', this route would not be possible.

The following are examples (see also table provided by Lord Steyn in *Ghaidan*).

- *R (Hurst) v North London Coroner* (2007): The governing statute required a Coroner to investigate ' how' a deceased came by his death. In the case of deaths prior to the Human Rights Act 'how' is construed narrowly to mean 'by what means'. In the case of post Human Rights Act deaths, 'how' means 'in what circumstances' thereby allowing a wider ranging inquiry into deaths in custody

- *R v Lambert* (2001): Under section 28 of the Misuse of Drugs Act 1971, it is a defence to a charge of possessing drugs for the accused to 'prove' that he neither knew of nor suspected nor had reason to suspect some fact alleged by the prosecution. This conflicts with the presumption of innocence (Article 6(2)). The House of Lords gave the phrase 'to prove' the unusual meaning of 'to give sufficient evidence'. Thus the prosecution still has the general burden of disproving the accused's claim. Lord Hope emphasised (at 604) that great care must be taken to make the revised meaning blend in with the language and structure of the statute. 'Amendment' seems to be possible as long as it does not make the statute unintelligible or unworkable (compare [80] and [81]. See also *R (H) v London North and East Region Mental Health Review Tribunal* (2001): reverse burden of proof but no room for manoeuvre).

- *R v A* (2001) (perhaps the most radical example): The Youth Justice and Criminal Evidence Act 1999 prohibited evidence in rape cases of the alleged victim's previous sexual experience without the court's consent, which could be given only in specified circumstances (s.41(1)). It was held that the court could construe the Act so as to permit evidence necessary to make the trial fair since that was the general object of the Act. Thus additional provisions, 'subject to the right to a fair trial', could be implied into unambiguous language beyond the normal limits of statutory interpretation even if this strained the normal meaning (see Lord Steyn's speech). However the court cannot override provisions that specifically contradict convention rights.

- *S (children) (care plan)* (2002): The power of court to intervene in local authority care proceedings could not be added to the Children Act 1989: court cannot depart substantially from fundamental feature of a statutory scheme particularly if it has practical consequences which the court cannot evaluate (s.38). Similarly *Poplar Housing and Regeneration Community Association v Donoghue* (2001): the term 'reasonable' could not be inserted into a statute which gave a landlord an absolute right to evict a tenant.

▷ *Bellinger v Bellinger* (2003): A statute could not be interpreted so as to treat a transsexual as female for marriage purposes since this raises wide social issues that a court is not equipped to confront (compare Gender Recognition Act 2004).

▷ *Cachia* v *Faluyi* (2002): A provision in the Fatal Accidents Act 1976 that not more than one 'action' shall lie in respect of the same subject matter arose when a firm of solicitors issued a writ in respect of the death of the claimant's wife in a road accident but then disappeared before it could be served. A second firm issued a new writ several years later. Under domestic law the second writ would probably be invalid. However under the HRA the Court of Appeal read 'action' in an unorthodox way to mean 'served process'. Brooke LJ remarked that this was a very good example 'of the way in which the 1998 Act now enables English judges to do justice in a way that was previously not open to us' [20].

Section 3 seems to assume that the meaning of the Convention is a given against which UK law can be measured. However even though the decisions of the European Court give some assistance, the meaning and scope of a convention right is often vague. Indeed as a 'living instrument' (above) the meaning of the Convention is always evolving. Thus interpretation is against a moving target. The enterprise may be self defeating since a convention provision could be 'read down' to conform to existing UK law as well as a UK law 'read up' to conform to the Convention.

20.3   Declaration of Incompatibility

Where it is not 'possible' to interpret primary legislation in line with a convention right, a higher court (High Court and above) may – but is not required to – make a 'declaration of incompatibility' (s.4). This is at the heart of the accommodation between law and democracy. A declaration of incompatibility has no effect on the validity of the law in question and is not binding on the parties (s.4(6)). A declaration of incompatibility invites Parliament to consider whether to change the law. It triggers a 'fast-track' procedure that enables a minister, by statutory instrument subject to the approval of Parliament, to make such amendments as he or she considers necessary to remove the incompatibility. A declaration of incompatibility is a last resort (*R* v *A* (above) [108]) and should not be used in order to avoid the task of interpreting the statute to comply with the Convention (*Ghaidan* (above) per Lord Steyn [39]).

The fast track procedure can also be used where an incompatibility arises because of a ruling by the European Court of Human Rights and a minister considers that there are 'compelling reasons' for proceeding (s.10). It does not apply to measures of the Church of England. Also subordinate legislation that conflicts with a convention right can be quashed by the court and reinstated in amended form under this procedure. Ministers are not bound to obey a declaration of incompatibility and judicial review may not lie in respect of a refusal to do so (below).

20.4   Remedies

The HRA must be applied by all courts. By virtue of section 6(1) 'it is unlawful for a public authority to act in a way which is incompatible with a convention right' except where (a) 'as a result of one or more provisions of primary legislation, the authority could not have acted differently' or (b) 'in the case of one or more provisions of, or made under, primary legislation which cannot be read or given effect in a way which is compatible with the convention rights, the authority was acting so as to give effect to or enforce those provisions'. For this purpose an 'act' includes a failure to act but does not include a failure to introduce or lay before Parliament a proposal for legislation nor make any primary legislation or remedial order (s.6(6)). This effectively adds another ground to judicial review in connection with the exercise of discretionary powers or the application of a statutory duty. It links with the interpretative obligation in section 3 (above) in that an action which is required by a UK statute or a Prerogative Order in Council is not unlawful on human rights grounds although a declaration of incompatibility may be made in relation to the primary legislation.

Section 7 entitles a 'victim' to bring proceedings in respect of an act which is unlawful under section 6 and also to rely on convention rights in any legal proceedings. However the Secretary of State can make rules designating an appropriate court or tribunal for particular purposes (ss.7(1)(a), 9(1)(c)). The Secretary of State has exercised this power principally in relation to special tribunals concerning immigration, asylum and other cases involving national security matters (Chapter 21). Reflecting the concerns of judicial independence, in relation to the judicial functions of a court or tribunal, proceedings must be by appeal or judicial review or otherwise as provided for by rules made by the Lord Chancellor or Secretary of State.

The onus is on the claimant to show that a law or decision does not comply with the Convention (*Lambeth Borough Council* v *Kay* (2006) and that he or she is a 'victim'. 'Victim' has the same meaning as in cases brought before the ECHR (s.7(7)). The claimant or a close relative must be directly affected, or at least very likely to be affected, by the action complained of (see *Klass* v *Federal Republic of Germany* (1979); *Open Door and Dublin Well Woman* v *Ireland* (1992)). There is no standing for Non-Governmental Organisations (NGOs) representing collective or public interests unless possibly the NGO is composed of victims (*Director General of Fair Trading* v *Proprietary Association of Great Britain* (2001)). Thus in a judicial review case an NGO can challenge a decision only on domestic grounds (s.7(3)). It appears that a public authority cannot be a victim against another public authority since in ECHR terms both are part of the 'state' (see *Aston Cantlow Parochial Church Council* v *Wallbank* (2003)). However this seems to assume a unitary theory of the state, which as we have seen is not recognised in English law (Chapter 6). The HRA does not refer to the state and in ordinary judicial review law the courts can certainly review decisions of central government against other public bodies such as local authorities.

Under Section 8 the court can award any of the remedies normally available to it 'as it considers just and appropriate'. Damages can be awarded only by a court which has power to award damages or order compensation in civil proceedings (for example not by criminal courts and other specialist courts) and then only if the court is satisfied that 'the award is necessary to afford just satisfaction to the person in whose favour it is made' (s.8(4)). The phrase 'just satisfaction' is part of the jurisprudence of the ECHR and the court must take into account the principles applied by the ECHR in awarding compensation (ibid.). However apart from insisting that there must be substantial loss or injury these do not give clear guidance and the court has considerable discretion (see *Z* v *UK* (2001); *Damages under the Human Rights Act 1998*, Law Com. No. 266 (2006); *Cullen* v *Chief Constable of the RUC* [2004] 2 All ER 237, 262). In order to safeguard judicial independence, where an action for damages is brought in respect of a judicial act, meaning in this context an act of a court, there is no liability in respect of an act in good faith except for an unlawful arrest or detention. The action must be brought against the Crown with the judge concerned being made a party (HRA 1998 s.9(3)(4)).

20.5   Public Authorities

The European Convention on Human Rights applies to states and some of its articles, notably Articles 8 and 10 are directed explicitly to public authorities. The Human Rights Act can be directly enforced only against a public authority (s.6(1)). For the purposes of the HRA 'public authority' includes a court or tribunal (s.6(3)). A public authority also includes any body 'certain of whose functions are functions of a public nature' (ibid.). However Parliament or a person exercising functions in connection with proceedings in Parliament is not a public authority except the House of Lords in its judicial capacity (s.6(4)). An individual can be a public authority (*A* v *Head Teacher and Governors of Lord Grey School* (2004)).

There are two kinds of public authority. Firstly there are bodies such as central and local government and the police which are inherently public. These are known as 'core' public authorities. All the activities of these bodies fall within the HRA. This can be contrasted with the approach taken in domestic judicial review law which is primarily functional so that some activities even of the central government may be considered to be private functions and so not subject to judicial review (Chapter 18). Secondly there are 'functional' public authorities. These might include private or voluntary bodies, the activities of which interrelate with those of the government. Functional public authorities may perform some functions on behalf of the government but also perform private functions. The 'private acts' of bodies of this kind do not fall within the Act (s.6(5)). Thus in the case of functional public authorities the court must look at the particular function which is claimed to invade a convention right.

On the one hand it has been argued that a broad view should be taken of what is a public function so as to subject a wide range of powerful bodies to the Act. This has been endorsed by the Joint Committee on Human Rights (Seventh Report, 2003–04, HL 39, HC 382). On the other hand it has been suggested that private bodies should be subject to less onerous obligations than public bodies narrowly defined (see Oliver, 2004; compare Sunkin, 2004, *Public Law*, 643).

The European Court of Human Rights has not addressed directly the question of what is a public function. Its approach seems to be based on whether the particular act is carried out under the control of the government or on behalf of the government (see *Sigurjónnson* v *Iceland* (1993)). The UK courts have broadly followed this approach. They have also been influenced by the belief that a body which is a public authority cannot itself claim human rights against another branch of the government (above). This is particularly significant in relation for example to religious bodies and charities that protect vulnerable minorities.

In *Aston Cantlow and Wilmcote with Billesley Parochial Church Council* v *Wallbank* (2003) the House of Lords held, overruling the Court of Appeal, that a parochial church council of the Church of England is not a core public authority even though the Church of England has a close connection with the state and has many special legal powers and privileges. A core public authority must be 'governmental' in the sense that its activities are for the benefit of the general public interest, whereas the Church of England primarily benefits its own members. However some aspects of the Church of England might fall into the category of *functional* public authority, for example functions in connection with marriages and funerals since these involve public rights. The case itself concerned the statutory right of a parochial church council to force a house owner to pay for the repair of a church roof under an obligation acquired with the property. A majority held that this was a private function, being the enforcement of a property right for the primary benefit of churchgoers. Lord Scott, dissenting, thought that this was a 'public' function in that it involved historic conservation for the benefit of the community enforced by special powers. *Wallbank* therefore illustrates the artificiality and uncertainty of attempting to distinguish between the public and the private and that the matter depends on a combination of factors. These include in particular public benefit and the operational connection between the body in question and another acknowledged public authority.

YL v *Birmingham City Council* (2007) is the other main authority. The House of Lords held that a privately owned care home was not exercising a public function in relation to a resident who was placed there and financed by a local authority acting under a statutory duty to care for the vulnerable. (This case was discussed in Chapter 19 in relation to the analogous approach taken in domestic judicial review cases; contrast *Weaver* v *London and Quadrant Housing Trust* (2008).) The majority took the view that there was not a sufficiently close connection between the home and the government to attract the Human Rights Act. The home had no special powers, was not acting as the agent of the government and the relationship between the home and its resident was the same whether or not the resident was supported by the local authority. The local authority funded the individual resident and not the home as a whole.

Lord Bingham and Lady Hale dissented taking a fundamentally different approach. This was based on the principle that the state had taken on itself the function of caring for the elderly and that it should make no difference so far as human rights were concerned whether this was done through a private agency or directly by the state itself. Lady Hale emphasised the positive duty of the state to ensure that Article 8 rights were protected, arguing that this can best be achieved by imposing liability directly on the private agency. This leads to the question of 'horizontality' (below).

20.6 Horizontal Effect

Even though the primary liability under the HRA is that of a public authority, it is arguable that the Act also has substantial 'horizontal effect' in the sense that private persons as well as public bodies may be required to respect human rights. Even private legal relationships are created and defined by the state, which could therefore be regarded as responsible for ensuring that the law meets the minimum standards appropriate to a democratic society. For example it would be anomalous if there were a right of privacy against an NHS hospital and not a private hospital. On the other hand the purpose of the HRA is to give effect to the ECHR which is enforceable only against a state (Article 34). It can therefore be argued that by their nature Convention rights are directed only against the state (Buxton, 2000). Moreover the Act does not include Article 1 of the ECHR which requires states to 'secure to everyone within their jurisdiction' the rights and freedoms conferred by the Convention.

The main cases of horizontal effect are as follows:

- All legislation must be interpreted according to the Convention even that applying to private relationships. In *Ghaidan* v *Mendoza* (2004) the House of Lords applied Article 14 (discrimination) to legislation which discriminated against homosexual couples occupying property owned by private landlords (see also *Wilson* v *First County Trust* (2003)).
- By virtue of section 6 the courts are public authorities. It is arguable that a court would act 'unlawfully' if it did not apply convention rights in every case before it, even between private persons (see *Douglas* v *Hello!* (2001) per Sedley LJ). The victim's right would be against the court itself, not directly against the other private party. It is therefore difficult to see how the court could award damages. However section 6 could also be interpreted as applying only to the court's own practice and procedure.
- A less extreme version of the above is that while section 6 cannot create a new cause of action against a private body, it can require the court to apply convention rights in the context of *existing causes of action* or in respect of the court's own powers to make orders and grant remedies (see *Wilson* v *First County Trust* [2003] 4 All ER 97 [174]; *Campbell* v *MGN* (2004) [133] per Baroness Hale). The matter would therefore have to arise in the course of other legal proceedings into which a human rights dimension could be implied. For example a court might be entitled to refuse to give a possession order to a private landlord who attempted to evict a tenant from her home (*R (McLellan)* v *Bracknell Forest Borough Council* [2002] 1 All ER 899 [42]). The weakness of this approach seems to be that it is random in that it depends on the matter falling into an existing category of UK law. In *Kay* v *Lambeth LBC* (2006) the House of Lords specifically refused to decide whether the Act would apply in cases involving a private landlord.
- Particular convention rights may include a positive obligation imposed on the state to protect the right and to require private persons to respect it (see *Kroon* v *Netherlands* (1995)). This has been recognised in the case of Article 2: right to life; Article 3: torture and inhuman or degrading treatment – *Z* v *UK* (2002); *X and Y* v *Netherlands* (1985); *A* v *UK* (1998); Article 8: privacy – *Douglas* v *Hello!* (2001) [91], *Thompson* v *News Group Newspapers* (2001) [25]; Article 9: freedom of religion – *R (Williamson)* v *Secretary of State for Education and Employment* (2005) [4, 86]; compare *Re GA (a child)* (2001). However this positive obligation is not absolute and the court will give the government a substantial margin of discretion in relation to the measures it takes (below).
- Particular provisions of the Act itself may have horizontal effect in their own right, notably section 12 which requires the court to have regard to the interests of press freedom (Chapter 20).
- The courts might develop the common law on the basis that the ECHR encapsulates values of general import. In *Campbell* v *MGN Ltd* (2004) the House of Lords used Articles 8 and 10 of the ECHR to reconfigure the common law of breach of confidence in relation to press freedom. The majority did not seem to think that the matter strictly fell within the Human Rights Act (see [17], [18], [19], [26], [49]).

20.7   Overriding Protected Rights

Any workable code of fundamental rights must be expressed in general language and with sufficient filters or exceptions to permit governments to act in the public interest or to resolve conflicts with other rights. Several methods are available to accommodate competing concerns and to adjust the law to changing circumstances. The ECHR has been described as a 'living instrument', meaning that the rights themselves and their ranking against other factors change with the times (for example *Ghaidan* v *Mendoza* (2004): homosexual partners).

It is tempting to seek an overarching principle that would combine the human right with the competing interest under some overall concept of common good or to find a 'balance' – a concept which itself presupposes some overriding objective measure. However it is doubtful whether any such overriding principle is possible and even if it is, it is not self evident that courts are well equipped to find it. Indeed in *R (S)* v *Chief Constable of South Yorkshire Police* (2004) Sedley LJ in the Court of Appeal pointed out that the notion of 'balancing' individual rights against the public interest means that the latter will always prevail (see also Lord Steyn in *Brown* v *Stott* [2001] 2 All ER 97 at 118).

Moreover there are competing approaches as to what human rights are about. On one view, that of liberal individualists, human rights concern a zone of individual freedom which might exceptionally be overridden in the public interest but recognising the sacrifice involved. On the other hand communitarians and republicans, favouring 'positive freedom', might argue that human rights in themselves are valuable only by virtue of their contribution to some greater good. For example in *Gough* v *Chief Constable of Derbyshire* (2001) Laws LJ said:

> rights are divisive, harmful, ultimately worthless, unless their possession is conditional upon the public good. (321)

> it is inherent in the nature of the right itself that the individual who claims its benefit may have to give way to the supervening weight of other claims . . . the right's practical utility rests upon the fact that there can be no tranquillity within the state without a plethora of unruly individual freedoms. (320)

From this perspective, accommodating human rights and the public interest would be less difficult since rights would be conditional upon conforming to whatever happens to be the particular preference as to what constitutes society's 'good', thus raising Isaiah Berlin's worries about authoritarianism (Chapter 2).

There are two ways of accommodating competing public interest considerations. These operate differently. Firstly the right itself could be narrowly defined. Secondly many of the rights are made subject to specific justifications for overriding them (overrides).

In *R (Begum)* v *Head Teacher and Governors of Denbigh High School* (2006) the House of Lords held that a ban on the wearing of a strict form of Muslim dress at school was not an unlawful interference with freedom of religion (Article 9). Two lines of reasoning were used. A majority held the right to religious freedom was not infringed. The child concerned had chosen to attend the school in question and could have attended other more flexible schools. Perhaps uncomfortable with the reality of this, Lord Nicholls and Baroness Hale held that the right had been infringed but that the decision was 'objectively justified' under one of the prescribed overrides, namely 'the rights of others', these being the social purpose of fostering a sense of community by means of a dress code. This case provides an illustration of the subjective and impressionistic nature of the balancing exercise and also the importance of mainstream opinion. Thus it was stressed that great weight should be given to the professional judgement of the head teacher and mainstream Muslim groups [34]. (See also *Copsey* v *WBB Devon Clays Ltd* (2005)).

The technique of defining the right narrowly can also be seen in respect of the meaning of 'discrimination' and that of 'deprivation' of liberty as opposed to 'restriction' of liberty (above). Sometimes this works against the claimant since the onus is on the claimant to bring him or herself within the scope of the right in question whereas in the case of the separate public interest overrides it is for the state to justify interfering with the right. On the other hand sometimes this might work in the claimant's favour since, as Lord Hoffmann pointed out in *Secretary of State for the Home Dept* v *JJ* (2008) [44], a narrow definition of deprivation of liberty may make it more difficult for the state to justify overriding it.

As regards the mechanisms for balancing interests, firstly some rights are 'absolute'. These include the prohibitions on torture and inhuman and degrading treatment (Article 3), slavery (Article 4.1), the right to a fair trial (Article 6) and discrimination (Article 14). Any accommodation with other interests must be found as suggested above by exploiting the meaning of the right. For example what counts as 'torture or inhuman and degrading treatment' might be redefined according to changing sensibilities (*Chalal* v *UK* (1996); *Z* v *UK* (2002)) and 'fairness' and 'discrimination' in themselves embody the notion of a reasonable balance between competing concerns. In *R (Williamson)* v *Secretary of State* (2005) the House of Lords refused to define 'religion' in a restrictive way or pronounce on the validity of a religion but indicated that the 'manifestation' of religion, meaning the interaction with others, was subject to implicit limits based on 'seriousness, cogency and compatibility with human dignity' [64, 76].

Other rights are limited in ways specified in the particular article, sometimes to the point of having little meaning (for example Article 12: right to marry in accordance with the laws of the particular state). Thirdly the court may be required to balance the right against a specified override which might be another right or a more general public concern. Articles 8–11 provide characteristic examples. The overrides vary with the particular article but in all cases include public safety, public order, the prevention and detection of serious crime, the protection of health and morals and the protection of the rights of others.

Sometimes one human right may conflict with another, for example freedom of expression and privacy but the Convention contains no guidance as to any ranking order. It seems clear that the right to life (Article 2), prohibition of torture (Article 3), personal liberty (Article 5) and right to a fair trial (Article 6) are given especially high importance. Freedom of expression is often said to have special importance but in practice it readily seems to give way to other rights (Chapter 21).

There are certain threshold requirements. Firstly the restrictions must be 'prescribed by law' or 'in accordance with the law', terms which apparently mean the same (*Malone* v

UK (1984)). This imports traditional rule of law ideas (Chapter 7). Thus the restrictions must be clear, must not involve wide discretion and must be made in accordance with a regular, democratic and accessible lawmaking process and preferably not by judicial extension of the law (*R (Laporte)* v *Chief Constable of Gloucestershire* (2006) [52]; *R (Gillam)* v *Secretary of State* (2006) [31]). The applicant must be able reasonably to foresee that the conduct in question would be unlawful and there must be adequate safeguards including independent and accessible courts. The common law is particularly vulnerable to claims of uncertainty (see *R* v *Goldstein* (2006); *Sunday Times* v *UK* (1979); *Klass* v *Germany* (1979)).

Secondly the restrictions must be 'necessary in a democratic society'. The concept of 'necessary' and 'democratic' are vague, inviting the judge to impose his or her personal views. They take their meaning from the context. Necessity is closely related to proportionality (below) in the sense that the more serious the interference with the right, the stronger must be the justification. It usually means an important interest, sometimes called a 'pressing social need,' which is more than merely 'useful', 'reasonable' or 'desirable' (*Handyside* v *UK* (1976); *R (Laporte)* v *Chief Constable of Gloucestershire* (2007) [52]); for example *Brown* v *Stott* (2001): combating drink driving; *R (Williamson)* v *Secretary of State* (2005) [79]: child welfare). In some cases, notably the question whether a state is entitled to derogate from a particular article of the Convention, it may come near to meaning 'indispensable' although the court may defer to the government's judgement as to whether this is the case (below).

20.7.1   Proportionality

We considered proportionality briefly in Chapter 17. In the human rights context the main role of proportionality concerns how the 'fair balance' is struck between a right and the public interest or between two competing rights. Proportionality also applies where the state has a positive duty to protect a right in order to avoid placing undue burdens on the government. This seems to apply even to the 'absolute' rights (*R (Pretty)* v *DPP* (2002) [90]). Proportionality asks whether the legislative purpose is sufficiently important to override the right in question, whether the measures are properly related to the purpose in question and whether they can be achieved by less intrusive means.

The court will ask:
1. Whether the restriction is imposed for a proper and practicable purpose, to meet a 'pressing social need'. In most cases the court will accept the government's view as to the existence of such a need. In particular an international treaty is unlikely to be questioned (*R (Bermingham)* v *Serious Fraud Office* (2006)).
2. Whether the interference with the right is a rational way of achieving the purpose. For example in *A* v *Secretary of State for the Home Department* (2005) legislation authorising the indefinite detention of non-British terrorist suspects was not only discriminatory (above) but not sufficiently focused upon the emergency which the government claimed to be tackling, namely the threat posed by al-Qaeda. The measure went too far in some respects and not far enough in others. On the one hand it included people who were not necessarily a threat to the UK or whose activities did not relate to al-Qaeda. On the other hand British terrorists were no less a threat than foreign ones.
3. Whether less restrictive means could have been employed, in particular whether there are safeguards to protect the individual (see *R* v *Shaylor* (2002); *Gaskin* v *UK* (1990);

Chapter 21). For example in *McVeigh* v *UK* (1983) the European Court held that an emergency restriction on personal freedom, while necessary to meet a pressing social need, did not justify a refusal to let the claimants contact their wives. In *A* (above) lesser measures such as surveillance might have been used. Proportionality also requires that the restrictions must not be discriminatory in the sense that like cases must be treated alike (*Marckx* v *Belgium* (1979)).

Proportionality might require restricting the right but not destroying it completely. For instance an important aspect of freedom of expression is whether there are alternative outlets for what the claimant wishes to communicate (Chapter 20; see also *R (Szluk)* v *Governor of Full Sutton Prison* (2004)). The social need might also be compromised. For example in *RJR Macdonald* v *Canada* (1995) the Canadian Supreme Court was divided over the extent to which tobacco advertising should be restricted in order to meet the public interest in health (see also *R (British American Tobacco UK Ltd)* v *Secretary of State for Health* (2004)).

It has been held that in dealing with legislation concerning matters of general social or economic policy, the question of proportionality should be decided at the macro level of the legislation in general and other than in exceptional circumstances not the micro level of the facts of the individual case (*Wandsworth London Borough Council* v *Michalak* (2002); *Harrow LBC* v *Qazi* (2004); *Wilson* v *First County Trust* (2003) [74], [75], [76]). However it is arguable that judgements at this level are best made by the legislature, which can seek a practical accommodation based on public opinion, and that courts are best equipped to deal with the individual case.

Sometimes the competition is between two individual protected rights, for example privacy (Article 8) and freedom of expression (Article 10). In such cases a comparison might plausibly be made by looking in turn at the consequences to the individual and the public interest of violating each right and choosing the lesser evil. This may amount to no more than the judge's gut reaction to the case as a whole.

In *Campbell* v *MGN* (2004) the *Daily Mirror* had published information and photographs about the treatment for drug addiction undergone by a famous fashion model. The newspaper's and indirectly the public's right to freedom of expression was balanced against the claimant's right to privacy. The House of Lords regarded these rights as of equal importance and looked closely at all the circumstances with the aim of producing the least harmful outcome. It was held firstly that the fact the claimant had been a drug addict was not protected since she had repeatedly told the media that she was not on drugs thus putting the matter into the public domain. However it was also held that the information about the details of her treatment should not have been published since this was inherently confidential in nature. Importantly there were no political or democratic values in issue of a kind which supported press freedom. Lords Nicholls and Hoffmann dissented, taking a wider view of press freedom, that a newspaper should be able to add colour and detail to its reporting and that journalists should be entitled to some latitude in the wider interests of a healthy press. A restrictive approach might inhibit the press and so hamper democracy. Thus in the end proportionality is a subjective judgement, raising the question whether the courts are in the best position to make it.

Margin of Discretion

As we saw in Chapter 19 the concept of the 'margin of appreciation', sometimes called the discretionary area of judgement, was developed by the European Court as a safety valve in cases where there are significant national differences in political, religious or moral values or legal practices. When asking whether state action is proportionate the European Court will not substitute its views for those of the state but asks itself only whether the national authorities were reasonably entitled to think that the interference complained of was justifiable (see *Handyside v UK* (1976); *Open Door and Dublin Well Woman v Ireland* (1992); *Buckley v United Kingdom* (1997)). Different communities may have different but justifiable blends of values and attitudes and if an international tribunal intervened it might forfeit respect.

The doctrine of margin of appreciation as such therefore has no application within domestic cases. Indeed the Act on its face requires the court to strike the balance between the human right and any competing interest. However, by whatever name, the courts sometimes leave a discretionary area of judgement to ministers and Parliament. This is analogous to the problem of reasonableness and justiciability in judicial review. The courts do not wish to exceed their proper constitutional role nor to interfere in matters where they have no experience or expertise or to which legal processes are unsuited.

In *R (Mahmood) v Secretary of State for the Home Department* (2001) [38], Lord Phillips MR said that

> the court will bear in mind that, just as individual states enjoy a margin of appreciation which permits them to respond, within the law, in a manner that is not uniform, so there will often be an area of discretion permitted to the executive of a country before a response can be demonstrated to infringe the Convention . . . The court will ask the question, applying an objective test, whether the decision maker could reasonably have concluded that the interference was necessary to achieve one or more of the legitimate aims recognised by the Convention.

The margin of discretion is sometimes described as involving 'deference' to the elected branch of government. In *R (Pro-Life) Alliance v BBC* (2003) Lord Hoffmann criticised this usage. He pointed out that the concept reflected the separation of powers' distinction between the role of the courts and those of the other branches of government. According to Lord Hoffmann, the courts are deferring to no one but are upholding those roles, which is their constitutional function (also Lord Bingham, *A v Secretary of State for the Home Department* (2005): 'institutional competence').

The margin of discretion does not apply to the initial question of whether the convention right in question applies at all. Nor does it apply when the contest is between two private rights as in *Campbell* (above). It applies primarily to the question whether the government is entitled to override the right on a public interest ground (*R (S) v Chief Constable of South Yorkshire Police* (2004) [27, 64]). It also applies to the government's positive duty to ensure that human rights are protected (see *R (Pretty) v DPP* (2002) [15]; *Rees v UK* (1986): transsexuals). To some extent it meets the common criticism that courts have limited information and may ignore wider questions of the public interest, giving spurious certainty to matters where there is legitimate disagreement. Its width varies according to the importance of the right, the importance of the public interest in question and the democratic content of the decision (*Huang v Secretary of State* (2007)). In *Gough v Chief Constable of the Derbyshire Constabulary* (2001) it was said [78] that the margin of

discretion is greater, perhaps akin to the *Wednesbury* test, when the decision maker is the primary legislator. In *R (S) v Chief Constable of South Yorkshire Police* (2004) [16], Lord Woolf said:

> I regard it as being fundamental that the court keeps at the forefront of its consideration its lack of any democratic credentials.

The margin is particularly strong in areas involving controversial political or ethical issues which depend on subjective judgements or predictions on which opinions can reasonably differ (for example *R (Countryside Alliance) v Attorney-General* (2008): hunting; *R (Pro-Life Alliance) v BBC* (2003): disturbing broadcast; Chapter 20). It is also strong in public order, defence and immigration matters which are regarded as especially the concern of the executive (*International Transport Roth GmbH v Secretary of State for the Home Department* (2002)) and in relation to legislation intended to meet general welfare goals such as the provision of social housing, these being matters of priority appropriate to democratic decision. In *Poplar HARCA v Donoghue* (2001) the Court of Appeal refused to condemn section 21(4) of the Housing Act 1988 which gave social landlords an automatic right to possession of a dwelling house in certain circumstances. Lord Woolf LCJ remarked [69] that:

> the economic and other implications of any policy in this area are extremely complex and far reaching. This is an area where in our judgement the courts must treat the decisions of Parliament as to what is in the public interest with particular deference.

(See also *R (G) v Barnet LBC* (2004) [69].) On the other hand some matters are so fundamental or closely related to legal issues as to fall outside any margin of discretion. Here the court will do the interest balancing itself. These include discrimination (*Ghaidan v Mendoza* (2004), Baroness Hale), the right to a fair trial (*R v A* (2001), personal liberty (*A v Secretary of State* (2005), Lord Bingham [39]–[42]) and serious restrictions on freedom of political expression (Chapter 20) (see Lord Bingham in *R v Secretary of State for the Home Department ex parte Daly* (2001)). In *A v Secretary of State* (2005) (above) a majority of the House of Lords deferred to the government as to whether the current terrorist threat amounted to an emergency so as to justify derogating from the detention without trial provisions of the ECHR since this was matter of political judgement (Chapter 21). However it was held, Lord Walker dissenting, that the court can decide whether the detention powers themselves were proportionate since personal liberty was directly in issue. This case prompted a suggestion by the Prime Minister that the Human Rights Act should be amended to strengthen government powers (see *Liberty*, press release 5 August 2005).

The margin is not applied automatically. The government must provide some rational support for its actions (*R v Shaylor* (2002) [61]); *Matthews v Ministry of Defence* (2003)). The European Court has emphasised that it may depend upon whether the matter has been subject to considered democratic deliberation as opposed to 'unquestioning and passive adherence to a historic tradition' (*Hirst v UK (No. 2)* (2004); Chapter 12). If this were to apply in domestic law, it would strengthen the position of the legislature. The court may be influenced by the extent to which a controversial government decision has been debated in Parliament, or is supported by international conventions, expert opinion and so on (see *R (Williamson) v Secretary of State* (2005)).

Summary

⯈ The HRA 1998, while not incorporating the Convention as such, has given the main rights created by the ECHR effect in domestic law. UK legislation must be interpreted to be compatible with convention rights and public bodies other than Parliament must comply with convention rights. The courts must take the decisions of the ECHR into account but are not bound by them. It is unlawful for a public authority to act in a way that is incompatible with a convention right. Victims can bring proceedings under the Act against a public authority and rely on convention rights in any legal proceedings.

⯈ The HRA can be directly enforced only against public authorities and by a 'victim' defined in accordance with the case law of the European Court. 'Public authority' includes all the activities of government bodies proper and courts and tribunals but in relation to bodies that have a mixture of public and private functions (for example social landlords) only to their public 'acts'. The courts seem to be taking a similar approach to the question of what is public function as in judicial review cases.

⯈ 'Horizontal effect' may be direct, where the court is required to enforce a right against a private person, or indirect, where the state is required to protect against violations by private persons. It is not clear how far the Act has horizontal effect although there are several devices that might enable it to do so.

⯈ Parliamentary supremacy is preserved in that convention rights must give way where they are incompatible with a statute. The courts have taken a moderate approach in relation to the obligation to interpret statutes, 'so far as it is possible to do so', to be compatible with convention rights. However there are differences of emphasis between judges as to the assumptions on which interpretation should be approached, in particular the extent to which established English law should be respected.

⯈ Where primary legislation is incompatible the court can draw attention to violations by making a declaration of incompatibility. There is a 'fast track' procedure available in special circumstances to enable amendments to legislation to be made. The government must be explicit as to any intention to override convention rights.

⯈ Some convention rights can be overridden by prescribed public interest concerns or other rights and a principle of fair balance runs through the Convention as a whole. The courts are guided by the concept of proportionality. While these devices help to structure and rationalise decision making they do not remove the need for the court to make a subjective political judgement.

⯈ The courts have applied the notion of 'margin of appreciation' or margin of discretion particularly in the context of decisions made by elected bodies. The width of the margin depends on various factors, chief among which are the importance and extent of the particular right that is violated in relation to the seriousness of the public harm if the right were not overridden, and the extent to which the matter involves controversial political, social or economic choices.

Exercises

20.1 What is meant by describing the Human Rights Act as creating a constitutional dialogue? Do you agree with this description?

20.2 'Rights *under* the Convention differ from rights created by the 1998 Act *by reference to* the Convention' – Lord Bingham in *R (Al-Skeini)* v *Secretary of State* (2007). Explain and critically discuss.

20.3 'My impression is that two factors are contributing to a misunderstanding of the remedial scheme of the 1998 Act. First there is the constant refrain that a judicial reading down or reading in would flout the will of Parliament. The second factor may be an excessive concentration on linguistic factors of the particular statute' (Lord Steyn in *Ghaidan* v *Mendoza* (2004) [40–1]). Explain and critically evaluate this statement.

20.4 'The court will bear in mind that, just as individual states enjoy a margin of appreciation which permits them to respond, within the law, in a manner that is not uniform, so there will often be an area of discretion permitted to the executive of a country before a response can be demonstrated to infringe the Convention' (Phillips LJ in *R (Mahmood)* v *Secretary of State* (2001)). Explain, illustrate and discuss critically.

20.5 Explain the constitutional significance of the declaration of incompatibility.

20.6 The Commune of the Many Names of the Lord is a religious community which believes that all life is sacred and that animal life is as valuable as human life. It cares for a number of animals at a small sanctuary. Among these animals is Clive the Golden Eagle. Under the imaginary Animal Health Act 2009 the local authority has power to order the slaughter of any bird which displays a positive reaction to the test for Avian Flu. Clive has tested positive and the local authority has ordered his slaughter. The Commune has evidence from a number of expert vetinarians that Clive could be successfully isolated and treated for the condition. Jobsworth, the responsible local official gave the following reasons for the decision to order the slaughter: (1) In her opinion Clive's condition represents a serious threat to human health; (2) An outbreak of Avian Flu would have disastrous effects for the local economy. Advise the Commune as to the possibility of challenging the Order in the courts.

20.7 Advise on the chances of success of challenges to each of the following under the Human Rights Act 1998:
(i) A decision by the NHS to refuse a life extending drug to elderly people suffering from certain terminal illnesses on the grounds that the cost is not worth the benefit and the funding is desperately needed for medical supplies in support of military interventions against non-democratic states.
(ii) A decision to deport a family to a country where they claim that their child who has learning difficulties will be compulsorily detained in a mental hospital and subject to electric shock treatment rather than receive behavioural therapy in the home which is available in the UK.
(iii) The policy of a private hotel not to accommodate gay couples.
(iv) The ransacking of a hotel in Iraq by British soldiers during a counter insurgency operation and the beating up of several of its staff for refusing to provide the soldiers with food and drink.

Further reading

Buxton, R. (2000) 'The Human Rights Act and Private Law', *Law Quarterly Review* 116:48.

Campbell, T., Ewing, K.D. and Tomkins, A. (eds) (2001) *Sceptical Essays on Human Rights*, Oxford University Press, Chapters 2, 5, 6.

Clayton, R. (2004) 'Judicial Deference and Democratic Dialogue: the Legitimacy of Judicial Intervention under the Human Rights Act 1998', *Public Law* 33.

Ewing, K., Than, J. (2008) 'The Continuing Futility of the Human Rights Act', *Public Law* 668.

Fenwick, H., Phillipson, G., Masterman, R. (eds) (2007) *Judicial Reasoning under the Human Rights Act*, Cambridge University Press.

Gearty, C. (2002) 'Reconciling Parliamentary Democracy and Human Rights', *Law Quarterly Review* 118:248.

Gearty, C. (2006) *Can Human Rights Survive?* Cambridge University Press (Hamlyn Lectures).

Harvey, C. (2004) 'Talking about Human Rights', *European Human Rights Law Review* 500.

Hickman, T. (2005) 'Constitutional Dialogue, Constitutional Theories and the Human Rights Act 1998', *Public Law* 306:317.

Hickman, T. (2008) 'The Courts and Politics after The Human Rights Act', *Public Law* 84.

Hickman, T. (2008) 'The Substance and Structure of Proportionality', *Public Law* 694.

Jowell, J. (2003) 'Judicial Deference and Human Rights: a Question of Competence', in Craig, P. and Rawlings, R. (eds) *Law and Administration in Europe*, Oxford University Press.

Kavanagh, A. (2004) 'The Elusive Divide between Interpretation and Legislation under the Human Rights Act 1998', *Oxford Journal of Legal Studies* 24:259.

Kavanagh, A. (2006) 'The Role of Parliamentary Intention in Adjudication under the Human Rights Act 1998', *Oxford Journal of Legal Studies* 26:179.

Klug, F., (2007) 'A Bill of Rights: Do we need one or do we already have one?', *Public Law* 701.

Lester, A. (2005) 'The Utility of the Human Rights Act: a Reply to Keith Ewing', *Public Law* 249.

Lewis J. (2007) 'The European Ceiling on Human Rights', *Public Law* 720.

Masterman, R. (2005) 'Taking the Strasbourg Jurisprudence into Account: Developing a Municipal Law of Human Rights under the Human Rights Act', *International and Comparative Law Quarterly* 907.

Nicol, D. (2006) 'Law and Politics after the Human Rights Act', *Public Law* 722.

Oliver, D. (2004) 'Functions of a Public Nature and the Human Rights Act', *Public Law* 329.

Poole, T. (2005) 'Harnessing the past? Lord Hoffmann and the Belmarsh Detainees Case', *Journal of Law and Society* 32:534

Steyn, Lord (2005) 'Deference: a Tangled Story', *Public Law* 346.

Sunkin, M. (2004) 'Pushing Forward the Frontiers of Human Rights Protection: The Meaning of Public Authority under the Human Rights Act', *Public Law* 643.

Young, A. (2005) 'A Peculiarly British Protection of Human Rights', *Modern Law Review* 68:858.

Young, A. (2002) 'Remedial and Substantive Horizontality: The Common Law and Douglas v. Hello! Ltd' *Public Law* 232.

Chapter 21

Freedoms of expression
and assembly

A free press is not a privilege but an organic necessity in a great society. Without
criticism and reliable and intelligent reporting, the government cannot govern.
(Walter Lippmann, journalist, 1889–1974)

Key words

- Instrumental and intrinsic value
- Democracy
- Self expression
- Reputation
- Privacy
- Responsible journalism
- Reportage
- Harm and offence
- Breach of the peace
- Imminence
- Police discretion

21.1   Introduction: Justifications for Freedom of Expression

A range of arguments can be advanced in support of freedom of expression. These have
been placed into two broad groups (Dworkin, *Freedom's Law*, Oxford University Press,
1996, pp. 199–201). The first identifies freedom of expression as an end in itself as a
defining characteristic of a human being. Dworkin argues that freedom of expression is
an essential and 'constitutive' feature of a just political society in which the government
treats all its members, except those who are incompetent, as responsible moral agents.
Those upon whom the right to freedom of expression is conferred are regarded as capable
of 'making up their own minds about what is good or bad in life or in politics, or what is
true and false in matters of justice and faith' and are properly entitled to 'participate in
politics' and to 'contribute to the formation of [their] moral or aesthetic climate'. Like Kant
who uses 'reason' in much the same way Dworkin seems to regard freedom of expression
as a badge of moral worth (see also Freeden, *Rights*, Oxford University Press, 1991, pp.
8–59). This might be regarded as merely a recital of liberal faith (Chapter 2) and easily
rejected for example from a religious perspective. It is moreover uncomfortable for those
whom Dworkin regards as incompetent.

The second group of justifications regards freedom of expression as instrumentally
valuable, that is, valuable as a means by which to pursue some other valuable end. This
approach, popular among the professional elite in the UK, could make freedom of
expression conditional upon the approval of some authority designated to decide what

the valuable end is and whether it is being sought. The ends in question were identified by Mill (Chapter 2) as democracy, self fulfilment and the testing of truth.

As regards democracy Lord Steyn in *R v Secretary of State for the Home Department ex parte Simms* (1999) emphasised freedom of expression in informing debate, as a safety valve to encourage consent and as a brake on the abuse of power. Democracy can only flourish in circumstances where a free press with access to government proceedings can offer information and comment and which the public has a right and perhaps a duty to receive. Lord Bingham in *McCartan-Turkington Breen v Times Newspapers Ltd* (2001), 290–291, stressed the importance of a free, active, professional and inquiring media to a modern participatory democracy pointing out that ordinary citizens cannot usually participate directly but can do so indirectly through the media. Free expression requires not only the right to criticise government and challenge orthodoxy but also fair opportunities at elections and other public debates (*Handyside v UK* (1976); *Bowman v UK* (1998); *Castells v Spain* (1992)), access to official information and to the proceedings of public bodies including courts in order to ensure that they are properly impartial. In *Hector v Attorney-General of Antigua and Bermuda* (1990) at 106, Lord Bridge said that 'in a free democratic society . . . those who hold office in government must always be open to criticism. Any attempt to stifle or fetter such criticism amounts to political censorship of the most insidious and objectionable kind.'

The liberal argument that freedom of expression provides a means to the end of self actualisation has been advanced by, among others, John Stuart Mill and Thomas Emerson. Its starting point is the proposition that the proper end of humanity is the realisation of individual potential which cannot flourish without freedom of expression. A variation on this theme has been advanced by Joseph Raz. He argues that freedom of expression provides a means by which the styles of life we adopt can, through public portrayals and representations, be validated (Raz, 'Free Expression and Personal Identification', 1991, *Oxford Journal of Legal Studies*, 11(3):303).

Mill was concerned that people should be free to experiment with different lifestyles provided only that they did not harm others. Mill distinguished between causing harm and causing offence which should not be prohibited. Indeed being offended or shocked might be considered good, as stimulating thought. In this argument we hear echoes of the Romantic movement. According to the Romantics, 'we find truth within us' and come to understand it in the course of giving expression to our 'inner voice' (Taylor, *Sources of the Self: The Making of the Modern Identity*, Cambridge University Press, 1989, Chapter 21). However it is not clear what counts as harm. Mill took harm to mean interfering with someone's rights or interests but of course this begs the questions of what counts as a right and who decides? Am I not harmed for example if I am seriously upset or offended by someone attacking my religion?

The argument that freedom of expression facilitates the pursuit of truth and the acquisition of knowledge suppressed by official orthodoxy has a long history. It was expressed in the seventeenth century by John Milton in his *Areopagitica*. Mill supported it, arguing that 'truth' can best be discovered and preserved by constant questioning. However Mill's utilitarian stance (Chapter 2) provides relatively weak support since there is no reason to suppose that truth is always conducive to the general welfare. On the other hand according to the philosopher of science Karl Popper, free critical discussion provides a means by which to eliminate errors in our thinking and thus to move towards ever more plausible working hypotheses but never incontrovertible truths (*The Open Society and its Enemies*, Routledge, 1996).

In the early twentieth century, the truth argument was advanced by many American judges, notably Holmes in his dissenting judgment in *Abrams* v *United States* (1919) at 630:

> the best test of truth is the power of a [given] thought to get itself accepted in the competition of the market [place of ideas].

In *Whitney* v *California* (1927), 357, 375, Brandeis J wrote that:

> freedom to think as you will and to speak as you will are means indispensable to the discovery and spread of political truth.

Brandeis J does not offer a definition of 'political truth'. In the political sphere, at least from a liberal perspective, the point of freedom of expression is arguably to keep diversity and disagreement alive. Moreover in the marketplace of ideas is there any reason to suppose that truth rather than the loudest and best paid voice will prevail?

A liberal approach illustrated by Bollinger suggests that freedom of expression facilitates 'the development of [a] capacity for tolerance' ('The Tolerance Society', 1990, *Columbia Law Review*, 90(1): 979). A capacity for tolerance weakens 'a general bias against receiving or acknowledging new ideas' (ibid.). Secondly as Locke recognised (*On Tolerance*, 1698) it is particularly valuable as a means of keeping the peace in large and complex societies containing people with varied beliefs and interests.

However it is widely accepted that freedom of expression is not absolute and not all aspects of it are equally important. This leads to the danger, identified by Berlin (Chapter 2), of freedom of expression being regarded as a 'positive freedom' conditional upon those in power assessing its worthiness.

The interests with which freedom of expression might conflict are open ended and difficult to define. Ultimately they depend only on the wishes of the particular lawmaker or public opinion. They include security, public order, confidential relationships, the fairness and independence of court proceedings, the protection of children or of reputation and personal privacy which is also a human right. 'Hate speech' is particularly controversial since it can be justified on all the grounds outlined above. It has often been emphasised that in a liberal society, freedom of expression is especially important where it involves controversial statements which might shock and offend, for example in relation to the religious, moral or cultural susceptibilities of others (see *Handyside* v *UK* (1976); Hoffmann LJ in *R* v *Central Independent Television plc* (1994)). On the other hand tolerance requires a certain degree of respect for the values of others. A further issue is whether it is possible to protect other interests without inhibiting the public interest in press freedom. Vaguely defined limits to freedom of expression might have a 'chilling' effect on the press by discouraging bold investigations (see *Campbell* v *MGN* (2004)).

The protection of free expression has other dangers. In the political context it could be argued that freedom of expression without constraint allows the loudest voice to prevail thus risking the 'tyranny of the majority'. It has been suggested that protection against state interference encourages indirect censorship by commercial and social forces which are intolerant of minority opinions. A free press is necessarily influenced by commercial concerns: the need to sell newspapers or advertising space. This leads to the press including trivial or sensational personal stories to attract customers or to publish material that suits the prejudices of the majority. According to this view society is polarised between a deeply conformist majority and marginalised dissenters and the protection of minorities might be improved through greater state intervention. A utilitarian argument also sometimes presented, for example by Lord Hutton in *R v Shaylor* (2002), is that freedom of expression might weaken confidence in those who govern us.

That there should limits on freedom of expression does not mean that they should always be imposed by law. This is because we may not be able to trust lawmakers or officials to exercise the delicate power of censorship wisely or honestly. Moral constraints are equally important and we might question whether we should entrust any public official with large power in relation to so fundamental a matter as freedom of expression. For example in relation to press freedom there is reliance on self regulation by means of the Press Complaints Commission (See Blom-Cooper, (2008) 'Press Freedom: Constitutional Right or Cultural Assumption', *Public Law*).

21.2 The Legal Status of Freedom of Expression

Article 10: Freedom of expression

This includes '*freedom to hold opinions and to receive and impart information and ideas without interference by public authority and regardless of frontiers. This article shall not prevent states from requiring the licensing of broadcasting, television or cinema enterprise*'.

Among the rights protected by the European Convention on Human Rights some judges have claimed that freedom of expression has an especially high status (for example *Attorney-General* v *Guardian Newspapers Ltd* (1987), Lord Bridge (dissenting); *Derbyshire County Council* v *Times Newspapers Ltd* (1993); *R* v *Secretary of State for the Home Department ex parte Simms* (1999) 407–8, Lord Steyn: 'the primary freedom'; *R (Pro-Life Alliance)* v *BBC* (2003), Lord Nicholls [6]). Because of its connection with democracy it also has an element of duty, this being realised in the idea of 'responsible journalism' which has recently been developed by the courts. The link with democracy also includes the notion of a right to receive information not just to impart it.

The extent of freedom of expression is influenced by the sort of expression approved of by the state thus attracting the notion of 'positive freedom' which was considered in Chapter 2. Thus some kinds of expression are given greater weight than others. The greatest weight is given to political expression through the media since this is regarded as essential to the processes of democracy (see Lord Bingham in *McCartan Turkington-Breen* v *Times Newspapers* (2001), 290–1). Less weight is given to forms of commercial expression such as advertising and possibly the least weight is given to lifestyle matters such as pornography. In *R* v *Secretary of State ex parte Simms* (2000) a prisoner was held entitled to have access to a journalist in order to publicise his claim that he was wrongly convicted. Lord Steyn thought that he would not have had such access to indulge in pornography or even in a general political or economic debate (see also *Campbell* v *MGN* (2004) [1006]; *R (British American Tobacco UK Ltd)* v *Secretary of State for Health* (2004): advertising; '*Miss Behavin*' v *Belfast City Council* (2007): sexual services). It is not clear how much weight is given to non-political cultural matters such as theatre and works of art. However where these conflict with religious susceptibilities, at least those of influential sections of the community, it seems that the latter carries greater weight. Moreover a distinction is often drawn between banning expression entirely and regulating the time and place at which it can be carried out (see for example *R (Pro Life Alliance)* v *BBC* (2003)).

Parliamentary supremacy prevents the existence of a right to freedom of expression as such. We have only such freedom as Parliament has not removed. However freedom of expression particularly in its political form is treated as a fundamental right that requires clear statutory authority to restrict (*R* v *Secretary of State ex parte Simms* (1999)). This is reinforced by the ECHR as incorporated in the Human Rights Act 1998 which accommodates freedom of expression with other concerns by providing a list of overrides to that freedom. Article 10 confers the right of freedom of expression subject to 'duties and responsibilities'. These entitle the state to limit freedom of expression for the following purposes:

- national security
- territorial integrity or public safety
- prevention of disorder or crime
- protection of health or morals
- protection of the reputation or rights of others. In particular freedom of expression may have to be compromised by the right to a fair trial (Article 6), privacy (Article 8; below, Chapter 21) and freedom of religion (Article 9).
- preventing the disclosure of information received in confidence
- maintaining the authority and impartiality of the judiciary.

Numerous Acts have restricted freedom of expression for the following main purposes: security, public order and safety, religious and sexuality based hatred and the independence of judicial proceedings (Contempt of Court), in particular restraining press comment on pending trials that create a 'substantial risk' that the course of justice will be seriously impeded or prejudiced (Contempt of Court Act 1981 s.2, see *Re Lonrho plc* (1990)). There is an important defence in contempt of court cases, namely that the publication contains a discussion in good faith of public affairs where the risk of prejudice is merely incidental to the discussion (see *AG* v *English* (1983)). Contempt law indirectly restrains free expression when it requires the identity of press informants to be disclosed (below). Other restrictions on freedom of expression include sexual morality (Obscene Publications Act 1959), reputation, personal privacy and confidentiality, the protection of children (Children Act 1989 s.97(2); Magistrates Courts Act 1980 s.69 (2) (c); see *Pelling* v *Bruce-Williams* (2004); *Re Webster (A Child) No. 1* (2006)), protection against misleading advertising and professional claims and intellectual property rights such as copyright. These purposes seem to comply with the overrides outlined above. However whether the law satisfies the test of necessity is more questionable.

There is probably a positive obligation on the state to protect freedom of expression (see Lord Scott in *R (Pro-Life Alliance)* v *BBC* (2003)). Some statutes give specific protection. The main examples are the Bill of Rights 1688, the Parliamentary Papers Act 1841 and the Defamation Act 1952 which protect parliamentary proceedings and related reporting (Chapter 11) and the Education (No.2) Act 1986 which imposes a duty on universities to protect freedom of speech on their premises. Sometimes statute protects freedom of expression against some general restriction (for example Environmental Protection Act 1990 s.79(6A): noise in street; political demonstrations).

21.3   Press Freedom and Censorship

As we have seen political expression is widely regarded as especially important so that attacks on the government are subject to restriction only in extreme cases. Therefore the media enjoys a high level of protection because it is a watchdog over government on behalf of the public (see *Castells* v *Spain* (1992); *Jersild* v *Denmark* (1994); *Lingens* v *Austria*

(1986); *Attorney-General v Punch* (2003) [27], Lord Nicholls. For example in *Re Webster (A Child) No. 1* (2006) the press but not the public were permitted to attend a high profile case involving child care proceedings (see *Openness in Family Courts: A New Approach* (2007), Ministry of Justice CP 10/17). The European Court has consistently emphasised the importance of press freedom including the need to give some journalistic latitude in order to prevent the chilling effect of legal restrictions discouraging frankness and openness (see *Thomas v Luxemburg* (2003), 373; *Fressoz v France* (1999), 656; *Selisto v Finland* (2006), 161. It should be emphasised however that press freedom is not a separate right but is an aspect of the general right to freedom of expression whereby the media exercise the right on behalf of the public. There is a two way relationship in that the public have a right to receive information and the press a duty to give it. It is also important for democratic participation and for liberal pluralism that there should be a wide variety of media outlets (see *Informationsverein Lentia v Austria* (1993)). To this extent the state may have a positive duty to promote freedom of expression.

In the eighteenth century Blackstone promoted the distinction between censorship in advance by requiring government approval and punishing the speaker after the event (*Commentaries*, 1765, III, 17). Prior restraint is regarded as an especially serious violation of freedom of expression because it removes from the public sphere the possibility of assessing the matter, whereas punishment may be regarded as a legitimate compromise between competing goods. Prior restraint should therefore be resorted to only as a last resort. The ECHR subjects prior restraint to a high level of scrutiny particularly in the case of news 'which is a perishable commodity' (see *Observer and Guardian Newspapers v UK* (1992)). Indeed in *Open Door and Dublin Well Woman v Ireland* (1992) five judges thought that prior restraint should never be tolerated. In *VGT v Switzerland* (2002), a ban on political advertising was condemned.

In *R (Laporte) v Chief Constable of Gloucestershire* (2006) [32] Lord Bingham emphasised that prior restraint in the context of public demonstrations should be subject to careful scrutiny (below). On the other hand where Parliament has established a special regulatory censorship mechanism the courts are reluctant to impose their own judgments, short of reviewing unreasonable decisions (*R v Broadcasting Standards Commission ex parte BBC* (2001)). Offence alone can justify suppression even of political speech although the courts are reluctant to impose their own views of what is appropriate.

In *R (Pro-Life Alliance) v BBC* (2003) the House of Lords was asked to decide whether an obligation imposed on the BBC to ensure that its programmes do not offend 'good taste and decency' overrode the right to freedom of expression of the Alliance who wished to include in an election broadcast vivid but accurate and unsensationalised images of the process of abortion. A majority of the House refused to intervene on the grounds that deciding the limits of good taste is not appropriate to a court and that the BBC has a margin of discretion which it had exercised reasonably. By taking this line the court accepted the principle that free expression could be restricted on the ground of taste alone. Indeed Lord Hoffmann emphasised the pervasive influence of television with the implication that protective measures are especially justified. A distinction was drawn between banning someone altogether from what he or she wished to say and refusing to give someone a platform to disseminate offensive material (see also *Appelby v UK* (2003); *DPP v Collins* (2006)). Just as no one has a right to have his or her work published by a particular publisher no one has a right to appear on TV. This analogy may seem unreal given the importance of television as a medium of political communication and the state's positive duty to ensure the dissemination of opinion. Lord Scott dissented on classical liberal freedom of speech grounds. The difference between his approach and that of the majority was that he gave greater weight to the democratic importance of an election broadcast. Far from wishing to protect the public against offence he thought that 'the public in a mature democracy are not entitled to be offended by the broadcasting of such a programme' and that a ban would be 'positively inimical to the values of a democratic society to which values it must be assumed that the public adheres' [98]. His Lordship also remarked in the context of 'voter apathy' that:

> a broadcaster's mindset that rejects a party election television programme on the ground that large numbers of the voting public would find the programme 'offensive' denigrates the voting public, treats them like children who need to be protected from the unpleasant realities of life, seriously undervalues their political maturity and can only promote [voter apathy]. [99].

Since the abolition in 1695 of state licensing of printing presses the government has no censorship powers over the printed word although in characteristically British fashion there are non-enforceable mechanisms presided over by committees of insiders for the purpose of self censorship in security matters (the 'D' Notice Committee). There are also provisions intended to protect competition in media ownership (Fair Trading Act 1973 ss.58, 59; Communications Act 2003). Broadcasting raises particular problems because of the variety of broadcast media that now exist at an international level and the ease with which material can be pirated (see for example *Autronic AG v Switzerland* (1990)). There is significant state regulation over broadcasting (but not the internet) including a general power to require announcements or to ban broadcasts exercisable by the Secretary of State (Broadcasting Act 1990 s.10, BBC Licence Agreement). There are also specific requirements including impartiality and taste policed by the Office of Communications (OFCOM) which replaced a variety of other bodies (Communications Act 2003). Under the Cinemas Act 1985 local authorities have a power to license cinema performances. There are also controls over the distribution of videos and DVDs (Video Recordings Act 1984).

The courts have prior restraint powers in the form of an injunction, disobedience to which attracts imprisonment for contempt of court. The Attorney-General can seek an injunction in the name of the public interest, most notably in the case of publications that risk prejudicing legal proceedings such as newspaper comments on matters related to pending litigation (contempt of court) and in the interests of government confidentiality or national security (Chapter 21). A temporary injunction pending a full trial can be granted on the basis that there is an arguable case, since once material is published there is no turning back. A temporary injunction prevents anyone, whether a party or not, publishing the material with the intention to impede the court's purpose in granting the injunction (*Attorney-General v Observer Ltd* (1988); *Attorney-General v Times Newspapers Ltd* (1991)). However an injunction will be granted only if it serves a useful purpose. Once material becomes public, even if unlawfully, the press has a duty to disseminate it and comment on it and further restraint cannot be justified (see *Observer and Guardian Newspapers* v *UK* (1992)).

UK law violated the ECHR because injunctions have been used in a manner disproportionate to the risk of harm. In *Attorney-General* v *Times Newspapers Ltd* (1974) the House of Lords held that it was a contempt for a newspaper to comment on the merits of civil litigation concerning the victims of thalidomide for the reason that 'trial by newspaper' was undesirable in itself, irrespective of whether the publication might influence the outcome of the trial. In *Sunday Times* v *UK* (1979) the ECHR held that contempt law could inhibit freedom of expression only where this was necessary to ensure a fair trial, for example to prevent influence on juries or witnesses. The test is whether there is a 'substantial risk' that the course of justice will be impeded or prejudiced (Contempt of Court Act 1981 s.2; see *Re Lonrho plc* (1990): appellate judges, no risk).

In *Attorney-General* v *Punch* (2003) a magazine published a series of articles by David Shaylor, a former member of the security services against whom a prosecution under the Official Secrets Act was pending for disclosing information about intelligence operations. An injunction prevented publication of any material obtained by Mr Shaylor in the course of or as a result of his employment in the security services. Although critical of this wide injunction because of its chilling effect on freedom of expression of restrictions that are not precisely targeted [61–3], nevertheless the House of Lords upheld it, rejecting the editor's argument that he did not intend to damage national security on the ground that this was irrelevant to the court's purpose in granting the injunction and the editor should have realised this. Moreover this was not censorship by the Attorney-General who, under the terms of the injunction could clear publication, since the matter was in the control of the courts.

The importance of press freedom has been reinforced by section 12 of the Human Rights Act 1998. This provides firstly that a court order limiting the 'Convention right of freedom of expression' cannot normally be granted in the absence of the respondent. This affects interim injunctions which might be sought as an emergency measure against the media. Secondly section 12 prevents an interim order being made unless the applicant is likely to establish that publication should not be allowed. Thirdly section 12 requires the court to have particular regard to freedom of expression and,

> where the proceedings relate to material which the respondent claims or which appears to the court to be journalistic, literary or artistic material (or to conduct connected with such material), to (a) the extent to which (i) the material has, or is about to, become available to the public; or (ii) it is, or would be, in the public interest for the material to be published; and (b) any relevant privacy code

(for example, that made by the Press Complaints Commission).

Section 12 does not privilege freedom of expression above other convention rights. In *Douglas and Zeta-Jones* v *Hello! Ltd* (2001) the Court of Appeal held that it merely ensures that the competing rights in question are taken into account at the interim stage. In *Cream Holdings* v *Banerjee* (2004) the House of Lords held that where section 12 applies the normal threshold is that the applicant would 'more likely than not' succeed at the trial. However the approach must be flexible so that for example if publication would cause serious harm, a lower threshold would be justified. In *Thompson and Venables v News Group Newspapers Ltd* (2001) the claimants (the notorious killers of James Bulger) sought indefinite injunctions restraining the press from disclosing their (new) identities on release from custody. Since the circumstances of the case were exceptional in that they involved the right to life, Dame Butler-Sloss granted the injunctions. She stated that it will only be necessary to grant injunctive relief where it can be 'convincingly demonstrated' that the requirements of Article 10(2), as to overrides, can be satisfied.

21.4 The Free Flow of Information

The European Court has held that the public has a right to receive information, ideas and opinions, so that the state has a positive duty to safeguard the free flow even of offensive information and opinion.

Jersild v *Denmark* (1994) concerned a television interview with representatives of an extremist political group. The interview was edited to highlight abusive remarks made about ethnic groups within Denmark. The TV interviewer, who did not challenge the racist remarks, was charged with aiding and abetting the offence of 'threatening, insulting or degrading a group of persons on account of their race, colour, national or ethnic origin or belief'. The court held, with seven dissenters, that the interview was protected by Article 10 because of the duty of the press to report controversial opinions in its role of public watchdog and the corresponding right of the public to be informed. It was not for the court to decide how journalists presented their material, provided that taken in its whole context the broadcast did not support the views put forward. In these circumstances restricting the press was not necessary in a democratic society as required by Article 10 (see also *Castells* v *Spain* (1992), para. 43; *Lingens* v *Austria* (1986) [41]; *Observer and Guardian* v *UK* (1991)).

It is important that the confidentiality of those who supply information to the press is protected. In *R* v *Central Criminal Court ex parte Bright, Alton and Rusbridger* (2001) the Court of Appeal quashed a production order sought by the Crown against the editors of the *Guardian* and the *Observer* to disclose information received from David Shaylor (above). It was held that disclosure would inhibit press freedom without there being a compelling reason for the disclosure.

The press also has statutory protection. Section 10 of the Contempt of Court Act 1981 protects the anonymity of a publisher's sources of information except where the court thinks that disclosure is necessary on the grounds of the interests of justice, national security or the prevention of crime and disorder. Section 10 enables the court to exercise a discretion between the competing concerns. Before the HRA the courts interpreted the exceptions broadly against the press, influenced by the common law idea that the press should have no special privileges (for example *X Ltd v Morgan Grampian Publishers Ltd* (1991): commercial interest outweighed press freedom). This was strongly criticised by the European Court in *Goodwin* v *UK* (1996) on the ground that the protection of journalistic confidentiality is crucial to press freedom, interference with which requires the most careful scrutiny. It has also been held that where national security or wrongdoing is involved the court will usually order disclosure (*X* v *Morgan Grampian* (1991); *Ashworth Hospital* v *MGN Ltd* (2001)). However in *John* v *Express Newspapers Ltd* (2000) which concerned the leaking of legal advice, it was held following *Goodwin* that a confidential source should be publicly disclosed only as a last resort.

Press Freedom and Reputation: Defamation

Defamation concerns the protection of reputation which is an aspect of the human need for self esteem (see *Reynolds* v *Times Newspapers Ltd* (2001) at 201, per Lord Nicholls: 'reputation [as] an integral and important part of the dignity of the individual'). Apart from its role in ensuring that those who rule us are accountable, freedom of expression is also part of individual dignity. Moreover both interests secure autonomy by providing protection against arbitrary interference. Hence those who have the task of accommodating these values within the law must make agonising and politically controversial choices. In general the press is subject to the law of defamation in the same way as anyone else. Indeed English law is widely regarded as relatively unsympathetic to the press and English courts are often chosen as a forum for defamation actions as opposed for example to the US where freedom of expression has a higher level of protection as enshrined in the Constitution. The main relevant difference is that in English law the defendant media have to prove the truth of any allegations they make whereas more usually the onus is on the claimant to prove that the allegation is false.

Material is defamatory if it:

1. Reflects on the claimant's reputation so as to lower him or her in the estimation of right thinking members of society generally (*Sim* v *Stretch* (1936))
2. Would tend to cause the claimant to be shunned or avoided (*Youssoupoff* v *Metro-Goldwyn-Mayer Pictures Ltd* (1934))
3. Would bring the claimant into ridicule or contempt (*Dunlop Rubber Co. Ltd* v *Dunlop* (1921)).

A claimant must prove that the relevant material is (i) defamatory, (ii) has been published and (iii) refers to him or her. Publication means merely communication to another person. Defamatory publications take one of two forms: namely, libel and slander. Material is libellous if it is published in a permanent form, for example writing or another recorded media.

It is slanderous if it takes a less than permanent form, for example word of mouth.

Defamation law recognises the importance of freedom of expression. To this end there are various defences. These include:

1. **Truth** (or justification): subject to an exception under the Rehabilitation of Offenders Act 1974 (s.8) this defence can be pleaded even in circumstances where a defendant has been actuated by malice (that is, spite or ill will).
2. **Absolute privilege:** liability for defamation cannot be imposed in the course of:
    (a) parliamentary proceedings (Chapter 11)
    (b) judicial proceedings
    (c) official communications (as between ministers of the Crown for example (*Chatterton* v *Secretary of State for India* (1895)).

3. **Qualified privilege:** traditionally this defence applies where a defendant who honestly believes what he or she says to be true meets the following two requirements (see *Reynolds* v *Times Newspapers Ltd* (2001) at 194–5 and 200, per Lord Nicholls):
   (a) the defendant has an interest or a duty (legal, social, or moral) to communicate the relevant material to another or others
   (b) the recipient of the material must have a corresponding interest or duty to receive it.
   However the defence of qualified privilege may recently have been modified as far as the press are concerned to one of 'responsible journalism' without the requirement of a specific interest/duty relationship. This important defence is discussed further below.

4. **Fair comment:** this defence protects honest expressions of opinion on matters of public interest. Judges sometimes identify it as a bulwark of free expression (see for example *Slim* v *Daily Telegraph Ltd* (1968), 170, per Lord Denning MR). While fair comment protects expressions of opinion, defendants have to establish that their views were based on a substratum of fact that was true at the time of publication (*Cohen* v *Daily Telegraph Ltd* (1968)). As with qualified privilege a plea of fair comment can be defeated by a showing that the defendant was actuated by malice.

5. **Reportage.** A person is liable if he or she repeats a defamatory statement made by another. This applies to the press as much as to anyone else .However there is a defence if it can be shown clearly that when read as a whole the author did not in any way associate himself with or support the statement in question. Thus very careful journalistic writing is required (see *Chapman* v *Orion Publishing Group* (2008); *Galloway* v *Telegraph Group* (2006)).

Two further features of the law protect freedom of expression. First the institution of the jury and second the limited availability of an injunction. Defamation actions (which are heard in the High Court) are usually tried with a jury which is regarded as providing a safeguard against official repression (see Fox's Libel Act 1792). However in *Grobbelaar* v *News Group Newspapers Ltd* (2001) the Court of Appeal took the (apparently) ground breaking step of overturning a jury's findings of fact on the ground that they were perverse and unreasonable.

The judiciary has long been reluctant to grant injunctions in defamation cases. Hence this remedy will not be granted unless the plaintiff can satisfy a number of exacting conditions. He or she will for example have to show that there is no real ground for supposing that the defendant may avoid liability by pleading the defences of truth, privilege or fair comment (*Bonnard* v *Perryman* (1891)). Further judges are particularly grudging in their readiness to grant interim (or interlocutory) injunctions which restrain the offending expression pending a full trial (ibid.). Such injunctions are only granted where (i) a court is satisfied that publication will result in immediate and irreparable injury and (ii) damages would not provide an adequate remedy (see *Monson* v *Tussauds Ltd* (1894); see also HRA 1998 s.12 above).

21.5.1 Public Bodies

In recent years three features of defamation law have been modified by the judiciary with a view to establishing a balance between press freedom and reputational interests compatible with the ECHR. These concern public bodies, damages and qualified privilege.

In *Derbyshire County Council* v *Times Newspapers Ltd* (1993) the House of Lords held that a local authority and other public bodies cannot sue in defamation. The Council sued following the publication in *The Sunday Times* of an allegation of impropriety vis-à-vis the management of pension funds. Lord Keith explained their Lordships' decision by stating that: 'it is of the *highest public importance* that a democratically elected body . . . should be open to uninhibited public criticism' (1017, emphasis added). Hence the law could not be allowed to exert a 'chilling effect' on expressive activity. Such an effect manifests itself in circumstances where liability rules encourage writers and other commentators to censor themselves rather than risk the (potentially negative) consequences of litigation. The House of Lords did not base its decision on the ECHR but found support in 'the common law of England'. Lord Keith did however conclude that English common law was 'consistent' with the ECHR's requirements. The same principle applies to political parties (see *Goldsmith* v *Bhoyrul* (1997)). One feature of the case suggests that Lord Keith's commitment to democracy may be half hearted. Lord Keith indicated that *individual* public officials can sue in defamation on the same basis as private individuals. The House of Lords has been criticised for failing to follow the US Supreme Court's lead in *New York Times Co.* v *Sullivan* (1964) by introducing the 'actual malice' rule into UK defamation law in relation to individuals. This rule protects statements against both public institutions and individual public officials made in the absence of malice with knowledge that they are false. This would have helped to protect politically significant expression and brought the law of defamation into closer alignment with the jurisprudence of the European Court of Human Rights. This treats Article 10 as requiring three distinctions, namely political figures should receive less protection from defamation law than private individuals and governmental bodies (and political parties) should receive even less protection from the law than political figures (see *Lingens* v *Austria* (1986); *Castells* v *Spain* (1992); *Oberschlick* v *Austria* (1995)).

21.5.2   Damages

Damages are the principal remedy for defamation. Plaintiffs are entitled to damages for both reputational and economic injury, for example loss of employment. Juries determine the amount and until recently they were not furnished with clear guidance as to the appropriate sum to award. This sometimes led to very large awards. Such awards are open to objection on at least two grounds. Firstly they are a disproportionate response to a defendant's wrongdoing. Secondly the prospect of having to pay such a sum may exert a powerful 'chilling effect' on expressive activity.

Objections such as these have prompted a change in the law. Under the Courts and Legal Services Act 1990 section 8 the Court of Appeal has the power, where a jury has awarded 'excessive' compensation, to substitute a lower sum. This power was first exercised by the Appeal Court in *Rantzen* v *Mirror Group Newspapers Ltd* (1994) where the Court substituted an award of £110,000 for the jury's award of £250,000. While the Court of Appeal based its decision on the Act, it also justified it by reference to Article 10 of the ECHR. Neill LJ stated that (994) the Convention required that damages should not exceed the level 'necessary to compensate the plaintiff and re-establish his reputation' (see also *Tolstoy Miloslavsky* v *UK* (1995)).

In *John* v *Mirror Group Newspapers Ltd* (1996) the Court of Appeal restricted the range of circumstances in which a plaintiff can recover exemplary or punitive damages. The Court stated that awards of this sort could only be recovered where the plaintiff offers 'clear' proof of the two following things (58, per Lord Bingham): first the defendant knowingly or recklessly published untruths; second the defendant proceeded to publish the relevant untruths having cynically calculated that the profit accruing from the publication would be likely to exceed any damages award made against him or her. The Court buttressed its decision by reference to Article 10 which, according to Lord Bingham, requires that 'freedom of expression should not be restricted by awards of exemplary damages save to the extent shown to be strictly necessary for the protection of reputations' (ibid.).

21.5.3   Responsible Journalism

We noted above that defendants must stand in a relationship of reciprocity, meaning (a) that they have an interest or duty (legal, social or moral) to communicate the material and (b) that the recipient(s) of the material had a corresponding interest or duty to receive it. Newspapers have experienced difficulty in establishing reciprocity vis-à-vis material communicated to the public at large. This is because judges have been reluctant to bestow on newspapers and other media organs an open-ended 'public interest' defence.

In *Reynolds* v *Times Newspapers Ltd* (2001) the House of Lords held that qualified privilege can in some circumstances be pleaded where political material is disseminated to the general public. However their Lordships emphasised that such material would still have to fall within the criteria for reciprocity (200 and 204, per Lord Nicholls). Their Lordships also rejected the gloss placed on the qualified privilege defence by Lord Bingham LCJ in the Court of Appeal, who stated that the press would have to satisfy an additional condition, namely what Lord Bingham termed 'the circumstantial test' (909). To satisfy this test defendants were required to show that 'the nature, status and source of the material and all the circumstances of its publication' were such that the publication should 'in the public interest' be protected (912).

However their Lordships (rather equivocally) identified 'circumstances' as a highly relevant consideration. Lord Nicholls stated:

> through the cases runs the strain that, when determining whether the public at large had a right to know the particular information, *the court has regard to all the circumstances*. The Court is concerned to assess whether the information was of sufficient value to the public that, in the public interest, it should be protected by the privilege in the absence of malice. (195, emphasis added)

To this his Lordship added a (non-exhaustive) list of considerations relevant to the question whether the qualified privilege defence should be available, namely (i) the seriousness of the allegation(s); (ii) the nature of the information and the extent to which the matter is a matter of public concern; (iii) the source of the information; (iv) the steps taken to verify the information; (v) the status of the information; (vi) the urgency of the matter; (vii) whether comment was sought from the claimant; (viii) whether the relevant publication contained the gist of the claimant's side of the story; (ix) the tone of the article; and (x) the circumstances of the publication (205).

Reynolds is open to at least two criticisms. First where judges draw on the considerations listed by Lord Nicholls they will be defining standards of good journalistic practice. It is far from obvious that this is a task that they are well equipped to undertake. Second the House's decision can be expected to produce uncertainty and so the chilling effect. By contrast in *Lange* v *Atkinson and Consolidated Press NZ Ltd* (1998) the New Zealand Court of Appeal, invoking Article 10 of the ECHR, held that defendants can plead qualified privilege vis-à-vis politically significant material communicated to the public. As well as expanding the qualified privilege defence, the Court also sought to forestall the danger of chilling effects. To this end it stated that plaintiffs must, in order to defeat a plea of qualified privilege, prove that the defendant lacked an honest belief in the truth of his or her statements. The decision was subsequently appealed to the Privy Council. The Privy Council remitted the case to New Zealand for rehearing, thus affording the New Zealand Appeal Court the opportunity to consider *Reynolds* (*Lange* v *Atkinson* (2000)). While prepared to 'amplify' its earlier decision the New Zealand Appeal Court declined to follow *Reynolds*. One of the reasons it gave for this decision was the greater readiness of the New Zealand press, as compared with the British press, to behave responsibly (398).

Later cases have perhaps redefined the *Reynolds* defence as in effect one of 'responsible journalism' and have emphasised that the law should be regarded as liberalising in favour of press freedom. It has been suggested that there is no longer a need to show a reciprocal duty- interest relationship in relation to the particular material. The public can be assumed to have a general interest in receiving material from the media and the press a corresponding duty to disseminate it. There is however no agreement as to whether *Reynolds* should be regarded as signalling a completely new defence or is merely an extension of the traditional qualified privilege defence with all its baggage. It has been emphasised that the Reynolds list of the requirements of good journalistic practice should not be regarded as an obstacle course nor applied strictly and pedantically but should be treated as providing general guidelines, importantly allowing latitude for editorial judgement (see *Jameel* v *Wall Street Journal Europe* (2006), [46] [50] [57]; *Chapman* v *Orion Publishing Group* (2008)). It also seems that the defence is available to anyone not only to the media (*Seaga* v *Harper* (2008)).

21.6   Press Freedom and Privacy

Article 8 of the ECHR states that 'everyone has a right to respect for his family and private life' (Chapter 19). There is therefore a clash with Article 10. Privacy relates to dignity, independence and self respect and the desire to control personal information. English law had no separate right to privacy, regarding privacy as a value that influences specific causes of action, most importantly breach of confidence (see *Wainright* v *Home Office* (2003); *Kaye* v *Robertson* (1991)). Breach of confidence protects secrets and personal information. It concerns wrongful disclosure of true information and relates to a range of concerns, some being matters of efficiency, for example commercial and professional confidentiality, others relating to dignity, for example intimate relationships and feelings. Newspapers are privately owned so that the protection of privacy against the press is an example of a positive obligation imposed on the state. In recent years the law of confidence has become stronger and more flexible and arguably is no longer separate from privacy. Confidentiality and privacy have been given increased weight in relation to freedom of expression.

An injunction can be obtained for breaches of confidence where the following three conditions are satisfied (*Attorney-General* v *Guardian Newspapers (No. 2)* (1998)):

1. The information is confidential in character. In *Campbell* v *MGN Ltd* (2004) the House of Lords held that privacy lay at the root of breach of confidence. It was suggested that information is confidential whose disclosure violates 'a reasonable expectation of privacy'. This test was preferred to the stronger one used in some jurisdictions that the disclosure be highly offensive to a person of ordinary susceptibilities (see [21], [22], [83], [134], [135]). This includes not only the content of the information but also the situation or relationship in which it is revealed, for example in the home or in a diary. A matter might still be protected even in a public place (see *Campbell* v *MGN* below).
2. The information must have been imparted in circumstances imposing an obligation of confidence: for example it was imparted for a limited purpose. Earlier cases requiring a specific confidential relationship such as family or employment no longer apply (see *Campbell* v *MGN* (2004)) although such a relationship for example between ministers and civil servants will still be sufficient (Chapter 21). Thus confidentiality is now more strongly linked to privacy and the courts have acknowledged the influence of the ECHR. The claimant must however establish that the relevant information was acquired in circumstances where a reasonable person would have realised that it was confidential. For example in *HRH Princess of Wales* v *MGN Newspapers Ltd and Others* (1993) photographs acquired by the press of the plaintiff exercising in a semi public gymnasium were held to be subject to a duty of confidentiality.
3. There must be an unauthorised use of the relevant information by the confidant or a third party with knowledge of the confidence and for a purpose other than that for which it was imparted (for example *Prince of Wales* v *Associated Newspapers* (2006): diaries written by the prince making disparaging remarks about overseas dignitaries).
   There is a defence that disclosure of the relevant material was (a) in the public interest and (b) that this outweighs the interest in preserving confidentiality. In cases involving press intrusion privacy is currently given a high level of protection (see *Von Hannover* v *Germany* (2004)). Privacy must also be balanced against freedom of expression. As we have seen (Chapter 19) the courts treat the competing rights equally. We must therefore ask what are their underlying rationales in the particular context and how strongly they apply, taking all circumstances into account. As usual the judges must make a subjective choice. The uncertainty generated by this risks inhibiting freedom of expression.

Recently, stimulated by the Human Rights Act, the law of confidence has been moving towards the general goal of protecting privacy as such, as opposed to protecting particular confidential relationships. The clash with freedom of expression is acute in that there seems to be no overarching general principle capable of comparing the two so as to balance the harms caused when one violates the other. Thus the familiar proportionality principle seems to be of little help. The main technique used by the courts when a conflict arises, for example in relation to press intrusions on the personal lives of public figures, is to look at the impact on each right in turn, asking whether the harm done to the privacy interest is *in its own terms* more serious than the harm done to freedom of expression taking all the consequences into account. Again this rough utilitarianism founders upon the problem that there is no common denominator against which to compare the harms.

It seems clear however that, contrary to the case with defamation (see previous section), privacy has been strengthened at the cost of restricting press freedom.

The following cases illustrate the main issues and show that the tests used are so broad that the matter depends substantially upon the subjective preference of the judge. *Campbell* v *MGN Ltd* (2004) concerned press reports relating to drug dependency therapy undergone by a famous model. These included photographs of the model in the street entering a clinic. A majority of the House of Lords held that the reports breached the claimant's right to privacy. This was because the photographs were particularly likely to cause upset and the information had no public importance. The minority (Lords Nicholls and Hoffmann) thought that freedom of the press should prevail. They favoured some journalistic licence in support of a free press, particularly as their Lordships did not consider that the material published seriously affected matters of dignity and self respect. All agreed however that the bare fact that the claimant was drug dependent could be published. The claimant had courted publicity by publicly denying that she was on drugs and to that extent had given up her privacy. Importantly however it was not suggested that she forfeited her privacy completely. Lord Hoffman remarked [51] that the law had shifted in emphasis from the notion of good faith to that of protecting autonomy and dignity and the control of information about one's private life (see also *Von Hanover* v *Germany* (2004).

By contrast, in *Re S (a child)* (2004) the competition was between press freedom in reporting the identity of the parties in court proceedings and the privacy of a child in care whose mother had been convicted of murdering his brother. The Court of Appeal preferred the press interest. It held that the importance of open justice and drawing public attention to child abuse outweighed the child's interest since the additional publicity would cause relatively limited upset over and above that which had already occurred.

In *HRH Prince of Wales* v *Associated Newspapers* (2007) the Court of Appeal prohibited the press from publishing extracts from the personal journals of the Prince of Wales. These contained his impressions of the appearance and character of the Chinese leaders during an official visit to China. The court held firstly that the right to privacy arose where there is a 'reasonable expectation' of privacy; secondly that the test is 'whether in all circumstances it was in the public interest that the duty of confidence be breached'. It is not enough that the matter is one of public interest. Factors to be taken into account include the fact that the information was leaked by an employee in breach of contract. It is a matter of public interest in itself that confidential employment relationships be protected. It was also relevant that the information made only a 'minimal' contribution to the public interest.

Breach of confidence protects privacy up to a point but it may be undesirable to shoehorn privacy law into the category of breach of confidence since the two serve different purposes, breach of confidence being to protect the information, privacy to protect the person. For example the quality of confidence is lost once the material has been released into the public domain so that the claimant cannot get an injunction in respect of publication after that time (*A-G* v *Guardian Newspapers (No. 2)* (1998)). However a claimant might still be awarded damages, for example where photographs that have been published with the claimant's permission are stolen and republished without permission (see *Douglas and Zeta-Jones v Hello! Ltd (No. 3)* (2005)). This is more consistent with a general privacy law than with breach of confidence.

21.7 'Hate Speech'

Hate speech involves attacks on racial, ethnic, religious or cultural groups including lifestyle matters such as sexuality. Freedom of expression therefore comes into particular conflict with Article 8 (privacy), Article 9 (thought, conscience and religion) and on a secondary level Article 14 (discrimination). Hate speech also involves matter that shocks or offends, thereby raising the overrides of public morality and the rights of others and providing a hard test of the rationales for freedom of expression. It could be argued along with Mill that being offended or shocked is not harmful since it challenges orthodoxy and does not limit freedom. On the other hand there is an argument for suppressing the expression of opinions that offend others where there is a risk to public safety or the welfare of vulnerable groups. However this leads to oppressive or lazy enforcement since it is often cheaper and easier to suppress a speaker rather than police those who cause a disturbance because they are offended.

The notion of ideas and information as underlying freedom of expression has enabled it to be claimed that some forms of hate speech should not be protected since they contain no worthy ideas (see *Otto Preminger Institut v Austria* (1994) (below)). Pornography is also susceptible to this argument. For example the publication of material that is likely to deprave and corrupt a significant proportion of those exposed to it is prohibited (the 'harm' principle) but subject to a defence of literary or artistic merit (Obscene Publications Act 1959). However this elevates the truth rationale for freedom of expression at the expense of that of self fulfilment and comes close to Berlin's fear of 'positive freedom' (Chapter 2).

As usual the law must find an accommodation. One way of achieving this is by attempting to distinguish between expressing opinions, however distasteful, and inciting unlawful or harmful behaviour. However in the case of particularly vulnerable groups this line is breached and some forms of expression that are offensive to such groups are also prohibited. The law is sensitive to particular historical circumstances and is not entirely consistent. For example there is protection in respect of racial or ethnic hate expression and to a lesser extent in respect of religion but not in relation to gender or class hate expression as such. There is no known rational solution and public opinion is the ultimate arbiter.

21.7.1 Racism and sexual orientation

Racism has been so widely condemned throughout Europe as to amount to a special case. Freedom from discrimination as such is not protected under the ECHR which expressly prohibits discrimination only in respect of the other protected rights (Article 14; Chapter 19). However the International Convention on the Elimination of All Forms of Racial Discrimination (1965) (CERD) has been ratified by most members of the Council of Europe (not Ireland, Lithuania or Turkey). Article 4 of this Convention requires signatories to create offences in relation to all dissemination of ideas based on racial supremacy or hatred, incitement to racial discrimination, as well as acts of violence or incitement to such acts against any race or group of persons of another colour or ethnic origin.

Article 4 also requires states to have 'due regard' to (among other things) the right to freedom of opinion and expression.

Racist expression is not entirely outside the protection of Article 10 but has a low level of protection, usually being outweighed by the need to protect the rights of others and prevent disorder. In *Jersild* v *Denmark* (above) the objective reporting by the media of racist abuse was held to be protected by Article 10. The reason for this is the role of the media as a watchdog against obnoxious elements in society. Measures to combat racism are reinforced by Article 17, which aims at preventing reliance on a convention right in order to undermine another. It is unlikely therefore that UK law contravenes the ECHR.

The main offences are contained in sections 17 to 23 of the Public Order Act 1986: a person is guilty if he or she uses

> threatening, abusive or insulting words or behaviour or displays written material which is threatening, abusive or insulting if (a) he intends to stir up racial hatred or, (b) having regard to all the circumstances, such hatred is likely to be stirred up thereby. (s.18)

Race includes colour, race, nationality, ethnic or national origins (s.17). An ethnic group can be defined by cultural as well as physical characteristics (see *Mandla* v *Dowell-Lee* (1983): Sikhs; *Commission for Racial Equality* v *Dutton* (1989): gypsies but not other travellers).

The offence can be committed in public or private places except exclusively within a dwelling (s.18(2)(4)). Public disorder is not required nor is the presence at the time of any member of the targeted racial group. For example the offence could apply to an academic paper read to an audience in a university or club. However there is a defence if the accused did not intend to stir up racial hatred and did not intend his or her words or behaviour to be, and was not aware that it might be, threatening, abusive or insulting (s.18(2)(5)). It is also an offence to publish or distribute written material in the same circumstances (s.17) and to possess racially inflammatory material (s.23). Similar provisions apply to a public performance of a play (s.20), to distributing, showing or playing recordings and to broadcasting or cable services except from the BBC and ITC (ss.22(7), 23(4)). Broadcasting bodies are governed by special systems of regulation (above). Contemporaneous reports of parliamentary, court or tribunal proceedings are excluded (s.26).The police have wide powers of entry and search (s.24).

There are increased sentences for offences of assault, criminal damage, public order and harassment committed wholly or partly with religious or racial motivations (Crime and Disorder Act 1998 ss. 28, 32). At the time of committing the offence or immediately before or after the offender must demonstrate hostility towards the victim based on the victim's membership (or presumed membership) of a racial or religious group.

21.7.2 Religion

In the context of religion, causing offence seems to justify restricting freedom of expression. Religion is defined to include any spiritual belief but its 'manifestation' must be cogent, serious, cohesive and important. It is not confined to belief in a supernatural entity (*Campbell and Cozens* v *UK* (1982); *R (Williamson)* v *Secretary of State for Education and*

Employment (2005)). This invites the decision maker to impose his or her own view as to what is important. Article 9 of the ECHR concerns freedom of religion. This overlaps with Article 10, freedom of expression but the two may conflict where freedom of expression is used to pressurise a religion or its supporters. The HRA 1998 requires courts to have particular regard in matters involving religious organisations to the importance of freedom of thought, conscience and religion (s.13). This could be read as authorising religious organisations to violate other rights such as privacy or to discriminate on religious grounds.

The European Court appears to give states a wide margin of discretion in respect of religious matters. In *Otto Preminger Institut* v *Austria* (1994) the state seized a film depicting Christ and his mother as in league with the devil which offended the Roman Catholic majority in the Tyrol. The Court held that the seizure was lawful for the purpose of protecting the rights of others. Recognising that there are differences in religious sensibilities between states and regions, the Court said that:

> in the context of religious opinion and beliefs . . . may legitimately be included an obligation to avoid as far as possible expressions that are gratuitously offensive to others and thus an infringement of their rights, and which therefore do not contribute to any form of public debate capable of furthering progress in human affairs.

This seems to come close to censorship based on majority sentiment. (See also *Wingrove* v *UK* (1997): homoerotic imagery discomforting to some Christians, ban upheld with strong dissent.) However in this kind of case it is difficult to see how such images prevent a person from manifesting or practising a religion as required by Article 9 but seem to give religion a privileged status (compare *Choudhury* v *UK* (1991): state not required to criminalise attacks on Islam).

Although the Church of England is closely associated with the state Christianity as such is not part of English law (*Bowman* v *Secular Society* (1917). However the main restriction on freedom of speech concerning religion was the offence of blasphemy. This ancient common law offence penalises attacks upon Christianity. It was originally used to enforce loyalty to the state. The common law offences of blasphemy and blasphemous libel were finally abolished by the Criminal Justice and Immigration Act 2008 (s. 79).

The Racial and Religious Hatred Act 2006, adding Part 3A to the Public Order Act 1986 creates various offences of intention to stir up religious hatred similar to those already applying to racial hatred (above). Religious hatred means hatred towards a group of persons defined by reference to religious belief or lack of religious belief. Thus atheists are protected by the Act. Religion is not defined (see *R (Williamson)* v *Secretary of State* (above)). Threatening words or behaviour are required and as with other public order offences, conduct taking effect entirely within a private dwelling is excluded.

The Act attempts to protect freedom of expression by stating that

> nothing in this Part shall be read or given effect in a way which prohibits discussion, criticism or expressions of antipathy, dislike, ridicule, insult, or abuse of particular religions or the beliefs or practices of their adherents, or of any other belief system or the beliefs of its adherents, or proselytising or urging the adherents of a different religion or belief system to cease practising their religion or belief system.

Since the offence requires threatening words or behaviour it may be that this provision limits the offence to personal abuse. Can threats of hellfire be used as part of an evangelising recruitment drive? Moreover it is arguable that the other public order offences (below) adequately protect religious groups (see Hare, 'Crosses, Crescents and Sacred Cows: Criminalising Incitement to Religious Hatred', 2006, *Public Law* 52).

Under the Anti-Terrorism, Crime and Security Act 2001 the penalties for certain offences involving assault, property damage, public order and harassment are increased where there is a religious motivation along the same lines as those applying to racially aggravated offences (s.39).

Under the Criminal Justice and Immigration Act 2008 s. 74 this group of offences has been extended to stirring up hatred on the ground of sexual orientation. Again there is some protection for freedom of expression. By virtue of Schedule 16 the discussion or criticism of sexual conduct or practices or the urging of persons to refrain or modify such conduct or practices shall not be taken of itself to be threatening or intended to stir up hatred.

21.7.3   Political Protest

The old common law offence of seditious libel consists of publishing material with the intention to incite hostility towards the government or its institutions or possibly to promote hostility between different classes of 'Her Majesty's subjects' (*R* v *Burns* (1886)). During the eighteenth century, which was punctuated by fear of popular uprising, seditious libel was used as a tool of state control in that judges had a wide power to decide what was seditious. Under Fox's Libel Act 1792 this was made a matter for the jury thus providing a safeguard for the individual in that judges cannot direct a jury to convict and juries do not have to give reasons for their decisions.

There is an important limiting factor in that the accused must intend to incite violence or disorder either in ordinary people or in the particular audience, for example if it includes extremists (*R* v *Burns* (1886); *R* v *Aldred* (1909)). There need not actually be violence. In *R* v *Chief Metropolitan Stipendiary Magistrate ex parte Choudhury* (1991) which concerned a novel that was offensive to Muslims, it was held that sedition applies only to incitement against the government (including however any person exercising public functions) and not to attacks on religious groups (compare *R* v *Caunt* (1947): anti-semitism). Under the ECHR the limits of permissible criticism are wider with regard to the government than in relation to a private citizen or even a politician (*Castells* v *Spain* (1992), para. 46). Therefore if prosecution is limited to cases of serious disorder it is unlikely that a proportionate response would fall foul of the HRA 1998.

There are other offences related to sedition that are little used but because of their vague language remain potential threats against political dissenters. The Incitement to Disaffection Act 1934 makes it an offence maliciously and advisedly to endeavour to seduce any member of the armed forces from his or her duty or to aid, counsel or procure him or her to do so. The Police Act 1996 creates a similar offence in relation to the police (s.91) and the Aliens Restrictions (Amendment) Act 1917 prohibits an alien from attempting to cause sedition or disaffection and also from promoting or interfering in an industrial dispute in an industry in which he or she has not been employed for at least two years immediately before the offence. It is questionable whether these provisions, particularly the latter, are HRA-compliant.

Anti-terrorism legislation imposes wide restrictions on political expression by virtue of its broad definition of terrorism (Chapter 22). In particular the Terrorism Act 2006 outlaws the publication or dissemination of a statement which directly or indirectly encourages terrorism (ss.1, 2). Encouragement includes 'glorifying' (which includes praising or celebrating) the commission or preparation (whether in the past, or in the future or generally) of acts of terrorism in such a way that members of the public could be expected to infer that they should emulate the conduct in question in existing circumstances. However the accused must intend or be reckless as to the consequences of publication and there is a defence that the statement did not express his or her views and did not have his or her endorsement. The offence can be applied to internet service providers (s.3).

21.8 Demonstrations and Meetings

Article 11 confers a right to freedom of assembly and association with the following overrides: national security or public safety, the prevention of disorder or crime, the protection of health or morals, or the protection of the rights and freedoms of others. This article shall not prevent the imposition of lawful restrictions on the exercise of those rights by members of the armed forces, of the police or of the administration of the state.

Freedom of assembly should also be given high protection, being closely related to freedom of expression. However public order issues are closely related to freedom of association in respect of which the executive is often conceded a wide discretion (below). Moreover it appears that freedom of assembly applies mainly to assembly for political purposes but not to assemblies for sports or other recreational purposes (R (Countryside Alliance) v Attorney-General (2008) [58], [119]; see also Anderson v UK (1997)).

The law has developed as a series of pragmatic responses to particular problems and political agendas and has become relentlessly more restrictive in recent years. The Public Order Act 1936 was a response to fears of fascism and communism. It was superceded by the Public Order Act 1986 which was provoked by race riots. Further legislation has been aimed at miscellaneous targets of the government of the day. These included anti-nuclear demonstrations, hunt saboteurs, travellers, 'stalkers', football hooligans, anti-war demonstrations, terrorists and animal rights groups (see Criminal Justice and Public Order Act 1994 ss.60, 60AA; Protection from Harassment Act 1997; Crime and Disorder Act 1998; Football (Offences and Disorder) Act 1999; Football (Disorder) Act 2000; Serious Organised Crime and Police Act 2005). Whether or not all of these are legitimate causes for concern the legislation may be drafted loosely enough to include wider political activities, thereby attracting human rights arguments based on uncertainty, proportionality and discrimination.

This illustrates the weakness of the traditional residual approach to liberty under which according to Dicey the right to hold a public procession is in principle no different from the right to eat a bun. The development of this subject is an example of the creeping erosion of civil liberties of a kind that Dicey did not anticipate. Taken individually each provision may be desirable but taken together they amount to a range of restrictions which, being loosely drafted, could be used for purposes other than those for which they were originally intended.

The notion that everything is permitted unless forbidden is particularly ironic in the case of public meetings. All meetings and processions take place on land. All land, even a public highway, is owned by someone, whether a private body, a local authority, the Crown or a government department. Holding a meeting without the consent of the owner may be a trespass (see Harrison v Duke of Rutland (1893)). Trespass as such is not a criminal offence. However the offences of 'aggravated trespass' and 'trespassory assembly' (below) put a powerful weapon into the hands of the police to remove demonstrators from land. The police can also remove 'travellers' from land under pain of criminal penalties (Criminal Justice and Public Order Act 1994 ss.61, 61A; see *R (Fuller)* v *Chief Constable of Dorset* (2002)).

The essential question is what are the public's rights in relation to the highway (which includes roads and their verges, footpaths, bridleways and waters over which there is a public right of navigation)? The traditional view has been that the public has a right only to 'pass or repass' on a highway (that is, to travel) and also to stop on the highway for purposes that are reasonably incidental such as 'reasonable rest and refreshment' (*Hickman* v *Maisey* (1900)). In *Hubbard* v *Pitt* (1976) for example the Court of Appeal held that peaceful picketing by a protest group who distributed leaflets and questionnaires was not a lawful use of the highway. Dicey thought that a procession, but not a static meeting, would usually be lawful because processions comprise a large number of individuals exercising their right to travel at the same time. However the procession could become unlawful if it paused.

In *DPP* v *Jones* (1999) the House of Lords upheld a right of peaceful demonstration in a public place although the limits of this are not clear. The defendant was part of a group of environmentalists who were arrested during a demonstration at Stonehenge. The demonstration was peaceful and nobody was obstructed. Lord Irvine LC held that the law should now recognise that the public should have a right to enjoy the highway for any reasonable purpose provided that the activities did not constitute a nuisance and did not obstruct other people's freedom of movement. Lords Hutton and Clyde agreed but took a narrower approach emphasising that not every non-obtrusive and peaceful use of the highway is necessarily lawful. Lord Hutton said:

> the common law recognises that there is a right for members of the public to assemble together to express views on matters of public concern and I consider that the common law should now recognise that this right, which is one of the fundamental rights of citizens in this country, is unduly restricted unless it can be exercised in some circumstances on the public highway.

Lords Hope and Slynn dissented, Lord Hope because of the effect of such a right on property owners who were not before the court to defend their interests, Lord Slynn because of a reluctance to unsettle established law. The law of trespass might be used to restrict political activity in premises such as shopping malls. Although the public has access to these places, they are not in law public places and are privately owned, often by commercial companies. The owner can therefore require anyone to obey whatever restrictions the owner wishes to impose and can exclude anyone from the premises. Whether the Human Rights Act applies to impose a positive duty on the state to protect freedom of expression in such places is questionable. In *Appelby* v *UK* (2003) the European Court held that the owner of a shopping mall could prevent environmental campaigners from setting up a stall and distributing leaflets. However the court stressed that they had other means of communicating their concerns. Moreover restrictions must have a rational justification.

Under the Serious Organised Crimes and Police Act 2005 it is an offence to trespass on a site in England and Wales or Northern Ireland designated by the Secretary of State (s.128). Except in the case of land owned by the Crown, which covers most central government land, and by the Queen or the immediate heir to the throne in their private capacity, this power can be used only in the interests of national security. However the courts are reluctant to interfere with the government's view as to what national security requires.

21.8.1 Police Powers

The police have wide powers to regulate public meetings and processions. These are supplemented by powers relating to particular places (for example Seditious Meetings Act 1817: meetings of 50 or more people in the vicinity of Westminster when Parliament is sitting (s.3); Serious Organised Crime and Police Act 2005 (below)). The main general police powers are as follows:

▷ The organiser of a public procession intended (i) to demonstrate support for or opposition to the views or actions of any person or body of persons, (ii) to publicise a campaign or cause and (iii) to mark or commemorate an event must give advance notice to the police (Public Order Act 1986 s.11). There are certain exceptions. These include:

   (i)   processions commonly or customarily held in the area. This only applies if the route remains the same. It is not enough that the time and place of commencement are the same (*Kay* v *Metropolitan Police Commissioner* (2007): mass cycle ride through London);

   (ii) funeral processions organised by a funeral director in the normal course of business;

   (iii) cases where it is not reasonably practicable to give advance notice (for example a spontaneous march).

   If a 'senior police officer' reasonably believes (a) that any public procession may result in serious public disorder, serious damage to property, or serious disruption to the life of the community or (b) that the purpose of the organisers is to intimidate people into doing something they have a right not to do, or not doing something they have a right to do, the senior officer can impose such conditions as appear to him or her to be necessary to prevent such disorder, damage, disruption or intimidation, including conditions as to the route of the procession or prohibit it from entering any public place specified in the directions (ibid. s.12). A senior police officer is either the chief constable, Metropolitan police commissioner or the senior officer present on the scene (s.12(2)). Intimidation requires more than merely causing discomfort and must contain an element of compulsion.

▷ All public processions or any class of public procession can be banned if the chief constable or Metropolitan Police Commissioner reasonably believes that the power to impose conditions is not adequate in the circumstances (ibid. s.13). The decision is for the local authority with the consent of a Secretary of State (in practice the Home Secretary) thus injecting a nominal element of democracy.

▷ There are police powers to impose conditions upon public meetings for the same purposes as in the case of processions (ibid. s.14). For this purpose a public assembly is an assembly of 20 or more people in a public place which is wholly or partly open to the air (s.16). Unlike processions the police have no general power to ban a lawful assembly but can control its location, timing and the numbers attending.

▷ The Criminal Justice and Public Order Act 1994 section 70 (inserting ss.14A, B, C into the Public Order Act 1986) confers power on a local authority with the consent of the Secretary of State to ban certain kinds of assembly in a place to which the public has no right of access or only a limited right of access. This includes private land and buildings where the public is invited, for example ancient monuments such as Stonehenge, meeting rooms, shops, sports and entertainment centres and libraries. The chief constable must reasonably believe that an assembly is (a) a trespassory assembly likely to be held without the permission of the occupier or to exceed the limits of his or her permission or of the public's rights of access and (b) may result in serious disruption to the life of the community or, where the land or a building or monument on it is of historical, architectural or scientific importance, may result in significant damage to the land, building or monument. A ban can last for up to four days within an area of up to five miles. The ban covers all trespassory assemblies and cannot be confined to particular assemblies.

The Serious Organised Crime and Police Act 2005 adds further controls in the case of areas designated by the Secretary of State within one kilometre of Parliament Square (ss.132–138). These are ostensibly intended to protect access to Parliament but also deter effective political protest. In view of the proximity of Parliament this power has a special symbolic resonance as an act of governmental arrogance. It is an offence to organise or take part in a demonstration within a designated area without police permission, for which written notice must be given if reasonably practicable at least six clear days in advance and in any case not less than 24 hours in advance. In relation to 'taking part' a demonstration can be by one person. If proper notice is given the police must give authorisation but this can be subject to conditions including limits on the number of people who may take part, noise levels and the number and size of banners and placards. These provisions do not apply to public processions which fall within the Public Order Act 1896 (above) nor to lawful trade union activity. The Constitutional Renewal Bill proposes to abolish this power.

Where a breach of the peace is taking place or imminent, the police have a summary common law power to arrest anyone who refuses to obey their reasonable requirements (*Albert* v *Lavin* (1982)). A charge of obstructing the police is also possible (Police Act 1996 ss.8, 9(1)) and magistrates can 'bind over' a person to keep the peace. The meaning of breach of the peace is probably confined to violence or threatened violence (see *R* v *Howell* (1982); *R (Laporte)* v *Chief Constable of Gloucestershire* (2006) [27]). However in *R* v *Chief Constable of Devon and Cornwall Constabulary ex parte Central Electricity Generating Board* (1981), 832, Lord Denning MR said that there is a breach of the peace 'wherever a person who is lawfully carrying out his work is unlawfully and physically prevented by another from doing it' (protesters lying in front of a drilling machine). Thus passive resistance might be a breach of the peace. The power to prevent a breach of the peace includes a power to remove a speaker (*Duncan* v *Jones* (1936)), including a right of entry to private premises (*Thomas* v *Sawkins* (1935)).

In the case of antisocial behaviour, under section 30 of the Anti-Social Behaviour Act 2003 a police officer of the rank of superintendent and above can make an order valid for up to six months within an area defined in the order. An order can be made where the officer has reasonable grounds to believe that the presence or behaviour of any persons is likely to result in any member of the public being intimidated, harassed, abused or distressed where there have previously been complaints of such behaviour. An ASBO empowers a constable to disperse any group of two or more people where the constable has reasonable grounds to believe that the behaviour of those persons is likely to result in any member of the public being intimidated, harassed, abused or distressed. There are exceptions for lawful picketing under trade union legislation and for lawful processions under section 11 of the Public Order Act 1986 (above). This power is mainly directed at hooligans but has also been used against political protestors.

Where there is a protest, itself peaceful but which becomes the focus of disturbances among its audience, should the police protect freedom of expression by attempting to control the audience or can they put public order first by taking what may well be the most efficient course of action by breaking up the meeting under the powers outlined above?

Beatty v *Gillbanks* (1882) is often cited as an endorsement of freedom of assembly. A temperance march by the Salvation Army was disrupted by a gang, known as the Skeleton Army, sponsored by brewery interests. The organisers of the march were held not be guilty of the offence of unlawful assembly (replaced by the Public Order Act 1986, below) on the ground that their behaviour was in itself lawful. However the issue was essentially that of causation and the more general question of the powers of the police to prevent a breach of the peace was not raised (compare *Duncan* v *Jones* (1936)). Nevertheless the Human Rights Act 1998 may embody a similar principle in order to show that the response is proportionate. We saw earlier that the ECHR has held that the state has a positive duty to attempt to protect freedom of expression and assembly. Moreover because it is indefinite, the police common law power may fall foul of the principle that a violation of convention rights must be 'prescribed by law'.

Before the Human Rights Act the courts were reluctant to interfere with police discretion. The main consideration was efficiency in giving the police the power to control the disturbance as they saw fit within the resources available to them. Therefore even where a peaceful and lawful meeting is disrupted by hooligans or political opponents the police may prevent a likely breach of the peace by ordering the speaker to stop in preference to controlling the troublemakers (*Duncan* v *Jones* (1936)). *Beatty* v *Gillbanks* (above) can be distinguished on the basis that police preventive discretion was not involved in that case.

Although the police must act even-handedly (*Harris* v *Sheffield United Football Club* (1988) at 95) there is a risk that they will exercise their discretion in favour of interests supported by the government or at least supported by public opinion. For example during the miners' strike of 1983 the police restricted the activities of demonstrators in order to protect the 'right to work' of non-strikers, going as far as to escort non-strikers to work and spending vast sums of money on police reinforcements. A cheaper and less provocative policy would have been to restrain the non-strikers (see also *R* v *Coventry City Council ex parte Phoenix Aviation* (1995): duty to protect business interests). On the other hand in *R* v *Chief Constable of Sussex ex parte International Traders Ferry Ltd* (1999) and *R* v *Chief Constable of Devon and Cornwall ex parte Central Electricity Generating Board* (1981) police restrictions on lawful business activities favoured animal rights and anti-nuclear protestors respectively. In both cases it was held that the matter was one of discretion (in the *Sussex* case this resulted in a breach of EC law).

Under the Human Rights Act, the police are required to give higher priority to freedom of expression. In *Plattform 'Arzte fur das Leben'* v *Austria* (1988) the ECHR held, in the context of an anti-abortion demonstration, that there was a positive duty to protect a peaceful demonstration even though it may annoy or give offence to persons opposed to the ideas and claims which it is seeking to promote (see also *Ezelin* v *France* (1991); *Steele* v *UK* (1999)).

In *R (Laporte)* v *Gloucestershire Chief Constable* (2006) the House of Lords reviewed the police common law powers to prevent a breach of the peace (above). The police had stopped, searched and then turned back with a police escort a coachload of anti-Iraq war protesters who were travelling to a demonstration at a military site at Fairford. Although this took place several miles from the site, the police claimed that their powers extended to taking action whenever they reasonably anticipated that a breach of the peace was likely, whether committed by the persons in question or by others. The House of Lords, invoking the importance of freedom of expression and emphasising the increasing legislative constraints on public protest, held that the common law power to prevent a breach of the peace was confined to a situation where the breach of peace was actually taking place or was imminent. If this was not the case the police had no power even to take lesser action. It was also held that the police action was disproportionate, in that freedom of expression should be limited only as a last resort. Lord Bingham was critical of *Piddington* v *Bates* (1960) and regarded *Moss* v *McLachlan* (1985), where demonstrators were also turned back, as a borderline example of imminence, recognising that the police must have some discretion.

Laporte was followed by the Court of Appeal in *Austin* v *Metropolitan Police Commissioner* (2008). The police detained a crowd including bystanders behind a cordon on the highway for two hours in conditions of discomfort in order to prevent a violent demonstration. It was held that the actions of the police were lawful. It was stressed however that the lawful exercise of rights can be curtailed only as a last resort and in extreme and exceptional circumstances. The action must be reasonably necessary and proportionate. However once this power is justified the actions of individual policeman can be challenged only if they are unreasonable in the *Wednesbury* sense (see Chapter 17). Moreover the court held that temporary detention of this kind does not amount to deprivation of liberty so as to attract the stronger protection of Article 5 of the ECHR (*Guzzardi* v *Italy* (1980)). At most it concerns freedom of assembly which can be overridden by public order considerations. It may also be a restriction on liberty subject to Article 2 Protocol 4 of the Convention which the UK has not ratified. It is also unclear how far the police have a margin of discretion, in particular the extent to which police resources can be taken into account in assessing the necessity of the police action. Finally it was left open whether an arrest can be justified under Article 5 (1) b (to fulfil an obligation prescribed by law) on the basis that there is a general obligation to obey police orders.

21.8.2   Public Order Offences

Specific public order offences strike primarily at people who intentionally cause violence, but sometimes go beyond that. They overlap, allowing police discretion in relation to the penalties. Even minor punishments or disciplinary measures might be condemned under the ECHR as disproportionate or uncertain and so 'chilling' the right of assembly (*Ezelin* v *France* (1992)). The main offences are as follows:

1. Under the Highways Act 1980, it is an offence to **obstruct the highway** (s.137). It is not necessary that the highway be completely blocked or even that people are inconvenienced. The accused's intentions are also irrelevant (*Arrowsmith* v *Jenkins* (1963); *Homer* v *Cadman* (1886); *Hirst and Agu* v *West Yorkshire Chief Constable* (1986)). However as a result of *DPP* v *Jones* (above) a reasonable peaceful demonstration would probably not be unlawful. There are also numerous local statutes and bylaws regulating public meetings in particular places.

2. The Public Order Act 1986 creates several offences, replacing a clutch of ancient and ill defined common law offences (rout, riot, affray and unlawful assembly). They are as follows (in descending order of seriousness):

   ▷ **Riot** (s.1). Where 12 or more people act in concert and use or threaten unlawful violence for a common purpose, each person using violence is guilty of the offence.

   ▷ **Violent disorder** (s.2). At least three people acting in concert and using or threatening unlawful violence.

   ▷ **Affray** (s.3). One person suffices. Using or threatening unlawful violence is sufficient, but threats by words alone do not count.

      The above offences may be committed in public or in private and the conduct must be such 'as would cause a person of reasonable firmness present at the scene to fear for his personal safety'. No such person need actually be on the scene. The defendant must either intend to threaten or use violence or be aware that his or her conduct may be violent or threaten violence (s.6). 'Violence' is broadly defined to include violent conduct to property and persons and is not restricted to conduct intended to cause injury or damage (s.8).

   ▷ **Fear or provocation of violence** (s.4). This offence is wider. A person is guilty who uses 'threatening, abusive or insulting words or behaviour or distributes or displays any writing, sign or visible representation that is threatening, abusive or insulting'. The offence can be committed in a public or a private place except exclusively within a dwelling or between dwellings (s.8). The meaning of threatening, abusive or insulting is left to the jury (see *Brutus* v *Cozens* (1973)) but the accused must be aware that his words are threatening, abusive or insulting (s.6(3)). The act must be aimed at another person with the intention either to cause that person to believe that immediate unlawful violence will be used or to provoke that person into immediate unlawful violence. Alternatively the accused's conduct must be likely to have that effect even though he or she does not so intend.

      In *R* v *Horseferry Road Metropolitan Stipendiary Magistrate Court ex parte Siadatan* (1991) Penguin was prosecuted under section 4 in relation to the publication of Salman Rushdie's book *Satanic Verses*. It was alleged that the book was likely to provoke future violence because it was offensive to Muslims. It was held that the violence must be likely within a short time of the behaviour in question. However whether the other person's reaction is reasonable is irrelevant, so that the principle that a speaker 'takes his audience as he finds it' seems to apply. Thus provoking a hostile or extremist audience as in *Beatty* (above) would be an offence, provided that the words used or act performed is to the knowledge of the accused threatening, abusive or insulting to that particular audience (*Jordan* v *Burgoyne* (1963)).

   ▷ **Threatening, abusive or insulting behaviour** or disorderly behaviour with intent to cause harassment, alarm and distress where harassment, alarm or distress is actually caused (s.4A) (inserted by the Criminal Justice and Public Order Act 1994).

This offence and section 5 below threaten freedom of expression in that they move away from the important safeguard that the conduct in question must be threatening, abusive or insulting, applying also to 'disorderly behaviour', an expression which is not defined.

▶ **Harassment, alarm, or distress** (s.5). Section 5 also applies to threatening, abusive or insulting behaviour or disorderly behaviour. It requires only that a person who actually sees or hears the conduct must be likely to be caused harassment, alarm or distress and does not require an intent to cause harassment, alarm nor actual harassment, alarm or distress. Violence is not involved. However there are the defences that (i) the accused had no reason to believe that any such person was present; (ii) he did not intend or know that his words or actions were threatening, abusive or insulting, or disorderly (see *DPP* v *Clarke and Others* (1992)); and (iii) his conduct was 'reasonable'.

The police have a summary power of arrest in relation to all the above offences but under section 5 must first warn the accused to stop. The conduct before and after the warning need not be the same.

It is unlikely that the offences under sections 1–4 are contrary to the ECHR in that they aim at preventing violence. Sections 4A and 5 are more vulnerable. In addition to 'threatening' behaviour they target abusive, insulting and disorderly behaviour which leads to no more than distress. This arguably runs counter to the view of the European Court that conduct which shocks and offends is a price to be paid for democracy (above).

3. Section 1 of the Public Order Act 1936 prohibits the wearing of political uniforms in any public place or public meeting without police consent, which can be obtained for special occasions. 'Uniform' includes any garment that has political significance, for example a black beret (*O'Moran* v *Director of Public Prosecutions* (1975)). Political significance can be identified from any of the circumstances or from historical evidence.

4. **Aggravated trespass**. Aimed originally at anti-hunting protestors, this occurs where a person who trespasses on land in the open air does anything (such as shouting threats, blowing a horn or erecting barricades) which in relation to any lawful activity that persons are engaging or about to engage in on that land or on adjoining land is intended to have the effect (a) of intimidating those persons or any one of them so as to deter them or any one of them from engaging in that lawful activity; (b) of obstructing that activity; or (c) of disrupting that activity (Criminal Justice and Public Order Act 1994 s.68). For this purpose a lawful activity is any activity that is not a criminal offence or a trespass (s.68(2)). There is no defence of reasonableness and violence is not an ingredient. The police can order a person committing or who has committed or who intends to commit an offence to leave the land (s.69). The police can also order two or more people who are present with the common purpose of committing the offence to leave the land. In both cases it is an offence to return within three months. Given the above examples, it is not clear whether passive conduct such as lying down would be an offence.

5. **Harassment**. Under the Protection from Harassment Act 1997 as amended by the Serious Organised Crime and Police Act 2005, a course of conduct (meaning conduct on at least two occasions relating to one person or on one occasion relating to each in the case of two or more persons) which the perpetrator knows or ought to know amounts to or involves the harassment of another is an offence. The test is whether a reasonable person in possession of the same information as the accused would think

the conduct likely to cause harassment (s.1(2)). Aimed originally at animal rights activists, this provision can be used against political demonstrations in general. Harassment is a wide term. It includes a course of conduct intended to persuade any person not to do something lawful or to do something unlawful and can include 'collective' harassment by a group (Criminal Justice and Police Act 2001 s.44). Thus the anti-abortion protesters in *DPP* v *Fidler* (1992) who were acquitted because they intended to persuade rather than to prevent women entering an abortion clinic would now probably be convicted. There are defences of preventing or detecting crime and acting under lawful authority and a broad defence of 'reasonableness' (s.1(3)(c)). This may allow the press to claim that its duty to inform the public overrides the victim's right of privacy. It may also allow religious enthusiasts to evangelise (compare Human Rights Act 1998 s.13; Chapter 19).

Summary

▶ The justifications for freedom of expression concern the advancement of truth, the protection of democracy and the rule of law and self fulfilment. Press freedom is particularly important in a democracy. Freedom of expression involves the state not only abstaining from interference but in some cases, particularly in relation to the press, taking positive steps to protect freedom of expression.

▶ Freedom of expression may conflict with other rights, notably religion and privacy. It may also be overridden by public interest concerns such as the integrity of the judicial process.

▶ We distinguished between prior restraint (censorship) and punishments after the event. UK law has some direct censorship by the executive in relation to the broadcast and film media. More general powers of censorship are available by applying to the courts for injunctions. These may be too broad in the light of the Human Rights Act 1998.

▶ Defamation protects a person's interest in reputation. Public bodies are not protected by the law of defamation although, perhaps unjustifiably, individual public officials are. The protection of qualified privilege is available to the press although its scope is uncertain.

▶ English law has no distinct right of privacy which protects interests in self esteem, dignity and autonomy. Breach of confidence covers some but not all of the ground. Protection for press freedom is based on establishing a public interest in disclosure. A governmental body must establish that secrecy is in the public interest.

▶ The relationship between freedom of expression and offence is particularly difficult. Although offence is generally not protected against freedom of speech, this may not apply to religious feelings.

▶ There are specific protections against hate speech in relation to race, religion and sexual orientation. These have savings to protect freedom of expression but the line is difficult to draw.

▶ The law relating to public meetings and processions sets freedom of expression and assembly against public order. This is characterised by broad police discretion. A range of statutes responding to perceived threats have created various offences that restrict freedom of expression and give the police extensive powers to regulate public meetings and processions and demonstrations by individuals and groups. The police also have wide common law powers to prevent imminent breaches of the peace. Under the Human Rights Act these powers must be exercised in accordance with the principle of proportionality in order to safeguard freedom of expression and association.

Exercises

21.1 'Freedom of expression is a trump card that always wins' (Lord Hoffmann). Does this reflect the present state of the law?

21.2 'In the context of religious opinion and beliefs may legitimately be included an obligation to avoid as far as possible expressions that are gratuitously offensive to others and thus an infringement of their rights, and which therefore do not contribute to any form of public debate capable of furthering progress in human affairs' (*Otto Preminger Institut* v *Austria* (1994)). Discuss the implications of this for freedom of expression.

21.3 'The common law recognises that there is a right for members of the public to assemble together to express views on matters of public concern and I consider that the common law should now recognise this right, which is one of the fundamental rights of citizens in this country, is unduly restricted unless it can be exercised in some circumstances on the public highway' (Lord Hutton in *DPP* v *Jones* (1999)). Discuss whether there is such a right and what its limits are.

21.4 'A function of free expression is to invite dispute. It may indeed best serve its purpose when it induces a condition of unrest, creates dissatisfaction with conditions as they are and even stirs people to anger' (Mr Justice Douglas in *Terminiello* v *Chicago* 337 US 1 (1949)). To what extent does English law recognise this?

21.5 While on holiday in Scotland the Prime Minister accidentally leaves his personal diary on a train. Another passenger finds it and is delighted to see that it contains disparaging remarks including crude obscenities about the Prime Minister's Cabinet colleagues. He hands it in at the Office of the Sunday Stir. The Editor informs the Prime Minister's Office that extracts from the diary will be published in next Sunday's edition. Advise the Prime Minister as to any legal remedy he might have.

21.6 A prominent Bishop of the Church of England has been invited to address a rally which the local diocese holds each year at various locations throughout the area following a procession. This year the rally is to be held in Phear Park. Police permission has not been sought. A press release announces that the Bishop will argue that homosexuality is a sin and that homosexuals should be expelled from the Church. A rival group, 'Christians for Tolerance' (CT) proposes to attend the rally. CT hires a coach for the occasion. The local police are short of resources to police the rally and procession adequately. Fearing that there may be violence at the rally, the police stop the CT coach at a motorway service area some five miles from Phear Park. They refuse to allow any passengers to disembark and detain the coach for about three hours by which time the rally had finished. Discuss the legality of these events.

21.7 Members of the Freedom for Peace Party distribute leaflets in a shopping mall in Westchester every Saturday morning. The leaflets, which are also published on the internet, include appeals to the armed forces to refuse to fight in Iraq and praise the seventeenth century Leveller movement which was prepared to fight for equality and democracy. Last week security guards employed by the owners of the mall, an insurance company, ordered the leaflet distributors to leave and when they refused to do so removed them by force. Discuss the legality of these events.

Further reading

Ahdar, R. and Leigh, I. (2005) *Religious Freedom in the Liberal State*, Oxford University Press.

Barendt, E. (2005) *Freedom of Speech* (2nd edn) Oxford University Press.

Greenawalt, K. (1989) 'Free Expression Justifications', *Columbia Law Review* 89(1):119.

Lester, A. (1993) 'Freedom of Expression', in MacDonald, R., Matscher, F. and Petzold, H. (eds) *The European System for the Protection of Human Rights*, Dordrecht, Nijhoff.

Loveland, I. (1998) *Importing the First Amendment*, Oxford, Hart Publishing.

Morgan, J. (2004) 'Privacy in the House of Lords Again', *Law Quarterly Review* 120:563.

Nicolson, D. and Reid, K. (1996) 'Arrest for Breach of the Peace and the ECHR', *Criminal Law Review* 764.

Chapter 22

Exceptional powers: security, state secrecy and emergencies

The words 'national security' have acquired over the years an almost mystical significance and the mere incantation of the phrase of itself instantly discourages the court from satisfactorily fulfilling its normal role of deciding where the balance of public interest lies. (Sir Simon Brown, 1994)

Key words

- Minimum standards and safeguards
- Variable levels of review
- Derogation
- Reduced role of Parliament
- Fair trial
- Special advocate
- Hierarchy of rights

22.1   Introduction: Security and the Courts

The rule of law requires that government powers be defined by clear laws and that there should be safeguards for individual freedom. Liberal democracy requires that laws be made by means of a democratic debate and that citizens should be fully informed as to what government is doing. As against this the Hobbesian minimum duty of the state is to safeguard human life by keeping order (Chapter 2). This may involve facing unpredictable events and acting quickly. Hobbes believed that the people must entrust open ended and absolute powers to government. He thought that the risk of government abusing its power was a price worth paying for security.

Wide emergency powers are particularly prone to abuse. For example political pressures may encourage a government to introduce legislation that removes normal legal safeguards on the ground that the seriousness of the threat requires speedy and decisive action. The 'precautionary principle' developed in relation to environmental protection applies to other risks by insisting that a lack of certain knowledge should not inhibit the taking of steps to combat serious or irremediable harm. This could be a cloak for satisfying the mob, particularly where the emergency involves threats from outsiders or minorities. Moreover it is easier and cheaper to enact laws than to raise policing standards. History tells us that governments may use the excuse of an emergency as a means of reinforcing their own positions. Marshal J (in *Skinner* v *Railway Labor Executives' Association* 489 US 602, 635–6 (1989)) remarked:

> When we allow fundamental freedoms to be sacrificed in the name of real or perceived exigency, we invariably come to regret it.

Emergency laws may violate the rule of law and democracy in several respects:

- Parliamentary scrutiny of legislation may be rushed or truncated so that the laws are effectively made by a small group within the executive without the wide process of consultation and checks and balances which both the rule of law and democracy require.
- Vaguely defined powers may target ill defined groups because the needs of an emergency favour flexibility. The judicial review doctrine that powers must be used reasonably and for proper purposes may be frustrated by the wide terms in which the powers are conferred.
- Safeguards such as judicial review might be restricted.
- Requirements of secrecy in court proceedings: exclusion of the press.
- Evidence in legal proceedings may be restricted, for example by allowing evidence taken by oppressive means, uncorroborated statements by anonymous informers or altering the burden of proof.
- Jury trial has been removed in some cases (Northern Ireland (Emergency Provisions) Act 1978).
- Random stop and search powers.
- Intrusive surveillance.
- Extended powers of detention without going before a court.
- Minorities might be targeted on the basis that those who do not support majority values are a security risk. For example Lord Rooker, a Home Office minister, stated that:

  > in a tolerant liberal society, if we are not guarded we will find that those who do not seek to be part of our society will use our tolerance and liberalism to destroy that society. (HL Deb. Nov. 27 2001, col. 143)

- Measures originally introduced to meet an emergency become permanent. Typically emergency measures are temporary and should contain a 'sunset clause' under which the measure expires on a given date unless renewed by Parliament.
- The executive is given power to alter existing laws.
- Measures intended to deal with serious threats are used against trivial offences or for political purposes. Laws cast in wide terms are not necessarily ambiguous so that ministerial reassurances about the scope of the legislation cannot be used as an aid to interpretation under the *Pepper* v *Hart* doctrine (Chapter 8).

The rhetoric of human rights that there must be a 'proportionate response' (Chapter 19) expresses a benevolent aspiration but does not rule out any particular violation of individual rights. The rhetoric of 'balancing' the interests of security and the rights of the individual is also of limited assistance since there is no objective measure to tell us where the balance should be struck. This has led to famous judicial disagreements (for example *Liversidge* v *Anderson* (below)).

A state can derogate from some articles of the European Convention on Human Rights in times of war or other public emergency threatening 'the life of the nation' (Article 15; Human Rights Act 1998 ss.1(2), 14, 15). The state must show that the threat is current or imminent, that the measures do not go beyond a necessary response to the emergency and that other international obligations are not violated. There must also be the safeguard of judicial review by an independent court (*Chahal* v *UK* (1996)). However protection ultimately depends on the extent to which the court is prepared to accept the government's word as to the needs of the situation. Article 2, right to life, cannot be derogated from except in respect of deaths resulting from lawful acts of war, nor can Article 3 (torture and inhuman and degrading treatment), Article 4(1) (slavery), Article 7 (retrospective punishment) and Protocol 6 (capital punishment).

The definition of emergency is not clear. The European Court has given a wide margin of discretion to member states (see *Brannigan and McBride* v *UK* (1993)). The criteria are that the threat be actual or imminent, that its effects involve the whole nation, that the organised life of the community is at risk, and that the crisis be exceptional so that normal measures are plainly inadequate (see *Lawless* v *Ireland (No. 3)* (1961); *A* v *Secretary of State for the Home Department* (2005)). The last criterion suggests that the crisis must be temporary although it might be indefinite. The UK had previously derogated in respect of measures in Northern Ireland. It recently derogated from Article 5, liberty and security, in order to enable it to detain those suspected of terrorism for relatively long periods without being tried before a court.

In *A* v *Secretary of State for the Home Department* (2005) a majority of the House of Lords were prepared to defer to the government on this point. However they held that because the measures went beyond those related specifically to the threat claimed by the government, the test of necessity was not satisfied (see Chapter 19). Lord Hoffmann took a different view. He suggested that an emergency existed only when the basic principles of democracy and the rule of law were threatened and that a high risk of terrorist attack was not in itself evidence of this. Indeed he suggested that government measures of the type in issue were a greater threat to democracy.

Derogation is from the ECHR as such. If as is often suggested the ECHR reflects rights that are inherent in the common law (Chapters 7, 19) then derogation would not necessarily prevent the courts applying similar principles. However common law rights can be overridden by clear statutory language short of the 'impossibility' principle that applies to convention rights under the Human Rights Act (Chapter 20).

In deciding whether an exceptional interference with a convention right is justified, the courts are particularly concerned with safeguards to prevent an abuse of power. These try to strike a balance by requiring certain non-negotiable standards based on the rule of law. These include:

- Powers being defined in detail by clear publicly announced laws (see *R (Gillan)* v *Metropolitan Police Commissioner* (2006) [31]).
- The safeguards of access to a lawyer and judicial supervision.
- Right to a fair trial including the right to challenge evidence (*Secretary of State for the Home Department* v *MB* (2008)).
- On the other hand the courts are prepared to accept evidence given in secret and the use of 'Special Advocates', state approved lawyers appointed to act on behalf of suspects. The suspects themselves may be denied access to witnesses and evidence.

The courts have traditionally been reluctant to interfere with national security matters. The European Court has emphasised the need for safeguards against abuse, as being necessary in a democratic society, but has given a wide margin of discretion and been reluctant to attribute improper motives to a government (see *Lawless* v *Ireland* (1961); *Klass* v *Federal Republic of Germany* (1979); *Malone* v *UK* (1984); *Aksoy* v *Turkey* (1996); *Brogan* v *UK* (1989)). Traditionally the UK courts have regarded matters of national security as non-justiciable relying on ministerial accountability to Parliament as a safeguard. According to Lord Diplock in *Council of Civil Service Unions (CCSU)* v *Minister for the Civil Service* (1985), 'national security is par excellence a non-justiciable question. The judicial process is totally inept to deal with the type of problems which it involves'. (See *Liversidge and Anderson* (1942): in which Lord Atkin's famous dissent in favour of individual liberty is now widely acknowledged as preferable to the views of the majority; see *A* v *Secretary of State* (above)) . However even in the CCSU case the government had to show that it was acting in good faith and that the matter, (the effectiveness of GCHQ, the government's interception of electronic communications centre) was genuinely one of national security.

In recent years the courts, often with a dissenting element, have been more willing to interfere with national security powers at least on the level of broad principle. This has been encouraged by the Human Rights Act 1998 which introduced the ECHR notion of minimum standards such as the right to a fair trial and provisions against indefinite detention. The jurisprudence of the European Court of Human Rights has invited the courts to apply the proportionality principle thus increasing the intensity of review. On the other hand at the level of detail the 'margin of discretion' enables the courts to defer particularly to the government's use of information, its assessment of risk and its use of secrecy since these are matters with which judicial experience is not comfortable (see Poole (2008)). For example in *A* v *Secretary of State* (2006) the House of Lords held that in principle, evidence obtained by torture was not admissible, regarding this as a 'constitutional principle'. However their lordships disagreed as to the standard of proof. A majority held that it must be shown on balance of probabilities that the evidence was tainted whereas the minority thought that it was enough to show that there was a 'real risk.' *(See also Secretary of State* v *Rehman* (2002); *R* v *Secretary of State for the Home Department ex parte McQuillan* (1995); *R* v *Secretary of State for the Home Department ex parte Adams* (1995).)

22.2 Access to Information

There are two aspects to state secrecy. The first concerns a right of access to information held by government. This concerns the general accountability of government and also, acutely, the right to a fair trial when government withholds relevant information in court or inquiry proceedings. Arguments in favour of 'open government' include the following:

- **Democratic accountability:** officials should be accountable to well informed public opinion.
- **Autonomy:** people should be able to exercise informed choice in relation to their own affairs.
- **Justice:** in being able to correct false information.
- **Direct public participation:** in decision making as an end in itself.
- **Public confidence:** in government.

Arguments in favour of government secrecy are primarily efficiency based and include the following:

- Release of certain kinds of information might cause serious harm, for example national security, crime prevention, childcare and some economic information.
- Expense and delay, bearing in mind that seekers of information may be cranks, enemies or maniacs.
- Freedom of information could weaken ministerial responsibility to Parliament.
- Frankness within government, for example the danger of policy making being inhibited by premature criticism or the quality of debate being diluted by the temptation to play to the gallery.
- Public panic if disclosures are misunderstood.
- Self importance and self protection by public officials; without secrecy it might be more difficult to make public appointments.
- The mystique of government emphasised by Bagehot as a source of stability.

Apart from cases where the principles of natural justice apply (Chapter 17) the common law gives no right to information. Indeed in *Burmah Oil Co. Ltd* v *Bank of England* [1980] AC 1090 at 1112, Lord Wilberforce did not believe that the courts should support open government. There are however certain statutory rights to information of which the Freedom of Information Act 2000 is the most general. This came into force in 2005. There are also particular doctrines such as public interest immunity (below) and the absence of a general duty to give reasons for government action (Chapter 17) that reinforce state secrecy. Similarly the ECHR does not give a right to government information as such. However such a right could be generated by those Articles that impose a positive duty on the state, notably Article 2 (right to life) in relation to investigations into deaths and Article 8 concerning environmental risks or access to personal information such as family records (see *Guerra* v *Italy* (1998); *Gaskin* v *UK* (1990); *Leander* v *Sweden* (1987)).

The second aspect of secrecy concerns claims by the state to suppress information held by others such as the media. Here the state is interfering with common law rights and also the right of freedom of expression under Article 10 of the ECHR. The onus is therefore on the state to justify its intervention. In relation to government information secrecy is re-enforced by statutes, notably the Official Secrets Act 1989 forbidding disclosure of certain information, by the civil law of breach of confidence and by employment contracts. There is also a culture of voluntary secrecy generated by the priority of efficiency over accountability and perhaps by the personality traits of persons holding public office. Contemporary policies of privatisation and encouraging public bodies to follow commercial practices including 'commercial confidentiality' also militate against openness in favour of a protective, defensive culture.

Access to government information as such is not protected by the ECHR. Article 10 has been said to protect people who wish to disclose information and does not force anyone to do so (see *Leander* v *Sweden* (1987)). However this takes no account of the democratic interest in the free flow of information which the ECHR has recognised in the context of press freedom (Chapter 20). There may however be a right to information under Article 6 (right to a fair trial) and Article 8 (respect for family life; see *Gaskin* v *UK* (1990): adoption records; applied restrictively in *Gunn-Russo* v *Nugent Care Housing Society* (2001)).

The Freedom of Information Act 2000

The scope of the Act is potentially wide. Subject to many exemptions, the Freedom of Information Act 2000 requires public authorities to disclose information on request and also to confirm or deny whether the information exists (s.1). This is supervised and enforced by an Information Commissioner who also has advisory and promotional functions. The Act does not prevent an authority from disclosing any information (s.78).

Under Schedule 1 central government departments (but not the Cabinet, the royal household or the security services), Parliament, the Welsh Assembly (but not the Scottish government, s.80), local authorities, the police, the armed forces, state educational bodies and NHS bodies are automatically public authorities, as is a long list of other specified bodies including companies which are wholly owned by these bodies (s.6). The Secretary of State may also designate other bodies, office holders or persons as public authorities which appear to him to be exercising 'functions of a public nature' or who provide services under a contract with a public authority, the functions of which include the provision of that service (s.3(1)). This might include a voluntary body acting on behalf of a government agency. The Secretary of State can however limit the kind of information that the listed bodies can disclose (s.7).

The Act gives a right to any person to request in writing (s.8) information held by the authority on its own behalf or held by another on behalf of the authority (s.3(2)). The person making the request is entitled to be told whether or not the authority possesses the information (duty to confirm or deny) and to have the information communicated to him or her (s.1(1)). Reasons do not normally have to be given for the request. However disclosure can be refused if the applicant has not provided such further information as the authority reasonably requires to enable the requested information to be found (s.1) although the authority must provide reasonable advice and assistance (s.16). A request can also be refused if the cost of compliance exceeds a limit set by the Secretary of State or where the request is vexatious or repetitive (s.14). A fee regulated by the Secretary of State can be charged (s.9). The authority must respond promptly and within 20 working days (s.10). However if the matter might involve an exemption there is no time limit other than a 'reasonable' time to make a decision. Thus the right is far from absolute and there is considerable scope for bureaucratic obfuscation.

The Information Commissioner can require the authority to disclose information either on her or his own initiative (enforcement notice, s.52) or on the application of a complainant whose request has been refused (decision notice, s.50). Reasons must be given for a refusal and the Commissioner can where appropriate inspect the information in question and also require further information. An authority can refuse to disclose to the Commissioner any information which might expose it to criminal proceedings other than proceedings under the Act itself. Both sides may appeal to the Information Tribunal on the merits, with a further appeal to the High Court on a point of law (s.57). The right to information can be enforced by the courts through the law of contempt but no civil action is possible (s.56).

The right to information under the Act is subject to many exemptions (Part II). These apply both to the information itself and usually to the duty to confirm or deny. Most are absolute exemptions for whole classes of information. Some require a 'prejudice' test relating to the particular document. However this is less onerous for the government than the 'substantial prejudice' that was originally envisaged in the White Paper (*Your Right to Know: Freedom of Information*, 1997, Cm 3818). Some exemptions are vague, encouraging delaying tactics by officials.

The absolute exemptions are as follows:

▷ information which is already reasonably accessible to the public even if payment is required (s.21)

▷ information supplied by or relating to the intelligence and security services (s.23). A minister's certificate is conclusive, subject to an appeal to the Tribunal by the Commissioner or the applicant, which in respect of the reasonableness of the decision is limited to the judicial review grounds (s.60)

▷ information contained in court records widely defined (s.32)

▷ information protected by parliamentary privilege (s.34)

▷ information that would prejudice the conduct of public affairs in the House of Commons or the House of Lords (s.36)

▷ certain personal information, although some of this is available under the Data Protection Act 1998 (s.40(1)(2))

▷ information the disclosure of which would be an actionable breach of confidence (s.41)

▷ information protected by legal obligations such as legal professional privilege or European law (s.44).

In other cases the exemption applies only where it 'appears to the authority' that 'the public interest in maintaining the secrecy of the information outweighs the public interest in disclosure' (s.2(1)(b)). The balance is therefore tipped in favour of disclosure. However because this test is subjective the Commissioner's powers may be limited to the grounds of judicial review. The main exemptions of this kind are as follows:

▷ information which is held at the time of request with a view to be published in the future (s.22). No particular time for publication need be set although it must be reasonable that the information be withheld.

▷ information required for the purpose of safeguarding national security. There is provision for a minister's certificate as under section 23 (above).

▷ information held at any time for the purposes of criminal proceedings or investigations which may lead to criminal proceedings or relate to information provided by confidential sources (s.30). This would include many inquiries into matters of public concern.

▷ information the disclosure of which would or would be likely to prejudice defence, foreign relations, relations between the UK devolved governments, the House of Commons or the House of Lords, law enforcement widely defined to include many official inquiries, the commercial interests of any person including the public authority holding the information, or the economic interests of the UK. Nor does the duty to confirm or deny arise in these circumstances (ss.26, 27, 28, 29, 31).

▷ audit functions

▷ communications with the royal family

▷ health and safety matters

▷ environmental information (this is subject to special provisions (below))

▷   information concerning the 'formulation or development' of government policy (s.35). This includes all communications between ministers, cabinet proceedings, advice from the law officers and the operation of any ministerial private office. It also seems to include advice from civil servants. However once a decision has been taken statistical background information can be released.

▷   other information which 'in the reasonable opinion of a qualified person' would or would be likely to prejudice collective ministerial responsibility or which would or would be likely to inhibit 'free and frank' provision of advice or exchange of views or 'would otherwise prejudice or be likely to prejudice the effective conduct of public affairs' (s.36). This would again ensure that civil service advice remains secret. A 'qualified person' is the minister or other official in charge of the department. Because the test is subjective it appears that the Commissioner would have no power to intervene except where the qualified person's decision was 'unreasonable'. A question here would be whether the minimal *Wednesbury* version of unreasonableness would apply.

Ministers also have power to override the Commission's enforcement powers. In the case of information held by the central government, the Welsh Assembly and other bodies designated by the Secretary of State, an 'accountable person' (a cabinet minister, or the Attorney-General or their equivalents in Scotland and Northern Ireland) can serve a certificate on the Commissioner 'stating that he has on reasonable grounds formed the opinion' that there was no failure to comply with the duty to disclose the information (s.53). Reasons must be given and the certificate must be laid before Parliament. The certificate would also be subject to judicial review.

22.2.2   Other Statutory Rights to Information

Other statutory rights to information are characterised by broad exceptions and weak or non-existent enforcement mechanisms. None of them gives access to the contemporary inner workings of the central government. The most important of them are as follows:

▷   Historical records (see Cm 853, 1991). These are, subject to exceptions, made available after 30 years (Public Records Acts 1958, 1967, 1975). The 1993 White Paper on open government (Cm 2290) proposed that records be withheld beyond 30 years only where actual damage to national security, economic interests or law and order can be shown or if disclosure would be a breach of confidence or cause substantial distress or danger. The Freedom of Information Act 2000 removes exemptions for communications within UK government departments, court records, decision making and policy formation, legal professional privilege and trade secrets contained in historical records. Information relating to honours is to be protected for 75 years and law enforcement matters for 100 years.

▷   Personal information relating to the applicant held on computer or in structured manual records (Data Protection Act 1998). However the Act exempts much government data including national security matters, law and tax enforcement matters and data 'relating to the exercise of statutory functions'.

▷   Local government information. The Local Government (Access to Information) Act 1985 gives a public right to attend local authority meetings including those of committees and subcommittees and to see background papers, agendas, reports and minutes. There are large exemptions which include decisions taken by officers, confidential information, information from central government, personal matters excluded by the relevant committee and 'the financial or business affairs of any person'. The Act appears to be easy to evade by using officers or informal groups to make decisions. It is not clear what counts as a background paper.

> The Public Bodies (Admission to Meetings) Act 1960 gives a right to attend meetings of parish councils and certain other public bodies. The public can be excluded on the grounds of public interest (see *R v Brent Health Authority ex parte Francis* (1985)).

> The Access to Personal Files Act 1987 authorises access to local authority housing and social work records by the subject of the records and in accordance with regulations made by the Secretary of State (see also Housing Act 1985 s.106(5)).

> The Environmental Information Regulations 1992 (SI 1992 no. 320) implementing EC Directive 90/313 require public authorities to disclose certain information about environmental standards and measures. The information must be made available on request but there are no specific requirements as to how this is to be done. A charge can be made. Requests can be refused on grounds including manifest unreasonableness or a too general request, confidentiality, increasing the likelihood of environmental damage, information voluntarily supplied unless the supplier consents, international relations and national security. Under the Aarhus Convention *Access to Information, Public Participation in Decision Making and Access to Justice in Environmental Matters* (1998, Cm 4736) the government is required to make regulations giving a general right to environmental information subject to exceptions on public interest grounds. These will replace the present regulations and be integrated into the machinery of the Freedom of Information Act 2000 under section 74 of that Act.

22.3 Disclosure of Government Information

22.3.1 The Official Secrets Act 1989: Criminal Law

The Official Secrets Act 1989 protects certain kinds of government information from unauthorised disclosure. It was enacted in response to long standing and widespread criticism of the Official Secrets Act 1911 section 2 which covered all information, however innocuous, concerning the central government (see Franks Report, 1972, Cmnd 6104). A series of controversial prosecutions culminated in the Ponting trial in 1995 where a civil servant who gave information to an MP concerning alleged governmental malpractice during the Falklands War was acquitted by a jury against the judge's summing up. Section 2 required the Crown to show that the disclosure was not made under a duty to the 'state'. The judge emphasised that civil servants owed absolute loyalty to ministers and held that the 'state' meant the government of the day (see Chapter 6), thus making it clear that the 'public interest' could not justify disclosure. However Ponting's acquittal meant that the government could no longer resist reform.

Section 1 of the 1911 Act which concerns spying activities remains in force but section 2 has been repealed. The Official Secrets Act 1989 is narrower but more sharply focused. It identifies four protected areas of government activity and provides defences which vary with each area. The aim is to make enforcement more effective in respect of the more sensitive areas of government. In each case it is an offence to disclose information without 'lawful authority'. In the case of a Crown servant or 'notified person' (above) this means 'in accordance with his official duty' (s.7). In the case of a government contractor, lawful authority means either with official authorisation or disclosure for the purpose of his or her functions as such, for example giving information to a subcontractor. In the case of other persons who may fall foul of the Act, such as a former civil servant, lawful authority means disclosure to a Crown servant for the purpose of his or her functions as such (ss.7(3)(a), 12(1)), for example to a minister or the Director of Public Prosecutions but not a member of Parliament not the police since these are not Crown servants. Alternatively lawful authority means in accordance with an official authorisation, presumably by the head of the relevant department (ss.7(3)(b), 7(5)).

The protected areas are as follows:

1. **Security and intelligence** (s.1). This applies (i) to a member or former member of the security and intelligence services; (ii) to anyone else who is 'notified' by a minister that he or she is within this provision; (iii) to any existing or former Crown servant or government contractor. In the cases of (i) and (ii) any disclosure is an offence unless the accused did not know and had no reasonable cause to believe that the information related to security or intelligence. The nature of the information is irrelevant. In the case of (iii) the disclosure must be 'damaging' or where the information or document is of a kind where disclosure is likely to be damaging (s.1(4)). 'Damaging' does not concern the public interest generally but means only damaging to 'the work of the security and intelligence services'. This might include for example informing MPs that security agents are breaking the law. It is a defence that the accused did not know and had no reasonable cause to believe that the disclosure would be damaging.

In *R v Shaylor* (2002) the House of Lords held that section 1 did not violate the right to freedom of expression. The accused, a former member of the security services, had handed over documents to journalists which according to him revealed criminal behaviour by members of the service, including a plot to assassinate President Gadiffi of Libya. His motive was to have MI5 reformed in order to remove a public danger. The House of Lords held that the interference with the right to freedom of expression was proportionate. The main reason for this was that the restriction was not absolute. It allowed information to be released with 'lawful authority' (above) thereby inviting the claimant to approach a range of 'senior and responsible crown servants' such as the Metropolitan Police Commissioner and the Security and Intelligence Commission [103]. The consent of the Attorney-General is required for a prosecution although again it is questionable whether this provides independence (Chapter 8).

Lord Hutton [99–101] went further than the others in stressing that the need to protect the secrecy of intelligence and military operations was justified as a 'pressing social need' even where the disclosure was not itself harmful to the public interest (compare Lord Scott [120]). This was to protect confidence in the security services both among its own members and those who dealt with them. Moreover an individual whistleblower may not be sufficiently informed of the consequences of his actions. Lord Hutton [105–6] also rejected the argument that senior officials or politicians might be reluctant to investigate complaints of wrongdoing, holding that the court must assume that the relevant legislation is being applied properly. By contrast Lord Hope [70] asserted that 'institutions tend to protect their own and to resist criticism from wherever it may come'.

Their Lordships also stressed the safeguard of judicial review and that a reviewing court would apply a strong proportionality test to a refusal to disclose. Lord Bingham [34] said that he could not envisage circumstances where disclosure would be refused to a qualified lawyer on a claimant's behalf even where this had to be limited to a special counsel appointed by the court (see also Lord Hope [73], Lord Hutton [108–16]). The Court of Appeal had left open the possibility that a defence of necessity might apply to the Official Secrets Act 1989. This would apply only in extreme circumstances where disclosure was needed to avert an immediate threat to life or perhaps property. The House of Lords did not comment on this issue.

2. **Defence** (s.2). This applies to any present or former Crown servant or government contractor. In all cases the disclosure must be damaging. Here damaging means hampering the armed forces, leading to death or injury of military personnel, or leading to serious damage to military equipment or installations. A similar defence of ignorance applies as in 1.
3. **International relations** (s.3). Again this applies to any present or former Crown servant or government contractor. Two kinds of information are covered: (i) any information concerning international relations; (ii) any confidential information obtained from a foreign state or an international organisation. The disclosure must again be damaging. Damaging here refers to endangering the interest of the UK abroad or endangering the safety of British citizens abroad. The fact that information in this class is confidential in its 'nature or contents' may be sufficient in itself to establish that the disclosure is damaging (s.3(3)). There is a defence of ignorance on the same basis as in 1 (s.3(4)).
4. **Crime and special investigation powers** (s.4). This applies to present or former Crown servants or contractors and covers information relating to the commission of offences, escapes from custody, crime prevention, detection or prosecution work. 'Special investigations' include telephone tapping under a warrant from the Home Secretary and entering on private property in accordance with a warrant under the Security Services Act 1989 (see below). Section 4 does not require that the information be damaging as such because damage is implicit in its nature. There is however a defence of 'ignorance of the nature' of the information (s.4(4)(5)).

Section 5 makes it an offence to pass on protected information, for example by the press. Protected information is information falling within the above provisions which has come into a person's possession as a result of (i) having been 'disclosed' (whether to him or another) by a Crown servant or government contractor without lawful authority; or (ii) entrusted to him in confidence; or (iii) disclosed to him by a person to whom it was entrusted in confidence. This does not seem to cover someone who receives information from a *former* Crown servant or government contractor. If this is so the publisher of the memoirs of a retired civil servant may be safe, although the retired civil servant herself will not (but see *Lord Advocate* v *The Scotsman Publications Ltd* (1990) where section 5 was applied). Nor does the section seem to apply to a person who accidentally finds protected information (for example a civil servant leaves her briefcase in a restaurant). Could this be regarded as a 'disclosure'? It is an offence for a Crown servant or government contractor not to look after the protected information and for anyone to fail to hand it back if officially required to do so (s.8).

The Crown must prove that the accused knew or had reasonable cause to believe that the information was protected under the Act and that it came into his or her possession contrary to the Act. In the case of information in categories 1, 2 and 3 (above) the Crown must also show that disclosure is 'damaging' and that he or she knew or had reasonable cause to believe that this was so.

22.3.2 Civil Liability: Breach of Confidence

As we saw in Chapter 21 information given in confidence can be prevented from publication by means of an injunction. As a legal person the Crown can take advantage of this. However a public authority must show positively that secrecy is in the public interest, which the court will balance against any countervailing public interest in disclosure. Conversely a public authority can rely on a public interest in disclosure in order to override private confidentiality even where the information has been given only for a specific purpose (see *Hellewell* v *Chief Constable of Derbyshire* (1995); *Woolgar* v *Chief Constable of the Sussex Police* (1999).

A civil action for breach of confidence may be attractive to governments since it avoids a jury trial, can be speedy and requires a lower standard of proof than in a criminal case. Indeed under the common law a temporary injunction, which against the press may destroy a topical story, could be obtained from a judge at any time on the basis merely of an arguable case (see *Attorney-General* v *Guardian Newspapers* (1987)). However section 12 of the Human Rights Act 1998 (Chapter 21) may have shifted the balance.

In *Attorney-General* v *Guardian Newspapers Ltd (No. 2)* (1990) (*Spycatcher*) the House of Lords in principle supported the interests of government secrecy. Peter Wright, a retired member of the security service, had published his memoirs abroad revealing possible malpractice within the service. Their Lordships refused to grant a permanent injunction but only because the memoirs were no longer secret, having become freely available throughout the world. It was held that in principle publication was unlawful since the relationship between the member of the security service and the Crown was inherently one of confidence and that the Crown could probably obtain compensation from Wright and from newspapers in respect of publication in the UK before the memoirs had been published abroad. This was confirmed by the ECHR as proportionate. In *Observer and Guardian Newspapers* v *UK* (1992)) the ECHR, with a strong dissent from Morenilla J, held that in the area of national security an injunction is justifiable to protect confidential information even where the content of the particular information is not in itself harmful (see also *Sunday Times (No. 2)* v *UK* (1992); *Attorney-General* v *Jonathan Cape Ltd* (1975)).

Spycatcher also confirmed that members of the security services have a 'lifelong duty of confidence'. In *Attorney-General* v *Blake* (1998) a former civil servant had been convicted of spying but escaped to Moscow where he published his memoirs. The House of Lords held that even though the content of the memoirs created no danger to national security and were no longer confidential Blake was liable to account for his royalties to the government on the ground that he should not be permitted to profit from his wrong. The exposure of 'iniquity' (serious wrongdoing or crime) by government officers can justify disclosure (see for example *Lion Laboratories* v *Evans* (1985)). In *Spycatcher* serious iniquity was not established and it remains to be seen whether 'iniquity' overrides national security. The method of disclosure must be reasonable and the discloser must probably complain internally before going public (*Francombe* v *Mirror Group Newspapers* (1984)). This suggests that a high standard of evidence is required, given that *Spycatcher* involved allegations of criminal activity against security service members including a plot to destabilise the Labour government. A common response by UK officials to those who disclose official wrongdoing is to condemn the whistleblower (see Committee on Standards in Public Life, consultation paper, *Getting the Balance Right*, 2003). For example Steve Moxon, a civil servant who had revealed irregularities in the processing of immigration visas to the press leading to the resignation of the responsible minister, was dismissed for 'an irretrievable breakdown in trust' (*Independent*, 2 August 2004).

The Public Interest Disclosure Act 1998 (Employment Rights Act 1996 Part 4A) protects employees against unfair dismissal in certain cases. 'Qualifying disclosures' are those which the whistleblower reasonably believes relate to the commission or likelihood of commission of any of the following: criminal offences, breaches of legal duties, miscarriages of justice, danger to health and safety or danger to the environment. Internal disclosure in good faith to an employer or responsible superior is protected and also disclosure to a minister or to a person prescribed by a minister. However there is no protection where the disclosure is an offence, for example under the Official Secrets Act 1989 (above) and employees working in national security areas can be excluded (s.11). Exceptionally, an employee can make a disclosure to another person or even to the press. However this must be 'reasonable' and applies only where either the matter is exceptionally serious or the discloser reasonably believes either that she or he will be victimised or that evidence will be concealed, or there is no prescribed person or the matter has already been disclosed to the employer. In the public sector the Act has mainly been used by NHS employees.

22.3.3 Public Interest Immunity

An important aspect of government secrecy concerns the doctrine once called 'Crown privilege' and now 'public interest immunity' (PII). A party to a legal action is normally required to disclose relevant documents and other evidence in his or her possession. Where PII applies, such information need not be disclosed. In deciding whether to accept a claim of PII, the court is required to 'balance' the public interest in the administration of justice against the public interest in confidentiality. At one time the courts would always accept the government's word that disclosure should be prohibited. However as a result of *Conway* v *Rimmer* (1968) the court itself does the balancing exercise.

Public interest immunity applies both to civil and criminal proceedings (see Criminal Procedure and Investigations Act 1996 ss.3(6), 7(5)). Any person can raise a claim of PII. Claims are often made by ministers following advice from the Attorney-General ostensibly acting independently of the government. It appears that a minister is not under a duty to make a claim even if he or she believes that there is a public interest at stake but must personally do an initial balancing exercise. In *R* v *Brown* (1993) the court emphasised that it was objectionable for a minister automatically to accept the Attorney-General's advice.

Where a PII certificate is issued the person seeking disclosure must first satisfy the court that the document is likely to be necessary for fairly disposing of the case, or in a criminal case of assisting the defence, a less difficult burden (see *Air Canada* v *Secretary of State for Trade* (1983); *Goodridge* v *Chief Constable of Hampshire Constabulary* (1999); Criminal Procedure and Investigations Act 1996 s.3). The court can inspect the documents at this stage but is reluctant to do so in order to discourage 'fishing expeditions' (see *Burmah Oil Co. Ltd* v *Bank of England* (1980)).

The court will then 'balance' the competing public interests involved, at this stage inspecting the documents. Grounds for refusing disclosure include national security, the protection of anonymous informers or covert surveillance operations (*Rogers* v *Secretary of State for the Home Department* (1973); *D* v *NSPCC* (1978)), financially or commercially sensitive material, in particular communications between the government and the Bank of England and between the Bank and private businesses (*Burmah Oil Co. Ltd* v *Bank of England* (1980)), the protection of children and relationships with foreign governments. It has also been said that preventing 'ill-informed or premature criticism of the government' is in the public interest (*Conway* v *Rimmer* [1968] AC 910 at 952). There is no automatic immunity for high level documents such as cabinet minutes but a strong case must be made for their disclosure (see *Burmah Oil Co. Ltd* v *Bank of England* (1980); *Air Canada* v *Secretary of State for Trade (No. 2)* (1983)).

The desire to protect candour and frankness within the public service is arguably not a sufficient justification (*Conway* v *Rimmer* (above) at 957, 976, 993–4, 995; *R* v *West Midlands Chief Constable ex parte Wiley* (1994); *Williams* v *Home Office (No. 2)* (1981), 1155; *Science Research Council* v *Nasse* [1980] AC 1028 at 1970, 108: candour a 'private' interest; but see *Burmah Oil Co. Ltd* v *Bank of England* [1980] AC 1090 at 1132). The courts also consider the purpose for which the information was given. Information given in confidence for a particular purpose will not be disclosed for another purpose unless the donor consents in circumstances where disclosure would not be harmful to the public interest (*R* v *West Midlands Chief Constable ex parte Wiley* (1994); *Lonrho plc* v *Fayed (No. 4)* (1994); compare *Peach* v *Metropolitan Police Commissioner* (1986): nothing to lose).

A distinction has been made between 'class claims' and 'contents' claims. In a class claim, even if the contents of a document are innocuous, the document should still be protected because it is a member of a class of document of which disclosure would prevent the efficient working of government, such as policy advice given by civil servants or diplomatic communications.

In *R* v *West Midlands Chief Constable* (above) it was claimed that evidence given to the police complaints authority was protected by class immunity. The House of Lords rejected this blanket claim, holding that immunity depended on whether the contents of the particular document raised a public interest, which on the facts they did not. It is not clear whether the notion of a class claim as such survives this decision since their Lordships rejected the claim only in relation to that particular class of document. However Lord Templeman remarked (at 424) that the distinction between a class and a contents claim loses 'much of its significance'. A successful PII claim means that there could be unfairness to the individual. Moreover before the HRA, at least in civil cases, the court did not give special weight to the interests of justice but applied a balance of probabilities test. In both respects therefore PII may violate the right to a fair trial in Article 6 of the ECHR. Article 6 contains no overrides except to the extent that the press or public may in certain circumstances be excluded from a trial. Indeed in *R v DPP ex parte Kebeline* (1999) Lord Bingham remarked that 'I can conceive of no circumstances in which, having concluded that that feature rendered the trial unfair, the court would not go on to find a violation of Art. 6'.

In *Kostovski* v *Netherlands* (1989) the European Court of Human Rights refused to allow the state to protect the anonymity of witnesses. It applied a test of whether the exclusion placed the accused at a substantial disadvantage. The Court emphasised that the right to a fair trial 'cannot be sacrificed to expediency'. Nevertheless PII as such has been held not to violate the Convention provided that the trial overall is 'fair' (*Edwards and Lewis* v *UK* (2003); R*owe and Davies* v *UK* (2001); *Jasper* v *UK* (2000); *Fitt* v *UK* (2000)). In *R* v *H and C* (2004) Lord Bingham asserted that PII must 'never imperil the overall fairness of the trial'. However unless the information to be protected is trivial or irrelevant, it is difficult to see how PII can be anything other than a departure from fairness.

In *R* v *H and C* (above) the House of Lords specified principles that must be applied, at least in a criminal case, to minimise unfairness. The government must show a pressing social need that cannot be met by less intrusive means. The parties must be given an opportunity to argue the reasons for the claim in open court and also for the procedure to be adopted. However this may not be possible without revealing the information itself. As much as possible of the material must be disclosed, although there may be extreme cases where it cannot be revealed even when a PII application is being made. Where a criminal conviction is likely to be unsafe as a result of PII the trial must probably be discontinued. Lord Bingham remarked that it is axiomatic that if a person charged with a criminal offence cannot receive a fair trial, he should not be tried at all.

22.3.4 Special Advocates

In PII cases and other proceedings involving secret evidence, for example undercover agents or informers, such as security cases decided by the Special Immigration Appeal Commission (SIAC), terrorism cases and hearings by the Parole Board the court can appoint a special advocate. This is a lawyer who acts on the accused's behalf and might see the material but without disclosing it to the parties. A special advocate has no duty to give information to the claimant nor to take instructions from the claimant. This device creates serious problems of fairness and raises ethical issues relating to the confidence inherent in the lawyer–client relationship.

In *M* v *Secretary of State for the Home Department* (2004) the Court of Appeal required the Secretary of State to show that he had properly considered all relevant factors. The appellant was a Libyan asylum seeker. There was evidence that some of his associates might be involved with al-Qaeda, a terrorist organisation, but none linking the appellant himself with al-Qaeda. The Court of Appeal held that the SIAC was justified in overturning the Home Secretary's certificate. It was not enough to show suspicious circumstances. The Home Secretary had to take a broad overall view based on all the circumstances and supported by evidence. However the court endorsed the process itself. Lord Woolf remarked (at 868) that the undoubted unfairness involved in this secretive procedure can be necessary because of the interests of national security but that so far as possible the disadvantage must be avoided or, if it cannot be avoided, minimised by the appointment of a special advocate who can object to evidence and to the need for secrecy. The courts accept that the Home Secretary is entitled to rely entirely upon 'closed' evidence that the defendant is prohibited from seeing on the basis of national security. If closed material is under consideration, the SIAC will sit as a closed court. This does not sit comfortably with the earlier case of *Murray* v *United Kingdom* (1996) which held that the Secretary of State must not use 'closed material' as the only source for suspicion.

In *R (Roberts)* v *Parole Board* (2006) the House of Lords upheld the use of special advocates in principle but with strong reservations. It could not be decided as a general principle whether the use of a special advocate satisfied the right to a fair trial but depended on the particular circumstances. An accused person must have the opportunity to challenge all the evidence against him. Lord Steyn thought that the special advocate was always a violation as being conspicuously unfair. Lord Bingham described the device as 'taking blind shots at a hidden target' [18] and thought that it could be used only where no serious unfairness was involved, for example where the relevant information could be edited or was not relied upon [19]. (See Commons Constitutional Affairs Committee, *The Operation of SIAC and the Use of Special Advocates*, Seventh Report, 2004–5, HC 323–1.)

22.4 The Security and Intelligence Services

The 'secret services' comprise the security services, the intelligence services and the government communications centre GCHQ. Traditionally they have operated under the general law without special powers other than the possibility of royal prerogative power. They were in principle accountable to ministers, ultimately the Prime Minister, but there was no formal mechanism for parliamentary accountability. Their role has been primarily that of information gathering. Where powers of arrest or interference with property were required, the assistance of the police was requested. However the *Spycatcher* litigation (above) brought to a head recurrent concerns that security agents were out of control and unaccountable and they have now been placed within a statutory framework. This relies heavily on the discretionary powers of ministers but contains certain safeguards, albeit judicial review is restricted.

The security services (formerly MI5) deal with internal security (Security Services Act 1989, 1996). They report to the Prime Minister. Their responsibilities include

the protection of national security and, in particular, its protection against threats from espionage, terrorism and sabotage, from the activities of agents of foreign powers, and from actions intended to overthrow or undermine parliamentary democracy by political or violent means. (s.1)

Section 1(3) includes the safeguarding of 'the economic well-being of the UK against threats posed by the actions or intentions of persons outside the British Islands'. This is extremely wide and could extend for example to the lawful activities of environmental non-governmental organisations (NGOs). The Security Services Act 1996 extends the functions of the security services to include assisting the police in the prevention and detection of serious crime. This includes the use of violence, crimes resulting in substantial financial gain, or conduct by a large number of persons in pursuit of a common purpose or crimes carrying a sentence of three years or more. This is wide enough to include political public order offences and industrial disputes and may violate ECHR notions of clarity and proportionality.

The Intelligence services (formerly MI6 and GCHQ; Intelligence Services Act 1994) deal with threats from outside the UK. They are under the control of the Foreign Office but also report to the Prime Minister. Their functions are 'to obtain and provide information relating to the actions and intentions of persons outside the British Islands' and 'to perform other tasks relating to the actions and intentions of such persons'. Reflecting the ECHR their powers are limited to national security with particular reference to defence and foreign policies, the economic well being of the UK in relation to the actions and intentions of persons outside the British islands and the prevention and detection of serious crime (ss.1(2), 3(2)). The services must not take action to further the interests of any political party (Security Service Act 1989 s.52(2); Intelligence Services Act 1994 s.2(3)). GCHQ monitors electronic communications and 'other emissions' and can provide advice and information to the armed forces and other organisations specified by the Prime Minister.

22.5   Surveillance

The problem of the state amassing information about individuals is of increasing concern because of computer technology which enables large amounts of information to be stored, collated, speedily accessed and transferred without apparent safeguards. Thus proposals innocuous in themselves, such as the introduction of identity cards (Identity Cards Act 2006) are viewed with suspicion not only because of the risk of abuse of power but also because of the risk of errors and accidents.

There is no common law right to privacy as such (Chapter 21). Provided that no trespass occurred the use by the police of telephone tapping and other covert surveillance devices were therefore lawful (*Malone* v *Metropolitan Police Commissioner* (1979). Moreover even unlawfully obtained evidence is admissible in court subject to a test of reliability (Police and Criminal Evidence Act 1984 s.78; *Schenk* v *Switzerland* (1988); *R* v *Sang* (1979); (*R* v *Khan* (1997), *Jones* v *University of Warwick* (2003)). Evidence obtained by telephone tapping cannot be used in court (see below).

The European Court of Human Rights held that under Article 8 of the ECHR (privacy) there must be safeguards in respect of surveillance. These must include clearly defined limits on the power and supervision by an independent court (*Malone* v *UK* (1984); *Khan* v *UK* (2001)). Moreover retaining data falling within Article 8 after it has been used for the authorised purposes is a violation unless there is a particular reason for suspicion against that person (*Amman* v *Switzerland* (2000)). In *Halford* v *UK* (1997) it was held that the UK was in breach of Article 8 by failing to regulate the use of interception devices by employers. In *JH Ltd* v *UK* (2001) the European Court held that bugging in a police station was a violation of the right to privacy.

The Regulation of Investigatory Powers Act 2000 (RIPA), which largely supersedes the Interception of Communications Act 1985, responds to the ECHR. It includes not only the police and intelligence services but also the revenue and military services and can be extended by the Secretary of State to other public bodies. RIPA authorises telephone tapping and intercepting electronic data such as emails and websites both on public and private systems. It also creates new powers of surveillance by making clear that certain forms of interception and uses of information are lawful including bugging devices. However notwithstanding the Act, eavesdropping upon lawyer-client communications may still be unlawful as an abuse of court process (see *R* v *Grant* [2005] 3 WLR 437 [52]).

RIPA does not apply to CCTV cameras, these being outside specific statutory regulation. The use of CCTV cameras by local authorities is authorised by the Criminal Justice and Public Order Act 1994 s.163. The use of CCTV cameras by private persons might be arguably be restricted in particular circumstances by the developing law of privacy on the basis that there may not be a sufficiently strong public interest supporting their use (Chapter 21; see *Campbell* v *MGN* (2004); *Peck* v *UK* (2003)). On the other hand the Human Rights Act does not apply directly to the acts of private persons.

RIPA distinguishes between 'directed surveillance' which is covert surveillance undertaken as part of a specific operation to obtain private information about a person (s.26) and 'intrusive surveillance'. Intrusive surveillance is covert surveillance carried out in relation to anything taking place on residential premises or a private vehicle where there is an individual planted or a covert surveillance device is used. Intrusive surveillance can be carried out only in the interests of national security or for preventing or detecting serious crime or in the interests of the economic well being of the country. RIPA also regulates the use of covert human intelligence (s.26, s.29). This includes undercover officers, spies and informers.

Intrusive surveillance must be authorised by the heads of the government agency in question. In the case of the police and customs agencies there must also be the approval of a Surveillance Commissioner (ss.36)). Authorisation by the armed services, the intelligence services and the ministry of defence require the approval of the Secretary of State. The authorising officer can appeal to the Chief Surveillance Commissioner against a refusal by a commissioner, but not by the Secretary of State to approve an authorisation. A person 'aggrieved' by an authorisation can complain to the Investigatory Powers Tribunal (s.65).

Directed surveillance and use of covert human intelligence can be authorised by a range of public bodies designated by the Secretary of State including government agencies, the police and local authorities (see SI 2003 No.3171). It can be used if 'necessary' and 'proportionate' for a wide range of purposes within the overrides to Article 8 of the ECHR (s.28). These purposes include national security, the prevention and detection of serious crime, the safeguarding of the economic well being of the country and – but only in the case of conduct other than interception – the safeguarding of public health, public safety, tax collection, emergencies protecting life and health and 'other purposes specified by the Secretary of State' (s.22). There is evidence that low level public bodies such as local councils interpret these purposes loosely and use surveillance powers to combat relatively trivial cases of anti-social activity such as dropping litter.

By virtue of RIPA s.1(1) is an offence, intentionally and without lawful authority to intercept a communication while it is being transmitted by means of a public postal service or a public telecommunications system including email. It is also an offence intentionally and without lawful authority to intercept a communication transmitted through a private telecommunications system (for example a company network, cordless phone or pager) except by the controller of the system or with his or her consent (see *R* v *Sargeant* (2003)).

The obtaining and use of 'communications data' can be authorised by a wide range of officials without prior judicial control (RIPA Part 1, Chapter 2). Communications data does not include the content of a message as such but includes 'traffic information' such as billing data and the source and destination. The Secretary of State can require persons operating public postal or telecommunications systems (which includes internet service providers) to keep a reasonable 'interception capability' (s.12(1)) and provide traffic data to designated public officials on demand (s.22(4)). Under section 102 of the Anti-Terrorism, Crime and Security Act 2001 the Secretary of State can issue codes of practice authorising retention of communications data and making it admissible in court for the purposes of safeguarding national security, the prevention and detection of crime or the prosecution of offenders. However blanket storage of personal information unrelated to a specific investigation may violate the ECHR.

RIPA empowers anyone in lawful possession of intercepted information to require the disclosure of the key to protected (encrypted) data on the grounds of national security, serious crime and, more dubiously, that it is necessary for the performance of a public function (s.49). The UK is the only leading democracy to allow this. A disclosure notice must be authorised by a circuit judge who must be satisfied that there is no other means of obtaining the required information and that the direction is proportionate to what is sought to be achieved. A disclosure notice requested by the police, the security services or the customs and excise commissioners can also contain 'tipping off' provisions imposing a lifelong secrecy requirement as to the existence of the notice (s.54).

The ordinary courts are largely excluded. Evidence cannot normally be given suggesting that there has been telephone tapping, lawful or otherwise (RIPA ss.17, 18). Information obtained by telephone tapping is not therefore admissible, thus encouraging the government to seek to detain terrorist suspects without trial (below). Information obtained from telephone tapping can be used in police interviews and presumably by the executive for other purposes (*R* v *Sargent* (2003)). Information obtained from overseas surveillance is admissible (*R* v *P* (2001)) as is information obtained by bugging devices, CCTV and undercover agents (*R* v *Khan (Sultan)* (1996)).

There are limited independent safeguards. The Secretary of State is responsible for ensuring that interception warrants are issued for proper purposes (s.15). The directors-general of each of the security and intelligence services are responsible as both poacher and gamekeeper for the efficiency of their service and for making 'arrangements' for securing that information is neither obtained or disclosed 'except in so far as is necessary for the proper discharge of its functions' or, in the case of disclosure, for the prevention or detection of serious crime. There is an Intelligence Services Commissioner who reviews the exercise of the various powers of investigation and use of material under the legislation (Regulation of Investigatory Powers Act 2000 ss.57, 59). The Commissioner, who must be its senior judge, has no enforcement powers and reports to the Prime Minister who must lay its annual reports before Parliament. Interception Commissioners and Surveillance Commissioners have similar status and functions. There is also an Intelligence and Security Committee composed of backbench members of Parliament, which examines the spending, administration and policy of the intelligence services (Intelligence Services Act

1994 s.11). However this is appointed by and reports to the Prime Minister and is not strictly speaking a committee of Parliament with a duty to Parliament itself. Its annual report is laid before Parliament but can be censored by the Prime Minister after consultation with the committee.

RIPA also creates an Investigatory Powers Tribunal to hear allegations of misuse of power by the security and intelligence services and also in relation to the interference with property, interception of communications, covert surveillance or misuse of information by the police and other bodies (s.65). The Tribunal is also concerned with claims based on human rights for which it has been designated as the only forum (see Human Rights Act 1998 s.7). It may award compensation and quash warrants or authorisations and order records to be destroyed (ibid.). The Tribunal is required to apply judicial review principles (s.67). In view of the wide powers involved this affords only a low level of review although it probably satisfies the ECHR. Decisions of the Tribunal and the commissioners (above) cannot be questioned in the courts even on jurisdictional grounds (Intelligence Services Act 1994 s.5(4); RIPA s.67(8)). In the case of the intelligence services, the Tribunal may, where it does not decide in favour of the complainant, refer a matter to the commissioner to investigate 'whether the service has in any other respect acted unreasonably in relation to the complainant or his property'. The commissioner may then report to the Secretary of State who can make an award of compensation (Schedule 1(7)).

The use of covert surveillance devices by the police is also regulated by the Police Act 1997 and the two regimes overlap. Part III of the 1997 Act authorises the police to interfere with property for the purpose of preventing or detecting 'serious crime'. For this purpose serious crime means crimes involving the use of violence, crimes resulting in substantial financial gain or conduct by a large number of persons in pursuit of a common purpose (s.93(4). Thus political demonstrators may be vulnerable. In a gesture towards human rights language the action must be 'necessary' and 'proportionate'. The action taken can include maintaining or retrieving surveillance equipment authorised under RIPA. The exercise of the power must be authorised by a designated senior police officer, military officer, customs and revenue officer or officer of certain other law enforcement agencies. In certain cases the authorisation must be by a Commissioner (above). This includes dwellings, hotel bedrooms and offices and matters likely to involve legal professional privilege, confidential personal information or confidential journalistic material. Where residential premises are involved these would also constitute 'intrusive surveillance' under RIPA. The 1997 Act also imposes duties on private communication providers such as internet service providers to cooperate with the authorities.

22.6 Emergency Powers

As we saw in Chapter 20 the police have a general power to prevent a breach of the peace. There is no legal obstacle to the armed forces or indeed anyone else being used in support of this. Indeed perhaps everyone has a duty to aid the civil power in quelling a disturbance (*Charge to the Bristol Grand Jury* (1832)). An individual whether policeman, soldier or private person in self defence is however liable for the excessive use of force, thus illustrating Dicey's version of the rule of law (Chapter 7). The force used must be no more than is reasonable in the circumstances for self defence or the defence of others (see Criminal Law Act 1967 s.3). In deciding what is reasonable the court will take into account the pressure of the circumstances (see *Attorney-General for Northern Ireland's Reference*

(No.1) (1975); *McCann* v *UK* (1995)). However obedience to orders as such is probably not a defence (*Keighley* v *Bell* (1866)).

Under the royal prerogative the armed forces can be deployed at the discretion of the Crown and the Crown can also arm the police (Chapter 14). The Crown may also enter private property in an emergency but must pay compensation for any damage caused other than in wartime (War Damage Act 1965; *Saltpetre Case* (1607); *Attorney-General* v *De Keyser's Royal Hotel* (1920)). The Secretary of State for Defence is politically accountable to Parliament for the use of these powers.

Beyond this is the possibility that where there is such a serious disruption to public order that the courts cannot function, the military may assume control under a state of martial law. Dicey denied that martial law is part of English law (1915, Chapter 8). However the concept has been used and indeed applied where the courts were still sitting in relation to colonial territories (*Marais* v *General Officer Commanding* (1902)). Martial law was declared in Ireland in 1920 and the House of Lords accepted the possibility that the courts could in principle control the activities of the military under martial law (*Re Clifford and O'Sullivan* (1921)). It is arguable that martial law is no more than an application of the broad doctrine of necessity which justifies the deployment of the armed forces. The courts are unlikely to interfere with such decisions (*Chandler* v *DPP* (1964)).

Exceptional executive powers can be conferred by emergency regulations (Civil Contingencies Act 2004). This might override any overlapping prerogative powers (Chapter 14). Regulations can be made by Order in Council (or if this would cause serious delay by a senior minister) if the relevant authority is satisfied that an emergency exists or is imminent, that there is an urgent need to deal with it and that existing legislation is inadequate for the purpose. The regulations must be in 'due proportion' (ss.20, 21). Thus there need be no declaration of a formal state of emergency nor approval by Parliament to trigger the powers.

An emergency is more widely defined than for the purpose of derogating from the ECHR (above). An emergency means:

> an event or situation which threatens serious damage to human welfare or the environment in the United Kingdom or in a part or region, or war or terrorism which threatens serious damage to the security of the United Kingdom. (s.19(1))

These threats are widely drawn. Human welfare includes loss of life, illness or injury, homelessness, property damage, disruption of supplies of money, food, water, energy and fuel, disruption of a communication system, facilities for transport or health services. Environmental damage is limited to biological, chemical or radioactive contamination or disruption to or destruction of plant or animal life (s.19(2)(3)). An emergency might include for example a general strike, a natural disaster or epidemic or terrorist threat.

Parliament must meet within five days and the regulations lapse unless approved by Parliament within seven days and in any event after 30 days. In both cases they can be renewed (ss.26, 27).

The Act allows ministers to alter statutes. It confers powers to deploy the armed forces, to require people to perform unpaid functions and to provide information, to restrict freedom of movement and assembly assemblies, to take or destroy property without compensation (s.22) and to extend the power to detain without trial. There are safeguards based on the ECHR. These include proportionality and compliance with convention rights. The powers can be used only for the specific purpose of dealing with the threats created by the emergency. There can be no military conscription or outlawing of industrial action. No offence can be created except one triable summarily by magistrates or the Sheriff's Court in Scotland nor punishable with more than three months' imprisonment. Criminal procedure cannot be altered nor the Human Rights Act 1998 (s.23). Judicial review is not specifically preserved but 'regard' must be had to its importance (s.22(5)). The emergency regulations are delegated legislation and as such are subject to the general law of judicial review and to the Human Rights Act 1998.

22.7 Anti-terrorism Measures

The UK's anti-terrorism laws illustrate on the one hand the phenomenon of 'creep' as increasingly wide powers introduced in response to specific events become absorbed into the general law but on the other hand the value, albeit haphazard, of safeguards comprising access to independent courts, monitoring bodies and parliamentary mechanisms. However these reassuring forms may help to legitimise harsh laws. Since terrorist actions usually constitute ordinary crimes such as murder there is a problem in treating terrorism as a special case calling for special powers, even though certain features of terrorism, notably large scale undiscriminating attacks carried out in conditions of uncertainty call for exceptional investigation and enforcement activity and for offences to be defined so as to prevent harm in advance. The problem lies in giving terrorism a political dimension in order to justify special measures. The rhetoric of 'war on terrorism' is substituted for that of law enforcement. This rhetoric may encourage the very terrorism that it seeks to combat. It has been widely recognised that:

> situations involving mass and flagrant violations of human rights and fundamental freedoms ... may give rise to international terrorism and may endanger international peace and security. (UN General Assembly Resolution, A/RES/40/61 (1985), 9 December 1985, para. 9)

Raising the political temperature may lead to hasty impetuous dramatic gestures that result in inadequate evidence for a successful prosecution and may create martyrs. For example in 2008 a failure to obtain a conviction in relation to an alleged plot to bomb aircraft was at least partly the result of US agencies prematurely detaining a suspect currently under surveillance by British police (see *Guardian* 10 September 2008). Moreover the width of the powers mean that they may be used against non-violent people whose activities the government dislikes or whom the police or local officials find it convenient to target. For example anti-terrorist legislation was used to remove a member who objected to the invasion of Iraq from a Labour Party conference (see *Guardian* 8 October 2005). Special anti-terrorism laws were originally enacted as emergency provisions in response to the conflict in Northern Ireland. The Northern Ireland (Emergency Provisions) Act 1978 (EPA) and the Prevention of Terrorism (Temporary Provisions) Act 1974 (PTA) created new offences and wider police investigation powers. They created two distinct anti-terrorism regimes in the UK; there were additional measures in Northern Ireland that did not exist in the rest of the UK (search, arrest, detention, trial by judge, detention without trial). The EPA and PTA were intended to be temporary and only apply to terrorism cases but between 1973 and 2000 these Acts were repeatedly re-enacted, extended and modified. The PTA 1984 was expanded to cover international terrorism (but was not extended to domestic terrorism other than that associated with Northern Ireland) and further offences and police powers were added. During this period some of the powers in the PTAs and EPAs were mirrored in new laws to deal with ordinary crime: the extraordinary powers had become ordinary.

In response to the peace process in Northern Ireland a review of the anti-terrorism laws was undertaken to ensure they were suitable for countering future terrorism threats. In 1996 the Lloyd Report (Cm 3420) recommended wide ranging changes including the harmonisation of anti-terrorism laws across the UK, the expansion of these powers to all domestic and international terrorism and a new definition of terrorism. Many of these recommendations were enacted in the Terrorism Act 2000 (TA). After the attacks in the US in September 2001 the TA was considered to be inadequate. In 2001 the Anti-Terrorism, Crime and Security Act 2001 (ATCSA) was enacted in unseemly haste. It was controversial, in particular introducing indefinite detention of non-UK nationals (s.23) and not all the powers were restricted to terrorism investigations. Because of its controversial nature, indefinite detention was subject to a 'sunset provision', automatically expiring after a prescribed time (see s.29: 15 months). This is one of the fundamental safeguards against the misuse of emergency powers since it ensures democratic debate.

The government's inability to secure the re-enactment of indefinite detention led to the enactment of the Prevention of Terrorism Act 2005 (PTA 2005) which introduced an alternative – control orders. However these have proven almost as controversial (see Lord Carlile of Berriew QC, *First Report of the Independent Reviewer Pursuant to Section 14(3) of the Prevention of Terrorism Act 2005*, 2 February 2006). The retreat from human rights norms that typifies anti-terrorism legislation has been continued in the legislation introduced after the London bombings in July 2005, the Terrorism Act 2006 (TA 2006). This has extended pre-charge detention (s.23) and introduced new offences that are widely feared to restrict free speech (ss.1–3) (Chapter 20). It has also introduced the offences of preparation of terrorist acts (s.5) and training for terrorism (s.6). The Treasury has power to make an order, subject to laying before Parliament, to freeze the assets of persons whom the Treasury 'reasonably believes' to be a threat to the UK's economy or to the lives or property of nationals or residents (ATCSA 2001). The hasty and panic fuelled manner in which anti-terrorism legislation has been enacted since 2000 repeats the way legislation was introduced in the 1970s. The Counter Terrorism Act 2008 introduced measures which largely tightened up existing powers.

22.7.1 Definition of Terrorism

The definition of terrorism (TA 2000 s.1) is complex, 'sweepingly broad and extraordinarily vague' (per Richards J in *R (Kurdistan Workers' Party)* v *Secretary of State for the Home Department* (2002)). It has three elements. Firstly there must be an act or the threat of an act that falls into one of five categories:

- serious violence against a person
- serious violence against property
- endangers life
- serious risk to the health or safety of the public or a section of the public
- seriously disrupts or interferes with an electronic system.

Secondly the action must be intended to advance a political, religious or ideological cause. The Counter Terrorism Act adds 'racial' to this list. Thirdly the action must be designed to influence the government or coerce the public or a section of it or an international governmental organisation (added by TA 2006 s.34). It is not necessary for the action to be carried out on UK soil, against a UK citizen or property owned by a UK citizen.

The breadth of the definition means that attacks or threats against any government anywhere can be investigated by British police. This would include people resident in the UK who are active political agitators against other states. Thus it is possible that the TA could be used to police international politics, raising grave questions of traditional liberties. The vagueness of the definition means that it could include a wide variety of actions and persons, some of which might not necessarily be a significant threat to national security. This breadth of definition would permit the use of the legislation in situations where the low threat of violence does not justify specialised powers and offences. During the Terrorism Bill's passage through Parliament, Jack Straw, the Home Secretary, conceded that the definition granted considerable discretion to the enforcement agencies (HC Deb. 1999–2000, vol. 341, col. 162; Standing Committee D, 18 January 2000, col. 22). Given the breadth of the definition, the police have the key role in deciding who is or is not a terrorist.

22.7.2   Proscription

One of the key elements of the anti-terrorism regime is the banning of terrorist organisations. It is an offence to belong to or to support a proscribed organisation (TA 2000 ss.11–12). The proscribed organisations are listed in Schedule 2 of the TA 2000 or have the same name as one listed or are proscribed by statutory instrument. The organisation remains proscribed irrespective of any change in name (TA 2006 s.21). The Home Secretary can add other organisations to the list if she or he believes the organisation is 'concerned in terrorism' (TA 2000 s.3, TA 2006 s.21). This means committing or participating in acts of terrorism, preparing for terrorism, promoting, encouraging or unlawfully 'glorifying' terrorism or otherwise being concerned with terrorism. Glorifying terrorism, which includes praise or celebration, is unlawful if it can reasonably be inferred to refer to conduct that should be emulated in present circumstances. The Home Secretary does not apparently have to show reasonable grounds for her or his belief. Currently there are 59 proscribed organisations (45 international groups including 2 proscribed for glorifying terrorism and 14 concerning Northern Ireland proscribed under earlier legislation; see www.homeoffice.gov.uk/security/terrorism-and-the-law/terrorism-act/proscribed-groups). It is an offence to be or to profess to be a member of a proscribed organisation (s.11) or to invite support for a proscribed organisation (s.12) (see *Attorney General's Reference No. 4 of 2002* (2005)).

In the case of Northern Ireland a statement by a senior police officer that in his opinion the accused belongs to a proscribed organisation, although it is not sufficient by itself is sufficient supporting evidence to justify a conviction (s.108). However this may contravene the right to a fair trial under the Human Rights Act.

The organisation or someone affected by the proscription can apply to the Secretary of State to deproscribe the organisation. There is a further right of appeal to the Proscribed Organisations Appeal Commission (POAC) established under the TA 2000 but this appeal can only apply the rules of judicial review (s.5). The POAC is appointed by the Lord Chancellor and includes an appellate court judge. The Lord Chancellor can make rules permitting its proceedings to be held in secret and for evidence to be withheld from the parties and their representatives (TA 2000 Schedule 3). There is a further right of appeal to the Court of Appeal but this requires the permission of the Court (s.6). In *R (Kurdistan Workers' Party)* v *Secretary of State for the Home Department* [2002] EWHC 644, three proscribed organisations sought permission to apply for judicial review in order to contest the lawfulness of the proscription process. Richards J refused permission on the ground that Parliament intended that the POAC be the appropriate court. The applicants sought to have the process challenged under the ECHR but the POAC does not have the power to issue a certificate of incompatibility under the HRA 1998 and so could not provide the remedy the applicants sought.

It is an offence to express support or invite support for a proscribed organisation, to address a meeting (of three or more persons) with the purpose of encouraging support for a proscribed organisation or furthering its activities, to arrange or help to arrange a meeting which the person knows supports or furthers the activities of a proscribed organisation or which is addressed by a person who belongs to or professes to belong to a proscribed organisation, irrespective of the subject of the meeting (s.12). In the case of a *private* meeting there is a defence that the person has no reasonable cause to believe that the address would support a proscribed organisation or further its activities. A remnant of the legislation's roots in the Northern Ireland conflict (where mass parades were held with men and women in paramilitary uniforms of flak jackets and berets) is the crime of wearing clothing or an item in public that would arouse reasonable suspicion the person is a member of a proscribed organisation (s.13). These laws on proscription are serious restrictions on freedom of expression and were controversial when they were first enacted but have come to be viewed as necessary and are among the least problematic of the anti-terrorism laws.

22.7.3   Arrest and Pre-charge Detention

A constable may arrest without warrant and search a person whom he reasonably suspects to be a terrorist, that is someone who has committed a terrorist offence or is concerned in the commission preparation or instigation of acts of terrorism (s.41, s 43 (2)). It is not clear whether 'reasonably suspects' has the same meaning as 'suspects on reasonable grounds' which is the text for an ordinary arrest. Arguably 'reasonably' in this context refers only to the broad test of *Wednesbury* unreasonableness (see Chapter 17). Unlike ordinary powers of arrest this power does not tie the arrest to a specific offence (*R* v *Officer in Charge of Police Office Castlereagh Belfast ex parte Lynch* (1980)). Significant in the context of liberal values of human dignity, the officer does not need to disclose to the arrestee the grounds for his suspicions (*Oscar* v *Chief Constable RUC* (1992)). Once the person has been arrested he or she can be detained for questioning without charge for up to 28 days (Schedule 8 as extended by TA 2006 s.23). Parliament rejected the government's police inspired proposal for 90 days' detention.

Extended pre-charge detention originated under the Northern Ireland legislation where the police could detain a suspect for up to seven days with permission from the Home Secretary. In *Brogan* v *UK* (1989) the European Court of Human Rights held this power to be in breach of the Convention requirement that a suspect must be brought promptly before a court (Article 5). The court decided that a suspect should be brought before a judge within a maximum of four days after their arrest. The UK therefore derogated from the ECHR.

The Terrorism Act 2000 as extended by the Terrorism Act 2006 section 23 was intended to end this difficulty. The Act creates a series of increasing powers. A suspect can be detained for up to 48 hours by the police alone. To detain a person from 48 hours up to 14 days, the police may apply to a senior district judge or his deputy in England, a sheriff in Scotland or county court judge or designated resident magistrate in Northern Ireland. For detention up to 28 days they must apply to a High Court (Senior) judge (Schedule 8). Permission can be granted if the detention is necessary to obtain or preserve evidence or to carry out an examination or analysis and the investigation is being conducted diligently and expeditiously (ibid.) but again the police investigation does not need to be tied to a specific crime. The detention must be kept regularly under review. The accused is entitled to legal representation but can be excluded from any part of the hearing and sensitive material can be withheld from the accused and his or her advisors (Schedule 8) see *Ward v Police Service of Northern Ireland* (2008). Thus the new detention power is in accordance with a strict legal interpretation of the *Brogan* judgment. However the continued ability to detain a suspect for up to 28 days flouts the intention of the ruling. This narrow interpretation of the ruling illustrates the state's ambivalence towards protecting terrorist suspects' human rights. There is a weakly democratic 'sunset' provision in the Act (s.25) under which the 28 day extension from 14 days ceases to have effect after one year unless the Secretary of State renews the extension for a further period of one year.

The Counter Terrorism Bill (see Government Response to the Ninth Report from the Committee on Counter-Terrorism Policy and Human Rights (HC 199, 2007–8) Cm 7344)) originally proposed a further extension of pre-trial detention for up to 42 days. This was withdrawn following a defeat in the House of Lords. However the Act includes provision for questioning a terrorist suspect after being charged (ss.22–4).

22.7.4 Stop and Search

Under Section 43 a constable may stop and search anyone whom he reasonably suspects to be a terrorist. Under sections 44–45 of the Terrorism Act 2000 a policeman in uniform can stop and search at random any person within an area authorised by a senior officer for articles of a kind that could be used in connection with terrorism. Reasonable grounds need not be shown. By contrast except after an arrest search powers normally require a warrant specifying the nature of the material to be searched for (see Police and Criminal Evidence Act 1984 Part II). Safeguards include a requirement for confirmation by the Home Secretary and a provision that the order has a limited life of 28 days. Moreover the police must use the power circumspectly and only in relation to terrorism. No more than outer clothing can be removed in public. However there are serious questions whether the police are misusing this power to monitor and disrupt political demonstrations and the lengthy life of orders (www.liberty-human-rights.org.uk/issues/6-free-speech/index.shtml). In *R (Gillam)* v *Metropolitan Police Commissioner* (2006) a policeman used this power against a student demonstrating against an arms sale fair supported by the government. The House of Lords held that this limited and temporary restraint did not amount to a deprivation of liberty within Article 5 of the ECHR. Moreover the view was taken that the proportionality test should be applied with latitude in terrorist cases.

Under section 42 a magistrate may issue a search warrant for the search of any premises if a constable has reasonable ground to suspect that a person whom the constable reasonably suspects to be concerned with the commission, preparation or instigation of acts of terrorism is to be found there. Under the general law a search can be carried out in premises where a person is arrested or occupied or controlled by a person who has been arrested (Police and Criminal Evidence Act 1984 (PACE) ss.18,32). The Counter Terrorism Act adds a power to remove documents including electronic data for examination and retain them for up to 96 hours (s.1).

Under s.89 a member of the armed forces on duty or a constable may stop any person so long as is necessary in order to question him for the purpose of ascertaining that person's identity or movements and what he or she knows about a recent explosion or incident.

22.7.5   Control Orders

Except in prescribed cases (children, health risks, the mentally ill, alcohol or drug abuse, vagrants, deportation) detention without trial violates the ECHR (Article 5). 'Internment' was introduced in Northern Ireland in 1971. It was an unmitigated disaster, creating far more violence than had previously occurred. Nevertheless indefinite detention for certain foreign terrorist suspects was reintroduced by the Anti-Terrorism, Crime and Security Act 2001 (ss.21–23). For this purpose the UK was obliged to derogate from Article 5 (SI 2001/3644). The government attempted to justify this on the basis of *Chahal* v *UK* (1996) where the European Court held that if there was a real risk that a person's Article 3 (freedom from torture, degrading and inhuman treatment) rights might be abused they could not be deported to their home country even if they were a risk to national security. The UK argued that indefinite detention was necessary because *Chahal* had made it impossible to deal with suspects who were too dangerous to be at large but against whom no criminal charges were brought.

The necessity of the system was called into question by the independent reviewer, Lord Carlile of Berriew. He suggested that the government was overplaying the threat to the suspects if deported in order to detain them (see Anti-Terrorism, Crime and Security Act 2001, Part IV, Review by Lord Carlile of Berriew, February 2003).

The indefinite detention regime was condemned in *A* v *Secretary of State for the Home Department* (2005). In a landmark judgment widely regarded as vindicating the rule of law, an 8 to 1 majority of the House of Lords held that indefinite detention was disproportionate and discriminatory. The House quashed the derogation order and issued a declaration of incompatibility. Firstly the power was not legally confined to al-Qaeda (who posed the main threat); secondly it only applied to non-UK nationals but UK nationals could also be members of al-Qaeda and an equal threat to national security; thirdly if these people were so dangerous they had to be detained without charge it was irrational to allow them to leave the country where they would be free to continuing plotting. Thus the regime

> was failing to adequately address the problem . . . while imposing the severe penalty of indefinite detention on persons who, even if reasonably suspected of having links with al-Qaeda, may harbour no hostile intentions towards the United Kingdom. (per Lord Bingham at para. 43)

Indefinite detention ceased in March 2005 when a 'sunset clause' ended the life of the provisions and new, alternative powers were enacted under the PTA 2005.

Control orders were introduced as an alternative to indefinite detention as being less restrictive of human rights. A control order is an order against an individual that imposes obligations on him for purposes connected with protecting the public from a risk of terrorism (Prevention of Terrorism Act 2005 s.1). The obligations that can be imposed are any obligations that the Secretary of State or court as the case may be (below) considers necessary for the purposes connected with preventing or restricting involvement by that individual in terrorist related activity. There need be no evidence related to a criminal charge. However before making an order, if it appears to the Secretary of State that a terrorist related offence may be involved he or she must consult the relevant chief constable about whether there is evidence available that could realistically be used for prosecution for an offence related to terrorism (s.8 (1)) . This is not however a condition of making the Order (*Secretary of State* v *E* (2008)). If a control order is made the Secretary of State can also require the Chief Constable to keep the investigation under review with a view to prosecution (s.8 (4).

The obligations that can be imposed by a control order include the following (s.1 (4):

- prohibition or restriction on the possession or use of specified articles or substances
- prohibition or restriction on use of specified services or carrying out specified activities
- restrictions on work occupation or business
- restrictions on communication and association
- restrictions on residence or persons with access to residence
- exclusion from particular places
- restrictions on movement
- requirement to surrender passport or anything in his possession covered by the Order
- requirement to give access to his residence to specified persons
- requirement to submit to searches and removal of articles for the purpose of enforcing the order
- requirement to allow himself to be photographed (the Counter Terrorism Act 2008 adds fingerprinting and non-intimate samples)
- monitoring requirements
- the provision of information to a specified person
- to report to a specified person at a specified time and place.

There are two types of Control Order: derogating orders and non-derogating orders. There are different legal rules for each (PTA 2005 s.1). Both derogating and non-derogating control orders can be imposed against nationals and non-nationals. Non-derogating orders impose obligations and restrictions on the controllee that do not amount to a breach of Article 5 of the ECHR (deprivation of liberty). A derogating control order is one that violates Article 5. The application of other Articles of the ECHR is not affected but most of the relevant rights can be overridden by the state on grounds including national security. Article 3, torture or inhuman or degrading treatment and Article 6 (fair trial) cannot be overridden (Chapter 19).

A non-derogating control order is made by the Home Secretary if she or he has reasonable grounds for believing that person to be involved in terrorism-related activity and the order is necessary to protect the public (s.2). Except where she or he certifies that the matter is urgent the Secretary of State must apply to the court for permission to make the order (s.3). However the court's power is limited to deciding whether the order is 'obviously flawed'. The meaning of 'flawed' refers to the standards of judicial review (s.3 (11). If it gives permission to make the order the court must give a direction for a further hearing as soon as reasonably practicable. If an order is made without permission it must be immediately referred to the court which must consider the matter within seven days, again as to whether the order is 'obviously flawed', and give directions for a further hearing. However the certificate that the matter is urgent can be quashed if it is 'flawed' thus requiring the court to go into greater depth (s.3(8)). On a further hearing the court must also go into greater depth and consider whether the order is 'flawed' (s.3(10)). The court can either quash or alter the order. The order can last for 12 months and can be renewed indefinitely.

To date no derogating control orders have been issued. A derogating order can only be made by the High Court (s.4). The Court will hold a preliminary hearing and can issue a derogating order if there are reasonable grounds for believing that the order is necessary for the protection of the public and the obligations are reasonable. This hearing can be held in the absence of the person in question but a full hearing can only confirm the order if on the balance of probabilities the person is involved in terrorism, the obligations are necessary, there is a risk of a public emergency and a legal derogation from the ECHR covering the control order. The orders last for six months and can be renewed by the High Court. Derogating orders require more rigorous proof of involvement in terrorism and risk to public safety than non-derogating orders.

Non-derogating control orders have been issued against nine of the 16 men indefinitely detained under the ATCSA. In his 2006 Report (above) Lord Carlile commented that these orders were 'extremely restrictive' and fell 'not very far short of house arrest, and certainly inhibit normal life considerably . . . the controllee's situation is tantamount to a reinstatement of detention without trial'. However the legality of the regime has recently been undermined.

In *Secretary of State for the Home Department* v *JJ and Others* (2008) the House of Lords, upholding rulings of the lower courts, held that obligations imposed under what purported to be a non-derogating control order were so severe that the order violated the ECHR as a deprivation of liberty contrary to Article 5 (Chapter 19). House Arrest was imposed for 16 hours per day, visitors and people met had to be authorised by the Home Office and the victim was confined to designated areas. These restrictions meant that the order was a nullity and so it could not be amended but must be quashed. The majority took the view that the meaning of deprivation of liberty was a matter of degree. The proper approach was to decide whether the restriction was so severe as to deprive the victim of a normal life in the context of his or her particular lifestyle. Lord Hoffmann dissenting took the view that nothing short of complete detention should count his argument being that anything broader would require the court to give the state leeway as to derogation from Article 5 [44]. Lord Brown thought that nothing less than 16 hours per day house arrest should count [105]–[108]. In *Secretary of State* v *MB* (2008) and *Secretary of State* v *E* (2008) the House held that lesser restrictions on visitors and movement and a 12 hour curfew did not violate a Convention right.

Control Orders are likely to be made on the basis of secret evidence which is not disclosed to the person concerned.

In *Secretary of State for the Home Department* v *MB* (2008) the Secretary of State had made a Control Order against the claimant under the Prevention of Terrorism Act 2005 (below) restricting the claimant's movements. The Secretary of State relied on powers in the Act to exclude the claimant and his lawyers from the proceedings and to exclude material and without giving full particulars of his reasons. The House of Lords held that the power to make Control Orders was not a criminal matter so that Article 6 of the ECHR (fair trial) was to be applied less rigorously. Article 6 did not confer absolute rights but allowed a 'fair balance' to be struck between the interests of the community and those of the individual. The use of a Special Advocate was justifiable on that basis. Nevertheless there was probably an irreducible minimum of fairness so that if access to the excluded material was essential to enable a person to defend him or herself the court is entitled to quash the Control Order. In *Secretary of State for the Home Department* v *AF* (2008) the Court of Appeal gave guidance on when a trial would be unfair where evidence was not disclosed in respect of a Control Order. However the approach taken by their Lordships seems to make the matter largely one of discretion. It was held that that as much information as possible should be disclosed but that there was arguably no irreducible minimum beyond which a trial would automatically be unfair. The overall test was whether the person concerned would be exposed to significant injustice. A special advocate can be used. Relevant factors include the nature of the case, what steps had been taken to explain to the controlled person the detail of the allegations and a summary of the closed material, how effectively the special advocate was able to act on behalf of the controlled person and what difference disclosure would make.

22.7.6 Terrorist Assets

Under the Anti-Terrorism, Crime and Security Act 2001 (ATCS) s.1 a magistrate in civil proceedings brought for the purpose can order the forfeiture of cash which is intended to be used for terrorist purposes or which belongs to a proscribed organisation or which is or represents property obtained through terrorism. Under the ATCS ss.4, 5. the Treasury can freeze the assets of any person resident in the UK or any UK citizen or company if it reasonably believes (a) that action to the detriment of the UK economy (or part of it) has been or is likely to be taken or (b) action constituting a threat to the life or property of one or more UK nationals has been or is likely to be taken, in both cases either by an overseas government or an overseas resident. The freezing order can prevent benefits being paid to the government or resident in question or to any person the Treasury reasonably believes has assisted or is likely to assist them. These powers are therefore not limited to terrorists but could for example be used to protect trade interests against overseas competition. They include power to require public bodies to disclose confidential information again not limited to terrorist offences (s.17).

By virtue of Orders in Council made under the United Nations Act 1947 the Treasury has power to give directions for the freezing of terrorist assets in order to give effect to various United Nations Conventions. This drastic power can involve placing serious restrictions as to every spending upon the persons concerned other than for essential needs. The order can be made without judicial permission. The Counter Terrorism Act 2008 introduces special High Court proceedings for setting aside the use of these powers. These provisions include what has now become commonplace powers to exclude parties and sensitive evidence and for using the device of a special advocate. However the Treasury is obliged to disclose to the court all relevant material both for and against its case. The Court is limited to applying judicial review principles.

Where a person has been convicted of certain funding and money laundering offences the court concerned may order assets connected with the offence to be seized (Terrorism Act 2000 s.23). The Counter Terrorism Act has extended this power and introduces provisions for compensating the injured out of the convicted person's assets.

22.7.7 Other Terrorist Offences and Powers

1. The Encouragement of Terrorism and dissemination of terrorist publications (Terrorism Act 2006 ss. 1, 2 (see Chapter 21).
2. Preparation of Terrorist Acts (ibid, s.5). This is not confined to a specific act of terrorism but could include for example buying materials capable of being made into bombs.
3. Giving or receiving instruction or training for terrorism (ibid. s.6). This is also wide including the use of any method or technique for doing anything that is capable of being done for the purpose of terrorism (s.6 (3) b). For example it could include IT skills. However the instructor must know that the pupil intend to use the skills for terrorist purposes.
4. Attendance at a place used for terrorist training.
5. Offences relating to radioactive devices or materials for terrorist purposes (ss. 9–11).
6. The Secretary of State can authorise the taking of land or a road closure or restriction if he or she considers it necessary for the preservation of peace or the maintenance of order (ss.91,94). A member of the armed forces on duty or a constable may order a road closure or restriction if he considers it immediately necessary for the preservation of peace or the maintenance of order (s.92).
7. The Counter Terrorism Act 2008 introduces increased penalties for any offence with a terrorist connection.
8. The Counter Terrorism Act 2008 confers wide powers on any person to disclose information to any of the intelligence services for the purpose of its functions (s.19) with a corresponding power given to the intelligence services also to disclose information. This does not appear to be limited to terrorist offences.

Summary

▶ The courts give the executive a wide margin of discretion in relation to security matters. Under the ECHR there is also a wide margin and states can derogate from some of its provisions in the event of an emergency. However the courts protect fundamental rights by requiring safeguards in particular independent judicial supervision.

▶ There is no general right to the disclosure of governmental information. The Freedom of Information Act 2000 confers a right to 'request' the disclosure of documents held by public authorities. However this can often be overridden by the government and is subject to many exceptions particularly in relation to central government policy.

▷ There are certain statutory rights to the disclosure of specified information but these are outnumbered by many statutes prohibiting the disclosure of particular information.

▷ Under the Official Secrets Act 1989 certain categories of information are protected by criminal penalties. Except in the case of national security, the information must be damaging. There is also a defence of ignorance.

▷ The law of confidence requires the court to balance the public interest in openness against the public interest in effective government. The balance is struck differently according to context. The courts have endorsed the importance of freedom of expression and a public body is required to show a public interest in secrecy. The main remedy is an injunction. Third parties such as the press are not directly bound by an injunction but might be liable for contempt of court if they knowingly frustrate its purpose.

▷ Public interest immunity allows the government to withhold evidence. The court makes the decision on the basis of 'balancing' the public interest in the administration of justice against the public interest in effective government. The courts' approach to public interest immunity is affected by the Human Rights Act 1998 which requires that any claim preserves the essentials of the right to a fair trial. The device of a special advocate might be used in PII cases and in other cases such as terrorist trials or parole hearings where confidential information is involved. It is questionable whether this satisfies the EHCR.

▷ The security and intelligence services are subject to a certain degree of control, largely outside the ordinary courts.

▷ There is regulation of electronic and other forms of surveillance by the police and other law enforcement agencies, also outside the ordinary courts. The overlapping regimes of the Police Act 1997 and the Regulation of Investigatory Powers Act 2000 give the government wide powers of interception and surveillance subject to procedural safeguards and to limits derived from the ECHR as to permissible purposes and proportionality.

▷ In an emergency the police supported by the armed forces may take action to keep the peace and can use reasonable force in self defence and the defence of others. It is questionable whether martial law as such is part of English law. The Civil Contingencies Act 2004 gives the executive wide powers to deal with an emergency. These are subject to control by Parliament and safeguards based on the ECHR.

▷ Increasingly restrictive anti-terrorist measures have been introduced in response to a series of threats and incidents. These have sometimes required derogation from the ECHR protection for personal liberty. They also involve restrictions on the right to a fair trial. The courts have condemned a significant number of these powers and criticised others. However there is no consensus on how to accommodate security and respect for freedom.

Exercises

22.1 'We have moved from a discretionary open government regime under a voluntary Code of Practice to a statutory open government regime in which the power to decide what is to be disclosed lies within the discretion of government and is denied to independent bodies' (Nigel Johnson, 2001, *New Law Journal* 151, p. 1031). Explain and discuss critically.

22.2 Tony, a US citizen, and Gordon, a UK citizen, are arrested by the police on suspicion of being associated with an international terrorist group. The police suspect that certain incriminating information which they received from the US may have been extracted from Tony by torture.

Gordon is released but Tony is detained under a certificate issued by the Home Secretary stating that he is suspected of being a terrorist. Tony demands to see the evidence against him. He also asks for a lawyer but the request is refused. He is offered a special advocate as a representative. Discuss.

22.3 Simon is the leader of an animal rights campaigning organisation. The police receive an anonymous message that the organisation proposes to enter the headquarters of a drugs company (known to donate large sums to the ruling political party) in order to distribute animal rights leaflets. A policeman stops Simon in the street and searches him but finds nothing relevant to the allegation. The policeman then arrests Simon on the ground that he is a terrorist. Simon is detained for 14 days without charge and without going before a court. The Home Secretary who knows Simon as a prominent critic of the government makes a Control Order against Simon 'as a matter of urgency'. This requires that neither Simon nor any member of his group carry out any political activity anywhere nor enter within 100 metres of any medicine related establishment without police permission.

Advise Simon as to the legality of these actions.

22.4 Derek, a civil servant in the Department of Health, believes that the cabinet minister in charge of his department has been ordering government statisticians to alter the latest NHS performance figures in order to show that government policies are bearing fruit. Derek gives this information to the editor of the Daily Whinge who contacts the relevant minister for his comments. The Attorney-General immediately applies for a temporary injunction and commences an action for breach of confidence against Derek. Derek requests the production of letters between civil servants and the minister (the existence of which he learned from an anonymous email) which he claims would support his version of events. The government issues a PII certificate on the ground that the information is in a category the disclosure of which would inhibit free and frank discussion within the Cabinet. The minister who signed the certificate did not examine the information personally but relied on advice from the Attorney-General that the 'certificate will cover us for all Cabinet-level documents'.

(i) Advise Derek.

(ii) Advise the Attorney-General whether he can prosecute Derek under the Official Secrets Act.

22.5 Tom has recently retired from a senior post in the intelligence services. He possesses recordings of conversations by service officials which suggest that senior ministers have requested them to fabricate evidence supporting a proposed invasion of an African country. He wishes to pass the recordings to Jerry, a journalist. Advise Tom whether he and Jerry are at risk of conviction under the Official Secrets Act 1989.

22.6 'Terrorist threats and actions test the Executive's commitment to the rule of law and good governance. Because of the extreme powers given by such extraordinary legislation, there is an incumbent requirement to provide limits to its terms, scope and life span' (Thomas, 'Emergency and Anti-Terrorist Powers 9/11: USA and UK', 2003, *Fordham International Law Journal*, 26(4):1993). Does the current law meet these requirements?

Further reading

Akdeniz, Y., Taylor, N. and Walker, C. (2001) 'Regulation RIPA 2000 (1): Big Brother.Gov.UK: State Surveillance in the Age of Information and Rights', *Criminal Law Review* 73.

Arden, M. (2005) 'Human Rights in the Age of Terrorism', *Law Quarterly Review* 121:609.

Austin, R. (2004) 'The Freedom of Information Act – a Sheep in Wolf's Clothing?', in Jowell, J. and Oliver, D. (eds) *The Changing Constitution*, Oxford University Press.

Bonner, D. (2006) 'Checking the Executive? Detention without Trial, Control Orders, Due Process and Human Rights', *European Public Law* 12(1):45–71.

Brandon, B. (2004) 'Terrorism, Human Rights and the Rule of Law: 120 Years of the UK's Response to Terrorism', *Criminal Law Review* 981.

Dickson, B. (2005) 'Law versus Terrorism: Can Law Win?' *European Human Rights Law Review* 12.

Feldman, D. (2005) 'Proportionality and Discrimination in Anti-Terror Legislation', *Cambridge Law Journal* 271.

Feldman, D. (2006) 'Human Rights, Terrorism and Risk: the Roles of Politicians and Judges', *Public Law* 364.

Gearty, C. (2005) 'Counter Terrorism and the Human Rights Act', *Journal of Law and Society* 32(1):18.

Gearty, C. (2005) 'Human Rights in an Age of Counter Terrorism: Injurious, Irrelevant or Indispensible?' *Current Legal Issues* 58:25.

Ip, J. (2008) 'The Rise and Spread of the Special Advocate', *Public Law* 717.

Oliver, D. (1998) 'Freedom of Information and Ministerial Accountability', *Public Law* 171.

Palmer, S. (1990) 'Tightening Secrecy Law', *Public Law* 243.

Scott, Sir R. (1996) 'The Acceptable and Unacceptable Uses of Public Interest Immunity', *Public Law* 427.

Walker, C. (2007), 'The Legal Defintion of Terrorism in the United Kingdom and Beyond', *Public Law* 331.

White Paper (1997) *Your Right to Know: Freedom of Information*, Cm 3818.

White Paper (2004) *Counter Terrorist Powers: Reconciling Security and Liberty in an Open Society*, Cm 6147.

Zedner, L. (2005) 'Security Liberty in the Face of Terror: Reflections from Criminal Justice', *Journal of Law and Society*, 32(4):507.